Data Mining Solutions
Methods and Tools for Solving Real-World Problems

CHRISTOPHER **W**ESTPHAL
TERESA **B**LAXTON

WILEY COMPUTER PUBLISHING

John Wiley & Sons, Inc.
New York • Chichester • Weinheim • Brisbane • Singapore • Toronto

Publisher: Robert Ipsen
Editor: Robert M. Elliott
Managing Editor: Erin Singletary
Electronic Products, Associate Editor: Mike Sosa
Text Design & Composition: Benchmark Productions, Inc.

This book is printed on acid-free paper. ∞

Published simultaneously in Canada.
Published by John Wiley & Sons, Inc.

This publication is designed to provide accurate and authoritative information in regard to the subject matter covered. It is sold with the understanding that the publisher is not engaged in professional services. If professional advice or other expert assistance is required, the services of a competent professional person should be sought.

Library of Congress Cataloging-in-Publication Data

0471-253847
Printed in the United States of America.

10 9 8 7 6 5 4 3 2 1

CONTENTS

FOREWORD

The term *data mining* can be used to describe a wide range of activities. A marketing company using historical response data to build models to predict who will respond to a direct mail or telephone solicitation is using data mining. A manufacturer analyzing sensor data to isolate conditions that lead to unplanned production stoppages is also using data mining. The government agency that sifts through the records of financial transactions looking for patterns that indicate money laundering or drug smuggling is mining data for evidence of criminal activity. An automated search through a document archive (or the World Wide Web) for articles on a certain topic may be thought of as data mining as well.

With so many different activities all going by the same name, there is ample room for confusion. Talk to two self-described data miners, and you may find that they work with completely different kinds of data to address completely different problems using completely different tools and techniques. Recently, at a data mining conference, I went to dinner with several other data mining practitioners. Over a delicious and elegantly prepared meal of sushi and sashimi, we discussed our work. By the time the second pot of green tea arrived it was clear there was very little overlap in our experience. One of us had worked on systems to tell the difference between whales and submarines in SONAR data, another had studied property insurance claims from areas hit by earthquakes and hurricanes in order to help plan federal disaster relief programs. My own project at the time involved studying data from several printing plants in order to get a better understanding of the factors contributing to paper waste for a publishing company. It was fascinating to hear each other's stories. It was also clear that we were all using the same term to describe very different activities.

How can we make sense of such an amorphous topic? Taking a cue from the online analytic processing (OLAP) world, we can impose some order on the field by thinking of it as a three-dimensional space defined by the following axes:

- Underlying task

- Nature of goal

- Degree of structure in the data

By locating a given data mining project along each of these axes, we can place it in a box with other similar projects. Each box calls for a different mix of data mining algorithms and approaches. Let's take a closer look at each of these dimensions.

Data Mining Tasks

There are many ways that data mining tasks could be classified. In fact, Gordon Linoff and I present a slightly different classification of data mining tasks in our book *Data Mining Techniques for Marketing, Sales and Customer Support* (John Wiley & Sons, 1997). To keep our model simple, we want a small number of broadly defined tasks that can be used to categorize the underlying activity in a data mining project. For this purpose, I have given our data mining task dimension four members each of which is defined below:

- Classification
- Estimation
- Segmentation
- Description

Classification

A classification task consists of placing labels on records. The labels come from a small pre-defined set (good/bad or red/white/rosé). The job of the data miner is to build a model that will successfully route incoming records into the correctly labeled bucket. Prediction is simply a special case of classification where you may have to wait a bit longer to find out if your classification was correct.

Estimation

Estimation is the task of filling in a missing (usually, but not always, numeric) value in a particular field of an incoming record as a function of other fields in the record. The usual statistical regression techniques are most often employed for estimation. Estimation is also a popular application of artificial neural networks. Figuring out who is likely to respond to a credit card balance transfer offer is a classification task. Figuring out the likely size of the transferred balance is an estimation task.

Segmentation

It often happens that, in a large population, there are so many competing patterns that they cancel one another. In order to see what is really going on, you have to break the population into smaller sub-populations having similar behavior. Within these sub-populations, all kinds of predictions may be possible. Various cluster detection, affinity grouping and link analysis techniques can be applied to segmentation tasks.

Description

Data mining can also be employed to give the analyst a clearer idea of what is going on in the data. Visualization techniques that allow clusters and linkages that would be imperceptible in a table or textual display to be spotted quickly and intuitively by eye fall under this heading. Descriptive data mining can be used to perform classification tasks even when the classes themselves are not well defined. In fraud detection, for example, a decision tree classifier can only be built based on known examples of fraudulent behavior. A good link analysis program coupled with visualization can turn this problem into one that humans perform very well—looking at a picture and spotting the anomalous or "interesting" bits.

Predictive and Descriptive Data Mining Goals

The next axis of our data mining cube puts data mining activities into one of two bins depending on whether the primary goal of the exercise is to produce *models* or *information*. On the predictive end of the spectrum, the goal of data mining is to produce a model, expressed as executable code, that can be used to score a database, route claims, or perform some other classification or estimation task. On the descriptive end, the goal is to gain understanding by uncovering patterns and relationships. For example, this book contains numerous examples of forensic data mining where the goal is to uncover evidence of criminal activity.

Structured and Unstructured Data

Structured data is the kind of thing found in most computer databases—fixed length, fixed format records with fields that contain numeric values, character codes or short strings. The data mining techniques that work well for this kind of data are often incapable of coping with less structured data such as free text or data that are structured very differently such as pixel maps derived from photographic images.

The Book You are About to Read

Now that I have constructed this cubic conceptual framework for data mining, I can see that my own work is concentrated in the corner where the primary task is classification or prediction, the goal is a predictive model and the data are highly structured. It was refreshing to read a book written by people whose primary practice is at the opposite corner of the cube where the tasks are largely descriptive, the goal is to gain understanding, and much of the data are unstructured.

Christopher Westphal and Teresa Blaxton have expanded my view of the data mining landscape with their wide-ranging coverage of topics such as phonetic name matching, visual methods for analyzing data, and the distinction between procedural and declarative knowledge. Their extensive coverage of data mining software tools will also prove valuable to readers who are planning to set up their own data mining environments. This book covers ground that has not been explored in any other book geared to a general audience. Enjoy it!

Michael Berry

ACKNOWLEDGMENTS

As two people who have worked as data mining practitioners for the past several years on a variety of projects, we have been struck by the fact that there are no clear and accepted approaches for conducting data mining analyses. Most of the books on the subject describe issues relating to the presentation of results rather than to analytical methods and tools that may be used to produce those results. As we have done this work over the years, we have developed our own set of general methods and approaches that we have applied in a variety of settings ranging from criminal investigations to the design of marketing campaigns to epidemiological studies. We wanted to share some of the lessons that we have learned along the way that might be of use to others facing similar tasks. We have tried to write a book that will be useful to people involved at all levels of data mining work. Our target audience includes system developers who actually do the implementation, technical managers who need to oversee the progress of the application, and analysts who will use data mining tools to perform analyses. We have aimed much of the text at readers in the business community, but the general principles apply to any domain where data mining is being used.

In an undertaking of this sort there are always many people whose contributions are valued and appreciated. In particular we would like to thank Bob Elliott, our editor at John Wiley and Sons, and his assistant Brian Calandra who have worked with us from the beginning of the project. Their inputs have been instrumental in shaping the style and focus of the book, and we are grateful for the many insights that they have shared with us. We also want to thank the Managing Editor, Erin Singletary, for her diligence, patience, and support on the production of this book. For their technical inputs, advice, and general support throughout this project we are indebted to Lou Kallis and Al Brandenstein from the Office of National Drug Control Policy (ONDCP), Mike Kling from Booz-Allen & Hamilton Inc., Vladimir Prupes from SPSS, Garry Robinson from GR-FX Pty Limited, Barry Engel from Inxight Software, Sandy Montgomery, Kevin Greer, and Jamie Houchens from Presearch Corporation, Tim Hendrickson from the National Ground Intelligence Center (NGIC), Kea Beaudry from Amtec Engineering, Inc., David Clarke from Perspecta, David Krider and Troy Whisenhunt from Visualize, Inc., Michael Monaco from Mitre Corp., and Dan Schoenbaum from Mercury Interactive.

A number of people were especially helpful to us when we were putting together the data mining product reviews discussed in Section III. We would like to personally thank Nancy Mancini and Max Stevens-Guille from Visible Decisions, Inc., John Blattner from Imagix Corporation, Ronny Kohavi, Aydin Senkut, and Mark Olson from Silicon Graphics, Inc., Carolyn Warburton and Shepherd Smith from I2, Inc., Dave Snocken from ALTA Analytics in the UK, Anthony Standifer and David Bikle from Visual Insights (Bell Labs New Ventures), Beverly Stockstill, Wally Maczka, and Mark Brown from SAS, Jim Ong and Jeremy Pool from Belmont Research, and finally David O'Connor, Ginny Keech, Colin Furtaw, and Nick Brown from United Information Systems, Inc.

Along similar lines, we wish to thank the following individuals for spending the time to talk with us about their own work that is described in the case studies presented in Section IV. They include Steve Lassagne and Ingrid Akerblom from Incyte Pharmaceuticals, Susan Osterfelt, Bryan McNeely, and Charles Mainer from NationsBank, Bob Heffernan from A.T. Kearney, Inc., Paul Marshall and Ed Zahos from Maxus Systems International, James Miller from Daisy Analysis, Bernice Rogowitz and Ed Murphy from IBM, Dave Baize from the Arizona Attorney General's Office, Rey Wong from the Financial Crimes Enforcement Network (FinCEN), and Kevin Hohn from the Internal Revenue Service (IRS).

Since this book emphasized the role of visualization in data mining, we tried to include as many examples of visual displays used in data mining applications as possible. In many cases these images were provided by companies that do business in this area, either selling commercial tools or developing data mining applications for clients. We could not have put together the CD-ROM or many of the book figures without the help of many other people. We want to especially thank Bennett McPhatter for his dedication and hard work in pulling together the CD-ROM. We want to thank Janet Reese and Darrell Olson for producing the image which appears on the cover and on the CD-ROM. Thanks to Dana Miletic for producing several of the figures contained in this book. Additionally, we want to thank Andrew Anoshkin for allowing us to use his PicViewer program on the CD-ROM. We would also like to thank Randy Woodson, Dennis McQuerry, and Jim Thomas from PNNL (Batelle), Bernard Buelow from Advanced Visual Systems Inc., Tamara Munzner from Stanford University, Timo Honkela, Samuel Kaski, Teuvo Kohonen, and Krista Lagus from Helsinki University of Technology, Christopher Ahlberg from Spotfire, Inc., Jim Lewis from Micro Logic Corporation, Dodie Bump and Imogen Holbrook from Harlequin Inc., Yoelle Maarek and Michal Jacovi from IBM Haifa Research Lab, Jason Mallen and Patricia Hughes from Integral Solutions Ltd., and Phil Parsons from ORION Scientific Systems, Inc.

Finally, we would like to thank all of our friends and family for supporting us through this effort.

INTRODUCTION

Our work within the field of data mining had convinced us that there is an overwhelming demand for a resource text that addresses all aspects of how to best perform a successful data mining endeavor. Although the enterprise of data mining has been part of the information technology vernacular for several years, many people still view the process as black magic. This is partly because no established road maps or procedures have been formally identified for guiding analysts to profitable outcomes. Thus, data mining activities often proceed in a haphazard fashion with mixed results. This book will lead you through a set of methodologies and related technologies that address all phases of the data mining process and bring together issues that have never before been discussed in the context of data mining. Our vision is that this book will become an invaluable resource for people engaged in analyzing patterns and trends within complex data sources. Therefore, the book is designed to provide value to curious students, sophisticated investigators, programmers and system designers, as well as corporate management personnel.

In this book, we describe how best to prepare environments for performing data mining and discuss approaches that have proven to be critical in revealing important patterns and trends in large data sets. From our experience, one of the best data mining technologies available is *visualization* because graphical display methods often offer superior results compared to other more conventional data mining techniques. Visual tools have traditionally been used by high-end intelligence agencies but have recently become accessible and useful as a practical, cost-effective approach for many businesses and corporate settings. In the interest of providing a complete picture of data mining, this book contains descriptions of a variety of approaches and tools that offer useful capabilities for the solution of pattern detection problems in data sets. As the use of visualization techniques becomes more mainstream, we feel confident that many nonvisual tools will be extended to include the use of visual display interfaces.

This book will further provide you with a comprehensive review of the principles, techniques, and applications that can be used to perform data mining. It is our expectation that once you have completed this text, you will be able to initiate a data mining activity effectively. *Data Mining Solutions* is a text that can be used by a wide range of readers, from beginners wishing to learn about the enterprise of data mining to analysts and technical programmers who will be engaged directly in the process. This book reviews some fundamental methods that can be used to structure and analyze large quantities of data derived from multiple sources. It also discusses a wide array of technologies and products that have been developed to support data mining analysis. Although it is easy to focus on the technologies, as you read through the book please bear in mind that technology alone does not provide the entire solution. Rather it is the methodologies you use for applying the technologies to specific problems that is of paramount importance in determining the success of data mining activities. No tool, no matter how advanced, will produce useful results unless it is applied with the proper methodological approach.

It is our expectation that after reading this text, you will have the requisite knowledge to tackle all phases of the data mining process. To this end, the book is constructed along two broad dimensions. First, we present a set of methodologies for approaching the data mining process. These are based largely on the theories and processes that we have developed and found useful over the past several years while implementing visual data mining systems. We have addressed all aspects of data mining, including formatting and extraction of data, the creation of models to be applied to extracted data, selection of display techniques, and interpretation of patterns revealed by the process.

The second aim of the book presents a comprehensive overview of data mining as it is currently being done with a variety of technologies with heavy emphasis on the use of data visualization. There is presently no other publication of this length and detail that allows the user to make comparisons among systems and/or techniques in order to choose the one(s) that provides the most appropriate solution for a given application. Our philosophy is that it is highly unlikely that any single product or approach can handle the entire data mining process. Rather, solutions are based on a combination of *technologies* and *methodologies*. Therefore data mining practitioners must consider the organizational requirements, available data sources, and corporate policies and procedures pending on every project. This book provides the background information necessary to evaluate options and make informed decisions at all phases of the data mining activity. All topics discussed have real-world examples provided to make understanding the process simple, straightforward, and transferable to the reader's own domain of interest.

The book consists of four sections with sixteen chapters written by experienced authors who have been performing advanced data mining using information visualization technologies in such varied domains as narco-terrorism, money laundering, insider trading, claims fraud, retail sales, biomedical research, and telecommunications. We have worked with many different clients on all sorts of data mining applications to help them detect patterns, expose inconsistent or suspicious structures, and reveal criteria activities within their data sets. As you go through the book, you will see real-world examples that serve as illustrations of the ways in which data mining principles and technologies can be applied. These examples are drawn from actual engagements, many of which we have participated in directly. The various examples and tools were selected for their utility in addressing various classes of problems encountered during data mining activities. We have placed special emphasis on the utilization of visualization, but also discuss and contrast nonvisual methods where appropriate.

One of our goals in writing this book was to minimize the hype associated with data mining. Rather than making false promises that overstep the bounds of what can reasonably be expected from data mining, we have tried to take a more objective approach. We describe the processes and procedures that are necessary to produce reliable and useful results in data mining applications. We do not advocate the use of any particular product over another. Rather, we have tried to give you enough information to decide which data mining tools and techniques are most appropriate for your particular situation.

SECTION I: Defining the Data Mining Approach. This section addresses important principles about the nature of data. To be an effective data mining practitioner, you need to understand all aspects of the data that will be used in the analyses. Knowing how to exploit data effectively can help you to use available technologies to reveal the hidden patterns and trends contained therein. To some readers, this discussion may appear trivial; however, it is probably one of the most important sections of the book. This discussion provides you with an overview of many important factors and approaches to consider when performing data mining.

SECTION II: Preparing and Analyzing Data. The techniques used to manipulate data are based on a variety of analytical methodologies. There are indicators contained within every data set that will reveal patterns; the difficulty is in knowing what type of patterns are available, what the predominate cues are, and how to interpret the results. Although every domain is unique, many features contained within different sources of data will embody consistent traits that can be globally exploited. This discussion reviews many of these approaches and methodologies and is structured to reflect an intelligence production cycle for *accessing data*, *analyzing patterns*, and *presenting results*.

SECTION III: Assessing Data Mining Tools and Technologies. There are a host of software tools and technologies available to businesses interested in performing data mining; this section presents you with an overview of categories of such tools and a sampling of the approaches available. The intent is not to provide a feature-specific review of tools, but to discuss the effectiveness of different data mining solutions for specific types of problems.

In Section III we focus on the application of visualization technologies available in data mining tools. Visualization tools are becoming more and more popular among data miners, and you need to know what types of tools are available, when to use them, and how to use them appropriately in your analytical engagements. In this section we introduce a host of visualization systems and briefly discuss their unique capabilities and typical uses. We divide visualization paradigms into three categories —link analysis, landscapes, and quantitative displays. Each chapter provides you with relevant examples and screen captures, information about ease-of-use, and other factors that businesses need to consider when applying visual data mining technologies to their environments. (All tools presented in this section apply to both large and small business concerns.) The section concludes with a future trends chapter that provides insight into pending developments in data mining.

SECTION IV: Case Studies. To tie everything neatly together, we present a series of descriptions of actual data mining engagements. The examples provide you with explicit illustrations of the types of patterns that typically can be found within the application domains presented. Each chapter in this section provides the background knowledge necessary to understand the domain and its associated problems. In addition we have tried to include descriptions of the logistical difficulties that the analysts experienced during the engagement. Therefore each case study includes war stories about real problems that were encountered as well as the useful outcomes that were derived from the analyses.

APPENDIX: Tool and Technology Resources. This section has information on the tools referenced throughout the book. We strongly suggest that you consult directly with vendors if you are interested in applying any of these tools in an application of your own. As with all quickly progressing technologies, numerous enhancements and features will have been added to many of these systems by the time this book goes into press. Therefore, we ask that you check directly with them to learn about these changes before making any final decisions.

Our hope for this book is that it will a fulfill a need that has not been met previously by providing you with a roadmap for the data mining process. The information presented here was gleaned from years of experience with many real world data mining cases. We have tried to extrapolate general principles from those experiences that you can put to use in your own work. We believe that this book provides information that will put you ahead of the game when developing your own data mining applications. We hope you enjoy reading this book and learn from its content.

Section I

DEFINING THE DATA MINING APPROACH

We have gradually grown accustomed to the fact that there are tremendous volumes of data filling our computers, networks, and lives. Government agencies and businesses have all dedicated enormous resources to collecting and storing this information. Presumably, information is amassed because someone at some point in time imagined an important use for it. In reality, however, only a small amount of these data will ever be used because in many cases the volumes are simply too large to manage or the data structures themselves are too complicated to be accessed effectively.

How could this happen? The primary reason is that the original effort to create a data set is often focused on issues such as storage efficiency and does not include a plan for how the data will eventually be used and analyzed. Thus, by the time analysts wish to use a data set to answer questions, they often find themselves at a significant disadvantage with little hope for future success. Data mining methodologies are aimed at solving some of these problems. The ultimate goal of a data mining exercise is to discover hidden patterns in these complex information sources.

Making the Most of Your Resources

What data do you have available to you for analysis? Data warehouses, legacy databases, and corporate information systems are ideal information sources to be used for detecting patterns and trends through the application of data mining techniques. As you think about the sources of information that can be used to perform data mining, keep an open mind about what sorts of data might be useful. Of course your main customer-tracking databases, accounting systems, inventory control, and other very obvious and explicit data sets are good candidates. Now dig a bit deeper. Where else can you derive relevant data within your organization? If you are doing forensic accounting, you might be able to use phone-call data collected by the internal telephone switch at most corporations. Communication patterns may also be traced by accessing records of e-mail transactions maintained on your network servers. If your application question bears on issues concerning access to building facilities, consider that some security departments have badge reader data that record time and ID numbers of people entering and leaving certain locations. Your personnel department maintains all of the home address and phone data on nonexempt staff. Inquiries about embezzlement or collusion may benefit from the comparison of these data to those contained on suspicious vendor invoices. When you think about it, expense reports, corporate credit card statements, travel advances, insurance claims, equipment maintenance reports, point-of-sale charges, warranty records, damaged goods receipts, shipping invoices, merchandise sales and returns, weather reports, and just about any other piece of information collected can be used in a data mining application.

In the event that the necessary data are not available or do not yet exist, they can usually be generated. For example, suppose that your information is reported at a level of detail above what is needed for the analysis. Imagine that you had a medical application in which you were trying to trace the origins of a series of apparent adverse reactions to some combination of medications. You might have coded the names of all medications being taken for each patient case in your study, yet still fail to find a definitive link showing that a particular drug was consistently present in the adverse reaction cases. One approach might be to create a new data source by listing the names of all ingredients making up the individual medications included in your original data set. By doing this you would add a level of detail to the analysis that might then permit you to discover that it is actually a combination of ingredients that produces the adverse reactions.

We have often found it useful to generate new data sources to be used as supplemental information during an analysis. In one particular data mining engagement we manually created a list that categorized various military units according to a set of unique codes which we analyzed in terms of requests for certain types of support resources. In another application for law enforcement, we created a list of vehicle types and their corresponding price ranges to help determine certain income-to-asset ratios, which were then used to expose noncompliant tax filing patterns. Simple lists such as these may be added as extra data sources and can contribute enormous value and insight to the data mining process. Since data mining is an iterative process, sources can be introduced at any time throughout the entire engagement. This occurs frequently because as you progress in identifying patterns, you realize that there are certain dimensions that may be missing. The easiest way to resolve this is to create a new data set that contains the information needed.

Data Mining as Problem Solving

From this discussion you can see that the success of a data mining engagement can depend largely on the amount of energy and creativity that you bring to the table. You will get as much out of a data mining analysis as you put into it. In essence, data mining is like solving a puzzle. The individual pieces of the puzzle are not complex structures in and of themselves. However, taken as a collective whole they can constitute very elaborate systems. As you try to unravel these systems you will probably get frustrated, start forcing parts together, and generally become annoyed at the entire process. However, once you know how to work with the pieces, you realize that it was not really that hard in the first place.

The same analogy can be applied to data mining. At this point in time, you probably do not know much about the details of your data sources. Otherwise you would most likely not be interested in performing data mining. Individually, the data records seem simple, complete, and uncomplicated. But collectively, they take on a whole new appearance that is intimidating and difficult to comprehend, like the puzzle. As you will see, being an analyst requires creative thinking and a willingness to see problems in a different light. You cannot expect automatic answers. One of our goals in writing this book is to encourage analysts to think outside the box, letting their imaginations wander. Once you delve into the problem and are able to discover some interesting patterns and trends, data mining becomes less awe-inspiring and more routine.

An Overview of Section I

In this section we cover a number of issues that will expand the ways in which you think about your data and the types of analyses that might be most useful to you. In Chapter 1, "What is Data Mining?," we describe the data mining process and give examples of applications in which data mining methods have been used successfully. A large portion of this chapter is devoted to issues that should be addressed before any data mining activities actually begin. Chapter 2, "Understanding Data Modeling," provides an introduction to the modeling process, including a discussion of object-oriented modeling techniques. We describe the basic differences between descriptive and transactional models, giving examples of each. The importance of choosing models wisely is illustrated in the discussion of the distinctions between intra- and inter-domain pattern detection. Last, in Chapter 3, "Defining the Problems to be Solved," we present a set of conceptual frameworks within which you can consider your particular application problems.

Following this, we describe the differences between reactive and proactive modes of analysis, and how you can best use these in your own engagement. We hope that this section opens up your mind to new possibilities in terms of ways to approach your own data.

WHAT IS DATA MINING?

Data mining is one of the fastest growing fields in the computer industry. Once a small interest area within computer science, it has quickly expanded into a field of its own. Though you may have heard descriptions of data mining techniques, been exposed to knowledge discovery in databases (KDD), or read reports of successful applications, chances are that you may still have some basic questions about what data mining is and why is it useful. The purpose of this chapter is to clear up a number of uncertainties you may have regarding the definition of data mining and to provide some examples of applications in which data mining methods have been used successfully. We go on to describe the boundaries that set data mining apart from other information technology approaches. Finally, we present some practical advice that you should bear in mind as you begin any data mining engagement.

Data Mining Defined

How do we explain what data mining really is? Let us begin with a few basic facts.

- Many organizations ranging from private businesses to government bureaucracies have devoted a tremendous amount of resources to the construction and maintenance of large information databases over recent decades, including the development of large scale data warehouses.

- Frequently the data cannot be analyzed by standard statistical methods, either because there are numerous missing records or because the data are in the form of qualitative rather than quantitative measures.

- In many cases the information contained in these databases is undervalued and underutilized because the data cannot be easily accessed or analyzed.

- Some databases have grown so large that even the system administrators do not always know what information might be represented or how relevant it might be to the questions at hand.

- It would be beneficial to organizations to have a way to "mine" these large databases for important information or patterns that may be contained within.

- There are a variety of data mining methodologies that may be used to analyze data sources in order to discover new patterns and trends.

There you have it. This is what the general idea of data mining is all about. Unlike situations in which you might employ standard mathematical or statistical analyses to test predefined hypotheses, data mining is most useful in exploratory analysis scenarios in which there are no predetermined notions about what will constitute an "interesting" outcome. Data mining is an iterative process within which progress is defined by *discovery,* through either automatic or manual methods. Usually you begin by getting an overall picture of the available data. This is followed by a series of steps in which subsets of the data are modeled and analyzed. Based on the discovery of interesting patterns, there may be subsequent resampling of the data set along with the formulation of new models designed to emphasize particular aspects of the data, and so forth. You might continue iterations down one path for a time, and then retreat back out to a higher level and begin again with another modeling approach when the first path is exhausted. Data mining may occur within a single data source or across multiple sources. Whatever exact form the analysis takes, the key is in adopting a flexible approach that will allow you to make unexpected discoveries beyond the bounds of the established expectations within your problem domain. The most important strategy to keep in mind for data mining is to keep your options open—there are many occasions when interesting discoveries may be made only when the data are approached from multiple perspectives.

There are many technologies and tools available for data mining applications. From our perspective, there are certain technologies that have better track records than others in terms of ease of use and return on investment. Nevertheless, despite all of their attractive bells and whistles (which we describe in detail later), the tools alone will never provide the entire solution. There will always be the need for the practitioner to make the important decisions regarding how these systems will be employed. This analyst must decide how best to manipulate, exploit, and expose critical patterns and relationships in the data by using a combination of techniques. There are general lessons and principles that may be commonly applied to all application areas. No matter which data mining tool(s) the analyst may employ for a given engagement, the analyst will want to be guided by these general principles in deciding how to construct models so as to get the most out of the data mining exercise.

Using Data Mining to Solve Specific Problems

One of the greatest strengths of data mining is reflected in its wide range of methodologies that can be applied to a host of problem sets. Since data mining is a natural activity to be performed on a data warehouse, one of the largest target markets is the entire data-warehousing, data-mart, and decision support community encompassing professionals from such industries as retail, manufacturing, telecommunications, health-care, insurance, and transportation. In the business community, you can use data mining to discover new purchasing trends, plan investment strategies, and detect unauthorized expenditures in your accounting system. Further, you can apply data mining to improve your marketing campaigns, using the outcomes to provide your customers with more focused support and attention. As another example, you can apply data mining techniques to problems of business process reengineering in which the goal is to understand interactions and relationships among business practices and organizations.

Many law enforcement and special investigative units whose mission is to identify fraudulent activities and discover crime trends have also used data mining successfully. Data mining methodologies can aid analysts in the identification of critical behavior patterns, in the communication interactions of narcotics organizations, the monetary transactions of money laundering and insider trading operations, the movements of serial killers, and the targeting of smugglers at border crossings. Data mining techniques have also been employed by people in the intelligence community who maintain many large data sources as part of activities relating to matters of national security. Four examples of areas where data mining has been applied successfully follow.

Improved Marketing Campaigns

Marketing programs can cost a company a significant amount of money in terms of the design, production, and distribution of materials. If a marketing campaign is not designed for the appropriate client base, the response to the offering might suffer, not only in terms of the expenses required to produce the campaign but also in lost sales. Additionally, if distribution of marketing materials is not handled correctly, the campaign might not be as effective as it might otherwise be. Inconsistent data sets that include wrong names, outdated addresses, duplicated records, and other incomplete data fields will most often produce nonresponsive marketing targets. Clearly this is a waste of marketing funds and company resources.

Losses on marketing initiatives were such a problem in one automobile industry segment that some companies used to include a fee (about $500 or 3–5 percent of a car's price) for every car sold to help recover these marketing costs. It is perhaps fortunate news, then, that there are now several examples within the automotive industry in which data mining has been used to help improve this marketing process. The effectiveness of infusing data mining into marketing campaign design can be measured in terms of the observed response to the improved campaign. Companies have saved literally millions of dollars by better managing their marketing concerns using data mining techniques.

We performed an analysis of the new car sales database for a local car dealership to determine whether specific problem areas could be identified in their marketing activities. Almost immediately we discovered several situations that the dealership was able to act upon quickly. For example, we found that many of the addresses maintained for car owners were assigned to the post office box of the credit agency financing many of the vehicles. Obviously these addresses were recorded incorrectly from sales transactions and were useless for marketing purposes. Since this single dealership was spending tens of thousands of dollars each month marketing their clients, it was important for them to have a well-focused ad campaign, and the resources spent sending materials to these wrong addresses were completely wasted. On a grander scale, you can imagine what the larger retailers spend for their marketing efforts. Mailings, flyers, and letters can run several dollars a copy after the design, printing, postage, and handling costs are included. Thus, sending thousands of marketing packages each month to clients with an improper address, such as was discovered at this dealership, is a waste of time, resources, and money. Identifying this pattern helped the dealership clean up their data and do a better job at marketing to their clients.

Sometimes the discoveries that you make during a data mining engagement have narrower ramifications that nevertheless turn out to be useful. During this same analysis for the car dealership, we discovered several groups of individuals in the data set who shared the same business phone number. The client acted upon this information and designed a special marketing ad for these groups, offering them free rides to and from work if they scheduled dealership services (e.g., oil change or routine maintenance) on a specific day. The dealership was able to maximize the use of its shuttle-van operations while satisfying a select set of customers through a very focused offering. This was an unexpected result, and it illustrates how serendipitous discoveries can be put to good use.

Improved Operational Procedures

Another arena in which data mining can improve the way an organization functions is within the operations and communications of the organization itself. The organizational structure itself is, of course, one source of information. Organizational structures are typically very hierarchical and rigid. The CEO is at the top level with several supporting VPs at the next level down, and so on (see Figure 1.1(a)). But does this sort of hierarchy really give a complete picture of how an organization functions in operational terms? Usually not. Drawing on social network theories, there are all kinds of subnetworks and informal groups contained within any organization. These subgroups might be defined by how often individuals communicate with others in the group, who works with whom on projects, or where individuals go within the organization to get advice. Taken collectively, all of these form the operational structure of a company, as shown in Figure 1.1(b).

This information is not usually contained within any existing corporate database. Rather, it must be collected through well-engineered questionnaires and communications analyses. Were this information to be collected and analyzed, it could be used to derive a realistic model of the way an organization functions. In cases where this has been done, clients report that this type of information allows them to determine which key business processes are actually being hindered, rather than supported, within the current structure. We have seen many examples of unbalanced interactions among departments within companies that are detrimental to the overall performance of the organization. These include marketing and sales departments having very little interaction with one another, technical engineers dominating the advice-networks of the management staff, and top management in accounting having almost no direct involvement with the rest of the company. Discovery of these unhealthy situations can lead to restructuring that will allow your company to achieve its stated goals.

Figure 1.1 Organizational structures depicting formal and informal networks.

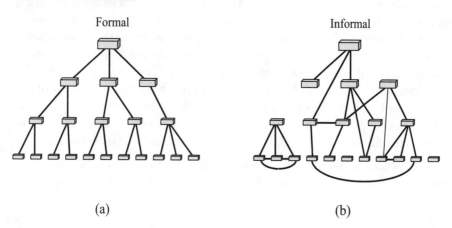

Formal   Informal

(a)   (b)

Identifying Fraud

Corporate security offices and law enforcement agencies have been applying data mining technologies to their data sets for quite some time. They have analyzed all sorts of data sets including telephone toll calls, narcotics operations, financial crime enterprises, criminal organizations, border crossings, street crime patterns, gang relationships, terrorist activities, tax evasion, embezzlement, insider trading, and a wide range of other activities.

In one particular data mining application that we conducted, the goal was to investigate the operations of a suspected money laundering operation. Money laundering is a term applied to any process that is used to take the monetary proceeds of illegal activities and transform them into assets that appear to have been obtained by legitimate means. Profit is the principal motive in such criminal activities, and usually involves cash transactions. In today's marketplace, money laundering is detected most easily at the point in which the funds enter a legitimate financial system.

Regulated financial institutions such as banks, savings and loans, and credit unions are required to comply with the federal statutes imposed on them as stated in the Money Laundering Control Act of 1986. These institutions collect various types of information about cash transactions that are over $10,000 including names, addresses, identification numbers, accounts, and amounts involved. The members of the particular group that we were helping to investigate were all foreign nationals and the monetary proceeds of their money laundering activities were suspected of being tied directly to narcotics operations.

The investigating organization had access to all of the forms listing the cash transactions of this particular group. It soon became apparent that one of the methods they were using to launder their money was to mix the funds in with the legitimate proceeds of a restaurant being run as a front company. Starting with a list of names provided by the law enforcement agency, we were able to identify an ongoing loan-back scheme. The loan-back scheme begins when a corrupt organization takes out a loan to cover business expenses. Collateral for the loan is usually property procured illegally with the original drug money. The approval of the loan serves to legitimize the source of the funds used to purchase the collateral property. The loan is then paid back using "dirty" money. We were in fact able to demonstrate this chain of events by applying data mining techniques to data sets containing information about the financial transactions of the individuals involved.

The investigation also exposed various illegal layering practices (also called structuring) of financial transactions. Recall that by law financial institutions must report any cash transactions of $10,000 or more. Money launderers often try to move money through a series of separate transactions, all falling beneath this $10,000 threshold. In this case we discovered numerous $9500–$9900 deposits made at various banks on the same days by members of this organization (see Figure 1.2). As it turns out, this form of structuring transactions to avoid documentation is a Federal crime that carries severe criminal penalties.

Examining Medical Records

Understanding medical data within a military environment can be particularly useful, especially when it pertains to the disposition and overall health of the troops. As a matter of fact, over 80 percent of the illnesses and incapacitation reported during wartime result not from physical injuries received on the battlefield, but from dysentery, infection, and disease. Planning for treatment of these conditions ahead of time can facilitate medical response and treatment during critical situations. In a medical application we performed for the U.S. Government, we analyzed data records of medical reports and diagnoses made onboard a set of military ships. Using data mining methodologies, we were able to identify several interesting patterns and trends. As an example, we discovered a relatively high incidence of chicken pox among young recruits between the ages of 17 and 19. As you may know, chicken pox in adults can be quite a serious health matter and identification

Figure 1.2 Structuring transactions under $10K in a money laundering operation.

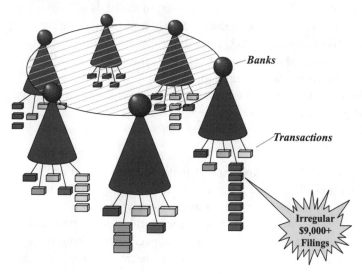

of problematic subgroups within the enlisted population can facilitate the establishment of policies and procedures aimed at minimizing this health threat. Another pattern revealed in our data mining analyses involved the detection of a specific secondary respiratory neoplasm (e.g., cancer) occurring in a set of military units whose soldiers all originated from the same recruiting location. The cases observed all had a particular set of attributes in common that allowed us to identify them as a group. Once the group was characterized, the client was able to perform further investigations of that particular location to determine whether the elevated incidence of this form of cancer could be attributed to the presence of chemicals or other carcinogens in the area.

What Data Mining Is Not

It is important always to bear in mind that the focus of the data mining process is to discover hidden patterns and trends. Once a particular pattern has been identified, it may contain certain characteristics that prompt the data mining practitioner to move forward along a path of further discovery. However, once that particular pattern is identified, it can be described as a known quantity. The pattern may be put to a multitude of uses including becoming the content for a standard report, serving as the training input to a neural network, or being encoded as a rule into an expert system. At this point, the process of discovering that particular pattern is finished. From the perspective of the data mining process, it may be regarded as a known pattern. Further inquiries about known patterns are made only if there is a need to confirm whether they are still valid or if variations of the patterns should be considered. Analytic approaches that search data sets on the basis of known patterns are *not* doing data mining, although they may use inputs from data mining exercises to form the basis of target matches. For this reason, we do not regard techniques that require implementation of rules, predefined training examples, or automated supervised learning to be data mining approaches. This of course does not mean that those techniques are not useful in many instances; it simply means that, in our opinion, those processes do not constitute data mining.

Analysis versus Monitoring

This brings up a distinction that is important to make in information processing between analysis and monitoring. The majority of data mining applications are focused on analyzing information that has been previously collected. For these cases, the data are static and represent the state of the world in some past interval of time. You may review the information at your own pace, confirming the accuracy of the data, making considered decisions about which patterns are important.

The data are not changing while the analysis is being performed. The results generated will therefore be reliable and consistent for that data set. Within reason, you do not concern yourself with the amount of time it takes to make a decision. Rather, you are in the mode of discovering new patterns and are more interested in following hypotheses wherever they may lead.

In contrast, monitoring often involves online pattern matching operations in which incoming data are compared against a set of conditions or boundaries. Monitoring often occurs in real time and involves the processing of data that are continually being updated. What is true one moment may abruptly become out-of-date and invalid the next moment. Monitoring systems have been developed for such application areas as financial markets, air traffic control centers, and nuclear reactors. Monitoring systems often make quick responses in order to take advantage of information as it is being presented. Thus, predictive models and forecasters can be used to help identify critical values, unusual behaviors, and criteria data. These systems are not usually performing data mining since they are not discovering new patterns or classifications. In most cases, the patterns of interest have been identified and generated during a previous analysis and the monitoring process involves detection of matches or violations of those patterns. True data mining is difficult, although not impossible in these types of environments. Several of the tools described in Section III support real-time data feeds and can achieve this level of analysis.

The following are publicized examples from industry that have been characterized as data mining applications. However, as you will see, they do not really fit the definition of data mining since they are dedicated to monitoring rather than discovery of new patterns and trends. They perform pattern matching rather than interactive discovery. Remember to keep in mind that once a pattern has been identified, it can be easily encoded into a rule or report which can then be run across a large quantity of information using other matching, correlation, or classification techniques. Once this stage occurs, data mining is finished and a new type of analysis has begun.

Monitoring Credit Card Transactions

As we all know, fraud is rampant within the consumer industry. In response to this problem, credit card companies have created elaborate systems to curb the misuse of their services. Many of us have been called at home by a credit card company representative inquiring about certain expenditures that do not appear to fit their normal client profile. The more unfortunate among us have endured the unpleasant experience of having a purchase interrupted by the revelation that our card actually has been suspended by the company based on an unusual pattern of recent buying activity. Credit card companies have a lot at stake and it is important for them to discriminate between good and bad transactions. What constitutes a "bad" set of transactions in this context? One example that is used by a large credit card company as a trigger for further analysis is the use of a card to make gasoline purchases more than a certain number of times in a given 24 hour period. As it turns out, criminals who steal credit cards often want to test the cards initially to determine whether they are valid before using them for a large purchase. One particular pattern that has been discovered is that credit card thieves will go to a gas station with pay-at-the-pump service so they can swipe the card to see if it has yet been reported as stolen. This initial test is structured to allow the thief a quick get-away in case the card gets identified as being lost or stolen. Once the thief has confirmed that the card is still operational, he or she usually visits another gas station, fills up the tank, and starts using the card for other purchases. So a small gasoline purchase quickly followed by a series of other gasoline and product purchases is often flagged as a questionable pattern that is identified for further inquiry.

Note that in this case the pattern of gasoline purchases is not being "discovered." Rather, this pattern is already known and is matched against incoming charge data. In cases such as these, the patterns of interest are discovered offline using data mining analyses and are then encoded into the systems for future classifications and matches, usually by a neural network. There is no actual data mining occurring within these online systems, only simple classifications, profile matching, or value boundary exception handling. All the hard work (and fun) of discovering and formulating the profile of the suspicious behavior was performed elsewhere and subsequently encoded into the matching system. (Just a word for the average credit card user—the credit companies know that one corrupt merchant can do much more damage than several individual card holders, partially due to credit card spending limits. Therefore, the companies often devote more of their resources to detecting merchant fraud than individual consumer fraud.)

Monitoring Medical Billing Fraud

One of the most common services provided by medical billing review companies is the ability to detect CPT (Current Procedural Terminology) code unbundling. CPT codes are an established list of five-digit numbers used to identify the medical procedures and services provided by physicians. The unbundling problem occurs when doctors submit their bills listing charges for routine procedures that should be classified under a specific CPT code, but instead are broken up and filed as a combination of several separate CPT codes. Physicians do this because they can get more reimbursement dollars for the sum of the individual procedures than for the single composite service. This behavior is illegal and constitutes insurance fraud, but it occurs on a regular basis. Companies performing review of medical billing for insurance purposes often claim to perform data mining on the submitted bills to look for these filing patterns. In actuality they usually are running some low-level expert systems or neural networks that have been programmed to look for specific types of known patterns. Again, the data mining involving the discovery of the suspicious patterns initially occurred offline and the known patterns were incorporated into a set of rules to be matched automatically against online data.

Marketing with Coupons

Think back to the last time that you bought groceries at the supermarket. Along with your receipt you may have received store coupons for items you purchased that day. You might also have noticed that you received coupons for items you did not purchase, but which might go well with some of the items in your cart. For example, you may have bought a case of soda and received a coupon for potato chips. How would the computer know to generate a potato chip coupon when you did not purchase potato chips that day? Is data mining being performed online as your groceries are being scanned? No. The discovery of sets of items that consumers tend to purchase together is a data mining activity that occurs offline using large data sets comprised of thousands of purchase transactions. Some supermarket chains spend a good deal of time looking at their data in order to understand these purchasing patterns more completely. Stores can take advantage of these known patterns by giving out coupons or placing associated items close to one another in the store in order to increase sales. When you go through the checkout line and receive coupons based on your purchases that day, the computer routine that selects your coupons is merely performing pattern matching on previously discovered patterns.

Avoiding the Oversell

It has been estimated that data mining services will become a $20 billion industry by the year 2000. As always the promise of an emerging field of technology brings excitement, but also the tendency on the part of some to make grandiose claims beyond the scope of the capabilities of the technology. Who can forget the claims in the 1980s that there would be a neural network in every toaster by now? Does anyone remember the promises of automated high-level language processing made by some in the field of artificial intelligence? Clearly these prophecies have not come to pass. This is not to say that either of those technologies was flawed—in fact, each has produced many wonderful innovations that have been a great help in a variety of application areas. The problem was in the overselling. Unfortunately the field of data mining will be no different.

Already we are bombarded with a host of new buzzwords that sound great, but in reality are old ideas being touted as part of the new data mining technology. Let us state from the outset that data mining is not just running correlations, statistics, or a set of sorted reports on a data set. Rather, data mining is a *process* of uncovering *new* patterns and trends within data that would not necessarily be revealed through traditional methods of analysis. Data mining is interactive discovery. You need to bear these caveats in mind as you decide whether or how to incorporate data mining into your arsenal of information technologies. You need to be well informed so that you can use this technology to your organization's full advantage and not be misled into adopting approaches that are not appropriate for your application.

Data mining is a very unique and challenging process. Although consistent principles regarding the data mining process may be identified, to some extent each data mining exercise has its own defining characteristics. There is currently no road map to follow for performing data mining, no cookbook of directions that can anticipate all starting conditions and guarantee a successful outcome. Anyone claiming to sell you a system as a silver bullet that will automate an analysis and always produce the desired answer should be regarded with caution. If it sounds too good to be true, it probably is. In actuality, the process of data mining almost never involves simply running a single application on your data set. Rather, it is a process in which the data mining practitioner utilizes combinations of technologies and methodologies. The person performing this task must be able to think creatively and be flexible in approaching a problem. Since data mining is a very iterative process, the practitioner will not simply be repeating a known scenario, but will constantly refine his/her approach based on outcomes or patterns discovered along the way.

Practical Advice before You Begin

The field of data mining shows exceptional promise in terms of its potential contributions to a host of analytical applications. We have seen our share of successful applications that have provided a significant return on investment. Presumably you have purchased this book in anticipation of learning more about this technology and perhaps using it in applications of your own. Before you begin, however, we would like to offer some cautionary words of advice on some real-world issues that can limit the utility of data mining engagements unless addressed directly.

Justifying the Data Mining Investment

How do you determine whether investment in a data mining system is justified? In some cases the math is fairly straightforward. Consider the amount of money an organization expends on marketing and service-related activities compared to what it gets in return. Given the difference between these numbers, you can derive a reasonable estimate on how much you would expect to improve this bottom line using data mining technologies (see the following sidebar). If there are methods that can be used to expand your marketing campaigns, to reduce fraud, or generally improve your profits, and the amount of improvement exceeds the cost of implementation, then consider it a good investment. Based on our experiences, companies usually look for the investment made in data mining to be about 15–20 percent of value of estimated losses or expected improvements made.

Evaluating Return on Your Data Mining Investment: A Sample Analysis

Sometimes an organization will have estimates of how much money is being wasted on expenditures. For example, in one data mining engagement our customers believed that there was a certain amount of fraud within the operating environment. They were spending over $350,000,000 each year servicing the merchandise that they produced and were receiving approximately 1,800,000 service claims per year. Using some simple arithmetic, the company was spending on average about $194.44 for each claim filed.

Clearly the identification of fraudulent claims within this context could quickly add up to big savings. The client estimated the percentage of fraud to be anywhere between 3 and 8 percent. Thus, the amount of money being paid for fraudulent claims every year was calculated to be between $10,500,000 and $28,000,000. If we take the middle of the road at 5 percent, this equates to $17,500,000.

Using data mining techniques, we were able to identify several critical patterns of fraud for this client very quickly. In this particular situation, one of the patterns found was based on the replacement of parts that were either removed, misplaced, or stolen while in possession of the distributor before the merchandise was actually sold. Since the part was a basic feature of the product and was both a functioning component as

Continued

**Evaluating Return on Your Data Mining Investment:
A Sample Analysis (*Continued*)**

well as a cosmetic feature, customers who eventually purchased the product wanted the part intact. The distributors did not feel obligated to replace the part since the product had not yet been sold when it was lost or stolen. Thus, the distributors decided to charge the cost of replacing the part back to the company as a basic warranty repair. Since these claims were relatively minor charges as compared to other types of work being performed, this fraud scheme was hidden easily among the larger number of legitimate warranty repairs.

Our discovery of this scheme put our clients in a position to save quite a bit on wasteful expenditures. They calculated that the resources spent on this data mining engagement provided at least a 50-to-1 return on investment. This calculation does not even take into consideration the future reduction of losses due to the identification of these patterns. This was not a bad return for a relatively small-scale investment.

Virtually any organization involved with communication, retail, insurance, finance, commerce, or transportation activities has areas of vulnerability in which fraud can occur. The previous example was just one aspect of one area within that particular company. Many frauds go undetected for years because they are hidden carefully among large numbers of normal business dealings. No wonder our insurance rates, car prices, and medical costs are so astronomical. As consumers, we are forced to cover the fraud, waste, and abuse of services through increased premiums and costs of products. This equates to billions upon billions of dollars lost every year by commercial businesses to fraudulent activities.

In many cases, fraud, malpractice, and malfeasance succeed because people do not know how to interpret their data sets or recognize the telltale symptoms. The stories we read in the newspaper about investors or accountants running off to Tahiti with large quantities of money are special cases and thankfully do not occur very frequently. So you should not be surprised if there are no million-dollar patterns exposed when you first apply data mining to your environment. The majority of theft and fraud is carried out in a large number of relatively small exchanges. Thus, instead of perpetrators trying to take advantage of organizations for millions of dollars at a single time, fraud usually is achieved through a series of frequent claims or transactions with relatively small amounts of money being stolen on any one occasion. Over an extended time period an organization may pay out millions of dollars, although not in one single chunk. This sort of fraud is of course subtle and not directly detectable through usual methods of oversight. Data mining approaches can be applied to these sorts of problems with great success at relatively low cost. The investment in data mining usually is repaid quickly with multiplicative returns when applied to these types of problems.

Working Efficiently: Timeliness Is a Virtue

A data mining engagement should not be a lifelong commitment. Although some engagements can go on for an extended period of time, you should expect to see tangible results within a period of days or weeks at the most. The only barrier that should reasonably bar you from this goal is lack of access to data sets. If you do not see discernible results within a reasonable period, it is time to go back to first principles. Perhaps the data mining tool being used is too limited in the features it provides. Perhaps the data are not being modeled in the most effective way. Perhaps the scope of the analysis is too broad or too narrow. Perhaps the whole analytical approach is inappropriate for the problem at hand. Or, finally, perhaps there just are not any interesting or surprising patterns in the data set.

On rare occasions we have analyzed data sets that contained no interesting patterns. This was due either to poor selection of the data extracted for analysis or to poor quality control in the original collection process. Typically these situations can be identified in advance and avoided, especially if you can help guide and control the initial identification and selection of the data to be used in the engagement. We have seen some self-proclaimed experts use the "bad data" excuse inappropriately. They often plead this defense either to stall for more time or to request additional data in the hopes of eventually producing an interesting result with the wrong methodology. In either case, the data mining practitioner should be able to explain and demonstrate the reasons behind a failure to produce usable results.

The beauty of data mining is that you begin to see patterns almost immediately if you apply the methodologies properly. In most of our data mining experiences, we have confirmed patterns of interest to our clients within several days of the start of the engagement. In one particular engagement, it took less than four hours to completely build and test models once we had the data. Furthermore, after producing our initial results we were able to reconfigure our models on-the-fly to search for other patterns of interest to the client. Does this mean that we are exceptionally brilliant people blessed with otherworldly intellect? We would like to think so, but probably not. More likely it is that we chose the most appropriate approach to the problem and so were able to produce the most usable results in a timely fashion. Remember, it is not always the army with the best weapons that wins the war, but the army that knows how best to use the weapons at hand.

Establishing the Limitations of Your Data Resources

Before you begin an engagement you should ascertain whether there are indeed sufficient data sources available to make the effort worthwhile. In the worst case, investigation of this question may reveal that very little of the critical information is coded into electronic format so as to be accessible to analytical tools. We noted one example of this problem during a counter-terrorism application performed for a U.S. Government agency. In one office that we dealt with was a lovely woman nearing retirement age who had a wealth of knowledge about the operations of a wide range of organizations important to the agency and, of course, to our national security. Stacks upon stacks of hard copy files were piled high on her desk and she knew exactly where everything was located. She could pull out any piece of appropriate information required to respond to a situation faster than you could conceive of doing it electronically. Perhaps you can think of similarly indispensable people within your own organization whose safety is no doubt prayed for every night. This is fine as far as it goes, but for obvious reasons it is preferable that the information be coded electronically and be made accessible to more than one individual in the group.

Before beginning any data mining exercise, you will need to determine from the outset that this type of roadblock will not hinder your progress. You must have accurate, well-coded, and properly maintained information in order to produce reasonable results. Additionally, you must make sure that the organization is going to give you permission to access all of the information that you will need to perform the analysis. If the organization has not already made an investment in this technology before you begin, it does not bode well for your chances of success. The two things we generally hope for are that the data are represented in an electronic format and that they are made available to the analyst. Once these two hurdles are overcome, at least some degree of data mining can usually be performed.

Keep in mind that you do not necessarily need online and interactive access to the data sources. In most cases, the data mining is not done in real time. Therefore, static extractions of data will satisfy the requirements of most data mining applications. In one particular engagement that we performed for a state agency, we needed to collect the real-property/assets records for a particular county. After several phone calls we jumped in a car, drove over to the county court records facility, and picked up a nine-track reel tape containing our requested information. This was subsequently loaded into our computing system as a local data set and we were able to perform our analyses successfully. Since property records are fairly stable and do not change significantly on a daily basis, we were able to use the information to produce reliable results for the better part of a year.

Defining the Problem Up Front

When performing data mining, you need to have an understanding of what things are of interest or importance. This allows you to set the boundaries of the problem space. If you set your focus too narrowly, you will miss the objective. Of course it is possible to err in the other direction as well, and in fact this is the more common mistake. Typically what happens with data mining projects is that the original scope is often very generalized and nonspecific in its definition. Sometimes in these cases the client may send you on a fishing expedition to find something "interesting." This is not necessarily a problem if the analyst is careful to narrow the scope continually as the engagement proceeds. One way to approach problem definition is to consider and discuss hypothetical examples with your client before analysis begins. By devoting time to these exchanges in the early stages of the process, you can develop a more accurate sense of the sorts of findings that are likely to be of interest in a particular application.

We have found that clients initially like to have a quick, definitive success in a data mining engagement before committing any additional resources to the project. As proof-of-principle successes are provided and the client becomes more educated about the potential usefulness of the data mining approach, new and more ambitious analyses will be requested. Thus, if successful early on, the data mining process will likely become iterative in its development. What usually happens is that you may start by looking for large-scale patterns that confirm that the approach selected is valid. Once the initial results have been presented, a more directed and focused effort can be initiated.

By taking the analysis in stages, hopefully you will avoid the pitfall of setting objectives that cannot be met. One mistake that is often made by analysts is in promising more insights and results than can be produced in a single engagement. If the application area is a complex one for which there are many classes of questions to be answered, you are well-advised to break the problem up into component parts. The best approach is to do a series of smaller-scale applications that might eventually be combined into a final system once useful results are produced. Do not bite off more than you can chew. Start small and make additions to the system only if they add value to the application. Your customer will see the potential of what is being done and will appreciate your approach.

Knowing Your Target Audience

One important issue that you will want to consider when formulating your approach to an engagement is the composition of the target audience. Who will be the recipient of the results? What will the results represent? What are the repercussions of the data mining engagement likely to be? Always keep your target audience in mind when performing your data mining activities. The approach used to solve the problem must satisfy the intended recipient. The data mining practitioner needs to know if the results are going to be used for internal review, informational purposes, formal presentations, or official publications. There are a wide range of issues to address when determining the target audience.

We have worked with everyone from high-tech computer programmers and intelligence analysts to corporate executives and members of a jury. Although we will not discuss presentation techniques until Chapter 5, we will point out that the degree of detail that is appropriate will vary among different types of target audiences. In some cases, the audience just wants a general overview of where, who, and how much. In other cases, the recipient will want to see every detail regarding the analytical process. Some audience members may even want to become collaborators in the analysis and may suggest alternative representation strategies, different analytical models, and what-if scenarios. You need to be careful and select the correct mixture of methods and techniques to match the requirements of your target audience.

In one application that we did for the banking industry, we had an interesting interaction with the corporate personnel who were responsible for collecting the data used in the analysis. By presenting the results in ways that made sense to them, they were able to contribute insights into how these data could actually be used in future data mining applications. This helped to increase their confidence in the process because they understood how their efforts were feeding into an analysis that had practical implications. We have also seen similar reactions in other industries where the results of the data mining efforts were used to justify existing data collection activities and, more importantly, help guide future collection efforts.

In another application, we were working with a set of nontechnical lawyers (could there be any other kind?) on a grand jury case involving the prosecution of methamphetamine dealers. In this application we had two target audiences. Our ultimate target audience was the jury. However, in the early stages of the project we had to work closely with the prosecuting attorneys and educate them about the analyses and presentation formats being used. In this particular case, we were looking at the telephone call patterns of the defendants—about 120,000 records. The attorneys needed to feel comfortable with the fact that the data were being accurately depicted and that nothing was being changed or altered in its meaning during our analysis. Once they accepted that our representation of the data was valid, the next step was to coach them on the different types of analyses that could be performed. Much of what we were doing was completely new to them, and they were not sure initially about what questions to ask. Since they were the ones who would eventually explain, justify, and defend the diagrams (e.g., patterns) to the jury, it was imperative that the information being presented be crystal clear to them. We started with very simple analyses and proceeded slowly. The more exposure they received, the more confident they became. When all was said and done, they had a very successful trial and will now be likely to use similar data mining analyses in future cases.

Anticipating and Overcoming Institutional Inertia

Because of the intransigence of established institutional policies and practices, it may be difficult for an organization to act on the results of data mining analyses, even when those results are quite dramatic and have serious implications for ongoing operations. During one data mining engagement, we worked for a major insurance company, helping them look for patterns of fraud within their claims database. This particular engagement was focused on the detection of corrupt doctors and lawyers who were submitting fraudulent claims for reimbursement. The insurance company personnel in charge of supporting this effort were from a Special Investigative Unit (SIU) within the company comprised of people with backgrounds in law enforcement, data analysis, and computer science. As the engagement progressed, we quickly discovered that fraud was rampant. Soon we were identifying high-value targets faster than the company could deal with them under their established procedures. Although there were literally millions of dollars at stake, the company was not in a position to expand the SIU and provide necessary resources to follow up on many of these leads, nor were they willing to change existing filing procedures to reduce some of the fraud. The rationale given was that they had identified enough targets to keep them busy for the foreseeable future and would focus only on the extreme cases. The company regarded the fraud as an annoying but calculated overhead cost.

Lest you think this is an isolated example, consider these events that occurred in a separate data mining engagement. We were using a database representing a large portion of the client base for a life insurance carrier and were looking at benefits paid for death claims. During the early stages of demonstrating a prototype data mining application, it became apparent that there were numerous people who had multiple claims submitted to the company. These individuals were not the family members or relatives of the deceased, but the actual (or shall we say alleged) people who were supposedly deceased. This was obviously a clear-cut form of insurance fraud. Nevertheless the company was not willing to endure the effort and expense of changing their existing policies to avoid these situations. Further, the company opted not to pursue many of the fraudulent claims identified since they believed that the cost of prosecuting the cases would have exceeded the returns.

Many readers may find these stories difficult to contemplate. However, take a step back and think about how your organization would respond if a set of threat patterns (e.g., fraud, embezzlement, and process improvement) were suddenly identified. If the problem is circumscribed you might be able to solve it by purchasing hardware, installing some new software, or changing specific vendors. In all likelihood, though, the problem would be more widespread and efforts to solve it would require changes in organization, personnel, and policy that are slow to be realized. Also, it would have to be determined whether the investment in these changes significantly offsets the cost of the damages or improvements identified in the first place. Thus you should be prepared to be realistic in terms of the benefits that can be derived by the use of data mining technology. Since our involvement with the different insurance companies, they have made some significant improvements and progress is occurring, albeit slowly.

In describing these events it is not our intention to discourage anyone from doing data mining analyses. Quite the contrary. As we will show throughout the book, data mining has been used in any number of problem sets to great effect. We simply present these vignettes as a reminder that, no matter how powerful an analysis, it will only be successful to the degree that its results may be put to some use. Thus, in making the decision to use data mining or any other form of analysis, you should give consideration to the types of data available for analysis and the types of outcomes that will be most useful within the context of the particular application area.

Summing Up

In this chapter we have given you a definition of data mining, provided some examples of the successful use of data mining in various application areas, and given examples of analytical information processing techniques that might be misconstrued as data mining approaches. In addition we have provided some cautionary information that you will want to consider before beginning any data mining engagements so that you can avoid potential pitfalls that might lie along your analytical path. Now that this background context has been established, you are ready to begin thinking about the mechanics of the real-world data mining exercise. In the next chapter we move into a more technical discussion of the process of data modeling which takes place at the start of all data mining analyses.

UNDERSTANDING DATA MODELING   2

Before you actually begin developing a data mining system, you will first need to think about how to model the data in order to get the most from your information sources. Data modeling is done in order to translate the raw data structures into a format that can be used for data mining. Developing a good data model is one of the most important aspects of data mining. The models you create will determine the types of results that can be discovered in your analysis. By characterizing your data in terms of types and formats, you will know from the outset what your data modeling options are, and therefore what types of discoveries you can expect to make. A good data mining practitioner should know what types and classes of patterns might be identified before the first data record is ever processed. The modeling process determines which features of the data will be made available to the user for analysis. If the data have not been properly modeled, then critical relationships contained within the data set will not be represented correctly and important patterns will go undetected, thus undermining the likelihood of success.

As it turns out, there are a few common themes and approaches that can be used to characterize most all data sets—you will soon realize how similar these characterizations can be across seemingly disparate domains. Once you understand these concepts, you can look at new data sets and immediately determine which methods of modeling are going to be the most beneficial. Once you master a set of modeling approaches, you will be able to mine virtually any domain that you encounter without having to reinvent new methods or techniques each time. Remember that *data are data are data*. At a certain level of abstraction, the particular domain of your problem is irrelevant. Given data of a certain type and format, there will be certain modeling approaches that are more appropriate than others.

In this chapter we review some of the basics of the modeling process. Before you can determine what type of models to build, you must first establish what kinds of questions are important in the analysis. Once you have some ideas about the initial direction of the analysis, you will begin to define your data model(s). You will first define object classes, or conceptual categories, as well as the relationships that will exist between them. Then you will refine object classes by assigning attributes that further describe and characterize individual objects. In building your model you can use data abstraction techniques as well as the representation of metadata. Although there are any number of ways you might choose to model your data for a given application, the models you build will generally fall into two categories—descriptive or transactional. The discussion on descriptive and transactional modeling explores the differences between the two, illustrating the types of information that may be derived from each. Finally, the type of model you choose for your analysis may depend upon whether you are looking for patterns within or across domains. To illustrate some of the differences between these types of engagements, we include an overview on discovering intra- and inter-domain patterns.

Establishing the Goals of the Analysis

When modeling the data, first consider the types of questions that need to be answered in the data mining process. Spend some time talking with the client to determine the initial direction of the analysis. Figure out what sorts of findings would be most helpful to the organization. In many engagements that we have done, the client has not had any specific goals in mind at the outset of the project but rather regarded the engagement as an exploratory exercise, hoping simply to receive some "interesting" results. In these types of cases, you can still do some initial work that can give you some guidance in the early stages of the analysis. Begin by examining the data structure itself and making a few observations. Some general-purpose questions to consider at this stage include the following:

- What kinds of potential relationships or trends might be considered interesting or important?

- Do questions tend to be formulated around any particular variables contained within the data set?

- Does the organization of the data structure contain any natural breaks among conceptual categories that might be of interest?

- Are some variables naturally nested within others?

- Can any variables be omitted from the model on the basis of too much missing data?

- Do certain variables contain too little variance to be useful?

- Can you characterize important variables in terms of how many discrete values they take on in the database?

- Will you need to merge data from more than one source in order to answer questions adequately?

Based on your initial answers to these (and other) questions, you can begin making decisions about which portions of the data to include in the modeling process and which to omit. Remember that as you proceed with the analysis, you can always go back and restructure your model(s) to include different components of the original data set. In fact you may even want to set up a series of models so that you can more precisely target different classes of questions. This is a very flexible process—you have a lot of options.

Conceptualizing the Problem: A Grocery Store Example

Suppose your data mining engagement involves analysis of retail records from a grocery store. You might begin by dividing the products sold in the store into conceptual categories. What conceptual organization should you choose? At a broad level you could begin by dividing the store goods into two categories of food and nonfood items. Within the food category, you could further divide items into perishable and nonperishable products. But suppose the client is interested in the more specific question of analyzing sales of store-brand versus name-brand goods. In that event, you would largely be concerned with only the nonperishable items, and you could exclude produce, dairy, and meat products from the analysis. Or suppose that the client wants to determine whether there are certain areas of the store that shoppers are less likely to visit. In that case you might create categories based on the position of items within a spatial grid, for instance coding items according to the aisles on which they are shelved within the store.

Imagine that the client does not care about the sales of particular types of products, per se, but is instead more interested in whether rates of sales vary throughout the day. In that case you might confine your analysis to the sales transactions themselves, creating categories of comparison based on hour of the day rather than on type of product being purchased. Taking the example one step further, imagine that the client wants to know whether certain products are more likely to be purchased on the weekend than on weekdays. To answer that question, you would need to model both the types of products being sold as well as the times and dates of the purchases.

These variations can go on and on. The point we are making here is that there will almost always be any number of ways in which you could impose a conceptual organization onto a problem. The one you choose should be determined by the questions that you are trying to answer. If the questions of interest cover a broad range of topics, you will likely need to formulate several approaches to address them all adequately.

Object Modeling

Our approach to data modeling assumes an object-oriented framework in which information is represented in terms of objects, their descriptive attributes, and the relationships existing between object classes. When you begin your modeling process, one of the first choices you will make is which records in your data set to designate as object classes, which to use as attributes of those object classes, and whether to designate any linked relationships among object classes. In this section we describe the types of information that may be represented at the three levels; object classes, attributes, and links.

Broadly speaking, object classes may be thought of as conceptual categories. Objects within a class can symbolize real-world entities such as people, places, and things. The decision of which variables to designate as object classes is critically important, and some choices are usually obvious. Typically, you will choose tangible entities for which descriptive information is represented in the data set. These entities can usually exert influence, be affected by some other entity, or interact with the world as measured by variables contained within the data set. Some examples of variables that might be set up as object classes include the following:

Individuals can be arrested.

The quality of **products** can be recorded.

Bank **accounts** can have a balance.

Telephone **calls** can be logged.

Contracts can be reviewed.

Credit ratings of **vendors** can be checked.

Sales figures for different **stores** can be compared.

Figure 2.1 shows several examples of the ways in which object classes can be used in data mining applications.

Object classes can also be more abstract in nature and may include titles, roles, values, dates, transactions, activities, or stages, to name a few. You should not necessarily limit yourself to the obvious choices, but rather think in terms of how to discover the relationships of interest in the data mining engagement. The use of more abstract object classes, where appropriate, can provide very powerful insights into the data because they impart a different perspective about what is being represented. Ultimately this allows you to model the events, behaviors, and processes about real-world entities.

Figure 2.1 Examples of real world and conceptual object classes.

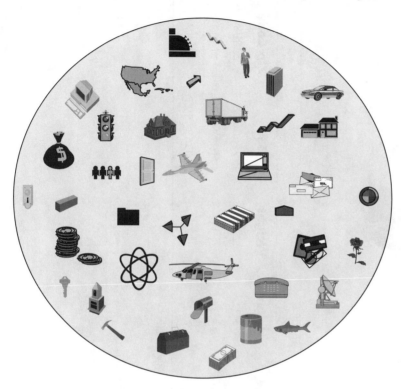

Assigning Attributes to Objects

Once an object class is designated, you will want to stipulate a set of attributes that may be used to describe it or characterize its behavior. For example, in the case of an object class containing information about individuals, one might designate such attributes as height, weight, age, gender, address, or whatever other descriptors are available for each individual in the data set. As the data are modeled, there will be a representation for each individual in the object class that contains a particular value for each of those attributes as extracted from the original data record. Attributes are primarily used to distinguish individual objects within a class from one another and help guide the subsequent analyses. The values applied to an attribute contain information about that object.

Say you want to explore the relationship between height and weight in men and women and you were given a data set that contains the types of data records shown in Table 2.1.

Table 2.1 A Sample Set of Data Records

Name	Age	Gender	Income	Height	Weight	SSN	Zip Code
Jim Brown	32	M	35,000	6'1"	220	499760022	22008
Sue Jones	45	F	100,000	5'4"	135	571023487	11398
Tim Green	55	M	98,000	5'11"	175	220358559	32097

You would probably begin with a model in which each individual was designated as an object class. Identifying labels for each class would be drawn from column 1 corresponding to name. To each object class you would assign attributes of gender, height, and weight, the values of which would be drawn from columns 3, 5, and 6, respectively for each individual object. Thus, Jim Brown would be assigned attribute values of M for gender, 6'1" for height, and 220 for weight in your model. In this case you would not bother to assign attributes based on age, income, SSN, or Zip code since these pieces of information are not relevant to the question at hand.

Suppose the direction of your analysis changed, however, and you became interested in the relationship between gender and income in your data set. Then the information about height and weight is no longer relevant. In that instance you would create a new model in which individuals had attributes for gender and income to be drawn from columns 3 and 4, respectively. That is, you would construct your model so as to include only the information that is relevant to your analysis. In many traditional business analyses, little thought is given to the possibility of representing the components of a data record as separate objects. Rather, the entire record is treated and processed as a single entity. For the purposes of data mining, however, you will need to rethink this approach. As the preceding examples illustrate, the information you choose to include from your records should depend entirely on the types of questions you are trying to answer.

Being Creative with Attribute Assignment

There are any number of ways in which you can define attributes so as to show relationships and similarities among objects. Consider the following example. Suppose we had a set of objects that includes a trash can, notebook binder, coffee cup, briefcase, and file cabinet. It might be hard to imagine that these diverse objects are related. However we can model them in ways that will allow us to capitalize on their similarities. For example, each has a related shape, size, material, and purpose. Some of these objects are cylindrical and some are cubic. The size of the coffee cup is small relative to the briefcase, trash can, and notebook, which are all medium sized. In turn, these objects are all smaller than the file cabinet, which can be characterized as large. The materials of the objects can also take on different values including plastic, leather, ceramic, or metal. Now think about the intended use of each item. A coffee cup holds liquids, a briefcase holds documents, a trash can holds wastes, a notebook holds papers, and a file cabinet holds folders. Thus, these items are all similar in terms of intended purpose, and this information can also be coded in terms of an attribute. The assignment of these attributes to these object entities will allow us to filter, cluster, and sort on these variables later during the analysis. Figure 2.2 shows how the objects can be clustered on the basis of shared attribute values.

Maintaining Nesting Integrity

Values of attributes must be completely nested within one instantiation of the object class. That is, for the purpose of describing a single object, an attribute can support only one value at a time within the model. For example, if your data set contains two or more different values of the weight of a particular person, there is no way for the system to resolve which of the two values is valid for that attribute. Such a situation might indeed occur if your data set contains a series of weight recordings

Figure 2.2 Clustering diverse objects by attributes.

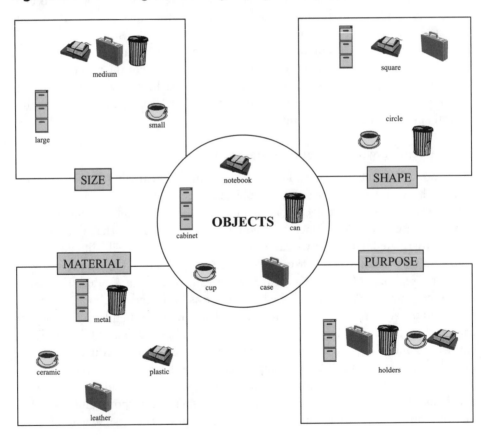

made at different time intervals for a group of individuals. If you simply assign an attribute of weight to individuals in your data set in this case, however, the actual weight recorded for each individual will simply be the last weight encountered in the raw data—the other weight recordings will be lost. An attribute may be assigned to an object class only if each member of the class has only one represented value of that attribute within the data set. Effectively, your model contains only the most recent belief state of the attribute.

At first this seems like a serious limitation. What if the representation of weight changes across time is important for the analysis? If that is the case, then we need to reconsider the entire analytical model. Apparently what we really need to represent is a one-to-many relationship between the object (individual person) and the attribute (values of weight). This may be achieved by designating weight as its own object class and then establishing a relation between the classes of persons and weight through other methods. This type of situation in which the actual value or the change in value is important to the outcome represents a *state-based analysis* (see Figure 2.3). You could also create the same identical records with the only difference being the weight. Alternatively you might set up two different weight attributes for each object in the class, weight-t1 and weight-t2, to correspond to these values.

Being Flexible in Attribute Modeling

The state-based example is interesting because it illustrates that the decision to designate a data field as an object class is, at some level, largely arbitrary. Any field in a data record can be used to create an object class. Furthermore, classes and their

Figure 2.3 Example of state-based modeling of attributes.

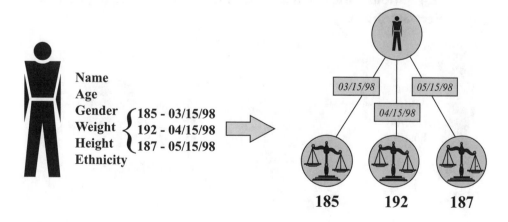

attributes can be intermixed to a large degree during the modeling process. You can have examples of a data field being designated as an attribute of an object class or as an object class all on its own, or both simultaneously (see Figure 2.4). It all depends on the goals of the analysis.

To illustrate, consider the representation of location information. You might want to create a model in which franchise stores for your company are designated as an object class with city as an attribute. In that case, the class will contain a separate object for each franchise, and each of those objects will have stored with it the city location of the franchise. On the other hand, if your analysis is going to be based on geographical location, you might want to represent location at a higher level. In that event you could create an object class of city which contains one object for each city represented in the data set. (Or you might want to do both at the same time.) It is important to keep these sorts of notions in mind so that you can adopt a very flexible approach to modeling.

Modeling Relationships among Object Classes

Once you have determined which parts of the data are to be designated as object classes and attributes, you can also establish links or relationships between object classes that are essentially objects themselves. Relationships allow you to associate two object classes based on some type of common characteristic found in your data. Since relationships are objects, they may also be assigned attributes. Assigning attributes to relationships can be a powerful tool in describing behavior. For example, associations between objects may be linked by such information as date, time, source, role, or activity type existing between them in the data set. Objects within a single data record may be linked or links can be established across

Figure 2.4 Various assignments of data fields to roles of object class and object attribute.

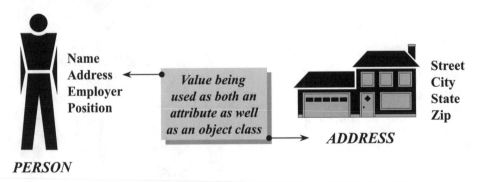

separate data tables. Multiple relationships can be established between any pair of objects and the values assigned to the attributes of the relationships can be unique for that particular connection. For example, a person can be connected with a location, say five times, but in each instance the connection could represent a different date. Thus, the role between the objects can be established through the relationships without violating the one-value-per-attribute rule.

Relationships are completely separate and orthogonal to one another. That is, a relationship is established or created without regard to any other links in the system. Links can be unique in their representation or can duplicate pre-existing information. We think of relationships as a form of abstraction and although some data mining tools do not explicitly support the representation of links between object classes, we have found this capability to be invaluable in many of our data mining applications. Links provide yet another dimension that can be analyzed for patterns and trends. This type of representation is especially important when creating models to be used in link analysis visualization systems.

Forming Composite Representations Using Data Abstraction

When representing the actual values that are used to comprise the objects and their attributes, it is important to keep in mind that the information can be abstracted from the low-level detail into composite representations. This technique is useful early on in the analytical process when you are trying to get an initial understanding of the classes of relationships and patterns existing within the data set.

Composite representations are formed by combining all objects with a similar user-selected characteristic (e.g., weights, dates, and locations) into a single object. The main attribute of the composite object then becomes the count of the number of underlying objects. Used appropriately, this can provide a top-down view of the range of diversity represented in the data set on dimensions of interest. This type of abstraction also permits the processing of more data at a time within the data mining application. Abstraction comes with a cost, however. The more abstraction you use, the less detail you will be able to access in the top level of the analysis. This is not a very serious concern since you can always drill-down to view the individual data elements that were used to construct the composite object if need be. Abstractions typically are used to help detect hot spots within the data to guide the selection of proactive slices of data. (Proactive extraction will be discussed further in the next chapter.)

Blending Actual and Abstract Values in Your Model

Sometimes you may want to include both actual and abstract attribute values in your model. We used this technique of blending actual and abstract values in a retail application. In this analysis we represented the customer and the individually purchased items as object classes within our data model. We then included the total dollar amount for the purchase rounded to the nearest $100 as an object (e.g., abstraction) in the model. This allowed us to determine quickly the distribution and volumes of individual product sales as subsets of entire transactions. This also provided us with the ability to look for subnetworks or classifications of buying patterns that might not have been thought of at the outset. These discoveries were possible because we included the abstract object class of "dollar amount" from the transactions.

Forming Abstractions Based on Attribute Values

Attribute values, especially numeric values, can also be abstracted into groupings (also called bins or categories). Thus, if the dollar amount of a purchase order or the age of a customer were used in a data model, it would be hard to find patterns when dealing with values as specific as $135.98 or 53. In these cases it is often useful to segment numeric attribute values into a set of predefined groups that permit more generalized pattern detection (for instance in groups of $0–$49, $50–$99, etc.). The original values should still be maintained or available for reference in a canonical data source, but the actual analysis would be performed on the abstracted values. These groupings occur most often for continuous valued data sets (e.g., numbers), but can realistically be applied to any type of data. Many OLAP systems use this type of structuring technique.

The range and size of the segments you choose will depend on the values represented in the data set and their distribution across that range. The number of segments should not be too small or too large. Suppose you wanted to form groups of dollar amounts less than $500. What intervals should you choose? In this case you would probably break the range into $25, $50, or $100 increments. If the range extended to $100,000 then it would be more appropriate to use $1000 or $5000 increments. You do not want to make the segments so small that every discrete value of the attribute forms its own grouping; that would defeat the purpose of doing the abstraction in the first place. On the other hand, if the segment size is too large you will miss critical patterns. One rule of thumb that we like to use is to look for a value that will generate about 10–25 natural groupings of reasonable size (ignoring outliers). Thus, if the majority of your values are between 1–100 with a few more values at 200, 600, and 700, then use 11 groups. Ten groups will represent values from 1–100 and one group will contain everything over 100. This concept applies for both upper and lower outlier bounds (see Figure 2.5).

Figure 2.5 Using abstraction to represent numeric attributes.

ORIGINAL	GROUPED
$149.98	$140
$109.99	$100
$126.60	$120
$113.43	$110
$143.35	$140
$105.14	$100
$352.49	$150+
$139.95	$130
$103.12	$100
$148.59	$140
$121.02	$120
$498.39	$150+

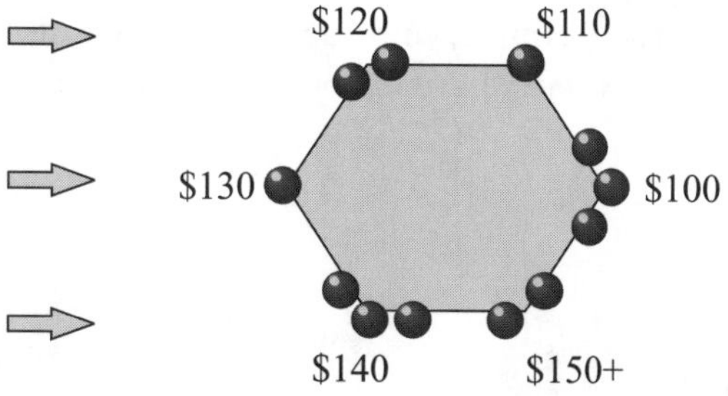

$120 $110

$130 $100

$140 $150+

This principle may also be applied to qualitative data for which there are natural levels of abstraction such as separate geographical regions. For example, stores are located in districts, districts are in cities, cities are in states, states are in regions, and regions are in zones. Many of the decision support systems used in OLAP applications provide facilities for modeling with this type of abstraction.

Working with Metadata

Using metadata is very important when performing data mining because metadata can add significant value to your analysis. Our definition of metadata is slightly different from that used in the context of AI and database systems descriptions. Basically, we refer to metadata as data *within* data as well as data *about* data. Part of becoming a good data mining practitioner is the ability to recognize this additional information and think of how to put it to use. The goal is to be able to exploit the metadata in a way that makes sense for your application and yields interpretable results. It would be impossible to list all of the different types of information and their related metadata, but there are a few in particular that occur commonly. Specifically, we will discuss the use of dates, values, names, and addresses.

Deriving Metadata from Dates

Many data records contain information about dates. In and of itself, a date is a very specific instance of time denoting when a particular event or set of events occurred.

The events could be anything from credit card transactions to phone calls to the submission of billing invoices. Analyses performed on these types of data normally include only the dates of the actual events of interest. With this approach we can quickly tell which events occurred on the same date, but this may not be adequate for data mining purposes. Instead, it may be necessary to abstract beyond the raw data presented. As an example, consider the following six dates. See if you can figure out what these six dates have in common, assuming a YYYYMMDD format.

19950228

19960220

19970211

19980224

19990216

20000307

As you think about this problem, you begin to realize that there is more information contained within a date than initially meets the eye. In fact we can derive well over 15 different types of metadata about dates, which can then be used to help correlate and refine the data for pattern detection and discovery. Many of these are illustrated in Figure 2.6. Not all of these dimensions are readily apparent from the

Figure 2.6 Metadata derived from date information.

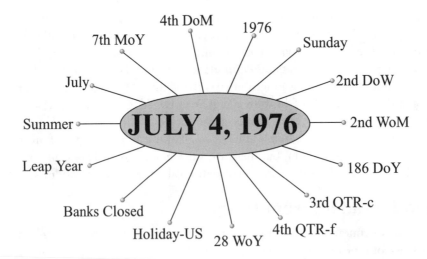

simple structure provided from a date and they must be calculated by alternative methods. Many database systems can help satisfy the conversion task, but in our experience conversion is usually conducted after the fact through external processing. The conversion algorithms are not very complicated and can be implemented quickly in most scripting or programming languages. There are also some commercial data translation software packages that can be used to support the metadata extraction process.

The abbreviations in Table 2.2 are used in Figure 2.6.

Extracting Month and Day Information

There are some very obvious types of metadata that can be extracted from a date to help expose patterns and trends. One of the easiest date decompositions to perform is based on month. In our example of 760704 presented in Figure 2.6, we can quickly determine that month of year (MOY) is July. If we were to sort a set of sales data by month in an analysis, we could quickly see what parts of the year contain peaks and valleys of activity, yielding a high-level picture of seasonal sales trends. We have used the MOY variable extensively in data mining applications. Some examples include the following:

- Looking for seasonal outbreaks of particular diseases in epidemiology applications.

- Determining whether financial filings correlate with cash-crop harvest periods in narcotics and money laundering applications.

- Understanding the replacement of warranted parts that have failed in inventory control applications.

Returning to our example, we can also determine the day of the week (DOW) by decomposing the date further. The DOW for 760704 is a Sunday. Note that the DOW must be calculated from the date rather than being obtained directly as we did for the month and year. Now we can start to expose more detail regarding potential patterns based on DOW. For instance, we could look at weekend versus

Table 2.2 Metadata Abbreviations Used in Figure 2.6

DOW—Day of Week	DOM—Day of Month	DOY—Day of Year
DOQ—Day of Quarter	WOQ—Week of Quarter	WOY—Week of Year
WOM—Week of Month	MOY—Month of Year	Year
QTR-f—Quarter Fiscal	QTR-c—Quarter Calendar	Season/Holiday/Leap

weekday calling trends, correlate purchases to pay periods, or review daily network traffic on a web site. It is interesting how something as simple as a DOW can be used to reveal behaviors that were previously hidden within the data. At this point you could also combine the MOY and DOW to get specific patterns over an extended time period.

Using Dates as Analytical Pivot Points

Date information may also be exploited as a pivot point during a temporal analysis. This is useful when you are trying to correlate events with respect to some significant activity. For some data mining work that we did on insider trading activities, the release date of an earnings statement for a company became the pivot point, and all trades performed on the stock during designated time periods before and after the announcement were reviewed for questionable activities. Patterns of stock sales revealed that certain key officials were trading illegally using insider information. Depending on whether the company was declaring profits or losses we saw corresponding buy and sell activities for these key people. These patterns would not have been identified if we had not used a date pivot method for analyzing the data.

So have you determined what the six dates in our example have in common? The answer is that they have all occurred in the first quarter of the calendar year, each on a Tuesday, and 47 days before Easter (our pivot date), which is the first Sunday after the full moon after the Spring Equinox. This of course locks us in on Fat Tuesday during Mardi Gras. For most of you, this was not an obvious answer and it shows that indeed there are a lot of data within data. Now, suppose that other significant events had occurred on all of these dates—we would be able to predict a similar event occurring at some future point in time. (In deference to the statisticians, it would be inappropriate to assign a confidence value to this prediction. More on this point later in Chapter 6.)

Deriving Metadata from Specific Values

The extraction of metadata from a value such as an identification number, dollar amount, or communication frequency will vary depending on the source information. Just about every type of number contains information in addition to its face value. For example, the Vehicle Identification Number (VIN) located on the dashboard, engine block, and frame of your car can generally be used to find out very specific details including make, model, manufacturing location, type, style, number of cylinders, and so forth of your automobile. VINs are also assigned with error checking built in so that it is quite unlikely that you would be able to make up a valid VIN unless you knew the correct sequence.

Similarly, information relating to validity and issue location can be ascertained from a social security number. The algorithms for determining the validity of numbers are obviously sensitive, but they do exist and can be used to generate metadata about the numbers. To use some other examples, if you know the communication frequency of a signal, you can derive information about the type of equipment used to generate the signal. Dollar amounts can provide information about the nature of financial transactions. Serial numbers can be used to determine where and when a product was made, which may lead to information about where it was sold. Invalid values of physiological measures can be identified out of prespecified ranges, and so on. To the degree that you can identify what sorts of metadata might be gleaned from the values of the attributes in your model, your data mining efforts can take advantage of the information.

Deriving Metadata from Names and Addresses

You can also generate metadata from the information contained within names and addresses. To begin, the names of people and organizations can easily be distinguished. Thus, if a car dealership sends out a marketing brochure to its client base, it makes sense to send materials only to individuals. Corporations will typically have separate maintenance agreements for their fleet vehicles and so would not be expected to respond to brochures tailored for individuals. The gender of a name can also, in many cases, be determined from its spelling to help focus various marketing efforts. Finally, the pronunciation of a name can also be utilized as a piece of metadata. String and word matches can be handled using internal phonetic indexing and conversion routines to take names that are similar in their pronunciation and/or spelling and associate them accordingly. Thus, data disambiguation can be accomplished through word matching techniques. More about this topic will be discussed in later chapters.

Addresses beyond their street, city, state, and Zip code breakouts can also provide valuable metadata. Locations can be compared to reference points, and through the use of modern geolocational positioning technologies, the distance between them may be determined. It is easy to tell how far apart 123 Elm Street and 321 Maple Avenue are using simple mapping techniques. Thus, using only a customer's address, a store can determine how far its clients have to travel to purchase goods and services. Many geographical information systems already provide this capability. Different social and economic demographics can also be derived from location information (e.g., based on Zip codes). A store can review the general makeup of its clients and adjust its inventory and prices to better reflect their needs.

Locations can also be used to detect certain types of situations that are largely considered uncommon in everyday activities. For example, although the Department of Motor Vehicles in many states prohibits the registration of vehicles to post office box addresses, it happens nevertheless. The cases that the DMV and other law enforcement agencies are particularly interested in are those post office boxes that have many cars registered to them since they might indicate a safe-house or some other type of unorthodox situation. Commercial facilities versus private residences are another distinguishing factor that can be gleaned from the structure of an address. If it is not always apparent, lookup tables can be purchased from third-party vendors who can provide this information. Despite the fact that this information is recruited from a separate data source, from our perspective this is still considered metadata and it can be very useful information to incorporate into an analysis.

Descriptive and Transactional Models

Virtually all data to be modeled in an analysis may be characterized as one of two types: descriptive or transactional. Descriptive data provide declarative information describing discrete objects via attributable values (e.g., the retail price of an item, the subscriber of a phone, etc.). Descriptive data typically represent state-based knowledge that is considered true only until replaced by a different value. Once replaced, the old value is usually not maintained nor is it used within any subsequent analyses. Transactional data, in contrast, contain episodic information about time and place of events. Much of the information within database systems represents transactions of some sort. You may have observed that the structure of transactions remains fairly static—it is the content or values stored in these structures that varies among instances. In general, transactional data contain a date/time component that can be used as a primary key to distinguish each discrete transaction. Transactional data may be used to represent recurrent or cyclic behavior of a specified activity through monotonically differentiated values.

When you begin a data mining engagement, you will need to decide whether you are dealing with descriptive or transactional data. Depending on the type of data you have, you will use either a descriptive or a transactional model. If your data are descriptive your analyses will be confined to the use of descriptive models. Transactional data, on the other hand, may be represented in either descriptive or transactional models. In these forthcoming passages we describe the model types and include examples of three ways in which the transactional information contained in phone call records may be modeled. As you will see, the types of results that you will be able to glean from your analysis depend in large part on the kind of model you select.

Defining Descriptive Data Models

Descriptive data structures tend to be used to represent declarative information such as organizational structures, credit reports, driver's licenses, vendor profiles, ingredients, network structures, and so on. When various classes of declarative information are represented in a model, you can show that relationships exist among them. For example, you might have a model in which there is a class of objects corresponding to people and another corresponding to vehicles with links between them indicating who owns which vehicles. Descriptive models tend to outline the overall structure of the relationships between the different objects contained within the data set. Descriptive data are useful for looking at networks and frequencies of connections, but are very difficult to use if the goal is to describe behaviors or events (see Figure 2.7).

Defining Transactional Data Models

To get a feel for transactional representations, consider the use of your credit card to purchase goods and services. No matter how many transactions are recorded for

Figure 2.7 Examples of descriptive data models.

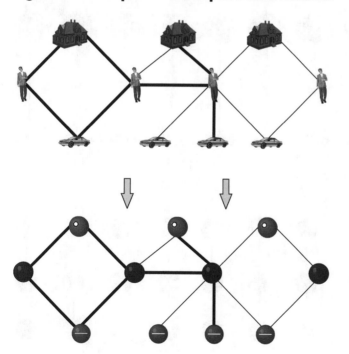

your card, the structure of the representation remains consistent. There is always a card number, a vendor, the merchandise, a price, and a date. What makes each use of the card unique are the values applied to each of these attributes for every transaction. Different vendors, products, and amounts will be paid during the lifetime use of the card. Even when you buy the same merchandise time and time again, each transaction will be unique just from the fact that it occurs at a different time and date. Since every transaction can be distinguished from every other by its assigned values, most importantly the date/time, you can start to perform data mining to look for explicit transactional patterns and related behaviors (see Figure 2.8).

In a transactional model, typically you can use links between object classes to represent traits or conditions of the event contained within the transaction. Thus, all of the conditions associated with the event can be applied to the link since they were derived as a result of the event. What this means is that any attribute applied to any link generated between any pair of objects derived using a transactional model can justifiably support any of the information used to describe the transaction. Is it not true that the amount, time, or date of a transaction can be used as an

Figure 2.8 Examples of transactional data models.

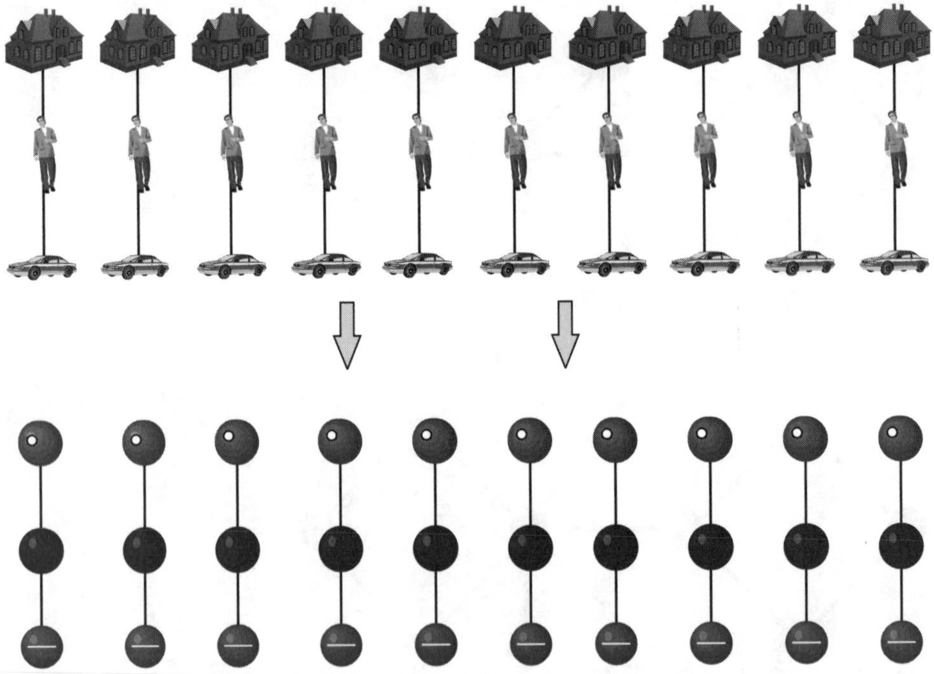

attribute to describe the link created between the transactor and the credit card as well as the link between the transactor and the merchandise? Also, the existence of many links between two objects indicates that many separate transactions occurred between the two and are each represented in the data set.

In a descriptive model, on the other hand, each of the links can have its own unique value used to describe the relationship between object classes. Thus, an individual person in a "people" object class might be connected to an "address" in another class because the information was listed in a credit application. However, that same individual can have a link with a particular automobile in a "vehicles" object class for a completely different reason, defined by a completely different set of conditions. This flexibility occurs in a descriptive model because the information that is used to specify the conditions of the relationship is distinct to the objects of interest. In a transactional model, on the other hand, the conditions represented in any relationship are generated from the transaction record and so are more focused on the event itself.

A Modeling Example: Phone Call Analysis

To help clarify the difference between descriptive and transactional models, imagine you are modeling a set of phone call data containing only five fields for each call: origination phone, destination phone, date, time, and duration. In fact, this corresponds very closely to the information that appears on your own home phone bill (with the exception that the originating phone is almost always your number on your own bill). There are several ways in which you could model these data. The type of model you choose will determine the types of findings you will be able to produce during the analysis. Figure 2.9 shows an example of this type of raw data.

Figure 2.9 A sample of telephone toll call data.

Origination	Destination	Date	Time	Duration
555-1234	555-1111	97/01/01	10:50	5
555-1234	555-2222	97/02/01	03:35	1
555-1234	555-3333	97/03/01	14:51	2
555-1234	555-2222	97/04/01	12:06	4
555-1234	555-4444	97/05/01	18:12	8

Using Simple Descriptive Models

How would you model these phone call data? Most people will designate originating phones as an object class and destination phones as another object class. They then create links between these two object classes to represent the individual phone calls. This is a descriptive model. In this model the links contain the information about the date, time, and duration of individual calls (see Figure 2.10). For every phone call made, a graphical link will be generated in the model. This model would work, but it would not be useful for performing data mining. The biggest flaw is in the designation of the originating and destination phone numbers as separate object classes. This overlooks the possibility that an originating number on one call might be a destination number on another call within the same data set. Should this happen you would never be able to tell which object class a particular number would belong to since the system will continue to reassign the number to the appropriate class as it is encountered in the data set. Remember what we said earlier about attributes being able to support only one value across the data set. Since the "class" of an object is technically represented as an attribute, it too may have only one value. Technically speaking, you could have two different data objects representing the same phone number, but that complicates the analysis and should be used only in special cases.

The solution to this problem is to take a step back and realize that, in the real world, these are all phone numbers, so they should be modeled as such. Thus,

Figure 2.10 Descriptive model of phone call data.

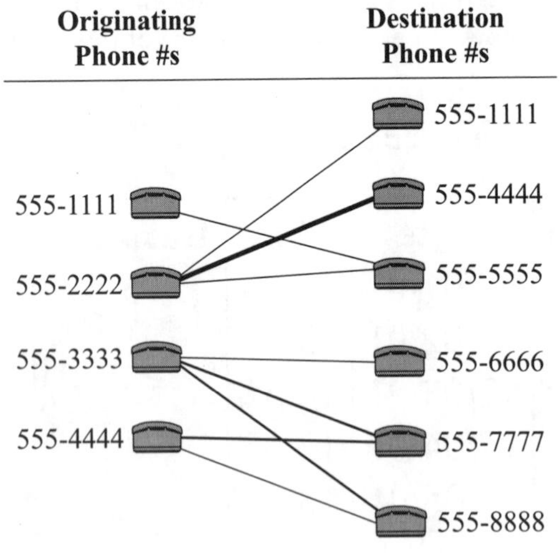

instead of having separate object classes for originating and destination phone numbers, we simply create one class to represent all numbers. You can always add a separate flag that signifies whether a phone has ever been used in an originating role. Again, this also represents a descriptive model. So we will amend our model of originating and destination phones to create objects of a vanilla type "phone," possibly using an attribute flag to distinguish these roles. The "role" of each phone within a call can now be determined based on the direction of the link. The resulting model is shown in Figure 2.11. It still represents individual calls as descriptive data between the phone objects. That is, we are showing the interconnections that exist among the phone numbers. Based on this, we can show a large number of situations including frequencies of connections, isolated networks, and pathways among different phone numbers (more about this in Chapter 5).

This is generally a good model, but it also turns out to be somewhat limited. Suppose you are asked to determine the call patterns among the phones in addition to their structures and relationships. Say you need to show the behavior and describe when the calls are occurring or how long they last. To do this you would have to access each individual link represented between any pair of objects and decompose them to expose the desired patterns. This is inefficient and impractical, particularly in a real phone analysis in which literally thousands of phone calls are included in the model. A better approach would be to represent these transactions themselves as objects that can have attributes. That is, move from a strictly descriptive representation of the phone calls to a more transactional one.

Using a Transactional Model

Our best and final model is presented in Figure 2.12. What we have done here is added another object class of phone calls in which each call is now represented as

Figure 2.11 Second descriptive model of phone call data.

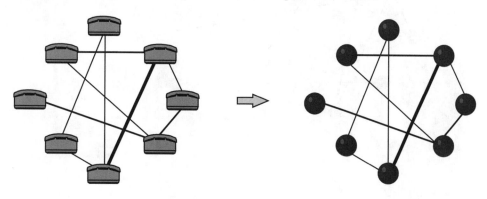

its own object, each having a link to the originating phone and a link to the destination phone. Information about time and duration are represented as attributes of the call objects. For this to work we edit the original data set to include a unique identifier for each phone call record, as shown in Figure 2.13. The easiest way to do this is to create a dummy variable by adding line numbers to the original data file. Each line number can be used as a unique identifier for each call. Now if we want to examine patterns having to do with call duration or time of day, we can simply cluster on those attributes and all of the call objects will automatically be sorted according to their values for those variables. Thus, we could immediately look at the results to determine whether there are any trends of interest with regard to these behavioral questions. You should note that although the transactional model is the most powerful alternative for examining behavior, it comes with a price. Transactional models often involve the proliferation of large numbers of objects and links that must be managed (see Managing Record Fan-Out). As a data miner, you will make decisions about how best to balance issues of analytical power with computational overhead.

Figure 2.12 A transactional model of phone call data.

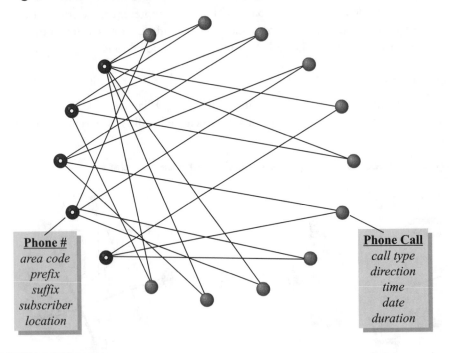

Phone #
area code
prefix
suffix
subscriber
location

Phone Call
call type
direction
time
date
duration

Figure 2.13 Revising the original phone call data set for transactional modeling.

Added Field →

Index	Origination	Destination	Date	Time	Duration
1	555-1234	555-1111	97/01/01	10:50	5
2	555-1234	555-2222	97/02/01	03:35	1
3	555-1234	555-3333	97/03/01	14:51	2
4	555-1234	555-2222	97/04/01	12:06	4
5	555-1234	555-4444	97/05/01	18:12	8

↑

Managing Record Fan-Out

You will consider many factors when deciding how to represent and model your data for a data mining engagement. One of the most important factors to consider is the degree of fan-out associated with the particular model you have selected. The term *fan-out* refers to the number of tangible entities (e.g., objects, links, and attributes) that will be created from a single record in your model. Consideration of fan-out is critical because it will determine, at least in part, how many records you can process at a time within a single application. Thus, you can have models with relatively low fan-out that allow you to deal with a larger number of records at a restricted level of detail. Alternatively, you can use models with a high degree of fan-out on a smaller number of records to expose more details. Figure 2.14 provides an example of four different data models showing the potential fan-out that can be achieved for a single data structure.

As you can tell from the previous discussion, the most common form of fan-out occurs within transactional data models. This is due to the fact that a unique transactional entity is created for every single record being analyzed. The fan-out is further compounded by the number of links/attributes that are going to be created for each record. The selection

Continued

Managing Record Fan-Out *(Continued)*

Figure 2.14 Record fan-out for four models of the same data set.

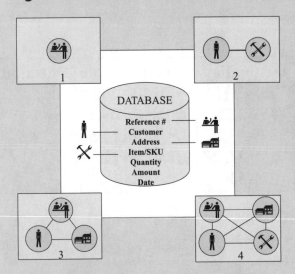

of a model with large fan-out can severely limit the number of records used in a data mining application. On the other hand, when dealing with descriptive models, a single representation of the same object can be reused over and over again. The only accumulation of information that can occur in this type of model is in the linkages being used to establish relationships among objects. Even this can be minimized if the links are not considered unique for each occurrence or if the level of detail required to represent information like time, date, transaction, and source is not required. We have often found it useful to begin a data mining exercise by using a low fan-out model to view most or all of the data to be analyzed. From this view we can determine trends and relationships that are likely to be of interest. We can then follow up with increasingly more detailed models that incorporate less data as we zero in on important patterns.

Intra- and Inter-Domain Patterns

One factor that determines the type of model(s) you will construct in your analysis is whether you expect to observe patterns within or across domains. Broadly speaking, the patterns detected in a data mining exercise may be divided into two classes, intra-domain patterns (horizontal) and inter-domain patterns (vertical). Intra-domain patterns are the most prevalent type encountered within analytical engagements. Intra-domain patterns typically are discovered during analyses that are focused on assessment of data sources derived from a single problem domain area. These types of problems might include such examples as understanding communication networks, interpreting transportation routes, appraising a supplier's available inventory, assessing sales by region, or detecting investment fraud. Because they are all derived from one problem domain, the data elements contained within intra-domain patterns are categorically consistent with respect to the types of real-world or conceptual entities they represent. For example, the same modeling conventions can be used within a domain to represent people and telephones for communication purposes, vehicles and road/railways for transportation issues, parts and equipment for suppliers, store locations and point-of-sale (POS) records for sales analyses, and records of stock transactions and tax payments for fraud cases. All objects within an object class in the domain will likely be modeled in the same way. Intra-domain patterns can thus be exposed solely on the basis of the shared values, relationships, or associations encountered within a unique circumstance or particular data condition.

Many different types of intra-domain patterns can be extremely useful (see Figure 2.15). Some interesting examples that we have encountered include patterns of communication events (e.g., telephone toll analysis), observations of cyclic-variants occurring within a transportation network caused by irregular aircraft arrival/departure time schedules, or the detection of articulation points (e.g., bottlenecks) within a manufacturing process that could severely affect production and

Figure 2.15 Intra- and inter-domain patterns.

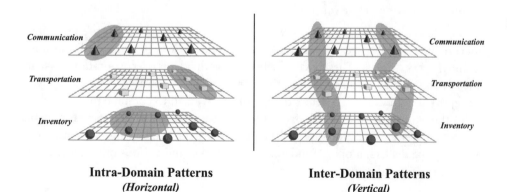

Intra-Domain Patterns
(Horizontal)

Inter-Domain Patterns
(Vertical)

delivery of goods. These and other intra-domain patterns can be identified, tracked, and used to establish a baseline of templates and models within a data mining system.

Discovering Inter-Domain Patterns

Suppose your data mining engagement involves analysis of patterns across domains. In these cases you will need to formulate your models so as to permit these discoveries. What this usually entails is using some of the data abstraction techniques previously discussed in order to formulate object classes that traverse the domains of interest. Combinations of data sources across different problem domains can reveal inter-domain patterns. An inter-domain pattern represents a set of conditions distributed across a set of information sources such that no one source contains the entire pattern. Inter-domain patterns involve more complex processing requirements, since most often multiple sources of data are being used to derive the results. Many of the same issues for detecting intra-domain patterns are encountered in detecting inter-domain patterns. The major difference rests with data integration problems that are largely a result of the inconsistent use of terminology across domains.

The methods of integrating disparate data sources can occur at many levels including string (name matching), spatial (geographic regions), temporal (time/date frames), structure-based (categorical clusters), or value-based (discrete ranges). Depending on the situation of the scenarios being monitored, a variety of approaches can be used to perform data mining under these circumstances. Examples of inter-domain patterns might include performing competitive intelligence for correspondence of a set of communication events (e.g., press releases), with transportation events from a warehouse facility (e.g., parts), along with observations of certain key individuals (e.g., business partners), all leading up to the announcement of a new rival product.

In one data mining application we developed that was heavily focused on inter-domain patterns, the agency was looking for situations that would indicate noncompliant tax filings. These occur when an individual or corporation has an extensive set of high-value assets that the filer is unlikely to be able to purchase given the reported net income. To detect these patterns we had to combine the filing data with other information available from separate sources. This type of inter-domain pattern implies a variety of sins and has been used in initial identification of tax evaders, drug dealers, money launderers, loan sharks, and various other individuals engaged in criminal activities.

In this case, the agency wanted to combine four intra-domain systems into a single inter-domain application. The data sources we used included income tax returns, real-property assets, department of motor vehicle records, and several money transfer data sets. All together, there were about ten different and unique data formats integrated to produce the inter-domain application. The types of patterns that were encountered were extensive and included such situations as people with three to four luxury vehicles (e.g., over $200K total) reporting less than $10K worth of income, people with several homes but no corresponding tax filing, and people with very large cash transactions from casino reports without corresponding reports of the income on their tax returns. These inter-domain patterns were used to identify potential starting points from which the agency decided whether to pursue full investigations.

In another application involving inter-domain patterns, a company was concerned that there were employees embezzling money through various loopholes in their expense reporting systems. The company's main interest was in determining whether there were any patterns of theft that could be detected without too much room for ambiguity with respect to the nature of the activity. In this particular application the inter-domain patterns were derived from two electronic data sources. The first data source was an online expense reporting system developed for internal use, which contained employee reports of business expenses, out-of-pocket charges, and travel reimbursables. The second data source contained actual charges incurred on the company-owned credit cards issued to company employees. Individually, each data source was mined to detect intra-domain patterns indicating personal use of the credit cards (for purchases in hardware stores and women's lingerie shops, for example) and for questionable business expense reimbursements such as very large phone call charges.

When the data sources were combined, one particular inter-domain pattern that stood out involved employee charges of airplane tickets to corporate credit cards. We correlated the online expense report and credit card data showing all reimbursements for air travel during similar time periods. In most cases there was a one-to-one correspondence of credit card charges and expense report reimbursements indicating that people submitting airplane ticket charges to the online expense reimbursement system were automatically compensated for their charges. All that was required was a copy of the receipt for the ticket. However, when we dug a little bit deeper and decided to include credit as well as debit transactions from the charge account data source, a whole new pattern emerged. For several particular employees, it was apparent that they were buying airplane tickets on the credit card, submitting for a reimbursement through the online expense system, and then returning the unused airplane tickets to the airlines for a credit back on their charge accounts. The net result was that they were pocketing the cost of the ticket at the expense of the company. Needless to say, this inter-domain pattern would not have been discovered without the combination of separate data sources in a single analysis.

Summing Up

Our goal in this chapter was to describe many of the decisions you will need to make when modeling your data set(s) for a data mining application. In particular we covered methods for establishing object classes, their attributes, and the relationships existing among classes. As we mentioned, you might choose to use meta-data in your analysis as well as combine information from disparate sources. Further, we described the fundamental differences between descriptive and transactional models, illustrating some of the pros and cons of each. This discussion has hopefully provided you with a framework for knowledge modeling in the context of data mining, whether your application involves intra- or inter-domain pattern detection. Having covered the basics of modeling, we now turn to the larger problem of explicitly representing your problem within a larger conceptual framework that helps you make important distinctions among the types of knowledge that you are trying to represent.

DEFINING THE PROBLEMS TO BE SOLVED

As the discussion of data modeling in Chapter 2 illustrated, the particular approach used by analysts for performing data mining will affect the types of patterns and trends discovered. As it turns out, the analyst's wider concept of the problem space can have implications beyond basic modeling issues of object classes and their attributes. When doing an analysis you need to have a broad sense of how to classify the types of information and knowledge that you are working with, and how to construct an analysis so as to move from one class of knowledge to another.

As you begin a data mining exercise, it sometimes helps to map your problem onto an explicit conceptual framework. The purpose of this chapter is to provide you with some ideas to consider in formulating a problem space of your analysis. To do this effectively, you will need to be flexible in your thinking, going outside the bounds to which you may be accustomed. To help you with this, we describe four possible frameworks that you can consider when thinking about your particular application. You can think of knowledge being represented in a hierarchy ranging from single objects all the way up to full systems; you can distinguish between "knowing how" procedures are accomplished as opposed to "knowing that" certain facts are true about a situation; you can characterize your problem in terms of metaknowledge and actual knowledge; or you can map your problem onto the orthogonal dimensions of situations versus parameter values. Once you have mapped your problem onto a conceptual framework, you can begin to think about whether your analysis will proceed in reactive mode, proactive mode, or whether you will use a combination of techniques.

The approaches to defining the problem space discussed in this chapter are meant to stimulate your thinking. We want you to think about your own application as well as the wide range of data mining applications in which you can use these methodologies. As you read through each section, try to imagine how your own data might fit within the framework being presented. We hope that the ideas discussed here will expand the ways in which you think about your data and the types of analyses that might be most useful to you.

Challenging Analysts to Think "Outside the Box"

In many organizations analysts are often provided with systems that force them to report findings in very limited ways. Usually these systems have been previously set up by database personnel and the analyst can choose only one of a limited number of options. Although the advent of data warehouses and decision support systems has helped to alleviate some of these restrictions, analysts are still fairly confined with respect to the types of output they can produce. As a result, analysts can become comfortable with having only a few, select, and limited choices to make. As time goes by and analysts continue to think of their data in this limited fashion, they grow more accustomed to "thinking in the box" and are less likely to conceptualize their data in novel ways.

Sometimes, however, finding a solution during a data mining exercise requires a fundamental change in perspective. The goal is to get analysts to think *outside* the box, to let their imaginations wander. This is sometimes a painful process, especially in those cases in which habits are deeply ingrained. Despite the best of intentions, adherence to established paradigms can often have the unintended effect of stifling curiosity and creativity.

We are reminded of an experience reported by a friend of ours who was a student in an undergraduate psychology course in which he studied learning in rats. Each student was provided with a rat that they trained personally during the course. By the end of the semester our friend was fond enough of his rat that he wanted to set it free rather than have it meet an untimely fate at the hands of a lab technician. So he took his rat, along with its cage, out to some nearby woods to give it the gift of a free life. He placed the cage on the ground, opened the door, and waited. He had assumed that the rat would be as thrilled about receiving its newfound freedom as he was in giving it. Instead, he was surprised to observe that the rat was extremely reluctant to leave the cage at all, much less bound off into the woods searching for new opportunities. For some length of time the rat repeated a series of behaviors in which it poked its head out of the cage, sniffed around, walked out cautiously, and then retreated back into the cage. After much coaxing the rat finally left the cage altogether, but it took much longer than our friend anticipated.

Learning to reconceptualize a problem domain for the purposes of data mining is very similar to the process of the rat leaving its cage. It can be daunting and it will not happen immediately. Experimentation is necessary. Some people will adapt more easily than others. We have observed that individuals who are comfortable using computers seem to fare much better when presented with different techniques for dealing with their data. One or two converts may be all that an organization needs in order to support a good data mining capability. You do not necessarily need to have a large number of people engaged in data mining activities. We have seen many examples in which a single dedicated analyst did great work, provided that that person is not over-committed on other projects. In situations in which the in-house analysts are having trouble making the transition, possible solutions might be to bring in someone new and train them in the business, or to consider outsourcing the data mining activities to a firm that specializes in your particular domain.

Driving without Maps and Cooking without Recipes

As previously stated, there is no road map to follow when performing data mining. To a large degree you will essentially make it up as you go along. The "outside the box" thinking that goes on in a data mining engagement is in some ways analogous to a southern cook in action. The cook begins with an array of simple ingredients such as flour, eggs, milk, flavoring, and the like. And since the cook is southern, it is quite unlikely that a recipe is on hand to provide a road map to the final product. Instead the cook begins combining whatever ingredients are available in various ways, adding "as much as needed" until the dish is complete. Talented cooks can form an endless variety of dishes from the same starting set of simple ingredients just by introducing minor variations. The final creation is a much more satisfying and complex system than the sum of the individual parts. Each dish is a new experiment and although some will not be successful, most will be.

As an inexperienced cook you might be frustrated with this process and initially may make the wrong choices in terms of proportion, consistency, cooking time, and so on. Once given the knowledge about how to combine ingredients, however, you realize that it was not really that hard in the first place. Regardless of whether you figure it out on your own or have someone show you, the solution is usually easy to understand and remember. This is also true of data mining. At this point in time, you might not have many ideas about how to combine the disparate pieces of your data in such a way as to yield interesting outcomes. As you learn more about analytical modeling, however, you will gain insights that you will be able to incorporate into multiple phases of the data mining process.

There's More than One Way to Slice a Bagel

Before we leave this section, let's do a little exercise to illustrate the importance of "out of the box" thinking. Suppose you are at a breakfast meeting with your best client and she asks you to cut a bagel in half. You clearly want to please her, so what would you do? Many of us would take the bagel and slice it horizontally all the way around yielding two halves, each with a hole in the middle. But is this really what you should do? Certainly it is the most obvious response, but there is more than one way to cut a bagel in half. You could make a vertical cut that bisects the hole, yielding two C-shaped halves. Or you could make a diagonal cut. Would you think to provide your client with these options or even determine if they were potential candidates for fulfilling the original task? Probably not.

This raises a much more basic question about why the client wanted the bagel cut in half in the first place. Did she want to make a sandwich out of the two halves? Perhaps she only wanted to share some food with her associate, in which case the best solution would have been to get her some more bagels. The point we are trying to make here is to find out what the real requirements are before taking any actions to complete an outstanding task. To do so often requires you to take a different tact and think about the situation from an alternative perspective. Be creative, be open to suggestions, and be careful to consider all angles of the problem—not just the obvious ones.

Mapping Your Problem onto a Hierarchical Framework

There are several levels of organization at which knowledge may be represented in a data mining application. As shown in Figure 3.1, these levels may be arranged hierarchically in terms of their increasing complexity. As complexity of the knowledge representation architecture increases, the corresponding complexity of the patterns and trends that may be represented by that architecture also increase. Depending upon your application, you may or may not need to utilize all of the knowledge levels represented in this framework. Nevertheless, it is useful to keep this framework in mind as you formulate your analysis so that you can choose a data mining tool that affords you all the flexibility you need in completely representing your problem. (We will discuss the various commercial data mining tools and the types of knowledge representation that they support in Section III.)

From Objects to Networks

As we discussed in Chapter 2, the most basic unit of knowledge representation is an object. At this level of representation, all patterns and trends are based on the

Figure 3.1 Hierarchical framework for knowledge representation in data mining applications.

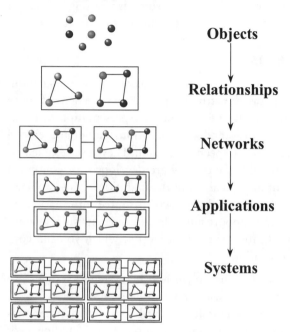

Objects

Relationships

Networks

Applications

Systems

specification, combination, and depiction of objects. From here we can add in the dimension of allowing simple relationships between objects. Thus we can now represent objects as well as their associations. Relationships, like objects, are mutually exclusive of one another. In fact, relationships are usually represented as objects. There is no dependency among relationships and each acts and functions as its own independent entity. Relationships may be considered abstract data types or they can be explicitly represented. This is a matter of preference in terms of what types of patterns you want to extract from your data sets.

Taken together, objects and relationships form networks of data. These networks can be used to represent simple patterns and trends. Most data mining tools support knowledge representation and analysis at this level. Network representations allow the analyst to establish pathways, identify important substructures in the data set, and identify a framework for more advanced analyses. Typically, many of these network systems represent only one source of information or one particular dimension of the problem space.

Many data mining efforts do not extend beyond this level of representation. In the case of simple analytical engagements, there is often no need to build a more complex knowledge representation. In the case of proof-of-principle exercises, it is easy to instantiate a problem up to this level of representation as a prototype system since it requires little effort but can still produce some interesting results. In practical terms, limitations in resources can force engagements to stop at this level.

Applications and Systems

The integration of one or more networks forms the basis of an application. Network integration also helps support the structuring and management of more complex intra-domain (horizontal) knowledge, leading to representation of intra-domain patterns. Applications are usually stand-alone solutions that are developed for a particular problem or targeted at a specific domain. They are designed to cover the target problem area thoroughly. Since they are developed for continued use, they usually provide a range of analytical support capabilities. Most applications offer methods to "walk the data" and drill-down to source information on data elements. In addition, they might support multiple data formats such as multimedia where appropriate. An application is the first level at which you can consider a data mining system to be operational.

As applications are brought together they form holistic systems. Systems are environments used by analysts to perform a wide range of data mining activities. A system supports a breadth of data mining capabilities as well as a suite of other analytical features and production mechanisms. Software programs including geographical information systems, word processors, e-mail, presentation graphics and the like are sometimes included in these environments. There are also automated methods for navigating the system, managing the data, and supporting accounting methods. Some of the more sophisticated systems can support multiuser access. Very few efforts make it to this stage, although there are several systems that support the infrastructure required to accommodate this type of functionality.

Distinguishing between "Knowing How" and "Knowing That": Procedural versus Declarative Knowledge

Many cognitive psychologists have long been interested in questions concerning knowledge representation in biological systems such as humans, monkeys, and rats. Based on experimental outcomes obtained across a wide variety of studies, many theoretical distinctions among types of knowledge have been proposed. One distinction that is particularly relevant to problems of data mining is one made between procedural and declarative knowledge. Procedural knowledge involves "knowing how" to do things; declarative knowledge, or "knowing that," represents factual information about the world. A procedural knowledge structure might contain information about how to ride a bicycle, how to predict stock prices, how to play the piano, or how to optimize output from a production facility. Declarative knowledge structures, on the other hand, are used to represent factual information such as the names of all fifty states and their capitals, mailing lists of all active customers, symptoms associated with a series of diseases, or the history of Supreme Court rulings on civil rights cases.

When you are in the early stages of your data mining project, you might want to consider whether the information you will be analyzing is procedural, declarative, or a combination of the two. Generally speaking procedural knowledge will contain information that must be maintained in sequence. For example, if you were analyzing information about a car factory production process, you might have information about construction of the frame or chassis, followed by installation of the engine, followed by installation of the interior, followed by assembly of the body, followed by application of the paint, and so on. Depending upon the goals of the data mining application, it may or may not be necessary to preserve this order information during the analysis.

You should play around with ideas about whether you should model procedural and declarative information differently. Chances are that the types of questions you will have regarding procedural information will differ from those generated for the declarative data sets. If so, you should structure the problem ahead of time so that you will be able to access each if needed. If you like, you can usually think of a way to represent procedural knowledge in declarative types of representations for the purposes of the analysis. You could just add a set of attributes describing where in the process a particular set of information applies.

Breaking Declarative Knowledge into Subcategories

In all likelihood, your data mining application will largely involve analysis of declarative knowledge. But within the category of declarative knowledge, we still can make important distinctions among knowledge types. One important distinction can be made between episodic and semantic information. Episodic knowledge is tagged with temporal and spatial information whereas semantic knowledge is not. For example, recall the discussion of descriptive and transactional models that we presented in Chapter 2. Both descriptive and transactional models represent declarative information, but it is the transactional information that is used to describe specific events in terms of time and/or spatial attributes.

On the whole, there are not tremendous differences in the qualitative nature of individual transactions. For example, all phone calls share certain traits or attributes in common. What is important in the analytical environment is that this episodic information can be used to distinguish one transaction from another. That is, you may not be so interested in *what* happened (since all events are fairly similar to one another) as you are in *when, where,* and *how often* it happened. In contrast, semantic or descriptive representations may or may not contain the same attributes. Patterns of interest within descriptive knowledge structures often center on similarities and differences in these attributes. Recall from our discussion in Chapter 2 that you can switch between transactional and descriptive models in order to represent episodic information so as to accommodate the goals of your analysis.

Distinguishing between Metaknowledge and Actual Knowledge

When you begin an analysis, start by asking yourself what kind of information you will be looking for in your data sets. Are you going to be describing known quantities? Are you looking for interesting relationships that might exist among classes of knowledge that you already know about? Are you prepared to discover classes of knowledge and patterns that you never even thought existed before? When thinking about the problem space of your application, it makes sense to segment classes of information along two dimensions. The first dimension is the actual status of information contained in the data sources available for analysis, in which case information can actually be known or unknown within the data set. The second dimension is your own metaknowledge about what information may exist in the data set. In this regard you may think that information is known or unknown a priori, and you may or may not be correct in your judgment.

The Information that You Know You Know (YKYK)

As shown in Figure 3.2, metaknowledge and actual knowledge exist along orthogonal dimensions. We can use these dimensions to construct a two-by-two matrix to describe the status of information available during a data mining engagement. In the simplest case, there is information that actually exists in the data set, and the user is aware that the information is there. We call this the YKYK (you know that you know it) cell. You know that a car will not run without gas; you know that water boils at 100°C; and you know that if you run a red light in front of a police officer, you will most likely get a ticket. Many of the things you know are self-evident, well established, and for the most part taken for granted. Many systems currently in use by corporations and industry depend heavily on this type of information because it is extremely reliable and can easily be encapsulated into rules. Basically, the YKYK cell contains information that organizations utilize in standard activities such as generating reports, running audit checks, or generically processing data. The YKYK information is what is typically used to think "inside the box" in accepted models that are already familiar and generally not questioned.

The Information that You Know You Don't Know (YKDK)

Just as you are sure of certain types of facts and information, there are also classes of knowledge that you know that you do not have. This introduces us to a category of things that you know that you don't know, or YKDK. You know you don't know the average rainfall in the vast upper regions of the Amazon (more than 78 inches every year); you know that you don't know the angle of the Earth's rotation on its axis on its orbit around the sun (23.5 degrees); you know that you don't know the exact height of the Empire State Building (1,453 feet) or the area of Central Park (843 acres). (In deference to our brilliant readers, some of you may have known several of these facts, but those who did not were probably sure that you did not.)

Now imagine events occurring within the context of your application area that fall into the YKDK category. Do you know what products tend to be purchased in conjunction with other products? Do you know if your sales promotions are effective and

Figure 3.2 Dimensions of metaknowledge and actual knowledge within the problem space.

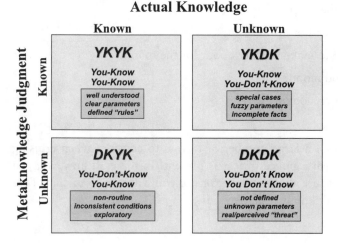

targeting the best market for your products or services? Do you know whether and what types of suspicious financial transactions tend to occur with temporal regularity? Do you know whether outbreaks of a particular disease tend to be more serious in certain parts of the world? Like the previous Jeopardy-style facts, chances are that you would have to do some research in order to find out this kind of information and add it to the data set since it does not already exist there. In essence, you can generate an answer if you have to, but it is not something that is typically available or readily accessible to your organization.

Many organizations have installed a firewall within their networks to protect themselves from outside intruders even though there was never evidence of any malicious behavior or damage to their systems. This is typically done as a precaution, in much the same way as we lock the doors to our homes or cars when we leave them unattended—you know you don't know if it will ever be tested. The YKDK cell can contain information about special cases that are out of the realm of normal analytical activity. Alternatively, information identified in this cell can be derived from alternative sources for an analysis if needed. Typically the technologies best suited for analyses in the YKDK category include neural networks, case-based reasoning, genetic algorithms, and expert systems since any of these may operate using a set of fuzzy parameters. For example, suppose we alter the parameters a bit in the red light violation scenario and make the light yellow instead. The question now becomes, if you run the yellow light, will the police officer give you a ticket? Chances are that you cannot say for sure. It depends on a variety of factors:

- Did the vehicle enter the intersection after the light turned yellow or was the vehicle already in the intersection when the light turned?

- Are there prevailing weather conditions that might discourage the police officer from leaving the comfort of his/her vehicle?

- Is the officer near the end of his/her shift?

- Does the officer need to make a ticket quota for the month?

- Is the officer in a good mood?

- Are you driving a sporty looking car?

- Are you young?

These are only a few of a large number of factors to consider when cruising through a yellow light when a police officer is present. In the end, however, you know that you are still not sure about whether or not you will receive a ticket. That is, you know that you don't know. It all depends.

The Information that You Don't Know You Know (DKYK)

Even though there is still uncertainty, both the red and yellow light situations are similar enough to one another that you can make some predictions about what will happen in each case. Now, consider the situation when the light is green and a stolen vehicle proceeds through the intersection. From the officer's point of view, all might first appear normal. However, suppose he or she is a bit bored and has time to run a routine check of the license plate on the system database only to discover that the vehicle is, in fact, stolen. This is a case in which relevant information was contained within the already established data source, and in fact was easily retrievable, even though the user had no metaknowledge guiding him or her toward a particular hypothesis. This is an example of the DKYK cell in Figure 3.2 containing information that you "don't know you know."

Any time that you are in a situation in which your metaknowledge status is "don't know," you are in a potential data mining space. Information in the DKYK cell is the type of information targeted in exploratory analyses in which you may not have definite ideas about what you expect to find. When you are in the DKYK cell, there is always the possibility that you may discover interesting information that is already contained within a data set although it is not currently being used. For example, you may not suspect that there are predictable patterns associated with a particular set of investment behaviors, although analysis of existing data may lead you to this discovery. Your organization maintains databases full of information and depending on what your area of business is, some very interesting results can be found. More sophisticated analysis of existing information sources could potentially reveal many patterns and trends that could be used to improve the quality of your operations. DKYK discoveries could lead to the forecasting of future behaviors, exposure of fraud, improved operational effectiveness, performance enhancement, and reduction of operating costs. The goal of the data mining practitioner with respect to the DKYK patterns is to move them as quickly as possible to the YKYK category. Thus, the patterns identified should be characterized clearly enough to be coded in a standard report or rule so that future recurrence can be detected readily and acted upon accordingly.

The Information that You Don't Know You Don't Know (DKDK)

Let's go back to our traffic cop. Now suppose that an unauthorized driver (e.g., intoxicated, impaired, unlicensed, etc.) is behind the wheel of a car passing through the intersection. Since the officer is only looking for red-light runners, and the vehicle is not stolen, this is a case that in all likelihood will be left unchallenged unless the officer's attention is grabbed by erratic driving behavior. The initial conditions of the case do not match an ongoing target pattern (the driver does not run a red light), nor is there information in the officer's database that identifies the driver as being incapacitated at that moment. This leads us into our fourth and final cell, the information that you "don't know you don't know" (DKDK).

Now, again, think about how the DKDK model applies to your operations. There may be important gaps in your data sources that you will not be aware of because you have no metaknowledge of them. This represents the most vulnerable situation you can face and it affects all governments, corporations, and industries throughout the world. For example, did you know that there is no method in place to trace the movements of convicted child sex offenders once they are released from prison, even though they are highly likely to repeat their crimes once released? In limited cases, officials within a state may trace the movements of these individuals within their own state boundaries, but there is no national network in place to coordinate monitoring efforts. This disturbing example illustrates the potential importance of the DKDK situation. The gaps in knowledge in the DKDK cell are not defined; they are based on yet unknown parameters, and therefore have never been noted. Thus, it is important for you to discover and interpret these gaps in order to deal with the threats against organizations, real or perceived. Detection of this missing information can help organizations in any number of ways.

Distinguishing between Situations and Parameter Values

There is also another way to look at the state of information contained in your data sources. We can recast the world into a different paradigm where instead of looking at metaknowledge and actual knowledge, we are looking at a set of situations and the parameters used to describe those situations. A situation represents an activity, a process, or some other function of interest. Different types of situations might include conducting a financial transaction, making a telephone call, buying groceries, or fixing a car. These situations may be described using a set of parameters, and each parameter may or may not have an established range of values for the situation in question. Parameters often used to describe situations can include dates, times, frequencies, weather conditions, account numbers, physiological measures, or any other attributable values used to describe the situation.

Using this approach it is very easy to construct a matrix of situations and parameters to describe the different types of data mining engagements that may occur (see Figure 3.3). On one axis, we place the situations and determine whether they are known or unknown. On the other axis we arrange the parameters according to whether there are established boundaries for the values that these parameters may take on for a given situation. The resulting matrix can be used to generally categorize different types of data mining scenarios. The following are brief summaries of what you would expect to find in each cell of the matrix.

Known Situation and Established Parameter Boundaries

Activities contained within this cell have known risks and probabilities. The exceptions can be easily flagged as being outside of established parameter ranges. For example, a mail-order catalog will carry only certain types of items to be sold and if an order is submitted with an invalid item number, the system will reject the entry. Similarly, if you try to exceed the charging limit of your credit card the system will automatically detect the violation of the established boundary, and your transaction will not be honored. These routine and known situations correspond to the YKYK

Figure 3.3 Characterization of knowledge in terms of situations and parameter values.

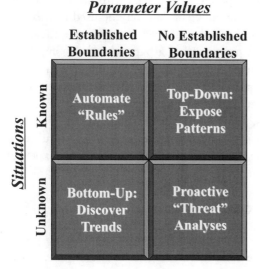

information described earlier. Routines for monitoring this information can easily be coded into automated detection and management schemes.

Unknown Situation and Established Parameter Boundaries

This cell characterizes "bottom-up" analyses. The goal of these data mining engagements is to detect patterns in existing parameter data that may be used to construct new categories of situations corresponding to important concepts within the application area. For example, examination of medical case reports might reveal patterns among various physiological measures in a geographical region during a certain period of time, allowing the user to infer that an outbreak of an infectious disease has occurred. That is, analysis of parameters having established boundary ranges can lead to definition of previously unknown situations. Consider another example in a retail sales application. You can take advantage of data falling out of known parameter ranges to detect exceptional rises and falls in sales of particular product lines that might not have been differentiated previously as a special category separate from other inventory.

Known Situation and No Established Parameter Boundaries

The data mining activities in this category are based on "top down" analysis and usually involve detection of discontinuous patterns. You start with the known situation, and the goal is to characterize the parameters that may be used to describe that situation so that its underlying causes may be inferred. For example, the question might be why the warranty repairs performed at a particular dealership have been above average during a recent time period. Analysis of parameter values may reveal that the increase in warranty repairs is associated with a decrease in other independent types of repairs being performed by that dealership during a time period leading up to the present. Thus, you can infer that the increase in warranty repairs may not reflect true failures in products, but rather may be the result of a dealership's dishonest attempts to generate revenue (at the corporation's expense) to make up for its own poor performance.

Unknown Situation and No Established Parameter Boundaries

This cell contains information about the most threatening set of circumstances that can affect organizations. These data mining engagements will seek to identify unknown patterns and practices, detect covert/unexplained practices, and will have the capability of exposing organized activity. The types of behavior that occur in this category are yet to be discovered. This final scenario is where many data mining practitioners live and breathe. We like to define working on these scenarios as a form of *proactive invigilation*. Invigilation is a variation on the word *vigilant*, which as you know means alert and watchful. As we explain in the next section, proactive analyses are those for which no clear targets are identified at the outset. Rather, the analyst is trying to discover patterns that no one knew about, but which might be important enough to be followed up with further investigation.

Performing Analyses in Reactive and Proactive Modes

Once you have thought about your application and have characterized your problem in terms of one of the conceptual frameworks previously outlined, you will be able to determine whether you will begin your analysis in a reactive or a proactive mode. In this section we describe each of these analysis modes, highlighting the differences between them.

Performing Reactive Analysis

You will choose a reactive mode if you have a concrete direct question to pursue. Reactive analysis occurs when an entity such as a person, organization, or location is targeted from the outset. In this event the focus of the analysis is placed on that entity, its behavior, and its relationships with other entities. A reactive analysis is basically a confirmation or verification of the data concerning a particular situation or subject. Through some prior event, the subject was selected as the focus of the analysis. These situations usually arise after a significant event has occurred, such as the decline in the price of a stock, the investigation following a murder, or the replacement of a faulty part.

In each case, a single, unique situation is designated for analysis and all information regarding that subject is acquired and presented for interpretation. Following the path of connections established in the modeling process, additional situations can be identified by virtue of their connection to the original subject. To maintain the context of the analysis, the new subject then becomes the source for the next level of inquiry. The analyst has the option to append or replace the current working data set with new data to control how much or how little information will be displayed for any given object. Reactive analysis tends to be a very efficient technique because the scope of the working data set is limited to the situation of interest and its related objects. Furthermore, the analysis is usually performed on indexed structures, making the access and recall of the data a considerably fast process. Reactive analyses performed using interactive data mining techniques such as data visualization can provide you with very timely results while processing large volumes of information.

One type of reactive analysis that we have done involved the tracking of behavior of individuals suspected of engaging in embezzlement activities. The company had suspicions that several of their employees were stealing funds from the company through the submission of false expense report statements. Very quickly we were able to confirm their beliefs by extracting all relevant information from several large computing systems regarding the activities of specific individuals. Another reactive analysis we dealt with involved the remote tracking of certain IP addresses (e.g., the unique identifiers of computing systems). In particular we were interested in finding evidence that users logged on from these IP addresses were traversing through unauthorized computer networks and systems. A clear pattern of behavior emerged from the analysis and the tracking agency was able to take effective counter-measures to minimize future breaches of security.

Performing Proactive Analysis

When you start an analysis in reactive mode, you are responding to crises or situations that have already occurred. Thus, the reactive analysis works well under circumstances in which something is already known about the data set and the analyst can generate hypotheses a priori. However, in those cases where a starting point is not known or cannot be defined, a different approach must be applied. Proactive analysis is used under these circumstances. Simply put, the goal during proactive analysis is to model the data in such a way as to be able to discover interesting, previously unknown patterns and trends.

In proactive mode, you generally start by trying to get a big picture of the overall scope and depth of the information contained within the data set. As familiarity with the data increases and interesting patterns are noticed, the scope of the search is refined to permit examination of emergent hypotheses. One example of a proactive analysis that we have done involved mining a database containing medical reports of head injury cases. The client had no hypotheses ahead of time concerning the types of patterns expected. (In fact, analysis using traditional statistical tests had yielded no interesting results.) By doing some high-level modeling, however, we uncovered several interesting trends in the data concerning relationships among such factors as the site of primary injury, accident type, age, and race of the patients that were not previously known by the client. Other secondary patterns included an observation in the rise of eye injuries that could be traced back to workers not wearing their required protective gear. This resulted in the reinforcement of procedures to ensure that all safety regulations were properly adhered to by the workers, especially those regarding eye protection. These findings turned out to be interesting and useful ones, and probably would not have been discovered other than by doing data mining in proactive mode.

Structuring the Proactive Slice of Data

You begin a proactive analysis by sampling a cross-sectional extraction from the entire data source. This extraction is sometimes termed a "proactive slice" of data. Proactive data slices can be identified using a variety of techniques ranging from the libraries created by case-based reasoning tools to the profiles defined in automated message handling environments. In many traditional database systems, these slices can easily be defined using temporal instances (days, weeks, months, or other date ranges), geographic regions (cities, counties, postcodes, or countries), or other data in particular value ranges. Examples might include people associated with certain assets, communications on specific frequencies, or financial transactions over a predetermined amount. Inductive learning techniques can also provide recommendations for various classifications or clusters of data that constitute valid slices of data.

Combining Proactive and Reactive Techniques

Proactive analysis will quickly reveal objects of interest either because a) they appear as unique and isolated structures; or b) they tend to occur with high frequency as compared to the rest of the objects presented. Once a target object or set of objects has been identified, you will want to view any additional data associated with the object(s) regardless of their origin. At this point, the analysis turns to reactive mode, guaranteeing that all information for the target set will be seen. This process of iteration between proactive and reactive modes can continue until the desired results are achieved. Figure 3.4 shows a graphical example of the different approaches for proactive and reactive analyses.

The combination of both reactive and proactive analytical techniques will allow you to work on terabytes of data because it manages the process that is used to interpret and analyze the data. For example, consider how the Internet is currently used. Typically, you can trigger an Internet search by specifying a set of keywords related to a topic of interest. The search generally will be conducted over a large quantity of processed HTML files, but can also be categorized by audio, images, newsgroups, and other file types. The results of the search are then passed

Figure 3.4 A depiction of reactive and proactive analyses.

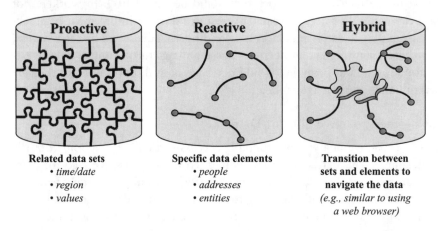

Proactive	Reactive	Hybrid
Related data sets • *time/date* • *region* • *values*	**Specific data elements** • *people* • *addresses* • *entities*	**Transition between sets and elements to navigate the data** *(e.g., similar to using a web browser)*

back and presented as a list of pointers. The system usually provides some type of relative ranking to help you decide which items were the best matches to your keyword request. You can think of the returned list of items as a proactive slice of data that was acquired from the system for analysis. At this point, you can review the list and select a single entry and follow the link to the targeted site. Once the single entry is chosen and supporting information about that item is requested, you have shifted into reactive analysis. From the current site, there will be other links to other sites, and so on. Thus, there is usually an inexhaustible list that can be used to navigate the World Wide Web (WWW). This is analogous to the data mining analysis models since any single entity can form the trigger or keyword for a new search. Unfortunately, as we all know too well, there are many dead ends and unqualified sets of information that get returned from Internet searches. The same can be true for data mining iterations. As you gain experience, you will be able to identify those entities that are most likely to yield interesting results within your problem domain.

Summing Up

In this chapter we have tried to emphasize the importance of thinking of your data in unconventional ways. We presented several conceptual frameworks within which you can characterize your data mining problem. At a high level of organization, you can distinguish among types of knowledge. Some of the distinctions among knowledge types include procedural versus declarative knowledge, episodic versus semantic knowledge. In another sense, you can characterize your problem solving space in terms of what is known, pitting metaknowledge against actual knowledge or juxtaposing situations and parameter values. Having characterized the problem space of your data mining activity, you can determine whether you will proceed in a reactive mode, in which you have well established hypotheses to test, or a proactive mode which involves more open-ended exploration. Once you have thought through all of these issues, you are ready to begin the next phase of the data mining analysis, namely getting the data into shape. That topic is covered in Chapter 4 in the next section.

Section II

DATA PREPARATION AND ANALYSIS

Having described the problem-solving approach of data mining in Section I, we are now ready to discuss the actual process of doing data mining. As shown in Figure S2.1, data mining can be broadly conceptualized as a multistep process. The aim is to go through a series of steps to transform your raw data into usable results.

The first step in the data mining process is to define the actual problem and then to access the data you need from original sources. Here you will face issues with formatting, conversion, clean-up, and extraction. Once you have accessed the data that you will need for your application, you must integrate across your multiple data sources and create one format that can represent all of the information consistently. Another step involves analysis and ideally is where you should spend most of your time. If you are using visualization methods, you will try out a number of models and different visualizations in order to discover interesting and important patterns. On the other hand, you might choose a nonvisual analytical method such as a statistical or neural network analysis. Chances are that interim results obtained during the analysis stage will dictate that you go back to your original data sources and get new data samples that allow you to pursue questions that arise along the way. Depending on the application and the size of the original data sources, you may traverse this feedback loop many times before your analysis is complete. When you have your final results, you will enter the last step of developing an effective means of presenting them to your target audience.

Overview of Section II

This section contains practical approaches and advice for getting through the steps outlined in Figure S2.1. We begin in Chapter 4, "Accessing and Preparing the Data," by discussing many of the issues that you will need to address when accessing data sets from original sources and formatting them for your application. We

[75]

Figure S2.1 A conceptual overview of the data mining process.

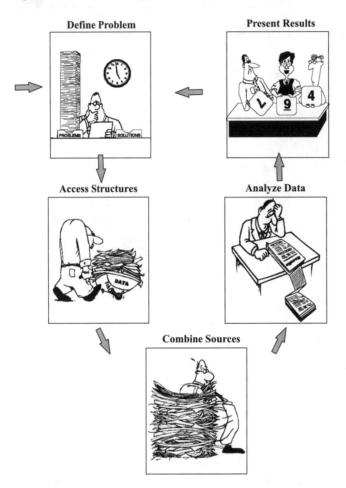

do not assume that you will always begin your data mining engagement with a data set perfectly formatted for whatever tool you are using. Rather, we discuss many of the problems that tend to arise when data are being imported into a system, with the hope that we can help you reduce the amount of time spent on this stage of the analysis. We provide guidelines for querying data sets and constructing proactive slices of data from which to begin an analysis. We describe approaches to integrating data from multiple sources so that you can create one virtual knowledge representation from which to run your data mining application. We discuss formatting and conversion issues such as manipulation of long and short data formats, name disambiguation, and handling textual information.

Once your data have been accessed and formatted correctly, you are ready to begin your analysis. Since the emphasis in this book is on visual data mining methods, we have devoted an entire chapter to this topic. In Chapter 5, "Visual Methods for Analyzing Data," we begin with an explanation of why visualization methods are so effective in the analytical process. Among other things, these advantages include the natural fit of visualization to human information processing capabilities. We next describe how you can best go about mapping your data onto a visualization scheme for analysis. The basic classes of positioning formats are described, including clustering, hierarchies, self-organizing networks, and landscapes. We then describe two classes of visual analytical approaches—analyzing structural features of simple displays and analyzing network structures. We provide descriptions of several classes of patterns that you can discover with each approach, along with the inferences that may be drawn from these findings. We provide further sections on discovering emergent groups and temporal patterns within data sets using visualization methods. Finally, we discuss issues that you should consider when presenting the results of a visual data mining analysis.

Many of the types of analyses conducted under the umbrella of data mining do not involve visualization. In Chapter 6, "Nonvisual Analytical Methods," we provide conceptual overviews of some of the more commonly used approaches including statistical tests, decision trees, association rules (market basket analyses), neural networks, and genetic algorithms. We describe the general approach of each and provide some examples of situations in which you might choose these methods of analysis for your application. Unlike visualization, these methods are not interactive and largely leave the analyst out of the loop.

Planning Your Data Mining Engagement

By the time you finish reading this section, we expect that you will have a very good idea about what is actually involved in a data mining engagement. We hope that this section includes enough preparatory information to prevent you from being blindsided by too many unforeseen problems in your data mining efforts. Use this section to assist your planning efforts before an engagement begins so that you can address as many issues ahead of time as possible. As you read this section, use it to help you answer such questions as:

- Will I have ample access to the data sources I need?

- Are the data in the proper format for the tool that will be used? If not, what must be done ahead of time to address this?

- How will I integrate data from multiple sources?

- Should I use visualization or a nonvisual analytical method?
- What visualization method should I use to display my data?
- How will I know what types of patterns are important?
- If I choose a nonvisual approach, what analysis will I be doing?

The following three chapters will help you to answer these and other questions before you ever begin. Remember that there are lots of options. Knowing how to choose among them is half of the battle.

ACCESSING AND PREPARING THE DATA

After the initial discussions, designs, and classifications, the next step in a data mining engagement is to access the data set(s) that you want to use and prepare them for analysis. This chapter provides an overview of a variety of issues that you may need to tackle in order to set up your data mining environment. Although most data warehousing applications should and do address many of the data formatting issues presented here, our discussion does not assume that you will always have an automated data management system available. In fact, our experience in data mining applications has usually involved the use of data derived from distributed locations, miscellaneous data extractions, and other third-party databases. The burden of acquiring, arranging, and integrating the data was left up to us. What we want to do in this chapter is to share some of the knowledge that we have gained, often painfully, from these experiences. We hope that some of the tricks of the trade that we have learned will be of benefit to even the most seasoned data hackers.

As you go through the phase of data preparation, you always need to keep the goals of the analysis in mind. The questions of interest in the application will dictate the ways in which you will model your data. These models, in turn, will determine the kinds of information you will want to extract for the analysis. Likewise, the format and content of the data sources will have a large influence on the types of models that can be developed. Under the data preparation phase there are a series of issues that will impact the modeling process later on. These issues fall within the categories of data collection and data integration.

We begin this chapter by presenting issues to be addressed early on in the data mining process when you are trying to gain access to data sources. This usually involves transfer of the data from some other source(s), integration and conversion into a format useful within the particular data mining tool being used. Along the way you will need to address formatting issues, especially if you are using data that are not in an electronic fielded format. Likewise, there are various cleanup operations that you will need to perform on the data set. If you are analyzing textual information, there are a host of additional operations that you may need to conduct before you are ready to begin. Once the formatting issues have been addressed, you will need to do sampling from the data source, constructing extractions that are appropriate for the set of questions you will be asking in your analysis. All of these preliminary steps are a vital part of the overall data mining process.

Accessing the Data

Before *any* system can be developed to analyze and report intelligently on data, the data must be made available. This basic requirement is not always easy to fulfill. If you are lucky, there will be online database systems and files that can be obtained directly without any special procedures, protocols, or access privileges. In many domains, most of the data are stored in relational structures that can be queried to access the desired information.

This may not always be true, however. Even though data warehouses have become very popular in recent times, they are very expensive to build and maintain properly. Chances are that if you are not part of a large commercial or government organization with a progressive information systems technology group, there will be no such reference structure to access. In the majority of the data mining engagements we have conducted, portions of the information used came from ad-hoc sources which had to be accessed, integrated, and presented using less advanced methods than a data warehouse.

Whether you are accessing data from an online data warehouse, or some less eloquent method, several issues must be addressed in bringing extractions into the data mining environment. The sidebar contains a list of methods you may need to perform during the access stage before querying and extraction begin.

Querying Data Sources

One of the first steps in a data mining engagement is to define a subset of data with which to begin your analysis. Recall from Chapter 3 that we refer to this process as extracting a proactive slice of data. You will want to structure your extracted data set to include a representative sample of the types of information you are analyzing. Sample extractions are one of the best methods for generating slices of data that can be fed into a data mining application. For example, you could generate data requests that will extract all records for a particular region, date frame, subject, port-of-entry, or even dollar value. Thus one of the first items of business is generating the queries to be applied against the data sources to which you have been granted access.

Helpful Operations to Perform during Data Access

There are a few operations that you will want to consider when beginning with a new data set. The following is a limited list of some functions that are virtually guaranteed to improve the quality of your data mining analysis.

Capitalization. Convert all characters in the data stream into either uppercase or lowercase. This helps avoid any variations that may occur due to case differences between various data elements. The names of people and organizations are good candidates for this procedure since they often include mixed cased letters. In the majority of our applications, we convert the data to an uppercase notation because it is easier to read in our graphic displays and yields a more consistent representation.

Concatenation. In many systems, data are stored as discrete fielded entries, such that the various components comprising a data object may literally be strewn across the entire record. Although this provides a powerful technique for modeling during the analysis, the individual components must be combined in such a way as to represent each data object uniquely. To do this you will need to have the capability of combining multiple fields into a single unit. For instance, fields involving lastname and firstname or street number, city, state, and Zip code will need to be concatenated.

Representation Formats. The formats used to represent certain types of information such as dates can be as varied as the data sources they come from. There seems to be no standard for representing dates and they can come in a variety of formats including 12/05/93, 05-DEC-93, 12-05-93, 120593, 93287, 93339, and so on. Our preference is to use a YYYYMMDD format because you can then sort or order your data entries by a date and be guaranteed that they will be represented in a consistent temporal order. This, of course, requires that all month and date values less than ten be entered with a preceding zero.

Augmentation. Data usually contain many different types of extraneous characters. Whenever possible these should be removed from the

Continued

Helpful Operations to Perform during Data Access (*Continued*)

data stream. These characters can include just about anything from !@#$%^&*(){}[];/.,<>?": to strings of letters (i.e., Mr., Mrs., Ph.D., unk, and, or, etc.). Getting rid of these extra characters can turn out to be very important to your application in terms of the choices of data types available to you for representation. For example if you have fielded values that you want to represent as a numeric data type, you might not be able to do so because extraneous symbols such as dollar signs, commas, or unit measurements would force the data into a string type.

Abstraction. It is sometimes useful to reduce the information represented in a field to a simple True/Yes or False/No value. This allows you to convey certain types of information without the overhead of representing every single unique value. Good examples of this include flagging people with criminal histories, marking products that sell internationally, or distinguishing medications with known side effects. If you are interested in the specific details about any particular item(s), you can drill down into the data to find out more as the analysis progresses.

Unit Conversion. You should adopt a standard unit for each field appearing in the data set. For example, if you have a field containing measures of distance, you should adopt one unit (say, meters) and make a standard conversion for all values represented in other units (i.e., converting feet and yards to meters). There are many examples for which unit conversion becomes an important issue. These include currency, weight, distance, and temperature, to name a few.

Exclusion. Because the processing of data takes up valuable computational time, you should have exclusion criteria for removing any unwanted file values. This process completely removes the record from the data set so that it never has to be processed or considered by the data mining application. Records containing empty or null fields that are critical to the analysis can usually be removed. Also value boundary violations (e.g., month = 99) that result in bad or dirty data can be discounted.

Since many data mining systems are usually third-party software programs, they typically are configured to accept their input through some type of flat-ASCII delimited file format. Although database drivers do exist and should be used wherever possible, the data streams that they create can be converted to a flat-file format. What this means is that any information used for data mining must be extracted from its holding source and placed into a temporary repository where it can be processed by the target data mining software. These data will eventually be used inside a data mining application. In that environment, you have the option of applying subfilters and other segmentation techniques that allow the extraction to be refined further. Additionally, updates to the working data set can be requested at any time should you find that they need to go back to the original data source for more information.

This takes care of the easy cases. Unfortunately, there are many situations in which the extraction you have does not contain the requisite information required for your analysis. For reasons beyond your control, you may be given only limited access to the data either because of copyright protections or related security issues. Additionally, many systems handle data access through front-end menu facilities that may have limited capabilities or limited access privileges. For example, the menu facilities might not allow you to perform the batch executions needed to extract large volumes of data. In many of these cases, manual efforts to cut and paste the data between systems are usually the only option. Furthermore, in a large number of systems, the report/query generation capabilities are limited and do not meet the requirements of the analyst. Precanned reports or fixed queries tend to serve the general population of requests, but they inevitably produce too much or too little information for your purposes in the data mining engagement.

Limiting the Scope of the Problem

The types of queries used to make extractions should reflect the types of patterns that you want to discover. Even though these patterns are unknown and hidden within your data sets, there are some general guidelines that you can use to help focus the analysis. Examples include restricting the extraction to predefined sets of geographical regions, time frames, or dollar ranges. You should limit the scope of the extractions using variables that can be identified through a range of specific values where possible (e.g., products, types, descriptions). Many OLAP systems use the concept of *dimensions,* which allows you to extract various subsets of the data. These types of systems can be used effectively to derive these slices of data.

When forming queries to be used in extraction, keep computational issues in mind. In particular, remember that the accumulation of values within standard relational databases is an expensive process to execute. For example, any of the following initial queries might be problematic even though they appear to be straightforward requests:

- All people who have visited your store more than three times during the past year

- All people who have spent more than fifty dollars total
- All people who have talked a minimum of 100 minutes

Queries such as these require the processing of accumulated values and are therefore likely to carry serious computational overhead with them. Typically, you would do better to save these sorts of filtering operations for the data mining environment. Accumulated values are represented as declarative data and are best calculated directly within most data mining tools or through their associated preprocessing systems.

If there is a general category of patterns that should be identified, consider structuring your proactive segmentation along values that will help expose those conditions. This is similar to planning a trip. Once you have selected a destination (or target site), you have several options for how you can get there. Sometimes you may feel like joy riding, so whatever direction you select will take you someplace, just not necessarily someplace interesting or new. (Remember the cautionary adage, however: If you don't know where you're going, you won't know when you get there.) If there are no clear segmentations within the context of your problem, you could consider generating the output by using inductive systems like decision trees or self-organizing neural network algorithms that can find specific breaks or segmentations within the data set (these approaches are described in Chapter 6).

Fortunately, the initial queries themselves do not have to be complicated. Since data mining is an iterative and cumulative process, the patterns are usually exposed after several refinements of the data used in the analysis. Some examples of proactive queries (e.g., data segmentation) might include:

- Showing a specific category of product repair to determine whether there are predictable sequences or questionable conditions under which the service was provided
- Looking at all purchase orders within a certain dollar range under a designated signature approval level to see whether any "structuring" is occurring (e.g., multiple small-dollar purchase orders are being generated to acquire an expensive item)
- Extracting corporate credit card purchase records with weekend-day charge dates (e.g., Saturday or Sunday) to determine if there is any repetitive, unusual, or suspicious activity suggesting corporate embezzlement

Structuring Extractions

Most data mining engagements begin in a proactive analysis mode in which you are simply searching around for interesting patterns as opposed to doing a directed analysis. Even so, some structure must be imposed from the outset when you decide what data to include in the extraction that you will use to begin your data mining engagement. The initial data extraction will be the first slice you use to begin your proactive analysis.

Depending on the type of technology you are using to do data mining, extractions can be very small or quite immense. Extraction size will largely depend on the level of abstraction you will use to represent data in your model. We have worked in many engagements where the entire data source was small enough to be put on a disk (e.g., 500–25,000 records). No initial data reduction is required in such cases. However, in those cases in which the amount of data being considered is simply too large to be maintained as a single entity, a subset must suffice. The way you go about choosing the subset(s) can be very important to the success of the engagement.

Extraction as Data Sampling

What you are doing with an extraction is taking a representative sample of the data set. This is similar to the way in which statistical sampling has traditionally been performed on large populations of observations. When surveyors acquire information from a general population, they sample only enough of that population to get a good approximation. You do not have to identify every single occurrence of a pattern within a data set in order to infer that the pattern exists. Once you lock onto a pattern you can get a feel for how extensive the pattern is throughout the entire data set through alternative reporting methods. Remember that you are performing data mining, not generating reports. Do not feel that you need to process the entire data set at one time. There will usually be more than enough results from the segmented data to keep you busy. We have found important patterns using as little as several hundred records. It is not the size of your data set that counts, but the way in which you use it. Keep in mind that in a well-constructed data mining environment, you will have access to all of the data that you need by making iterative extractions in a series of steps.

Walking the Data

Once you identify a particular entity of interest in your proactive slice of data, you can follow that lead by requesting that all additional information regarding this entity be brought forward from the original data source. This allows you to "walk the data" using a feedback loop so that you can constantly refine your viewpoint on the data. This method guarantees that you can work with all of the data you have available within your data sets, regardless of their sizes. When the new information regarding the target entity is made available from the system, you then have the option of either replacing or appending the current working set with the new information. By using this feature directly within the analytical environment, you will have the ability to control the size and focus of the analysis.

In many of the analyses we perform involving the use of a feedback loop, we also ensure that there is a method in place that allows us to know when the data slice was introduced. Usually, this is a simple counting mechanism tracking iterations from the original download. However, very elaborate methods are possible and can even include state-based environments where all information is kept in separate holding areas for detailed reconstruction (see the discussion in Chapter 10 "Future Trends in Visual Data Mining").

Maintaining Consistency and Integrity

When performing extractions, there are a few technical rules to follow. The contents of the data in the extraction must be structured to differentiate each fielded value and support a consistent layout format. This implies that the values contained within the fields of a particular table value will always support the expected definition and this information will always be available from the same place in the file. All supporting code lists or look-up tables must also be provided during the extraction. Any extraneous characters or field values should be dismissed. This includes information used for database administration purposes unless it is relevant to the analysis. All data requiring special handling (large text files or images) should be processed independently and separated from the main data files. This will make their integration for analysis straightforward as long as the data keys are maintained.

Transferring Data from Original Sources

We have made reference to several issues that we have encountered with respect to the transfer of data in prior sections of this book. The main objectives of transferring data from the host platform back to your data mining environment will be to make sure that the extraction is done properly and that the data can be moved from point to point. As we have previously stated, the transfer of data does not necessarily have to be done in real time. For the most part, most of our data sets come in electronic formats on high-density tapes, through e-mail attachments, or FTP bulk downloads. We occasionally even get a stack of paper documents that contain the data that are targeted for analysis. The following is a quick overview of several different repository types that can be used to transfer data out of the host system to the data mining platform.

Databases

When information is extracted and transferred out of a large relational database system, you are usually well advised to request the assistance of the database administrator (DBA). It is typically a matter of good politics (on any number of levels) to include the DBA in the process. The main issue to be addressed is the type of output format expected by the data mining tool(s). Most often decisions must be made about whether one large table will be created with all of the requisite data or whether there should be a series of small tables. The former format regularly requires a significant amount of SQL programming in order to join together all of the different tables needed to supply the full details of the target data. For example, if you are trying to reconstruct a credit card transaction, there may be three different tables that will have to be queried, accessed, and joined together in order to convey the contents of a simple store purchase completely. These tables would include the merchant reference table describing the type of business, the customer profile including items such as name and address, and the transaction itself which would have the item (e.g., SKU), times, dates, and amounts of the purchase. The integrating factor across each table is the card number.

For the most part, we request the information be extracted and transferred as a series of discrete tables. We have found that this is the easiest method for the DBA to handle and it rarely results in incomplete files. So in our example, instead of receiving one well-formatted data file, we would expect to receive three separate files. It is usually easier for us to let the data mining tools we are working with take care of the multiple data integration issues. This approach will also help to determine whether there are any missing data in your extraction. When we go to join up the files within the data mining tool and we see that the key-field is not properly matching up between the files, we know there is a problem somewhere. This mismatch could indicate several possibilities including inactive merchants, nonexistent customers, phantom credit card numbers, and other questionable instantiations of data.

You could also use micro-database programs (e.g., FoxPro, Access, LotusNotes) to help you perform data transfer. These types of programs are widely used throughout the business community to help manage data. Many of these systems have well-defined user interfaces and help wizards that assist with exporting functions. These systems tend to be very flexible with respect to exporting their contents to a flat-ASCII file format, which is usually sufficient for most data mining tools and supporting OLAP constructs. Since each program has a slightly different export method, you will have to make a few adjustments each time you gather the data from a different one of these systems.

Word Processors

Information used for data mining might come from the contents of a word processor. In this context, we are referring to a free-text document that contains a minimal amount of formatting, if any, to describe its content. The type of data usually found within a document could include abstracts, narratives, topic lists, and a variety of other relatively short entries. Their layouts almost always have some limited amount of formatting, which makes them amenable to low-level parsing. Documents can also contain large text passages (e.g., technical paper, annual report, etc.) that require different and more complex methods of extraction. For the most part, the extractions you can make from a file created by a word processor are fairly limited—you are largely restricted to the format used to save out the contents to a file. In our experiences, a straightforward "text" output without any formatting option is the best method of getting to the data. In all cases, we have had to write post-processing scripts in order to take the output and refine it into a format that was conducive for our data mining applications. This is not a difficult task, but it can involve many exceptions and special cases due to the nature of the formatted text. Once the scripts have been written, the word processing text extracts can be consistently processed without any additional overhead or development costs. (We discuss free-text issues more in a later section of this chapter.)

Spreadsheets

In those environments that do not support a large mainframe database system, we often find that people will use spreadsheet programs to help maintain and manage their data sets. These programs are attractive because they are simple to operate and require little set-up prior to data entry. Most spreadsheets provide some limited analytical capabilities as well, such as simple business graphic charts that can be generated to show certain dimensions of the data. The spreadsheets are often well structured due to the strict row/column format they impose on data. The transfer issues associated with spreadsheets simply involve the selection of the appropriate output format. They all have standard export functions that may be used to select the fields, format, and style of the data. We prefer to use a tabular data format without any quotation marks around stringed values.

The majority of problems we see with spreadsheets have to do with the inconsistent replication of data across cells. The concerns with name variations are very prevalent within spreadsheets. Inconsistencies tend to occur in punctuation usage, including such violations as extra spaces, periods or commas. The users/developers of these data sets usually retype the names into each cell, rather than copying and pasting the data. Regardless, spreadsheet databases are very efficient and easy to use when data sets are small (e.g., fewer than 25,000 records) and no complicated layout schemes are required (e.g., multiple tables).

Machine-to-Machine

Some data transfer issues arise because data are being moved from one computing architecture to another. The transfer of data rarely results in a format change, but can sometimes require an adjustment to the format or content depending on the character codes used. One client we recently dealt with was using a VMS machine to download some medical case records. Generation of extractions and performing data transfers were straightforward processes. However, the record separator characters imposed by the VMS system were not standard in this case. We received the information on our UNIX machine as one very long, continuous character stream. Needless to say, we had to create some translation scripts to parse through and insert the necessary breaks in the data in order to access this data source. In another case, the "binary" mode was not switched on as some WordPerfect files were being FTPed across a network between UNIX and PC machines. This resulted in an unexpected garble of text on our end of the data stream. Little events like these illustrate the importance of double-checking your formats as data are moved among computing platforms.

Integrating the Data

The data to be used in an analysis do not all necessarily need to be derived from the same sources. Once data are accessed, the logical and physical integration of disparate data sets is the next step required for development of a formal application. The analyst must decide what the *important* aspects of the data are in the different sources and how they will realistically be exploited to fulfill the objectives of the investigation. There are many ways to identify the structures that you will want to import from your array of data sources. There are a variety of informal techniques and methodologies that are capable of exposing the critical facts, similarities, or anomalies contained within and across data sets (see the sidebar on Data Integration Issues). This will force all underlying schemata to be managed in a consistent and useful manner. The combination of data representations and sources used in an analysis will influence how the data will be presented and interpreted by the end user.

Integrating Separate Data Sets: An Example

Let's assume that you have extracted information from multiple data sets and are now ready to integrate these data into one model. There will likely be overlapping

Data Integration Issues

A variety of concerns must be addressed during the integration of data sets derived from separate sources. Many of these can easily be resolved, but others will take some time to sort out. Some possible thorny issues that you should consider ahead of time before performing data integration follow. Hopefully your attention to these problems early on will prevent any from becoming show-stoppers in your application. Figure 4.1 provides an overview of these issues.

Multisource. Issues need to be resolved for handling Sybase, Oracle, M204, Informix, Excel, Lotus, ObjectStore, flat files, and so forth. As you can imagine, every single vendor has their own query, access, and reporting methods. Although the use of ODBC, CORBA, and most data warehousing environments greatly facilitate this process, there are always exceptions and exclusions that must be addressed. Furthermore, every database design supports different data schemata. The processing required to obtain the information needed will often depend on how complicated the structures are to control. Fortunately, we have yet to encounter a source that would not give up its contents for use in a data mining application, although some have not gone gently into that good night.

Figure 4.1 A list of data integration issues.

How do we get at the information?

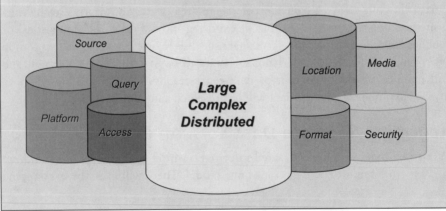

Multiformat. Relational databases, hierarchical structures, free-text, ASCII, field delimited, column based and many more format differences will affect how you will go about accessing information. The formats of each data source must be clearly understood in order to facilitate the access and retrieval of the data. Many formatting issues can be resolved through normalization routines that are applied to the data as they are prepared to be integrated and modeled into the target data mining application. Terminology differences, unit measurements, and code-list translations are among some of the topics we typically have to address in multiformatted data sets.

Multiplatform. There are a variety of operating systems (DOS, UNIX, VMS, etc.) and hardware platforms (PC, workstations, mainframes) that support different access protocols. Gaining entry to these systems and navigating their interfaces can prove to be a significant challenge. Additionally, the structure of the data can be affected by the operating system (e.g., end-of-line characters), especially with the introduction of special characters. Although these problems are relatively easy to overcome, they must be reconciled, if encountered. In our experience, this is more of an issue when dealing with special systems such as phone-switches, card-readers and other nonstandard (proprietary/customized) systems.

Multisecurity. Data can be classified using a variety of methods ranging from unrestricted to very specialized compartmentalization. At a national level the U.S. Government has established extensive guidelines and procedures for dealing with secure data. From a right-to-privacy perspective, data can also be considered very sensitive depending upon how they were originally derived. Copyrights, personal records, and other usage restrictions can limit what can legally be done with certain types of data. From a business standpoint, there may be other restrictions that a company may wish to place on the circulation of some types of information. If you are not cleared to access information, leave it alone. If you are not sure, leave it alone. The data mining world is one place where it is better to get permission than forgiveness.

Multimedia. Information can be represented using multimedia formats including free-text, images, audio, video, and other binary objects.

Continued

> **Data Integration Issues (*Continued*)**
>
> Usually these types of data are used as supporting materials to include in reports or to use as references during an analysis. Thus, if you want to see a picture, read a document, or hear an audio clip related to an object encountered during an analysis, you can set up links between those data sources and the relevant objects in the model. If properly applied, the use of multimedia sources can significantly enhance the quality of a data mining engagement. However, if the source materials are incomplete or inconsistently represented (e.g., not all objects within a given object class have a picture), their inclusion may present more problems than benefits. Since multimedia sources can also be expensive to incorporate, this issue should be carefully considered before the resources are committed.
>
> **Multilocation.** Local and remote data sources must be accessed via LANs, WANs, dial-up connections or wireless access services. When data are not readily available from a central repository or data warehouse, special consideration must be given to where and how the information will be acquired. This also typically means that the information will be controlled by another party and access will be limited by their approval. We have seen several instances in which data ended up not being utilized to the full benefit of the data mining analysis due to control issues on the part of the supplier. It is best to address these issues up front so that all parties are in agreement and supportive from the start.

field values contained in the extractions that can be used to facilitate the integration. Tables 4.1 and 4.2 provide examples of the content of two data sets. Note that there are spaces included in the data files shown as underscores "_". These will need to be cleaned up during integration. The particular approach presented here represents but one method of performing this task.

The first data file contains six fields; last name, first name, street number, street name, city, and state. In its current format, this extraction is not ready to be included in the analysis because each field contains only a portion of the information that will eventually comprise the objects modeled for the analysis. This is due in part to the way the original database designers structured their data schemata and implemented the load interfaces. As we mentioned previously, the design of a database rarely reflects how it will eventually be used because the architecture is usually more suited for efficient storage than it is for query and retrieval of data. To

Multiquery. You will need to determine whether the query format is consistent across data sets and whether the extraction of large numbers of records can be performed. Certain systems are not configured to permit the batch execution of queries, but rather force you to acquire data in small sets, either by the individual record or through screen captures. These tend to be remote access systems and can be difficult to accommodate. Screen scrubbers and "expect" scripts may be used to handle these situations, but they are not elegant solutions. Also, the schemes adopted for original storage of data may force the user to submit multiple queries in order to retrieve all of the desired information. Although not efficient, this problem can be accommodated through automated scripts.

Multiaccess. Subscription services have specific restrictions on the number of accounts that may be used at any one time. Your ability to use accounts set up for AOL, West Law, Lexis/Nexis, Reuters, DTIC, and other information providers will depend on the number of active subscriptions available to satisfy the task. Since data mining systems tend to be very specialized in their distribution and usage, this typically has not been a problem in the past. However, as the utilization of data mining tools becomes more commonplace, upper access limits may be reached and additional subscriptions will have to be purchased, no doubt to the delight of the service providers.

prepare the data for analysis, several of the fields need to be integrated together to form the model object types. To create a "person" object, the last name and first name fields will be switched and concatenated together with a space inserted

Table 4.1 Extraction from Data Set 1

LASTNAME	FIRSTNAME	STREET #	STREET NAME	CITY	STATE
Smith	John	123	_Elm_Street	Charlotte	NC
Jones	Bill__	_456	Maple__Ave	Chicago	IL
Williams	Mike	789	Main_Street_	San_Francisco	CA
Smith	Suzie	123	Elm_St.	Charlotte	NC
Brown_	Bob		Apt_B._59_Ave	Brooklyn	NY

Table 4.2 Extraction from Data Set 2

FULL NAME	ACCOUNT #	TRANS-TYPE	DATE	AMOUNT
Mr._Mike_Williams	43659493	Deposit	980414	50.85
Mr._Mike_Williams	54968584	Deposit	980418	74.16
Mr._Bill_Jones	54943920	Deposit	980422	29.69
Ms._Sue_Smith	88399493	Deposit	980501	84.94
Mr._John_Smith	43945920	Withdrawal	980512	95.33

between the values. The rest of the fields will also be concatenated with a set of spaces to produce an "address" object. Note: we would not want to use just the street number and name to produce an address because they can literally occur in many places throughout the county. Since there are also cities with the same names (e.g., Columbus can be found in Ohio, Georgia, Kansas, Texas, Wisconsin, North Carolina, and 12 other states), we need to include the state as well. So in order to ensure that an address is unique in its representation, we have to use the full street, city, and state notation.

The output of this set of transformations results in a new data format that reflects the full name, full address, street, city, and state. We have kept the street, city and state as separate fields because they will be used as attributes of the address in the model. At this point, we will exclude any extraneous characters from the records. This is done after any significant alteration of the fields themselves because as they are being concatenated or switched around, extra spaces may be inadvertently introduced because of the way the data were entered. When removing extra spaces, you need to ensure that all double spaces are reduced to a single space. Do not completely remove double spaces. Otherwise you will find values such as names without any break between the first and last names. The process of eliminating double spaces may require that you make several passes through the data because fields may have multiple double spaces (e.g., triple and quadruple spaces). Additionally, you want to make sure that any extra spaces at the beginning or end of a field are also removed. So for example if the delimiter between fields is a TAB, any SPACE-TAB or TAB-SPACE combinations should be reduced to just a TAB. The final step for transforming this data set is to change all entries to an uppercase notation. This is done to avoid conflict with integrating other data sets as well as any data load issues.

Depending on how elaborate you want to get with cleaning up and disam- biguating your data, a set of data standardization routines can be invoked. For instance, within the address fields abbreviations are used quite often including *St* for *Street*, *Blvd* for *Boulevard*, *Rt* for *Route*, *N* for *North*, and so on. Conversions along these lines can be performed for a wide range of field values including names of people and organizations, addresses, ID numbers (social security, vehicle identi- fication), license plates, diseases, and general merchandise descriptions, to name a few. The final product of our data adjustments is shown in Table 4.3. As you can see, a data set that appeared to be simple and straightforward in its initial repre- sentation can go through a fairly elaborate transformation prior to analysis.

The second data set (in Table 4.2) must also be processed through a set of cleanup filters as well. Since the first field represents the name of the individual and it is also the key to integrating the data files together, we must make sure that they are consistent. In this example, this is just a matter of removing the prefix on the names (e.g., Mr., Mrs., Dr., etc.). However, you can expect to see all sorts of varia- tions with respect to representing names such as misspellings, nicknames, and var- ious alternatives. The second field of this data file contains the number of an account where the first two digits indicate the type of account (43=savings, 54=checking, and 88=loan). This will be extracted, converted, and placed into its own field in the final version. The third field is obviously the type of transaction performed and will be reduced to a single letter to save space. The fourth field con- tains a date that will be decomposed into several components including the month

Table 4.3 Data Set Resulting from Cleanup of Data Set 1

NAME	ADDRESS	STREET NAME	CITY	STATE
JOHN_ SMITH	123_ELM_STREET CHARLOTTE_NC	ELM_STREET	CHARLOTTE	NC
BILL_ JONES	456_MAPLE_AVENUE CHICAGO_IL	MAPLE_AVE	CHICAGO	IL
MIKE_ WILLIAMS	789_MAIN_STREET SAN_FRANCISCO_CA	MAIN_STREET	SAN_ FRANCISCO	CA
SUZIE_ SMITH	123_ELM_STREET CHARLOTTE_NC	ELM_ST.	CHARLOTTE	NC
BOB_ BROWN	APT_B._59TH_AVE BROOKLYN_NY	APT_B._ 59TH_AVE	BROOKLYN	NY

and day of week. Additionally, the amount of the transaction contained in the last field will be rounded to the nearest $25 increment. The final adjustment made to this data set is to provide a unique identification number for each transaction given by the line number in the data set. These distinct identifiers for the individual transactions allow us to analyze the transactions as separate events.

The resulting transformations are shown in Table 4.4. As you can see, a lot of value was added through the employment of our meta-data techniques. At this point we are ready to model the data. Here we further decide what fields to make into objects, attributes, and linkages. Depending on what type of system we use, the data can be integrated directly through the data mining tool by providing a unique configuration load/model routine for each data format. This is the preferred method but it can also be done through the deployment of a simple join across the name fields in each file. The major difference is that you would be able to connect fields directly using the latter method. Figure 4.2 shows the resulting model. You can see how we created people, accounts, and addresses as object classes and linked them together through the key field that was the person. Quickly you can see that Sue Smith and Suzie Smith are indirectly connected to the same objects, indicating that they are probably the same person. You could then go back and clean up your data sets by changing one of the data files or you could use a merge/combine function in the tool (if available) to rectify this and other anomalies that might be discovered.

Performing Data Integration across Data Types

As we just described, the information used in a data mining exercise can come from virtually any source imaginable and the sources and types of information that can be used are essentially limitless. Information can be collected on tapes, disks, in hardcopy format, from questionnaires, generated from third-party programs, manually entered, extracted from the Internet, FTPed across networks, scanned, and so forth. Although we would always prefer to be able to extract our data from established databases, chances are that some nonstandard formats will be encountered during the course of an analysis. This need not be problematic. The data do not need to be pretty; they just have to exist. Broadly speaking, we divide nonstandard data types into three classifications: free-text, tables, and "other" types.

Free Text

The most common type of information not represented in fielded structures is free text. Textual format is best suited for small sets of data that can be read quickly and

Table 4.4 Data Set Resulting from Integration of Data Sets 1 and 2

FULL NAME	ACCT NMBR	ACCT TYPE	TRNS TYPE	DATE	MTH	DAY OF WEEK	AMT1	AMT2	INDX
MIKE WILLIAMS	43659493	SAVG	D	980414	APR	TUE	50.85	50	1
MIKE WILLIAMS	54968584	CHCK	D	980418	APR	SAT	74.16	75	2
BILL JONES	54943920	CHCK	D	980422	APR	WED	29.69	50	3
SUE SMITH	88399493	LOAN	D	980501	MAY	FRI	84.94	100	4
JOHN SMITH	43945920	SAVG	W	980512	MAY	TUE	95.33	100	5
JOHN SMITH	88399493	LOAN	D	980512	MAY	TUE	53.29	50	6

Figure 4.2 Model used for analysis of integrated data sets.

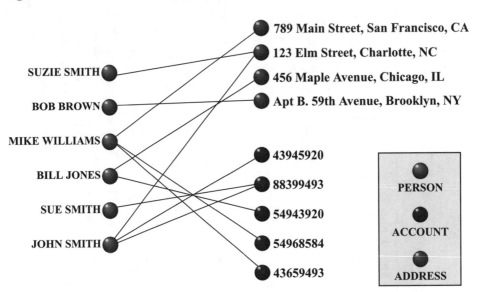

interpreted by the analyst. Even small selections of free text, however, contain a large amount of extraneous information that can obfuscate those aspects of the data set that are important for the application. Text is also a difficult format to integrate with other data types due to its informal structure. Although large amounts of data exist in textual formats, mostly in comment fields or description files, text can be condensed and summarized into more direct and meaningful styles. That is, categorical labels can be substituted for passages of free text in order to denote information about their content. Therefore, as text is interpreted and structured, it can be made to approximate a tabular format containing declarative descriptors. (We discuss issues of text processing at greater length later in the chapter.)

Tables

Tables provide better mechanisms for analyzing and presenting information due to the structure and formatting that they impose on the data. Tables can sort similar types of information into common regions or areas for quick identification and selection. Many of the existing database and spreadsheet systems currently in operation support this format. Tables can be used successfully when combining information from more than one source, since all common features are placed into their appropriate columns. However, tables do not convey large amounts of data very well. When more than a page of space is required for representation, the user has to switch back and forth between parts of the table. This switching dramatically reduces both efficiency and ease of analysis. (More about this topic will be discussed in Chapter 5.)

Other Formats

Other formats including pictures, sounds, videos, or graphics can also be used in data mining applications. These formats are not amenable to decompositional analysis. That is, they cannot be used to add declarative knowledge to your model since they would need to be interpreted and labeled within the model conventions. Nevertheless, these information sources can be quite valuable when contextually associated with declarative knowledge represented in the model. This can easily be done, for example, by including these information sources at the level of object attributes. Product pictures, blueprints, medical images, mug shots, fingerprints, scanned documents, surveillance videos, and wire-tap recordings are some of the types of alternative formats and media used within data mining applications.

Moving toward a Single Virtual Representation

Once all of the important facts and structures have been identified from the various data sources, they need to be integrated into a single coherent representation. To accomplish this, the data will be "normalized" as they are brought into the application. When performing data mining using multiple sources of information, you would ideally like to be able to use a single query that could be sent to all data sets in order to perform the initial extractions. This sounds easy in theory, but when it comes to real-world practice, it is often difficult to implement.

Consider the complexity of a simple query that requires information from two very distinct data structures such as "show all people with expensive homes in a certain geographical region (e.g., a public property database) who have purchased high-margin items at certain store locations (e.g., your centralized customer database)." Unless you have a fairly well-established data warehouse already built that contains the requisite information, you will most probably have to submit multiple queries to the different systems in order to get it. To deal with this query, different database tables need to be accessed and appropriate field values acquired from those tables. This produces several data files that have to be managed within the target data mining system. The challenge is to determine how best to integrate these files into a single coherent representation that contains the data of interest.

When combining multiple sources of information for use in a data mining application, it is important to consider the end-user models that are being populated. As data come together, you want to ensure as much standardization as possible. All unit measurements should be converted into the same scale, all terminology should be as consistent as possible and similar types of data should be represented together. If possible, data reduction techniques should be employed to represent similar concepts across data sources (see the sidebar on a Credit Card Example of Data Reduction). Thus, you are trying to condense or reduce the duplicated information as much as possible with respect to the number of unique records contained within a data set.

A Credit Card Example of Data Reduction

Suppose you were modeling a credit card transaction and wanted to use the "amount" of the transaction as an attribute in your model. There are several ways to represent this information. One method would be to create a new field for storing the amount. However, credit card transactions can also result in a posting or credit from returned merchandise. This amount would also have to be represented and could be expressed in a separate field indicating the amount returned. Therefore, one field is for expenses and the other field is for credits. This is a valid model, but does take a considerable amount of space just to represent a simple value. Since any one transaction can have only one value at a time, one field will always be null. (For these purposes, every unique occurrence of a debit or credit is considered a separate and unique transaction and therefore can support only one value.)

An alternative approach would be to combine the values from both fields into a single composite "amount." In this field, credits could be represented as negative numbers and debits as positive numbers. This single field could then serve to satisfy both values in a more efficient way. Not only does this save computational overhead, but this method will make data interpretation easier later on during the analytical phase. Where possible, you should try to think of ways to represent the most information in the most economical way that you can. This will also help to simplify the models that you will have to build.

Converting Data

Every engagement usually brings with it some unique or special case that has not been encountered in prior data mining activities. In many domains, it is undesirable to change the data set in any way, shape, or form since you may always need to reference the original. For the purposes of performing the analysis, the data can be manipulated and refined, almost as if performing "what-if" scenarios. As long as you can recreate or point to the original source and describe what alterations have occurred, there is usually no problem with converting the data to meet the needs of the analysis.

Working with Long and Short Record Structures

Unless you are working on an application in which you are processing free text, your data sets are going to be formatted in a particular way when you bring them into your data mining application. It turns out that the format of your data sets partially determines the sort of model you will be able to use in your analysis. The record formats used to represent data usually fall into one of two categories—long or short. Next we discuss some of the issues associated with processing each type of format so as to facilitate data processing.

Manipulating Long Record Structures

In almost all of the data sets we have used, the fields associated with each record are contained in one long sequence of values that are either separated by some type of delimiter or placed into a fixed column format. This is called a long or a wide record format. Figure 4.3 shows an example of this type of record structure and Table 4.5 shows some sample content. This is a long record format because all information about an entity is contained within the scope of that entity's record. Even when data are split across multiple tables within a database, long records are still implied. This occurs because the information is most likely merged across tables to generate a complete description of the entity. In most cases you can build data models in your configuration file directly from the long record data set so long as you specify the mappings of fields to object classes and attributes each time.

Long record formats almost always require customized configuration routines to accommodate their unique formats. When you construct your models using long records, you explicitly reference an absolute field position for each object class or attribute. In the example in Figure 4.2, field1 contains names of individuals, field2 contains addresses, field3 contains account numbers, and so on. Once you have

Figure 4.3 Example of a long record structure.

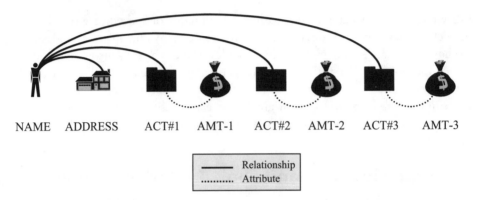

NAME   ADDRESS   ACT#1   AMT-1   ACT#2   AMT-2   ACT#3   AMT-3

———	Relationship
··········	Attribute

generated your model based on the long record format, you need to go back and change your configuration files if new fields are added or if the structure of the data changes. The long record format gives you access to all available types of information about entities of interest, but the price you pay for this functionality is that the process of building your model(s) may be a bit more complex.

The main disadvantage of the long record format is seen in cases for which multiple values of an attribute must be represented or for which there are repeating fields in the data structure. In one particular banking activity that we were involved with, we needed to represent up to six different types of bank accounts that could be involved in any one transaction. These included account types such as checking, savings, money

Table 4.5 Sample Long Data Record Structure

NAME	ADDRESS	ACT#1	AMT-1	ACT#2	AMT-2	ACT#3	AMT-3
Mr. Smith	123 Elm Street	449213	$55.32	449393	$12.43		
Mr. Jones	45 Maple Ave	449293	$94.43	882939	$20.20	495932	$33.50
Mrs. Smith	123 Elm Street	449394	$64.23				
Dr. Walters	239 Main St.	884949	$34.40	448858	$22.04		
Ms. Brown	501 E. 47th St.	450939	$94.95	440394	$12.40	449948	$43.42
Mr. Elliot	95 Broadway	883939	$13.49	499312	$93.02		

markets and loans. The data set contained six different account fields, each with a slot for the corresponding value of a transaction amount. In some cases more than six account types were involved and so a second record was generated with room for an additional six accounts. Our configuration files modeled the transactor (e.g., the account holder) and each of the accounts as object classes, and specified transactor-to-account links. Although this model worked, it was inefficient because the majority of records were assigned to only one or two account types used (e.g., savings and checking). Thus, the system was maintaining many account type fields to handle those few cases in which they were needed, even though this processing was superfluous in most cases. The added overhead and complexity consumed computing resources and slowed overall processing rates. Additionally, when multiple records were spanned, connections were repeated unnecessarily.

Converting Long Record Structures to a Short Format

One method that can be used to resolve representation problems with long records is to convert them into a series of short records (also called a narrow format). To do this, the data set must be parsed prior to being read by a configuration file. This parsing process generates a set of tuples (e.g., pairings, triples, etc.) that is a much simpler data schema than that used in the long record format. Looking back at the long record structure depicted in Figure 4.3, now imagine that the structure contains attributes with multiple values (i.e., multiple transaction amounts associated with a single account). Figure 4.4 shows how such a long data record can be transformed into a short record format.

Figure 4.4 Example of a short node record structure.

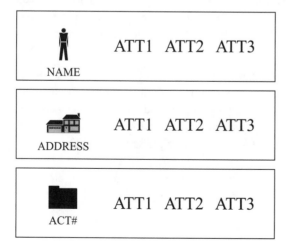

Assuming that your data are going to be parsed in a standard way, you could set up a generic configuration file to be used for virtually any data set being modeled. Within this configuration scheme, certain types of data could always be drawn from the same fields, allowing you to have just one model to be applied across multiple data sets. For example, you might designate the first field in the configuration file as the name of the entity (e.g., a unique key) paired with a description of its type (e.g., an account number paired with a type descriptor such as "savings"). Just this simple name/type pairing can handle many of the modeling situations you may encounter. Other approaches can use a third value that represents an attribute being defined for the object. In that event the third field becomes a value of the attribute rather than a node type. Thus, each record would be converted to a name-attribute-value structure. If you wanted to represent the values of several attributes for an entity, you would do this by creating as many separate tuples as there are attributes. Thus instead of constructing object classes that have many attributes (as in the long record format), you effectively create a separate object class for every kind of attribute that you need to include in the analysis.

To represent links between entities, you would create a configuration instruction that specifies two short node record structures as just described along with the type of relationship existing between them. Thus there would be three components to the short link structure—two node records (including type information if needed) along with the type of link used to associate the two. Figure 4.5 provides an example of a short link record representing this type of information. Table 4.6 shows what these data might look like after being parsed.

Using a short record format, the resulting number of lines processed to load a data set is increased significantly because data can be replicated within the file. That is, a given value can appear in more than one place. However, duplicated records can easily be removed if desired. Finally, you have only one configuration to deal with in the model. The short record essentially becomes a global configuration to be used in virtually any situation.

One of the biggest drawbacks of the short record approach is that the data must be presented to the configuration file in the exact format defined for the model. The parsing scripts that perform this task can become complex and usually need to accommodate many exceptions and exclusions. These data manipulations are often done outside the data mining program using such facilities as AWK, GREP, and SED (within a UNIX context) or PERL. As you can appreciate, this can require a significant level of preprocessing. A second thing to note about the short record format is that, although it offers consistency in modeling across data sets, you end up with a rigid format that

Figure 4.5 A short link record structure.

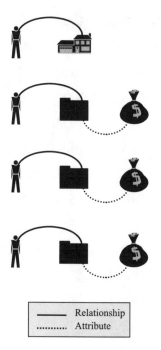

might not be appropriate for all data sets that you are using in the analysis. As always, the degree to which the short data format suits your needs depends entirely on the data processing requirements of your particular application.

Data Cleanup

There are inevitable problems that you will encounter as you begin to use a new data set. To some degree, the contents of virtually any database system will have inconsistent, incomplete, or erroneous data elements. As much as 80 percent of the time associated with the data mining process will be spent dealing with these problems. Errors arise for many reasons such as characters being transposed and/or misinterpreted at time of data entry, missing data, incompatible formats, improperly completed data entry screens, or even deliberate improper coding due to fraud.

As part of the data preparation process, a variety of actions can be performed on the raw data sources. These preprocessing routines help ensure that the data utilized for the data mining application are of high quality and integrity. Many applications benefit from front-end data scrubbers set up to identify and clean up some of the more

Table 4.6 Sample Short Data Record Structure

OBJ#1	OBJ#1-Type	OBJ#2	OBJ#2-Type	VALUE
Mr. Smith	PERSON	123 Elm Street	ADDRESS	RESIDENCE
Mr. Jones	PERSON	456 Maple Ave	ADDRESS	RESIDENCE
Mrs. Smith	PERSON	123 Elm Street	ADDRESS	RESIDENCE
Dr. Walters	PERSON	239 Main St.	ADDRESS	RESIDENCE
Ms. Brown	PERSON	501 E. 47th St.	ADDRESS	RESIDENCE
Mr. Elliot	PERSON	95 Broadway	ADDRESS	RESIDENCE
Mr. Smith	PERSON	4492932	ACCOUNT	$55.32
Mr. Smith	PERSON	4493934	ACCOUNT	$12.43
Mr. Jones	PERSON	4492932	ACCOUNT	$94.43
Mr. Jones	PERSON	8829393	ACCOUNT	$320.20
Mr. Jones	PERSON	4959320	ACCOUNT	$33.50
Mrs. Smith	PERSON	4493949	ACCOUNT	$64.23
Dr. Walters	PERSON	8849493	ACCOUNT	$304.40
Dr. Walters	PERSON	4488583	ACCOUNT	$22.04
Ms. Brown	PERSON	4509394	ACCOUNT	$94.95
Ms. Brown	PERSON	4403948	ACCOUNT	$112.40
Ms. Brown	PERSON	4499482	ACCOUNT	$403.42
Mr. Elliot	PERSON	8839392	ACCOUNT	$193.49
Mr. Elliot	PERSON	4993122	ACCOUNT	$93.02

common errors. (Our British readers should exchange the term "cleanser" for "scrubber" in this context.) What follows is a discussion of some strategies that you might use to address some of the more commonplace yet troublesome problems encountered during cleanup operations. These include approaches for name disambiguation, the use of translation and look-up tables for name matching, along with hybrid phonetic approaches, which take advantage of multiple techniques.

Naming Consistency and Disambiguation

One of the most troublesome problems requiring data manipulation occurs when names are changed slightly across records that are being analyzed. Keep in mind that to a relational database, any variation in the representation of data objects produces a unique instantiation of the object being represented. What this means is that small perturbations (e.g., periods, extra spaces, and other various annotations) in the spelling of a name result in multiple representations of the same entity. To a human it is obvious that the entries can all refer to a single entity. To a machine, however, these relationships can be very difficult to detect. For example, how would your system automatically determine that all of the name values in Table 4.7 are being used to represent a single individual?

The number of different combinations is essentially limitless. We did not even demonstrate spelling errors in this example, but there are some names that can be spelled in many different ways (e.g., Kadaffi, Khadafie, Quadaffy, Quaddafi). To find a good example of this problem, check your own mailbox. How many different versions of your own name appear on the junk mail you receive? In one particular data mining application involving the detection of money laundering patterns, we found an individual with roughly 35 different variations on his name in the data set. Of course he had deliberately altered his name across a series of financial transactions to avoid being detected. He was ultimately discovered, however, because these different versions of his name were all tied to similar values listed for his addresses, identification numbers, and accounts. We were able to discover a large network of interconnections that clearly showed that he was trying to avoid detection and hide his criminal behavior. Figure 4.6 shows a simplified example of this type of data disambiguation using a visual metaphor.

What can you do to clean up your name data? Before a name is processed, simple name cleansing routines can be applied to do preliminary cleanup such as removing single characters (e.g., middle initials) and name prefixes or suffixes (Mr., Mrs., Ph.D., Jr., III, and, or, etc.). This helps to normalize the names and provide a consistent representation. Following this, more sophisticated methods can be applied.

Table 4.7 Simple Name Variation Representing the Same Person

John Q. Smith	Mr. J. Smith	Mr. John Smith	Mr John Smith	Mr. Smith
Jon Smith	Mr. J.Q. Smith	John Smith	J. Smith	J.Q. Smith
Johnny Smith	Smith, John	Smith, J.	Smith, J.Q.	Smith J Q

Figure 4.6 Data disambiguation techniques to find duplicate names.

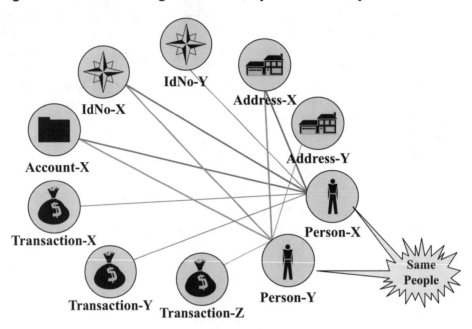

One approach to disambiguating name confusions is to create string and word aliases using internal sound indexing and inversion routines. These algorithms take names that are similar in their pronunciation and/or spelling and associate them accordingly. N-gram name matching routines offer another approach. Unlike sound-indexing techniques, which utilize the entire name or specific parts of a name to come up with a uniform value, n-gram routines will partially match names if some substrings that make up the targeted name are identical to some of the substrings that make up a different name (also see the sidebar on Soundex Algorithms).

For example, given the target word "smith", and using "@" to represent prepended and appended blanks, the trigram (3 character) segments in the word are: @sm, smi, mit, ith, th@. Each segment can be compared against other word segments for correlation. Different size n-grams (e.g., 2, 3, 4, etc) can be tested to determine which provides the best match for your data set. N-gram matching facilities provide analysts with the ability to identify significant name alterations, help target the use of aliases and alternative spellings, and help expose name variations that are not well suited for some of the other techniques. Its major drawback is that it is a relative matching technique. To determine if one name is similar to another name, each n-gram must be matched against every other n-gram in order to come up with a relative comparison or ranking between the two names. Although some work has been done with respect to the vectorization of n-grams (e.g., for use in calculating the thematic representation of a document), this methodology is still very much in the research stages.

Translation Tables

Name matching routines can be further enhanced through the use of name translators. Generally, alternative spellings of a name may sometimes use a variety of different structures. Depending on how diverse their representations are, name matching algorithms can sometimes produce very disparate results. For example, the pairing of the names Robert and Bob, Juan and John, Virginia and Ginny, or Richard and Dick would never provide a set of corresponding phonetic or structurally consistent values. Rather, the results would be quite varied and not very useful except to find exact spellings.

The easiest method of dealing with this problem is to construct special translation routines that convert these types of alternative spellings into a common representation. The only way to deal with this type of situation is to create look-up tables manually containing all known variations of the different names. It may not sound

Soundex Algorithms for Name Matching

You might consider using Soundex routines for integrating and disambiguating data. Soundex has been around for quite some time and has been used extensively in many different applications. Soundex is an "absolute" matching method allowing values to be precalculated, stored as attributable values, and globally referenced. When properly applied, it can add a lot of value to an analysis. A Soundex representation is an encapsulation of a name or stringed value into a numeric form to be used for matching on the basis of phonetic similarity. Using a phonetic matching rule, for example, matches could be found between Westphal and Westfall or Blaxton and Blackstone. There are many variations on the standard Soundex algorithm that are used to handle phonetic variations for Asian, Middle Eastern, and other nonstandard languages. Most of the popular commercial database systems include Soundex as part of their basic configuration capabilities. The most common types of Soundex routines remove all vowels (other than initial letters), any double letters,

Continued

Soundex Algorithms for Name Matching (*Continued*)

and all numbers. The routines make special conversions (e.g., ph -> f, kn->n, mn->n, k->c), and translate a certain number of the remaining characters to numerics. For example, using one particular Soundex technique, the string "elephant" becomes "elfnt" and then "e415". This value can then be used to search for all other occurrences potentially resulting in a matched name. Soundex functions work well under the right circumstances, especially if the names are consistently represented (e.g., last-name, first-name). However, if there is a wide range of variation, Soundex will perform poorly. In many of our applications, the use of Soundex values has formed the basis of clustering routines where all similar sounding names appear grouped together. This helps us to identify duplicate information or potential targets of interest quickly.

One of the most widely used Soundex techniques keeps the first letter of the name and drops all occurrences of A, E, H, I, O, U, W, and Y in all other positions. Values are assigned to the remaining letters except the first according to the following rules:

B, F, P, V	1
C, G, J, K, Q, S, X, Z	2
D, T	3
L	4
M, N	5
R	6

If two or more letters with the same value are adjacent, the first is kept and the rest are dropped. If there are less than four places in the resulting output, the remaining spaces are filled with zero (0).

There are some variations that can occur such as allowing K to equal N when K precedes N, otherwise letting K equal C. There are also alternative approaches to handling different ethnic names. For example, Spanish names contain multiple surnames that are derived from the patronymic (father) and matronymic (mother) names. The understanding of Spanish names can become quite complex due to the different variations on the construction of the names. Arabic names can also be complicated to work with because of their transliteration into a romanized representation. There are no hard and fast rules to use when making these translations, and therefore large variations can occur. This is further complicated by the use of particles and honorifics contained within the language. Chinese names are also typically romanized. However, with the establishment of the Standard Telegraphic Codes (STCs), numeric codes for the actual Chinese characters can now be mapped to their romanized name components. (There is a good deal of literature addressing the use of foreign naming conventions but their detail will not be covered in this text.)

The Soundex algorithm has been used for a wide variety of purposes in several states, the Department of Motor Vehicles uses a compound Soundex value for driver's license numbers. Phone companies use Soundex-like technologies in their information services such as 411 to help look up phone numbers based on the way names are pronounced. We have used the Soundex values extensively (when they apply) to perform clustering on the data elements to quickly see if there are similarly named entities within the data set and to determine whether they share common attributes. Additionally, we have used Soundex to help start a proactive analysis, where the data slice was derived from the resulting value supplied.

An important fact to keep in mind when using Soundex is that the phonetic similarity does not necessarily imply that two entities are the same. Where possible, you should consider the use of composite keys for representing data entities. These could include other information such as similar addresses, or identification numbers, or any other types of unique characterizations. Thus, you can feed composite keys to name-matching routines that are comprised of a combination of descriptive attributes.

We have found it useful to develop our own algorithms for name-matching on a number of occasions. In several data mining applications, instead of automatically combining records together, we have created a piece of value-added data that represents an ACB (Also Could Be) relationship between the two diverse records. We then expose the patterns of interest and confirm whether or not the entities are indeed the same. This type of approach is very powerful when selecting individual or small sets of entities matching a particular type of pattern.

like an efficient technique, but it is the only viable method for dealing with these types of situations. Of course, once a translation has been performed on a name, the result can be stored as an attributable value for future recall. By now it should be obvious that the translation must occur before any further processing is performed on the name. This guarantees that the maximum amount of normalization has occurred on the name before its representation is finalized.

Name permutation is another technique that can be used to process name data in a reactive search capacity by applying a word translator in reverse. This is a method you might want to use if you are trying to generate possible alternate versions of a name that might appear in a data set. The target name to be permutated is usually uniquely selected by the user as part of the front-end query or back-end feedback loop. In this search mode, a single name can be permutated to generate dozens of candidate representations.

A Hybrid Approach: Absolute and Relative Word Matching

One particularly innovative approach to performing word matching is a combination of absolute and relative name matching. The goal is to acquire the speed of an absolute match such as Soundex, with the resolution of a relative technique such as an n-gram (see the sidebar on Soundex Algorithms). The resulting hybrid approach can then be used to find all occurrences of names that may be similar.

More simply, these methods could be used to reduce data sets to eliminate potential duplications. As such, the approach would have to be changed to a heuristic process that would automatically combine the records based on a set of probabilistic calculations. Used in this way, the algorithm is a data cleanup technique, and not a data mining method.

The general approach is defined as follows. For every entity value presented to the system, Soundex-like values for all parts of the name are individually calculated. From the resulting set an alphabetically sorted combinatorial set of values is generated, such that every combination of each word segment is represented. For example, the name John Quincy Adams can be converted to JN QNC ADMS, then reduced to J500 Q520 A352. The set of values can be combined in the alphabetical ordering J500, Q520, A352, J500Q520, A352J500, A352Q520, and A352J500Q520. Names with two words produce three entries, three words produce seven entries, and four words produce thirteen entries, and so on. Expressions will produce $(n * n-1) + 1$ entries, where n is the number of words in the expression.

Next, each entry is loaded into an array for which every distinct entry is assigned to a single array bin. In each bin the source record and a pointer for the entry are also provided so we know where to find the data. If the entire string is present within the bin (e.g., the representation that comprises the complete original name, in this case A352J500Q520), a special flag is set on the bin and record source to indicate that a full-name key has been provided. This process continues for all the names contained within a single data set or across multiple data sets.

This technique is able to provide a match on other names or their subsets such as John Adams (A352J500), Quincy Adams (A352Q520), Martha Adams (A352M630), Adams John (A352J500), John & Martha Adams (A352J500M630). Since the representation of a name is consistently translated, normalized, sorted, and then structured into a common representation space, the resultant matches prove to be accurate and reliable. The only major drawback is that the size of the array can become quite large. This can be managed by controlling the size of the extracted data set. To help minimize computational resources, you can assign bins only to those entries containing more than one word. Allowable modifications of the approach ultimately depend on the level of specificity needed from the calculations to meet your data mining needs.

The hybrid method yields a fully populated structure that can be summarized, presented, and queried. Thus, before any decision about how to integrate the data sets occurs, the array can be queried to determine its suitability. A list of conditions that can be applied to the hybrid process in order to control the quality, focus and content of the matched records follows.

- Only allocate bins that contain at least two names. This avoids matching only first names, last names, or common words in an organization or address.

- Only use bins when there are multiple sources present. This can also be made specific to the number data sources integrated (e.g., 3 out of 5).

- Only allocate bins when there are matches and the full-name key flag has been set. This ensures well-qualified matches since at least one entire name will be available.

- Only allocate bins when there are less than 20 total matches. This can reduce the consideration of very common names like John Smith that may result in many bin collisions. The converse may also be desired for applications such as cleaning up the contents of a mailing list.

- Only use bins that have only one record entry. This can expose entries that do not have a known corresponding match from another source.

Once the initial calculations have been performed, they will remain resident in the array until the application has been terminated. This provides the freedom and flexibility to add in new data sources, remove existing sources, and generate numerous extractions to satisfy different analyses. The use of this hybrid model may initially seem resource intensive, but it provides for a very focused set of matches using an extremely fast and efficient mapping technique. Using this approach, you get the best of both name matching worlds.

Name Disambiguation in Data Integration

Names can be used to determine how multiple data files will be connected. Since there are two or more sources of data that are being considered, this provides us with at least three different integration strategies that can be used to produce a working data mining example. Figure 4.7 shows the overlap achieved by each data set integration scheme. The first method, and most widely used in our experience, is to include only those elements from each source that have been determined to be a match via the ACB (Also Could Be) algorithm. This intersection of data provides answers to requests such as "Show all customers using product-X (database 1) who are also using product-Y (database 2)." This would allow you to provide very targeted marketing offers to that set of individuals.

The next method is to pass in all of the data from at least one or more of the sources along with the value-added information about which items are considered to be the same (e.g., the ACB). This is typically used to determine where categories or segmentations occur within the data. Thus, requests such as "Show all people living within a certain geographical area (database 1) and highlight those who have purchased our goods and services (database 2)" can be accommodated using this method. Showing all of the first database with only those elements that match in the second database would identify hot spots or underserved areas within your marketing community. This approach allows you to see how the whole of one set is affected or influenced by the other set.

The third method is a slight variation on the second but it is used to pass through the data from one or more sets that do *not* match the ACB. We have used this approach to find answers to requests such as "Show all people with registered property (database 1) that do not match any of the people who have filed a tax return (database 2)."

Using Look-Up Tables

Where possible, the use of look-up tables should be used to help convey information to the end user. In many data sets, there are coded fields or abbreviations that are used to represent the information in the database efficiently. A look-up table converts a short representation into its longer descriptive definition. Thus, different store locations may be coded with a numeric representation (045 = Albuquerque) or certain sale codes may have a short abbreviation (XR = broken merchandise). Their direct translation may not be obvious to the user, and the use of a look-up

Figure 4.7 Three different data integration schemes.

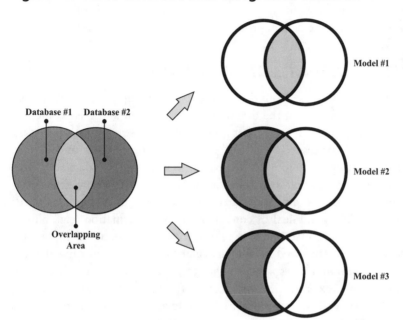

table makes interpretation that much easier. Note that this is not really a computational issue since automated data mining tools such as those described in Section III maintain a unique value for each entity. Rather the advantage is realized in the human/computer interface during analysis and presentation.

Look-up tables can also help support the ordering of certain values that you may want to have represented in a specific way. A good example of this is the use of day-of-week values. As we all know, there are seven distinct values that can be applied: Sunday, Monday, Tuesday, Wednesday, Thursday, Friday, and Saturday. However, these values are just a string-based abstraction of a sequence of days occurring in a specific order. So, as the information is presented within a data mining system, chances are that it will be sorted alphabetically so that these items will be presented in the order Friday, Monday, Saturday, Sunday, Thursday, Tuesday, Wednesday. Since the sorting of the string-value in this case does not reflect what the end-user would want to see, the use of a look-up table can help resolve this issue.

Typically, when information is encoded into a look-up table, the order in which it is entered will dictate the relative value of the entries. Essentially, the look-up table can be considered yet another data source. The relative order within the table would represent an attributable value (e.g., integer) of the entry. As we know, this value can then be used to sort or sequence the data appropriately, thus providing the desired results.

Handling Textual Information

For the most part, the previous sections discuss access and manipulation of relational structures. That is, we know what the different fields represent and their content is organized and structured in such a way that it generally makes finding the necessary data a straightforward process. These data are easy to manipulate and can be processed by most existing computing platforms. However, relational data structures are only one type of information available for analysis. As you know, some data sources are comprised only of text. Some text sources follow fairly rigid standards of creation and contain a good deal of consistent header information (e.g., almost approximating a relational format). However, this is more the exception than the rule. In many cases, text is not structured in any particular fashion—it is just like the text in this book, the articles in a newspaper, or the stories in a magazine. There is no consistent format. Some text might be written in a foreign language, some writing styles might be flowery while others are spare, some texts are poetic whereas others are technical. Thankfully there are approaches being researched that help you to accommodate these types of data sets.

In this section we take you through a few of the approaches used to handle textual information. We discuss the use of natural language processing techniques (such as is done on the Internet), techniques designed to provide thematic summaries of bodies of text, and finally an alternate method of coding text using the Standard Generalized Markup Language.

Natural Language Processing

Free text interpretation or, as it is more commonly referred to, natural language processing (NLP) is focused on understanding the contents of human communications. What this generally allows you to do is identify critical data contained within large, unstructured text sources for the purposes of performing data mining activities. One basic feature that must be supported before any data mining can happen is the detection of documents. Detection is the ability to locate documents based on the search parameters used by a free-text search and retrieval engine. A text engine is conceptually very simple. It takes the content of a document (e.g., the words) and breaks it up into a set of indexed structures with pointers back to the original source reference. When a specific word or phrase is requested, the engine can quickly find all occurrences of these terms within the documents and produce a hit set.

A good example of a mainstream application of this technology is the Internet. When you are using a web-based search facility to look for sites or documents that contain the key words you desire, what is really happening is that a free-text search engine is being invoked. This engine reviews all of the entries within the indexed data structure it has previously created, usually by sampling in HTML pages. The pages are identified for processing either by a URL address submitted directly to the engine or by invocation of special processes (soft-bots, intelligent agents, or web crawlers) that constantly seek out new sites and pages. The result is a very large index of terms, which represents the corpus of documents that can be searched for specific words or combination of words. Depending on the environment, the corpus can range from very isolated and focused domains such as the papers presented at a conference to very large and complex environments such as news wire feeds and open-source competitive intelligence systems. The analogy to the document corpus is the information contained in a relational database. It has a general overall focus and the extractions (e.g., data slices) can be used for subsequent analyses or recall.

Documents can be of any type and contain virtually any kind of information. The hit set returned by the engine is usually ranked based on a variety of factors including frequency of word matches, term co-occurrence, word proximity, and so forth. The more information that can be presented to the end user, the better the likelihood of a successful search. So part of the goal associated with NLP is to find the most relevant sequence of matching terms or phrases. There are certain words contained within text that you do not want to consider for searching purposes and which are typically removed from any processing activities. Examples of such *stop* words include "the", "and", "a", along with other strings that do not add value to the search. These lists can also be modified to reflect particular environments or situations.

Thematic Summarization of Text

The results returned by a search engine are sometimes too numerous to be realistically interpreted or read by the end user. Thus, beyond just providing a rank order associated with the document, new techniques have emerged that can produce a summarization as well. A summarization represents the semantic classification of a free-text document, sometimes called a thematic representation or topical similarity. Based on the actual contents of a document, a value or vector can be produced, which is used as an abstract approximation of its content. Other documents with similar values can be considered comparable in their content. If the resultant values are populated into a visual representation, you will see clusters appear based on the corpus selected. (See Figure 4.8 for an introduction to document visualization and Chapter 10 for more specific examples.) If you find a document with relevant information, chances are that the other documents appearing within the same cluster will have similar content. Thus, instead of having to page through documents 10 or 100 at a time in order to find the most relevant material, you can now present the documents using a classification vector and literally deal with thousands of references in a single display.

To facilitate the analysis of large quantities of data, you will need to abstract the most relevant topics of the document into tangible entities (see Figures 4.9 and 4.10 for examples). This might include identification of the names of people, organizations, locations, times, and dates. Some systems are configured to perform sentence parsing to interpret the contents of a file (e.g., nouns and verbs are used in sentences that are structured according to certain rules). Other approaches use different techniques that do not process any particular syntax or morphology.

Figure 4.8 Examples of document visualization techniques.

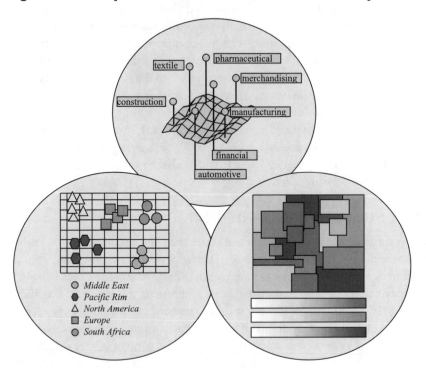

Figure 4.9 An example of word extractions from a structured free-text document.

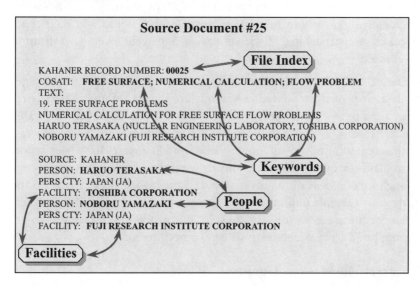

Some more advanced algorithmic methods currently in use by the NLP community take advantage of clues offered by the free-text structures themselves. Some approaches include large lexicon tables containing entries for first/last

Figure 4.10 A visualization of text from word extractions.

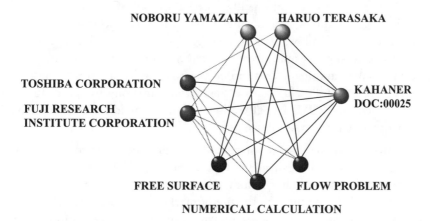

names, organization descriptors, title nomenclature, and delimiter words for various role types. Both upper- and lowercase words can be interpreted in addition to the punctuation and word ordering encountered in a document. Current systems can achieve classification rates in finding unknown proper nouns and their types (person, place, etc.) approaching 90 percent with 5 percent over-generalization (false positive) rates.

Recent research has also made breakthroughs in the detection of the linkages between the data elements themselves. So not only are the algorithms able to determine that the names of two people were referenced within a text, they are now able to derive the relationship of those two people. It may sound like a trivial process, but some of the greatest minds in computer science and linguistics have been working on this problem for quite some time and their efforts are now starting to pay off. Even though a good deal of interpretation and processing is occurring on the documents, the only tangible outputs are the names, links, and types of the objects that have been encountered. So you can consider this process necessary just to get you to a starting point from which analysis can be performed.

Standard Generalized Markup Language (SGML)

One other simpler form of text is the Standard Generalized Markup Language (SGML). SGML is a data coding format not too dissimilar to its more popular offspring HTML and the more recent XML format that allows the information in documents to be identified and shared. SGML provides a means for users to tag information within documents for later reference, representation, and reporting. It has been increasingly adopted as the international standard for data and document interchange in open environments. It is used in combination with advanced technologies to understand information quickly. The data in an SGML tagged document may include text, graphics, images, and even multimedia objects such as video and sound. Because SGML allows data to be tagged with useful, related information, it can be used to support innovative retrieval methods. For example, SGML can be used to facilitate automatic creation of hypertext webs of information that users can navigate freely, following trails of related information through the associated document elements. SGML can also allow systems to build documents on the fly out of networked databases of information.

SGML is invoked in the context of a model of the document format being processed. This model, called a Document Type Definition (DTD), describes what to expect within the format including names, addresses, dates, and times, for example. The entities are identified through the use of markup tags specific to the DTD being used. Thus, different associations, companies, or news sources can use their own terminology and structure, just as long as it is properly reflected in the DTD. The markup tags identify where the entities are located within the document. Of course, this means that someone has to specifically interpret what types of entities are being represented and then manually make the proper annotations. There are also methods in which attributes can be defined for the different entities.

The following is a simple example of a document that has SGML markup tags inserted into it for proper identification of the entities of interest.

```
<to>Accounting Division<\to>
<from>President/CEO<\from>
<date>29th February<\date>
<topic>Quarterly Sales Projections<\topic>
<conclusion>The earning projections for next quarter look
        good.<\conclusion>
```

Summing Up

In this chapter we have covered many of the issues you will face when trying to access data from disparate sources and prepare those data sets for analysis. We discussed issues involved in structuring queries so as to gain maximum benefit from the resulting data extractions. In addition we presented some practical considerations that you might face in transferring data from various formats and integrating multiple data types prior to analysis, including conversion from long to short data formats. Finally we presented some strategies for data cleanup including name disambiguation in fielded data as well as manipulation of textual information. Armed with these strategies, you are now ready to proceed to the next topic of using visualization methods to perform data mining analyses.

VISUAL METHODS FOR ANALYZING DATA

The methods available for analyzing data are virtually limitless. From our perspective, visualization offers a powerful means of analysis that can help you uncover patterns and trends that are likely to be missed with other nonvisual methods. As will be discussed in Chapter 6, data analyses are often performed using other nonvisual paradigms such as statistical testing, rule induction, and unsupervised neural network modeling. However, many of these approaches require that you analyze data in a hypothesis testing mode in which you have a priori notions about what the important results will be before the analysis actually begins. Results obtained with these methods tend to describe overall group trends, generalized differences, as well as broad categorizations. Although clearly useful for many purposes, global trends are not the most interesting or actionable outcomes in many cases. Visualization methods allow you to discover overall trends in your data set while also affording you an opportunity to discover smaller hidden patterns that can often be just as important within an application. Most of you will already be familiar with many of the more traditional analytical methods. Since visual analysis is such a different analytical paradigm, we devote an entire chapter to its exposition. As you read about visual analysis, please bear in mind that we are not advocating the use of this approach to the exclusion of other methods. Rather, we have often found it useful to combine multiple methods during data mining engagements so that we get the best of all worlds.

We routinely use data visualization to help mange diverse, intricate, and complex data sets. Visualization has proven to be reliable, easy to learn, and extremely cost effective. Additionally, visualization provides a natural method of integrating multiple data sets and has been used across a number of disciplines including commercial research, forensic accounting, and throughout the investigative community. As covered in Section I, any fielded values contained within a data set (e.g., age, race, gender, etc.) can be depicted graphically and their resultant values used to reveal patterns and trends. This chapter will review some of the many different visualization approaches that have been successful across problem domains. In an absolute sense there is no one type of visualization model that is better than another. The visualization method of choice will usually be determined by such factors as appropriateness for the application domain and preferences of the end user. As a matter of fact, most information can be visually presented using a variety of graphical schemes.

In this chapter, we begin by describing some of the main advantages of the visualization approach to data mining, including ways in which visual presentation methods take advantage of the strengths of human cognitive abilities. We then present the various classes of visual displays used for data mining and discuss the ways in which you can use the features of each to convey information during an analysis. We then move into a discussion of how to do visual analysis, including descriptions of characteristic patterns that can be observed for different display types. We include sections on emergent group and temporal pattern detection and discuss the ways in which these analyses may be conducted within a visual environment. Finally we end the chapter with a section on the issues that you should bear in mind when presenting the results from a visual data mining analysis.

Dynamic Observation without Preconception

Visual data mining techniques afford you the luxury of being able to make observations without preconception. What this means is that you do not necessarily have to know what you are looking for ahead of time. Rather, you can let the data show you what is important. During a visual analysis you can quickly see patterns of interest based on boundary violations, frequency of occurrence, and all sorts of data interdependencies. Visualization allows you to audit the analytical process, since you are examining the data directly and are making iterative decisions about what is being presented. Your intimate involvement in the twists and turns of the analysis will afford you a deeper understanding of your data set than you might otherwise achieve. This is much different than the black-box computations of many other approaches in which calculations are made by obscure algorithms that dispense results out of the back end of the system. We are not saying that these other approaches are not useful, but the results that they produce are sometimes difficult to interpret. Combining traditional analytical methods with visual presentation techniques can generate a very robust approach to data mining.

Applying visualization against most data sets lets you quickly find important patterns or emerging trends that might otherwise go undetected. Graphic depiction of data allows you to inspect larger quantities of information at a time than may be accomplished using many traditional techniques. Visualization is also an interactive technology that lets you dynamically adjust parameters to see how they affect the information being presented. In this paradigm it is easy to perform analysis in an exploratory mode, trying various "what-if" scenarios as you go. Additionally, visualizing the correlations and associations among data objects can quickly reveal patterns and trends implicit in the data, thus increasing the probability of a successful analysis.

Keeping Cognitive Demands in Mind

Perhaps the most important advantage of using visualization in data mining is that visualization methods play to the strengths of human cognition, rather than to its weaknesses. There are certain cognitive tasks that humans perform astoundingly well, and there are others that we do very poorly. The choice of an analytical method should include considerations about the types of information processing that the human analyst will be required to do during the course of an analysis. Where possible, the data mining approach should allow information to be represented and manipulated in ways that are easy for the analyst to understand and interpret. Visualization moves information out of unwieldy formats and allows the analyst to switch into a more efficient information processing mode.

Cognitive Limitations on Information Processing

In our opinion, most traditional formats of information presentation such as text and tables force the human analyst into the wrong modes of information processing. These formats make high processing demands on those aspects of cognitive function that are the most limited. By forcing the human to rely extensively on his/her own memory during an analysis, for example, the task is made very difficult, and errors are virtually assured. The activity of data mining can be cognitively demanding in terms of requiring users to understand complex data formats, combine information from multiple sources, and interpret and discover previously unknown patterns. To the degree that we can ease the cognitive burden by displaying information in formats that are easier to process, we will be doing the analyst a big favor.

Short-Term Memory Limitations

Imagine having to look at extensive results returned from a series of relational database searches or having to read through all of the documents identified through a key-word term search on the Internet. Most likely, it would take you a long time just to sift through the information. You would have to read portions of the text, page through to new sections while trying to remember what you just read, and then cycle backward to recheck information that you already encountered. Throughout this process, you would struggle to try to form insights about relationships and trends contained in the information. You would probably not be wildly successful, however, because this type of serial processing task is so difficult for humans to do.

Typical tabular or text-based formats of presentation force the user to process information in ways that the brain is just not designed to do well. One thing that the science of cognitive psychology has clearly shown us is that the human has very severe restrictions on the amount of information that can be held in short-term memory at any one time. Once this short-term memory capacity (usually seven to nine chunks of information) has been exceeded, any new incoming information displaces previously held items. Thus, when trying to page through documents keeping track of several things at once, performance is bound to suffer. You will quickly reach a point at which you will either be unable to add new items into your short-term memory queue, or you will lose track of items already being monitored. As a result you may "forget" about interesting results that you pass along the way, and may lose the opportunity to incorporate them into the final outcome.

Long-Term Memory Limitations

Even if there were some way of overcoming the attentional limitations just described, you would still have to deal with problems of retrieval from long-term memory. For example, say that you were examining a set of documents describing a topic that you already know well. That is, you already have information about this topic represented in your long-term memory. In some respects this will put you ahead in the game because you would already have a conceptual organization of this knowledge. This would allow you to interpret individual pieces of information within a broader context as they appear in your analysis. However, as we all know, retrieval from long-term memory does not always operate as reliably as we might like. For example, say you were examining sales figures from a set of franchise operations located around the country and you notice a slump in sales in the southwest. You might overinterpret this result at first because you do not remember that your franchises in that region tend to perform poorly on a particular product line. Had you remembered that fact, you could isolate that product line from the analysis. Alternatively, you may incorrectly "recall" that franchises in the southwest did poorly on a particular product line last fall, when in fact it was actually some franchises in the northwest that showed the poor sales. That is, you can "remember" something that never happened (even though you are very sure that it did), and this false retrieval can actually be a detriment to your current analysis. (This tendency for people to be confident in their memories even when they are falsely recognizing information is one reason that eyewitness testimony is often legitimately challenged in court cases.) Thus your analytical method should not force you to rely too heavily on retrieval from either short- or long-term memory, since there are so many ways in which this retrieval can fail.

Visualization Capitalizes on Cognitive Strengths

Although humans are limited in terms of attention and memory, they excel at the processing of visual information. Given a complicated visual scene, humans can immediately pick out important features in a matter of milliseconds. Our brains are structured so that visual processing occurs rapidly and in parallel. This is very different from information that is coded verbally and must be processed one item at a time. Furthermore, information presented in a visual format is learned and remembered better than information presented verbally.

The benefits of visualization can easily be seen in Figure 5.1. This example shows different methods of displaying phone call data during a specified time interval. The left portion of the figure shows a typical arrangement of tabular output derived from a database query. As you see, even though the query was constructed to retrieve only a portion of the underlying database, the query nevertheless produced several pages of information that the analyst must inspect. Contrast this representation with the one presented in the right portion of the figure. Here the same exact information is represented in a diagram in which relationships among objects are denoted by links in the display.

From the diagram on the right, you can immediately see that there is a lot of calling activity between certain pairs of telephone numbers, and little or none between others. Thick lines denote higher numbers of calls in the data set. By looking at this link diagram, an analyst could quickly determine which numbers were the most interesting prospects for further analysis. That is, all of the work of discovering these interesting relationships occurs automatically. Given the tabular format, on the other hand, the analyst would have to pore through the entries one by one, calculating frequency of representation, occurrence of links with other numbers, and so on. This would require extensive paging back and forth through the output, and many interesting relationships might be missed. This is a case in which visualization clearly gives the analyst an advantage in moving toward a useful outcome quickly.

Now look at the network diagram shown in Figure 5.2. This diagram shows those phone numbers in the data set that are linked together by virtue of the calling patterns included in the extraction. As you see, there are isolated networks of

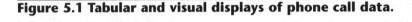

Figure 5.1 Tabular and visual displays of phone call data.

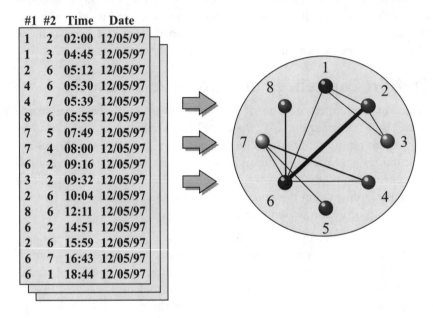

#1	#2	Time	Date
1	2	02:00	12/05/97
1	3	04:45	12/05/97
2	6	05:12	12/05/97
4	6	05:30	12/05/97
4	7	05:39	12/05/97
8	6	05:55	12/05/97
7	5	07:49	12/05/97
7	4	08:00	12/05/97
6	2	09:16	12/05/97
3	2	09:32	12/05/97
2	6	10:04	12/05/97
8	6	12:11	12/05/97
6	2	14:51	12/05/97
2	6	15:59	12/05/97
6	7	16:43	12/05/97
6	1	18:44	12/05/97

numbers that call each other but do not call the other numbers in the set. Higher frequencies of calls are again represented by thicker links. This representation is quite useful, because it not only denotes which objects (phone numbers) are the most active, but immediately conveys the extent of their connection to other entities in the data set. Using the tabular format, it might take an analyst weeks or months to arrive at the understanding that is produced immediately using visualization.

As you can appreciate, the benefits of these visualization methods increase dramatically as the size of the data set increases. For example, it is not uncommon for an analyst to work with tens of thousands of phone records at a time in a phone call analysis. Imagine how heavy that workload can be if the analyst were limited to tabular data. Figure 5.2 shows an example of a larger and more complex network diagram. Note that even though many more records are represented in this figure, you can nevertheless immediately see important patterns in the data that would be very hard to uncover using a straight tabular representation.

Why is visualization so helpful in these cases? In the phone call diagrams in Figures 5.1 and 5.2, the relationships between phone numbers are seen easily because the data were modeled appropriately before being read into the display environment.

Figure 5.2 Network diagram of a large phone call data set.

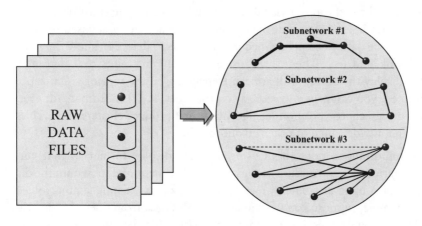

In all such cases, the models selected to represent the data (see Chapter 2 for a discussion on data modeling) determine the types of patterns that can be identified.

Mapping Data onto Visualization Schemes

The visualization method you choose for your analysis will depend upon the type of data you have and how it has been modeled. The level of data abstraction was minimized in the previous examples to show explicitly the relationships between the fundamental objects that were represented in the model (e.g., the phone numbers). We could just as easily have imposed abstractions to show regions, area codes, or even calling plans. In this section we describe various positioning algorithms and techniques you can apply to control the appearance and arrangement of data within analytical displays. We describe each class of display on its own, but there are many instances in which you might want to combine techniques in order to achieve a desired result.

As you consider which visualization techniques to use in an analysis, always bear in mind that you can easily switch among visual display types. Remember that the data mining process is iterative and cumulative. Nothing should be considered permanent. If a technique is applied to a data set, it can be reversed as easily as it is applied. Additionally, the world is full of systems, approaches, and techniques that can be used to analyze data. Undoubtedly there are techniques others than those discussed here that you will want to consider as well.

Positioning Algorithms

As data are being brought into a visualization environment, you must decide how to display the data in a fashion that makes sense. This activity is focused on using the attributes of the data elements defined in the models to determine how the information will look and feel. Thus, there are positional constraints that determine where in the display the objects will appear. Depending on the type of visualization being performed, you can generally expect to produce a (x,y,z) coordinate for every data point. You can choose positioning algorithms that produce clusters, hierarchies, landscapes, and a wide range of other layout formats.

What is important to note about using different display formats is that your data model determines the structure of the display. Placement of data within the display is based on object attribute values and on linkages existing among object classes. For example, suppose you were analyzing sales data from a set of franchises for some of your product lines. If you want to see relationships between franchises and product lines in the display, for example, you will have to designate franchises and product lines as object classes, specifying a link between them in your data model. Likewise, if you want to arrange product lines in your display according to revenue amounts, you will need to include revenue amount as an attribute of the product line object class.

What follows is a high-level overview of the different types of displays that can be generated using visualization techniques. This discussion is not comprehensive but is intended as an overview of the various display paradigms that can be used to present and analyze data. In Section III, you will find an overview of numerous data mining systems that can be used to generate visual displays.

Clustering

Objects are usually assigned a place in the display based on general descriptive values. Items will be clustered or grouped around shared values. Typically when these values represent an arbitrary set of descriptions (e.g., names, diseases, id-numbers, account types) you will see concentrations of data along shared values. Many two- and three-dimensional displays use this approach, especially with respect to generating scatter plots.

The clusters themselves can physically be mapped to a specific XYZ location or sequenced into a geometric display (e.g., circles, lines). The difference between these two types of cluster layouts results in absolute or relative object placement. In an absolute placement, the physical location of the objects determines how the clusters will look and, furthermore, the distance between different clusters can be measured.

Thus, a spatial component is introduced into the display space of the diagram. As you can imagine, missing values are easy to detect using this type of approach, but similar or exact values will be overlaid on top of one another. In a relative placement display, the clusters are differentiated by sequencing in a particular order using a geometric layout such as a circle or line. The major distinction between clusters is that each represents a different and unique value. Thus, if data were to be clustered according to the attribute "month" in a relative placement display, it would be hard to tell if the data were skewed other than by counting the number of clusters to determine that there were more or less than 12. The clusters could go from January, February, and March, to May and beyond, thereby completely missing April.

When should you pick relative clustering instead of absolute placement? Relative clustering is more beneficial when you are dealing with a variety of discrete value ranges, such as the dollar amounts associated with retail transactions. An absolute cluster physically has to accommodate the entire range of values (say $10 to $10,000). This results in a large cluster display if you wanted to have any type of resolution available. It also requires that every expected value be depicted in one of the cluster bins. In a relative placement display, the individual clusters represent each discrete value range and there is essentially no space conflict. This more closely approximates the format of the raw data source because it uses only the actual values encountered rather than including additional placeholder values as is done with absolute placement. Additionally, the clusters can be sequenced according to their values, number of cluster objects, or other attributes. Examples of displays formed by clustering on object attributes using absolute and relative placement are shown in Figure 5.3.

Hierarchies

When an object's position is based on its relationship to other objects, you can form hierarchies in the display. Some examples of hierarchical displays are shown in Figure 5.4. These displays are useful for data sets in which certain object classes and types are nested within others. The topmost portion of the hierarchy is called the root node. The selection of the root node determines how a hierarchy will be constructed for display purposes. Since each level is connected to the previous level (e.g., relative placement), there is no cross-level mixing of relationships assuming bidirectional linkages. However, there can be intra-level connections. Special care should be taken to show these types of relationships because they can affect the interpretation of the hierarchy. If the root node is not properly selected, the hierarchy can become lopsided and difficult to interpret. Also, depending upon the application, there can be more than one root node present within a display. In these cases, the root can represent a class of objects (e.g., top performers, sales over projection).

Figure 5.3 Examples of displays based on absolute and relative clustering by object attributes.

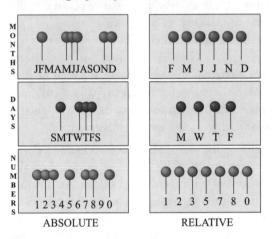

ABSOLUTE   RELATIVE

Hierarchies do not necessarily have to be formed on the basis of linked relationships. Some hierarchies are based on the values assigned to attributes of the objects that are in turn used to set up a layered architecture, which is a form of absolute placement. Using this approach for representing an organization, you might place the CEO at the root level, people with a title of vice president at one level below, directors at a sublevel, and staff employees at a bottom level. This structure reflects a formal organizational hierarchy; however, if the connections being presented reflect

Figure 5.4 Examples of hierarchical displays.

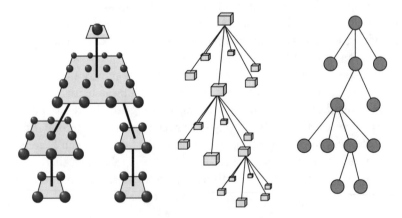

communication patterns or social interactions as opposed to direct supervisory relationships, then you can expect to have a mixture of inter-level connections. In these cases, the structure of the hierarchy does not accommodate the links and can result in a very cluttered diagram. Though perhaps not ideal, this type of display can be used to expose certain types of patterns, specifically hidden dependencies.

Self-Organizing Networks

There has recently been a wide range of interests in the use of self-organizing networks to present information. These should not be confused with the self-organizing networks used in neural network or latent semantic analyses (these are discussed in Chapters 6 and 10, respectively). The idea is very simple—objects repel and links attract. The concept is a variation of Coulomb's Law of spring kinetics where data objects push against one another unless connected together. Self-organizing network displays will organize data objects into discrete clusters of information. The general presentation is a very dynamic network of interacting objects that will remain in flux until a steady state is achieved through the most optimal placement of objects based on their relative connections (see Figure 5.5).

Depending on the data set used in a self-organizing network, the results can be quite interesting. When there is a good distribution of linkages among the objects, the networks will break apart and form discrete clusters. Additionally, they will

Figure 5.5 Examples of self-organizing network displays.

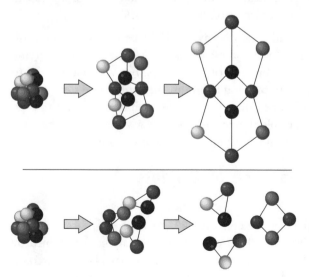

minimize their line-crossings, producing a very attractive layout of information. These networks become very easy to understand and require a minimal amount of repositioning. Three-dimensional self-organizing networks are also possible, but a bit more difficult to interpret.

When using self-organizing networks you should remember that models that are very well connected with all object classes linked to each other will not produce usable diagrams. The cohesion among the links will drive all of the objects into a central mass. Even though the objects will repel one another, the strength of the links will be overpowering because the data fan-out drives the behavior of the network. In order to produce an interpretable display you will need a model in which there are some object classes that are not connected to every other object class. Whether such a model makes sense depends entirely upon the nature of your application.

Geopositioning/Landscapes

Geopositional displays are formed by explicitly mapping the value of an attribute to a predetermined spatial structure or grid, which indirectly can be considered a form of clustering. This method of display is usually used to represent true spatial positioning information. Maps, blueprints, diagrams, and other physical structures are good candidates for geopositional object placement. In these cases objects are usually modeled to include information such as latitude/longitude or other coordinates that help guide the placement of objects within the landscape. The displays usually have some type of background to provide a context within which the data are being positioned. Vectorized outlines, GIF images, or other forms of media can be used as overlays to provide this information (see Figure 5.6).

Object placement within a landscape display need not be based on true positional information. You can map objects onto a landscape on the basis of attribute values that are not necessarily spatial in and of themselves, but which are easier to analyze in a spatial format. For example, you might use a coordinate system to map objects on the basis of values obtained on two or three attributes in order to classify objects along continuous variable dimensions. This is a variation on the clustering algorithms discussed earlier and is usually represented as a grid.

Controlling the Appearance of Objects within the Display

The display characteristics of data can be conveyed largely by the appearance of the individual objects themselves. The visual features of objects may be determined by attribute values. Objects may be varied in the display on the basis of shape, color, size, and style. Other more subtle display features such as intensity, textures, images,

Figure 5.6 Examples of landscape displays.

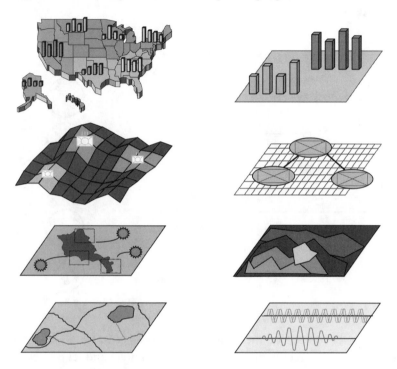

rotation, blinking, gyration, and orientation can be used to make certain values more noticeable, especially when time is involved. Further, objects may be labeled by attributes of interest. Figure 5.7 shows an example of how this mapping can be defined.

The particular attributes chosen for coding (e.g., selecting the key field) in the display will vary. For many objects, the value used to generate its unique instance will be used (e.g., name, address, symptom, identification number). However, when working in a transactional environment, the records are usually differentiated from one another by the use of a record number. This obviously does not produce an intelligible label that conveys information to the user. Instead, more descriptive details about the object (e.g., another set of attribute values) should be used in the display. In many systems that we have built using a transactional model where the "real" label of the object was a unique numeric key, we have labeled objects instead by using relevant attributes. For example, telephone calls can be labeled using time of day, date, or duration. Alternatively, financial transactions can be labeled with date, dollar amount, or direction of funds. Labels can quickly become complex within a display, however, so they should be used with caution. As an example, it is

Figure 5.7 Manipulating display parameters of objects in visualization systems.

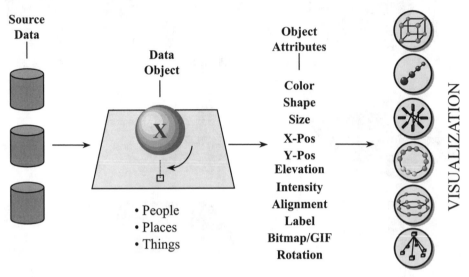

almost never useful to label objects on the basis of addresses since full address labels are long (e.g., street number, street name, city, state, zip, country) and tend to clutter the display. It would be better to select only a limited sample of the address, say the first 15 characters, for use in the display. Through drill-down methods, you can always get to the other details.

There are other important factors to consider when making the assignment of attributes to display characteristics. For example, the use of color should be applied only to an attribute that will have no more than a half-dozen unique values. Otherwise the rainbow effect in the display makes it uninterpretable (remember the chunking limits we discussed earlier). Additionally, you probably should not convey information about values in terms of object size unless you have very few possible values, for example three or fewer. There are, of course, exceptions to all of these guidelines. Just keep in mind that you do not do yourself any favors by making the display too busy. Make sure that each display manipulation adds to the understanding and interpretation of the data. *Don't do it just because you can.*

Keeping Displays Interpretable

The techniques just described for representing object information afford you great power in displaying data. However, as we just mentioned, you have to be careful not to go overboard. Depending upon how extensively you code attribute information into the display, you can represent anywhere from five to twenty (or more) dimensions. How does this happen? First you have the dimension of the extraction itself as a subset of the original data set. Next, based on the data model you have selected, a set of objects will be created to reflect the real world and conceptual entities contained within your data set. This further defines the analysis because your model necessarily will include and exclude certain portions of the extraction. Once the data have been brought into a visual display, the resulting objects may then be presented using a combination of positions (e.g., clusters based on object class), appearance traits (e.g., color or shape based on attribute values), and labels. Depending on how many of these dimensions you employ within the display, you can easily derive twenty or more pieces of information for each data object on the screen.

No analyst that we have encountered is capable of considering twenty dimensions at once. (Recall the seven to nine chunk limitation on short-term memory.) Clearly, a more measured approach is in order. When designing display configurations try and choose ones that will help you examine a few key questions at a time. As your analysis progresses and you become more familiar with the data, you will have less trouble dealing with hyper-dimensional visual displays. This is in large part because your analytical focus will increase as the analysis progresses. Thus, your questions will become more and more narrow, and you will be processing information from only a few dimensions at any one time.

As you gain experience with this method of analysis, you will become more skilled at dealing with comprehensive displays, but in the beginning you should try and keep it relatively simple. In the end you may need to present complicated results in a series of displays in order to show higher order relationships and patterns. Remember that the displays of your final results will be useless if they are too complicated for your target audience to understand.

Analytical Approaches

When using visualization methodologies the analysis occurs through interactions with the displays themselves. In this context there are classes of patterns that are revealed by the structures of objects and their relative values or positions within the displays. In cases for which network models are used, there is an added dimension of linkages among object classes. Network analyses can yield another set of pattern classes that reveal additional sorts of information. This section describes the kinds of inferences you can draw from simply viewing your data visually as a set of objects and their related connections. We realize there are also a host of landscape terrains and quantitative representations that can be used, but we subsume these under the link analysis paradigm.

In every data mining engagement that we conduct, there is always a discussion about which visualization paradigm to use in the analysis. The approach of choice will vary depending on the needs of the client. We pull bits and pieces from our cadres of tools and techniques to fulfill our obligations and produce tangible results. In this section we provide a brief overview of several techniques that have proven to be effective in a wide range of applications and domains. There are many others that are not discussed in this text. We recommend that you look at each of the tools presented in Section III to learn more about some of the other ways in which data can be presented and analyzed.

Analyzing Structural Features

Many inferences can be made by simply looking at the structure of a visual display itself. That is, before the names of any data elements are explicitly presented to the user for review, the diagrams themselves can show you where potential patterns may exist. Object placement and appearance can convey a large amount of information to the user. Unusual patterns can instantaneously convey information about data elements that exceed boundary conditions, data that are missing, or unexpected patterns. Additionally the mere appearance of the display can convey interesting anomalies such as data with illegal values, data groupings of unequal proportions and sizes, and a host of other facts. We always begin a visual analysis by doing an overview display of the data without any object labels or higher order appearance manipulations just so that we can see these more global features clearly.

Out-of-Bounds Values

Sometimes the display of outlier information is so noticeable that it can immediately trigger examination of the underlying data structures. In an engagement that we performed for a medical organization, we analyzed a set of several thousand emergency room admissions records. At one point we were interested in exploring the relationship between vital signs upon arrival and eventual patient outcome. Using a landscape display, we plotted systolic and diastolic blood pressure readings against a trauma scale score indicating the severity of the patient's overall condition. One of the first things we noticed when we examined the display was that we had some diastolic blood pressure values over 500 (see Figure 5.8). Since this is a physiological impossibility, we knew that we had bad data in those records. Further examination revealed that those records were corrupted in other ways as well, and so they were removed from the analysis. This also resulted in some refinements in the data preparation stages for this application. If we had used a nonvisual approach, such as computing statistics to

Figure 5.8 Out-of-bounds values can signify bad data records.

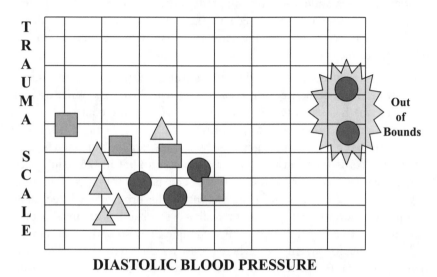

describe overall trends, this information might have been missed and might have skewed the analysis. It was only by having a means of viewing data for each individual record that we were able to discover this problem quickly.

Missing Data

Sometimes the goal of an analysis is to detect records that should be present but in fact are missing from the data set. As an example, consider the case of a cellular communications network in which information about individual calls is collected from several independent sources including the switch and billing systems. As it turns out, cellular communication companies need information from all sources in order to determine proper billing for every call. If any piece of information is missing for a call, we know that a system failure has occurred. Therefore, if we want to test whether the system is functioning properly at any point, we can collect the phone call data and determine whether any records are incomplete.

To do this evaluation, a test call matrix is generated to define the parameters of the test cases. The matrix will include entries describing the call disposition including all the service plans, times/dates, switching exchanges, VMAC levels, and signal strengths of each call. A standard testing matrix will contain information describing a few thousand cellular records. Test calls are generated using specialized cellular hardware technologies capable of recording all of the operating conditions under which the communication was made. A "master" control list is generated from the hardware which then becomes the basis for verifying how well the system responded to the hardware changes and/or software upgrades. This list (*control data*) is later compared with the various cell-switching logs (*switch data*) that are individually maintained by each switch in the cellular network, along with the billing information generated about the call.

By visually clustering the data according to a set of descriptive features, discrepancies can easily be identified between the control and switch data sets. What we look for in these diagrams is a consistent set of pairings between the control data and switch data based on the values used to perform the clustering. Figure 5.9 shows a display that reveals that data are missing in the application data set. Any missing data such as unpaired records found in the diagrams indicate a fault in the cellular network. Thus, the diagrams can very quickly reveal discrepancies for that configuration by exposing the missing data. Analysis of tabular data in this problem might be a long and arduous process; nevertheless, you can immediately see that data are missing once the data sets are sent to a visual display. This technique can also scale to accommodate the billing information system data where triples are expected. Thus, a complete cellular network programmatic test and evaluation can be conducted using visual techniques in a fraction of the time needed using customary methods.

Figure 5.9 Missing data within a test-pairing of cellular control and switch data.

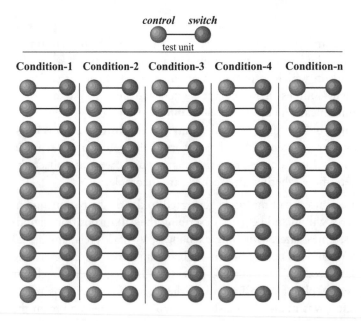

Anomalous Patterns

Some data sets contain representations that are very principled in their construction such that certain events trigger the occurrence of other events. Further, in many cases, events may be expected to occur in a particular order. When a series of events occurs in the wrong order, this constitutes an anomaly that may indicate an important pattern.

An interesting example of events occurring in unexpected order may be taken from the airline industry. As you know, many airlines structure their fares so that a discount is given for round trips that include weekend stays in the destination city. In fact, you usually pay substantially more for a round trip that does not include the weekend stay. Some clever frequent flyer travelers have devised a scheme that allows them to simulate weekend stays and take advantage of lower fares. Sometimes called a back-to-back scheme, this plan requires that the traveler take two trips scheduled such that there is a weekend between the beginning of the first trip and the end of the second trip. As seen in Figure 5.10, what the traveler is actually doing is taking two back-to-back trips, traveling from Monday through Friday on two successive weeks and coming home for the weekend in between. However, the traveler can structure

Figure 5.10 Scheme for disguising back-to-back flights.

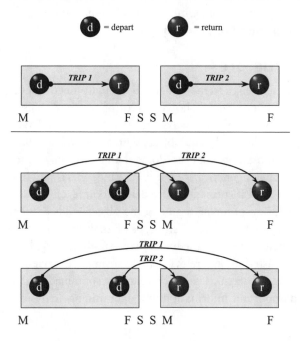

the airline ticket purchases so that credit is given for weekend stays for both trips even though no travel occurs over the weekend on either trip. How? The trick is to purchase the tickets as if one trip is nested within the other. So the original return leg (the first Friday in our example) is actually booked as the originating location of the second flight; both legs occurring after the weekend are booked as return flights for the two originating flights before the weekend.

This is a clever scheme that can save business travelers quite a lot of money. Although technically this is not illegal, the airlines would obviously like to identify these patterns when they occur. The reason that this nesting is detectable is that there are two originating flights without the round trip return in between, as would be expected in the normal scheme of things. That is, the nesting is the anomaly that can be detected when events occur out of their normal order.

Having read the preceding chapters, however, you should be able to come up with some ideas about how to avoid being detected under these circumstances. First, you could simply book the nested flight on a different airline than the outer flight so that the information would not appear in the same data source. If that is not an option, you could book the flights under slightly different names such as John Smith versus Mr. John R. Smith, in which case a simple name matcher would not identify them as the same person. If the flights are tied to your frequent flier number, you could set up separate accounts with the same airline, book the two flights on these two accounts, and so on. (Sometimes it pays to understand technology well enough to stay one step ahead of the other guy.)

Analyzing Network Structures

Many other types of analysis lend themselves to the visualization environment. In the examples presented throughout this book, we are showing a lot of network analysis paradigms. This is because the network is in many ways the most fundamental visualization paradigm. By modeling your data as linked objects with attributable values, you can represent information in most any analysis domain that you encounter. Furthermore data objects can be applied generically to a wide range of visual landscapes and quantitative displays (Section III presents more detail about each individual type of visual display). The inclusion of linkages among the objects adds another dimension to the equation. Thus, the most comprehensive type of analysis that can be performed includes a relational dependency (e.g., the links) between objects. Without the links, you tend to have simple clustering. Figure 5.11 shows a simple overview of a network structure. The following subsections describe features contained within network structures that can yield important information in a data mining analysis.

Figure 5.11 The structure of a network.

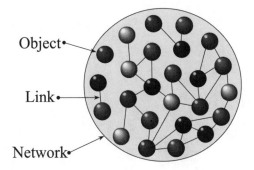

Object•

Link•

Network•

Interconnectivity

In one particular engagement we had with a U.S. government agency, we were at a disadvantage because we did not have the requisite security clearances permitting us to access their data sets. They needed our expertise, but could not get us cleared in time to help them analyze the data. We finally reached a solution that satisfied all of their requirements without compromising their security. We configured a visualization tool to load data in a certain format into a generic model. Next, we set up a display function to toggle on and off certain descriptive information (e.g., the labels) that might reveal the nature or content of their data. We operated the system in the "labels off" mode; our clients operated in the "labels on" mode.

Once the information was populated into the model, we were able to help them identify critical patterns and data elements within the display solely on the basis of the way the object structure looked. Using a link analysis tool, we easily identified objects that were highly interconnected (see Figure 5.12 for a conceptual example), had unusual relationships, or did not quite fit in with the rest of the data. Further, by clustering on various attributes, we showed where the strongest relationships existed in the data set. When our clients wanted to check the values of specific objects when we were not present, they could just turn on the toggle switch to display this information. Thus, we were able to perform a successful analysis strictly by examining the structure of the network, as opposed to its content.

There are certain types of structural patterns that show up in visual analyses across problem domains. This principle is illustrated in Figure 5.13 where two different link displays based on different underlying data sets are shown. Note that the displays are structurally similar, although the objects shown in the two displays represent different types of real world entities. The diagram on the left shows a data set used to expose an illegal loan-back scheme. As already described in Chapter 1, loan-back

Figure 5.12 An example of structural patterns within a link analysis diagram.

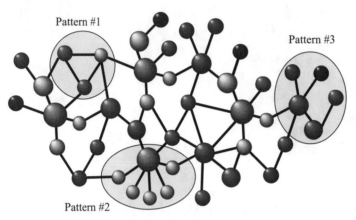

schemes are used in a variety of money laundering operations. In this scheme, loans from a business are repaid using monies obtained from illegal activities (usually drug sales). The use of the money to pay back a legal loan legitimizes or "launders" the funds. You can see in the loan-back diagram that there is an account that is being utilized by a wide variety of different people. The links represent each of the transactions between the people and the account. Since the type of account is "loan" it indicates that lots of people are paying down the account balance through deposits, most probably made at different branch locations. As you can imagine, this type of situation is most unusual and typically is observed for these kinds of illegal dealings.

The diagram on the right is structurally similar to that generated by the loan-back data, but is produced by slightly reorienting our analytical focus. In this diagram, the majority of objects represent bank accounts and the links represent transactions. You can easily identify the high-velocity account as the one with the most transactions. Thick lines represent multiple links such that link thickness corresponds to frequency of activity. Using this approach, you can quickly understand the financial transaction behaviors affiliated with certain accounts and follow the paths as money is moved among accounts via deposits and withdrawals. Taken together, then, the displays shown in Figure 5.13 illustrate how interesting patterns are revealed as similar kinds of configurations in data structures across analytical domains.

Articulation Points

One analytical approach that lends itself to visualization technologies is the detection of bottlenecks, or articulation points in the data set. For example, data objects

Figure 5.13 Using the structure of data to reveal important patterns.

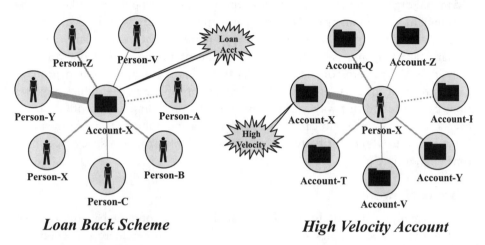

Loan Back Scheme   *High Velocity Account*

that connect two or more subnetworks may be important articulation points in the overall structure. The fact that an articulation point object exists within the networks most often indicates that the represented object has an important role to play. There may also be multiple articulation points within a network that may or may not serve similar functions.

An articulation point can also represent an object that has a large or inordinate number of connections. If the object were to be removed, the entire structure of the network would be significantly affected. What-if scenarios can be generated based on the inclusion or exclusion of this particular object. The importance of the object will be determined from the model used to represent the data.

Suppose that you were modeling the production and sale of consumer electronics products around the world. You could create an object class of "country" to represent the location in which products were manufactured. In such a network you might expect countries such as the United States, China, Japan, Taiwan, and Korea to all be articulation points within the model since these countries utilize a variety of raw materials to produce consumer electronics products. You could filter on particular types of products or sources of materials to examine any changes that might occur in overall patterns of articulation points that might indicate that certain pairs of countries tend to trade (or control) some products but not others. This analogy could also apply to other application areas such as arms sales and nuclear proliferation studies.

To take another example, suppose you were modeling phone call data within a criminal organization. You might discover one particular phone number that has incoming links from many of the participating phone numbers in the data set. That pattern would tell you that this particular number is a central articulation point in the organization, and is probably very significant to the overall operation. By examining the patterns of outgoing calls from this number, you could probably gain important insights into how the organization operates. Gambling organizations can be found this way during time intervals preceding high profile sporting events. Lots of people will call into a central clearing number to place their bets. What is unique about this pattern is that it occurs only around a specific period of time (e.g., a time pivot).

Discrete Networks

In some analyses it is useful to identify subnetworks contained in the data set. Within a large and complex network structure, inevitably numerous subnetworks will play an important part in your analysis. Each of these discrete or isolated networks can be analyzed independently to determine its configuration and makeup. Sometimes the goal of the network analysis is to discover subnetworks that exist with a larger organizational framework. As an example, the way that personnel interact within an organization may be modeled so as to reveal discrete networks. There may be discrete networks within the organization in which most individuals interact only with others in their own department and do not have any interdepartmental contacts. Each subunit works within the larger organization, but functions independently to some degree. A network analysis would reveal this behavior and this information might be used to formulate plans for reorganization, if desired.

In other instances, the goal is to build a network from a set of separate cases. For example, suppose that the police could build a data set containing information about all individual burglaries occurring within a metropolitan area including such information as their geographical location, modus operandi, and so forth. By filtering on particular attributes, it would be possible to isolate networks of crimes sharing critical features. These networks might reflect the crimes of particular burglars operating within the jurisdiction, each committing a series of burglaries. This information could then allow the investigators to tie together several separate crimes to be solved as a group rather than as individual cases.

Missing Connections

One interesting class of finding in a visual analysis is the discovery of entities that are detached from the main network structure. Missing connections can constitute a special form of discrete network, where the resultant subnetwork consists of a single object. Within virtually every network that is generated, there will be objects that do not fit or connect with the rest of the objects. Missing connections may reflect inconsistent or incomplete data and should be looked at carefully to make sure that they do not adversely affect the analysis in any significant way. If you have done filtering operations prior to display, however, you may have missing connections because specific values have been excluded from consideration within the network. For example, if the data set were filtered to include only credit card transactions occurring on a Tuesday or Wednesday, then all other data that did not pass the criteria would result in a missing connection. Single objects that are not connected to anything else in the data structure are often called isolates.

Strong/Weak Linkages

Examination of linkage patterns allows you to see the relative strength of relationships within the network. Objects can be associated with one another for a variety of reasons. The frequency of these connections usually is determined by the number of observations within the original data set presented for analysis. Objects with many links between them are easy to visualize in these systems. Numerous sales transactions, repeated calling of certain phone numbers, regular interactions with other people or organizations are examples of the types of information that can help show frequent connection.

We typically use the frequency analysis when looking at our network logs. However, keep the larger picture in mind as well. Since the frequency is just an attributable value with respect to describing a relationship, any other quantitative attribute can also be used to facilitate the accumulation of values (e.g., a running total). Suppose you wanted to represent the fact that a supermarket shopper is purchasing a certain product such as bread. The strength of the linkage between the shopper and the product can be established by a single transaction of that shopper making one bread purchase. Over a period of time you could establish a very strong link between shopper and bread for someone who comes in and buys fresh bread every day. Alternatively, you could consider the number of loaves of bread being purchased in any one transaction to be the discriminating factor of how strong or weak the shopper-bread relationship is within your analysis. The link could take on the value of the total number of bread loaves purchased during the data collection period. Therefore, using this reference model, the shopper who purchases ten loaves of bread a week has a stronger relative link value than the one who purchases only a loaf a day, even though the frequency of observation is less. The point is that you can be flexible in your use of linkages, using them to model relationships and behaviors that might not be obvious at first glance.

Fan-Out Frequency

The number and type of associations between the various data elements can be a good indicator of the level of activity that exists among the data objects. Using the sequencing or sorting capabilities inherent in most visual data mining systems, analysts can quickly distinguish those objects that tend to be connected to a wide variety of other objects. This is a form of fan-out that exists within data sets where an entity is observed numerous times with a variety of other different entities. These objects stand out because they have an inordinately large number of relationships to other objects within the system. (These objects may be articulation points as described earlier.)

Fan-out frequency can be a good indicator of unusual behavior for particular entities within a data set. We noted a good example of this when performing work for a federal agency in which we were analyzing a financial transaction data set. In a data set in which most individuals and addresses were represented only once, we quickly noticed that one particular address was represented quite frequently (over 250 times). The fan-out frequency of this item set it apart from the other addresses in the analysis, and it turned out to be information that the client pursued in a subsequent investigation.

Pathway Analysis

Sometimes the goal of an analysis is to determine whether a set of objects may be connected across a series of linkages. In these cases the path may not be a simple one and may contain several types of linkages. The goal is to determine if there are at least one or more pathways available that can be traversed to connect two specified endpoints. This can be done in a network analysis by isolating one end-object at a time and exploring the possible paths of connection between them using shed or isolate functions. Weighted pathway analysis networks can also be considered based on one of the quantitative attribute values associated with the relationship. Again, the nature of the data model used will determine the quality of the pathways that can be identified.

For example, many of you have played the parlor game called "How many steps to Kevin Bacon?" in which the goal is to find a chain of movie-actor connections that links Kevin Bacon and another actor in the least number of steps. It turns out that most well known actors can be linked to Kevin Bacon in five steps or less. For example a path may be traced between Kevin Bacon and Al Pacino in three steps: Bacon costarred with Meryl Streep in "The River Wild"; Streep starred with Robert DeNiro in the "Deerhunter" (and other films); DeNiro starred with Pacino in "The Godfather, Part II" (and "Heat"). Sometimes there are multiple paths that may be identified between endpoints and the goal is to find the shortest one. So in our Kevin Bacon–Al Pacino example, an even shorter path with only two steps exists: Kevin Bacon and Ellen Barkin both appeared in the movie "Diner," and Ellen Barkin starred with Al Pacino in "Sea of Love."

Commonality Linkages

Interesting information may sometimes be derived from the fact that a set of entities is connected to common elements. An example of commonality was described in Chapter 1 in which we discussed the insurance company's payout of multiple death claim benefits for the same deceased individual. Commonality can also be detected in the opposite direction in which otherwise disparate objects are shown to be linked to a common object. Commonality within a network is determined when two or more reference objects within a data model share a third object in common.

Some tools have automated commonality routines that allow the user to discover and expose quickly critical associations that would otherwise go undetected or consume hours of manual labor. There are many applications for which analysis of commonality linkages are key to making important discoveries. Some good examples of following commonality links in analyses include:

- Exposing fraud by showing people using common identification numbers

- Reducing unnecessary marketing costs by finding duplications of addresses within client mailing lists

- Minimizing transportation and delivery costs by identifying common locations to be visited across a set of sales transactions

Figure 5.14 provides a set of illustrations of the types of patterns you may obtain from a network analysis. As you can see, when the data are modeled appropriately, it is easy to appreciate each of these patterns in a visual display. Note that as you perform your own analysis, chances are that you may discover combinations of these patterns within a single data set. Thus, you could conduct a pathway analysis using a variety of factors regarding the strength and commonality of objects within the model to determine whether discrete networks form. These patterns are not mutually exclusive, and very complex patterns can be exposed when these techniques are used in combination.

Discovering Emergent Patterns of Connectivity

There are several techniques adapted from social-network theory that can be applied effectively to many network-based applications. One particular algorithm used in several systems exposes emerging patterns of connections. Emergent patterns show hidden "enterprise" structures comprised of closely interacting nodes. Emergent patterns of connectivity are revealed by grouping those nodes that share

Figure 5.14 Patterns revealed in visual network analyses.

Network Structure Patterns

Articulation Points - look for bottlenecks where one
particular entity connects two or more subnetworks

Missing Connections - expose entities that are
detached from the main network structure

Discrete Networks - identify all the different
subnetworks contained in the data

Strong/Weak Linkages - see the strength of
relationships within the network

Pathway Analysis - determine if a series of linkage
will connect a tuple of entities

Commonality - look for entities connected to common
elements

more linkages with each other than they do with nodes outside the group. Each group is cohesive by virtue of its shared linkages. The concept of emergent group is most meaningful in contexts in which relationships among entities are being analyzed, such as in the case of people and organizations.

Emergent Groups

Emergent pattern algorithms can be used to identify close-knit groupings of objects based on their relationships to one another (see the sidebar on the Emergent Group Algorithm). Some applications for which we have used emergent pattern algorithms to good effect include:

- Examination of published document abstracts, discovering networks of authors collaborating and publishing with one another

- Analysis of identification and account numbers to expose networks of individuals involved in fraudulent activities

- Inferring patterns of utilization of a web-site based on sequencing patterns of the HTML pages

- Describing the informal e-mail groupings within an organization based on communication events

The Emergent Group Algorithm

The algorithm is generic in its application and grouping typically is based on three criteria:

- The group must contain at least three candidate nodes.
- Each one of these entities must have a relationship with a minimum of two other nominated group members.
- At least a certain number (e.g., 50%) of the total relationships for each entity exist only with other nominated entities in the group.

In some tools, these parameters are not rigid and can be adjusted to better focus the analysis if desired. An illustration of emergent groups is shown in Figure 5.15.

To understand how emergent groups are defined, consider an example. Suppose you were looking at patent data and wanted to know if there were emerging groups of related technologies based on the individuals and organizations represented in your data set. When building your data model you could establish object classes for patent technologies, individual people to whom the patents are awarded, and the organizations with which the work is affiliated. Assuming that each record in the

Figure 5.15 Example of an emergent group.

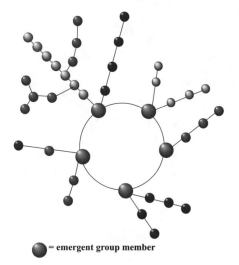

= emergent group member

data set contains information on each of these variables, each object would then have a relationship to every other object defined under the patent. The resulting model would form a fully connected patent-representation. Since individuals can have multiple patents, and organizations fund the development of different patents, and the technologies involved can overlap among several patents, a very large network of entities could be generated. Thus, it would be hard to get an understanding of the general layout and structure of the patent data without generating some type of imposed structure. By looking for emergent groups, however, you could immediately see selected subgroups of individuals, organizations, and technologies that were most closely interconnected. Each grouping could be considered cohesive, very tightly coupled, and would be the dominant force involved within the selected discipline you were interested in studying.

Key Components that do not Belong to Groups

Not all data elements can be uniquely classified into a group. Nevertheless, particular data elements might play other critical roles in an overall network structure. Depending upon your application, these roles may be very important in the understanding of the data structure. The following three additional roles comprise the majority of the classifications used for these types of objects (see Figure 5.16).

Figure 5.16 Structures not defined as emergent groups.

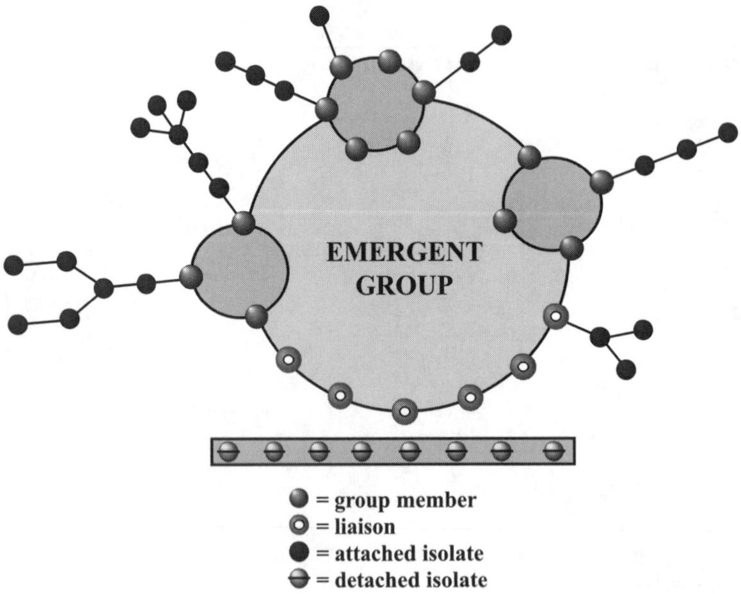

EMERGENT GROUP

● = group member
◎ = liaison
● = attached isolate
⊜ = detached isolate

Liaisons Liaisons are objects that are key components in the main network of entities. They might not be part of any particular group, but may be highly connected with most other nodes in the model. They are important because they can bridge the gaps, if any, between two or more groups within the overall structure. Thus, if you wanted to find out information about an organization, learn how the communications work within a network, or start a rumor, you would go to the liaisons. You would do this because they are connected to multiple groups and/or other liaisons and their breadth of connection is much more expansive than that of emergent group members. Thus a liaison is a great go-between that can be used to manipulate the network. Abstractly, you can consider a liaison to be an articulation point of sorts.

Attached Isolates These entities have an interesting role within the network because they are connected to other objects, one of which is eventually tied back to an emergent group member or liaison. Thus they tend to serve more of a support role to the different emerging groups or liaisons, but to only one particular group or liaison at a time. An example of attached isolates can occur in a phone call analysis in which a calling circle would form around a central set of numbers (e.g., the emergent group). The phone numbers may represent, for example, the friends and family members of a close-knit group of people. These core phones would in turn call other phones outside the immediate group for various purposes such as ordering pizza or speaking with a pharmacist. Since these numbers are not generally important or involved in the day-to-day calling patterns of the emergent group, they can be defined as attached isolates. A long stream or large number of attached isolates can form if the data permits.

Detached Isolates These entities are simply not part of any network that was constructed. They do not belong to any group nor do they have supporting connections to any other entity within the network. Thus, if you were doing an organizational analysis and identified a set of detached isolates, you would need to ask why these individuals are not an integral part of the company. The individuals might be isolated by virtue of having been out during the data collection interval and their responsibilities have been taken over by other individuals. These situations occur if someone is out on maternity leave, extended travel, or they have taken a sabbatical from work. More seriously, detached isolates might indicate dead weight within the organization. People who do not communicate or interact with the people in the rest of the organization in some tangible fashion, whether it is within their assigned group or not, might tend to be the least productive, depending upon the nature of the organization.

Analyzing Temporal Patterns

Having discussed structural, network, and emergent group pattern detection, we now turn to a fourth class of analysis, namely temporal pattern detection. All business transactions, whether related to finances or telecommunications, have a temporal component. Likewise, the passage of time is an important component in many other application domains as well. It is thus imperative that you are prepared to look for temporal patterns represented in your data set. Analysis of various classes of temporal patterns can be accomplished in a visualization environment.

In the simplest case, you can use date information as a means of representing the passage of time in a temporal analysis. To identify patterns in a time series, it is realistic to think of a time series as consisting of several different components:

Trend. Upward or downward growth (may be linear or exponential) that characterizes the data over a period of time (e.g., an increase in expenditures on a credit card account).

Cycle. Recurring up and down movement around trend levels. For example, the peaks and troughs of spending or expansion followed by contraction in the economy would constitute a cycle.

Seasonal. Patterns that complete themselves in a year or some other predetermined period (e.g., elections, natural resource constraints, and weather).

Irregular. Erratic movement in a time series that follows no regular pattern (e.g., leftover unaccountable expenses after considering trend, cycle, or seasonal variations).

In our experience in working in environments heavily dependent on time, the key to detecting a temporal pattern is to determine the cycle in which the pattern occurs. Many systems define *cycles of convenience*. These cycles tend to fall within intervals that we find easy to interpret. Convenient cycles include abstract temporal representations such as minutes, hours, days, weeks, months, and years. We understand, accept, and work within these cycles, and are therefore often predisposed to look for patterns within them. However, the interesting patterns do not always fall within these convenience cycles. Stock markets can have very irregular patterns of behavior that do not fit known cycles. Likewise criminals will often deliberately try to disguise their behaviors by acting at irregular intervals to avoid detection. This will disguise the cycles of convenience that typically are addressed by conventional analytical methods. Required are techniques that can be used to detect and expose the *hidden* patterns.

Establishing Classes of Temporal Patterns

We have generally defined two categories of temporal patterns—absolute and contiguous. Absolute time references specifically address the actual amount of time spent on any event or between a set of events. The value of an absolute time reference equates to the amount of elapsed real-world time. Contiguous time references are concerned only with the order in which events have occurred, such that one event precedes another event. There is no consideration of the amount of time that has passed between events, only their relative order. Figure 5.17 shows the high-level differences between these patterns. Either of these characterizations of temporal patterns may be used to define and detect cycle-event patterns within a data set. A cycle event can be defined as a particular association between two objects (e.g., people, organizations, locations, and accounts) that occurs with a certain frequency. In each case, we are looking for a pattern match between two or more events occurring at either absolute or relative intervals within the data set.

Absolute Time Cycle Events   To initiate a pattern-matching search for an absolute time cycle event, a trigger event needs to be defined, which forms the basis of the pattern match. This event may be a simple representation such as the occurrence of a certain object with a particular attribute value (for example, credit card transactions of more than $5,000). Alternatively, a more complicated trigger event made up of a composite representation as defined by more than one

Figure 5.17 Absolute versus contiguous temporal patterns.

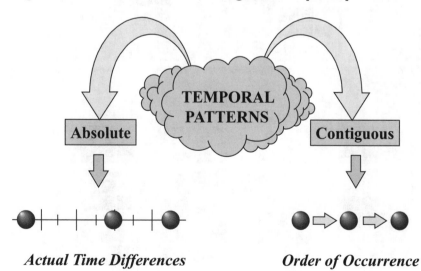

attribute across one or more object classes (for example, credit card transactions of more than $5,000 reported from certain department stores within a particular Zip code) can be generated. To the degree that the trigger for the time cycle event is made more complex, you increase the granularity of the search, giving it more resolution and focus. You can then define the boundaries of the search and the size of the time cycle to be inspected (see Figure 5.18).

A good method for detecting absolute time patterns is to decompose the cycle specified into a series of discrete time segments of equal length. For each segment, determine whether the trigger event has occurred. Repeat this process on successively smaller (or larger) time intervals, finally stopping at a preset boundary. Patterns can be reported for a given run if the number of time intervals in which the trigger event occurs exceeds the reporting threshold (i.e., 50%, 75%, etc.). The user

Figure 5.18 Absolute time cycle event.

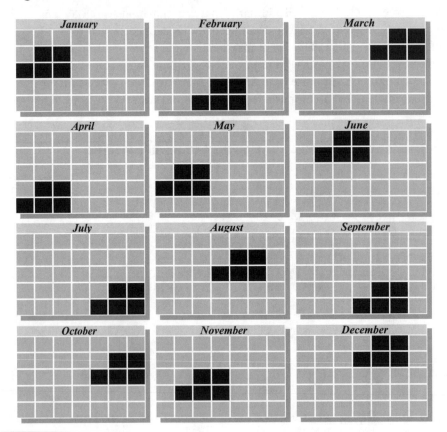

may then inspect these findings, run again with a more refined trigger event, and so on as desired. Any patterns detected can then be used to forecast events and establish relationships to other activities. Figure 5.18 shows an example of a pattern that fits an absolute time cycle model, where the pattern is occurring every month.

Contiguous Time Cycle Events In the approach just described, you are looking for the recurrence of a particular event across a measurable interval of time. Rather than searching on the amount of time passing between occurrences of a single event, however, you may be more interested in detecting the co-occurrence of two or more events within a nonstandard time interval. Thus the contiguous time cycle event is a simple extension of the absolute time cycle event in which the search is directed towards patterns of two or more events occurring across a series of time intervals. Contiguous pattern detection examples can include successive occurrences of telephone conversations, stock transactions, meeting contacts, or deposits in associated bank accounts.

As before, the user would define the trigger to be used in the search. The trigger is composed of the initial event and the user specifies the boundaries of the time intervals to be searched and the increments or decrements in interval size on each successive pass through the data. For every detection of the initial event, you would gather all data fitting within the bounds of the subsequent interval. This interval may be defined by the user as an interval following the trigger event, an interval before the trigger event, or both. Once a complete pass is made through the data, you search for events contained in common across all intervals included in the pass. A pattern is defined as the repeated recurrence of an event in conjunction with the initial trigger event across the defined time intervals.

Figure 5.19 shows a sample diagram of a contiguous time cycle event. In this figure, there are a series of shaded time intervals for which the trigger event is depicted by an upward triangle symbol. Each event has a corresponding time/date stamp that can be used to determine whether it belongs in the interval following the trigger event. In this example, a pattern has been detected in that the trigger event is consistently followed by two other events (circle symbols) that both fall within the shaded time interval.

Hybrid Time Cycle Events There may be certain applications for which you may wish to establish an interval as the period of activity between two cycle events or until the end of a cycle. All specification mechanisms defined for contiguous time cycle events can be used for configuring the hybrid time cycle events. However, the interval between events will be of varying duration that can be long or short in nature depending on the behavior of the object being

Figure 5.19 Contiguous time cycle event.

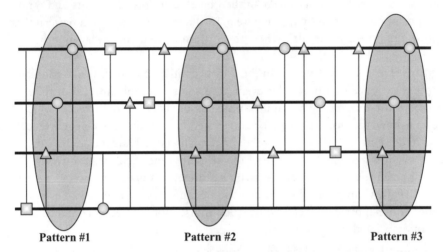

Pattern #1   Pattern #2   Pattern #3

reviewed. For example, when a certain amount of money is deposited into a specific account, it is observed that money is also removed from a different account within some specified time interval or preset number of observed events.

Visualizing Temporal Patterns

Once temporal pattern detection algorithms have been run on a data set, a set of output patterns will be generated, most likely in some kind of tabular format. Since this method of presenting the information is likely to be very difficult to interpret, you will need to think about ways in which to display the information for inspection by an analyst. There are certainly no hard and fast rules about which method to select, and you may want to experiment with a few methods in your own applications. Nevertheless, we will mention that we have had success with using 3-dimensional grid displays such as the one shown in Figure 5.20.

The data presented in Figure 5.20 are from a set of financial transactions of varying amounts (x axis), on different dates (y axis) filed by a set of individuals (z axis). Recall that one of the functions of the algorithm is to shrink and stretch these intervals until patterns emerge. In this example, an interesting pattern was discovered when amounts of the transactions were broken up into $5000 intervals, and time intervals were divided according to days of the week.

There are a few important things to notice about the grid. First, a cell in the grid is filled if there are any data points in the data set falling into it. The brighter the color of the cell, the more data points it has. So lighter colored boxes denote "hot spots" containing relatively more data points and show trends in overall

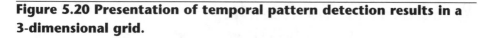

Figure 5.20 Presentation of temporal pattern detection results in a 3-dimensional grid.

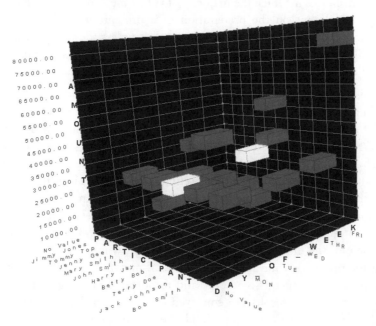

financial transaction activity. If a line of cells is filled all the way across the grid in any direction, then a pattern has been detected. In this particular example, there are a few patterns to notice. First, there are more transactions on Mondays than on any other day of the week. Second, there are more transactions filed with $25,000 amounts than any other amount. Perhaps the most interesting finding is that one individual has filed more transactions than any other individual in the data set and he has a very distinctive filing pattern. He files on Tuesdays and Fridays, usually for $25,000 at a time. So if we wanted to predict when this person is likely to file his next big transaction, we could wait for him in the bank on Tuesdays and Fridays.

In the event that you do not detect any interesting patterns in your display, you could alter the size of the intervals on dollar amounts or time, and get the next set of outputs. You could then redisplay the data to see whether a pattern has emerged. You could compare displays to determine whether you were going in the right direction in terms of shrinking or growing the intervals of interest. The point is that, just like any other form of visual analysis, temporal pattern detection is an iterative process that can be greatly facilitated by visualization technologies. The display itself is a tool that can be used to aid the analytic process.

Presenting Your Results

There will be many instances in which the majority of your time and effort is placed not on the analysis itself but on the preparation of a presentation. The results derived from analyses described in this chapter are useless unless they can be communicated effectively. Thus, visual data mining analyses include the presentation of results as a critical final step.

The types of visual analyses described in this chapter are often conducted using high-powered computational data mining tools and are designed to process very large quantities of data. We frequently work with systems that provide the ability to display tens of thousands of records in a single diagram. Needless to say, these diagrams can be very complex and can be quite difficult to understand without a lot of up-front training and instruction. If interpreting these displays is difficult for the analysts, you can imagine how opaque some of them must appear to other consumers of the information. In most cases the communication of results to a third party can be next to impossible without a significant amount of refinement. This section reviews some of the more important issues that you will want to consider when converting the results of your analysis into a final presentation. It is important that you be prepared to spend some time and resources on this part of your engagement to ensure that the results are conveyed effectively to the appropriate recipients. The displays of your final results should be interpretable by your target audience, should hold together as a cohesive narrative, and should be supported by documentation from the original data set.

Keeping the Target Audience in Mind

The target audience is perhaps the most important factor to consider when finalizing the presentation of your results. Always structure your presentation with the following considerations in mind:

- Who are the people in the target audience?

- What are their interests?

- What particular aspect(s) of the results are likely to be most important to them?

- What is their level of expertise?

We can state with certitude that some aspects of your results will be more important to some audiences than others. Every time you present your findings, rethink your presentation based on the nature of your audience. Spend the time it takes to revise the structure of your presentation to suit their interests and levels of expertise. It does you no good to make a presentation that your audience cannot understand or appreciate. In fact, it will probably do harm to your future prospects as a data miner if you cannot tailor your presentations to the needs of the target audience.

You want to lay out the sequence of events in a manner that will make the most sense to your target audience. Many of you may have heard the anecdote about a sales representative for a beverage company presenting a marketing idea to a middle-eastern client. The rep created a storyboard with the first frame showing a person in the desert who is very hot, thirsty, and generally miserable. The second frame showed this person gulping down the company's beverage. The final frame portrayed the person as invigorated, blissful, and very relaxed. Although this storyboard seemed promising, it did not have the desired effect. What the rep had forgotten to take into consideration was that his Arabic client read from right to left. Although humorous, this tale reminds us to make sure that results be presented with the listener's perspective in mind.

Suppose you conduct an analysis on some phone data that are to be used in a court case. How are you going to convey that information to the jury? Should you present displays showing thousands of objects and links corresponding to the individual phones and the calls made between them? That would be just about the worst thing you could do. Instead you should take the opposite tack, making the displays as simple as possible in order to convey the essence of the important relationships that you discovered in your analysis. On the other hand, suppose you were presenting this same analysis to the prosecuting attorneys who are trying the case. Would they want to see only the bare bones results, or would they want more detail? Chances are that they might be interested in those displays that contain the more complete picture of the entire data set. In other words, you have to consider the interests and needs of the recipient when deciding which method of presentation will be most effective.

Adopting the Audience's Terminology

Whenever possible, you should present information using conventions and terminology that are familiar to your audience. As you know, many specialized disciplines have their own sets of terms and styles of problem solving. The closer you get to speaking their language, the more effective you will be. (For an example of a presentation technique specialized for certain domains, see the sidebar on Anacapa Presentation Methods.) At the same time, you do not want to burden your audience with the jargon of the visual analysis world. They should not have to understand visual data analysis in order to understand your presentation. Speak English (or the appropriate native language of your audience). Do not overwhelm them with new terminology that is only incidental to their understanding of the big picture.

Anacapa Presentation Methods

One particular technique that was developed to help present results of investigative cases is the Anacapa format. Although originally targeted for the law enforcement community, Anacapa methods are now used in a variety of domains including the military, industry, and corporations. Established in the late 1960s, Anacapa is sometimes touted as an analysis technique. In our opinion, however, it is better characterized as a presentation method that supports limited analysis. When Anacapa was developed, the size, volume, and complexity of typical cases were not as expansive as the ones we are seeing today. You would very quickly run up against limitations with this technique if you tried to use it to analyze even 10,000 phone records. Thus it is better used as a standard presentation method for reporting the results of an analysis than as an analytical tool.

Using Quality Ratings. One of the most basic types of information conveyed in an Anacapa display are the quality ratings assigned to data and data sources. For the most part, you might regard your data as valid because they are derived from electronic sources or reliable systems. However, this is not always the case. In the real world when information is being collected and assembled in support of an analysis, the sources of information can be quite varied. In a law enforcement analysis, for example, data can come from confidential informants, undercover operations, previous investigations, legal statutes, physical evidence, personnel surveillance, technical surveillance, community interchange, open sources, overt references, interviews, interrogations, and debriefings. Clearly you would want to distinguish among these sources in characterizing the quality of data provided by each.

In the Anacapa system each piece of information used in an analysis is assigned a rating based on reliability of the source as well as validity of the information itself. These factors are used to determine how the information should be employed. Facts derived from reliable sources and deemed valid will be taken at face value. This type of information usually includes eyewitness testimony from other law enforcement agencies or from criminal records. On the other hand, information derived from unreliable sources will be discounted and removed from the investigation. Unreliable sources might include anonymous phone tips or reports from known criminal elements. This table summarizes the values assigned to source reliability and data validity. (Our British associates have modified this rating to include only four ratings for each factor: A, B, C, X, 1, 2, 3, 4.)

Index	Source Reliability	Index	Data Validity
A	Reliable	1	Confirmed
B	Usually Reliable	2	Probably True
C	Fairly Reliable	3	Possibly True
D	Not Usually Reliable	4	Doubtfully True
E	Unreliable	5	Improbable

Creating Association Matrices. One commonly used Anacapa format is the association matrix (see Figure 5.21). A version of a cross-correlational matrix, this display contains information about the relationships between known entities important to the analysis. As seen in Figure 5.21, the list of entities is entered alphabetically along the diagonal of a triangle. The relationship between any pair of entities is recorded in the (x,y) cell that forms the intersection point for those two entities in the matrix. In this way, all possible relationships between entities are represented in the cells of the resulting matrix. Standard symbols are used to represent strong (filled dot) and weak (circle) relationships. If there is no relationship at all, the cell will be left blank. If there are special factors to consider, for example, that an individual is the leader of an organization, then a plus sign will be used. Depending on your requirements, numbers can also be used within cells to show the actual number of connections between two entities.

There is also a version of the association matrix that conveys information about the direction of the relationships between entities. In these cases, a full square grid is used because the values above the diagonal might differ from those below the diagonal, depending on the direction of the relationship. This particular approach is used quite often when working with telephone numbers. Since a phone can act as both an originating as well

Continued

Anacapa Presentation Methods *(Continued)*

Figure 5.21 An Anacapa association matrix.

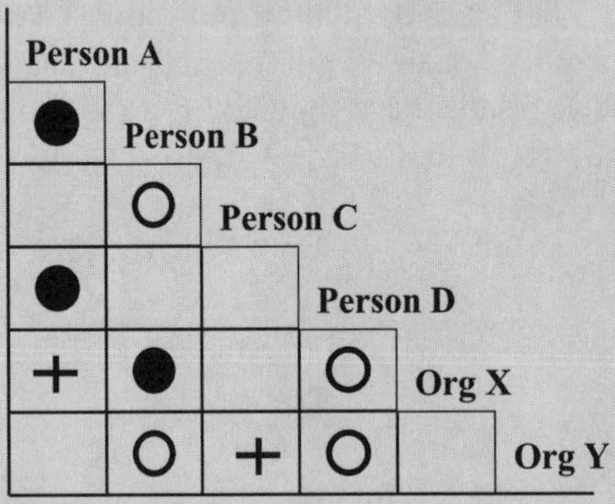

as a destination number, the full grid will be required to show all inbound versus outbound calls. Usually, the grid will be extended to include an attached row and column to present the total number of relationships for that particular entity. Figure 5.22 shows an example of this type of matrix being used to show telephone calls. A variation of this presentation technique is also used to show association rules in some commercial systems.

Figure 5.22 An Anacapa association matrix showing direction of relationships.

		TO						
		555-1111	555-2222	555-3333	555-4444	555-5555		
	555-1111				15		15	
F R O M	555-2222	5		6	3		14	T O T A L
	555-3333		1			12	13	
	555-4444	9					9	
	555-5555	11		8			19	
		25	1	8	18	12		
		TOTAL						

Creating Link Analysis Diagrams. In many cases the association matrix is just a prelude to the creation of a link analysis diagram. The representation of data within a matrix can be difficult to interpret, especially as size and number of relationships increases so that the matrix extends over more than one page. Converting either form of matrix into a link diagram is a straightforward process. Anacapa link diagrams are drawn so that the entity with the largest number of relationships is in the center. For law enforcement purposes, individuals are always represented as circles in these displays. Links conveying the strength of relationships are drawn between entities (strong=solid line; weak=dotted lines). Line crossings are avoided wherever possible. Figure 5.23 shows two displays, a preliminary diagram and its final formal Anacapa layout. (Note that these link analysis diagrams are significantly different from the other link displays presented earlier in the chapter and elsewhere in this book.)

To relate an individual to an organization, the circles depicting the individuals are enclosed by rectangles representing the organizations. All sorts of diagrams can be created this way, including individuals with membership in more than one organization, multiple organizations, and associations among individuals and organizations. Figure 5.24 shows some samples of

Figure 5.23 An Anacapa link diagram.

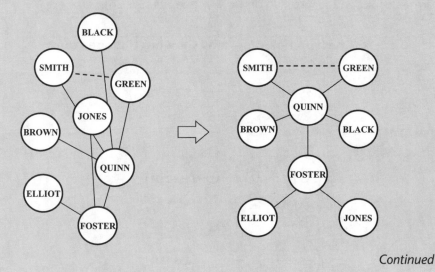

Continued

Anacapa Presentation Methods *(Continued)*

Figure 5.24 Anacapa link diagrams depicting organizational relationships.

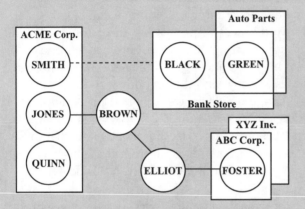

these different relationships. Additionally, when dealing with a full grid of data where there are counts showing the direction of the relationships, the diagrams' linkages can be extended to show these numbers (see Figure 5.25). There are variations on these link diagrams that can be produced to show event flows. The entities themselves are sequenced in order of the time in which the events occurred. Additionally, the linkages can have arrows depicting the direction of the flow (see Figure 5.26).

Figure 5.25 Anacapa link diagrams showing linkage counts.

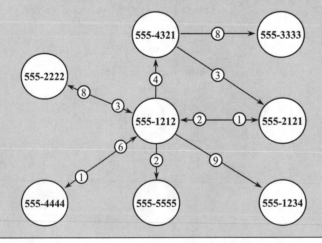

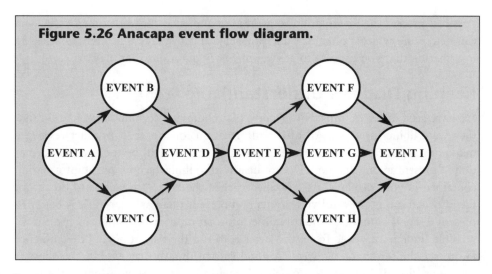

Figure 5.26 Anacapa event flow diagram.

Telling a Story

Presenting your results is very much like telling a story. What are the traits of a good storyteller? That person is capable of capturing the audience's attention and imagination and of keeping them interested in what is being said. Good storytellers entertain with suspense and conflict. Most importantly, they engage the listener with dialog, rhetorically soliciting feedback, and effortlessly guiding the listener down the path that they have chosen. The audience wants to know how the story ends and is therefore willing to wait until all the details have been presented. If the story is presented in a cohesive fashion, the audience is likely to be persuaded to the storyteller's point of view. However, if the narrative is incomplete or inconsistent and the audience has to work to understand your point, there will be questions and confusion that will undermine your effectiveness.

Maintaining the Flow of Information

Most good stories have a beginning, middle, and end. Your challenge is to prepare your story and arrange it frame by frame so that you maintain interest while keeping the narrative understandable. It is highly unlikely that you are going to be able to summarize your results in a single display that is readily understandable. Rather, you first need to explain the original problem and why the analysis was done in the first place. Then you will need to lay out the various stages of the analysis frame by frame. You will conclude by showing the set(s) of results that most directly impact on the audience to whom you are speaking.

As you construct your narrative, try and anticipate questions that will arise along the way. Fill in enough information to avoid gaping holes and weaknesses. If possible, present the information to a practice audience ahead of time so that you can determine which points are unclear. Make up displays that contain back-up information that you can use to answer ancillary questions that may arise.

Keeping Displays Understandable

We have seen many examples of displays that contained so much information that they were uninterpretable. All of the information for a case, a product review, a marketing report, or the disclosure of a fraud typically will be too much information to present in one diagram. Do not be afraid to limit the amount of information contained in your displays. As described earlier, the best approach is to break out the information into several viewpoints and present them as a series. It is better to present a small amount of interpretable information at a time than to present all possible findings at once. To do the latter is to run the risk of having the audience fail to see the forest for the trees. A good rule of thumb that we like to follow is that your display contains too much information if it takes you longer than five minutes to explain it fully.

Limiting the Scope of Displayed Information

Displays should be designed around the main point that you are trying to make. This seems obvious, but we have all seen many examples of displays filled with information that was only incidental to the main point being discussed. Information should not be included if it will serve to distract the audience from your narrative. You can see what we mean by looking at the two displays shown in Figure 5.27, which show findings from a fraud investigation. On the left is a link analysis display that shows all modeled connections between objects for an entire data set. Notice that there is a node at the 3:00 position in this diagram that has many more connections than any other object in the data set. As it turns out, this node represents a person that was tied to numerous suspicious activities, and it was this address that proved to be a key clue in uncovering a bank fraud operation.

Given that the 3:00 node represents the most important finding of the analysis, do you think that the display in the left-hand portion of Figure 5.27 adequately conveys this information? Probably not. That diagram contains too many extraneous objects and connections that distract the viewer's attention from the 3:00 node and undermine the salience of the pattern. The result is better presented in the format shown on the right side of Figure 5.27, in which only the node of interest and all of its connections are shown. Now there is no superfluous information to distract the audience from the main finding. Additionally, in this more streamlined display, there is room to include labels and increase the size of the nodes to facilitate communication of the results.

Figure 5.27 Two link analysis diagrams resulting from a fraud investigation.

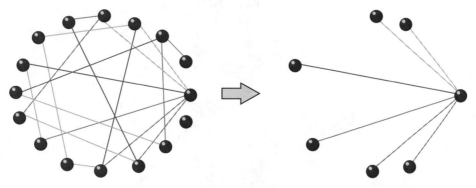

Highlighting Critical Information within the Display

Use techniques that will highlight the critical portions of the display. You can set important patterns apart by using any number of techniques including

- Coloring data points according to attributes or values of interest

- Highlighting or marking critical data points

- Framing portions of the display that are most important

- Shaping data symbols according to group or attribute values

- Labeling key data elements within the display

- Sizing critical elements differently to set them apart

- Grouping items by class membership

Although it may seem trivial to mention, the use of annotations, legends, and other references within the diagram can be critical to effective interpretation of displays. Compare the displays shown in the left- and right-hand portions of Figure 5.28. As you can see, the simple addition of a few pieces of support information greatly facilitates interpretation. Remember, the easier you make it for your target audience to understand your point, the more effective you will be.

Creating Summary Displays

Sometimes the goal in designing a display is to provide a cohesive summary of a broad topic or process. In that event you are not necessarily trying to create a narrative, but are producing a visual summary that can serve as a reference point for a

Figure 5.28 Using annotations to make displays more interpretable.

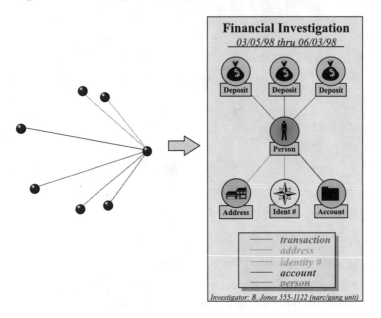

group of viewers. Summary displays present a special challenge because they require you to make many assumptions about the interests of the people who will view the information. You have to consider their interests very carefully so that you can make decisions about what facts you must include and those you can omit.

One technique that we have found very useful in creating summary displays is to divide the display space into separate areas, each of which is dedicated to the presentation of a single subset of the information of interest. Information usually can be partitioned into separate functional areas that make sense within the context of the application. Within each partition, you may want to employ different display techniques. Some information might be presented in textual format, some might be rendered in spatial grids, some might be conveyed in images, and so on. The formats you choose will depend upon the type of information you are presenting. To the degree that you can keep the partitions perceptually distinct from one another, however, your summary will be more effective.

We saw an excellent example of a summary display in a law enforcement facility we recently visited. There was a diagram presented on the wall that depicted information about a drug-bust to occur later that night. This diagram was composed of several components, each of which conveyed important information about the upcoming activity. The organizational hierarchy of the gang structure was presented in one area and included photographs of the key individuals. Another area of the display showed a spatial map of the house that was going to be searched with respect to its position in the neighborhood, along with its physical layout and critical features (doors, windows, closets). A third component of the display was composed of textual annotations of intelligence gathered regarding the types of drugs expected to be seized, the animals located in the house, and where the entry points were going to be established. Thus, in one diagram, using multiple display modalities, the entire plan of the night's events was clearly laid out and conveyed to the agents involved in the bust. There was supporting information regarding any aspect of the plan should anyone want further detail. What was most important about this presentation was that it summarized information gleaned from months of surveillance, information gathering, planning, and refinement and displayed it all as a well-structured diagram. The needs of the audience (in this case the personnel going on the raid) were met in that the display was used to plan a raid that was eventually well executed.

Backing Up Conclusions with Documentation

Visual outputs of analytical results always need to be backed up with supporting documentation. The process used to analyze data is not the same process used to present data. Thus, the supporting information used to generate the diagrams or draw a conclusion must be available for review. This supporting information is usually structured into table or textual formats that can easily be mapped into the visual diagrams. All information that has been utilized as part of the analysis needs to be available in a format that can easily be accessed and interpreted by the recipient.

The combination of diagrams and supporting text documents represents the final output of the data mining efforts. The patterns have been identified, presented, and backed up with the appropriate justifications. They can be replicated, confirmed, and universally interpreted. In the methamphetamine case we discussed earlier in the book, there were twelve diagrams presented at the trial. For each one of these diagrams, we gave the client a package of information that contained all of the text records that were used in the construction and development of the diagram. This provided the opportunity for anyone (including the judge and opposing counsel) to verify whether the displays presented to the court were indeed accurate depictions of the underlying data. The textual documentation also provided an alternative medium for people to reference if they were not comfortable with the visual displays.

Justifying Conclusions Using Drill-Down

Drill-down is commonly used to facilitate justification of data once it has been abstracted into a visual format. Drill-down functions provide methods for viewing alternative levels of analytical detail, including the raw data set itself. Drill-down procedures are very important to the analytical environment. To date, we have not yet used a tool that was not capable of supporting drill-down procedures. Keep in mind that when a drill-down is conducted on a specific data element, all you are viewing is the immediate data supporting that object. This will usually be reflective only of the subset of data that was brought into the analysis environment. Unless you have "walked" the data and have all supporting information available on an object, you will be looking only at a subset. Depending on the nature of the data set, drill-down can also introduce multimedia data formats. Thus, when you profile a data object, information can be presented about the specific characteristics of the object, including references to pictures, images, or audio clips.

Summing Up

In this chapter we have described some of the basics of analysis using data visualization. Visual data mining is a particularly useful method of presenting large and complicated data sets. It is effective primarily because it capitalizes on the strengths of human information processing capabilities, offering the analyst an opportunity for observation with preconception. As such it is ideally suited for exploratory analyses. We have covered some strategies that analysts can employ, looking for structural features as well as features that identify networks of interest within data sets. As a special case, we also discussed some of the special issues involved in detection of temporal patterns and trends. We ended the chapter with a discussion of the issues to consider when preparing results for final presentation. As you leave this chapter, please bear in mind that we are not evangelizing for visualization at the expense of all other analytical methods. Quite the contrary, we would contend that there are many instances in which visual data mining methods can be paired with more quantitative approaches, with each complementing the other. With this in mind, we now turn to Chapter 6, in which we briefly describe many quantitative data analysis methods that are widely employed in data mining engagements.

NONVISUAL ANALYTICAL METHODS 6

In the past few chapters we have outlined an approach for data mining using visualization. As we have stated from the outset, we believe that visualization is a very powerful technique. You have seen how visualization provides opportunities for users to discover interesting and provocative patterns in their data sets. Even more importantly, visualization provides the most flexibility for those situations in which users may not have a clear understanding of the scope of information contained within a data set, and therefore may not have specific hypotheses from which to begin an analysis.

For some situations, however, you may wish to employ other analytical methods during data mining. In this chapter we will introduce some of the most widely used alternative analytical methods including statistical testing, decision trees, association rules, neural networks, and genetic algorithms. We will briefly describe the conceptual approach of each. As you will see, each method can produce results that are both interesting and useful. Although complete descriptions of these analytical methods are beyond the scope of this chapter, this discussion should provide you with a basic understanding of each approach within the context of application problems. After reading this chapter you should have enough information to determine which of the alternatives, if any, is appropriate for your given data set and application questions. Note that in many cases you might still use visualization as a means of conveying the results of an analysis, even though the analytical method does not involve visualization, per se.

As you read about these analytical approaches you will notice that, unlike visualization, these methods are employed with the user largely out of the analysis loop. That is, the types of analyses described in this chapter are performed using a set of rules or algorithms that are computed automatically over an entire data set. The user decides what the initial conditions of the analysis will be, but beyond that the analysis is not an interactive process. As we begin we would urge you to keep in mind that, although we are presenting these quantitative techniques as methods separate from visual analysis, the line between the two camps is becoming blurred. As new full-scale data mining tools are developed and made available to analysts, the choice of analytical methods available in one environment will climb. This is already being seen through the offering of certain commercial data mining systems that seamlessly integrate these capabilities, and it is a trend that will no doubt continue, much to the benefit of all.

Statistical Methods

The use of descriptive and inferential statistics is by far the most standard approach to data analysis. Statistics are the preferred analytical choice in science, medicine, and even in business domains in which one of the goals of the analysis is to determine whether differences exist among predefined groups. Several of the largest commercial data mining products as well as most of the decision support system (DSS) providers are heavily invested in the use of statistical methods in one way or another.

Statistics involve mathematical computation, and therefore require the use of quantitative data. (You can sometimes use statistics on qualitative or nonnumeric data if you recode the information into a numeric format before the analysis.) Statistical tests can be used to compare values among various groups sampled in the data set. In the simplest cases, you can use descriptive statistics to provide an overview of the general characteristics of the groups sampled. Descriptive statistics include such measures as the mean (average value), median (middle value), mode (most common value), standard deviation (a measure of variance), range (low and high values), and distribution of the data sample. In this section we describe two other classes of statistical tests, those aimed at assessment of group differences and regression analyses used to provide predictive information.

Assessing Group Differences

At a more sophisticated level, statistical methods may be used in the context of hypothesis testing in which we predict differences between groups before the analysis begins ("a priori"). Consider the sales information presented in Figure 6.1. In this case we have plotted fictitious data describing sales patterns in a set of franchises during the months of November and December. One set of questions we might have about these data is whether there are overall differences in the magnitude of sales between the two months. If we have enough observations, we might even be able to do comparisons week by week or even day by day for the two months. In general, these kinds of questions are easily answered using statistical tests.

Figure 6.1 Graph showing hypothetical sales (in $100,000 increments) for franchises during the months of November and December.

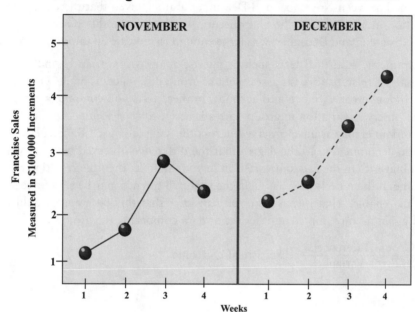

Hypothesis Testing

In the world of statistics, hypotheses about group differences are tested against the standard null hypothesis. The null hypothesis assumes that there are no real differences between groups. Thus, what we usually seek to do with statistical tests is to amass evidence that permits rejection of the null hypothesis in favor of a hypothesis of group differences. Taking the data in Figure 6.1 as an example, you might want to determine whether sales levels rose between November and December. Your experimental hypothesis would be that the December figures are in fact higher overall than the November figures. The null hypothesis in this case is that there is no reliable difference between sales levels during those two months, and that any difference you happened to observe in your particular data set was probably due to chance. More generally:

Experimental Hypothesis: H_1: Groups are different.
Null Hypothesis: H_0: There are no differences between groups.

In our example of sales figures, we would not expect that the numbers would ever be exactly the same from one month to the next. There is a certain amount of baseline fluctuation that occurs, but if it tends to balance out over time it is of no great concern. So the real question is not whether there is *any* difference in the numbers obtained between November and December. Rather, given that there is a baseline variation in sales figures, the real question is whether the difference observed between November and December was large enough to indicate an important trend.

In parametric statistical tests such as t tests, analysis of variance, and multivariate analyses (F statistics), the assessment of group differences is made while taking this random error variance into account. In these tests you compute a ratio in which the observed variation in group scores is assigned to the numerator and the overall random error variance observed across the sample is used to calculate the term in the denominator. To the degree that the difference observed between your groups is bigger than the random variation in your sample, then the resulting ratio will be large. If the ratio is large enough, the group difference may be said to be significant, or reliable. That means that you can infer that this difference would be observed again if you sampled another set of data comparing the groups.

$$\frac{\text{Group Difference(s)}}{\text{Error Variance}} = \text{Statistical Outcome}$$

Size of Statistical Effects

How large does the ratio need to be before an outcome is considered reliable? The answer depends upon a number of factors. The three most important factors are the probability level that you choose as your criterion for statistical significance, the number of observations included in your sample, and the number of groups being compared. The criterion level for statistical significance, referred to as the alpha level, usually is chosen to be either 0.05 or 0.10. If the results of a test are significant at the 0.05 level, for instance, that means that there is a 95 percent chance that the group effect observed was not due to random error. Rather you infer that you have observed a real group difference that you would expect to observe again if you were to collect another independent sample of data. As you might expect, you usually need to observe a fairly large difference in order to reach such a conclusion with an alpha level of 0.05.

You can still claim statistical significance with smaller differences, however, by changing the number of observations in your sample and/or the number of groups being compared in the analysis. Both of these directly impact the degrees of freedom associated with the ratio. Degrees of freedom are sort of like allowable deductions on income tax. The more degrees of freedom associated with your test, the smaller the ratio you will need in order to reject the null hypothesis and conclude that differences do indeed exist among the groups in your analysis. Increasing the number of degrees of freedom is most directly achieved by increasing the number of observations included in the data set. This last point is very intuitive. Of course your conclusion about differences between groups is made stronger as you compile more and more observations of those differences into your data set.

Predictive Regression Analyses

In some cases you may wish to make predictions about the numeric values of a variable(s) within the problem space represented in your data set. One approach to this problem is to perform a linear regression analysis, which yields a best-line fit to your data points. The outcome of this test has two important components. The first is the mathematical function for the line describing the best fit through your data set. Along with this line, there is also a correlational measure, which tells you how closely the data in your sample fit this function. Specifically, the correlational measure tells you how much of the variance observed in your sample is accounted for by the best-fit line.

As you can see in Figure 6.2, some fits are better than others. The function on the left shows the relationship between height and weight for a sample of young adults. There are a few things to notice about this graph. First, the best-fit line is drawn so as to minimize the distance from all data points. This line has a slope of about 45 degrees, showing that there is a strong linear relationship between these two variables—weight tends to increase as height increases. Note also that the data

Figure 6.2 Using linear regression to show relationships between variables.

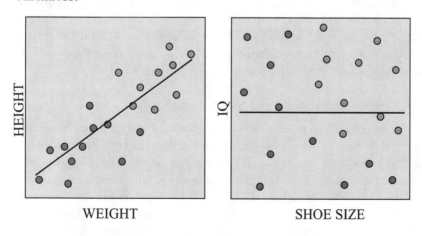

WEIGHT   SHOE SIZE

points themselves tend to fall relatively close to this line, with very little variance away from the best-fit function. Generally, the closer this line is to the diagonal, the stronger the relationship between the variables, and the greater their correlation. That is because correlations are computed in part by summing the squares of the distances of each point from the line.

Now look at the function represented on the right side of Figure 6.2. This function shows the relationship between IQ and shoe size in the same group of young adults. As we would expect, there is no predictive relationship between these variables, and the best-fit line drawn to minimize error distance from each point is horizontal. Having failed to find a relationship between these variables using a linear regression model, we might try a quadratic or logistic (nonlinear or multilinear) function, which would give us a curve through the space in order to improve our ability to make predictions. (Chances are that in this example, however, those approaches would also fail to show any relationship.)

When to Use Statistical Analysis

Several conditions must be met before you will be in a position to observe statistically reliable effects in your analysis. First, as we have indicated, your data must be in numeric form and be divided into groups for analysis. Next you must have some sort of hypothesis about what you expect to find in an analysis. That is, you must know ahead of time what sorts of differences you are interested in and must therefore know how to divide information in your data set into groups for comparison purposes. Ideally these issues should be worked out prior to any collection of data. In those cases, planned statistical comparisons can be made directly between groups. What often happens, however, is that situations arise in which you will want to do exploratory analyses on a set of data that have already been collected, perhaps for another purpose entirely. In such circumstances the analyst has to tread very carefully. When making a series of multiple comparisons on a single data set, you are obliged to "correct" your alpha level to a stricter criterion level so as to avoid the possibility of falsely identifying differences that are actually due to chance.

The Interplay between Variance and Sample Size

Variance can be an issue all on its own within a statistical analysis. If you happen to be working in a domain in which baseline error variance is high, this will work against you. For instance, if you are compiling data about sales figures, you could have a lot of baseline variance in your measure since the numbers involved can theoretically vary from zero to very high levels. On the other hand, if you are measuring a quantity with more bounded limits, for example the range of body temperature readings for people showing up to an emergency room, the baseline variance will be smaller. (Of course the absolute group difference sizes would be expected to be smaller as well in the case of temperatures.) If baseline variance is too high, you could compensate by increasing the number of observations in the data set. Failing that, you could try to come up with a different measure altogether.

If your variance is large and your sample size is small, you will run into problems concerning power. In the vernacular of statistical analysis, "power" refers to the ability to detect an effect that is really present. By estimating the expected size of the group effect along with the baseline variance, you can calculate the power of your test to detect an effect if one were indeed present. If power is low, adjustments can be made in terms of number of observations.

Even when you have defined hypotheses and determined that your baseline variance is manageable, you must still consider sample size. Increases in sample size increase the number of degrees of freedom that you are allowed to claim when assessing statistical significance. Furthermore, error variance tends to decline as number of observations increases, thus reducing the denominator of your test ratio. If you are working with a data set that has a very limited number of observations on the dimensions that are of interest to you, chances are that you will not be able to demonstrate any statistically reliable effects. Whether this is of critical importance depends entirely on the type of problem being investigated. If you are trying to demonstrate trends in sales figures, then of course you want as many observations as possible in order to be able to predict trends accurately. On the other hand, if your goal is to identify a pattern of insider trading, you are probably looking for unusual behavior of only a very few people represented in the data set. In that case you would not be concerned with overall number of observations because you would not be asking questions about overall group trends.

Keeping the Big Picture in Mind

This last point should be given particular consideration within the context of your own data mining application. What is the overall goal of your data mining activity? Is it to determine whether levels of measurement are different across groups in your data set? Are you trying to predict trends and future behavior? If so, then you probably do want to do a statistical analysis, and you would ideally plan this analysis prior to any data collection in order to adequately address the issues raised previously concerning sample size and power.

On the other hand, your goal might be very different. You might be working from a data set that has already been compiled and you may not have any idea what results are interesting or important a priori. You might just be looking for relationships that you did not know about ahead of time. Or in other cases, you might know which relationships or patterns are important to you, but you also know that these are likely to occur in only a very small portion of the data set. Thus, the patterns of interest to you would not represent overall trends of the data set and would never be identified by a statistical test.

Consider an example of a warranty analysis that we performed for a product distributor (see Figure 6.3). In that case we were looking at a very large data set containing information about warranty claims submitted by hundreds of distributors across the country. One particular finding of interest related to a series of suspicious warranty claims made by only a few distributors who were apparently working together in a scheme to defraud the manufacturer. As it turned out, this discovery was important to our client because the fraud was costing them millions of dollars a year. Only a few distributors were engaged in the fraud and the suspicious claims constituted only a small portion of the total claims submitted by those distributors. Thus, an overall statistical analysis of the data set would certainly have failed to identify this problem. By modeling the data appropriately, however, we were able to discover this pattern using visualization. Note that we are not trying to discourage the use of statistical analyses by this example. We are simply saying that whether a statistical test is the appropriate analysis depends entirely upon the type of question being asked in the application.

Figure 6.3 Statistical versus visualization analysis of warranty fraud.

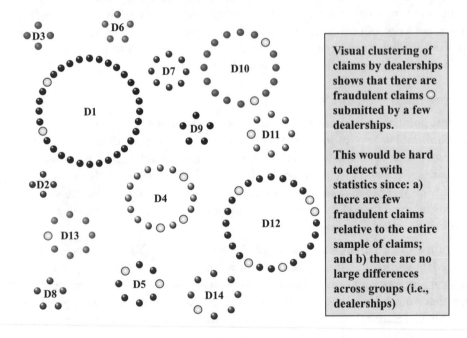

Visual clustering of claims by dealerships shows that there are fraudulent claims ○ submitted by a few dealerships.

This would be hard to detect with statistics since: a) there are few fraudulent claims relative to the entire sample of claims; and b) there are no large differences across groups (i.e., dealerships)

Decision Trees

Decision trees are analytical tools used to discover rules and relationships by systematically breaking down and subdividing the information contained in your data set. To get a feel for the type of information provided by a decision tree, consider the example shown in Figure 6.4. In this fictitious example, the goal is to make predictions about the car buying profiles of males and females. As you can see, the data set used to make predictions contains information about the characteristics of the vehicles being purchased as well as information about the buyers themselves.

Segregating the Data

The algorithms used to subdivide data in decision tree models seek to find those variables or fields in the data set that provide maximum segregation of the data records. In our example the top-level division is made with regard to the 2-door versus 4-door

Figure 6.4 Decision tree describing car purchase profiles of males and females.

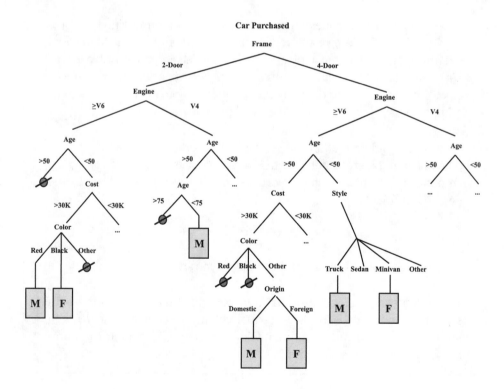

classification since this is the variable that most equally divides the records in the data set. Any field in the data set may theoretically be chosen, but the field is useful only if it divides the records. For example, we could have chosen the first cut based on whether or not the vehicle had air-conditioning, but since virtually all of the vehicles in the data set are air-conditioned, this variable would have done little to break up the data into

Information Theory

Suppose you look outside one morning and see that it is raining. You then turn on your TV and the weatherman reports that there is a 90 percent chance of rain in today's forecast. Is this prediction useful to you? No; the forecast provides you with no new information because you already know that it is raining. However, consider a different scenario in which you look outside and see sunshine. You then hear the weatherman predict rain for later in the day. In this case, the forecast is more useful to you because it provides information that you did not already have. Another way of putting it is that the forecast reduces your uncertainty about what the weather will be like later in the day.

Information theory provides a mathematical means of formalizing the transmission of information, or the reduction of uncertainty. In this framework information is represented in binary bit units. By defining the possible events and their probabilities within a problem space, we can calculate the amount of information transmitted for any event or transaction. Information is transmitted whenever the number of possible alternatives is reduced.

The amount of information transmitted corresponds to the ratios of alternatives before or after some event. When alternatives are equally likely, the amount of transmitted information is calculated using logarithms to the base 2 such that

$$H = \log_2 N$$

where H represents amount of information in bits.

To take an example, suppose that four basketball teams are in the NBA semifinals and that each has an equal chance of winning. How much information is transmitted in identifying the winner? We plug the numbers into our formula such that subgroups. In the vernacular of information theory, we would say that we want to choose a variable that provides the most information; that is, the variable that reduces the most uncertainty. Since there is very little uncertainty associated with the question of whether a particular vehicle is air-conditioned—virtually all of them are—this variable cannot help us to reduce uncertainty (see the sidebar on Information Theory). At

$$H = \log_2 4 = 2$$

and we see that two bits of information were transmitted. When alternatives are equally likely, one bit of information is transmitted each time the total number of alternatives is reduced by one half.

What about examples in which the alternatives are not equally likely? As you might expect, the situation becomes a little more complicated. In these cases, H is calculated as a weighted average of the individual events. For any individual event j,

$$h_j = \log_2 (1/p_j)$$

where p_j is the probability of event j and h_j is the "surprisal" value of event j. In our NBA example, imagine that the Chicago Bulls are one of our four semifinal teams and that both Michael Jordan and Scottie Pippen are still playing for the team and are healthy during the playoffs. Since this team has won the championship five times in six years, most analysts would assign them a relatively high chance of success, say on the order of 90 percent. Thus we could calculate how surprised we would be if the Bulls were to win another title by the formula

$$h_{Bulls} = \log_2(1/.9) = 0.15 \text{ bits.}$$

As you can see, this outcome would not be very surprising, yielding only .15 bits of information. Generally speaking, the most information is transmitted when alternatives are equally likely. When we know that some alternatives are more likely than others, we have less uncertainty about the outcome of events, and so less reduction of uncertainty is possible. The total amount of information associated with problems having unequally likely outcomes can generally be calculated as

$$H = \sum p_j \log_2(1/p_j) = -\sum p_j \log_2 p_j.$$

each level, the variables chosen to form the next child nodes of the tree will be those variables providing maximum segregation given the records contained in the training set. Note that this may or may not result in the same variables appearing all the way across a given level of the tree.

Using Decision Trees to Build Rules

In our example the frame variable (2-door or 4-door) represents the root node. The next division level of engine type (V4 or higher) is a child node of the root node, and so on. When a record enters the tree, it moves down until it reaches the point beyond which it can no longer move. Rules for discriminating among records can be articulated by following the path taken by the record through the decision tree. From Figure 6.4 we can see that there were some cases in which we can make pretty good predictions about buyer behavior. For example, looking at the left side of the decision tree, we can see that:

1. If the vehicle has a 2-door frame AND
2. If the vehicle has at least six cylinders AND
3. If the buyer is less than 50 years old AND
4. If the cost of the vehicle is >$30,000 AND
5. If the vehicle color is red, THEN
6. The buyer is highly likely to be male.

    Alternatively, looking at the right side of the tree we can see that:

1. If the vehicle has a 4-door frame AND
2. If the vehicle has at least six cylinders AND
3. If the buyer is less than 50 years old AND
4. If the vehicle is a minivan, THEN
5. The buyer is highly likely to be female.

    In other words, for those leaves of the tree that end up being filled with predominantly male or female records, we can directly construct rules describing the classification procedure. Recalling that this was the goal of our exercise, you can see that this is a very useful outcome.

Assessing Rules

Once the decision tree is in place, you will want to evaluate its performance. This is usually accomplished by testing the system with a new data set not used for training.

For each rule you can measure how often the submitted data records are properly classified. Additionally, you can compute the error rate of the entire tree as a weighted sum of the error rates for all of the individual leaves. Error rates and computational efficiency can be improved by pruning the tree, getting rid of the less useful rules.

At a more global level, you will want to think about the general utility of the rules represented by the decision tree. Some rules will be very important for your analysis, and will provide meaningful accounts of system behavior. On the other hand, other rules may be nonsensical in the context of your application, and so will be of little use. In these cases those rules can be eliminated from the tree manually if desired.

Gleaning Information from Rules that "Fail"

There are a few final things to notice about the decision tree and the rules it produces. First, the selection of variables may yield leaves of the tree for which there are few or no records. In our car-buying example, there were very few buyers over 50 years of age purchasing 2-door V6 engine vehicles (or at least the number of these cases was very small). The dearth of data in these cells may be informative in and of itself. Very often in data mining, you learn just as much from failing to find a pattern as you do from positive results. The client may find it interesting to learn about groups who do not make purchases of certain products. Armed with this new knowledge, the client might now be able to structure marketing campaigns to target groups that are underrepresented in the data set. Going in the other direction, the client can alter existing ad campaigns to better focus on the groups who are more likely to buy the product.

You may have also noticed in our example that it was not always possible to predict with any certainty whether a buyer would be male or female. For instance, in the case of 4-door V4 engine vehicles, there was no combination of fields that could be used to build a tree that would reliably discriminate between male and female buyers. Though at first disappointing, this failure may be telling us something. Perhaps this is evidence that the male/female distinction is not terribly important in the buying patterns for 4-door V4 engine vehicles. Maybe we were asking the wrong question all along, and analysis of other factors might prove more fruitful. Based on the failure to find a result, the direction of the analysis might change considerably.

Node Splitting and Fan-Out Effects

You will notice in Figure 6.4 that some of the divisions in the tree are binary whereas others are of a higher order. Some decision tree tools such as CART require that all splits be binary. Others such as ID3 and C4.5 are more flexible, allowing the number of branches per node to vary. Strategies for optimizing the number of branches represented at different node levels can be a bit tricky. On the one hand, the representation of all levels of a categorical variable at a node can be very helpful as in our example in which the breakout of style into four categories revealed two leaves that allowed us to discriminate between males and females. On the other hand, if a categorical variable has many values represented in the data set, then there will be a huge fan-out effect at that node of the tree, possibly resulting in very few records being sorted into the bins below these nodes.

In general you want to avoid situations in which records are sorted too broadly across one horizontal level of the tree, because this reduces your ability to assess accurately the predictive power of the rules contained in the tree. For example, imagine that a categorical variable with large fan-out was included and that this resulted in only two or three records falling into each of the bins. It might very well be the case that the tree could be used to sort all of the training data accurately, but it is highly unlikely that these divisions would work later on when new data were introduced into the tree structure. This is the same principle that we discussed earlier in the section on statistical methods—your confidence in your conclusion increases with the number of observations going into the test. Thus, you are unlikely to be confident in rules constructed on the basis of only a few records. To avoid this problem, you will need to be vigilant about fan-out effects.

When to Use Decision Trees

Decision trees are useful for problems in which the goal is to make broad categorical classifications or predictions. On the other hand, they are not useful in applications requiring specific predictions about the values of quantitative variables. It is probably best to use decision trees for applications in which there are questions identified a priori. However, as we have seen, it is possible to make useful unexpected discoveries using decision trees as well. Decision trees are most useful in domains in which values of variables can be broken out into relatively small numbers (in some cases only two values, depending upon the tool being used).

Association Rules

Association rules are derived from a type of analysis that extracts information from coincidence. Sometimes called "market basket" analysis, this methodology allows you to discover correlations, or co-occurrences of transactional events. In the classic example, consider the items contained in your shopping cart on any one trip to the grocery store. Chances are that your own shopping patterns tend to be internally consistent, and that you tend to buy certain items on certain days, for example milk on Mondays and beer on Fridays. There might be many examples of pairs of items that you tend to purchase together. For instance you might always buy champagne and strawberries together when you shop on Saturdays, although you only rarely purchase either of the items separately.

Apart from your own cart, now consider the carts of all of your neighbors who shop at the same store. In all likelihood they tend to buy many of the same products that you do. Since customers tend to shop at stores close to home, we can also make assumptions about income level and so forth based on known demographics describing the local population. Taking purchase records of all shoppers into account at once, there are likely to be many sets of items that tend to be purchased together across the group. Presumably this is information that the store manager could use to make decisions about where to place items in the store so as to increase sales. This information can be expressed in the form of association rules. From our example, the manager might decide to place a special champagne display near the strawberries in the fruit section on the weekends in the hopes of increasing sales.

The Cross-Correlation Matrix

Association rules are derived from analyses based on cross-correlation matrices in which the likelihood of each event occurring in conjunction with every other event is computed. A fictitious example of association rule analysis using data on grocery store purchases is provided in Figure 6.5. If desired, this matrix could be extended to compute correlations among n dimensions at a time. For the purposes of clarity, we will keep this example simple and stick to two dimensions. Figure 6.5 shows those pairs of items in our sample data set that are often purchased together (depicted using multiple circles), those sometimes purchased together (a single circle), or those showing no particular relationship in terms of purchase patterns (blank). We will consider only the portion of the matrix above the diagonal since the two halves are redundant. A full matrix can be used when there is a basis for distinguishing the occurrence (e.g., directionality or dependency) of one value with respect to another. For example, when strawberries are purchased, there are only a limited number of cases (out of the total set of strawberry purchases) where champagne is also bought. The most common correlations for strawberries will be other fruit, chocolates, cereal, etc. However, whenever champagne is bought, there is a much higher relevance with strawberries. Whichever approach you take will depend on the type of analysis you want to perform.

First you will notice that some of the stronger correlations make sense. For example, some pairs of items that tend to be purchased together include milk-bread, milk-cereal, and bread-eggs. This comes as no surprise since all of these are staple items that tend to be purchased frequently. Chances are that these relationships are

Figure 6.5 Example of a cross-correlation matrix used to infer association rules about the purchase of grocery store items.

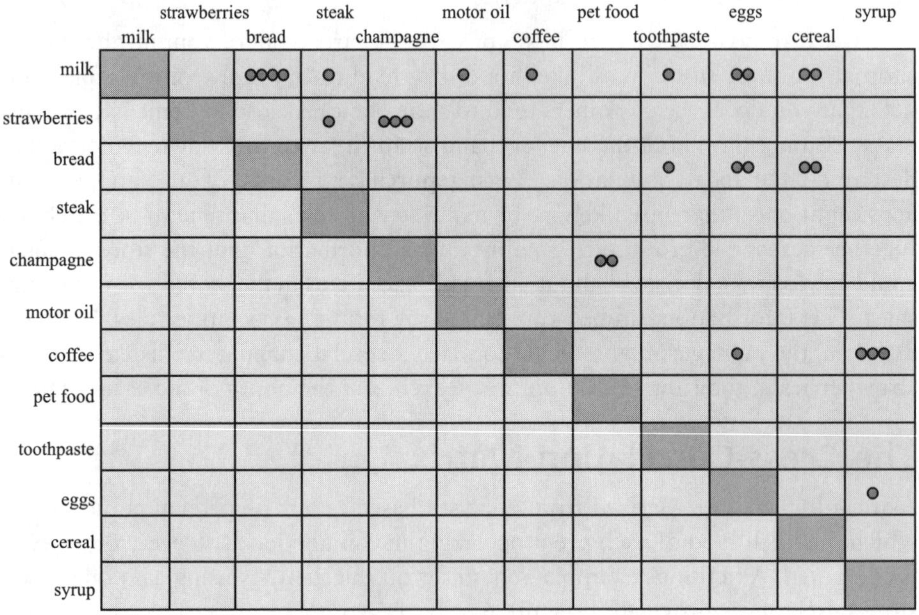

	milk	strawberries	bread	steak	champagne	motor oil	coffee	pet food	toothpaste	eggs	cereal	syrup
milk	▨		●●●●	●		●	●		●	●●	●●	
strawberries		▨		●	●●●							
bread			▨						●	●●	●●	
steak				▨								
champagne					▨			●●				
motor oil						▨						
coffee							▨			●		●●●
pet food								▨				
toothpaste									▨			
eggs										▨		●
cereal											▨	
syrup												▨

already well known to the grocer. There are also other correlations that are surprising, but which make sense such as the association between strawberries and champagne. It is these surprising but interpretable associations that are the payoff in the analysis.

As you can see in Figure 6.5, however, the use of correlation has its limitations. Although the champagne-strawberry association rule seems valid, there will likely be many association rules that will be of little use. Suppose that when you shop you also buy dog food every week. Unless you are quite unusual, you do not consume the champagne and the dog food together. You do not even associate the two in your own mind except that you can buy them both at the grocery store. Nevertheless, an association rule could be produced between them since they are purchased together with great regularity. We will go out on a limb and predict that the grocer will not see great increases in the purchase of either champagne or dog food were he or she to move the champagne to the pet food section. However, the system that produces the association rules will not be able to tell the difference between the "good" rules and the "useless" rules. It is looking for co-occurrences only. Unfortunately, correlation is no substitute for judgment. The grocer will have to review all of the association rules produced in order to determine which ones are worthwhile.

When to Use Association Rules

Association rule analysis will be most useful when you are doing exploratory analyses, looking for interesting relationships that might exist within a data set. To the degree that the associations identified are useful ones, they may be used to help predict behavior. As illustrated previously, however, the mere fact that two things occur in proximity to one another is no guarantee that the relationship is either meaningful or important. Thus, it is probably likely that the surprising associations identified by this type of analysis will need to be studied more carefully using another analytical method in order for the relationships to be interpreted.

Neural Networks

Neural networks are a type of computational methodology commonly used for pattern identification and classification. Neural networks are comprised of nodes that are interconnected by excitatory and inhibitory connections. Depending upon inputs presented to the network, any number of nodes may be activated at a given point in time. Patterns of activity are used to represent information in the network in a distributed fashion. That is, a piece of information may not be represented in one node, per se, but in the pattern of activated nodes.

Supervised Learning

In the most popular neural network paradigms, learning occurs in a supervised mode in which systems are trained on a known set of targets so that those targets are readily identified when presented as inputs to the system. On each trial during supervised learning, an input is presented to the system, the input activates certain nodes, and the system provides an output response based on the pattern of activation. If the output does not match the desired response during learning, the system is provided with feedback designed to modify the incorrect response. A variety of algorithms may be used to provide feedback to the system during learning trials so that the strength of connections between nodes are altered in such a way as to produce correct responses consistently. Once the system has learned the correct responses to the set of training inputs, the learning mode is finished and the neural net can then be used to detect and classify those patterns among new inputs. Thus, having been trained, the system can be used to automate pattern detection and alert the user when incoming patterns match a previously learned output response. This is the type of formulation at the heart of back propagation networks and other approaches used in supervised learning systems.

You can easily see how supervised learning in neural network systems can be useful when used in decision support and in tracking previously identified patterns. In fact they have been very successfully employed in a number of applications. However, as we noted in Chapter 1, supervised learning systems are not doing data mining because there is no new discovery taking place. The user determines ahead of time which inputs will be included in the training set, what outputs are allowed, and what the proper mapping between inputs and outputs should be. The neural network does not "discover" these things. Rather, the neural network functions as an automated pattern classification system and does not learn any new output responses once training is completed and the system is put into use. Supervised learning systems are appropriate in those cases in which input-output mappings are known ahead of time, but they cannot tell you anything new about your data.

Unsupervised Learning

The neural network models that can be used for data mining learn in an unsupervised mode. Unsupervised learning systems do not require that the set of permissible output responses and their mapping to inputs be defined a priori. Instead, what happens in unsupervised learning is that the network forms its own set of outputs during training based on features extracted by the network.

The most popular unsupervised learning approach is Kohonen's feature map. There are two layers in the feature map, an input layer and an output layer. Nodes in the output layer can have excitatory as well as inhibitory connections with neighboring nodes. Given an input, the nodes within the output layer go through a competitive activation process whereby activated nodes try and inhibit other nodes in order to "win" the competition. The winner of the competition is usually the node (or set of nodes) whose incoming connection weights most closely match the input. Having won the competition, the winner has its weights adjusted even further in the direction of the input pattern.

A feature map is created by adjusting not only the weights of the winner after every input, but also the weights of its neighboring nodes. Thus, over trials, the entire neighborhood of nodes will respond to some degree to the same input. Training usually progresses by reducing the size of the neighborhood eligible for adjustment until the "neighborhood" becomes only a single output node. At this point there may be one node that responds most strongly to a given input, but this node will be closely connected to a network of nodes that also have a high rate of response to that same input. This means that similar inputs will tend to activate the same neighborhood of nodes. We can then create a topographical map depicting the strength of these interconnections in terms of Euclidean distance, with highly connected nodes located close to one another in the space (see Figure 6.6). We may then extrapolate concepts represented by output nodes that end up being located together (and separated from other groups of nodes) within the map.

What is interesting about this from a data mining perspective is that you could feed inputs into an unsupervised learning network and use the competitive process to let the network determine which features might be used to separate classes of inputs into categories or clusters. Note that you would not need to specify these categories ahead of time—the network discovers them for you. The map may be segmented to divide data into subclasses for further analysis by another feature map or by some other method. Since the output from this neural network computation is represented in a set of vectors, you will usually need to combine this approach with other visualization methodologies in order to appreciate the results.

When to Use Unsupervised Neural Networks

What are the conditions under which the unsupervised learning approach will be an option? As in the case of statistical analyses, you will need to use stimuli that can

Figure 6.6 Topographical map produced by an unsupervised learning network.

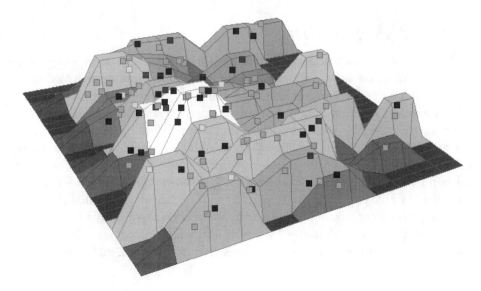

be represented in a quantitative format. Unlike statistical methods, however, neural network analyses do not provide you with information about how likely an outcome would be expected to occur by chance. There is no means of rigorously extrapolating the results beyond the data set used for training other than by actually doing direct testing with nontraining data. Further, there is no explanatory information available about why a neural net makes the classifications that it makes. Rather, the system is a black box. In some applications this may not be a problem, but there are circumstances in which justification for decisions and predictions must be provided. In those instances you are probably better off using a decision tree, visualization, or some other method. Perhaps the most important advantage of unsupervised learning over some of the other analytical methods is that you do not need to start with hypotheses about expected differences among groups represented in the data set. This can be used as an exploratory analysis.

Generally speaking, the neural network approach to data mining is most useful when you are searching for novel ways of segmenting the data set. This method can be used to discover subgroups of data that are defined in terms of some common feature(s) that separate them from other portions of the complete population. There are any number of reasons that you might wish to identify dimensions along which data may be classified in this way. Applications in which you might use such an analysis include identification of the types of customers who are most likely to buy certain products, designation of constellations of symptoms that might be used to classify various diseases, and characterization of features that might segregate suspicious stock trade patterns from a group.

Genetic Algorithms

The last class of analytical approaches that we will discuss in this chapter is genetic algorithms. All of the other methods that we have presented are concerned with classification and prediction problems. The utility of genetic algorithms lies more within the realm of optimization. Borrowing upon metaphors developed within evolution theory, genetic algorithms start with a population of items and seek to alter and eventually optimize their composition for the solution of a particular problem. Individuals within the population (for example candidate solutions to a problem) evolve over a series of generations. The genetic material or information represented by each individual can be passed on to subsequent generations in a variety of ways with optimization occurring in the process. Within this framework, there are three basic mechanisms by which information is chosen, altered, and passed on in order to achieve optimization—selection, crossover, and mutation.

Selection

The process of selection as implemented in genetic algorithms is analogous to the process of natural selection that occurs in evolution. Selection is based on the principle of survival of the fittest in which the individuals that are best suited for the environment are the ones that survive to pass their genetic material on to the next generation. Fitness values are calculated for all individuals or genomes in the population, and those with the highest values are allowed to reproduce. Genomes with low fitness values have fewer copies that survive to the next generation. The method of choosing genomes for successive generations is usually done probabilistically. That is, selection of the next generation is done randomly from a population in which number of individuals represented is proportional to fitness value. The higher the fitness value, the more copies of that individual in the population and thus the higher the chances that the information contained in that genome will survive to the next generation. There are also selection schemes based on other ranking and tournament methods.

In the simplest genetic algorithms, the entire population of individuals is replaced on every cycle and population size remains constant. However, in more sophisticated models, the population size is allowed to grow or shrink, more in keeping with natural events. In the case of the growing population models, individuals with lower fitness values may survive longer, thus having a greater chance of contributing to the optimization solution. This can be helpful in addressing problems encountered by systems that converge on solutions too quickly, perhaps missing the most optimal outcomes.

Crossover

Crossover occurs when two individuals chosen randomly from the population are joined or "mated" such that the resulting offspring contain partial replications of the information contained in each of the parents. The offspring then become full-fledged members of the population, competing for survival along with the rest.

As seen in Figure 6.7, all individuals within the population are represented as vectors of the same *n order* containing a sequence of bits. The order of the vectors is chosen to accommodate the representation of all information records contained in the data set. When a crossover cycle occurs, genomes are randomly paired together and reproduce according to an assigned crossover probability. This probability is a parameter that may be varied so as to affect the rate at which change occurs in the population. When crossover takes place, new offspring are created by combining subsets of information contained in these vectors from both parents. The amount of

Figure 6.7 An illustration of crossover in genetic algorithms.

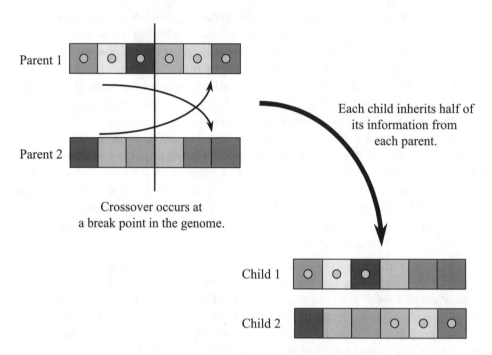

Parent 1

Parent 2

Crossover occurs at
a break point in the genome.

Each child inherits half of
its information from
each parent.

Child 1

Child 2

information to be copied into the child genomes is determined by the crossover break point, which is a parameter that may be set externally.

In this example, the crossover bits completely replace the destination bits in the mated vector. In the parlance of evolution theory we would say that the crossover bits are dominant—they are the genes that get expressed in the child vectors. In more complicated genetic algorithms, however, bits can be assigned dominant and recessive attributes that will determine how information is expressed in the offspring genomes. Additionally, you can even have diploid structures that contain two slots for every bit so that an individual's fitness function can change depending upon which genes are expressed during a given generation.

Mutation

When information is inherited through crossover there is a perfect transfer of information from parents to children. In this way there are gradual stepwise changes that occur in the population over time. In nature, however, evolutionary progress often occurs through sudden mutations in the genetic makeup of individuals in a population, which cause jumps in the rate of evolutionary change. Mutations can occur naturally when there is an error in the transmission of genetic information from parent to child. As with all types of change, mutations can have either good or bad effects. In some instances mutation may be the only way of introducing potentially useful traits into the population.

The metaphor of mutation can be realized in genetic algorithms. Genomes can be mutated by changing one or a few bits in the vectors of a few individuals. As a rule, only small mutations are used since even small changes can produce large effects within a few generations. Mutations effectively increase the search space for solutions that might not have been represented originally in the initial data set.

When to Use Genetic Algorithms

As we mentioned already, genetic algorithms are most useful in cases in which the goal is to find an optimal solution given a definable problem space. Furthermore there needs to be a fair amount of uniformity in terms of data to be analyzed since all data must be coded into vectors of the same dimensionality. For this reason, it is unlikely that genetic algorithms will be useful in situations in which you are combining data from several disparate information sources and types.

Genetic algorithms have been useful in certain problem areas such as maximizing profit and switchability by searching through combinations of product features. They have also been used successfully in applications involving scheduling and time series analysis. Genetic algorithms may also be combined with neural networks to good effect. Genetic algorithms have been used for training neural networks and decoding solutions produced by neural networks. Recall that the output from a neural net is a black box of connection weights among nodes. Since genetic algorithms produce symbolic outputs, they can be combined with neural nets to produce more useful symbolic representations of these weighting schemes.

Summing Up

In this chapter we have provided a conceptual overview of those analytical techniques that are used most commonly in nonvisual data mining applications. We covered several approaches including statistical analyses, decision trees, association rules, unsupervised neural networks, and genetic algorithms. We hope that these descriptions have given you a sense of those situations in which these methods might best be applied.

Having read through Sections I and II of the book, you should now have a good grasp of the basic ideas and principles behind the analytical approach of data mining. At this point we will switch gears from theory to practice. To give you an idea of the ways in which data mining analyses actually proceed in the real world, we turn to Section III where we provide descriptions of some of the commercial tools that are available for doing data mining analysis.

Section III

ASSESSING DATA MINING TOOLS AND TECHNOLOGIES

Having read the first two sections of the book, you are now ready to begin thinking about setting up a data mining application. One important issue that you will need to resolve at this point is how to choose the appropriate data mining tool(s) for your implementation. There are quite a variety of commercial tools available as fully fielded systems, along with countless others currently under development. Tools range in scope from small-scale systems developed for particular problem domains all the way up to high-end general-purpose systems that can be used on almost any data mining problem. There is a lot of variance in terms of cost, platform independence, and requirements for computer power among the tools you may consider. To help you start out on the road to making an informed decision, this section is devoted to the description of many of the state-of-the-art data mining tools that are often used in business and other application areas.

A host of systems are available to businesses interested in performing data mining, and this section presents a sampling of different approaches. The intent is not to provide an exhaustive review of available tools, but rather to discuss the effectiveness of different data mining systems for specific types of problems, with a focus on the application of visualization. Visualization tools are quickly becoming a commodity in the data mining marketplace. If you know what tools are available, when to use them, and how to use them, you will be more effective in your data mining efforts. This section introduces a host of visualization systems and briefly discusses their unique capabilities and typical configurations. We provide you with relevant examples and screen captures, information about ease-of-use and other factors that those in the business community need to consider when applying visual data mining technologies to their environments. All tools presented have direct applicability to both large and small business concerns.

Assessing Current Data Mining Systems

This section is divided into four chapters. The first three chapters describe tools that are heavily invested in one of the three visualization paradigms of link analysis, landscape displays, or quantitative analysis. Although most tools have capabilities in more than one of these paradigms, there is usually stronger functionality in one area than in others. We are using this taxonomy as a method of convenience to present the different tools and their unique capabilities in a reasonably systematized fashion. By dividing visualization paradigms into these three categories we do not mean to imply that there are necessarily hard and fast distinctions among them. Indeed we know of many examples where these paradigms have been combined to produce hybrid approaches that were very effective. In Chapter 7 we present descriptions of several link analysis systems including NETMAP, Analyst's Notebook, Imagix 4D, Daisy, and others. Chapter 8 presents discussions of several tools that make great use of landscape visualizations. Here we present descriptions of Mineset 2.0, Metaphor Mixer, In3D, and others. Chapter 9 is devoted to tools that focus more on quantitative analyses. Tools presented in this chapter include Clementine, Enterprise Miner, Diamond, and CrossGraphs.

Whereas Chapters 7 through 9 review existing tools, Chapter 10 provides a discussion of what we feel are some of the most important future trends in data mining technology. We focus on four primary areas of development: web visualizers, free text visualizers, full scope systems that embody many visualization paradigms, and visualization tools that are designed as overlays onto existing data management systems. We describe data mining tools that either have been or are being developed for each of these problems. The importance of each of these problems in the overall context of data mining analysis is discussed.

Two years ago there were only a handful of commercially available data mining tools. We now know of several dozen systems that support the use of visualization in one way or another. The textual descriptions of the tools described in the next three chapters are not intended to provide complete inventories of the capabilities provided by each. Rather, what we emphasize here are the features of the tools that can be exploited in visually based data mining applications. Complete and detailed descriptions are available in the documentation provided by the vendors of the tools, who are listed in the Appendix. You will note that the products presented throughout this section are not compared or contrasted with one another. We have opted not to do a head-to-head comparison for several reasons, not the least of which is that tools are updated so often that any such analysis would be obsolete before the book goes to press. In any event, head-to-head comparisons are not very meaningful in the abstract because your decision will no doubt be influenced by a host of factors. These might include the size of your budget, the scope of the project(s), the amount of time available for the project, the experience level of your staff, the quality of your data, and the infrastructure of your computing networks. For these reasons we present each tool on its own merits with no biases for or against any one tool. Additionally, we have not provided any cost information associated with any of the tools. The pricing structures of these systems are subject to change without notice and we would rather have you contact the vendors directly for this information.

Using the CD-ROM

Throughout the book our figures are presented in black and white although many were originally derived from color images. This is particularly true of the figures presented in this section, which were largely derived from screen captures of the tools being described. As you can appreciate, some information is lost in this translation since part of the power of data visualization is the use of color to code information within analytical displays. For this reason, we remind you that color versions of all figures may be viewed on the CD-ROM.

In a similar vein, trying to describe the operation of a data mining tool using text and static displays is a little like trying to convey the beauty of a Michael Jordan fadeaway jumpshot using only still photographs. Something gets lost in the translation. The real power of the tools described here often lies in their support of the user's dynamic analytical interactions with the system. Since the data mining process is better understood through demonstrations, we have included versions of as many tools as possible on the CD-ROM as well. (Unfortunately, not all manufacturers were able to participate.) We hope you will take the time to load up your CD-ROM and check out some of the demos that have been provided. This will go a long way toward giving you a real understanding of what interactive data mining analysis is all about.

There are many systems not included on the CD-ROM that can be downloaded directly from the Internet. Thus, we suggest that you also check out the Appendix and see what other systems are available within the visualization community. Many of these companies offer demonstration versions of their systems that you can try first-hand and determine whether they would work for you. We have tried to identify as many of these tools as possible in the Appendix, but no doubt missed some unintentionally. In any event, you should become accustomed to searching through the Web yourself to keep abreast of new developments in this field since things are moving at such a rapid pace.

Link Analysis Tools

Introduction

Link analysis is the process of building up networks of interconnected objects through relationships in order to expose patterns and trends. Link analysis uses item-to item associations to generate networks of interactions and connections from defined data sets. Link analysis diagrams have a variety of names ranging from entity-relationship diagrams and connected networks to nodes-and-links and directed graphs. Link analysis methods let you add dimensions to an analysis that the other forms of visualization do not support. By explicitly representing relationships among objects, you gain an entirely different perspective on how the data can be analyzed and the types of patterns that can be discovered. Link analysis systems were initially used primarily in the investigative world (e.g., law enforcement), but they have recently made significant inroads into a wide variety of commercial applications. One potential drawback of link analysis is that the aggregate number of data records that can be presented in most diagrams is somewhat limited, as compared to the other visualization paradigms. As a result, the analyses tend to focus on verifying subsets of large data sets. Nevertheless, link analysis provides a powerful means of performing visual data mining, particularly if you know how to take advantage of layout options, filter assessments, and presentation formats. Used properly, link analysis systems allow you to identify patterns, emerging groups, and generational connections quickly.

A variety of tools are available for visual data mining analysis that support representation of data in object-oriented structures that show links or relationships between individual objects and object classes. In this chapter we review some of the better established and fully developed link analysis tools that may be used to build data mining applications. Those who are already familiar with this area of data mining will likely note that there are several other link analysis systems that are available within the data mining community. We have included tools in this chapter that we feel give a representative overview of the types of capabilities you can obtain in commercially available products. Specifically, we describe NETMAP, Analyst's Notebook, Imagix 4D, and Daisy in some detail. We also include a brief overview of several other systems in a final section as well.

NETMAP

NETMAP is perhaps one of the most mature visualization systems available within the commercial data mining market. It has been around since the early 1980s when it was originally executed in batch-mode on mainframe systems, producing only hardcopy printouts of diagrams. Its primary use back then was to support the network mapping of social interactions within businesses and other organizations. As machines got faster and graphics got better, NETMAP quickly evolved into its current incarnation as a premiere link-analysis system. Since its early days, NETMAP has been deployed throughout a wide range of applications, far surpassing its creators' original expectations.

ALTA Analytics, a relatively small company headquartered in the Midwest, has been the chief purveyor and developer of the NETMAP system. NETMAP currently runs across all major UNIX environments supporting an X-Windows protocol. There is also an NT version that has been wrapped by NuTCRACKER. Although NETMAP has been written in the C programming language, it has an extremely detailed and powerful API (Application Programming Interface), which is currently supported through TCL (Tool Command Language) program extensions. TCL is a generic object-oriented programming language that can be run across a wide range of computing platforms, not too dissimilar to what Java has become. Since TCL is an interpreted language, it is easy to develop and test new scripts, modules, and functionality for NETMAP applications. The API literally allows you to control any aspect of the interface, the data structure, and even the control menus. This can be a very powerful feature when used appropriately, but it clearly requires programming expertise on the part of the user.

Accessing Data in NETMAP

Data access does not occur automatically in NETMAP because it does not have any native database access methods that support data acquisition. Any data feeds must be constructed externally and an intermediate set of transport files need to be created to supply the system with data. NETMAP reads all information in a flat ASCII delimited format. Through a set of configuration files, NETMAP converts the ASCII data into a format that is understood by its internal inference engine.

Through a very efficient translator called CRDB (for CReate DataBase), the flat files are converted into a set of integer node and link matrices. These matrix structures allow you to manage large quantities of discrete data that can be derived from multiple sources. Although this layout is not elegant for representing data, it provides a radically fast method for processing data, thus enhancing performance beyond levels possible with most other tools.

NETMAP's Support Functions

NETMAP also has a wide range of support facilities that may be used to help customize its environment. In addition to CRDB, there is a module called NETFRONT that helps to manage the different applications that have been produced, a shape generator used to extend the icons that are available in the display, a font creator to alter the presentation of labels, a dynamic legend-key builder, and a presentation tool called NPT that supports the annotation of the diagrams. NETMAP even includes its own language constructs for performing mathematical calculations, trigonometric computations, string comparisons, and various other functions. These facilities combined with the extensive number of other adjustable features allow applications to be extensively tailored to meet very specific needs.

Unfortunately, this level of freedom comes with a price. To use these support functions effectively, you will need to learn a good deal of detail about the low-level operations of NETMAP. This might be overwhelming to novice users. NETMAP is a serious tool for high-end data miners and its capabilities should not be underestimated. There is a lot of horsepower available under the hood when seasoned professionals use this product.

The Unconventional Displays of NETMAP

The look and feel of NETMAP has not changed much since its initial inception. The basic graphical rendering engine still uses vectorization methods for drawing the displays. What this means is that everything within a NETMAP display is represented as a line (e.g., a vector), including all text and shapes. The benefit of this approach is that the displays can be rendered instantly and manipulated through a variety of control parameters. Any of the display layouts described within this section can be zoomed, panned, windowed, and rotated very quickly. They are all derived from the same basic node and link matrices used to represent the data. Thus, assuming that your data have been properly modeled, there is no need to reload the data using a different configuration setting in order to achieve a desired result.

Navigating NETMAP's Node and Link Menus

The primary method of manipulating the NETMAP displays is through a pair of node and link menus. These menus have two distinct roles. The first is to filter the node and link matrices to include only specified elements from the main working set of data. For the most part, node selection within NETMAP is based on the union of values, whereas link selection tends to be based more on the intersection of values. The subsets of filtered data that are produced are only temporary and each new filtering is based on the way in which parameters are set within the menus at any given point in time. So it is easy to backtrack from an analytical path that leads to a dead end. The second role of the menus is to support manipulation of the appearance of the nodes and links within the display. Through various settings available on either of the menus, you can gain full control over what is being presented within the display to include the sizes, shapes, colors, and styles of the nodes and links. Since the menus are dynamically created when a new application is produced, the entries or selections available within them are derived from the actual values encountered within the data set being processed. This provides a way to discern what choices are available or valid for the different functions supported by the menus.

The node menu specifically controls which objects are included within the display, how they should be structured, and their general look and feel. Most of the features available within the node menu are independent of any link characteristics. Attributes defined in the configuration files determine the choices available in the menus for manipulating the displays. You can alter the position and placement (i.e., clustering) of objects on the basis of attribute values as well as their physical appearance such as color, size, or shape. Thus, an extensive number of displays can be generated just from making selections from this menu. Alternatively, the link menu only controls what links are presented and how they should be depicted. For the most part, the functions of the node and link menus operate orthogonally to one another. However, seasoned analysts realize that filtering out certain types of links will also remove certain nodes from the display, so there is an implied connection between the two menus through the common use of a single data set.

Variations of the NETMAP Display

NETMAP displays are very distinctive. They have been called everything from a ball-of-yarn to a wheel-of-fortune. The main shape of a traditional NETMAP display closely resembles a wagon-wheel format. This is usually depicted as a band of nodes that have been arranged in a circular format with links appearing across the center as a set of spokes. The visual representation within NETMAP is tied directly to the models that are used to symbolize the data. Figure 7.1 shows an example of a typical NETMAP display. In this case we are showing the relationships between people and accounts as would be used in a bank or credit card application. As you can see, there are many different dimensions being displayed within this one diagram. For example, the bands (or groups as they are called) represent the different values associated with a specific attribute. These are drawn in a counter-clockwise fashion starting at the three o'clock position to represent the lowest value assigned to the attribute. Within each group, the objects are sorted according to their value on another attribute. Their sizes, colors, labels, and secondary markings all provide additional methods for conveying the contents of attributes. We should note that the use of color to convey information is very important in NETMAP, as in many other tools. Thus, these black and white versions of NETMAP figures do not do justice to the displays generated in a real application. More realistic color examples are provided on the CD-ROM as they are for every tool profiled in Section III. Additionally, the clarity of the labels for each node has been reduced in these figures to emphasize the structural aspects and relationships of the data.

The NETMAP format also supports a wide range of other display characteristics. Depending on how the data have been modeled, certain unique structures will appear. Figure 7.2 represents the same information presented in Figure 7.1. In

Figure 7.1 A typical NETMAP display.

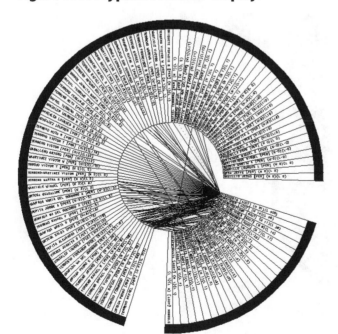

this version, the intra-group links are now being displayed in structures called satellites. If Figure 7.1 shows the data grouped by type to reflect the people and accounts, the lines crossing the center of the diagram reflect the inter-group connections (e.g., people are owners of accounts). However, when showing the relationships within a particular group (e.g., people to people or accounts to accounts), then the intra-group links are shown in the satellite structures as depicted in Figure 7.2. There is a one-to-one correspondence of the satellite nodes to the inter-circle nodes. They are presented outside as a visual convenience to help provide different perspectives on the data set.

In this application people can be connected to people if they share the same account or have co-signed on a loan together. Accounts can be related to accounts if money is transferred between them. Since the grouping of data can be controlled through the node menu, you need to be cognizant of how you are displaying your data. If the same data shown in Figure 7.2 are regrouped according to the location of the bank/person, the ethnicity of the person, the type of account, the amount in the account, or any other attribute defined in the data model, then a different set of displays can be produced, as shown in Figure 7.3. Notice that the number of groups

Figure 7.2 Representing satellite nodes in a NETMAP display.

Figure 7.3 Different grouping strategies within NETMAP.

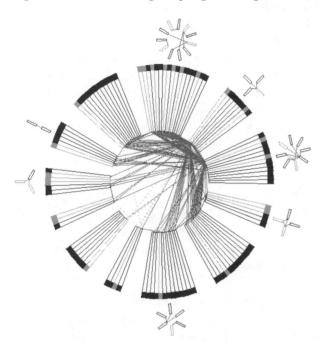

reflects the number of discrete values encountered for the attribute used to group the nodes. There will also be an additional group for NULL, to reflect those nodes that do not support a value for the attribute. The same number of nodes and links are represented within Figures 7.2 and 7.3, it is just the manner in which they have been presented that has changed.

Selecting a Display Layout in NETMAP

NETMAP supports several different display layouts. Since data placement within these layouts is based on a grouping strategy, you should be able to predict what the displays will look like before they are even generated. For instance, if the attribute "month" is selected as the primary grouping method, you will most probably get 13 groups, (1–12, plus the NULL group to handle nodes that do not support a "month" attribute). If anything else appears, it needs to be investigated and explained. Before a display layout is selected, you need to consider how your data are mapped into the defined grouping strategy. Otherwise, you may not be able to make sense of the resulting displays.

Overall, NETMAP supports seven different layouts. In addition to the traditional wagon-wheel NETMAP format, there are also Circular, Column, Row, Row/Column, Bullseye, and Cartesian options. These other options allow you to select object shapes other than wedges. The wedges in the baseline display cannot be manipulated or extracted independently from their group due to the way in which they are drawn. The other display formats use individual display nodes that can assume a position separate from the rest of nodes. These nodes can be dragged around the screen, assigned shapes, and presented in any manner defined through their underlying placement algorithms. A quick review of each layout is provided in the sidebar on NETMAP Data Layout Formats.

NETMAP Data Layout Formats

As already mentioned, NETMAP supports several positioning algorithms that allow you to arrange data within a display for link analysis (see Figure 7.4). These are briefly described next to give you an idea of the range of possibilities for presenting data during link analysis.

Circular. This layout format provides a similar placement to the NETMAP format. All nodes are grouped using a counterclockwise positioning technique in which the order is based on ascending value. The first group, the one with the lowest value identified in the attribute, is placed in the three o'clock position.

Figure 7.4 A sample set of NETMAP displays.

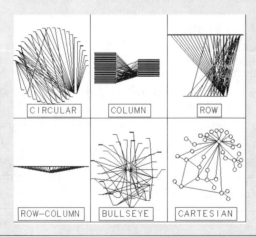

Using Step-Link to Show Pathways

In the examples provided in Figure 7.4, placement of objects within a display is based on the values contained within attributes used to describe nodes. This will handle a large majority of the analyses that you might want to perform. However, it does not cover them all. There are cases for which grouping needs to be performed based on the linkages among nodes. NETMAP supports the ability to group nodes according to the way they are connected. Thus, using a special feature called a Step-Link, NETMAP can display the levels of connection from target nodes to destination nodes contained in the data set (see Figure 7.5). This feature lets you group nodes based on the number of connection steps from a predetermined starting group. Most uses of

Column. Uses a left to right placement technique to control the display. This can be very powerful when showing a sequence of activities, assuming that you can get the groups to align properly. The links between nodes will still be drawn, so the display can become cluttered if you are not careful in your selection of groupings. The Column layout is fairly compact since it stacks the data elements. This layout is very useful for representing hierarchical relationships and is good to try with the Step-Link function.

Row. This layout algorithm uses the exact same approach to presenting nodes as does Column, except that items are positioned from top to bottom of the display space. Row displays imply a hierarchical structure, and are particularly useful with data sets that contain hierarchical elements. The use of Row also tends to expand the nodes on the screen since they now lie end-to-end rather than being stacked.

Row/Column. This is a unique combination of both the Row and Column formats. As the name implies, the nodes contained within the starting group are presented in a row across the top of the screen. For each subsequent group, they are presented as a series of columns. This can lead to very interesting display, but it has proven most useful when looking at distributions (e.g., times, dates, amounts) for selected nodes.

Bullseye. The group at the center of a Bullseye display is the starting group. Its nodes are laid out in a circular format. Each subsequent group is wrapped around the center group in a series of bands, similar to a bullseye target. The size of each group will have an effect on the way the diagram looks. Since the distances are greater the further out you get

Continued

> ## NETMAP Data Layout Formats (*Continued*)
>
> from the center, groups with a small number of nodes can be stretched quite thin. Alternatively, groups with a large number of nodes placed closer to the center usually appear to be compressed. Bullseye is another good format for use with the Step-Link function.
>
> **Cartesian.** This is an undocumented feature within the system because it does not work without some external programming support through the NETMAP API. A Cartesian layout provides the ability to place nodes anywhere on the screen according to a pair of x,y coordinates. Since these values are initially set to 0,0, there is no default placement technique used here. The upshot is that the Cartesian format can be used to introduce new layout algorithms into your NETMAP environment. Thus, if you are willing to program a new placement algorithm through the TCL interface, you can reap the benefits of new display designs. There have been several good third-party algorithms defined for use in this layout format.

Step-Link are based on the identification of a single node such as a person, organization, or address rather than a group of nodes. In NETMAP, a single node is still considered a group if it is the only node that supports the value or specified condition.

Step-Link can also be used to generate the shortest path between any two groups of nodes automatically. So in addition to specifying a starting point, a termination point can be defined. Step-Link will identify paths that can be established between two nodes, presenting only those objects directly supporting the connection (see Figure 7.6). Step-Link does not use any type of weighted calculations, so the results returned are based purely on the identification of the shortest number of connections between two points. This technique can be quite powerful especially when performing "what-if" analyses. As a method of testing a network for vulnerability, arbitrary removal of any node from the path will result in either the generation of a longer path or the failure of the system to establish a connection.

Figure 7.5 A NETMAP step-link example using a columnar format.

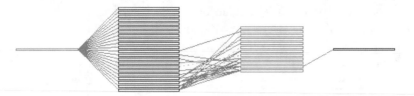

Figure 7.6 Showing the shortest path between two nodes in NETMAP.

The patterns contained in the data are often revealed in terms of differential frequencies among alternative paths. The relative frequencies can be used by a set of NETMAP filters that determine the strengths of the relationships identified in a path analysis. The total number of linkages between any pair of nodes can be set to meet a minimum threshold value before reporting will occur. For example, you could set a threshold for the minimum number of connections that each node within a path must have before that path can be included in the set of critical paths identified in an analysis. You can manipulate these thresholds as a means of increasing your confidence that the pathways identified in an analysis are indeed reliable.

Analyzing Emergent and Discrete Groups in NETMAP

There are other techniques that can be used to group data according to their links with other nodes. The basic NETMAP display format can be modified slightly to accommodate the results of some of these advanced analyses. In particular, NETMAP supports the emergent group algorithm. If you will recall from Chapter 5, an emergent group is defined as a highly interconnected group of entities that share more linkages with members of their own group than they do with any others. The trick is in defining what constitutes a group in the first place. The algorithm has special roles defined for categorizing the nodes as group members, liaisons, attached isolates, and detached isolates. The manner in which the nodes are connected through links will determine their role in the diagram. Unfortunately, the values used by the emergent group algorithm within NETMAP are fixed and cannot be adjusted. However they have been set to values that usually produce reliable results. An example of a display generated in an emergent group analysis is shown in Figure 7.7. In this display, the nodes in the main circle are banded into emergent groups by virtue of the fact that there are more connections to nodes within the groups than to nodes outside the groups.

NETMAP can also be used to detect discrete groups. A discrete group represents all of the nodes that can be connected to form a self-contained independent cluster. What this mean is that nodes are assigned to a group along with any other nodes to which they are connected. This continues until there are no longer any nodes that have not yet been grouped. Once all the pathways have been exhausted for a particular data set, it forms a discrete group. Figure 7.8 shows a sample discrete network display within the NETMAP system. Discrete groups are shown as satellite structures outside the main circular data array.

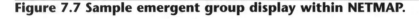

Figure 7.7 Sample emergent group display within NETMAP.

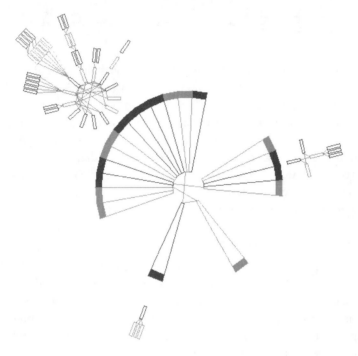

Identification of discrete groups is a little bit like untangling strands of holiday lights. You might not be sure how many different strands there are in the bundled mess until you start to unravel the different lengths of wires. There are as many groupings in the display as there are completely detached networks of nodes. Each group is completely self-contained such that any node within a particular group can be linked to any other node in the group through one or more levels. The nodes between groups cannot be connected because they are in separate groups. Thus, there are no links shown across the center of the NETMAP diagram when presenting a discrete group. All links are shown in the satellite structures associated with each group. The discrete group display is extremely useful for getting a quick understanding about various target entities, the extent of influence for certain nodes, and an overall picture of where the interesting subnetworks might be in your data set.

The NETMAP Presentation Tool

The NETMAP Presentation Tool (NPT) is a stand-alone module that supports annotation of displays and report generation within NETMAP. NPT emulates a large number

Figure 7.8 A discrete network grouping within NETMAP.

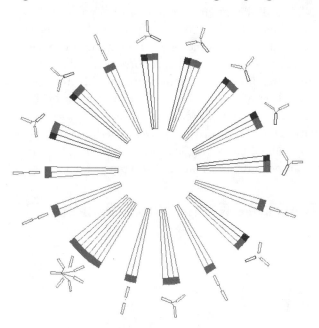

of popular drawing functions that can be used to adjust the contents of a NETMAP diagram. There are several basic features that are provided by NPT including line and shape drawing, text entry, line styles, color palettes, object groupings, grid alignment, and many more. NPT is typically invoked towards the end of an analysis when you want to make final displays to be used for presentation of results.

Using NPT for Data Modeling

NPT can also be used to create new nodes and links without editing the NETMAP configuration file. Using NPT you can drag out new nodes from a palette of choices, set their colors, assign shapes, and provide labels. Nodes can be linked together quickly by connecting the endpoints of a link to the designated nodes. NPT does not support creation of a formal data model in which entities can easily be distinguished from one another. Instead, NPT presents data elements as generic drawing objects and does not provide access to supporting information defining the attributable values of the nodes and links. Should any significant changes to the data need to be performed, these have to be done in the main NETMAP application This can sometimes be a challenge, especially for cases in which large numbers of changes are made to a diagram via NPT. It usually means that you have to start over and reinvest the effort to regenerate the diagram.

Using NPT for Storyboarding

NPT lets you load multiple NETMAP files at any one time so that you can show a series of discrete states in a storyboard fashion. The diagrams can be arranged to show a sequence of events, a breakdown of time periods, or general changes in activity. NPT produces a set of panels that are equally proportioned and positioned within the display (see Figure 7.9). This layout method can provide an effective means of presenting a complicated set of results. Since each panel within NPT acts as a placeholder, absolute time references can be used to generate empty screens representing periods of nonactivity. This can also be done over other discrete or continuous values such as dollar amounts, dates, frequencies, and so on. The printed results of this type of display can be quite informative as a reporting device.

Figure 7.9 Multiple NETMAP diagrams presented within NPT.

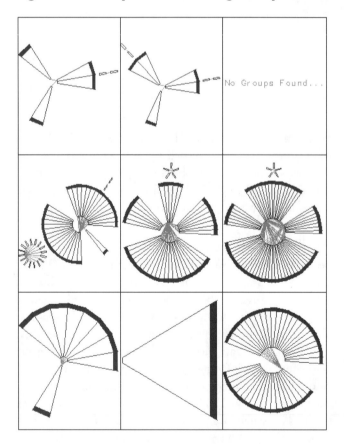

Analyst's Notebook

Perhaps one of the most widely distributed visualization systems within the investigative, intelligence, and law enforcement communities is the Analyst's Notebook. This is an easy to use system that enables you to perform various types of analyses that support an active case. The system provides different types of visualization displays, analytical components, data management facilities, and presentation graphics. It is based largely on a modernized link analysis version of the Anacapa methodologies presented in Chapter 5. The entire system is largely targeted at nontechnical users, so the approach is simple and intuitive. The charts produced by the Analyst's Notebook have become very popular throughout the investigative world because they can be generated effortlessly, shared, and interpreted by a large user community. In fact, many courtroom presentations are based on the charts produced using the Analyst's Notebook.

The Analyst's Notebook is being developed by i2 Ltd., which has sites in the United States, United Kingdom, and Australia. They have consistently made enhancements to the Analyst's Notebook to reflect the needs of their specific user community. Nevertheless, the methods and presentation techniques supported in the Analyst's Notebook are generally applicable to a wide variety of problem domains. Thus, the Analyst's Notebook is a package of well-defined software modules that can be used to generate results quickly for a target application. The suite of tools includes the Link Notebook, Case Notebook, iBase, iConnect, and several other supporting modules used for administrative purposes. The Analyst's Notebook currently is supported on a wide range of computing platforms including the entire Windows line of operating systems and several flavors of UNIX (X-Window/Motif). As part of making the Analyst's Notebook widely available to the end-user community, the software has been designed to run on common computing systems as opposed to high-end workstations that might not be readily available. This tool can be run on very stripped-down systems in the simplest of environments. This has partly been the key to the global acceptance and usage of the Analyst's Notebook.

Incorporating Data Sets into Analyst's Notebook

The Analyst's Notebook can be used either to look at existing sets of data or to dynamically create new information on the fly. The capability to support both ends of the data manipulation spectrum is important to the data mining process. The Analyst's Notebook can be dropped into virtually any situation and be put to use almost immediately. The data pipes supported by the Analyst's Notebook are used to connect to different databases to extract and import information. Currently, five different data pipes provide support for DDE (Dynamic Data Exchange), ODBC, Sockets, Sybase, and Oracle. The pipes all function identically to one another. Having a direct coupling to a data source is a very powerful capability because it foregoes the requirement to produce a transport file each time new information is required for presentation. This enables you to query the data directly from the chart in real time, sending requests for information from the visual representation to the underlying database. This feature has been very well developed and is one that you will appreciate when setting up your own environment with the Analyst's Notebook software suite.

Using the Link Notebook

The Link Notebook supports a set of functions used for link analysis. There are nodes and links that can be added manually or generated from structured data sources. Working manually, you add nodes to the chart to represent each item of interest in the investigation, draw links between the nodes, and add cards (e.g., a data profile) to the links to summarize the source details. Alternatively, you can quickly configure the Link Notebook to read in the data from a file or database and automatically create the corresponding nodes and links from each of the fields in the source data. Individual nodes on the screen are called entities within the Link Notebook. The entities can represent any type of object present within the data set, such as a person, organization, telephone number, or account.

The system supports drill-down of complete information not displayed on screen. Supporting information about an entity can include its name, source type, intelligence grade (Anacapa-based values), source reference, and general notes. For the most part, any number of attributes can be defined for any entity within the chart. There are, however, a fixed number of attribute types that can be generated including text, number, time, and flag. The information contained within an attribute can appear within the diagram, with an associated symbol (e.g., squares, circles, or text blocks). This makes interpreting the Link Notebook charts much easier since there is additional detail associated with each entity presented right on the display in a graphical format. Additionally, the entities can have an associated graphical icon that makes their content more explicit. There are icons to represent a wide range of node types including people, places, items, weapons, processes, events, and much more. The icons used by the Link Notebook are produced using an editor that allows you to create your own graphical representations.

Using Inter-Item Linkages in the Link Notebook

Entities can be connected through different types of links. Within the Link Notebook, three link types can be used to represent the connection between any two entities: single, directed, and connected. A single connection will contain only one link, with or without an arrow to show its direction. A directed connection has up to four subtypes including the source-to-destination, destination-to-source, both directions, and undirected (similar to the single connection). This provides a method to specify the level of detail necessary to justify what the links represent. The multiple connections may contain any number or combination of directed and undirected links. Taken collectively, the entities and their links can be assembled into a variety of diagrams as depicted in Figure 7.10.

Navigating in the Link Notebook

The overall structure of the Link Notebook is fairly straightforward. There are control options along the left-hand side. These are used to select entities, zoom in and out, add graphic annotations, change styles, create boxes, assign labels, and much

Figure 7.10 A sample display using the Link Notebook.

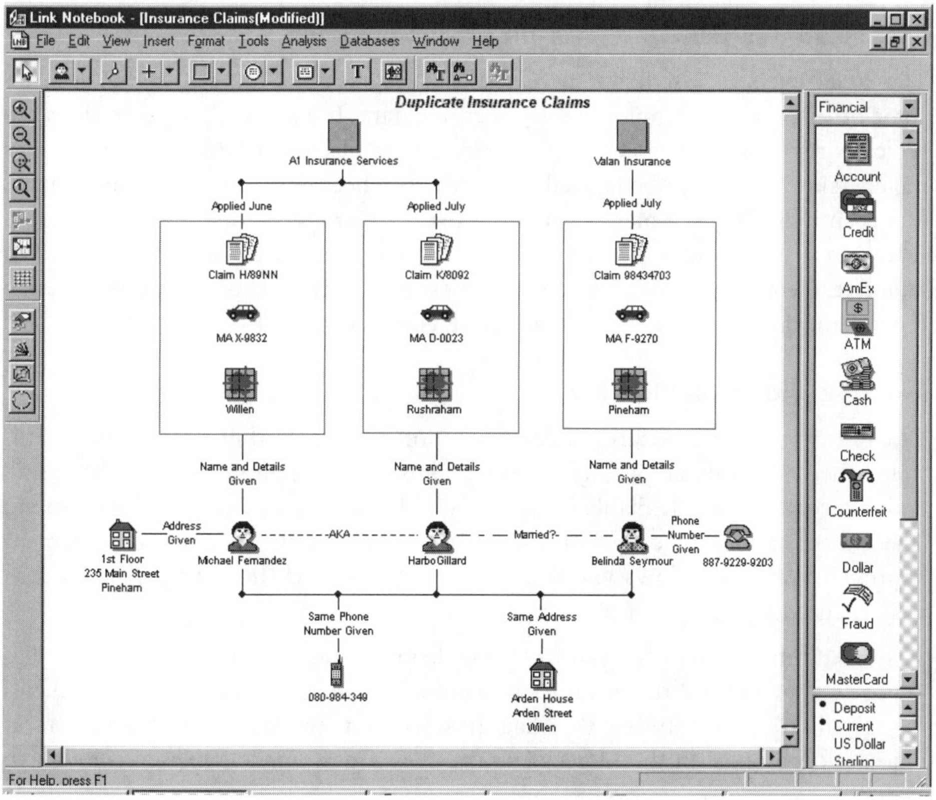

more. On the right-hand side is a panel containing icons representing the different types of entities defined for the application being built. Creating new instances of these classes of entities is a simple drag-and-drop operation from this panel. You can very quickly create or modify a data set by using the entities contained within this panel. These entities can then be linked together to form network diagrams. The link styles can be adjusted to include different labels, styles (dotted, dashed, solid), and can even be bent around a particular point. Recall that one of the requirements for presenting an Anacapa-like method is to minimize the line crossings. By being able to put bends in a link, they can be extended or drawn around objects to try to minimize the overlap. Multiple bends can also be applied to any link.

Construction of the chart is accomplished by dragging selected elements into position. A snap-to grid command makes it easy to clean up the appearance of the display by aligning elements in rows and boxes. Three automatic layouts can be applied to large charts to uncross the lines and move significant elements to the center of the chart. You can even add an attribute to chart elements to ensure that they keep their positions while the remainder of the chart is repositioned.

Special Annotation Options in the Link Notebook

The Link Notebook also has some special drawing options that are used to emulate some other Anacapa techniques for presenting data. If you recall, organizations are typically represented as boxes and individuals are placed within the box to signify membership. Boxes can be labeled manually to reflect the names of organizations. When an individual is a member of more than one organization, there are multiple boxes presented around the particular individual. There are also methods used to annotate the diagram with text boxes, lines, and circles. This can result in some fairly elaborate diagrams, as presented in Figure 7.11.

Working with Multiple Charts

One of the many nice features of Analyst's Notebook is its ability to maintain multiple active charts within a single session. Thus at any one time you can have several different displays available for analysis within a single execution of the system. The charts can be cascaded or tiled using a standard Windows management approach. This also allows you to compare and contrast different perspectives as well as cut and paste between them.

When information is copied from one diagram and pasted into a different diagram, you can control the integration of information. Generally the entities themselves will transfer between the diagrams without any additional definition. If objects do not exist in the target diagram, they are created. If they already exist,

Figure 7.11 A Link Notebook diagram with annotation.

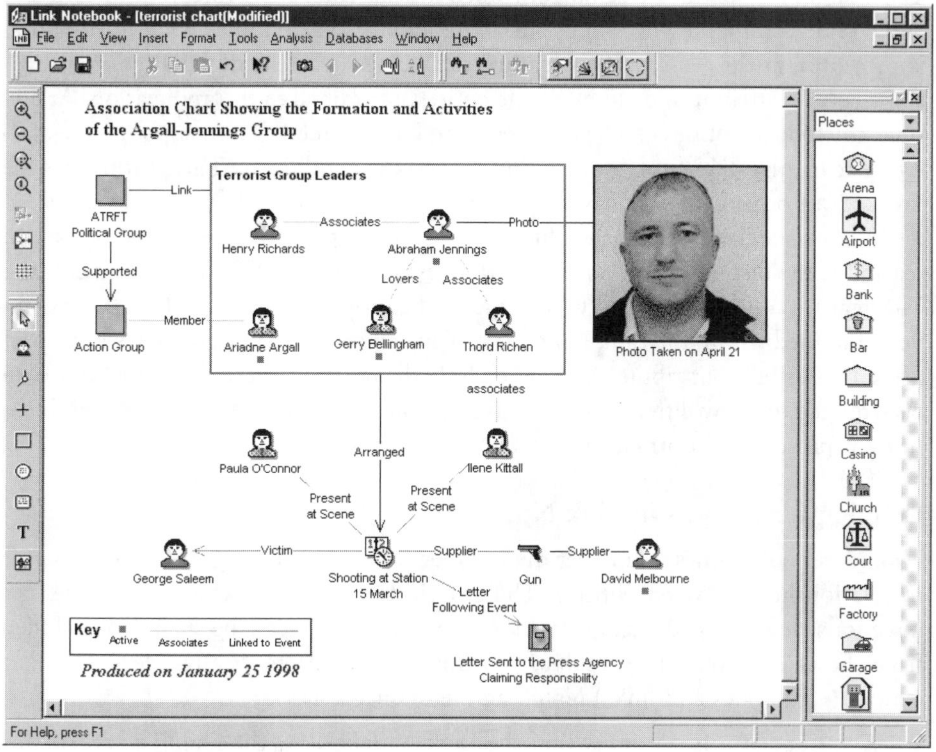

their links are transferred to the existing entity. On the other hand, the type of action performed when transferring links is based on the type of links used. For single links, the values on the links are combined; for directed links, the values on the links are combined in terms of their direction; and for multiple links, any links pasted are shown as new, distinct links between the entities.

Attributes are incorporated in conjunction with their corresponding objects and links, but this process is governed by a set of user-defined rules. For integer-based attributes, a wide range of calculations can be performed including sum-highest-lowest of both values, pasted-minus-existing, existing-minus-pasted, pasted-value, or existing-value. For text-based attributes, the system supports functions such as concatenation, pasted-value, or existing-value. Time can be expressed as existing-value, pasted-value, earliest, and latest. Finally, for flag attributes, you can do OR, AND, XOR, pasted-value, or existing-value calculations.

Setting the Visibility of a Node

The visibility of entities can be controlled within the Link Notebook. There is a Show/Hide command within the Link Notebook that determines what information is presented in the display. This feature can be applied to individual entities (e.g., show certain attributes) or to all of the entities contained in the application. At any time, the hidden entities can be restored. The Link Notebook also supports the ability to rearrange the display according to certain conditions. This feature can be invoked automatically whenever the Show/Hide command is used. Thus, as elements are being included or excluded from the display, the Link Notebook will rearrange the display so as to produce the best placement of the remaining entities. This feature can be combined with some of the more advanced analytical capabilities contained within the Link Notebook. You can create a series of views of a chart using the visibility attribute to show or hide different entities. The series can then be arranged to show different perspectives on the same data set. This is a useful feature for presenting information to others one step at a time.

Defining Link Levels in Link Notebook

Link Notebook allows you to set the number of levels of linkages to show *from* or *to* relationships between entities. The search-depth can be set to any value, the directions defined, and certain types of nodes or links can be included/excluded from the calculations. The results from this feature automatically select the other entities (e.g., nodes and links) matching the defined criteria.

A variant of this option within the Link Notebook is the ability to search for paths contained within the data structure. A path can be established as any connection between two objects. A path can be as simple as a direct connection or it can be very convoluted where there are multiple indirect connections between the two objects. The Link Notebook uses the selection of entities to define the start and end points. Figure 7.12 shows an example of a link chart where there are two nodes selected. Figure 7.13 depicts the resulting path that includes only those nodes in the pathway. This feature also allows you to accumulate the value of an attribute along the path. As an example, if the data set contains values regarding the transfer of funds between bank accounts, the pathway calculation could also produce a summation of every single transfer amount and present the total on the screen. There are also methods to find shortest paths, rearrange the chart for optimal placement, and include/exclude attribute values.

Generating Clusters in Link Notebook

The Link Notebook supports a cluster feature, which is used to show groups of entities that are more interconnected to each other than to other entities outside the

Figure 7.12 Selecting the endpoint for a pathway analysis (see highlights).

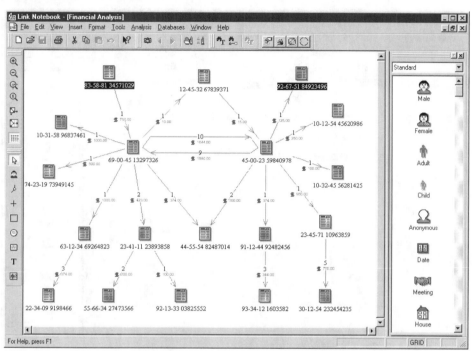

group. This is very similar to the emergent group techniques that were discussed in Chapter 5. Within the Link Notebook, clusters contain a minimum of three entities. Clusters may be defined on the basis of loose, medium, or tight connectivity. You can select the cluster members, hide noncluster elements, automatically rearrange the display, and add attributes to various components. Figure 7.14 shows an example of several different clusters identified within the Link Notebook where the labels associated with the links reflect the number of the cluster to which they belong.

Other Options in Link Notebook

The Link Notebook has an extended set of customizable features. There are methods for dealing with OLE (Object Linking and Embedding), fonts, styles, auto-saving, authorship, and so on. There are also a range of printing options and output devices that can be configured. The Link Notebook has an extensive set of printing capabilities to help prepare the final output. The page setup features provide a thumbnail outline of the diagram overlaid onto an outline of the paper size. Through some simple display manipulations, you can orient and restructure the

Figure 7.13 Showing pathways within the Link Notebook (see highlights).

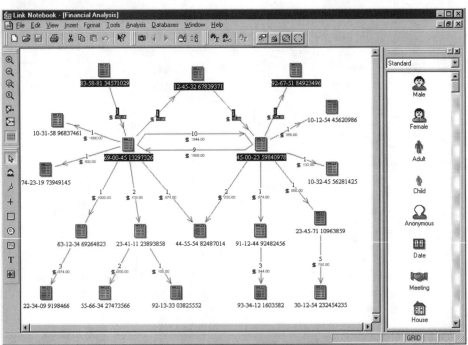

diagram to best fit the paper size. Additionally, if you do not have devices for generating large charts, this feature can be used to spread a chart across several standard-size pages. You can also use Link Notebook to customize the legend-key for the diagram. The legend can contain information about attributes, entities, element lines, fonts, and link-styles.

The Link Notebook also supports generation of customized reports. The reports present the details of the entities including their names, sources, comments, and any other attributes defined in their Note Cards. Information about the entities themselves as well as the links among them is reported.

Working with the Case Notebook

Another visual presentation module contained within the Analyst's Notebook is called the Case Notebook. This module is particularly useful when working with temporally coded information (e.g., time-based). The main focus of the Case Notebook is to help lay out progressive states of knowledge maintained during different stages of an investigation. As we discussed in Chapter 5, there are generally

Figure 7.14 An example of clusters within the Link Notebook.

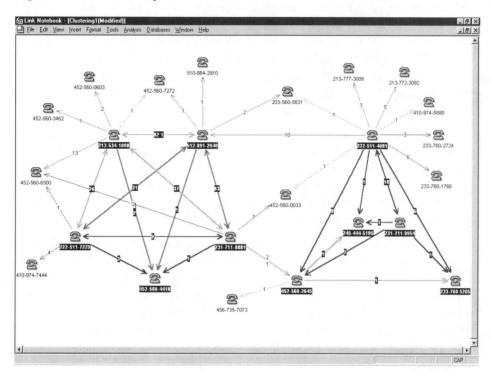

two forms of temporal patterns, absolute and contiguous, that can be represented in a data mining analysis. In the Case Notebook, these are referred respectively as proportional and nonproportional time periods. For proportional time periods, the distance between events corresponds to actual real-world time. For nonproportional events, the relative order of events is the critical feature represented as opposed to the amount of time actually separating the events.

Generating Case Charts in Case Notebook

The components that are used to generate case charts within the Case Notebook include themes, events, and links. Themes represent key elements of the analysis. For each case chart, there can be multiple themes represented. Themes might include people, organizations, locations, and so forth. Events are then associated to each theme. An event can represent a particular activity in which a theme element was involved for such things as phone calls, sightings, meetings, contacts, or any other type of observation. Each event has a title, a description, a source, and a time. Events can be associated with one another through the use of links.

The horizontal orientation of the Case Notebook is used to show the time axis. This axis is labeled in regular intervals and markers can be introduced to highlight intervals of interest. Themes are represented along the vertical axis. Events are then placed within the diagram accordingly along their respective horizontal and vertical axes. This approach produces a timeline of events that allows you to see which critical activities are shared in common among multiple themes. When an event is shared by more than one theme, horizontal lines drawn from the themes converge at the event to represent the commonality.

The portrayal of an event for a particular theme can be broken out into multiple pathways by adding burst points, creating flexible sections of the themes that can be joined to show that multiple actions have been performed at the same time. For presentation purposes, you may want to separate close events so they do not overlap in the display. Figure 7.15 shows an example of a case chart with several events that have occurred for the selected themes.

Unlike the Link Notebook, which summarizes information in terms of the links between objects, the Case Notebook enables the display of detailed information. The details are presented in a fashion where you can read the text contained within any event. This information can be searched at any time for particular terms, names, or values. Case charts, however, can become quite large and complex because they are usually used to keep track of detailed information during an analysis. To aid in the interpretation of this complex information, a summary mode can be invoked that will reduce the events to a simple circle with only the title presented. This significantly simplifies the interface by hiding the details of the events and allows you to peruse larger periods of time. This data reduction is particularly helpful when looking at a large number of nonproportionally related events, such as phone calls. The diagrams can be compressed to show sequences of events across a wide time interval. Figure 7.16 shows an example of a case chart presented using the summary mode.

Using this type of approach, the themes can be compared to one another within the Case Notebook and their differences or similarities highlighted. You can generate a derived-theme that contains the desired information. For difference functions, a derived-theme for each selected theme is created and it contains the events unique to that theme. For similarities, a single derived-theme shows all of the common events among all of the selected themes. This can prove to be a very powerful set of capabilities when looking at the behaviors of multiple themes. Figure 7.17 shows an example of both a theme difference and similarity.

Case flow charts can show links among events over a period of time, and in particular can be used to identify repeating occurrences of the same pattern of links.

Figure 7.15 An example of a case chart in Case Notebook.

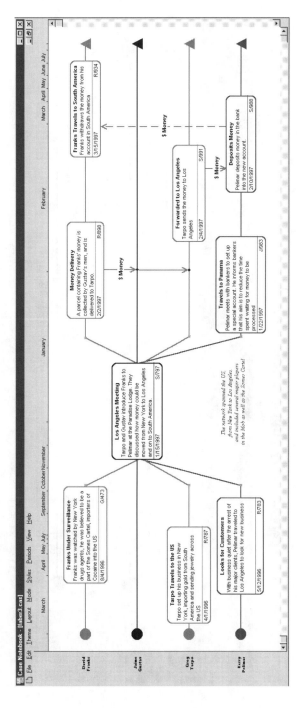

Figure 7.16 A case chart summary display format in Case Notebook.

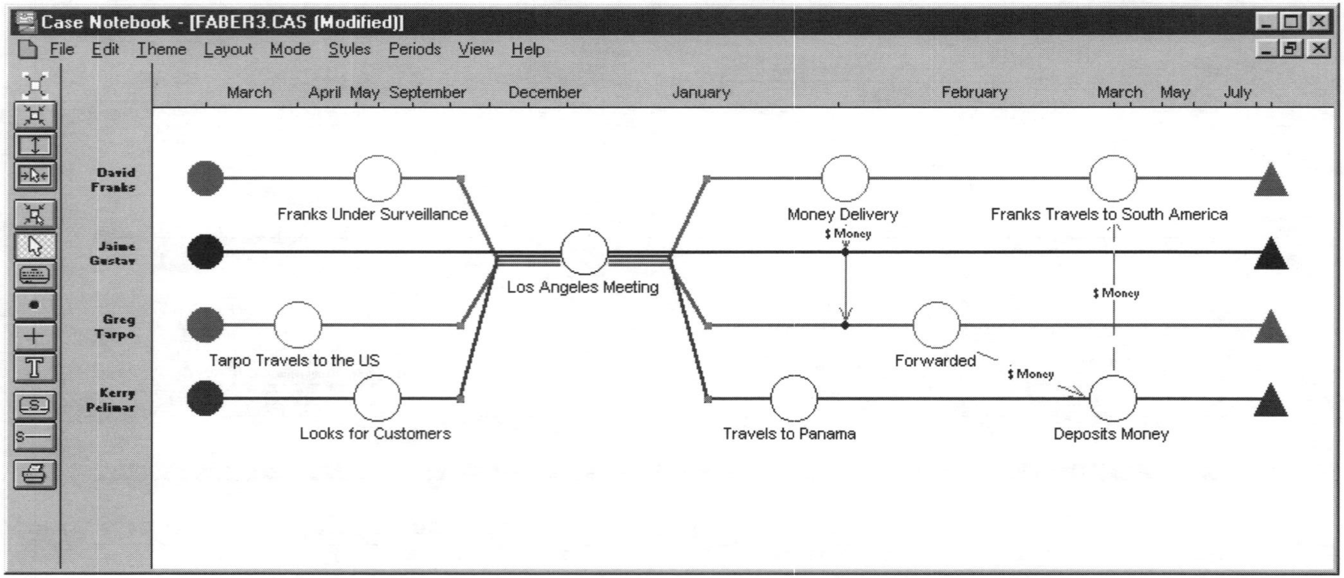

Figure 7.17 Case charts generated from derived-theme information in Case Notebook.

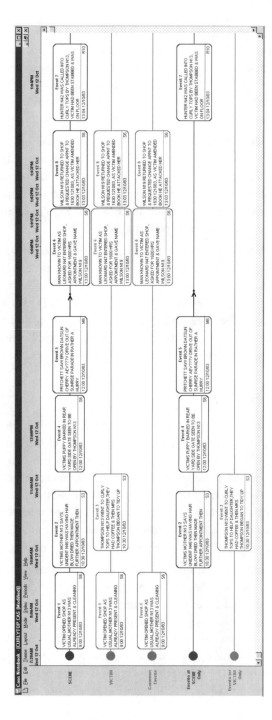

In this format, events are shown only as dots, and the emphasis is given to the links between the events. For telephone calls, the source event and the destination event occur at the same time, the dots are shown against their respective themes, and each connection is shown as a link. During automatic import of text files, you can specify the information you wish to have shown on the link, and the resulting chart makes it easy for you to discover unusual or repeating connections.

For analysis purposes, the Case Notebook offers the option to rearrange the chart automatically in an ordered fashion in which events are placed one after the other. Alternatively, you can opt for a chained format in which Case Notebook groups together all events that occur within a preselected time interval. This method reveals clusters of events occurring in close temporal proximity. Examples of temporally clustered events are shown in Figure 7.18.

Case Notebook lets you manipulate a wide range of parameters to customize your analysis. These include the start/stop dates, time increments, presentation styles, markers, symbols, and much more. Time periods can also be collapsed to hide information. As with the Link Notebook, there is also a comprehensive set of printing options. The Analyst's Notebook suite of products is constantly being improved to provide utility across a wide range of applications and we can expect to see many more updates over the next several releases.

Imagix 4D

One of the more interesting and abstract systems profiled in this chapter is Imagix 4D. Imagix 4D is a link analysis tool that was developed for use in the domain of software analysis. In particular, Imagix 4D shows the composition of a piece of software in terms of subcomponents and their interconnections. Despite the fact that software analysis may have little to do with your application problem, remember our mantra that *data are data are data*. The methodologies developed to represent information from a given problem domain can almost always be generalized to accommodate other problem areas. Imagix 4D is no exception to this rule.

In its original incarnation, the data used in Imagix 4D were derived from the structure and content of software programs where variable declarations, function calls, source files, and other components could be graphically represented. The point of this type of analysis is to make the dependencies and structures within a program explicit, which as you can imagine can become quite involved in large applications having many thousands of lines of code. The explicit representation of program structures within Imagix 4D provides support for a variety of purposes including software enhancement, maintenance, documentation, and reuse. Additionally, Imagix 4D has

Figure 7.18 Showing temporal clustering of events in a case flow chart.

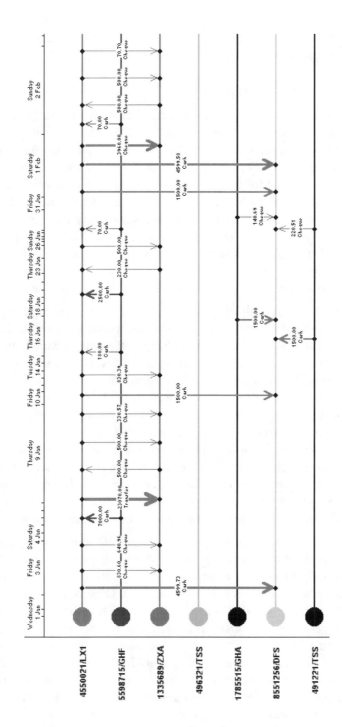

recently been outfitted to support the Year-2000 (Y2K) problems currently facing most businesses throughout the world.

Importing Data in Imagix 4D

Imagix 4D is produced by a small company located in California called Imagix. Imagix 4D has been built using a combination of C and TCL code. It runs in both a Windows environment and under UNIX. The system is primarily distributed through the Internet and license keys are issued through e-mail. The data processing requirements are a bit different for Imagix 4D than the rest of the systems discussed in this book. The source data to be visualized are not extracted from traditional databases per se; rather data are derived from the software programs themselves. As a result, you will not find any ODBC compliance within Imagix 4D. Instead you will see references to makefiles, file structures, and source code. Imagix 4D derives its data directly from parsing raw programming code usually stored as ASCII files. Imagix 4D converts the content of these files into its own internal format.

For those of you familiar with programming terms, objects within Imagix 4D can be composed of functions, procedures, declarations, variables, typedefs, header files, classes, macros, and so on. For example, Imagix 4D collects data from your makefiles to generate information about build dependencies (for more information see the sidebar on makefiles). Imagix 4D can be used to extract class, function, variable, and type information directly from your source code. This type of paradigm is analogous to that used in the other tools presented in this section. It really does not matter what the underlying data represents. The behaviors and structures exhibited by the objects and their inter-relationships are what is important to analyze. So whether you are looking at phone calls, Internet access logs, POS transactions, or the content of software programs, it is the underlying data models that determine the types of patterns that can be exposed. It just so happens that Imagix 4D has been specifically tailored to work exclusively in the analysis of software programs.

Although this discussion makes the utility of Imagix 4D seem limited, the system could actually be used to represent many types of information used within a corporate information processing environment. The data structures of Imagix 4D closely approximate a hierarchical link display paradigm. Objects are placed within the display based on their relative distance from a predetermined level. For use within software programs, this hierarchical visualization can be analyzed to expose critical modules, unused variables, duplicated code, and other issues that degrade the integrity of the software. The same principle holds true for other hierarchical networks that might be mapped into this visualization scheme. You can import non-program data sources into Imagix 4D using methods described in the section entitled "Working with Data Sources in Imagix 4D."

What Are Makefiles?

Imagix 4D can derive the knowledge structure that is used to represent a program from the corresponding *makefile* that was used to create the run-time code. Makefiles contain a set of descriptions that are used by the operating system utility called *make* to execute a sequence of commands. Makefiles are commonly used to help manage the creation of large software programs but can realistically be used for a wide variety of purposes where there are dependencies among files. The dependencies might reflect the order in which the files should be compiled, the sequence in which they should be joined together, or even a succession of different shell commands that operate on a set of files. Makefiles have even been used to coordinate the installation of software as well as to manage the formatting of documents.

Any one who has been involved with software development knows the utility and time savings that can be achieved using a makefile. One of the advantages of using makefiles is that if a single file is changed somewhere in the dependency hierarchy, it does not necessarily mean that the entire set of files comprising an application needs to be updated. When dealing with the compilation and linking of complex software code, it can take quite a long time to build an executable sequence, sometimes upwards of several hours. By using a makefile in these cases, only those files associated with the actual code changes would be recompiled and relinked accordingly. The ability to perform selective building makes it easy to incorporate changes in a large software development effort. The use of makefiles also facilitates parallel and distributed code development. Code can be developed in pieces, with multiple programmers assigned to separate parts of the overall task.

The structure of a makefile is fairly simple. There are targets that represent the outputs desired from executing a make. The targets are comprised of prerequisites or dependents that are based on the files identified in the makefile.

So the target of a makefile might be the generation of code from an automated billing program, which is comprised of many interdependent components represented as headers, C language code, libraries, and other

Continued

> **What Are Makefiles? (*Continued*)**
>
> related files. The actual syntax and structure of a makefile will not be covered in these discussions, but you can see how important a makefile can be to the management of software development. Being able to visualize and use the contents of a makefile to better understand your software is a very powerful concept.

Using Imagix 4D "Outside the Box"

Because Imagix 4D is such a departure from the standard class of data mining systems that you might normally consider, we wanted to take a little extra time to reemphasize the virtues of using these types of approaches in nontraditional applications. Adopting a system like Imagix 4D is a good example of thinking "outside the box," leaving yourself open to discover methods that might work better than ones you are currently using. The scope of Imagix 4D applications can be quite extensive and we have seen the tool applied to nonsoftware problems where the front-end data parsers were reconfigured to handle different sources of data. In particular this tool might be one to consider if your data structure is inherently hierarchical or sequenced, since true representation of hierarchical and sequenced structures including inheritance relationships is not readily handled by many of the other systems.

Imagix 4D provides a wide range of methods you can use to interact with your data and includes routines to browse, explore, analyze, and document the underlying data. It lets you look at file structures and data usage in order to build dependencies and class inheritance into your model. To help you become familiar with features, functions, and operations of the system, Imagix 4D provides a tutorial included with the basic package. This tutorial introduces you to Imagix 4D's features, and shows you how to use them to solve typical development problems. This tutorial is one of the better software training guides that has been produced for commercial packages because it is dynamic and actually uses Imagix 4D's processing engine to conduct the training. Thus, you can observe as menus get invoked or pulled down, entries are selected, and screens rotated to show the points of interest being made. A main control screen allows you to select the type of training that you would like to receive and the tutorial lets you interact directly with the screens. You can move at your own pace and replay sections until you are satisfied that you completely understand Imagix 4D's operations.

Context-sensitive help is also available on all of the different Imagix 4D screens. Every button, selector, and slider has relevant information about its assigned function within the current context. Certain features have dual use within Imagix 4D, and the help function quickly guides you along and aids you in learning the system within the context of your analysis. Imagix 4D also has a full set of help pages that can be searched or referenced through a help index. Additionally there is also a context sensitive legend depicting the different symbols and colors that are being used for each of the modes available within Imagix 4D. This makes it easier for you to keep track of the analysis while switching among the different modes.

Working with Data Sources in Imagix 4D

You have complete control over how much or how little information is imported and analyzed within Imagix 4D. There are two approaches for invoking the Imagix 4D parser on your source code. The first involves completion of a form that requires the directory path that points to where the source files are located, the names of the source files (using *.c style notation), and preprocessor flags. The second approach involves adding Imagix 4D targets to a makefile. Since makefiles are used to guide the construction of software programs, much of the requisite information already resides in the file itself. For those novice users who are just getting started with Imagix 4D, the forms-based approach will prove to be a bit easier to use than trying to create a makefile. All of the information derived from these data sources is then converted into a "project" that is stored in the file system. Since the types of information analyzed can vary at different phases of an analysis, you typically will create a number of different projects within which you can examine different parts of your data set.

Defining Data Types

Imagix 4D can support a variety of data types that can be defined into three basic categories: file systems, build rules, and software program elements. File systems are structured as a hierarchy of directories that starts with a top-level directory containing subdirectories that can be used to organize and store your data neatly. As you may know, these directory structures can sometimes become very complex and unruly. For each directory contained within the file system structure used to store related code segments, Imagix 4D will include its name, location, and any file attributes, such as owner, read/write permissions, and modification date. Imagix 4D directly collects this information from the file system and no manual intervention is required. The hierarchical nature of the Imagix 4D displays makes it an ideal choice for presenting this type of data. Figure 7.19 shows an Imagix 4D screen depicting a simple file hierarchy. You can probably think of several other nonsoftware applications that could use this form of presentation including web-site analysis, product descriptors, medical terminology references, or technical manual navigation.

The process of assembling software requires that you define all of the elements used to construct the system, much in the same way that a cook would follow a recipe. The makefiles themselves contain most of this information and they contain

Figure 7.19 A file hierarchy shown within Imagix 4D.

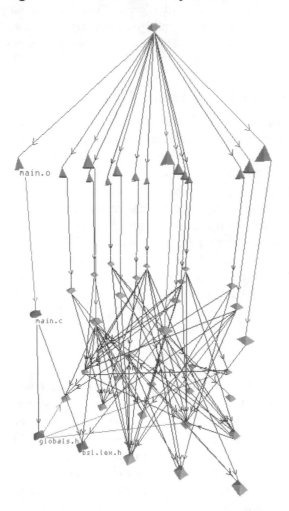

rules that tell the system how to build the software. Details about build targets and build dependencies, as defined in build rules, are collected directly from the makefiles defined for a program. If you recall from the sidebar, a makefile typically is used when there are multiple source code files that need to be compiled and linked in a certain order to ensure generation of a properly constructed executable program. The main components of a makefile include targets, prerequisites, and dependencies. For those that have never implemented a makefile, these build rules can become very complex depending on the nature of the application being built. Thus, they are crucial to any large software development project. Figure 7.20 shows an example of some build rules that were derived from a sample makefile. You could also use this technique to look at the processes associated with, for example, the production or manufacturing of products or equipment.

Software program elements represent the third data type used by Imagix 4D. As we already discussed, the original application domain for Imagix 4D was the analysis of software programs. Thus Imagix 4D has special features for parsing and representing individual function names, variables, declarations, and other program elements. These elements can then be linked to one another to show dependencies

Figure 7.20 Build rules shown with Imagix 4D.

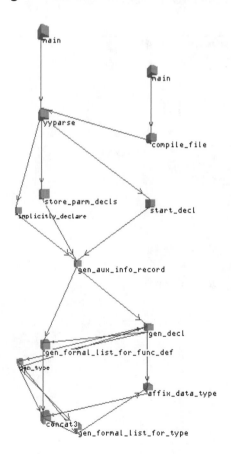

within the code (e.g., variables are used in functions, functions call other functions, and so on). The majority of the information is derived from C and C++ source files or from compiler-generated databases. Figure 7.21 shows the contents of source code within Imagix 4D. This type of representation can also be used to show relationships between people, places, and things.

As you can see in each one of these figures, all objects within Imagix 4D are coded according to a shape and color. For example, blue for functions, green for variables, orange for files, and purple for classes. Lines represent relationships among these objects and each has a direction, which is depicted as an arrowhead. The line can also have an associated color to indicate the type of relationship it represents. Once these networks of information have formed, they can be manipulated to expose or hide certain types of information to facilitate a better understanding of the data. (See the CD-ROM for color Imagix 4D images.)

Figure 7.21 Source code shown within Imagix 4D.

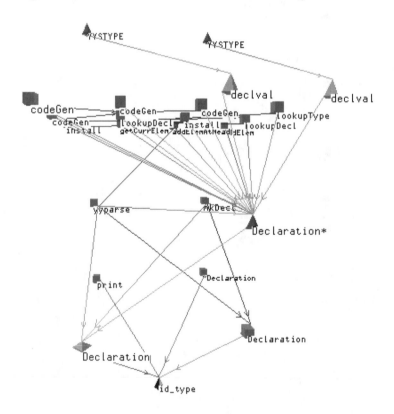

Navigating the Imagix 4D Displays

Since the data contained within an Imagix 4D display are presented in a three-dimensional space, there is a comprehensive set of navigation aids that facilitate interaction with the data. There are two main interface components built into the Imagix 4D displays (see Figure 7.22). On the left-hand side, there is the graph window that helps you view and understand the data structure by pictorially representing the object and relationship data. In the graph window, you can observe specific objects (also called symbols) and how they relate to each other. The display window also allows you to pan, rotate, and zoom in on the symbols and their relationships. On the right-hand side, there is a textual list of the symbols being presented within the graph window. Whereas the graph window shows the symbols and their relationships, the list window describes various characteristics of the symbols themselves. Within the list window, a gray background associated within any symbol indicates that it is visible in the graph window, and a yellow background indicates that the symbol is highlighted in the graph window. Each one of the symbols within the list window is placed into a hierarchical layout depending on its role

Figure 7.22 The navigational interface of Imagix 4D.

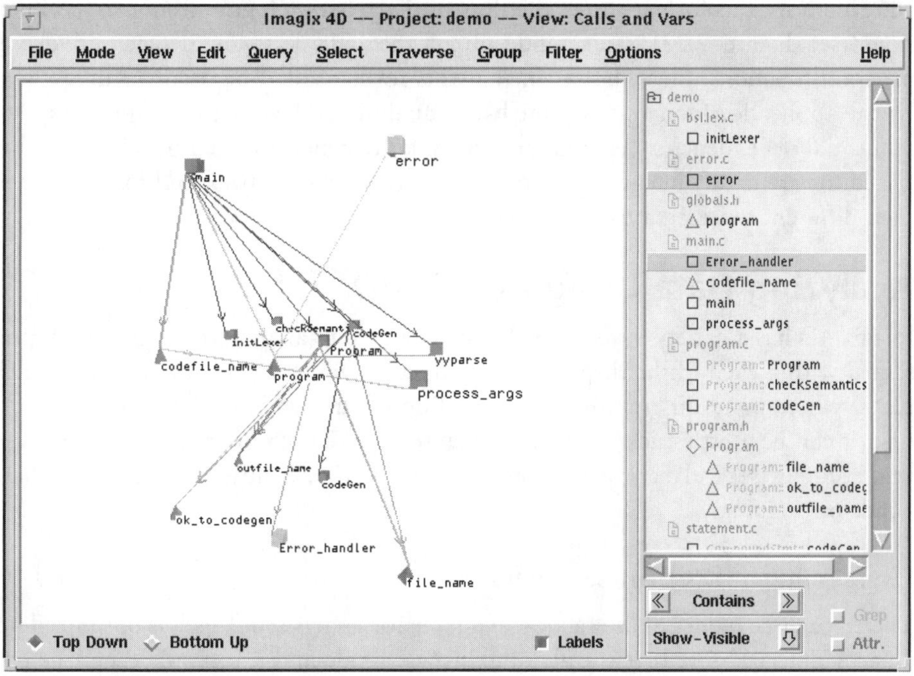

and relationships to other symbols. Selecting, querying and navigating operations all apply across both windows. An icon list appears across the top of the display to help facilitate these interactions and most any operation initiated within Imagix 4D can be reversed by using an Undo command.

Each symbol in the graph or list windows represents a data element in your source code. To see the context in which the symbol was used within the source code, you can request that the corresponding data segments be made available through a file editor window. This form of drill-down can be quite powerful. Once selected, the information derived from the drill-down can be brought directly into an editor if desired. The editor native to Imagix 4D provides you with navigation and query facilities that are integrated with the graph and list windows. (You can specify another editor of your own choice through an options window.)

There are other windows in the Imagix 4D interface that you can use in your analysis. There is a file browser used for listing all active files along with their respective members. There is also a class browser that you can use to navigate through your data set at a high level. Both of these browsers provide a window with symbols relevant to the information requested. By selecting any of the symbols within either of these browsers, the main display is adjusted automatically to reflect the selection.

One final window can be used for looking at flow charts. In the context of software analysis, this format shows the flow of the program logic within defined functions (see Figure 7.23). This rendition of the data lets you detect and debug program functions. Note, however, that this format could be used for many analytical application domains in which the analysis is geared toward detection of sequential dependencies. As with most Imagix 4D windows, the flow chart and the file editor are highly integrated, allowing you to transition back and forth between their different representations with ease.

Analyzing Data Using Imagix 4D

Imagix 4D has a variety of features that can be used to analyze the information presented within each of the displays. Depending on which mode you are in, the displays will respond differently to the selection of the symbols being presented. At first, it can be a little tricky to know when to invoke each of the modes. However, this becomes second nature with use of the tutorial, a little practice, and some hands-on training.

Using Imagix 4D's Browse Mode

There are three modes of interaction available for analysis and each is optimized for a particular task. The first is called the browse mode and it basically takes the last

Figure 7.23 A flow chart display generated in Imagix 4D.

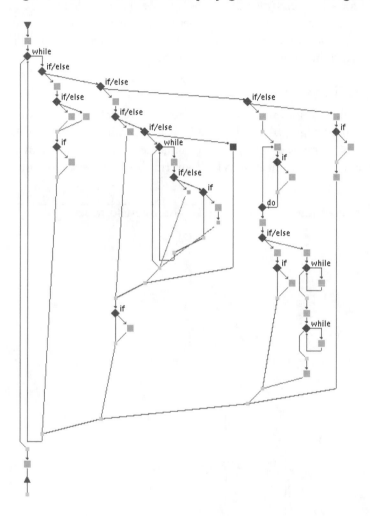

selected symbol and makes it the focus of the display. When you click on any symbol within the graph (or list) display while in the browse mode, only those symbols that are directly connected to it are shown. Depending on the directionality of the links, the symbols are placed as close to the middle of the graph as possible with anything above it in the hierarchy shown above it and anything below it in the hierarchy shown below. Additionally, the list display will update itself accordingly to reflect only those symbols that are present within the display.

Figure 7.24 shows a sample of an Imagix 4D display in the browse mode. This mode is very useful for selectively isolating symbols to see the immediate scope of their connections. It minimizes the amount of time you will spend managing your views of the data set. As with all Imagix 4D interactions, the system automatically responds as soon as a symbol is selected from either the display or list window.

Using the Explore Mode in Imagix 4D

The second mode is called explore and it is used to create more elaborate and extensive diagrams within the Imagix 4D display window than can be generated in the browse mode. The explore mode allows you to accumulate data into the display as you go. This lets you focus on as much or as little information as necessary in order

Figure 7.24 A sample Imagix 4D display in the browse mode.

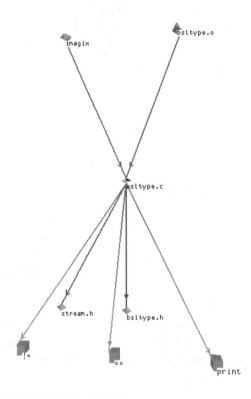

to understand the data set. The explore mode provides a set of navigational features that make these refinements easy to perform. These include methods for selection, traversing, grouping, and filtering the data. These functions work on the symbols that are visible in the display at any point in time. A separate filter function can be used to add or delete symbols from the display.

Selection of symbols in the explore mode can be done at several levels. There are methods in place that allow you to select either all, roots, roots/leaves, or none. The root and leaves selection functions are dynamically calculated based on what is presented within the display window. A root node in one display may become something completely different in another display, so these definitions are only temporary. Selection of a symbol remains in effect until it is either manually unselected or removed from the display.

Selection of a set of symbols will drive the behavior of the other refinement methods. For instance, the traverse routines base all of their calculations on selected symbols. This includes determination of paths existing between pairs of nodes and calculations of path distance. You can also use symbol selection as a starting point for difference calculations that identify those symbols that are not shared among connection paths. The difference calculations recurse up and down the structure to determine which ancestors or descendants of the selected symbol to include in returned results. You can also perform an intersection function on these paths in order to identify the symbols common to selected paths. A full up/down will respectively highlight everything either above or below the connected symbols until a root or leaf node is encountered. A step up/down will traverse only one level. These are very effective manipulation techniques for finding commonalties and differences within the data structure. Figure 7.25 shows an Imagix 4D diagram in the explore mode.

The explore mode also supports the ability to filter displays based on selected symbols. You can either isolate or hide selected symbols to refine the content of the display window. This makes it easy to focus your analyses on only those symbols that are important. There is even a way to filter on the relationships (e.g., by sets, calls, etc.).

Additionally, the explore mode allows you to group and ungroup selected symbols. When a set of symbols has been selected and they are grouped together, Imagix 4D requires you to name the new group. A single composite symbol (e.g., a superclass) will then be created to represent all of the symbols selected for inclusion in the group. All of the links connecting symbols in the group are assigned to the new superclass. At any time the grouped symbols can be reverted back to their original status by simply ungrouping them.

Figure 7.25 A sample Imagix 4D display in the explore mode.

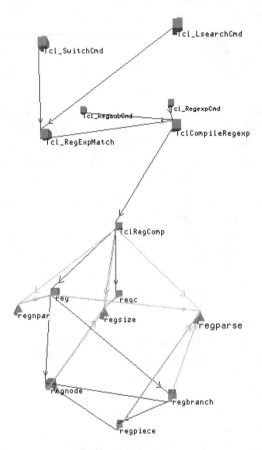

Using Imagix 4D's Analyze Mode

In Imagix 4D's analyze mode, you assume more control over what you view. You determine what portions of the database are relevant to your current problem and you focus the views on that information. Imagix 4D provides a series of analysis submodes showing the quantitative aspects of your data elements. These submodes include number of lines, complexity, number of calls, coverage, time, and frequency. The lines mode shows how many times a function was called; the blocks mode shows the complexity of each function; coverage mode shows how completely each function has been exercised; time mode shows how much time was spent in each function; and frequency mode shows how often each function was executed. Imagix 4D also provides a threshold adjustment method that will let you set the number or percentage of events encountered along with a related scaling factor depending on which submode is chosen. The types of features available in the analyze mode can be used in other domain contexts to help expose different types of patterns and/or unusual connections.

If you want to see a more traditional display format, Imagix 4D has the ability to draw its diagrams using both 3D as well as 2D formats. There are occasions when the 3D diagrams can become complicated and it is sometimes difficult to select individual symbols because of all the layers involved. Imagix 4D supports the ability to transform the inherent 3D formats into 2D representations. Essentially, the display is flattened, making the symbols easier to read. One potential drawback of the 2D renderings is that they occupy much more real estate

Figure 7.26 A 2D representation of an Imagix 4D display.

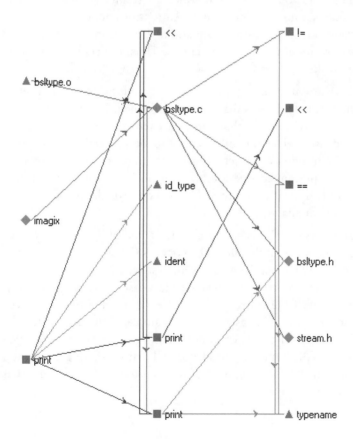

within the display, especially for large diagrams. Figure 7.26 shows an example of a 2D Imagix 4D display.

There are options you can use to define your own views within Imagix 4D by controlling what types of symbols and relationships are shown. There is a very comprehensive menu that allows you to select files, classes, data types, program types, and relationship types as well as connections. Thus, you can focus the displays to reflect exactly the information you need to see.

There is also an AutoQuery function that provides a means by which to instantiate predefined questions. AutoQuery provides a list of prestructured queries that have been defined for targeting different portions of your software (see the sidebar on AutoQuery options). The queries represent the most common types of questions that would typically be of interest during a software analysis or review. The AutoQuery facility can be operated in two modes. The first mode steps you through the selected query and allows you to see the intermediate results as they are generated. In this mode you can see how the individual menu actions build on each other, creating a focused view on the desired information. The second mode is fully autonomous and does not require many interactions. Thus, the results are generated in only a few keystrokes.

The concept of an AutoQuery is very powerful because it helps to put a set of boundaries around the types of analyses that can be performed. This provides more of a structured analytical environment that can be extremely useful for both the novice and experienced users. The capability can also be generalized into other environments where certain types of structural analyses (refer back to Chapter 5) can be encapsulated into precanned queries—all you do is seed it with a target entity of interest. Not only a great time-saver, this method provides a level of consistency while performing an analysis.

Imagix 4D also supports the ability to search through all of the source code to look for particular references within the files. The system's GREP function is encapsulated to make it easy to invoke and be used for analysis and navigation based on results. GREP inquiries can be controlled to include exact case matches, visible symbols, selected symbols, as well the entire project. A search capability of this type also has utility in other domain areas as well. For example, if there were textual abstracts or reports associated with a set of transactions (e.g., message traffic, open source), you could use the GREP function to identify all entities sharing a common set of terms. Thus, when the GREP is initiated, it will consider only those files that meet the defined search criteria.

AutoQuery Options in Imagix 4D

The following is a partial list of several AutoQuery selections available within Imagix 4D. They are grouped here according to their functions.

Function Exploration

What functions directly/indirectly call FunctionX?

What functions are directly/indirectly called by FunctionX?

What functions use TypeX?

What functions contain StringX?

How does main indirectly call FunctionX?

How does FunctionX indirectly call FunctionY?

If FunctionX is used, what files need to be linked?

Variable Exploration

What functions set/read/use VariableX?

What functions are directly/indirectly set/read/used by FunctionX?

What variables are of TypeX?

How does FunctionX indirectly set/read/use VariableY?

Class Exploration

What are the superclasses of ClassX?

What classes are derived from ClassX?

What are the virtual functions of ClassX?

What classes override FunctionX?

Which classes contain or declare a function named FunctionX?

If ClassX is used, what classes will be linked?

Build Exploration

What files include FileX?

What files are necessary to build TargetX?

Continued

AutoQuery Options in Imagix 4D (*Continued*)

What directories contain files to build TargetX?

What header files include other header files?

Why does FileX include FileY?

If FileX changes, what files need to be rebuilt?

File Exploration

What files are owned by UserX?

What files have changed since DateX?

What files owned by UserX have changed since DateY?

Which files contain a program element named Prog_ElemX?

Where are all the source files?

Where are all the header files?

Miscellaneous

Where are all the source browser databases?

Where are all the 4D projects?

Generating Imagix 4D Output

Part of the utility of a visualization system such as Imagix 4D is its ability to generate a set of report files. Many of the other systems described in this section rely solely on the output of their visual displays. Incorporating a set of formatted reports to complement the displays can dramatically enhance the interpretation and acceptance of the results by your target audience. Even though Imagix 4D is geared heavily towards the documentation of software code, this type of application can have far-reaching effects into other domain areas. Several different types of reports can be generated within Imagix 4D, including:

- File summary reports showing how many C, C++, and header files were used in the project broken down by directory structure.

- File information reports containing the name, location, size, owner, and dates of the different files in use.

- Class summary reports listing a high-level summary of class locations.

- Function information reports that have data on the names, complexity, locations, and calling routines.

- Several Year 2000 reports containing synopses of time and date related components within the source code. This is an effective way to see the extent of any programming changes for Y2K development efforts.

Documentation can be run against the entire project or it can be produced using only a selected subset. Both methods are specified using forms that tell Imagix 4D what types of reports to generate and how they should be formatted. Imagix 4D supports a rich text format (RTF) that is useful for generating hardcopy output. Thus, you can import the information into a word processor for further refinement or formatting purposes. Additionally, Imagix 4D can generate an HTML format so you can create online documentation. Since all of the relationships are defined within an Imagix 4D project, the HTML format can support hypertext links among the different files, function calls, class summaries, or whatever information is being documented. The format of the HTML output can be based on a section or symbol that lets you determine how to divide the document into files. Also Imagix 4D can produce a straight ASCII file format if desired. Many options are available within the documentation functions and they can be used to customize your reports.

Imagix 4D and the Year 2000

Since the data used within an Imagix 4D environment are derived from the software programs themselves, it forms a perfect environment for dealing with the Year 2000 date issues that are causing concern throughout corporate America. We have all become aware of how critical it is to update and modify existing legacy systems to handle the conversion from two- to four-digit century dates (e.g., 98 → 1998). Severe consequences could result from the misinterpretation of 00 as 1900 rather than 2000. This can lead to problems in virtually every industry, especially finance and transportation, which rely especially heavily on the use of schedules. Fortunately, this issue has already been addressed within the Imagix 4D environment. The Imagix 2000 tool is an add-on to Imagix 4D that addresses millennium-related problems in software systems. It helps users locate potential date-related types and variables in their software, assess whether they might cause a Year 2000 problem, determine how widely they are being used, and analyze how best to correct them.

Imagix 2000 leverages the existing Imagix 4D database, query, and visualization technologies. Imagix 2000 is specifically composed of several different add-on modules that extend the core capabilities of Imagix 4D including the Year 2000 filter, the Year 2000 browser, and the Year 2000 report. The Year 2000 filter is responsible for searching the source code (which is represented within the database maintained by Imagix 4D) for all symbols that meet user-specified name pattern criteria. The resulting symbols are then passed along for use by the browser and the reporter. The Year 2000 browser provides a variety of mechanisms for viewing the identified symbols. For a given symbol, you can see the composition of the symbol, the scope of the symbol's use, and where the symbol actually is directly or indirectly used. Results are viewable both in list form and as graphic displays. The Year 2000 report generates a summary for each of the identified symbols. The report can then be used to determine which symbols are most widely used, and thereby focus assessment. There is a section discussing the Imagix 2000 system within the online tutorial supplied by Imagix 4D.

Daisy

Daisy is a unique visualization tool that is very easy to use and requires little set-up to become operational. Daisy stands for Data AnalysIS InteractivelY and has been developed by a small firm located in England. The program was originally named for an English Setter owned by one of the company executives. Daisy (the software) has been around for several years and has been applied to a wide range of interesting problems. Some of these include analyzing delays in the London Underground, checking the relations among equipment faults in a large engine factory, analyzing the usage of telephone systems, looking at the results of wine tasting evaluations, reviewing faults within software programs, and finally predicting the outcomes of horse races.

In its current incarnation Daisy will run under all of the different Windows operating platforms. Daisy supports data access from ASCII files, Excel spreadsheets, Access, FoxPro, dBase, and Focus Master Files. There are several sized versions of Daisy available for use depending on how you expect to use the system. There is a full-fledged ODBC compliant version that provides numerous options and extensive processing capabilities, a standard version that supports creation of displays for visual analysis, and a Daisy-lite version that has been designed so that it works in conjunction (or is incorporated) with other programs. To provide a feeling for how much data can be processed by Daisy, the standard version can support up to 250,000 records and create 30,000 nodes with an equal number of links. There can be up to nine separate workspaces active at any one time within Daisy, thereby allowing you to generate multiple diagrams to compare and contrast where appropriate.

A tutorial supplied with Daisy will help you understand many of the features being offered. The tutorial is also intended to expose you to the many different variations of Daisy charts that can be generated. The tutorial is run as a separate application that manages the different scenarios presented within Daisy. It provides a good overview of what the tool can do and it depicts its use in a variety of applications. Daisy also has a fairly extensive set of help files that can prove useful when learning about some of the specific options and specialized features.

Manipulating Your Data in Daisy

Daisy supports the concept of projects in order to manage its data sets and related files. All data files, SQL scripts, and project descriptions are organized around projects. Projects can extend the contents of their data sets through a variety of commands including arithmetic values and field extensions. The application of arithmetic values to a field is fairly straightforward. However, you can get a lot more functionality and value-added if you use field extensions in the data set. There are over 80 field extension functions available within Daisy and they include features such as data cleansing, string replacement, uppercase conversions, selection of lowest/highest values, and the like. There are also over 25 logical functions that can be used within a project. Logical functions return true/false or 0/1 values when performing calculations such as alphanumeric comparisons, null field checks, and range bounding. A project also provides previous/next record functions that make it easy for you to skip ahead or go backwards in the data file. There are also functions contained within this list that are used for cleaning up the data set.

Data values can also be manipulated with mapping functions. Table 7.1 shows the functions that are available for performing mapping (e.g., translating, transforming, and adding value to data). When you review this list, you will notice that many of these functions perform a metadata extraction. Thus, when a new field is created based on the output of one of these functions, its value represents a tangible new piece of information rather than just some scaling factor or combination of values. You may recall the date and address examples that we described in Chapter 2 in which metadata were created from similar abstractions.

Information Layout in Daisy

The overall concept of Daisy is fairly simple. You can use it to create charts that enable you to see relationships between different groupings of data records. The formats used by Daisy follow a circular layout of nodes that are interconnected with linkages. For each node, there can also be an associated histogram that is presented around its perimeter. Figure 7.27 depicts a typical Daisy chart. The nodes that are used to create the bands or groups that form the circle are based on the fields that have been mapped into the application. Each band represents a different field from

Table 7.1 Daisy Data Mapping Functions

AfterChars	AllAlpha	AllNumeric	AMPM	BeforeChars	Billions
Currency	Day	DayofWeek	EMailAccount	EmailAddress	EMailDscripton
EMailDomain	FileExtension	FileName	FirstCharacter	FirstName	FirstWord
Fixed	Fraction	Hour	Hundreds	Initials	Integer
LastCharacter	LastDigit	LastTwoDigits	LastWord	LeadAlpha	LeadNumeric
LongDate	LongTime	MediumDate	MediumTime	Millions	Minute
Month	MonthYear	OddEven	PhoneArea	PhoneCountry	PhoneExchange
PostcodeArea	PrviousMonday	PrviousSunday	QtrYear	Scientific	Second
ShortDate	ShortTime	ShortPostcode	Sign	Soundex	Standard
StreetName	StreetNumber	StrippedName	Tens	Thousands	TrailAlpha
TrailNumeric	VehRegLetter	VehRegYear	Year		

Figure 7.27 A sample Daisy chart (without histograms).

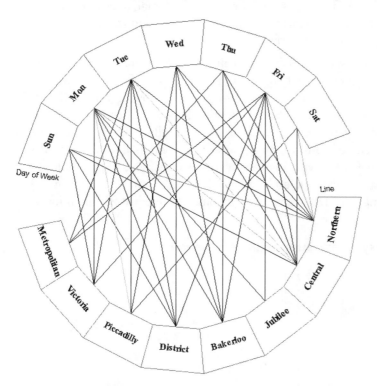

the selected data set and each node within a group depicts a unique value for that field. Thus, there are as many nodes in a group as there are discrete values for a field. The number of groups is controlled through a display options menu.

Links are established within a Daisy chart when two values are concurrently observed within a single data record. The number of observations in the data set can determine the style of the links. For example, Daisy supports the ability to set the lowest 10 percent valued links to a gray color, which essentially emulates a dotted line, as well as to show the top 10 percent as a double-thick line that is easily distinguishable within the display.

Aggregating Data in Daisy

Within the standard charting window there is also an option for aggregating values. Since any node within a Daisy chart will usually be comprised of multiple records, the aggregated value is the statistical function (e.g., largest, median, average, negate, etc.) applied against all of the values for all of the records used to comprise the node. This information is used to construct the histograms that appear on the outer perimeter of the nodes. Through the histogram options window you can take any aggregated value and present it in the chart.

A variety of options are available for scaling and displaying aggregated values. In addition to any user-defined aggregations, there are two that are system-defined—number-of-records and number-of-links. The presentation styles of the histograms can also be altered to meet your specific needs. There are methods for merging histograms together into a continuous graph, filling the histograms with a color, adding borders to the histograms, presenting them as lines instead of bars, and even annotating them with their associated values. The height, radius, and scales of the histograms can also all be adjusted as well. Figures 7.28 through 7.31 show several examples of Daisy charts using some of these histogram options.

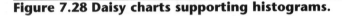

Figure 7.28 Daisy charts supporting histograms.

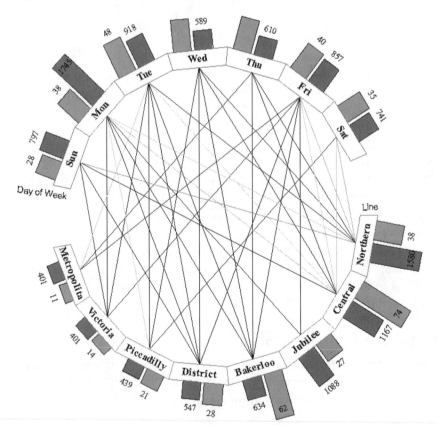

Figure 7.29 Daisy charts with extended histograms.

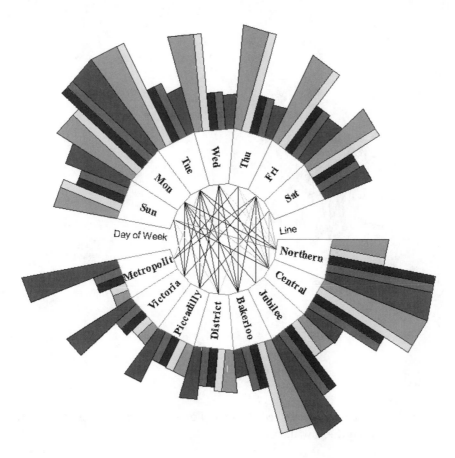

Navigating the Daisy Display

The Daisy displays can be manipulated by zooming, panning, and fitting to screen. Any node within a Daisy chart can be investigated or profiled by simply selecting it to show a summary of its makeup. A profile window contains the name of the selected node, its associated grouping, how many records and links it represents, plus any aggregated values (e.g., total duration, distance, amount, etc.). Keep in mind that any node presented within a Daisy chart represents an index to all of the records that share that value, so node data reflect an aggregated value. There are also buttons that allow you to move on to the next node (clockwise) or visit the previous node (counter-clockwise) within the circular display. Additionally, there are buttons that can be selected to show both the underlying records and links in

Figure 7.30 Daisy charts using line connections.

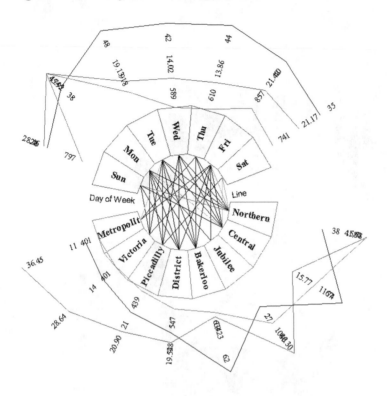

separate windows using a spreadsheet format. For the record entries, all of the fields contained within the raw data are shown.

Using the Standard Draw Option in Daisy

There are essentially two methods that can be used to generate the charts—a standard draw and a quick draw. The standard draw presents a menu that manages all of the different charting commands. The main emphasis of this menu is on the selection of what are called mapping fields. These fields are the attributes or column entries defined for each record within the data set. Daisy charts can be generated with the selection of at least one but no more than ten mapping fields. Each mapping field is displayed according to its type (e.g., text, date, time, or numeric) and a format used to display the node labels.

A range of display formats can be used depending on the type of data being presented. Many of these are based on the mapping functions previously presented

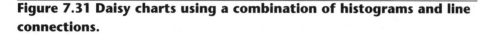

Figure 7.31 Daisy charts using a combination of histograms and line connections.

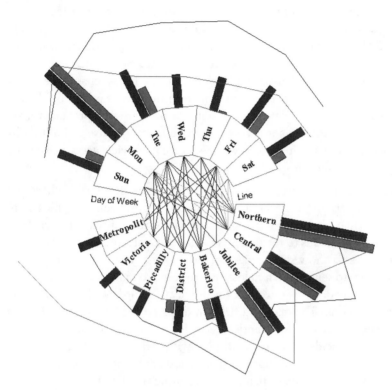

within the table. Control of the look and feel of the nodes is accomplished through a subwindow. Depending on the type of data being presented, you can control the display of missing or erroneous values, the case of the label, the length of text, value limits, and several other options. The process of mapping fields is very straightforward and can be accomplished with the click of a button.

The information within a chart can also be filtered to show more focused data sets. Through a variety of node and link filters within the standard draw options you can set the number or percentages of records and links to display within the chart. These can have both lower and upper bounds associated with them in addition to weights. Records can also be selected from the command menu through point-and-click interfaces, simple queries based on type of data, and whether or not they are displayed. The results of these actions produce a spreadsheet of data showing the processed record formats, or through other methods they can be hidden from the display.

Using the Quick Draw Option in Daisy

The second method of generating a Daisy chart is through a quick menu inter-face. The quick menu takes you through an uncomplicated set-up procedure, in much the same way as an agent or wizard would help you define parameters in other programs. The quick menu requests that you create a new chart, use an old chart, or base your display on a preexisting template. Since there are many options that you have control over while generating a Daisy chart, the quick menu makes it very easy to specify how the resulting diagrams should look through a few simple menu selections. The quick menus are comprehensive, yet they are easy to understand. This is a very attractive feature to use when initially setting up a project or generating a new Daisy chart. Novice users can create some elaborate charts using this method.

One of the first things that the quick menu asks for is the type of chart you want to create. There are five general options you can choose from including stan-dard, duplicate, circular, date/time, and summary. The standard selection will pro-duce charts that map the fields to the nodes arranged in an arc and it will draw links in between the nodes to show the strength of the linkage. In a submenu, you are given the opportunity to select which fields you are going to map into the chart. The duplicate selection provides a way to look for duplicate records within the data set that match certain criteria. The mapping fields in this scenario are combined into a single text string used to search for identical records. Thus, the node key represents a composite of all the fields selected for display within the data set. The circular selection provides some additional options that include drawing one node for each record, drawing a selected database field, or aggregating the data to a set of nodes. The date/time summary will generate a chart that is based on the day of the week and the hour of the day. The summary selection is similar to the duplicate selection function, except that is uses all records within the data set.

Customizing Displays in Daisy

There are many other features that can be customized within Daisy. For example, you can customize the initialization screen. There are options to set the screen sizes, check international spelling, manage operating system differences, and sev-eral others. There are also summarization interfaces that give you an overview of your current project. These provide entries for such things as the database names, mapping fields, aggregation fields, number of records, number of linkages, and total nodes. Font styles and sizes can all be adjusted in terms of their alignment to the displays.

Other Link Analysis Systems

In this section we present brief descriptions of a few more link analysis systems. Some of these were developed for specialized applications such as law enforcement, insurance fraud, or telecommunications. Nevertheless, by now you should be able to appreciate that this does not necessarily limit the utility of a tool in other application areas. These tools are viable data mining systems that should be considered if you are interested in performing link analysis functions. The list of tools presented in this section in no way completes the list of link analysis packages available within the marketplace. There are undoubtedly systems being developed within university environments, research facilities, and by commercial vendors that perform similar tasks, and you should always keep an eye out for new developments.

ORION Systems

There is a suite of products offered by ORION Scientific Systems that were developed for use within the law enforcement community. They are configured to run under different operating platforms including the Web, Windows, and UNIX. The ORION line of products has been designed largely with the nontechnical user in mind. The interfaces are simple and their operations are straightforward. There are several different products offered by ORION including GangNet, NETLEADS, and ORIONLEADS (Law Enforcement Analysis Data System). There is also ORIONQA, which is a remote data entry application for collecting information while in the field. The following are descriptions for several of the tools being offered by ORION.

ORIONLink

ORIONLink follows an Anacapa format (see Chapter 5) where people are represented as circles and connected with edges to other circles, squares, diamonds, and triangles. The color-coding used in ORIONLink is unique because it colors the circles based on shared attributes, such as group/organizational membership or event association. Thus, every person who is a member of multiple groups or who has been involved in the several events will have several different colored pie-wedges in the display. Objects sharing the same color share the same value of an attribute. ORIONLink can be used to draw boxes automatically around nodes to show cell, intra-group or incident functions, and relationships. The ORIONLink displays are fully interactive and objects can be moved, grouped, and the diagram annotated with text and symbols. ORIONLink has also been outfitted with several special features including an "associations" mode that will highlight all of the associates of a selected person, a "what if" mode to hide/restore various objects and their connections, and the "show articulations" mode that is used to highlight all "keynodes" in the display which, if removed, would have a significant impact on the connectivity of the structure. Figure 7.32 shows an example of an ORIONLink display.

ORIONPhoneToll

ORIONPhoneToll focuses exclusively on the analysis of telephone data. It comes configured with a set of filters for the most common telephone company toll data and Dialed Number Recorder (DNR) formats, but you can also customize your own filters (e.g., data load formats). ORIONPhoneToll uses a datasheet tool, similar to a spreadsheet, to sort the phone calls and display their content. This provides a way to create reports using histogram representations to show the frequency of counts between pairs of phone numbers. Frequency counts can be

Figure 7.32 A sample ORIONLink display.

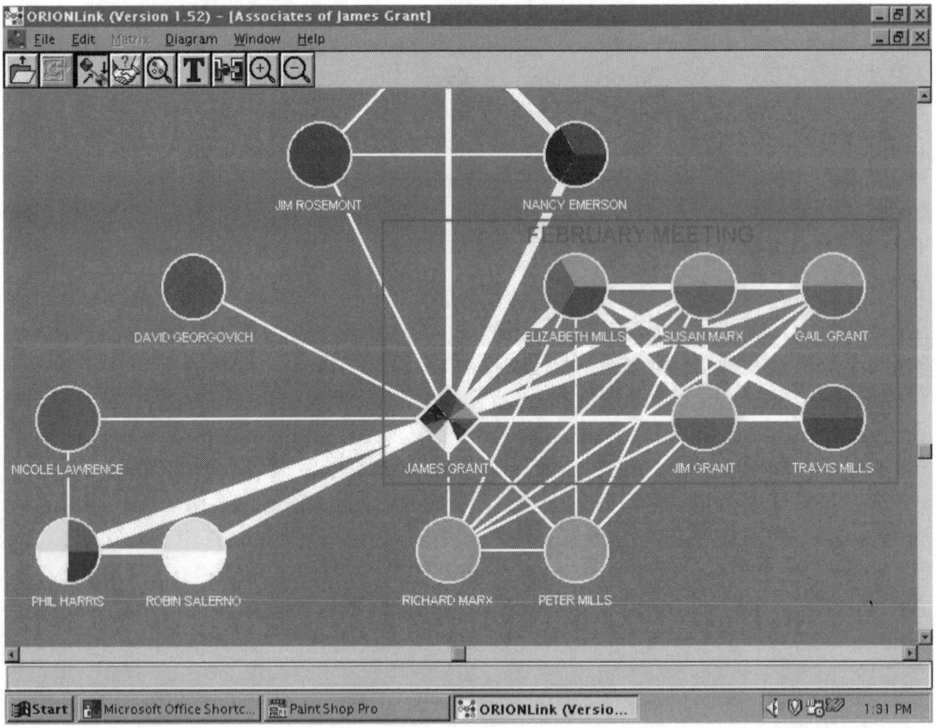

based on area codes, times of day, days of week, and so forth. Several other features supported within ORIONPhoneToll include a variety of parsing routines for supporting caller id, credit card calls, pager numbers, international calls, long distance access calls, and more. There are also interfaces to several "Subscriber CD" libraries, which provide automatic name (white pages) lookup on all published numbers. ORIONPhoneToll can import data from ASCII files, FOIMS, and DBF formats. ORIONPhoneToll has been designed to work with ORIONLink so that you can produce link charts based on the results of your analyses.

ORIONInvestigations

ORIONInvestigations is a tool for tracking and analyzing crimes based on case information collected about different events, groups, people, and vehicles. It is mainly a database application that collects and stores details about known facts and leads relating to a crime scene. ORIONInvestigations uses a series of forms to solicit its input and it comes configured with three security levels (supervisor, clerk, and data entry) to control how data sets are created and accessed within the system. It also has a filter wizard that looks for related records based on similar selection criteria. There is a reporting facility that generates various outputs including materials related to a specific crime or contents of any specific record (e.g., form). ORIONInvestigations can also be combined with ORIONLink to visualize the content of the database.

ORIONVIA

Visual Investigative Analysis (VIA), also called ORIONVIA, is used to chart the series of events associated with a crime. These charts are based on plotting the known facts or descriptive summaries along a time line for different data elements (e.g., people, groups, vehicles, etc.). Figure 7.33 shows an example of an ORIONVIA diagram. Its main purpose is to help investigators analyze the connections among fragmented bits of data to see where there are missing values, unknown facts, or common patterns that exist among different events. ORIONVIA employs standard charting symbols such as triangles to represent the first/last events of an activity, circles to represent entities, and diamonds to signify the point in time in which a decision was made. There are a variety of features offered by ORIONVIA including the ability to create what are called "bursts", which correspond to the initiation of multiple events and "merges" which combine several activities into a single event. The ORIONVIA diagrams can be annotated with text, symbols, and icons. Collateral information such as graphics, photographs, video images, sounds, documents, and databases files can be attached to the charts.

Figure 7.33 An ORIONVIA diagram.

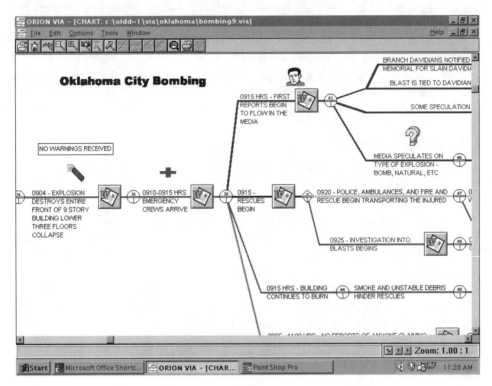

Watson

The Watson system developed by Harlequin Group plc., in the United Kingdom, is a visualization approach targeted largely at the law enforcement community. Watson currently runs across all Windows-based platforms and it supports several connection and import features that are used to acquire data from a variety of sources. The system supports a diverse set of features including a Visualization by Query (VBQ) methodology, which means that you graphically specify your target object such as a person, event, organization, vehicle, and so on. The system then checks its underlying data set to supply all of the relevant information regarding the specified object(s). This is analogous to the reactive analysis approach discussed in Chapter 3. Any selected data are then presented in charts that show the different objects and their relationships to each other. All objects are represented from a large selection of icons that are included as part of the system. See Figure 7.34 for a sample screen generated by Watson.

Figure 7.34 A Watson link analysis chart. (Copyright ©1998 of Harlequin Group plc. Reprinted with permission.)

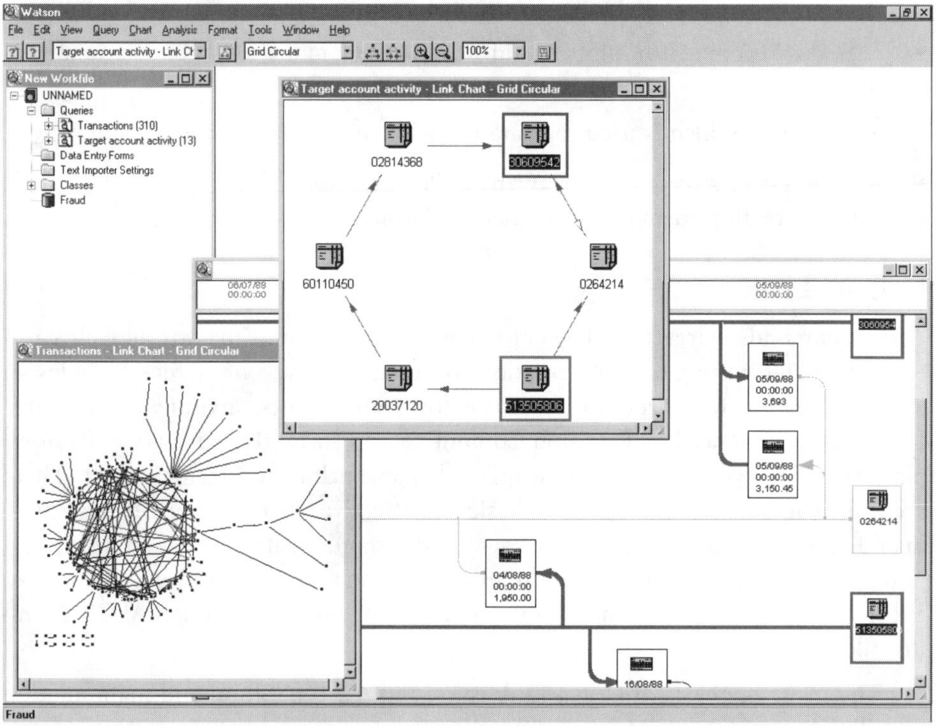

Watson supports the definition of attributes associated with the objects within a chart. These attributes can be used to set one of the display styles for the objects, such as color or icons. They also form the foundation for searching the data for specific conditions. Any objects or links present within the display that match the desired conditions can be selected and/or isolated. Manipulation of display features based on attributes allows you to control the focus of your charts and present as much or as little information as you need. There is also a feature to generate the most direct link (e.g., shortest path) that exists between two objects. Watson is also outfitted with the ability to present a complete audit trail for any analysis. This is very important because you can use it to justify how conclusions were reached as well as to try out alternative scenarios by backtracking to prior states or avenues previously explored. Furthermore, Watson contains a timeline representation that allows you to see when events occurred and if there is commonality among the charted objects.

Watson can be seamlessly integrated with other Harlequin Intelligence products:

- CaseCall, used to manage telephone information
- PowerCase for managing the information and resources of an investigation
- Watson Mapping for plotting information on maps and geopositional diagrams
- Watson Pro, which is used for data modeling and database integration

(Harlequin Intelligence, Watson, Watson Pro, Watson Mapping, CaseCall, and PowerCase are all trademarks of Harlequin Group plc.)

Crime Link

This system is also targeted at law enforcement organizations that are actively gathering data and putting case information together. This type of system provides an ideal application for corporate security offices and related investigations. Crime Link is being produced by Precision Computing and currently runs under Windows platforms. The system uses an Anacapa-style approach to representing data. There are link diagrams, matrices, and a basic yet effective set of options by which to manipulate the data. Crime Link is structured around creating a case that can support illustrative details such as case number, investigator, and description. Data can either be created manually through its interfaces or imported though ASCII delimited files.

The main emphasis of Crime Link is around the generation and manipulation of its link diagrams. Any of the objects (defined to be people) present within the display can be moved around easily, linked together, or removed from view. Keeping with Anacapa representation styles, people are represented as circles and can be related to one another through different types of linkages. Confirmed links are depicted as solid lines, suspected links are dashed lines, and they can be drawn with an arrowhead indicating the direction of the link. Within Crime Link, a person can have a name (last, first, middle), an alias, a deceased flag, and a short descriptive text field. Simply selecting a person or any object within the display will bring up its profile so you can see these values. If an alias is being used, it is displayed inside a new intersecting circle and it will contain the alias name identified.

Entities within Crime Link are considered to be anything that does not represent an individual. So things like organizations, identification numbers, locations, and so forth are represented as rectangles. Individuals related to these entities are shown inside the rectangles. If there is more than one person within a rectangle, they are assumed to be related and therefore no linkages are shown. One interesting feature of Crime Link is that when a person object is being moved around the screen and it is contained within a rectangle, the rectangle will resize itself according to where the object is moved. Thus, people always remain inside their respective boxes. Figure 7.35 shows an example of a sample Crime Link diagram with several people and entities being depicted.

When a Crime Link diagram is generated, there is a set of rules that it tries to enforce with respect to how the data objects are presented. Positioning algorithms avoid crossing lines and overlapping objects. Objects violating positioning rules are displayed in red. There are also several filter features available within Crime Link that can be used to manipulate the link displays. The filter selection is done using a list of available data elements.

Another feature available within Crime Link is the ability to generate a two-dimensional cross-correlational matrix that is often used to show more detailed relationships between people. The cells of the matrix show symbols representing the type of relationship existing between the cells' corresponding column and row elements. A filled circle is used if the relationship is known, whereas a hollow circle signifies that the nature of the relationship is suspected. Implied relationships are shown with filled squares. Figure 7.36 shows an example of a cross links matrix in Crime Link.

Figure 7.35 A Crime Link display showing people and entities.

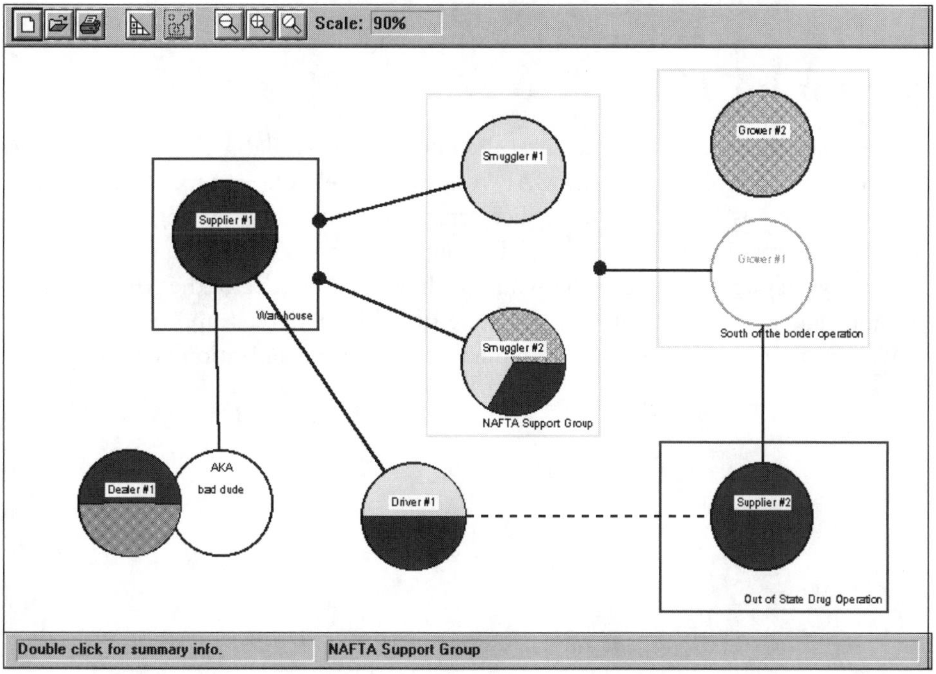

Figure 7.36 An example of a cross links matrix in Crime Link.

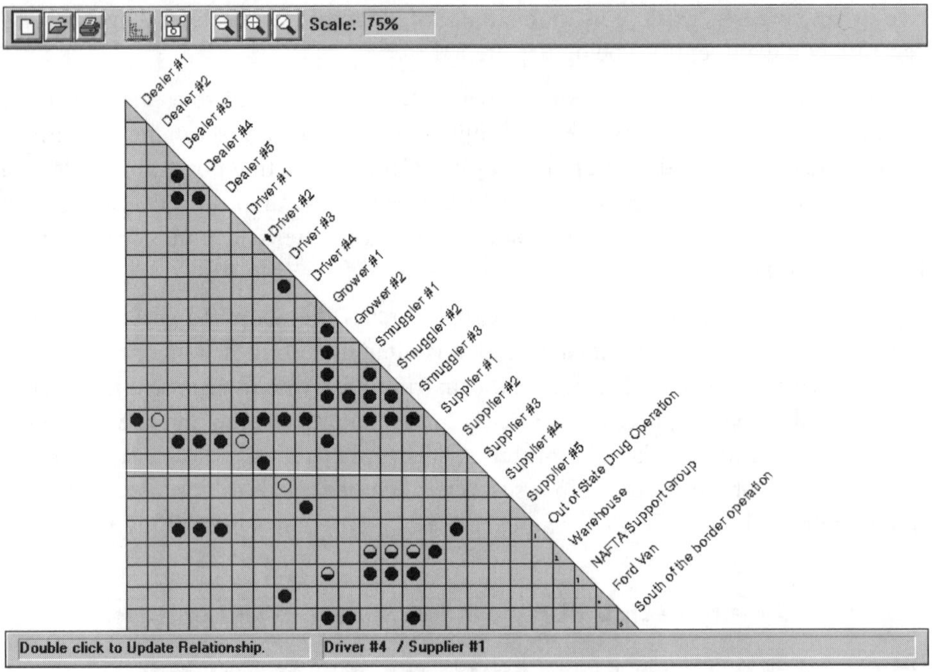

Summing Up

In this chapter we have covered several commercially available link analysis tools, placing special emphasis on NETMAP, Analyst's Notebook, Imagix 4D, and Daisy. All of these tools have been used successfully in visual data mining engagements across a variety of problem domains. Having seen the types of displays available in link analysis systems, we hope that you now have a better idea of the types of analyses and data structures that are well suited to this analytical approach. We now move on to our next class of tools, namely landscape visualization systems.

LANDSCAPE VISUALIZATION TOOLS

Introduction

The second class of visualization tools that we are covering in this section are ones that emphasize the use of landscape visualization schemes in order to support data analysis. When we use the term "landscape" we do not simply refer to geospatial maps, although maps are one form of landscape visualization. Rather, we use the term more generally to describe environments in which data are placed within geometrically bound terrains. A critical feature of landscape visualizations is that the relative positioning of data elements within the geometric terrain is used to represent information that is important to the analysis. Landscape visualization systems typically use abstract representations in interactive, immersive, 3D virtual environments to display large quantities of data. Landscapes can be used effectively in a proactive analysis mode to expose high-level trends within complex data sets. This is usually accomplished by navigating the landscapes and visually orienting the data to reveal hidden biases. As it happens, some of the tools that have been developed using landscape visualization paradigms are also geared toward support of real-time applications. The displays created for real-time data feeds are often very powerful in their presentation of parametric values using animation and simulation techniques. In this chapter we cover what we believe to be the most fully developed and fielded systems currently available in the commercial market. As always, our list is not exhaustive, but the descriptions of these tools should give you a good overview of the types of systems available to support landscape visualizations for data mining. In this chapter we review MineSet 2.0, Metaphor Mixer, In3D, and other similar tools.

MineSet 2.0

Silicon Graphics is the developer and manufacturer of the MineSet tool suite. This is a system that supports the analysis of information by integrating a wide variety of analytical approaches and visualization. MineSet is based on a client-server architecture that supports scalability and fast database access. Although the capabilities of MineSet are quite extensive, we focus here on its visualization capabilities, particularly with respect to landscape visualization. A more complete list of capabilities is provided in the sidebar "Analytical Functions Supported by MineSet 2.0." (For an overview of the complete scope of MineSet's capabilities not covered in this chapter, see the MineSet 2.0 documentation provided by Silicon Graphics.)

Analytical Functions Supported by MineSet 2.0

Although this section focuses on the visualization capabilities of MineSet, there is an extensive set of other analytical functions that may be invoked during a data mining engagement using this tool. Many of these functions are used to prepare the data for use within the visualizations provided by MineSet. In fact, these functions are responsible for a variety of tasks that include figuring out what type of data to present and determining how to present it (e.g., layout of the data). The majority of these functions are:

- Association rule generation
- Classifier induction of decision trees and evidence (Simple Bayes classifiers)
- Automatic accuracy estimation (holdout and cross-validation)
- Automatic attribute discretization (binning)
- Integrated input from data access and transformation facility
- Node-splitting criteria for decision tree induction
- Pruning factors for decision tree induction
- Laplace correction for evidence induction
- Automatic feature selection for evidence induction
- Data holdout percentage for accuracy estimation
- Loss matrices
- Lift curves
- Scoring and weights

MineSet's visualization capabilities are very impressive. The overall look and feel of MineSet as well as the functionality it provides makes it a well-integrated environment for performing complex data analyses. The MineSet system takes full advantage of the high-end graphics available on Silicon Graphics workstations by providing extremely interactive 3D visualizations of the data. The system offers at least five unique visualization methods that can provide multiple views onto the data being analyzed. Additionally, there are a variety of analytical data mining tools that generate models that can be viewed using MineSet's visualizers. Many of these are listed in the previously mentioned sidebar. MineSet is not just a collection of attractive visualizations; rather, think of it as a comprehensive data mining environment where many of the underlying data preparation and feature extraction functions are built right into the system.

MineSet currently runs only on Silicon Graphics workstations, which are specialized, high-end, graphic machines. There have been discussions of porting MineSet to other platforms. However at the time of this writing, no other platforms were supported. MineSet can be run using a client/server interface in which a Silicon Graphics server is coupled to your network running some type of X-Windows emulation software that supports OpenGL. This allows the MineSet screens to be posted or broadcast to PC displays. Notwithstanding, the Silicon Graphics hardware still has to be present somewhere in the loop. The system also requires a significant amount of memory to operate, upwards of 96 megabytes.

There are a wide range of functions to work with in MineSet, and Silicon Graphics has done an excellent job of integrating all of these separate components into a single analytical environment. MineSet is composed of three primary software subsystems that are used to control, manipulate, and display data. The Tool Manager is a centralized control module that helps manage the invocation of the other tools within MineSet. There is also a DataMover that coordinates the access and manipulation of the data being analyzed. The data mining and visualization tools make up the rest of the system. MineSet supports a range of different analytical approaches that have been encapsulated under a single interface control that can be used within a data mining context. Although each of these systems could realistically be operated independently of one another, say for specialized applications, together they form a well-integrated system to support complex data mining activities.

Operating the Tool Manager and DataMover

The Tool Manager controls the entire MineSet system and user input to each of the different modules. It has been designed to coordinate access to data including submission of queries, and supports some data transformations. The Tool Manager is also responsible for creating the specific configuration files required by each tool to utilize the data. It is the central launch point for any of the other modules available within MineSet. Figure 8.1 shows a sample of a typical Tool Manager interface. As you can see, there are a wide range of features and functions supported by the Tool Manager, although detailed descriptions are not within the scope of this discussion. We provide brief descriptions of the more important features offered by the Tool Manager.

To start interaction with MineSet, connection is established with the DataMover. The DataMover is a process that runs on the server where the data are stored to retrieve the information requested by the Tool Manager. There are five different data-format access mechanisms. As in all data mining systems, data can be accessed from binary and flat ASCII files. Additionally, there are special drivers for Oracle, Informix, and Sybase. These drivers are very specific to the databases they interact with and are specially designed to connect to MineSet. To function properly, there can be good deal of overhead involved in setting up these drivers, their environments, and the secondary databases so that the DataMover can function properly.

Figure 8.1 MineSet's Tool Manager interface.

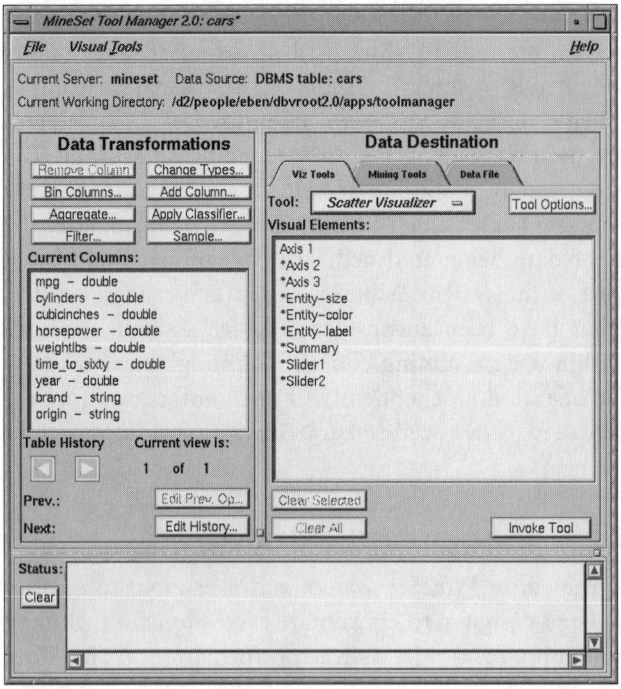

Once the data are identified, extracted and returned by the DataMover, the Tool Manager can be used to clean up the raw data before it is processed by one of the other modules. The Tool Manager has several data transformation methods that can be used for these purposes (see Figure 8.1). There are methods available to remove columns of data, bin columns to group values of data, aggregate values (sum, min, max, average), filter to select subsets of data, change data types, add new columns based on mathematical expressions, and sample a random subset of data. These data transformation methods are important for fine-tuning your data set to better reflect patterns expected in your application.

From here, the Tool Manager can be used to select the destination application targeted for the data. There are a variety of choices to be made including saving the intermediate results to a file, passing them off to one of the visualization methods, or further refining them through one of the algorithmic data mining subsystems. There is no preset course of action to follow when using the Tool Manager. It is up to you to determine what data to acquire, how it should be processed, and how to finally present it. Depending on the choices made, the Tool Manager keeps a history log to track all of the actions performed within the system. This log shows the different operations performed on the data and even depicts the resulting data structures. This log is visually represented within the Tool Manager in a flow diagram that can be used to regenerate or justify the analytical process. Essentially, it provides a visualization of the analysis process so you can see what transformations have occurred and which subsystems were invoked for any of the results produced by MineSet.

Interacting with Visual Displays in MineSet

MineSet takes full advantage of the graphical power offered by Silicon Graphics workstations. A variety of visual tools can be used to depict data, ranging from tree-structures and pie-diagrams to data-grids and spatial-mappings. The power of MineSet comes from its ability to support different visualization formats in an environment that includes interfaces that provide simple control and navigation of the data. All of the visualization tools in MineSet require their own unique configuration files that are used to map raw data into a format understood by the respective tool. We will describe each tool as if it were invoked from the Tool Manager, but bear in mind that any one of these can be run independently from the rest of the system as well.

Each tool supports many customization options in terms of relative size, height, width, and color manipulations. There are also facilities for filtering, range selection, threshold definition, value aggregation, and other classification methods.

There are just simply too many support options to cover within this text. For the record, Silicon Graphics was very thorough when they designed the MineSet visualization tools, as is reflected in each of the following descriptions. The following subsections describe the Tree Visualizer, Scatter Visualizer, Map Visualizer, Splat Visualizer, and Evidence Visualizer. There are also Statistics and Record Viewer modules, but they are used more for administrative or verification purposes. A detailed description of their capabilities will not be presented here.

Using the Tree Visualizer

The Tree Visualizer is a three-dimensional display that depicts the information contained in your data set in a hierarchical fashion (see Figure 8.2). The Tree Visualizer can be invoked from the Tool Manager's main screen. It is here that the different display dimensions are selected and configured. You are responsible for setting each of the options to an available variable. Once generated, each branch point in the tree represents a node within the data structure that can have a subset of variables (or attributes) displayed as bar charts. These bar charts convey summary information in terms of height and color for all data points represented by all subsumed structures of the branch. The summary statistic can be set as the average, minimum, maximum, or count of a selected variable. Depending on what variables are being shown, you can quickly ascertain a picture of the distribution of data points within

Figure 8.2 A Tree Visualizer hierarchy in MineSet.

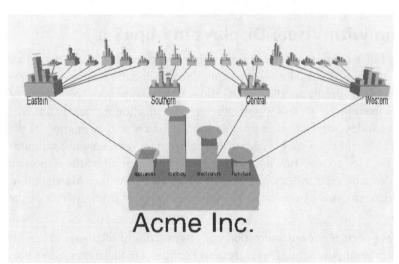

the tree structure. The Tree Visualizer uses dynamic expansion, which allows it to handle large trees. The tree will continually expand itself to show more detail as you approach its endpoints (or leaf-nodes). Thus, for very large trees, the degree of resolution presented is dependent on your viewpoint within the display. This visualization method supports 3D rotation, drill-down, and a host of other features. Some of the options available in the Tree Visualizer are listed in the sidebar.

Options Available in MineSet's Tree Visualizer

Key-Bar. Represents the way that the bar charts are specified on each of the branch nodes. For each unique value encountered within the variable selected, there is a corresponding bar within the chart produced on top of each node. An example of a variable used here might include categories of foods found in a supermarket (e.g., fruits, vegetables, cheese, meats, etc.).

Height-Bar. Specifies the height/length of each individual bar within the chart. The bigger the value, the higher the corresponding bar. This option could be assigned to the actual sales figures for a particular month, stock performance, and so on.

Height-Disk. Supports the value used to fix the height of the floating disks that can optionally be associated with each of the bars in the chart. As an example you could assign projected sales estimates to the height of the disk to see if the actual values are above or below expectations.

Height-Base. The size of the branch-node can convey value information as well. The height of the node corresponds to the value associated with this display element.

Color-Bar/Disk/Base. The colors of each of the different display elements can be assigned to a particular variable.

Sort By. Allows a particular column to be selected where its values are used to sort the layout of the display nodes.

Hierarchy Root Level. Controls which data element is used as the seed point from which to grow the hierarchy. There are also additional controls for defining any of the subhierarchies within the tree structure.

The Tree Visualizer also has the ability to "spotlight" objects within the display. This is a very interesting technique that gives the appearance of beacons of light shining down from the heavens (e.g., from the top of the display). Spotlighting is used to display the results of either a search (colored yellow) or the selection of an object (colored white). There is a separate interface used to define the parameters of a search. Figure 8.3 shows an example of a Tree Visualizer display utilizing the spotlighting feature to show a set of objects that have been identified through a search. As you can see, the use of spotlighting can quickly make objects of interest noticeable within the display.

The Tree Visualizer can also provide an overview of the landscape it produces. Some of the hierarchies displayed within the Tree Visualizer can become quite large, depicting hundreds of branch nodes. Navigating these large structures in a head-on fly-by sequence can be time consuming and arduous. This limitation can be overcome by switching to the overhead view. In a separate window, a complete overview of the entire hierarchy is presented as a flat two-dimensional display, with an X marking your current spot within the main Tree Visualizer display. All objects are active within this overview display and selecting them will drive your main Tree Visualizer interface to respond accordingly. Finally, you can mark an object with a flag. Thus you can identify important locations that you may want to utilize later on. Figure 8.4 shows the use of marking within the Tree Visualizer display.

Figure 8.3 Spotlighting in a Tree Visualizer display in MineSet.

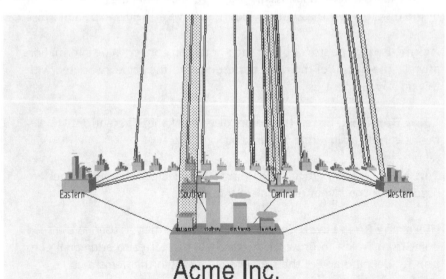

Figure 8.4 Marking objects in MineSet's Tree Visualizer.

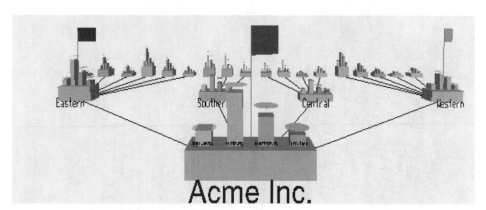

Invoking the Scatter Visualizer

The Scatter Visualizer is one of the most basic and simple display types within the MineSet system. This display type is a three-dimensional grid where the columns of a database are mapped onto the grid dimensions. Each crossing point supported by a record or data row will show in the grid. These three dimensions combined with size, color, and labels for each displayed data object can provide a fairly complex and powerful diagram to interpret. Figure 8.5 shows an example of a Scatter Visualizer screen. As you can see, each dimension is made up of a set of regular intervals, shown as grid lines that span the interval being mapped. The individual filled-squares or cubes within this figure represent the data being presented. Any of these squares can be selected to show more detail about what information constitutes that particular cross-section of the grid. The Scatter Visualizer is an efficient display method for smaller data sets where only a limited number of data elements are being considered.

There are several other types of information that can be associated to the objects being presented within the grid. Sliders can be defined that map onto other variables within the selected data set. As these sliders are manipulated, either as integer-based or discrete value-based entries, the grid objects will respond accordingly. Thus an animation effect can be produced in the Scatter Visualizer by putting the values identified and selected though the sliders into motion. The appearance, colors, and sizes of the objects will reflect the values defined in the sliders. If one of the animation values is set to a grid value, then it will appear to slice the grid across that dimension, thereby clearly showing the structure of each segment. This is an effective method to use when you are looking for patterns and trends. Combined

Figure 8.5 A sample Scatter Visualizer screen in MineSet.

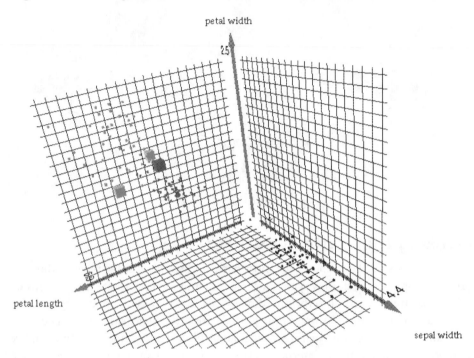

with various filters, scaling factors, and other visual display characteristics, the Scatter Visualizer can provide powerful analytical support. Descriptions of some of these functions are described in the sidebar.

There are some other important features available in the Scatter Visualizer. Not all of these are necessarily unique to this tool. One feature in particular is the ability to execute an external command when an object is selected. Since MineSet runs within a UNIX environment, the types of commands available can be quite extensive. When the grid is being used to represent products, people, or other tangible entities, and an external command is executed, one of several actions could occur. For example, an external viewer or web browser could be invoked that would provide additional detail regarding the selected object, especially multimedia items such as pictures and audio clips. Alternatively, any one of the other MineSet visualization tools could be invoked with data specific to only the object selected. The options in this case are essentially limitless in terms of what you could do with this discriminating feature.

Options Available in MineSet's Scatter Visualizer Displays

Axis 1, 2, and 3. For each of these three variables, a corresponding column from the data set is required to be identified. At least two of the axes need to be defined in order to produce a usable diagram. If only two are specified, then a basic X-Y chart is produced. If all three values are provided, then a full 3D chart is generated.

Entity-Size, -Color, -Label. Additional information may be added to the display by manipulating the appearance of objects according to these parameters.

Slider1/Slider2. Provides the ability to map variables directly to one or two animation sliders that are used to adjust the way the Scatter Visualizer displays look. These are dynamic-response sliders that act as local filters to fit the data into ranges that have been interactively specified. The data type required for a slider is either integer or binned (e.g., discrete values).

Normalization. Can be used to scale the entire grid or selected walls.

Working with the Map Visualizer

Another way to view data is by arranging objects in three-dimensional spatial proximity with respect to other data objects. MineSet supports this type of display through the Map Visualizer interface. The landscapes can represent virtually any type of terrain including geography, logical networks, manufacturing designs, building structures, and other physically aligned data sets. The spatial location with respect to the other data elements is determined in the arrangement of the landscape. Figure 8.6 shows a Map Visualizer display depicting the individual elements of these landscapes. Examples of data elements that can be represented effectively in this format might include cities and states within a geographical map, computers and routers within a logical network, parts within a manufacturing process, or rooms within a building. These can all be shown as irregularly shaped bar charts. That is, the shape of the chart can be made to reflect its real-world physical counterpart. The height of the bar chart can then be associated to a variable describing the object of interest. Color can also be assigned to a variable as well. A summary of some of these and other features is provided in the sidebar.

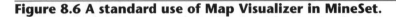

Figure 8.6 A standard use of Map Visualizer in MineSet.

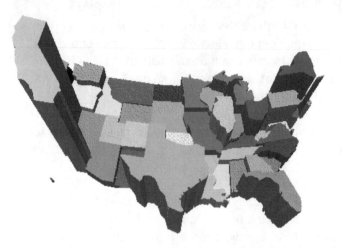

Setting Display Parameters in MineSet's Map Visualizer

The Map Visualizer requires a set of input parameters including the geographical object and corresponding numeric values for assignment of its height and color. The following parameters can be adjusted from the Tool Manager interface.

Entity-Bars. Represent the variables that are used to define the spatial mapping. This value must have a corresponding set of mappings in order for the Map Visualizer displays to function properly.

Height-Bars. Contain the variables that are used to specify the heights of the graphics, cylinders, or lines on the map.

Color-Bars. Make color assignments to the different regions, cylinders, or lines.

Slider1/Slider2. Animation sliders that act as local filters to fit the data into ranges that have been interactively specified. The data type required for a slider is either integer or binned (e.g., discrete values). Through VCR-like controls, the speed and resolution of the sliders can be controlled independently. This animates the screen to filter the data visually to reflect only the value being stepped through the animation. This function allows you to evaluate the data set for bad data, dependencies, or patterns of interest. The VCR can be set to play once, loop continually, or swing (reversing direction when an endpoint is reached).

The resulting landscape diagrams can also be rendered as two-dimensional outlines in which cylinders rather than real-world entity shapes are used to display variable values. This helps make the value distinctions more obvious than the prior method because larger shapes do not obscure smaller shapes. Figure 8.7 shows a flat landscape using cylinder shapes. Using this method, you can also mix and match levels of abstraction. The original map outline used in Figure 8.6 is still being shown in Figure 8.7. However, the individual cities within each of the states are being shown as cylinders. In the original Figure 8.6, the size of the state represented an aggregation of all the values for each of the cities being shown in Figure 8.7. Since the interfaces used to define the contents of a Map Visualizer display are very flexible, different combinations can be generated to accommodate specific analytical needs.

The Map Visualizer interface also lets you generate landscapes showing the relationships between specific point locations. The relationships are shown as lines, each having a specific width and color to denote information about the data. Figure 8.8 shows a sample Map Visualizer display with various lines connecting

Figure 8.7 A flat landscape with cylinder shapes in MineSet's Map Visualizer.

endpoints. Some very interesting displays can be generated with this option, depending on the underlying landscape selected.

Using Drill-Down and Drill-Up Features in MineSet

Map Visualizer also has the unparalleled capability to support a drill-down or drill-up on any one of the spatially positioned data elements. This provides a method by which to implement the different levels of abstraction we discussed earlier. The information at one level can be aggregated up into more abstraction or broken down into more detail. This capability is implemented through the hierarchy files used to construct the maps. Each file entry has a column name reflecting the graphical object to be displayed, which also corresponds to the name used within the data files. Each column name has an associated mapping file used to describe the location and shape of its corresponding graphical object. Finally, there is an optional description regarding the hierarchical relationship of the graphical objects. It is here that the drill-down and drill-up functions supported within the Map Visualizer are realized.

View Modes in the Map Visualizer

The Map Visualizer interface supports two types of view modes. The first mode, grasp, is used to navigate the display. As with all MineSet displays, the Map Visualizer can be rotated, zoomed, or panned from virtually any angle or viewpoint. The second mode, select, can be used to gain information about any object present within the display. The level of detail is dependent on the level of abstraction being shown at that time. Through simple mouse-clicks you can drill-down and expose

Figure 8.8 A MineSet Map Visualizer display with lines connecting specific endpoint locations.

more detail about a single object, drill-down on the entire scene to show the next level of detail for all objects, or drill-up to return to a higher level of detail.

Using Built-in Maps

MineSet comes with a variety of prebuilt maps, including the shapes that describe the outline of all 50 United States. This was used to create the Map Visualizer diagrams shown here. There are abstractions contained within these files to support drill-ups for regions (Southwest, Northeast, etc.), as well as East/West breakouts. Conversely, there are files that can show the individual counties within a state, should that level of detail be necessary. The drill-downs and drill-ups are managed through the Map Visualizer interfaces. The layout definition for creating new maps is fairly straightforward. So if there is a different type of map or some other physical placement of data that currently is not available within MineSet, you should be able to generate it quickly without too much added overhead. To help get your application up and running within the Map Visualizer interface, MineSet ships with the following maps:

- The individual states, counties, area codes, and five-digit Zip codes of the United States.

- The individual provinces and territories of Canada.

- The individual states of Mexico and Australia.

- The individual countries of Western and Central Europe.

- Regional subdivisions of both France and the Netherlands.

Interacting with the Splat Visualizer

Conceptually, the Splat Visualizer is not too dissimilar to the Scatter Visualizer. Each uses a set of three dimensions to logically plot out the data—the difference is in the way the individual points are represented. Whereas the Scatter Visualizer shows the individual cross-points where the fields within a data record converge, the Splat Visualizer imposes a level of abstraction before the results are presented. The abstractions are called *splats* and represent the aggregation of a set of data points. This allows the Splat Visualizer to represent much larger data sets than the Scatter Visualizer because much of the detail has been abstracted into a composite representation. If more than one data point is placed within a single bin (e.g., a 3D cross-section), these are aggregated and drawn as a single point. Depending on the number of points being aggregated, the resulting splats will have a related size, opacity, and color. Refer to Figure 8.9 to see an example of a Splat diagram. Be sure to view these figures on the CD-ROM to see how color and opacity are used in a splat.

The color of a splat is determined by averaging the values of the data set that have been mapped into a specific bin. The opacity is based on a weighting of the number of data points that fall into the bin. If there is no particular variable mapped to the opacity visual trait, then the actual record counts are used instead. Silicon Graphics has created some very elaborate methods of calculating the opacity of a splat. Unlike the Scatter Visualizer where every single data point must be managed within the display, the Splat Visualizer only has to deal with derived numbers. Therefore, the performance of the Splat Visualizer is not tied directly to the size of the data set (e.g., the number of records processed). Rather is it based on the number of bins represented along each dimension. For clarity, a bin can be defined to represent a range of integer values such as 1–100 divided into 20 unit increments resulting in five bins. Bins can also be based on the values of discrete data elements such as strings (e.g., product names, locations, and descriptions). Each unique occurrence of a stringed value produces a different bin. If a numeric variable selected for display within the Splat

Figure 8.9 An example of a Splat diagram in MineSet.

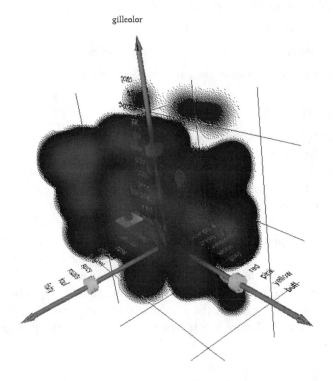

Visualizer has not been binned, the system automatically will create a uniform binning by arbitrarily producing equal segments.

As with all of the MineSet tools, the Splat Visualizer has a group of parameters that can be set from the Tool Manager. The color and slider parameters are very similar to those used in the Scatter Visualizer. You can also control opacity. There are some other unique options available within the Splat Visualizer. One in particular is the definition of the shape of the splat itself. There are several shape options that can be selected including constant, linear, Gaussian, texture, or sphere. Each one has subtle differences in the way that it draws its shape. Shapes range from single, large pixels, and texture mapped rectangles to sets of small triangles and opaque spheres based on a cubed root of the count. Other options include the ability to adjust the size of the grid, define colors, and change label sizes. The animation provided through the sliders can reveal a good deal of insight into the data set. Since the Splat Visualizer does follow formats closely associated with the Scatter Visualizer, the learning curve for understanding these splat displays should be minimal.

Using the Pick Dragger

Perhaps one of the most interesting features of the Splat Visualizer is in the way it lets you navigate and interrogate its data points. The viewing mode supports a special 3D-pick dragger that provides a method to select an area within a dense cloud. A summary of the area that has been selected is provided. The pick dragger has several modes that can be used to profile the data. Along each axis of the grid, there are cylinders fixed at a particular value. If you select and drag one of these cylinders, the drag motion is constrained to that particular dimension (e.g., it remains parallel to the dimension). The cross-point of all three dimensions is then summarized. In a different select mode, a square appears in the center of the grid within the splats. Its orientation determines its movement behavior such that it moves only in the plane defined by the square. This square can be adjusted into three different planar positions (e.g., XY, XZ, YZ) to affect its movement. Figure 8.10 shows an example of a Splat Visualizer with an active selection box. Again, please refer to the CD-ROM for color versions of this figure.

Understanding the Rules Visualizer

The information required for operating the Rules Visualizer comes from patterns that are expressed via association rules used to indicate the frequency of occurrence of two or more variables. This type of data is most often used in market-basket analyses such as those described in the association rules section of Chapter 6. The Rules Visualizer has been developed to show the relative frequency of different pairings of items (e.g., their frequencies) within a data set.

Figure 8.10 An active selection box within MineSet's Splat Visualizer.

avg_hrs_worked_bin

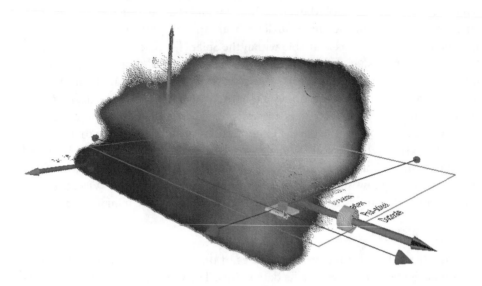

The method used to present the data in a Rules Visualizer is a hybrid of several of the other MineSet displays. It has grid characteristics of the Scatter Visualizer mixed in with the bar charts of the Map Visualizer combined with the aggregation capabilities of the Splat Visualizer. The diagrams created are not necessarily complex, but are extremely powerful in showing associations among the presented data elements. Figure 8.11 shows an example of what a Rules Visualizer display looks like for a supermarket basket analysis. The display layout is fairly straightforward and easy to interpret. Where the row associated with any particular product intersects with the column of any other product, the diagram shows the relative frequency of the two products observed in the dataset. The height of a bar graph is used to show the value associated with their frequency of occurrence. Since the rows and columns are usually mirrored, the entities are the same on both sides of the diagonal axis. Their frequencies, however, can be different (see the processing requirements defined later for more detail).

Calculating Association Rules in MineSet

To populate the Rules Visualizer display, the raw data must be converted to a special format. An Association Rule Generator is used to process the data and produce the results. For the purposes of this discussion, we consider this to be

Figure 8.11 A sample Rules Visualizer display in MineSet.

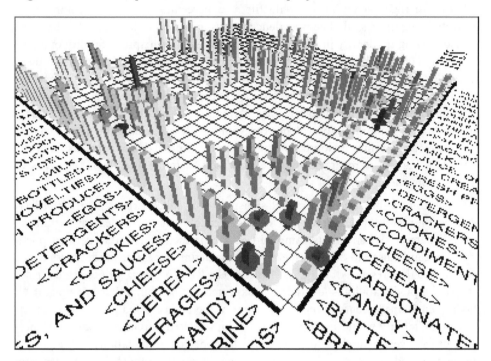

part of the Rules Visualizer display. A frequency matrix is calculated based on the observation of different data elements. Since transactional data elements are being abstracted or aggregated into a set of simple counts, large quantities of data can be processed by the Rules Visualizer. What determines performance is the number of unique entities encountered within the data set, since each one has a relative frequency of occurrence with all other entities. As the data preprocessing is done, a set of three values are defined for use within the Rules Visualizer to generate a set of low-level association rules.

The first value is used to define the *predictability* of the rule. Association rules take the format of "if LHS then RHS." The left-hand side (LHS) and right-hand side (RHS) parts of the rule are based on the values encountered within the data set. Thus, an example of this format can be represented as "if Soda then Chips." Acceptance or belief of this rule is partially based on how frequently these two items are purchased together as a percentage of the total number of times they are bought. What this represents is how often the LHS and RHS occur together as a fraction of the number of records in which the LHS occurs. The Rule Visualizer has a minimum predictability threshold set at 50 percent, but it can be adjusted upwards to meet specific analytical needs.

The second value is called *prevalence* and it tells you how often the LHS and RHS occur together within the data file as a percentage of the total number of records being processed. The prevalence of a rule is a good indicator to use when you are trying to identify predominant patterns. Even if the predictability of a pair of items being purchased together approximates 100 percent, it is of little value to a retailer if it occurs only a few times. What is of greater interest is whether frequently occurring patterns are predictable. This is why the prevalence of a rule in combination with its predictability is so important. The Rules Visualizer has a method to set a minimum prevalence threshold while processing the data such that all associations falling below this threshold are discarded from the display. The default value is 1 percent, but can be increased to refine and focus the types of association rules generated.

The third value used by the Rules Visualizer is called *expected predictability*. This value represents the frequency of occurrence of the RHS element within the overall dataset. When this is compared to the predictability value defined previously, it can be used to derive a measure of the definitiveness or randomness of the rule due to the presence of the LHS element. The Rules Visualizer does not use rules where the predictability is less than the expected predictability. For example, if "if Soda then Chips" occurs in only 12 percent of the Soda-related purchases, its relative predictability would be 12 percent. If Chips-related purchases occur in 15 percent of the overall purchase transactions, the expected predictability will equal 15 percent. Based on these values, the rule would not be reported because a predictability of 12 percent is less than the expected predictability of 15 percent. This is just another way of helping to cull the large number of potentially irrelevant association rules that can occur by chance.

The association rules produced from the data sets can then be placed into the Rules Visualizer to show what items tend to co-occur. The LHS entities are placed on one axis and the RHS entities are placed on the other axis. Where they intersect within the grid is where the attributes of the rule are displayed. Depending on what pairs of entities are used for the LHS and RHS of the rule, the resulting values are specific for that particular pairing. The converse of the rule does not necessarily hold true. For example, the "if Soda then Chips" may be a very highly valued rule, but "if Chips then Soda" may result in a poor outcome. Thus, the different sides of the diagonal line within the Rules Visualizer will most likely have different values being presented by the height of their respective bar charts. Figure 8.12 depicts this difference in the supermarket example presented earlier. You will notice there is a big variation in the pairings among the objects when using different LHS and RHS pairings of products.

Figure 8.12 Different LHS and RHS values presented in the Rules Visualizer.

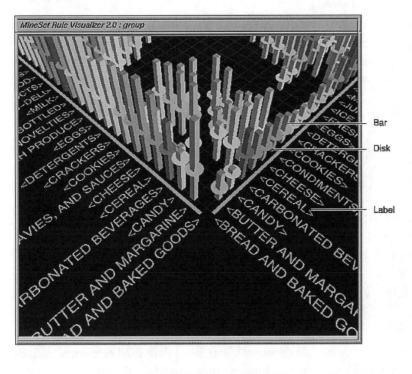

As with all of the MineSet displays, the Rules Visualizer also requires that a set of input parameters be specified from the Tool Manager interface. The number of parameters and options available to support the Rules Visualizer are fairly extensive because it also includes the Association Rule Generator. Some of these are summarized in the sidebar.

Options Available for Display Manipulation in the MineSet Rules Visualizer

The Rules Visualizer has methods to define binning, ways to map the data into the grid, prevalence and predictability thresholds, output sorting control, and many other parameters. Our interest is in describing the variables used to control the display. The types of parameters used in the Rules Visualizer are very similar to all of the other displays and include:

Continued

Height-Bars. Used to set the variables mapped onto bar chart heights. The most obvious value selection for this parameter is the predictability rating. Large bar charts will immediately draw your attention to those entities that frequently are observed together.

Height-Disks. Just as in the Tree Visualizer, disks can be set on the bar charts to show additional information. The values assigned to the disks are most likely going to reflect the expected predictability rating. This way you can compare the bar chart heights to the disk heights to see if the rule is well qualified.

Color-Bars/Disks. These parameters allow you to set the colors of the bar charts and the floating disks. By default, these are both set to the prevalence value.

Label-Bars. Provides the ability to vary the factor represented by the bar labels.

The Rules Visualizer can also process hierarchical data used to control various levels of abstraction. This allows you to direct the focus of the data being processed. In the market basket example, if the data presented are represented down at an SKU level where the brand name, quantity/size, and packaging are all available, you are going to get very few, if any, patterns. The degree of resolution is so fine using this representation that there most likely are not going to be any tangible results that a retailer would care to use. However, the data can be abstracted into larger bins. So instead of representing, for example, the different types of beer such as wheat, honey lager, stout, ice, or draft independently within the Rules Visualizer, there could be a generic category called "beer" that comprises all the different types of beer sold by the retailer. There could also be intermediate categories such as dark/regular/light, import/export, or country of origin.

Using the Evidence Visualizer

One of the last major visual interfaces supported by the MineSet system is called the Evidence Visualizer. The display is based on the output of an Evidence Classifier that tries to predict the value of an attribute based on the values of other attributes. The focus of this module is on describing the display formats used by the Evidence

Visualizer rather than the characteristics of the Evidence Classifier itself. There is a considerable amount of detail describing how the classifications work, and we refer you to the Silicon Graphics User's Guide for additional explanation.

The displays produced with the Evidence Visualizer are unique because they reference and use two different display panes as shown in Figure 8.13. The right pane of the Evidence Visualizer is called the Label Probability Pane and is used to present the *prior probability* for a single attribute selected from the data set. The resulting pie-chart represents the different breakouts for each discrete value encountered in the sample set for the selected attribute. These are sometimes called class-labels. The wedges of the pie-chart are respectively based on the number of records matching the distinct value of the attribute divided by the total number of records within the data sample. Basically, this is just a simple distribution of values presented as a set of percentages. A legend appears within this pane to identify what the different parts (e.g., the class-labels) of the pie-chart represent through a color-coded scheme. It is important to keep in mind that the discrete value attributes represented within this right pane of the Evidence Visualizer should have a finite set of unique values; otherwise, the display is going to be difficult to interpret. Continuous attributes are binned automatically into regular intervals.

The left pane of the Evidence Visualizer is called the Evidence Pane. This pane contains a set of rows, each with a value label, to represent the other attributes defined within the data set. Within each row, a series of pie-charts are presented, one for each unique value supported by the attribute. These individual pie-charts

Figure 8.13 A sample Evidence Visualizer display.

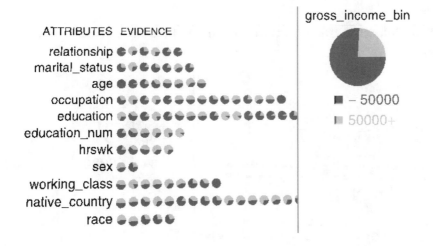

represent the *conditional probabilities* of the Evidence Visualizer, since they are used to support the evidence presented in the Label Probability Pane. The colors of each of the wedges correspond to the color associated with each class-label. Additionally, the size of the wedges displayed in any of these pie-charts reflects the level of observations made regarding each of the prior probability (e.g., the class-labels). What this indicates is how many times the value was used to support one of the class-labels defined on the right-hand side. Obviously, if the wedges for a conditional probability are equally distributed, they are not going to be useful in making a distinction regarding the identification of a class-label.

The height of the pie-chart within a row is usually based on the number of records supporting the specific value associated with the attribute. If the data set is complete and consistent in its content, the sum of the heights of all of the rows should be equal. There are also two sliders contained in the bottom part of the Label Probability Pane that can be used to magnify the heights of these pie-charts. The first slider is used to adjust the *importance threshold,* which can be useful for removing attributes that are less effective for classification. The second slider can be used to adjust the *percent counts threshold* to remove any pie-chart where the number of observations falls below a certain percentage of the total number of records in the data set. Furthermore, the individual pie-charts within each Evidence Pane can be selected manually and combined to show different aggregate classifications. For each pie-chart selected, the main probability pie in the Label Probability Pane is adjusted to reflect the total distribution. Figure 8.14 shows an Evidence Visualizer where several pie-charts have been selected to alter the main probability pie.

The main probability pie displayed in the Label Probability Pane can also be used to help refine the information presented within the Evidence Visualizer. The

Figure 8.14 Selective classification within the Evidence Visualizer in MineSet.

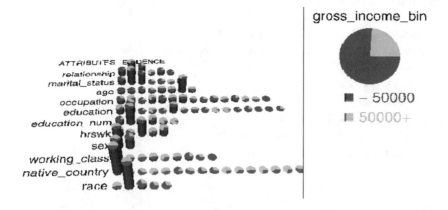

buttons associated with the class-labels presented below the pie can be selected to activate the label. Immediately, the probability of predicting the label is displayed in the text output region at the top of the display. Additionally, the pie-charts displayed in the Evidence Pane on the left change to bar charts, as shown in Figure 8.15. The height of the bar charts reflects the degree of the evidence in favor of the selected class-label. This can also be switched to display the evidence against the prediction of a class-label. Using these viewpoints, certain patterns will stand out that may have been missed by looking at all of the data at once. Thus, those values most directly related to predicting a particular class-label can be discovered easily in this kind of display.

This previous description was focused exclusively on MineSet 2.0. SGI has recently released their version of MineSet 2.5 and it contains some enhancements that will be briefly mentioned. The newest feature is the use of clustering algorithms to break your data up into related segments. The output is presented as a matrix of bar-charts (based on field values) that reveal the composition of each cluster. MineSet 2.5 also supports parallelization, boosting, regression trees, and ROI curves. To learn more about their latest release, please consult SGI using the information identified in the Appendix.

Metaphor Mixer

Metaphor Mixer is designed and marketed by a company called Maxus Systems International, Inc., located in the metropolitan New York City area. They have

Figure 8.15 Relative degree of support for variables within the Evidence Visualizer in MineSet.

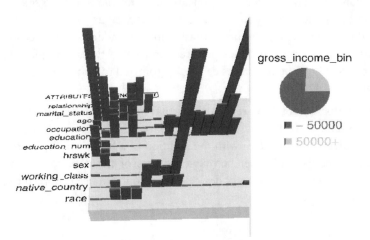

managed to create a highly interactive environment that is one of the few systems designed to support real-time data feeds. Metaphor Mixer has matured into a very impressive system that was originally derived from exclusive use within the financial markets, and has recently spread out to include an extensive set of other applications. Maxus works with a diverse set of partners, including universities and commercial businesses, to integrate the Metaphor Mixer (MM) decision visualization paradigm into a variety of domains. (As a side note, the recent novel *Trading Reality* by Michael Ridpath describes a system called "Bondscape" that is based in part on the MM design.)

The underlying processing engine used in MM was originally derived from a previous system built by Maxus that supported the ability to process real-time financial news and market data feeds. Thus, they already had the ability to acquire information on the fly and were able to integrate it with the historical information (fundamental, technical, and derivative) defined within their underlying data structures. If you recall from Chapter 1, we indicated that monitoring does not constitute data mining since monitoring does not involve discovery of new patterns. What Maxus has done with MM is to integrate historical data (descriptive) with real-time data feeds (transactional). This provides both a method to support the reporting of real-time data feeds such as stock prices or any other sensor input while also sustaining the decision-making process necessary to support data analysis in real time. Thus, MM provides an effective way to support real-time data mining.

MM currently runs on several platforms including Windows and UNIX. The methods used to get data into MM are fairly standard and include support for flat ASCII file formats. MM also provides support for OLAP (specifically Arbor Essbase), DDE, and proprietary real-time financial feeds (Reuters, DBC Signal, and Knight-Ridder), as well as Maxus' proprietary financial analytic engine, CAPRI. As part of defining the configuration of an MM application, a mix-file is used to select the textures that can be applied to any of the data points as well as to the borders represented within the terrain. These textures are read in as standard GIF/JPEG so that company logos, books covers, product pictures, and so forth can be placed within the MM displays. Thus, the interfaces can be customized to handle virtually any type of application.

The main interface displays of MM reflect 3D virtual information terrains that can be used to map out large quantities of multifaceted data. The navigational interfaces closely model a video-game interface with the addition of a heads-up display to represent the locations, details, and other pertinent features of the data contained within the terrain. MM even supports a set of device drivers so it can been coupled to gaming joysticks to help facilitate navigation of these terrains. MM is built on top of Sense8 Corporation's WorldToolKit, one of the leading virtual reality library tool kits.

Defining the MM Displays

MM consists entirely of a single visual paradigm, the information terrain. However, you can derive a variety of different displays from MM by adjusting its parameters. You can instantiate different models within the displays at the push of a button. The information presented by MM can take on a completely different perspective depending on how you decide to set these display parameters. The following describes the different components and approaches that may be used to customize the MM displays.

Designating Border Elements

MM furnishes the big picture of the data set while supporting the ability to drill down to the details of individual data elements. These individual data elements, such as stocks and bonds, can be presented in the terrain in a manner that maximizes their interpretation according to the display parameters selected. The main MM display consists of a planar, categorically-defined surface intersecting a continuous numerical axis. The cross-sectional 2D base of the MM terrain is constructed from a pair of information dimensions, or attributes values, called border elements. Examples of border elements can include industry groups (e.g., automotive, textiles, electronics, etc.), market segments (e.g., technology, finance, construction, etc.), geographic regions (Asia, Europe, North America, etc.), and so forth. There is a different column or row for each discrete value encountered within each of the border elements selected. Cells formed in the intersection of this 2D matrix contain all of the data elements that correspond to the specified values on the x and y dimensions. This unique representation is what distinguishes MM from other landscape visualization tools.

You can represent various levels of abstraction using the border elements by defining categories within the range of attribute values represented in the data set. Within each dimension there is typically a hierarchical (or other) relationship among items. For example, countries can be placed into regions, products into categories, or companies into technology areas. Any combination of these values can then be paired together to produce a corresponding terrain. Indirectly, the choice of border elements also acts as a filter because only those data elements that contain attributes specified by the selected border elements are displayed within MM. Figure 8.16 shows an example of a sample MM information terrain.

Figure 8.16 A Metaphor Mixer information terrain.

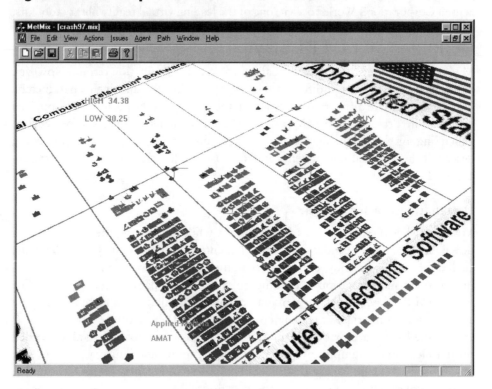

Controlling the Appearance of Individual Data Elements

A configuration dialog is used to map the different dimensions against one another within the MM terrain. Through simple interface techniques, an unlimited number of new terrain types can be configured automatically. Through the same dialog box, you can also set the triggers that invoke blinking, spinning, sliding (left-right jitter), quaking (pole movement), shape, height, arrows, and color of the data elements themselves. Within each cell on the terrain, the selected elements can be normalized to reflect the different statistics being mapped to the heights and colors of the objects assembled on the terrain. This provides the smooth curves or transitions generated through the placement of the individual data elements regardless of what statistics are being mapped.

Display characteristics assigned to individual data elements in an MM display can be changed through simple interface parameters. You can filter elements from the display based on attribute values. Additionally, you can assign display characteristics to elements based on their value relative to other items in the display. For example, you could designate that those data elements in the top percentage of some attribute value be given a certain appearance in the terrain. You could have elements corresponding to products in the top 10 percent of sales revenue rotate and have those items in the bottom 20 percent of the distribution blink. Thus, you could look at the combination of blinking and rotating data elements and very quickly determine that there is a potential problem with the marketing of particular products. Since MM supports blinking, rotating, sliding, and quaking in addition to the shape, height, image, label, color, arrow vector, and a set of border elements for each data element, there are many combinations of display characteristics that can be generated within a single terrain.

Using Arrow Displays to Describe Trends

Information about the value of data elements relative to some standard can be represented dynamically in MM using arrow displays. Although the arrow displays were initially developed to show changes in stock prices for particular financial applications (see the sidebar), they are useful in any number of problem domains. When large amounts of data are presented within a display, it can sometimes be difficult to see small differences in colors, shapes, or sizes of individual data elements. However, by assigning an arrow vector to reflect a certain set of conditions, important changes in behavior as well as differences among data elements can quickly be seen. As an example, suppose that an airline wanted to monitor patterns of activity across airports throughout the course of a day relative to other competing airlines. Assuming that arriving and departing flight information was available in real time from the airports, arrow vectors could be used to show the relative frequency of flights for that airline at each individual airport. In such a display, you could quickly identify changes throughout the day in market share across the individual airports sampled. Similar applications could be developed to show changing behaviors and trends in other industries including retail, manufacturing, health care, telecommunications, and pharmaceuticals.

Special Metaphor Mixer Displays for Stock Information

Since MM originally was designed to show changing market values within the financial communities, it was specially outfitted with an arrow vector display feature. The arrow vectors compress a stock's price history into one discrete object. For example, this feature can be set to indicate a certain analysis run on a stock's price. If the stock is above or below its 30-day

Continued

Special Metaphor Mixer Displays for Stock Information (Continued)

moving average by a predefined amount, it could be shown by six phases of a clock arrow, with each degree representing how far above or below the moving average this particular stock is according to the last data available.

Depending on the orientation of the arrows in this case, the direction of the arrow would indicate its technical attractiveness. In a rapidly declining market, the arrow vectors become increasingly important. For example, stocks tend to get oversold in a panic market. The stock drops through all kinds of technical points that the analyst may be interested in, such as where the current price is relative to its moving average. The price may have dropped significantly below its moving average as a result of a panic sell-off and therefore the arrow vector would begin to turn up or maybe point directly up to indicate that a lot of selling has occurred. On the other hand, oversold stocks might be valued at far less than their moving average, and this information could be conveyed by a downward pointing arrow (see Figure 8.17).

Figure 8.17 Using arrow vectors within Metaphor Mixer.

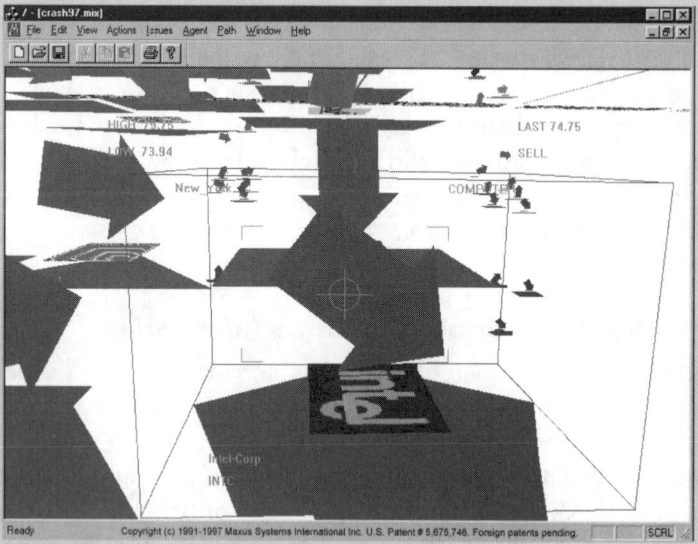

> The terrain floor of the display can also be adjusted to reflect any one of the application variables such as the market index, price change, P/E ratio, or any other global reference. This equates to a ground-zero point against which gains and losses can be assessed. The data elements themselves do not change their relative locations but adjusting the baseline typically will change the colors of the elements accordingly. The use of color within MM is graded according to a value range where red is low, gray is zero, and blue is high. The use of color is also reinforced by the height of the data elements above or below the baseline.

Defining MM Navigation Techniques

MM has many features that are designed to help you navigate through data sets and interact with its displays. Some of these are described here.

Flying through the Data

As previously mentioned, Maxus has spent a considerable amount of time thinking about different ways in which to navigate 3D information spaces. One particularly innovative approach they have created is the ability to define flight paths that can be traversed through a data set. This saves you from having to explore the data manually through a traditional mouse navigation process. All flight paths are precalculated as the data sets are loaded into MM. Thus, they reflect the content, size, and layout of the data sets themselves rather than some fixed orientation. Flight paths can take you above, below, or through any designated level of the information terrain. The predefined flight paths include an orbit path (elliptical), figure-eight path, sidewinder path (back-forth, top-bottom), crop-duster (left-right and up-down), and the air-raid path (zigzag/strafe across display). When engaged in a flight path, the system continually flies you through the loop so you can take time and observe the data from different perspectives.

Flight paths can also be created dynamically and saved to a file that can be utilized by other users to replay various journeys through a data set to show the results of prior analyses. Thus, you could create a set of flight paths at one location, ship them to a client in a different location, and they could see the intended results and different perspectives in a hands-free display scenario. This can also double as a training aid to introduce new users to the software. This feature forms the basis for establishing a collaborative analytical capability that will be exploited in future MM releases.

Navigating via Playback

MM has also been outfitted with a VCR-like capability that is used to play back the data events across different time periods. The idea is that you play the data like a "market-VCR", with the data elements moving day-by-day to their respective values (e.g., percent changes). Based on the degree of increment selected within the VCR, the data elements will quake, vibrate, change color, blink, or spin depending on the specific conditions applied during the particular time interval represented. By sequencing the data across time, a user can replay a set of events to see if there were specific indicators that led up to an important result or decision. This makes justifying the decisions made during a MM engagement much easier since they can be reviewed for accuracy and checked for consistency. The VCR can also be used to play back a flight path that you have defined or created by the system. This provides a good way to view different segments of the data with different degrees of specificity.

Navigating in Wire-Frame Mode

The system can be placed into a wire-frame mode while navigating the display. The wire-frame mode helps speed up execution of MM when using low-throughput processors or memory-challenged systems. This provides minimal degradation when moving around the terrain due to the reduction of rendering and texturing time that is being performed. When your movement stops, all display characteristics are then reapplied to the final state. When the flight paths and VCRs are not being utilized, you can navigate the terrain using the three buttons present on a standard mouse. These control the zoom, azimuth, and tilt perspectives associated with your viewpoint.

Working with the Interactive Agent

Although we have emphasized its visualization capabilities, MM is not just a data visualization system. It also has a unique method for detecting specific types of information through the use of an interactive data agent (nicknamed LIA). Most interestingly, this agent has been outfitted with voice responses that are used to help convey its actions. The agent offers two distinct operating modes. The first mode runs autonomously in the background in combination with the underlying processing engine. In this mode the agent is programmed to look for explicit conditions you have defined such as a news story reporting lower than expected earnings for a certain stock, the recall of a product due to faulty parts, or even specific price increases in certain commodities markets. When the matching values are encountered in the real-time data stream, the agent automatically notifies you that critical information is available for review. In a second mode you can employ the agent more interactively, looking for data elements with certain characteristics via simple text references.

In either mode, the agent is shown as an abstract geometric object (e.g., a dodecahedron) that persistently rotates within your field of view. Depending on how you want the agent to identify its target data elements, one of two navigation techniques can be used. The most direct approach is to have the agent move you to the object of interest. Essentially, the agent takes control of your viewpoint and pulls you along the shortest distance path to the data element. It is a no-frills process that works very effectively. The second approach is more of a following mode in which the agent generates a series of neon-frames as it independently moves from your viewpoint out towards the target in an elliptical path. The frames are placed along the path traversed by the agent, resulting in the appearance of a tunnel that you can follow if desired. At this point, you have the option of flying down through the tunnel to the target data element for further analysis. Figure 8.18 shows an MM diagram with such a tunnel appearing in the display. Use the CD-ROM to see the neon frames more clearly in a color figure.

Figure 8.18 A tunnel showing the path traversed by an agent within Metaphor Mixer.

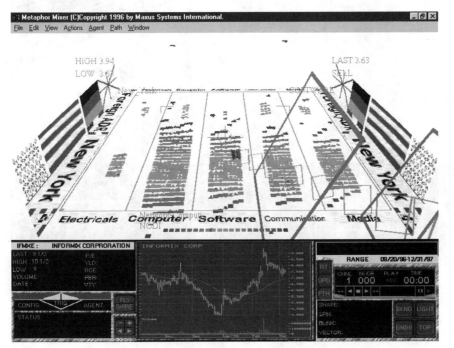

Controlling the Environment

MM has a control panel that can be used to manage all of the different variables represented within a terrain. When a data element is profiled within MM, a hypertext drill-down on the individual attribute information is presented within the main console. These might include P/E, low, close, volume, yield, return-on-equity, price-to-book, volatility, and other various financial decision support statistics that may be relevant for a portfolio manager or trader. In addition to the standard attribute values used to describe a data element, multimedia can be inserted to show more complex views. These might include stock charts (real-time snapshots), pictures, or other forms of related data. Figure 8.19 shows an example of the multimedia support offered by MM. The control panel also contains a status window that depicts the current selections and actions you have taken. These might include current agent actions, indications when switching configurations, control settings, flight paths, and so on. A history log of actions taken during a session is shown in this

Figure 8.19 Multimedia representations within the MM display.

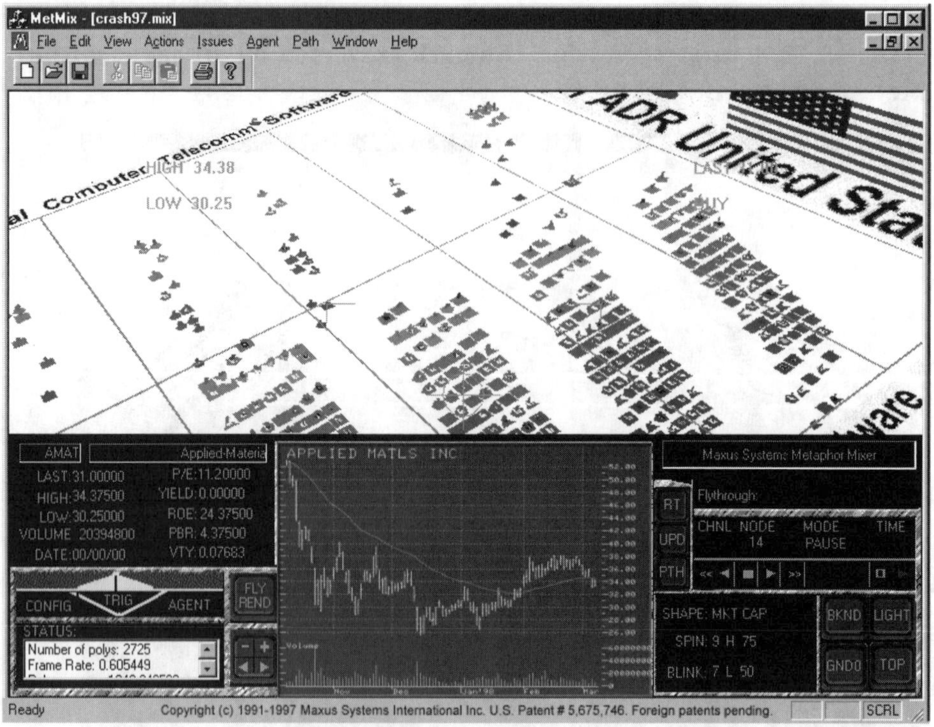

way. This log can then be recalled at a later point either to replay the analysis or to justify the actions taken. The control panel also has features to set the configurations listed in the mix-file, which are the various defaults.

Future Directions of MM

There are a variety of new features that will be included within the MM in the next several version releases. Specifically, the developers at Maxus are focused on including additional OLAP support because MM is based on the use of multidimensional modeling. The dimension tables, fact tables and star schemas typically associated with OLAP systems provide a natural mapping to the MM terrain. Maxus will also be providing different shapes, outlier parameters, terrains, and voice control/feedback for a smoother interface. MM is also going to be outfitted with an Internet telephone capability. This feature is initially targeted at the financial sector but could realistically be used by anyone working within a collaborative environment.

The use of Internet telephone support will be embedded directly within MM so the client can have a system operating, click on a stock and have the system present the home-page for the stock. This feature will also act as a tool for the brokerage houses to present new opportunities and services to their clients. Thus, the main broker could be talking with a client while sending the flight paths of a new stock via a preprogrammed VCR flythrough. Since MM will have an Internet telephone hook up, the broker can call the client through the display over the Internet and converse directly though MM. This will help various users working with MM to collaborate with each other by identifying hot stocks, looking at the flythroughs, and talking about opportunities.

Additionally, Maxus will further investigate the use of neural networks and fuzzy logic to program agent behavior. In all, the system is focused on providing better business situation awareness by supporting mechanisms to observe the behavior of data across a variety of dimensions, which often includes time. This directly supports what Maxus and other businesses refer to as their OODA loop (i.e., observe, orient, decide, and act). Thus, the faster you can turn around this cycle, the quicker you can move past your competitors within the marketplace. This is obviously a critical advantage in the fast paced world of today's financial markets and MM provides a well-defined paradigm for supporting this process.

Visible Decisions In3D

Visible Decisions Inc. (VDI), is a firm located in Canada that has been able to produce a visualization engine that can be customized to address a wide range of data mining engagements. VDI was originally started with an earlier product called Discovery, which was primarily used within the financial community for doing risk management and related types of analyses. Unfortunately, the Discovery product included a proprietary language that limited its appeal with IT departments. While using Discovery, extensions typically would be necessary to tailor the system to meet specific requirements identified within the client's operating environment. This required the creation of one-off extensions to Discovery, and obligated VDI to perform an extensive level of consultation and maintenance to keep their clients operating properly. However, VDI smartly generalized their offering with the creation of the next-generation visualization system. Their latest products are based on In3D, which is a visualization API consisting of C++ that can be used to create a variety of data landscapes.

Like several of the other visualization systems, In3D does not directly support any data access mechanisms. Through the In3D API methods, customized routines must be created to populate its internal data structures. Thus, it has been designed to work in almost any development environment including spreadsheets, C++, Visual Basic, Visual J++, VBScript, Web Scripting, and even Java. In3D provides a set of classes for storing, organizing, and accessing data within the system. In fact, In3D can support real-time data feeds if it has been specifically programmed to do so. Third party data modeling tools such as STL, Rogue Wave, and ObjectSpace can easily be integrated with In3D. Thus, an In3D visualization layer can be applied on top of many other environments for better data management and analysis. This produces what VDI calls "best of breed" applications in which you can select the most appropriate technologies and have them work together in order to meet data processing and analytical needs.

In3D is currently supported on the Windows 95 and NT operating systems as well as by several flavors of UNIX. It is based on a cross-platform rendering library called Orca, which sits on top of OpenGL and is VRML 2.0 compliant. Also, VDI has created an In3D Studio, which has been designed to allow nonprogrammers to prototype visualizations quickly using a drag-and-drop environment. In3D Studio is very interactive and provides a way to create entire standalone applications or new modules for existing applications. Its concept is similar to developing web pages where you select the components you want to use, drag them out onto the display, and immediately see their effect. Parameters associated with each component can be used to customize their behaviors and look-and-feel. In addition to all of these capabilities, In3D also has a lightweight C-like interpreter called Eye for handling run-time expression evaluation.

Working with In3D

The other visualization systems described in this chapter provide predetermined methods and functions that are well defined and circumscribed. On the one hand this is a good thing because you know what the environment is like and can access capabilities automatically within clearly defined limits. On the other hand, users may often have to make do with functionality that is not entirely appropriate for every application. You may have to live with systems that may not offer all desired capabilities for given applications. In3D is the answer to this particular problem. When using In3D, you construct your own visualization environment by drawing from the various components available through the API library. Since In3D provides an extensive set of features that can be combined in an unlimited number of ways, the potential for flexibility and customization is enormous. However, as is always the case with visualization environments, the options selected will only be useful to the degree that they map onto a problem space that is well suited to the particular application. Thus, it is important to think out the types of displays you will need and how they will behave with your particular data set before initiating an In3D application.

You work with In3D in what is called a Model-View-Controller paradigm. The data sets (Model) are separated from the visualization (View), which are both manipulated using various filter operations (Controller). Generally, the data are stored within In3D as containers represented as arrays. This makes slicing the 3D data into 1D and 2D arrays very efficient and it also provides the foundation for creating hierarchical abstractions. Figure 8.20 shows data slices that may be specified for an In3D application. In3D provides the ability to navigate data in a 3D space through zoom, rotate, and pan features including keyboard and mouse interactions. Additionally, other important data mining capabilities such as drill-downs, local filtering, and detail resolution (image rendering) are supported by In3D using some very clever user interface techniques.

Viewing the Data

Within In3D, the visual representations of the data are called *views* and each view has a set of properties (also called attributes) that define how it looks and where it is placed. In3D offers a number of different views such as boxes, triangles, lines, surfaces, grids, prisms, spheres, cylinders, cones, and text. There are many different kinds of views available within In3D (e.g., single, multiple, and 2D multiple) and they are characterized by the amount of data they represent. Single views are the

Figure 8.20 Defining slices of data within In3D.

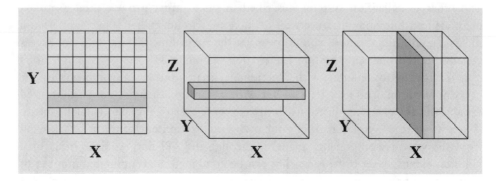

basic primitives from which the visualizations are composed and usually represent individual data elements as would be found in a link analysis system. Multiple views represent single arrays of data. Instead of just representing a single element, the multiview is focused on processing an array of like-elements. The elements can be depicted as discrete boxes or text as would be found in a single view, or they can be connected through the use of ribbon and wire display characteristics. 2D multiviews are composed of two-dimensional arrays of data, so they tend to form surfaces. Figure 8.21 shows an example surface generated by In3D.

Constructing Compound Views

As applications are being built with In3D, the views used to convey the data can be combined to create compound views. Basically, a compound view groups one or more views into a single entity, presenting a uniform set of properties as its combined interface. You can thus construct a framework that presents different levels of detail within a single display. Consider a compound view to be a stacked set of subcomponents, where each subcomponent represents a specific level of detail. Depending on where you are in the stack, you will see different types of data. The way a compound view is associated with the display is through the use of "distances," where each subcomponent can be associated with a distance from your viewpoint. So as you zoom in or out from a compound view, it changes its appearance to reflect the appropriate level of detail. As you can imagine, in complex environments you would want to show more detail as the viewpoint got closer to a compound view and less detail further out.

A compound view can also be used to magnify certain display characteristics when the viewpoint is far away from an object. For example, suppose there is a critical value that always needs to be displayed for a certain class of display element.

Figure 8.21 A surface generated by In3D.

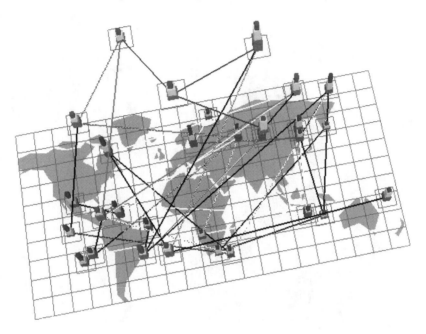

Ordinarily, as you would move further out, the salience of this feature would become small relative to everything else being rendered within the display. However, by amplifying the value, it could remain consistent in its perceptual distinctiveness. Within In3D, a compound view can support up to 16 different levels of detail.

Using Multiple Perspectives

One particularly powerful feature associated with In3D is its ability to maintain multiple data landscapes within a single display. What this means is that different perspectives can be applied to the same data set and be viewed within their own representative space. Thus, instead of having multiple windows that can quickly cover up important data or force you to switch back and forth between the displays, In3D can actually place different landscapes within a single display (see Figure 8.22). So you could maintain the same data elements in two different displays and filter on both, all in one operation.

Manipulating In3D Display Characteristics

A variety of visual display properties can be associated with any view constructed in In3D. Unlike other graphic APIs that only perform their rendering

Figure 8.22 Multiple views within an In3D landscape.

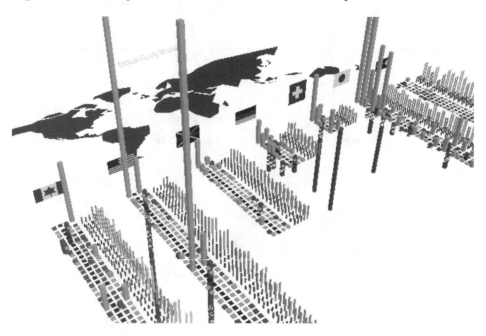

based on a static definition of the data, In3D can dynamically associate display characteristics with data to create individualized presentations. The most basic physical dimensions for conveying information about data include color, width, height, depth, and radius. Individual objects can also be shaped in any number of polygons.

Using Materials, Textures, and Lighting Effects

In3D can display material properties and textures, as well as lighting effects to the data landscapes. Materials can be applied to any view and they are used to define how the display elements reflect light from various viewing angles. In3D comes with a palette of predefined materials that can be selected for use in a view. Several display parameters can be set to define the material properties, including ambient intensity, specular intensity, specular color, emissive color, and transparency. Each material within the palette has a combination of values that give them their individual look such as glossy, metallic, and translucent. In3D also provides a materials editor that allows you to create new types of materials or change the existing ones in the palette.

Textures can be used to customize views and give an In3D application a very unique look and feel. The textures for a view, like materials, are also derived from a palette within In3D. The texture formats currently supported by In3D include JPEG, GIF, and BMP formats. So when a view has been created, a texture can be applied to its surfaces thereby providing some very distinctive display characteristics. Textures are defined in a 2D coordinate system so that they can be mapped or warped onto the different shapes selected for the views. If a texture and material are combined together within a view, the texture is modified according to the lighting selected.

Lighting is very important within In3D because it is an integrating display characteristic that gives a data landscape its overall presentation style. In order for materials to reflect light, there must be a light source available. One basic form of lighting can be derived from the use of a "headlight" that is always shining in the direction from which the scene is being viewed. Depending on the type of visualization being generated, other forms of directional light can be used. A directional light is independent of the viewing position and it simulates light from an infinite point, thus, its source can never be seen.

Interacting with In3D

As we have seen with most visualization systems, there are methods in place that are used to navigate and interact with the displays. Within In3D several distinct sets of commands are used to manipulate the views to provide further detail about the underlying data elements. The selection of these commands is based on the use of the mouse, keyboard, or some combination thereof. These are, of course, customizable so you can define the specific behavior of the interaction. Since In3D is a visualization API, the functionality of some of these features must be programmed by the application developer. The sidebar describes some of the interaction features currently supported by In3D. Finally, In3D supports several different output formats. Since In3D has been built using Orca, it can write out a file corresponding to a VRML 2.0 format. Additionally, In3D can generate a JPEG or GIF image file corresponding to the state of the data landscape being presented in the display. In3D can also generate postscript files, bitmaps, as well as pixmaps.

Other Landscape Visualization Systems

There are several other landscape visualization tools that you may want to consider when planning your application. We briefly describe a few of these systems here. More complete descriptions are available directly from the vendors who are listed in the Appendix.

Interaction Functions Supported in In3D

Selection. Selection within an In3D display can occur by simply clicking the mouse on a view or set of views present with any display. This causes a highlight box to appear around the view, indicating it has been selected. View selection within In3D provides a method for forcing the system to respond to a direct request for more information. Since the selection can be programmed through the In3D API, different responses can be generated depending on the situation. Within a data landscape, for example, details can be hidden until a view is selected, alternative views can be presented upon selection, and operations can be conducted on the selected view. In3D can also distinguish between five different types of selections.

Brushing. The use of brushing within In3D provides a dynamic way to expose additional detail regarding certain views in the display. When you brush or point at a view, an overlay can be presented (e.g., a chart or textual summary of the details of the region brushed) or the actual contents of the view can be adjusted to show different information. The use of brushing has been widely adopted in other contexts to provide, for example, context-sensitive help (also called ballooning), or to highlight features as has become popular on many web pages. When you exit a view activated through a brushing, the display will revert back to its original configuration. A button can be held down while brushing thereby causing additional behavior to be invoked if so desired. If you click the mouse while brushing a view, then a selection is conducted. Figure 8.23 shows a sample of what a brushing event can show when activated. In this case, a simple grid overlay is used to show some of the underlying data.

Controllers. To interact with the data presented in an In3D display, a set of controllers must be made available. The controllers defined by In3D reflect standard buttons, levers, and sliders that can be programmed to do a wide variety of tasks including setting the resolution of a chart (e.g., changing the scale) or actually filtering the underlying data. The interactions with a controller usually are presented immediately within the display and can either function on a single value or be used to adjust multiple values. For example, suppose you were adjusting a control slider that was tied to the height variable defined for a view. As soon

Figure 8.23 Showing detail through brushing in In3D.

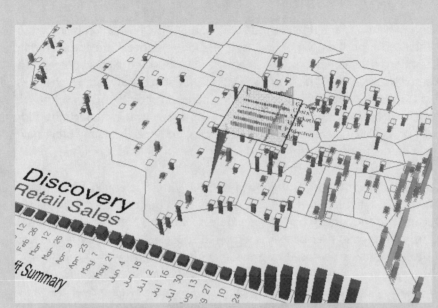

as the slider was moved, the heights of the view would change accordingly. Thus, you can try out all sorts of controller combinations to determine whether there are interesting patterns contained within the data. Controllers can be used to define such things as watermarks where a baseline within an In3D display can be moved up/down among the different views being presented. Controllers can also be assigned to filter out data to show only those views meeting certain conditions, top/bottom percentages, or even ranges of values.

Navigation. In3D supports the concept of a hemisphere navigation where you can tilt, pan, or zoom through the display. Tilting within the hemisphere is limited to 180 degrees of latitude and 360 degrees of longitude. Zooming can be applied up to 1000 percent of the optimal viewing distance and panning is limited to the size of the landscape itself. By applying these restrictions on the navigation VDI ensures that you will not get lost within the In3D display—which can easily happen in a 3D environment. The displays can also be set to a planar view thereby showing only

Continued

Interaction Functions Supported in In3D *(Continued)*

two dimensions at a time. In this configuration, the navigation is limited to either an x position, y position, or the zoom-distance from the scene. In addition to the interactive movements, In3D supports the ability to perform automatic fly-bys of the landscape using predefined viewpoint paths. This can also support navigation around a particular point on the landscape while maintaining a constant distance. The speed of the interactions, rendering quality, guidance limits, key bindings, and just about any other navigation control can be configured through simple interface methods.

Sensors. To make In3D a truly interactive visualization, VDI has implemented a set of features called sensors that can be positioned in the landscape and triggered when you navigate over them. An event is generated every time you enter or exit a region in space as defined by a 3D box. These events can be used to provide additional detail within the display. For example, a sensor is placed on a view that contains information regarding the sales of a certain product. As you navigate over the view and enter the proximity of the sensor, additional detail can then be displayed automatically regarding the regions where that product is sold. Alternatively, images could be presented, charts rendered, or even sound- or video-clips played.

Commands. Within any type of visualization application there is sometimes a need to invoke commands to act on the state of the application. These commands could be as simple as changing the color of a view to a complex events such as saving the contents of the display to a file. Commands are extremely useful when they are sequenced into a set of actionable events that can be encoded into a macro. All applicable commands executed within In3D support undo and redo functions. This makes it easy to back up and try different approaches as well as establish an audit trail on the analysis being performed.

Spotfire

Spotfire is an interactive visualization system that has been used for an extended variety of applications. Spotfire is currently a Windows 95/NT application, although an experimental Java version is in the works. The interfaces are very intuitive and responsive, so it is easy to get a quick understanding of your data using the Spotfire displays. Getting information into Spotfire is a matter of using flat ASCII files and ODBC connections. You can use this tool to display data along with supporting background information. In its current version Spotfire accepts maps generated from MapInfo, which means you can overlay your data onto map displays to show geopositional relationships. Spotfire has a very clean and intuitive interface that can be configured to meet your specific analytical needs. Figure 8.24 shows an example of a graph produced by the Spotfire system.

The methodology employed by Spotfire uses set of sliders located on the right-hand side of the screen to represent the variables that are available to the system. Adjusting these sliders changes the data displayed in the main window. Thus, you

Figure 8.24 A graphical representation produced by Spotfire.

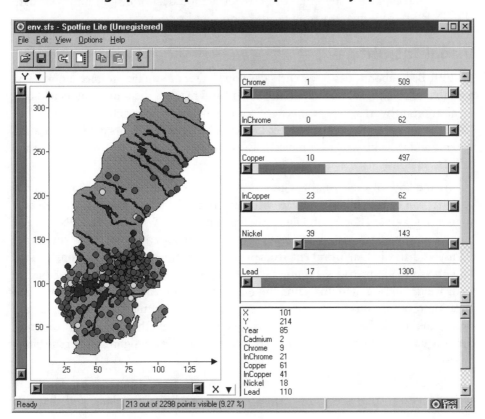

can adjust the values on these sliders to reflect a wide range or combination of values by which to focus your analyses. The data are represented as symbols or markers and their size, color, rotation, glyphs, and labels can all be associated with various descriptive values (e.g., attributes) contained within your data. Spotfire can handle numerical, string, and categorical data types.

The presentation of data by Spotfire emulates scatterplots, geographic maps, and bar-chart visualizations. Since the displays are interactive, you can drill-down using a brushing technique to expose the underlying data. Additionally, if more than one viewpoint of the data is being displayed within Spotfire, these can be linked together. Thus, when you select markers in one viewpoint, the corresponding markers in every other view are immediately marked as well. This provides a very effective technique for comparing different filter settings (via the sliders) to see what commonality is present across the associated data set. Spotfire can export its views/data into spreadsheets, files, SQL queries, and bitmaps. Spotfire is a very effective and capable system that can provide a good deal of insight into your data with little up-front investment in terms of time and resources.

Visual Insights

In 1991, Bell Laboratories researchers developed a set of visualization technology systems that allowed AT&T to better understand and manage the growth of its telecommunications networks. In September 1996, Lucent Technologies and its R&D unit Bell Laboratories were spun off from AT&T. Lucent has now refined its data visualization systems and is making them commercially available through a new venture company called Visual Insights.

At the core of the Visual Insights system are its components, which are modules that can be reused to build new visualizations. The Visual Insights components support a C++ class library and most can be used in both Windows and UNIX operating environments. Visual Insights' software provides features that support a robust and flexible environment from which to create new visualizations. Visual Insights' software provides a unified view of a database. Methods are available for navigating, filtering, and analyzing the underlying data. All of the interactive visualization tools are linked so that changes (e.g., selections) made in one display are propagated to all the other displays. Thus, you could view the same data from multiple displays in which several perspectives are created by assigning different filters or visual layouts to the different screens.

Visual Insights' software represents all data elements using glyphs. These are symbols used to represent abstractions of the contents of the data, and they can have different shapes, sizes, and colors. Visual Insights provides interactive filters that can be used to refine the displays so that they only reflect those values of interest for the type of analysis being performed. There are animation features that can be used to reveal hidden relationships in data. Animation is particularly useful when dealing with data sets that have a temporal component, since the feature can be used to replay knowledge states as a function of defined time intervals. The Visual Insights product contains several interactive visualization tools that are described next.

Using the Text Patterns Tool

The Text Patterns tool has been developed for providing visualization of the content of software programs. Each line of code is represented as a row within a rectangle. The code can be colored based on a variety of attributable values including dates (age), programmer, or its intended functionality. It can even be used to look at the execution sequence of the code. Thus, you could quickly see where the majority of computational time is spent within a program, identify unused variables, reveal unexecuted code, and even spot unreachable functions. The Text Patterns tool also uses a browser to display the original code segments. Figure 8.25 shows an example of the Text Patterns display. This type of visualization can also be used in a Difference Patterns tool to look for changes within the content of files, or to look at the directories/files to see if there are any structural differences.

Using the Event Trails Tool

Visual Insights also has developed the Event Trails tool, which may be used to analyze streams of time-stamped, typed messages. Within the Event Trails tool displays, each message is represented with a color-coded tick mark. These are positioned within a grid representation where time is presented along the x-axis and type along the y-axis. Figure 8.26 shows an example of the Event Trails display. This type of display can be used to see the correlational relationships contained within time-oriented data.

Using the Data Constellations Tool

Another component of the Visual Insights software is the Data Constellations tool, which displays data as networks of interconnected nodes. Placement of the nodes in the Data Constellations displays is based on their interactions. The linkages also support various display characteristics that can be assigned to attribute values as well. When the nodes are aligned or positioned within a map, then the Visual Insights displays can be used to show geopositional information as depicted in Figure 8.27.

Figure 8.25 The Visual Insights Text Patterns display.

Contributed by Visual Insights, a venture of Lucent Technologies.

Visual Insights software has been used to show the structure of a large relational database used in maintaining and developing software code for the 5ESS switch. A custom-built interactive visualization tool is used to display the associations between tables explicitly, mappings between the database and application code, physical representations of relations, schema information, and paths through a specific database. This type of representation introduces the use of link analysis techniques and forms the basis for the other types of displays that are part of the Visual Insights product.

AVS/Express

Advanced Visual Systems has been involved in data visualization for quite some time. They have an extensive suite of software tools that covers just about any type of application you might ever want to build, and offer the services to actually build the application if you wish. AVS/Express can be run under Windows and a range of

Figure 8.26 An example of the Visual Insights Event Trails display.

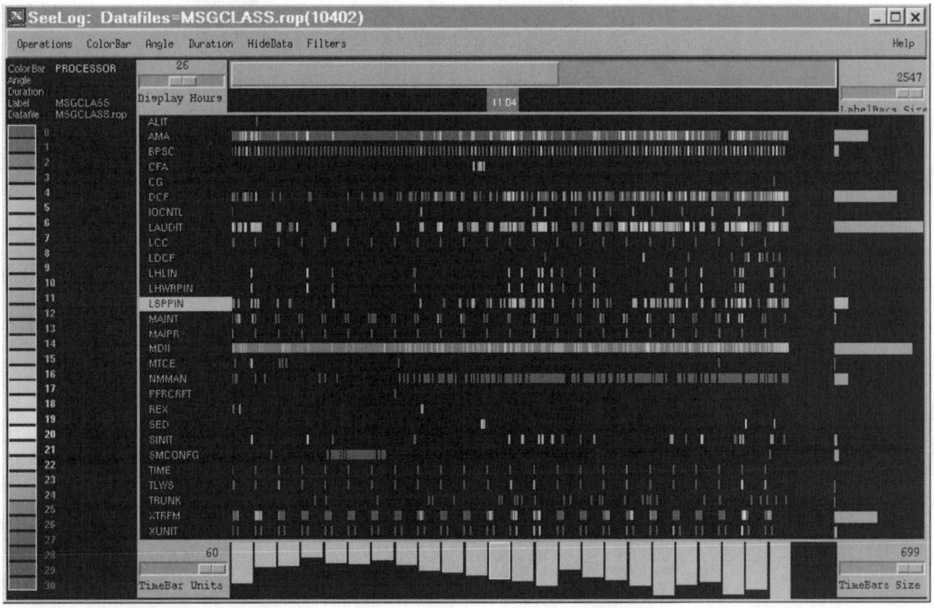

Contributed by Visual Insights, a venture of Lucent Technologies.

UNIX platforms. Their approach is to provide an environment with a set of libraries, data structures, and other support software, which gives you the flexibility and power to create your own customized visual data mining environments. Traditionally, AVS/Express has been used to visualize scientific data sets. However, with the recent emergence and interest of data mining technologies, they can easily support many unique and innovative applications using their current configuration. AVS/Express is being used today in a wide variety of industries including defense, telecommunications, engineering, energy (oil and gas), financial services, pharmaceutical, medical imaging, and environmental cleanup.

The methods used to create systems within AVS/Express are based on a flowchart-like approach where you construct the type of visualization that is to be generated. There is a suite of objects, called modules, available within AVS/Express that are connected together in order to build a visualization network. The network actually represents the application that is used. These networks are easy to share, modify, or distribute within the AVS/Express user community. New objects can be created through various programming language constructs including C, C++, and

Figure 8.27 A Visual Insights tool used to show geopositional information.

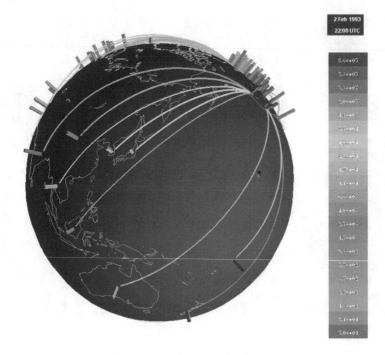

Contributed by Visual Insights, a venture of Lucent Technologies.

FORTRAN. So if there happens to be a very specific type of feature that is not available within the comprehensive set of AVS/Express objects, it is easy enough to create it using a very straightforward process. Additionally, the objects tend to be what AVS calls "polymorphic." This means that the objects are not specific to any particular type of data and they can be reused over a wide range of data types including integers, floats, doubles, and characters. There is even a Data Import Tool that is available within AVS/Express to help access and load your data sets into these object constructs.

There are many features offered in the AVS/Express libraries that can be used to create 2D and 3D visualizations. There is support for setting the views, camera, and lights within the displays to give the proper perspective on the data elements. AVS/Express provides basic rendering primitives such as images, polygons, lines, and text in addition to various display parameters such as colors, fills, transparency, shading, and much more. There are pick-operators for probing the data (e.g., drill-downs and brushing), annotation mechanisms, and interactors (e.g., those methods of manipulating the displays). AVS/Express lets users run animations on data sets to show timelines. Figure 8.28 shows a sample diagram of an AVS/Express screen showing a J.P. Morgan mortgage application. Keep in mind this is only one of many different models that can be presented within AVS/Express.

AVS/Express can be applied to virtually any type of data. AVS/Express has been utilized by a large number of third-party vendors to create unique standalone visualization applications for a variety of different domain purposes. In addition to AVS/Express, Advanced Visual Systems, Inc. also supports several other visually oriented tools such as AVS5, Gsharp, and Toolmaster. Each one of these can be used to develop unique visualization systems. We refer you to the company for more detail regarding their visual products.

Figure 8.28 A sample AVS/Express display.

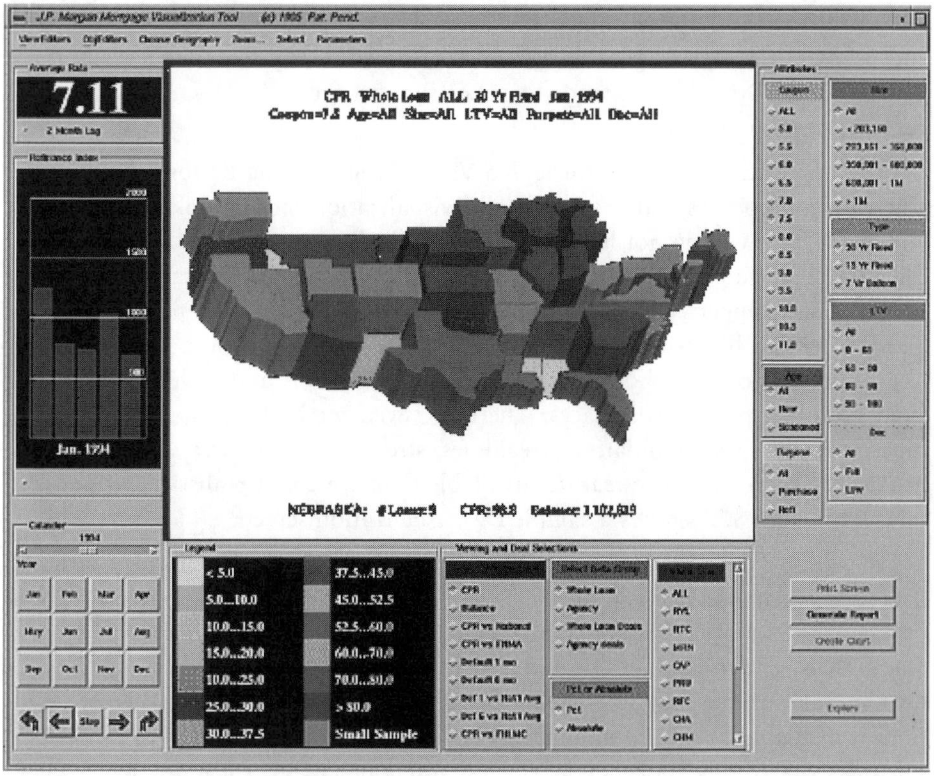

Image courtesy of Advanced Visual Systems, Inc.

IBM Visualization Data Explorer

The Data Explorer (DX) is a generic data visualization system that can be used to create a wide range of applications. It is currently supported on Windows as well as UNIX platforms. The approach used to create the visualization within DX is through the construction of networks, similar to several other systems already presented within this section. Through a set of simple interfaces, you can drag-and-drop different display modules ranging from annotations to import functions. The resulting networks are easy to understand and can quickly be changed to produce alternative types of visualizations. There is a wide range of support for generating very powerful displays without any programming. Should you need to customize your interface, however, DX does support a high-level scripting language and programming API.

In the past, the DX has been used heavily to view scientific data sets. However, the system modules and interfaces are easily adapted for use in most any visual data mining application. In fact, there is already a wide range of fielded systems using DX for just these purposes. Since you control how the displays are going to look and behave, it is easy to get the right mix of functionality for your level of focus and analysis. Through an extended level of support facilities, DX makes it easy to generate new applications.

DX applications are built through a Visual Programming Editor, which creates a network of modules that define how the visualization should look and behave. If you decide that you do not like the look of a display, you can just clip the link or use a different plug-in module. The DX supports a variety of interactors including sliders, dials, steppers, selectors, and so forth. There are color maps available and a sequencer can be used to animate the data, for instance along a time scale. DX has the ability to create both 2D and 3D representations and includes everything from vector glyphs to isosurfaces. There are even methods for defining ribbons, tubes, axes, meshes, boundaries, streaklines, streamlines, and arrow plots to name just a few. There are more features available than we could realistically discuss in this text. Figure 8.29 shows a sample DX visualization screen.

In terms of data management, DX's support modules understand the different data types that are being processed. Thus, there is no reason to worry about whether the data are represented in integer or string format when using the system. Since DX is very comprehensive and easy to use it can be extended to include your own modules or those modules created by other users. Thus, a wide range of extensions is available for the community of DX users. A full description of DX is outside the scope of this book but we suggest you contact IBM for more detail.

Figure 8.29 An example of a DX visualization display.

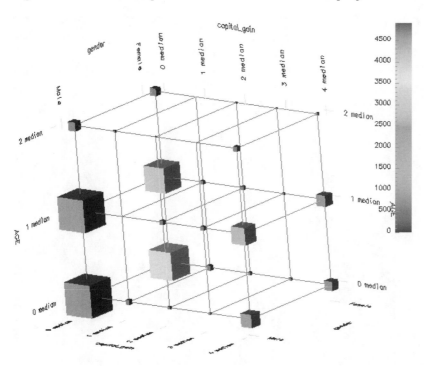

Summing Up

In this chapter we reviewed several data mining tools that take advantage of landscape visualization paradigms. We presented MineSet 2.0, Metaphor Mixer, and In3D in some detail and briefly described several others. Having read through these descriptions and seen the screen captures from these tools, we hope that you have gained a wider appreciation of the wealth of ways in which landscape visualization paradigms can be used effectively in data mining applications. With this in mind, we now turn to Chapter 9 where we present tools fitting into our third category of visualization, namely quantitative displays.

Quantitative Data Mining Tools

Introduction

In the previous two chapters we covered tools that emphasized link analysis and landscape-based terrains. These methods are certainly powerful, but there may be some occasions in which you will want to place more emphasis on quantitative analyses such as those described in Chapter 6. Quantitative approaches are preferred and often required, for example, when you need to obtain estimates of significance or reliability in a statistical sense. In addition, quantitative analyses can provide summary information about overall group differences and trends that can be used to provide first cut analyses of large data sets. As you know from our earlier discussions in Section I, you do not always need to have numeric data in order to conduct quantitative analyses. You can create quantitative descriptors of qualitative data using data abstraction techniques to create dummy variables or count information from aggregation routines.

Quantitative diagrams can handle extremely large volumes of data. The diagrams of most quantitative data mining tools tend to have a traditional look and feel to them for clustering, summarization, and range comparisons. Recent implementations have pushed the limits of these diagrams to perform hyper-dimensional analyses (an extended level of attributable characteristics). These added features provide ideal environments for identifying linear or exponential trends occurring within data sets. There are many quantitative data mining systems on the market, but we have selected a set for inclusion in this chapter that we believe will give you a feel for the types of possibilities that are currently available in commercial systems. Specifically, we present discussions of Clementine, Enterprise Miner, Diamond, and CrossGraphs. As with the previous two chapters, these descriptions are meant to give you an overall sense of each tool as opposed to detailed descriptions of their operation.

Clementine

Clementine is a system named for the famous song about the daughter of a gold miner, and can be considered the "darlin" of quantitative data mining tools. This next generation system has a variety of data manipulation features and powerful analytical capabilities provided within a single, well-designed and engineered interface. Clementine was created for use by nontechnical analysts who have a reasonable amount of knowledge about their own data sets. The system supports a range of functions, from generation of simple graphs and visualizations to neural network analyses and rule induction. Clementine has a visual programming interface that is used to build up analytical models by dragging and dropping icons, connecting them together, and invoking procedures.

Although Clementine is not entirely a visualization-based data mining system, its impressive capabilities merit its inclusion in our discussion of data mining tools. Clementine is currently being developed and serviced by ISL (Integral Solutions Limited), which is an independent company based in the United Kingdom. Clementine is a very versatile data mining system because it provides support for many of the phases of the entire data mining engagement including data access, integration of multiple data sets, modeling, analysis, and presentation of results. Modules have been developed to address each particular phase, and switching among these functions is transparent from the interface. In our experience, Clementine is only one of a few commercial systems that support this level of integrated functionality. Many other systems address selective pieces of the data mining process, but Clementine provides a broad set of functions that allows the analyst to get up and running in a short time period.

The Clementine system runs on a variety of platforms including UNIX, VMS, and NT. Although the NT port is not native because they have encapsulated the system in a NuTCRACKER wrapper, we noticed no degradation in performance or functionality on the NT. NuTCRACKER is a shell that provides facilities for building Windows applications from UNIX source code. NuTCRACKER provides seamless access to UNIX libraries, commands and utilities, as well as an X server. NuTCRACKER displays Motif applications directly with a Windows look-and-feel without any rewriting of Motif code. Additionally, NuTCRACKER facilitates tight integration of UNIX and Windows NT by allowing Windows networks to appear as extensions of existing UNIX networks for system administration and interoperability purposes. Several other commercial tools also use this method for extending their range of platform support.

Clementine's Graphical Interface

Clementine's graphical user interface is very easy to use. All of the functions available to the end-user are presented in a palette of icons at the bottom of the screen. Figure 9.1 shows a sample screen of a typical Clementine display. Several general categories of icons are used to identify the available data sources, perform data manipulation, and generate output. Icons in each category are distinguished in the display by their different shapes and user-generated labels.

All you need to do to use Clementine is to drag and drop these icons onto the main panel of the display to construct a model of the analysis. Your model graphically represents the set of instructions specifying the process by which the analysis is to proceed. The icons, referred to as "nodes," are linked together to form an ordered network model of the analysis. The outputs of each node are directed to the inputs of other nodes through a directed link. The resulting model is called a "stream" because it reflects the overall processing flow of the analysis.

The graphical presentation of the stream, which resembles a link-chart, is displayed in real time as it is created. The data sources are typically the starting point of the stream diagrams, where the flow of information is always outbound. The process does not need to be serial, however. Almost any module can send its output to more than one other module. Thus, you are not stuck with a model in which you are testing only one hypothesis at a time. Because you can create multiple paths of data flow within the Clementine displays, it is very easy to have several different hypotheses being tested at once where the outputs can easily be compared with one another. In all cases, it is up to you to determine what nodes to use and how they are connected. In other words, you can easily switch among data sources to be used, types of analyses to be performed on those data, and format of displays to be produced from the analyses.

The entire Clementine interface is very clean and visually appealing, consistent in its functionality, and easy to use. As ISL continues its development of Clementine and releases new versions, you can expect to see more features being added under the different palettes. These are easily integrated into the existing interface design.

Data Formatting in Clementine

To access data using Clementine, you can use either a flat ASCII file format or invoke its ODBC drivers. Since Clementine includes a full ODBC interface, data can be pulled directly from existing tables or views within a data source. The ODBC drivers in Clementine can support access to databases including Oracle, Informix, Sybase, Ingres, Access, and SQL Server. When special access is required or a unique

Figure 9.1 Clementine's main interface.

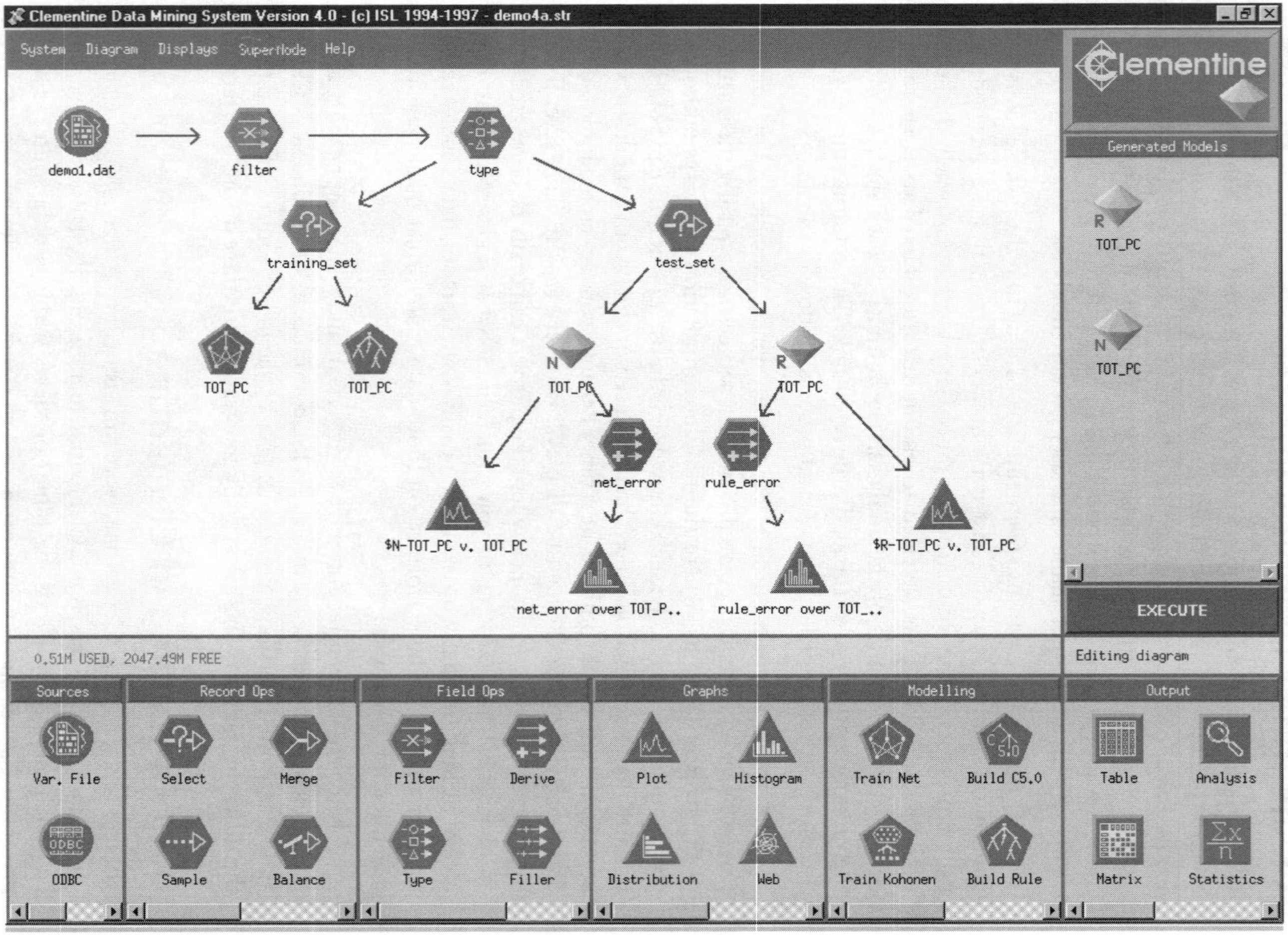

query must be imposed, the Clementine interface supports the submission of a user-generated SQL statement. When the source data are not derived from a database, they can be loaded in through a flat ASCII format. An ASCII file structure is fairly standard as far as data import facilities go. Information can be either delimited with a special character (e.g., tabs, spaces, commas, etc.) or it can be based on fixed-length records.

The different data formats supported by Clementine are limited to four categories—integers, real numbers, strings, and flags (true/false)—in addition to several data and time formats. One interesting aspect of Clementine is that it supports an autotyping feature that sets the data type of a field based on observed values. This can really help speed up the process of importing and preparing data.

Manipulating Data in Clementine

Clementine offers a suite of data manipulation functions. Recall from Chapter 4 that a large majority of time performing data mining is spent dealing with the various styles, content, and structure of data. Special routines are often created to clean up raw data sets and convert them into a format that is conducive for data mining. Simple functions such as excluding certain records or joining tables together can take a substantial amount of resources and time to execute, especially if you are just temporarily testing out different hypotheses. What you could end up with are directories full of different data sets, each with a slight variation in its content to reflect a certain approach or belief being tested. Fortunately, the Clementine system has many of these data manipulation functions already built in as a series of record and field operations.

One other important point to make is that Clementine has a very comprehensive language called Clem that allows you to perform low-level calculations on your data sets. These calculations can significantly assist in the creation or extraction of metadata within an application. There were over 200 different functions, comparators, and operands included in the Clem language at the time of this writing. Clem supports type testing, arithmetic operators, mathematical functions, trigonometric functions, string comparisons, string tests, bitwise integer operators, time and data functions, logical operations, and various other special functions. For the most part, you should be able to find what you are looking for when performing special operations on your data set. The Clem language can be used in almost all of the Clementine data manipulation functions.

Another powerful feature is that Clementine makes a distinction between record and field level operations. This gives you a lot of leeway in defining functions to manipulate your data in a variety of ways to satisfy the goals of your analysis. Each of the basic node types has a set of parameters that can be set to customize Clementine to your processing requirements. The following sections describe each of the functions available for performing these low-level operations.

Performing Record Operations in Clementine

One set of procedures available for data manipulation within the Clementine system is contained in the Record Ops palette. Here, high-level record manipulation is performed by one of seven functions. These functions are used to direct the types of records to be selected and processed by the system. The functions available in this area perform operations only at a record-level, so out of every data feed presented to a Record Ops node, the resultant output is some type of subset or combination of the records processed. The invocation of these functions is optional if the data sets being processed do not need any further refinement. The operations performed by the nodes contained within the Record Ops basically act as high-level filters and are processed through the entire record. That is, no field value manipulation occurs at this stage. The sidebar on pages 324–326 describes each of the nodes available under the Record Ops palette.

Record Operations Supported by Clementine

As stated in the main text, several functions can be invoked in Clementine to manipulate data records when importing them into an application. They are as follows.

Selection nodes. Used to include or exclude records based on conditions defined through the specification of Clem constructs. This function can perform broad filtering operations on the records being processed through the system. Using the selection node, you can filter on strings, value ranges, or date/time ranges to narrow the focus of your analysis. Selection nodes can be used to filter out those records that do not match your defined criteria. The use of selection nodes helps you to focus your analysis quickly.

Record sampling nodes. Used to support an efficient method of slicing data into segments that can be used to represent the breadth of values contained within your source data. These nodes allow you to sample a block of records to be passed on or passed over for processing. More precise sampling can be done as well, for example, including every tenth

Performing Field Operations with Clementine

Another set of data manipulation features available within Clementine is geared toward performing individual field operations. Whereas the Record Ops palette contains nodes that are exclusively focused on managing the data records, the Field Ops palette contains specialized nodes that operate on the individual field values. The major difference between the two is that the field operations can alter the structure of the data being processed. Field operations can be used to change values, remove unnecessary fields, add new fields, and perform a variety of low-level conversions. As opposed to the Record Ops that act more as gating filters, the Field Ops are responsible for fine-tuning and refining the data elements to be used in an analysis. The field operations currently supported in this palette are described in the sidebar "Field Operations Supported by Clementine."

Displaying Data in Clementine

Clementine supports a variety of different output formats for presenting data. The Graphs and Output palettes contain all of the nodes used to generate these displays. Since the outputs are used to confirm the contents of simple data manipulation or

or twentieth record in the data set. Finally, parameters can be set so that a random sample (e.g., 25 percent) of the data set is selected for processing. These features are quite useful, especially when you are working on a large data file that has been sorted in some fashion, for example to alphabetize last names in a particular field. If you were to take the first thousand records and conduct an analysis, you might get to work on only those records where the last name began with an A and miss some of the other patterns that more broadly represent the trends of the entire data file. On the other hand, if you sampled every tenth record you would not be subject to this bias. Clementine gives you the options you need to make these sampling decisions.

Merging nodes. Invaluable when integrating records from multiple sources with a common field. The type of join currently performed passes to output only those records that have corresponding record values (e.g., a key) between the different source files. (The ability to conduct an outer-join is not yet supported in Clementine.) Other features offered by the merging node also support a sequence merge where the nth records from

Continued

Record Operations Supported by Clementine *(Continued)*

all sources are combined to form a new nth record. This type of merge is based purely on the ordering of the records within the file and can come in handy when times, dates, or transactional data are being used.

Sorting nodes. Provide support for some of the other Clementine modules. The main role of these nodes is to sort records into ascending or descending order based on the values contained in one or more of the fields. Although the ordering of records should not matter when performing an analysis, this feature can help with sampling as well as with formatting the output for some of the graphs. It is important to keep in mind that these nodes can be used throughout the Clementine model and not just necessarily on the raw data stream. So, for example, the output of another module can be run through a sorting node in preparation of generating a final report.

Aggregation nodes. Help support data abstraction in the Clementine models. The primary function of this node type is to aggregate records across a specified field or combination of field values. For each unique value encountered in the target fields, summations and averages can be included in the aggregated record, along with the number of records actually consolidated. This feature makes it possible to generate high level models of the data to support activities such as performing an evaluation on medical diagnostics, conducting a demographic trend analysis, or even summarizing point of sale data.

Data balancing nodes. Offer a special type of capability for specific types of analyses in which there are missing data in certain cells or an insufficient number of observations to conduct a statistical analysis or provide input to a neural network. The data balancing node either reduces or replicates records within your dataset to provide a more even distribution of values. Note that this feature actually changes your data since it involves dropping data out or replicating already existing observations. We advise you to use caution with this function, particularly when asking the system to replicate records. Statistical outcomes derived from analyses where data were replicated to fill sparsely populated cells will almost certainly not be valid.

Field Operations Supported by Clementine

Filter nodes. Include or exclude fields from data records. This feature can provide significant time savings when parsing through files with a large number of descriptive fields. By being selective with respect to the different fields, very focused data streams can be generated for the different displays, reports, or machine learning facilities. Additionally, fields can be renamed at any point within Clementine, thereby providing more customized output.

Type nodes. Primarily, a type node acts as an automatic data dictionary, determining the type of data being processed. For example, it determines whether a field is a symbolic (categorical) type or if it is an integer and what its range of values represent. The type node also supports Clementine with managing noisy/dirty data. Missing values can be identified as being of type "blank" and special processing can then be applied.

Derive nodes. Provide an interface for dynamically creating new fields. This node type can operate using the results of any regular Clem expression, results from the application of Boolean flags (e.g., true/false), and can produce a set of values with a default entry (e.g., a fixed value), and other expressions based on specified conditions (e.g., make assignments based on the content of other fields). This function can also keep a count of the number of times a condition has occurred and can switch between states depending on conditions.

Filler nodes. Used to fill in missing values that may appear within a data set. This condition can occur when there is a blank, whitespace, NULL, or other specified values (e.g., "99") that need to be altered. The replacement value can either be calculated as a result of a Clem statement or be set to be a constant default. The use of fillers can help make a data set more consistent in its presentation and analysis.

History nodes. Allow historical changes in a field to be collected and presented to a modeling algorithm. This feature is particularly useful in time series analyses where changing historical values over time need to be modeled and analyzed.

are used to verify more complex calculations, they tend to act as sinks (e.g., the terminating portions of the data model). Typically, you will not take a graph or table and redirect it into another module because these outputs do not alter the underlying data. The different outputs produced are generated within their own presentation windows to ensure that the main Clementine display remains uncluttered. A benefit of using these outputs is that they can be invoked at any point in an analysis to produce a tangible product, diagram, or report. This also makes it convenient to check intermediate results as they are being generated. The types of output nodes available in Clementine are described in the sidebar.

Output Formats Supported by Clementine

Table nodes. Generate outputs in a spreadsheet-like layout with appropriate cell formatting and heading definitions. As is obvious, there is no graphical visualization in a table per se, but the contents of a table can be exported to other third-party programs if more advanced visual analyses are required.

Matrix nodes. Can provide a cross-tabulation of values between two variables. These values can also reflect summed or averaged values for a third field where pairs of value coincide.

Distribution nodes. Provide information using more of a traditional statistical look and feel. A distribution represents a combination of graphics and text to display the relative proportions and absolute frequency values for various fields as represented in the data set. As you can see in Figure 9.2, a typical Clementine distribution contains the raw value, horizontal bar-graph proportion, numerical percentage, and number of occurrences of the value of interest. The display of the distribution of a data set can provide insight as to the shape of the distribution (e.g., Gaussian, exponential, binomial, etc.) and whether there is any skewness present.

Plot nodes. Produce two-dimensional graphs from a set of pairs of numeric values (see Figure 9.3). These X, Y plots (sometimes called scatterplots in other tools) can be viewed as either point plots or line plots. Depending on what values are selected for the different axes, various types of displays can be generated including those approximating a time series. A plot display can also have an optional third overlay of a symbolic field.

Modeling Data in Clementine

The Clementine system supports several methods that can be used to help detect patterns through more sophisticated methods. The technologies used for building the decision support modules within Clementine include neural networks (supervised and unsupervised), rule induction, and statistical analyses including regression modeling. In all cases, you can simply invoke an analytical technique through the interface. Thus, you do not have to worry about the details of the underlying algorithms. You need only specify a connection between an input stream and the appropriate

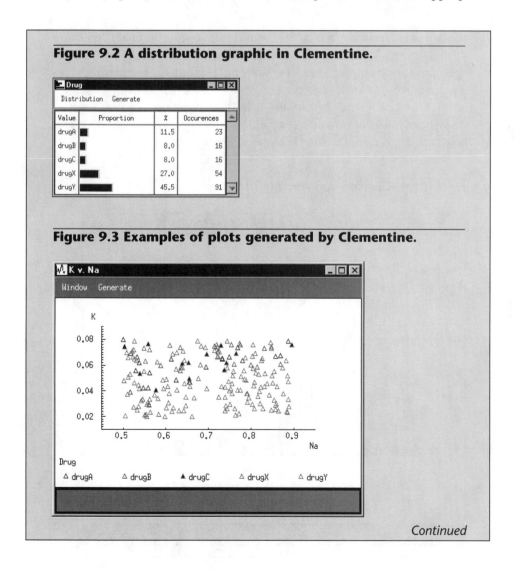

Figure 9.2 A distribution graphic in Clementine.

Figure 9.3 Examples of plots generated by Clementine.

Continued

Output Formats Supported by Clementine *(Continued)*

A plot node can be used to generate *multiplots,* where multiple Y fields are plotted against a single X field. The multiplot can also be normalized thereby scaling the different Y values into a common representation space (e.g., 0 to 1). One particularly impressive feature about these diagrams is that rectangular regions can be selected with a mouse so as to define samples to use in generating the plots. These selections can then be used by other parts of the Clementine system.

Histogram nodes. A typical histogram display can be produced using a single numeric field to show the distribution of values. This diagram type also supports the option of overlaying a symbolic field that provides for the normalization of the data by scaling the proportions to percentages. A special type of histogram called a "collection" can be used to show how values of one numeric field vary across those of another. This helps to support multivariate analyses where larger numbers of variables

Figure 9.4 A histogram display in Clementine.

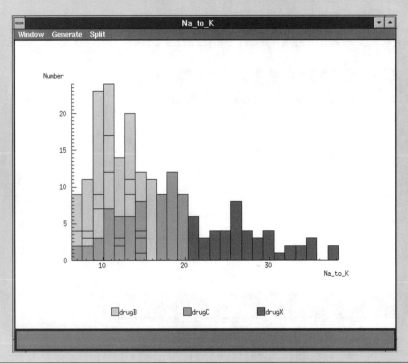

are present in the analysis. The histogram displays also support the definition of thresholds and bands through interactive mouse controls. Figure 9.4 shows a histogram display generated by Clementine.

Web nodes. For each variable presented within a web diagram, the number of distinct values encountered for each variable are presented as a band of points. For each co-occurrence of values being presented within a corresponding data record, a line is drawn between the respective endpoints. Line thickness is based on the number of observations within the data set for two value pairing where the thickness can be set to either absolute values or proportional values. A web diagram can show different line strengths (weak/dotted, medium/dashed, strong/solid) based on user-defined inputs. The lines can be profiled through interaction with the mouse to show strength and the number of records being represented. These profiles can form the basis of a selection operation. Figure 9.5 shows a sample web diagram.

Figure 9.5 A web diagram in Clementine.

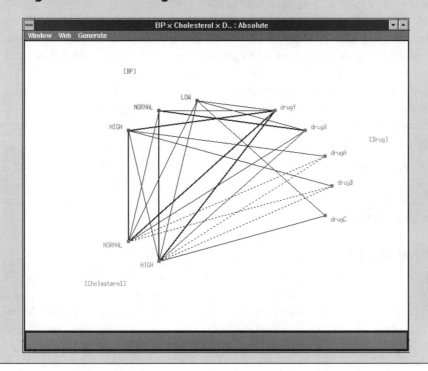

modeling node. Clementine will take care of the necessary details. Of course, for those more knowledgeable about the inner workings of the system, there is always the option to override the selections made by Clementine. For the purposes of this text, we will not go into the different implementations of these technologies, although they do represent a significant capability within Clementine. But what we will say is that for supervised learning via a neural network, Clementine uses a Multi-Layer Perceptron (MLP) network trained through back propagation. Clementine also uses a Kohonen neural network for unsupervised learning by clustering the data into a two-dimensional grid. Decision trees are produced in Clementine with rule induction based on both the ID3 algorithms as well as the C4.5 algorithm. Clementine V4.0 now has two new association rule induction algorithms (GI and Apriori) that are used to discover patterns called affinities or associations. C4.5 has recently been updated to C5.0 to include more robust rule induction techniques. Finally, the regression-modeling module provided in Clementine builds equations using numeric input fields to estimate the value of a numeric output field. (The basics of each of these analytical methods were presented in Chapter 6.)

Enterprise Miner

The Enterprise Miner is a system that can be used for quantitative data mining analyses. The system is produced by SAS Institute, Inc. in North Carolina. This is the same company that produces SAS, which has long been one of the most popular statistical analysis systems on the market. The designers of Enterprise Miner envision an archetype of data mining that they call the SEMMA process. The SEMMA sequence of analytical steps includes data *Sampling*, *Exploratory* analysis, *Modification*, *Modeling*, and finally *Assessment* of modeling results. The modules and functionality of Enterprise Miner have been constructed to support these activities as they occur in an analytical engagement.

Enterprise Miner is a client/server application that runs on Windows 95/NT clients and on popular UNIX server platforms. The current version requires 250 MB of disk space, a CD-ROM drive, and a system that has a communication protocol in place between the client and server platform.

Accessing Functions in Enterprise Miner

The interfaces in Enterprise Miner are a combination of windows, dialog boxes, and pull-down menus from which you can access the various types of information and processing options needed to do your analysis. When using Enterprise Miner, you construct a process flow diagram (PFD) of your model in the DataMining Workspace window. This flow diagram is composed of connected nodes, each representing a discrete function in the overall analytical process. In a manner similar to that used in other tools, you design the analytical stream of the analysis by dragging and dropping items from the Nodes window, and arranging and connecting them in the Workspace window.

Three primary classes of tools are used to construct these models. The data preparation tools are used for applying transformations, detecting outliers, handling missing values, selecting variables, group processing, data partitioning, and taking data samples. The statistical tools perform functions such as clustering, associations and sequences, generating decision trees, applying regression, and instantiating neural networks. The visualization tools can be used to perform a wide range of multi-dimensional analyses. There are also tools for comparing models and predictions from any of the modeling tools. These tools allow you to manage, edit, export, and execute scoring code generated by the mining process. A special tool enables you to incorporate new or existing SAS code into process flow diagrams developed with Enterprise Miner. Figure 9.6 shows a sample of what the DataMining workspace would look like when performing a reasonably complex analysis task.

The Nodes window contains a node palette that displays all data mining processing functions that are available for use in constructing the overall process flow diagram. You can drag and drop icons from the nodes window palette into the data mining workspace window in order to create the model for the analysis. Information flows from node to node in the direction indicated by connecting arrows that you specify. The interface is designed so that you can easily change

Figure 9.6 A sample DataMining workspace display within the Enterprise Miner.

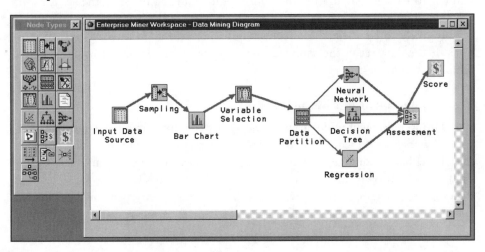

connections, add and delete nodes, and so forth. Functions are broken out into individual modules invoked by the nodes so that you can easily modify your analytical models on the fly with very little difficulty. There are also tools for embedding a diagram within a diagram and also for adding control points within diagrams.

Sampling Your Data in Enterprise Miner

The first step in defining your analytical model is to tell the system which data set is going to be loaded for analysis. Therefore the first node in your process flow diagram is always the input data source node, which specifies the data source to be used in the analysis. The particular data set or table to be used is selected through a series of dialog windows. You can use a data set that is stored in one of the SAS libraries, or you can generate a data set from an SQL query of a data table. The input data can also reside in one of over 50 different proprietary data stores including Excel, Sybase, Oracle, and others. There are also options allowing you to create a data mining database that is stored in a specialized SAS database format. The SAS code node enables you to incorporate new or existing SAS code into process flow diagrams developed with Enterprise Miner. You may choose the data set(s) to be processed by the node, view details about data sets, automatically compute a new data mining database from the training set, and view the macro variable name assigned to each data set. You may directly enter program code or import an existing SAS program to be run when the diagram is executed. Results or data sets generated from the SAS code can then be exported for use by subsequent nodes in the diagram.

Analyses can be conducted either on entire data sets, random samples, or on partitioned subsets of data. For very large data sets, you may want to use sampling in order to reduce computation time during the modeling phase of the analysis. As the name implies, random samples are constructed with each data element being equally likely to be selected for inclusion. To preserve certain categorical proportions of the data set in the sampled data, you have the option of using stratified sampling techniques.

Data Replacement in Enterprise Miner

The Data Replacement node provides the ability to impute missing values for interval and classification variables. You can choose to use one of the default statistics (mean, median, midrange) to replace missing values for interval variables, or you can specify your own value. You can ascribe missing values for class variables with the most frequently occurring level of the variable or specify your own value. The Data Replacement node also allows you to trim or truncate values for interval variables. For example, if you wish to cap the values of an interval variable at some maximum value, you can do that with this node. Similarly, if you wish to set all negative values for a variable to zero, you can do that as well.

Filtering Outliers in Enterprise Miner

The Filter Outliers node enables you to apply a filter to your data to exclude extreme values or other observations that you do not want to include in further data mining analyses. The node provides you with the option to filter observations automatically from the data set based on eliminating rare values, and/or eliminating extreme values based on the standard deviation from the mean, extreme percentiles, the modal centroid, or the median absolute deviation (MAD). The node also incorporates an enhanced visual interface for manually defining the acceptable range for interval variables.

Transforming the Data in Enterprise Miner

There is also a set of preprocessing operations that you can invoke prior to analysis. The Transform Variables node facilitates the creation of transformed variables to be used in the modeling process. The node supports log, square root, inverse, square, and exponential transformations of numeric variables. It also allows you to standardize numeric variables and create new variables from existing variables in the data set. For each variable, several simple statistics such as the mean, standard deviation, skewness, and kurtosis are displayed. A graph of the distribution of any variable may also be displayed from within the node by selecting the variable name and choosing View Distribution from the pop-up menu. Additionally, the node supports user-defined formulas for transformations and provides a visual interface for segmenting interval-valued variables by creating buckets or quantiles. Transform Variable nodes allow you to make transformations such as log, arcsine, or square root on the data. Additionally you can filter out data elements of particular values or eliminate outliers from the data set. You can select which of the variables represented in your data set to include in the analysis. Finally, you can eliminate records that have missing values.

Partitioning Data in Enterprise Miner

Once a sample of data has been specified, the sample is usually partitioned before you begin the modeling phase of the SEMMA paradigm. In particular, you may want to partition your data into training, validation, and testing subsets that can all be invoked independently to test the generality of results obtained with analyses. You can specify proportions of observations to allocate to each of these subsets.

Exploratory Analysis Options in Enterprise Miner

The Input Data Source node enables you to define the name of a data source to be used for the data mining process and to enter details about the variables in the data. When a data source is imported into SAS Enterprise Miner via the Input Data Source node, meta-information is created automatically for each variable in the data set. Initial values are set for the measurement level and model role of each variable. You can change these values if you are not satisfied with the automatic selections made by the node. For each interval-valued variable, summary statistics are created automatically, and for each classification variable, the number of class levels is computed and displayed. The Input Data Source node also incorporates the SAS Query window for importing data sets. This feature provides you with additional functionality such as the ability to join tables and create new columns directly from the Input Data Source node.

The Insight node enables you to explore and analyze your data interactively using SAS/INSIGHT. SAS/INSIGHT is designed for the exploration of your data through graphs and analyses linked across multiple windows. SAS Enterprise Miner passes a sample of your data to the node to be used with SAS/INSIGHT. You can then use this sample to analyze univariate distributions, investigate multivariate distributions, create scatter and box plots, display mosaic charts, and examine correlations. You can also fit explanatory models using analysis of variance, regression, and generalized linear models. However, you should use the SAS Enterprise Miner modeling nodes to create predictive models from large data sets.

Early on in the analysis you may want to get an overview of your data set, looking for general patterns and trends and identifying outliers. Enterprise Miner supports several visualization methods including bar charts and cluster diagrams that can be very useful when invoked during exploratory analysis. We present a few of these next.

Using Bar Charts in Enterprise Miner

Enterprise Miner can be used to create three-dimensional bar charts. By selecting the bar chart node from the Nodes Window and dragging it to any place in the process flow diagram after the input data source node, you can get an overview of the data at that point in the model. You can customize bar charts using the multidimensional histograms window. Here you can designate which variables are represented on the x, y, and z axes of the bar chart. You have the option of setting minimum and maximum ranges for variable values as well. Several examples of the types of 3D bar charts that can be produced in Enterprise Miner are shown in Figure 9.7.

Figure 9.7 Three-dimensional bar charts created in Enterprise Miner.

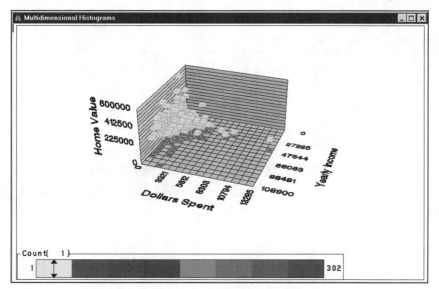

Clustering in Enterprise Miner

The visual clustering option can be used to give you an overall picture of how the data set might be segmented into groups. Sometimes this method is useful in identifying subgroups that may be contrasted in further analyses. The clustering methods compute Euclidean distances from one or more quantitative variables and seeds that are automatically calculated by the system. You can specify the threshold distances that the algorithm uses to specify clusters as well as the maximum number of allowable clusters in the analysis. Descriptive statistics about each cluster can be reported separately for comparison purposes. Graphical representations of the clusters across levels of specified variables can also be generated as shown in Figure 9.8.

Modeling Your Data in Enterprise Miner

The Variable Selection node provides you with several methods for reducing the number of variables to be used in your data mining modeling activities. You may remove variables unrelated to the target, remove variables in hierarchies, remove variables with large percentages of missing values, or remove class variables that have more than a specified number of levels. The first method utilizes the DMINE procedure, which provides you with a fast preliminary variable assessment and facilitates the quick development of predictive models with large volumes of data.

Figure 9.8 Example of a clustering analysis in Enterprise Miner.

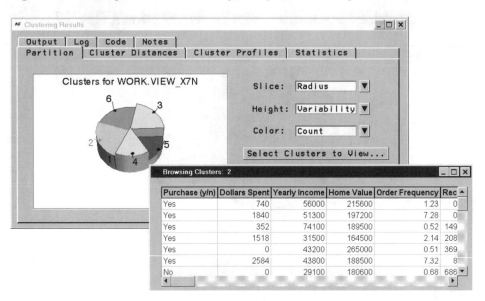

Using this method, you can quickly identify input variables that are useful for predicting the target variable based on a linear models framework. You have the option of including all possible two-way interactions in the variable selection process. DMINE also offers an option to create 16 variables for each interval-valued input variable. These variables are constructed by creating 16 equally spaced bins from the interval variable. The new variable can account for some degree of nonlinear relationship with the target. Additionally, DMINE can collapse the levels of categorical variables based on the relationship of the variable to the target.

The second variable selection method (Remove variables in hierarchies) looks for variables with hierarchical relationships and gives you the option of keeping the variable having the most detail or the variable having the least detail. The third method (Remove variables with large % missing) identifies and removes variables with large percentages of missing values. You can supply the percentage to be used as the cut-off criterion. Class variables that have many levels, such as Zip code, can be related to the target, but eliminating these variables tends to speed the processing time of the modeling nodes, often without a great loss of information. The fourth method identifies and removes these variables. The Variable Selection node can be run prior to any other analysis. After the most important variables are identified, they are passed to any subsequent modeling nodes in the PFD (Process Flow Diagram).

The Group Processing node enables you to define group variables for which you can obtain separate analyses for each level of the variable(s). This process is sometimes referred to as "by-group processing." Also, if you defined more than one target variable in the Input Data Source node, then a separate analysis is performed for each target.

As previously mentioned, various types of quantitative modeling options are available that may be specified in the process flow diagram. Depending upon the goals of your analysis, you may want to use several of these methods to determine the degree to which the results agree, and to decide which approach yields the most useful information. You can construct your process flow diagram so that multiple modeling approaches are used. Additionally, you can create subdiagrams that collapse portions of the larger process flow diagrams into a single unit that might include the steps needed to invoke a modeling approach and its assessment. As a side note, Enterprise Miner does not offer extensive support for time series analyses, although you can invoke SAS routines devised for this purpose. What follows are brief descriptions of the quantitative modeling approaches supported in Enterprise Miner.

Using Regression Models within Enterprise Miner

Perhaps the most commonly used modeling approach is the regression analysis, which allows you to make input-output predictions by finding best fits of either linear or logistic regression models to your data. This module can analyze either discrete or continuous variables as inputs. It will automatically create any dummy variables needed for handling classification variables as inputs. It allows you to use stepwise, forward, and backward model selection techniques and provides you with the ability to force variables into the model. This is a very basic analysis, and its results may be presented in tabular, graphical, or chart format.

Association Rules/Market Basket Analyses in Enterprise Miner

As described in Chapter 6, association rule analyses allow you to discover pairs or groups of items that tend to occur together in your data set. Association rules are usually based on the relative frequency with which items tend to occur together within records across the data set. Associations imply co-occurrence but not causation. Enterprise Miner takes the association rule analysis one step further to include sequence discovery, which takes the ordering of associated events into account. Binary sequences are constructed automatically, and an event chain handler allows you to construct longer sequences based on the patterns discovered by the algorithm. This analysis assumes that a time stamp is available for the data records.

You can set several parameters in an association rule analysis including reporting thresholds for frequency of co-occurrence, confidence values, and number of items in the association. The results of association analyses are presented as lists of associates and the rules describing their relationships. They can also be graphed as shown in Figure 9.9.

Decision Tree Analyses in Enterprise Miner

As described in Chapter 6, decision tree analyses can be used to construct rules for categorizing data elements and predicting classifications of new data. A hierarchical tree structure is built up from the elements contained in the data set. Splits in the tree are based on nominal, ordinal, or interval inputs. (In the case of interval splits, you must define the splits before modeling begins.) Once the splitting criteria are specified, control can be exercised over such factors as number of leaves produced in the tree. You choose among several options to designate the splitting criteria to be used in creating the tree. Training can occur either automatically or interactively.

Various quantitative methods are available for evaluating the rules created by the modeling procedure including statistical tests and profit/cost assessments. Assessment displays include tabular outputs, ring diagrams, and graphs. The tree ring diagrams are particularly interesting because they show successive degrees to which the data set is split as you traverse down the decision tree (see Figure 9.10).

Figure 9.9 Display of association analysis results in Enterprise Miner.

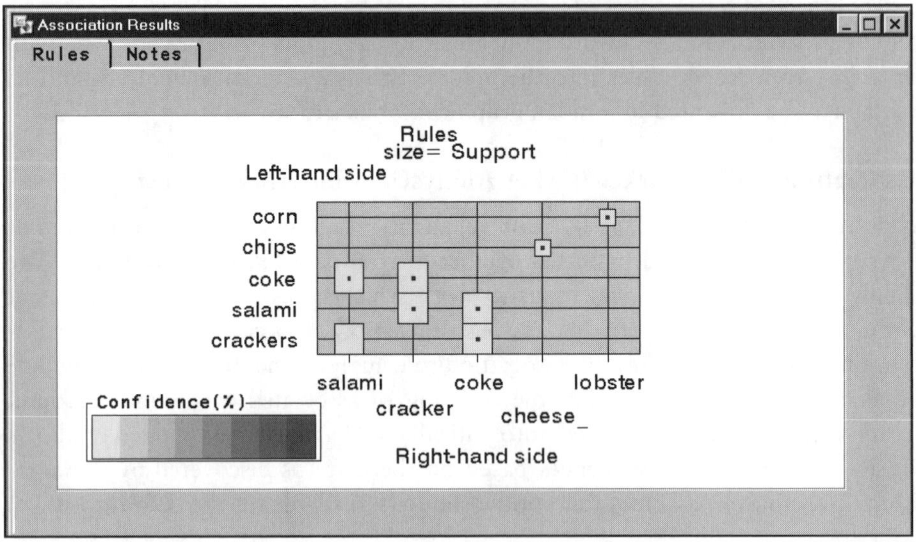

Figure 9.10 Example of a tree ring diagram in Enterprise Miner.

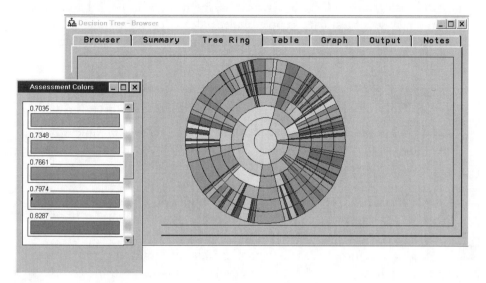

Neural Network Analyses in Enterprise Miner

Enterprise Miner supports a fairly impressive neural network modeling capability. You can specify any of several types of neural net models, all of which are supervised learning networks (see Chapter 6 for a discussion). The main thing to note about supervised networks is that you must specify the categories of inputs and their associated outputs a priori. That is, the analysis models the predictive relationships existing between input and output variables. The network does not *discover* new categories among which outputs can be divided—all possible output categories are known ahead of time and are based on known categories already existing in the data set.

The types of neural network models supported by Enterprise Miner are summarized in the sidebar. The system supports iterative specification, testing, and revision of models. You can specify which items to use for training, which variables to include in the model from the data set, and what the outputs should be. You must also specify activation functions, but some candidate functions are provided as defaults depending upon the type of neural network model being used. You can specify the training technique, maximum number of iterations, and maximum CPU time for the training process.

Neural network models can be displayed in a process flow window very much like the DataMining Workspace window. You can add hidden layers, manipulate activation functions, specify connectivity configurations, and so on using pull-down menus and dialog boxes. Once a network has been trained, it can be saved and tested on a new set of test data sampled independently of the training set. Results of tests are generally reported in lists or tabular format, although simple plots are available for displaying training functions.

Neural Network Models Supported by Enterprise Miner

Using Enterprise Miner, you can invoke any of a number of varieties of supervised neural network models. They include the following options, which are presented in order of increasing complexity.

Simple Networks. Formed from a single input and single output layer, these models effectively compute a linear regression function.

Perceptrons. These use linear combination of inputs to form a net input. An activation function is then applied that equates to the computation of a multiple linear regression model (i.e., predicting more than one output variable).

Hidden Layers. Simple networks and perceptrons may be expanded to include hidden layers that apply an added transformation to signals in the input layer. An activation function is applied to the hidden layer. You can add as many hidden layers as desired, and different activation functions may be applied to each. A special version of a hidden layer model is the Radial Basis Function, which is a network that has one hidden layer between the input and output that uses a radial combination function in the hidden layer.

Multilayer Perceptrons. These models usually employ hidden layers that have nonlinear activation functions. Weighted connections are computed and adjusted between the input and the first hidden layer, between hidden layers, and between hidden and output layers. The nature of these connections is under your control.

Assessing Results in Enterprise Miner

The Score node enables you to manage, edit, export, and execute scoring code that is generated from the data mining process. The scoring formulas are created in the form of a single SAS data step, which can be used in most SAS environments. Score code is accumulated in the process flow based on the path traced by the training data set. Operations on only the validation or test data sets are not recognized as part of the score code.

Modeling nodes generate different scoring formulas when operating on subsets of the data, as defined by a Group Processing node. The Score node merges the scoring code for each group into a single data step by logically dividing the data into IF THEN/END blocks. Any node that modifies the observations of the input variables or creates scoring formula generates components of score code. Transformation, Data Replacement, Clustering, Group Processing, Regression, Neural Network, Decision Tree, and SAS Code nodes all generate components of scoring code.

Results obtained in regression, decision trees, and neural network analyses are evaluated by invoking either assessment nodes in the DataMiner Workspace window or the model manager in each of the modeling nodes. Assessment nodes must be preceded by any of the modeling nodes in the process flow diagrams since they utilize results from modeling operations. Results may be presented in tables or in graphical charts. Enterprise Miner supports color-coding of variables in the chart displays. 3D versions of some charts are also available. Results can be printed to bitmap files for inclusion in presentations or saved to HTML or VRML files for delivery and viewing on the Web.

Usefulness of models is conveyed in several ways including profit charts, which contrast actual and expected profit values, receiver operating characteristic curves, diagnostic classification charts, identification of top-ten marginal impact variables, and threshold-base charts that display agreement between expected and actual values across a range of threshold levels. An example of a profit chart display is shown in Figure 9.11.

Diamond

Diamond is a quantitative visualization package that was developed by the Exploratory Visualization Group at IBM research and is currently licensed to SPSS for distribution. Since the input format for Diamond is a plain ASCII file, it is easy to use in conjunction with other data analysis tools. For example, Diamond forms a natural front-end analytical tool to OLAP systems because it follows a similar multidimensional modeling format using visualization. Diamond is available through SPSS on AIX, OS12, and Windows platforms; an enhanced version available as a library of embeddable cross-platform function calls is nearing completion at IBM. This section describes the functionality of SPSS Diamond. (Additional features of the

Figure 9.11 Examples of assessment results in Enterprise Miner.

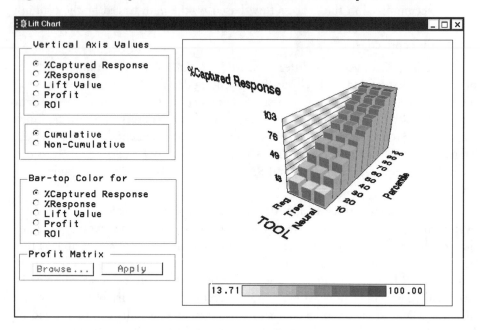

API are described in the case study reported in Chapter 14 in Section IV.) Within a single invocation of the Diamond software, you are restricted to one particular data set. If a new data set is loaded into an existing invocation of Diamond, it will overwrite the one currently in memory. The way to compare and contrast information derived from different sources is to launch several versions of Diamond or to join all of the data sets into a single file prior to the analysis.

Like a real-world diamond, this tool provides many different facets for viewing your data, each with its own unique characteristics. One impressive feature of Diamond is its coordination of all of these facets in the evaluation of the same selection of data. Diamond can interactively support the selection of points within a display and have all of the other active displays reflect the same selection. This is a unique form of drill-down where visual selections are used to drive the target points of interest.

Formatting and Loading Data in Diamond

The data structure used by Diamond is fairly straightforward and closely emulates those representations usually found in a spreadsheet application. The basic layout is to put variables denoted by titles in columns with corresponding values for each case in rows. When you are loading a data set it is easy to select a range of cases or choose the specific variables you want to analyze. The native worksheet system distributed with Diamond arranges data in this format. This worksheet is very simple in its construction and usage because it simply requires you to specify the titles of the columns followed by rows of values separated by blanks or tabs. If Diamond detects that there are not enough values to map into the titles provided, the fields are left blank and will return NULL values. Titles are important because they become the names of the variables within the visualizations supported by Diamond. If there are no titles present, the worksheet will default to a simple sequence of terms such as v_01, v_02, up to v_NN. The cells within the worksheet contain the actual values assigned to each title (e.g., column) and they may be either numerics or strings. The maximum size of any cell is 20 characters, so any long descriptions are trimmed accordingly. The content of any cell can be changed, copied, cut, or altered in any way to satisfy the type of analyses to be performed.

Other input formats supported by Diamond include simple ASCII files (variously delimited), Excel and Lotus spreadsheets, DIF, and dBase. You can also create files in a special Diamond format. The import dialog recognizes the select data import source format and puts the requisite information into the Diamond worksheet. You can then verify that the information is correct before saving it out into the Diamond format. There are upper bounds to the number of records that Diamond will handle. Currently, there are limits of 500 columns and 5000 rows that can be loaded into a Diamond data set.

Defining the Proactive Slice of Data in Diamond

When actually loading your data into Diamond, there are also several parameters that can be set to refine and focus the types of analyses that can be performed. There are options to load the entire data file or to load only a subset. As we discussed in Section I, it is sometimes important to slice your data into workable segments in order to perform an analysis. Data subsetting is supported by Diamond through a dialog that requests the starting record number and the number of records to load. This helps you focus your analysis and manage the performance of the system. If there are too many records being processed, response times are going to be slower. Additionally, there are parameters to rearrange the ordering of the variables, include/exclude variables, and add defined variables and equations (e.g., x: y*z).

Diamond also provides a feature that lets you test out different approaches and subsets of data through a "reinvocation" procedure. A new instance of Diamond is invoked with the subset of data that was selected for review. The subset can be defined through dialog boxes that provide the ability to reinvoke based on select cases by colored groups (e.g., sets of data you have interactively selected), by a selection of variables, or by some combination. The invocation feature essentially provides a method by which to set up checkpoints to further explore different analytical contingencies without interrupting the current analysis. This can be used to look at more detail about a particular area through instantiation of different models or to get rid of variables that do not support the current analysis. This type of capability is a high-level form of drill-down where the information is being presented as a separate invocation. The new instance of Diamond is completely independent of the one that spawned it.

Manipulating Your Data Set in Diamond

When working with the data in a Diamond application, there are times when additional information can be generated from the variables selected from the data being analyzed. Diamond does support a single scaling function to any variable, but more often you will want to perform more complex types of calculations. Diamond lets you define new variables in order to add value to the existing data. Any time you create a new variable, it is instantaneously available for visualization and manipulation. The types of value-added capabilities currently supported by Diamond are quite extensive. There are functions that help deal with missing values, integrate and differentiate, compute distribution functions, perform principal components analysis, and even deal with time. Any defined variable equations can be saved in files that can be loaded when a data set is opened. The range of functionality is quite extensive and the sidebar gives a quick overview of each of the different types of data manipulation functions available in Diamond. A full description of each is provided in the Diamond Help Facilities. There is even an assist function that will support you in the selection and parameter definitions for any function.

Data Manipulation Functions Supported by Diamond

In keeping with its emphasis on quantitative manipulation and computation, Diamond offers a number of data manipulation functions that can be evoked directly from the interface.

Casewise. Transforms data by absolute value, arccosine, arcsine, arctangent, cuberoot, ceiling, cosine, cube, derivative, exp, floor, high, in, log, low, power, rd^2, sign, sine, squareroot, square, and tangent.

Color. Allows you to set colors by value rather than by using the mouse. Color choices are limited.

Before you begin your analysis, you will want to address issues concerning the use of color within the Diamond environment. There are features provided to set colors by data type, value, and so forth. Initially, all display points are presented as gray until a color scheme has been selected. The most common way to select and color subsets of data is by brushing the data dynamically with a mouse-driven brush. Assignment of color can also be done through a dialog box that asks you to choose which variable to associate with the colors. Alternatively you can use a rainbow brush to subdivide selected regions into unique colors. There are also several other color features contained within Diamond not covered here.

Displaying Data in Diamond

Once you have identified the types of data you are using and the functions that are being applied to the data, Diamond redisplays its main interface screen. The initial display contains a summary of the information that has been loaded including the number of variables, the number of records, primary color selection, derived values, and several other facts. This main interface also contains a toolbar from which to launch into Diamond's visualization methods. At this point you can either use one of the graphic representations or view your data using one of the textual presentation methods. There are seven different display types and three textual displays. Each one is discussed next.

Diamond's Directory Displays

The first display type is called "Directory" because it provides an overall view of all combinations of variables that have been selected for presentation. The Directory

---

Distribution. Lets you describe the distribution of the data set as flat, index, normal, saw, spike, step, steps, triangle, vector, or wave.

Miscellaneous. Computes a number of functions including closest, density, and radius.

Missing Value. Identifies missing values using such functions as miss, missing, reveal, unmiss, valid, and values.

Ordering. Includes diffuse, find, in, jumble, reverse, select, sortdown, and sortup.

Continued

> **Data Manipulation Functions Supported by Diamond** *(Continued)*
>
> **Periodic.** Describes and imposes periodicity onto the data set through such functions as cycles, lags, leads, phases, rotates, shifts, and warps.
>
> **Primitive Arithmetic.** Includes basic operators such as +, ñ, /, %. *, <, <=, >, >=, =, /=, |, and &.
>
> **Statistical.** Computes various descriptive statistics such as cluster, correlation, geometric, harmonic, kurtosis, length, maximum, mean, median, minimum, mode, nonlin, powered, range, rsquared, skew, slope, spread, standard deviation, and total.
>
> **Tessellating.** Includes change, diff, product, ratio, run, smooth, and sum.
>
> **Transforming.** Transforms data sets according to various rules such as conform, derivative, derivs, dissim, fuzz, hump, integ, merge, normalize, perim, principal, project, quantize, residual, scale, and unmask.
>
> **Unique.** Identifies lone, twin, and unique values.

display shows a matrix of thumbnail scatter plots of paired variables. The rows and columns of the matrix are formed from the variables. For each one of these scatter plots, best-fit regression lines can be computed and displayed. Associated with each variable are two rows of histograms, which are discussed in the Pairwise display description.

As you move the mouse around the matrix, the information box at the bottom of the directory screen will show you the points that are currently active. This can be used to give you a quick overview of the paired relationships represented within the matrix. Figure 9.12 shows an example of the Directory display using some sample data. You will notice that the diagonal shows a linear diagram because those cells pair variables with themselves. Additionally, the two sides of the diagonal are redundant with one another within the default sorting scheme. There are commands that can be used to change sorting preferences within the Directory display.

Diamond's Pairwise Displays

From the Directory display you can double-click on any one of the panels and it will automatically take you into the Pairwise display. The Pairwise display is a

Figure 9.12 A sample Directory display in Diamond.

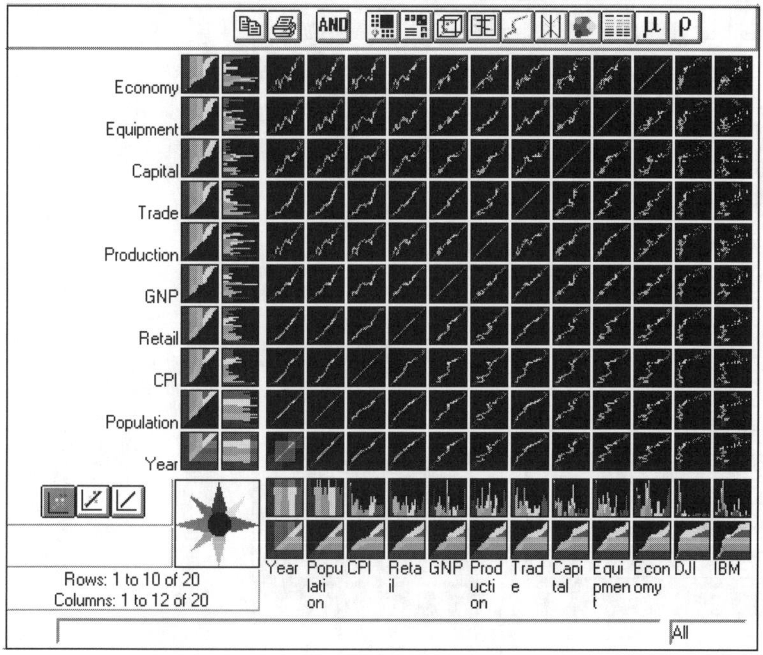

close-up of the two variables that were selected from the Directory display. If invoked directly from the command bar, an intermediate dialog box will appear requesting the selection of two variables to plot. The resulting display is used to show the relationships between the selected variables. The Pairwise display has several features of interest. The first is the use of histograms across the bottom and the left-hand side of the display. The inner-histograms are used to show the minimum and maximum values for each variable. The outer-cumulative histograms (e.g., first left, last bottom) are used to show the total number of cases supporting the variable. As you move the mouse over any point within the Pairwise display, it will present to you the color and values associated with any point or band selected. The Pairwise display also contains an area where there are bivariate statistics presented in a tabular format showing the case, slope, correlation, r-squared, and clustering values for each of the different color bands presented within the display. Figure 9.13 provides an example of a sample Pairwise display.

Diamond's Triplewise Displays

Triplewise displays are logical extensions of Pairwise displays, in which a 3D transparent cube is used to display a scatter plot of three variables. Data for the

Figure 9.13 Pairwise displays generated in Diamond.

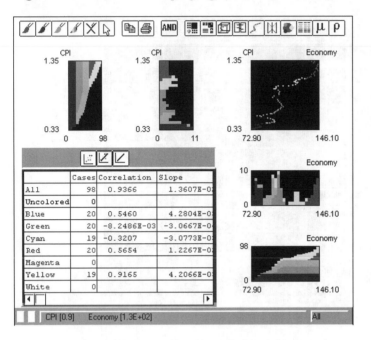

variables selected are normalized relative to one another before being plotted so that the size of any side of the cube remains consistent. Colors can be assigned to the grid points to code variable types and values. A point within the display is generated only when there are valid values for all three variables. Invocation of the Triplewise display function brings up a dialog where you can select the three variables that are to be plotted.

There are several unique features associated with Triplewise displays, one of the most interesting being animation. You can navigate the cube to inspect points fully that might otherwise be obscured from view. Thus, Triplewise has the ability to tilt, spin, and work across the x, y, and z axes. There are also features for zooming, perspective definition, and animation rates. Once you put the cube into motion, it rotates around the defined axes providing a very lively view of the data. Figure 9.14 shows a Triplewise display where the grid has been captured from one perspective. Remember that it would actually be rotating around within the display in actual operation.

Diamond's Quadwise Displays

Taking the Triplewise displays one step further, Quadwise displays can be used to present four variables simultaneously using two separate scatter plots. The variables

Figure 9.14 A Triplewise display showing a cube of data within Diamond.

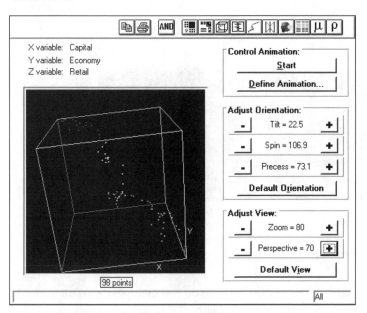

used in a Quadwise display are acquired through a standard dialog box. Each scatter plot defines two of the four dimensions and each point within a scatter plot is connected through a link with its corresponding point within the other scatter plot. A Quadwise display draws a point within a scatter plot only if there is an analogous point in the other scatter plot. Thus, there may be a different number of points in the Quadwise than there would be in some of the other display types. There is a gray area in the middle to provide some spacing between the scatter plots so that links may be differentiated. Quadwise also supports a variety of transformation functions that let you adjust the appearance of the display. Figure 9.15 depicts an example of a Quadwise display in Diamond.

Diamond's Parametric Snake Displays

One additional animation display is called the Parametric Snake. This unique display is derived from three different variables specified through dialog boxes. The first two variables are used to define an x,y scatter plot. The third variable represents the parametric value used to connect (e.g., draw lines between) the points (e.g., the cases) in increasing value. In order for a line to be drawn, the case has to support values in all three variables, otherwise it will not appear. There are animation parameters that can be set to control the look and feel of the Parametric Snake

Figure 9.15 A Quadwise display showing four variables and their corresponding linkages.

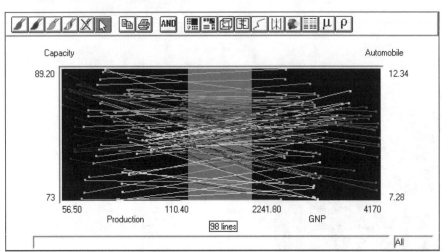

as the connecting lines are drawn in the display. You can manipulate animation rate and percentage of points to connect. By switching on a segmentation parameter, you can control how many links are displayed at a time and the rate at which the display changes to show links among progressive subsets of data. The animated effect looks like a snake traversing through your data. As a side note, the Triplewise display can also be used to generate a Parametric Snake through a simple mouse select. The x and y dimensions transfer directly and the z dimension is used as the parametric value. Figure 9.16 shows a Parametric Snake display.

Diamond's Parallel Coordinates Displays

Perhaps one of the most powerful display types offered by the Diamond system is the Parallel Coordinates display. The layout of this display provides a way to view all of the variables contained within your data set simultaneously to determine if there are any biases or dependencies. No dialog box is required to specify the variables targeted for use within the display because by default all variables are included. A Parallel Coordinates display normalizes all values with respect to one another so that relative trends can be observed, although you can plot raw values if desired. Each axis within a Parallel Coordinate supports a different variable and includes its label and minimum and maximum values. A line is drawn between the axes when there are values coinciding with a case in the data set. Thus, you do not have to have complete records available in order to use a Parallel Coordinates display. The axes can be sorted

Figure 9.16 Parametric Snake display shown within Diamond.

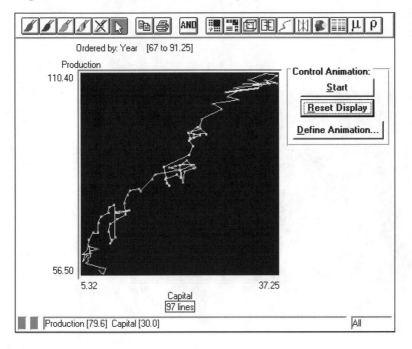

according to a number of conditions including titles and statistics. You can grab any axis and drag it to a new location in the display and all connections to the axes on either side of its new position will then be shown. The scale of the axes can also be changed through the interface if desired. Figure 9.17 shows an example of a normalized Parallel Coordinates display.

Diamond's Fractal Foam Displays

One final form of visualization supported by Diamond is called the Fractal Foam display. This abstract display is based on the representation of bivariate and univariate statistics for a related group of variables. Figure 9.18 shows an example of a Fractal Foam display. Its concept is relatively straightforward since the diagram is seeded with a single variable selected from a dialog box. This focus variable is represented within the center of the display as a circle using some preselected color. For each variable encountered within the data set, a corresponding set of bubbles appears around the focus variable. Their size is at least one half the size of the focus variable (for strongly correlated variables) and varies downward from that point depending on degree of correlation. This display format provides a quick rendering

Figure 9.17 Sample Parallel Coordinates generated by Diamond.

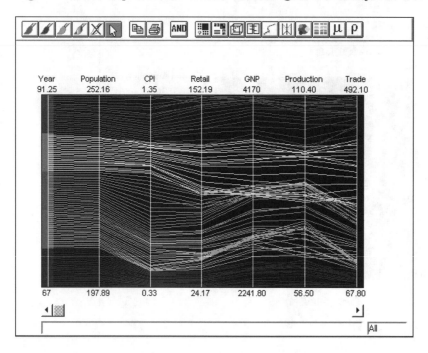

Figure 9.18 A Fractal Foam display within Diamond.

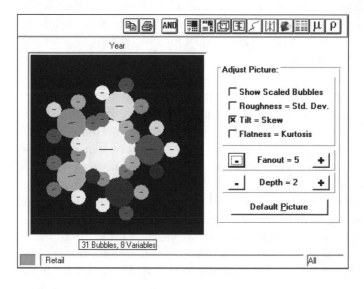

of those variables in the data set that are correlated. As an added bonus, the shapes of the bubbles carry information about the univariate statistics of the individual variables. The degree of jaggedness of a bubble is proportional to the standard deviation of the group represented by that bubble. Furthermore, tilt is used to depict the skew of the distributions of the variables in the data set.

CrossGraphs

CrossGraphs is perhaps one of the most flexible commercial data visualization systems available for performing multidimensional quantitative analyses. The system was originally developed for the government for use in clinical cancer research studies. Since then, significant enhancements have been made that have elevated it to a mainstream analytical system. CrossGraphs is developed by Belmont Research, an emerging technology company out of the New England area and now a wholly-owned subsidiary of Pharmaceutical Product Development, Inc. Like many other statistical systems, CrossGraphs supports a wide array of univariate statistical analyses. What makes CrossGraphs unique is its approach to combining cross-tabulation and statistical graphics to produce graphical arrays of data. Using this approach you can quickly review and compare these arrays of data as different rows, columns, and diagonals all within a gallery of graphics. The graphical arrays provide the ability to view hyper-dimensions of data, taking you well beyond the two or three dimensions associated with traditional business graphics. The CrossGraphs interfaces are easy to understand and require a minimal level of effort to use. All functions are invoked through a drag-and-drop interface. In its current release, there are more than a dozen different graph types that can be used to display data.

Platform Support and Development Environment of CrossGraphs

The CrossGraphs system configuration is supported on a variety of platforms including UNIX, NT, PowerPC MacIntosh, and the family of Windows configurations. CrossGraphs is written in CG++, which is a Belmont-defined programming language similar to Java. CG++ is a simplified version of C++ used for rapid application development purposes. This language can be used to program specific customizations or to extend many of the basic capabilities contained within CrossGraphs. CG++ has a wide range of features and supports many of the standard string manipulation procedures, mathematical operations, and trigonometric functions. CG++ syntax must be used when defining variables, filter expressions, or statements to be parsed by CrossGraphs. All in all, CG++ is a straightforward language that is not too difficult to understand if needed within your CrossGraphs application. It helps to have some programming background, however, especially when you are first getting started.

Importing and Processing the Data in CrossGraphs

CrossGraphs has a variety of data access methods that can be used to couple to data sources. It is ODBC compliant and also has special interfaces for SAS data sets, ASCII files, and dBase. This makes transferring data to CrossGraphs a fairly straightforward process in most cases. It can be run in a real-time interactive mode or through a batch execution to support those situations where frequent or periodic reports need to be generated automatically. Additionally, CrossGraphs has the ability to merge multiple sources of information by designating matching fields among data sources. This is done using graphical metaphors so it is easy to see how the different sources have been combined to form the current working model.

Creating Metadata Description Files in CrossGraphs

To couple CrossGraphs to your data sets, Belmont Research has skillfully crafted a set of front-end data access and processing protocols that are used to translate raw data into a format readable by the system. For ASCII files a corresponding metadata description file must be produced to tell the system how to read and interpret the data. The type and characteristics of the data are already known if you are using ODBC and the other drivers. The format of the metadata description files used by CrossGraphs is fairly straightforward and includes methods for specifying the types, names, locations, ranges, defaults, and various other formatting options. There are also several date/time styles that can be invoked to help you work with unconventional formats. Once a metadata description file has been created, it is automatically checked for errors and the design and the data set are then compiled into a binary format specific to the CrossGraphs system. This provides efficient representation and facilitates transportability among different CrossGraphs packages running on different machines or platforms. When necessary, this binary file can be updated or replaced to reflect new data formats or requirements. There are also methods available in the load functions to translate data sets from multi- to single-column descriptions (see Chapter 4), and to provide indices on certain fields to help address performance issues. You can also generate unique identification variables for data sets that can be especially useful for reporting purposes.

Using TableTrans in CrossGraphs

Belmont Research also produces a product called TableTrans, which is used to support data cleansing, data migration from one schema used by the legacy system to a new schema, data extraction into analysis data sets, data conditioning prior to data mining, and complex queries that require multiple SQL statements. TableTrans is a visual database transformation system that can be used to manipulate and refine the contents of data sources. It uses a palette of icons that can be connected together to form complex transformation models. The transformation details are specified using a graphical interface. A wide variety of features are supported within TableTrans including facilities to select a subset of the rows or columns in a data set and the ability to derive new columns or insert/delete rows. Other transform steps let you compute the union, intersection, or difference between rows in different tables. TableTrans can also compute natural and outer joins, and append columns from matching records. It can be used to summarize data and detect outliers by calculating aggregate column statistics, frequencies of distinct column values, or distributions of continuous column values. TableTrans along with CrossGraphs and the CG++ language provide a powerful suite of tools to support the data mining process. Figure 9.19 shows a sample of a typical TableTrans display.

Creating a CrossGraphs Design

Once all of the data sets have been identified, integrated, and combined with their corresponding metadata description files, you are ready to begin your analysis. To do so, you will need to create a design specification. The term "design" refers to the experimental design context in which data are gathered. Within this framework,

Figure 9.19 A typical TableTrans display in CrossGraphs.

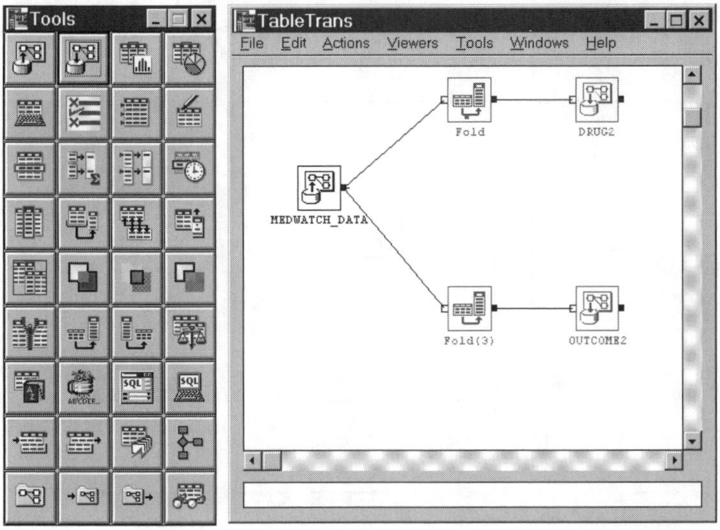

independent and dependent variables are identified and a priori hypotheses generated. However, in nonexperimental applications, you can consider a design to be a specific viewpoint of your data. The basic intent of a design is to define what data to process, what graphs to use, and which variables to display for partitioning and reporting purposes. The designs can be stored and recalled in either an interactive or batch process to regenerate the same reports.

The design window shown in Figure 9.20 is used to support the creation of CrossGraphs designs and is composed of four primary areas. The variable list on the left-hand side is used for displaying the fields defined from the underlying data sets. The list is either presented alphabetically or grouped according to the source data set. To select a variable for display, you drag the name from the list and drop it in the central design area in the middle of the display. The variable can be placed into one of three positions in the central design area. It can be applied to the rows or columns, or as the layer (e.g., outer) variable. The design area is used to construct and configure the types of displays that are produced. Here the set of variables and a single graph type are specified. The configuration of these parameters determines how the resulting displays will look. The graph palette on the right side contains icons for all of the different types of statistical graphs that can be selected. These graphs are also selected by drag-and-drop methods for placement in the

Figure 9.20 CrossGraphs design window.

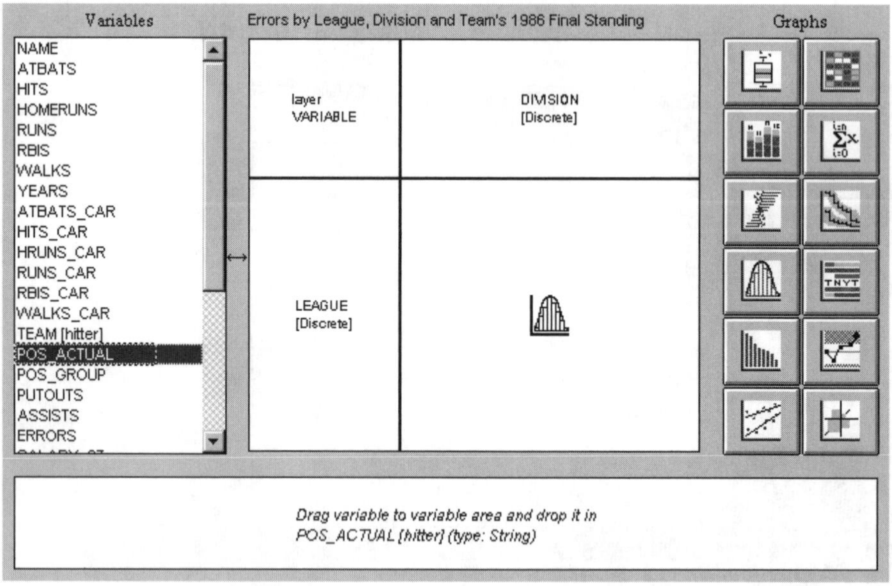

graph area in the central display. Only one graph can be functioning at a time and when it is selected, it prompts you to specify any additional information it requires. The final part of the CrossGraphs screen is the message area. It is here that feedback and help messages are displayed.

A dozen different graphs are available in the CrossGraphs system. Many of these graphs also support *inner breakdown variables*, which are used to further refine how the diagrams look. These are usually defined as subgroups within the graphs where the colors, symbols, line types, or positioning of data is used to distinguish the subgroups. These breakdown variables are where the hyperdimensional display capabilities of CrossGraphs are introduced.

One important point is that CrossGraphs treats discrete and continuous data differently. Discrete variables are composed of values within a predefined set of entries. Virtually any variable used to represent stringed values is discrete. Discrete variables might include such classes as seasons of the year (of which there are four), gender (with two levels), or brand of detergent in a marketing study (of which there would be as many levels as the number of detergents being compared in the analysis). Continuous variables, on the other hand, are necessarily numeric and have values that fall within a predefined range. Continuous variables might include such factors as time, age, height, and total sales. Continuous values are segmented by default within CrossGraphs into three equal-sized groups according to their values. In many cases, continuous variables can be converted to discrete variables through manual grouping methods. The converse is not true, but for most analyses, the classification of data into discrete categories is sufficient to provide insightful information.

Presenting Data Using CrossGraphs

Although CrossGraphs is not very interactive from the point of view of dynamic simulations or animated 3D displays, it does produce static graphs that are calculated on demand. Any graph can be adjusted to meet your specific needs by changing the labels, size parameters, and color scales. Drill-downs are available on most of the CrossGraphs displays where a cell from the graphical array can be extracted and profiled in a separate window. This provides you the opportunity to analyze the cell contents in more detail or compare them to the content of other cells in the display. For those graphs that do support drill-down, individual points can be selected within the diagrams and their variable values displayed. There are also custom features that can sort or limit the types of information presented in a drill-down. Additionally, all graphs support a text-only format where the details are presented textually instead of graphically.

Using the Report Viewer Window in CrossGraphs

Once you have specified all of the display parameters, you can generate the output. All output in CrossGraphs is presented to a report viewer window. This is a separate window from the main design window and it contains specialized navigation controls. For any single design, there can be only one corresponding display presented at a time. However, CrossGraphs does let more than one design be open at a time thereby allowing multiple displays to be compared and contrasted. The report viewer has an extended level of customizable features. These include definition of text characteristics, axis labels, print designs, cell layouts, line styles, and fonts, to name a few. Additionally, for each type of diagram produced, you usually have the option of drilling down to the original data as well as displaying a range of secondary variables (called Inner Variables or Breakdown Variables).

Generating Graphical Displays in CrossGraphs

Appropriate selection of the graph type within CrossGraphs has a significant effect on the range of patterns that can be discovered. To better understand the types of information conveyed by the different graphical formats, a high-level overview of several types is provided next. These descriptions are not meant to explain all of the features of each graph fully, but rather to introduce capabilities and give a sense of their general look and feel. Readers familiar with statistical analysis will recognize many of the different formats. What is unique about CrossGraphs displays is the number of dimensions being presented through the rows, columns, layers, and inner breakdown variables (layered dimensions are not shown in the following figures). The term "analysis variable" used in any one of the descriptions refers to the primary variable used to produce the associated graph.

Box-Plots in CrossGraphs Summaries of information contained within one continuous variable can be represented as a box-plot. The general structure of a box-plot is laid out in a two-dimensional grid, where one axis is used to display the distribution of values for the target variable from min to max, and the other axis is used to map the target variable itself. If there are subgroups or bins defined for the target variable, then a set of box-plots will appear for each discrete grouping. Continuous variables are usually subdivided into three groupings to represent the lower, middle, and upper third of the values sampled. The information from the values associated with the target variable can then be converted into a set of graphical display elements used to construct the box-plot for subsequent analyses. Figure 9.21 shows a sample set of box-plots.

Figure 9.21 Sample set of box-plots created within CrossGraphs.

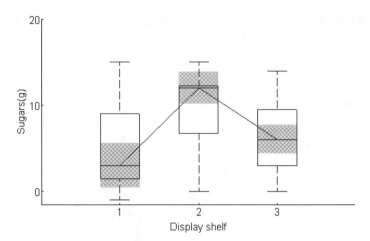

Box-plots are constructed to convey several types of information. Boxes (rectangles) in the diagram are drawn around the *interquartile range* (IQR) encompassing 50 percent of the observations for a given value grouping. Within each IQR box, shading is used to indicate the median of the grouping. Examination of the distance from the median to the top and bottom of the box allows you to infer the shape of the distribution for that grouping. Using this technique, you can compare the distance between the median and either end of the rectangle to see whether your data are evenly distributed or skewed more toward one end of the distribution than another. The *adjacent* values, or two remaining quartiles, are represented using vertical lines extending from either end of the IQR rectangle. (Outliers are plotted separately using a symbol.) The box-plots do support a drill-down capability within CrossGraphs.

Contingency Table Graphs in CrossGraphs These graphs are used to display the types of information usually included in a Chi-square analysis in which contingencies between two variables each having two levels are examined. The finding of interest in this type of analysis is a pattern of unequal volumes in the four cells of the two by two matrix. When all cells are equal, you can infer independence between the two variables. Inequalities indicate that there are dependencies between the variables, the nature of which is usually a matter for further analysis. As shown in Figure 9.22, the frequency of observations appearing in each cell of the matrix is represented by the size of the squares originating at the center of the matrix. In this example, the size

Figure 9.22 Examples of contingency table graphs in CrossGraphs.

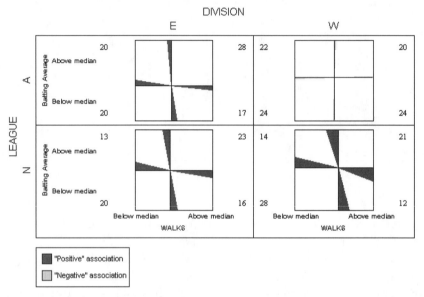
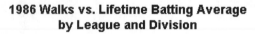

of these squares is not equal, indicating a dependency between the two variables being examined.

Counts Graphs in CrossGraphs These are very simple diagrams that can be used to summarize the number or percentage of elements observed within the data sample for a particular category or binned set of values. Several display formats are available from within the counts graphs including bar graph, pie chart, symbol, or text representation. Their structure is defined based on the type of count being performed. Three types of counts can be used to summarize the data. A basic count is just the number of observations made for a particular category regardless of the number of duplicates encountered. A unique count removes any duplicates from the total. A weighted count offsets the number of observations with a weighted variable where the result represents the sum of the weighted variable values. If desired, counts graphs can represent the relationship between the levels of two or more variables. Figure 9.23 shows a sample of several count graphs. Drill-down is available for the counts graph.

Figure 9.23 Several different counts graphs produced by CrossGraphs.

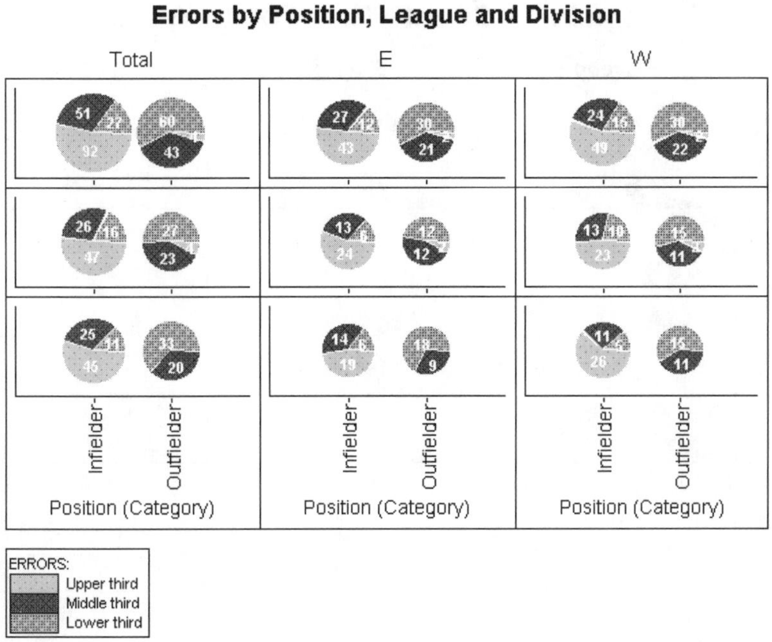

Errors by Position, League and Division

Delta Graphs in CrossGraphs Delta graphs display information about the change in the value of a variable across two separate observations on a set of entities. In this type of graph, a horizontal line is drawn for every pair of beginning and end observations. Each line represents the magnitude (length) and direction (negative-left, positive-right) of the difference observed between the start and endpoint for each pair of observations. Line color may be manipulated to display which cases show increases and which show decreases. There are two types of delta graphs supported by CrossGraphs. The tree style places all starting points at a zero value on the x axis; the Carr and Yang style (default) plots the actual starting and ending values without any adjustments. Observation pairs can be ordered along the vertical dimension (individual cases are usually represented in the y axis) in terms of original value, magnitude of difference, experimental variable, and so on. You might use a delta graph to convey information about the effectiveness of a drug treatment in a study in which you measured some physiological variable before and after treatment. Alternatively, you could use a delta graph to convey sales information in a series of franchises before and after a particular marketing campaign. Figure 9.24 shows examples of delta graphs plotting the efficacy of a drug treatment. The points on each line represent the end-

Figure 9.24 Set of CrossGraphs delta graphs.

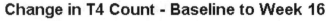

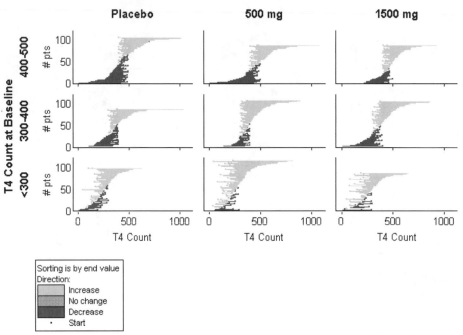

ing observation and are used to better distinguish which way the change has been recorded for the particular case. Drill-down is supported in delta graphs.

Histograms and Bar Graphs in CrossGraphs The use of histograms and bar charts is well known within the business and statistical communities. Within CrossGraphs, these types of graphs are used to present statistical information for a single continuous variable. A histogram is used to show the frequency distribution of values and a bar graph shows the value of a computed statistic. The height of a bar graph represents the relative quantity of the statistic computed, which can be a single value, mean, median, interquartile range, minimum, maximum, standard deviation, variance, coefficient of variation, and skewness. As a side note, the analysis variable is displayed along the x axis for a histogram and along the y axis for a bar graph. Figure 9.25 shows an example of histogram displays of errors made by baseball players. Histograms and bar charts also support drill-down on their respective data sets.

Figure 9.25 Histograms in CrossGraphs.

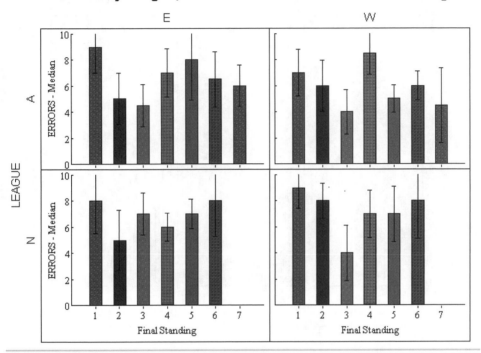

Errors by League, Division and Team's 1986 Final Standing

Picket Fences in CrossGraphs Picket fences are a special form of bar graph where a thin bar is generated for every single element within a data set to show the variable's cumulative distribution. The analysis variable is placed along the y axis and the series of bar graphs for each data point fills the x axis. The height of each bar graph reflects the value of the analysis variable. This produces a vertical bar called a *picket*. The data points are sorted in descending order so that larger values appear on the left of the diagram. If the placement of the pickets is equalized then the x axis is converted to a percent, which makes comparing different sized data sets easier. Figure 9.26 shows an example of picket fence displays using the percent approach. The width of each picket in the middle and right hand displays are wide enough to give it the appearance of one continuously filled diagram. Alternatively, the individual pickets can be replaced and only their top markers shown or lines can be used to connect the tops of the data points. Picket fence diagrams for more than one experimental group may be presented in the same graph for comparison purposes. Drill-down is supported for picket fence graphs.

Figure 9.26 Using CrossGraphs to create picket fence graphs.

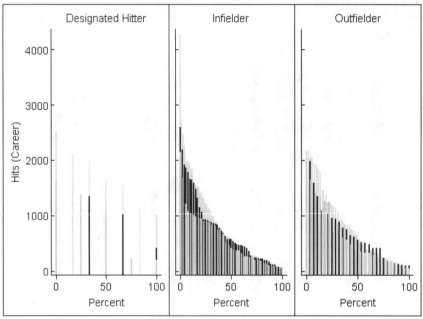

Career Hits by Position and Team's 1986 Final Standing

Position Category

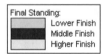

Final Standing:
Lower Finish
Middle Finish
Higher Finish

Scatter Plots in CrossGraphs Most readers are familiar with this form of presentation. A scatter plot basically shows the relationship between a pair of continuous variables in which observation of the value of both variables has been made across a set of entities. In CrossGraphs, scatter plots can become hyperdimensional. The x axis is usually fixed to represent a specific variable. The y axis can support multiple variables (up to six), to be distinguished using different symbols, shapes, or colors. The intersection of values along the x and y axis variables are shown as a set of data points. Very quickly you can see clusters of data, linear relationships, or outliers. Figure 9.27 shows a sample set of scatter plots. Straight lines associated with each y axis variable can be placed within the diagram to help show general trends in the data. These lines represent the solutions to linear regression analyses (see Chapter 6) which seek to find the best fitting line through a set of data points (i.e., the line that minimizes

Figure 9.27 Set of scatter plots generated within CrossGraphs.

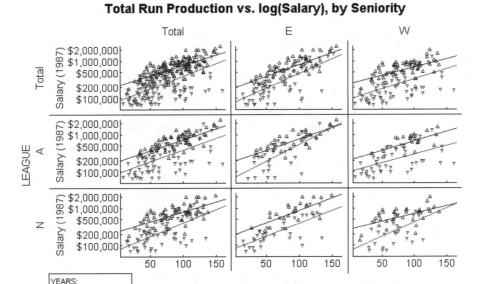

the distance between the points and the solution). Many people find the use of these lines helpful when trying to get a general overview of the direction of the data. Scatter plots can also be converted directly into line graphs in which the data points are connected through a series of lines and the individual symbols are removed from view. When the x axis represents time using a line graph, then a time series graph is produced. Scatter plots also support the ability to perform drill-down.

Spatial Maps in CrossGraphs This method can be used to display the relationships among three variables at a time. Two of the variables are represented along the axes of an x,y grid. Even if the variables are continuous, they are broken down into discrete categories in this display, creating a checkerboard effect. The values of the third variable are represented using color coding in the cells formed in the x,y grid. The third variable is also broken down into discrete intervals, each of which is represented by a different color in the display. Because there are likely to be multiple observations falling into each cell of the matrix, the color of the cell codes some summary statistic such as mean, median, number of observations, and so on. So by examining the pattern of color placements across the grid, you can discern patterns of relationships and dependencies among the three variables. Figure 9.28 shows an example of a spatial map within the CrossGraphs system. Unlike some of the other displays, the spatial maps do not support drill-down on data subsets within the graph.

Statistics Graphs in CrossGraphs CrossGraphs supports a wide range of univariate statistical analyses, the results of which may be represented in any number of ways within the system. At the most basic level, CrossGraphs supports all the basic forms of statistical analyses for presentation as a textual list. The use of a statistical graph is based on the selection of one or more standard statistical options. It requires the definition of a standard analysis variable for which the statistics are to be performed. The types of statistics currently supported by this feature include count, missing count, mean, median, interquartile range, standard deviation, variance, coefficient of variation, sum, minimum, maximum, and skew. For the most part, these statistics are computed on continuous data. If a discrete data type is used for the standard analysis variable, then only the count and missing count are available for processing. Figure 9.29 shows an example of what the

Figure 9.28 Spatial map within CrossGraphs.

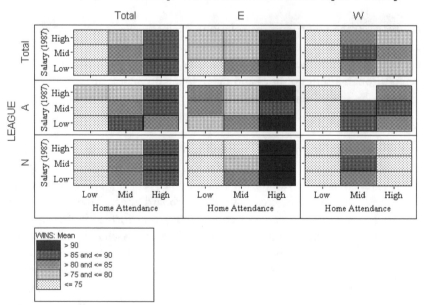

Figure 9.29 Elements of a statistical graph using CrossGraphs.

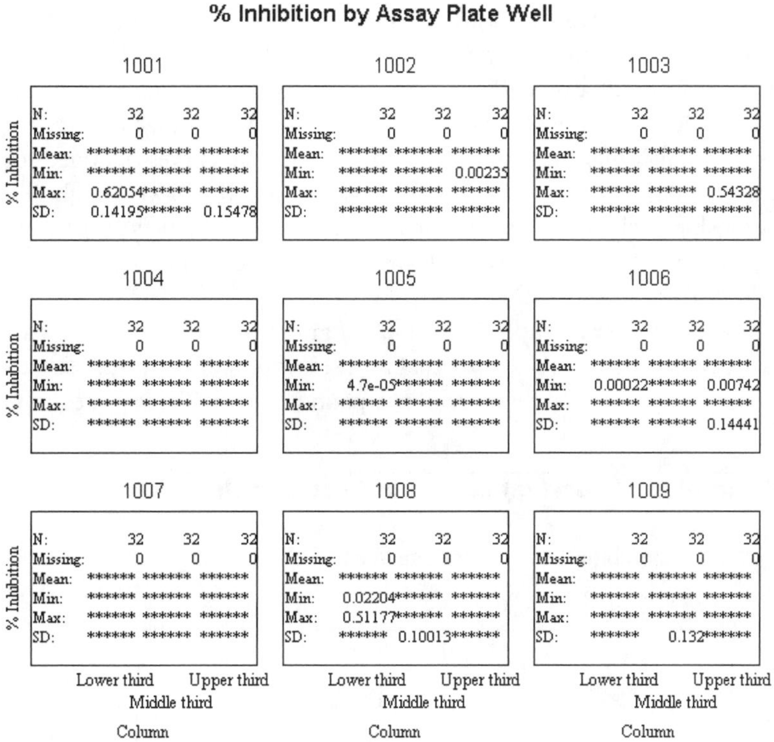

% Inhibition by Assay Plate Well

textual list output looks like from the use of a statistical graph. There is obviously no drill-down supported for this type of presentation.

Survival Curves in CrossGraphs Survival curves can be used to represent information about the percentage of surviving cases (y axis) versus temporal interval (x axis) starting from some beginning point for one or more groups. In the beginning of the observation cycle, all cases are present (they are "surviving") and the time passed is 0 units. So the highest point on the graph is the upper left-hand corner (100 percent cases remaining, time interval is 0). Everything goes downhill from here. As the time interval increases, the proportion of cases still present and surviving declines. The survival curve shows the rate of this decline of the surviving population of cases in the data set. Survival curves for multiple groups can be plotted side by side on the graph, with error information represented as the width of the curves. To the degree that there is open space between curves, this indicates different rates of survival for the groups (see Figure 9.30). This kind of graph is used frequently by insurance companies to present actuarial data and by medical researchers studying changes in physiological symptoms during drug trials. However, this presentation format is not necessarily restricted to bad news scenarios. All you need is a temporal variable on the x axis and a predefined goal as the criterion for inclusion in the data set. So you might plot survival curves for the time (in years) that it takes for graduate students to finish their dissertations, and compare the curves obtained for computer scientists as opposed to students in the business school. Or you might use it to plot a relationship such as the time needed for franchises to achieve a particular profit margin based on whether they are located in urban or rural areas.

Timeline Summaries in CrossGraphs This type of graph is often referred to as a flag chart. This 2x2 matrix allows you to visualize a set of parameter values associated with a particular individual or category over a period of time. There is a column

Figure 9.30 Examples of survival curves in CrossGraphs.

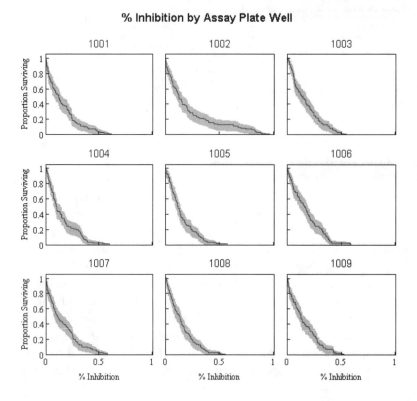

in the chart for every time unit that you are analyzing. For all practical purposes, the time dimension (e.g., x axis) could realistically be set to any other type of discrete or binned value. The individual variables being measured across the intervals are presented in rows along the y axis. What forms is a cross matrix of information, in much the same way as the spatial map is constructed. The types of graphs that can be produced using a timeline summary can be either a "simple" format where color is used to code the statistical summary of each cell or a "fancy" format that includes both the color and the value for each variable. By using color rather than y axis position to show values, the timeline summary graph lets you visualize the values of many variables at once, even if the ranges of the variables differ and cannot be overlaid onto the same y axis. Figure 9.31 shows an example of this type of display. Drill-down is supported within the use of a timeline summary. There is also a key specification that can be used with this type of graph.

Trend Graphs in CrossGraphs Trend graphs in CrossGraphs are used to represent information about changes in the values of a set of variables for a given set of individuals over a series of observation episodes. Data are usually displayed separately for

Figure 9.31 A sample CrossGraphs timeline summary graph (flag chart).

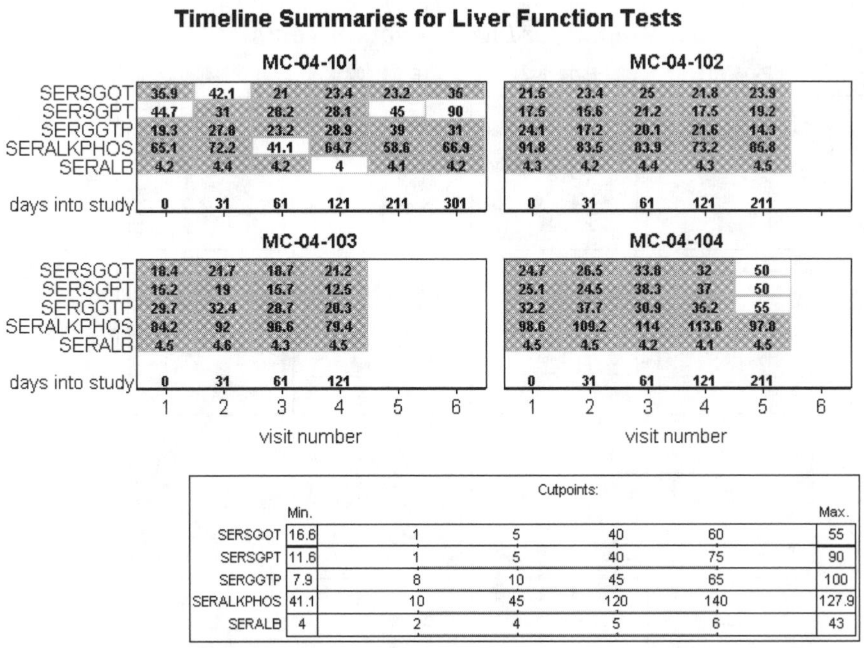

Timeline Summaries for Liver Function Tests

individuals. A matrix is formed in which time is represented on the x axis and individuals and tests are represented on the y and z axes. One common way to use the graph is to plot trends separately for individuals (i.e., putting individuals in the z dimension) so that the changes in test values over time can be observed easily on a case by case basis. You can define normal ranges for each of the test variables and deviation above or below those ranges can be depicted in the graph using special symbols. Beginning (baseline) values of test variables can be represented as dotted lines extending across the entire time interval so that deviations from normality can be more readily observed. You can instruct CrossGraphs to draw a border around graphs containing unexpected data values (e.g., values that are out of their normal range or deviate significantly from their baseline). This graphical highlighting helps you spot graphs that contain interesting data that deserve closer examination. Drill-down is supported in this display. An example of a trend graph is shown in Figure 9.32.

The next release of CrossGraphs (v 2.0) will have several enhancements including new graph types. These include starplots (sometimes called radar graphs) that plot multivariate data in the form of a star, where the radius-length of each of the star's points reflects the magnitude of a single continuous variable. The shapes of

Figure 9.32 Trend graph example using CrossGraphs.

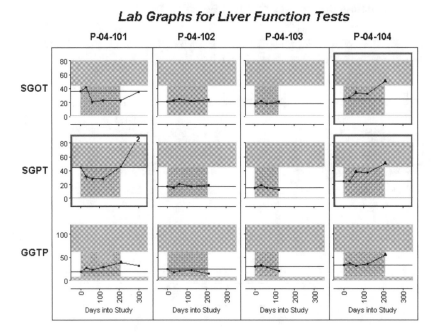

stars can be compared visually to examine multivariate relationships in the data set. There is also a scatterplot matrix that shows all of the two-way combinations among a set of continuous variables as an array of scatterplots. Graphs may be brushed with the mouse to select points in one graph and then highlight the corresponding points in the other graphs in the matrix. In this next version, CrossGraphs also provides more powerful sorting, layout, and annotation functions. The primary breakdowns (layer, row and column) now support nested breakdowns. In addition to the previous options for ordering the levels of a breakdown variable, you can now order the levels by the value of another variable. This lets you prepare graphical reports where the most "interesting" graphs are presented at the beginning. Each cell in a report can now be optionally annotated by the value of a variable associated with the cell. Annotations can be multi-line and can be flexibly positioned with respect to the associated cell. Cell annotations support auto-wrapping. For more information about CrossGraphs 2.0, please consult with Belmont Research.

Other Quantitative Visualization Systems

Since the quantitative paradigm is by far the most common among data mining tools, we cannot feasibly present a complete listing of all available options. This is partly because, in some sense, you could regard the entire body of DSS (decision support systems) and statistical approaches as quantitative analysis systems. However, in our view, most straight statistical analysis systems are not particularly well suited for exploratory data mining investigations. In this section we briefly describe two other visualization tools that have a heavy emphasis on quantitative analysis and that are useful in the data mining discovery mode. These synopses should furnish you with enough information to determine whether these tools may be feasibly applied to your data mining applications. See the products reference section for a more comprehensive list of similar systems.

Graf-FX

Graf-FX is a shareware application that has been written in Microsoft Access. It therefore has many of the features you would expect to see in this type of environment. It is an easy system to use, so for those who want to explore the use of visualization without the hassle of training and setup, Graf-FX might be a good option. Graf-FX was designed as an open front-end application that can be layered on top of any Access system or data import. To get data into Graf-FX, you only need to attach your tables to an Access/ODBC database. Once the data are made available, you can start to take advantage of the Graf-FX features. Graf-FX supports up to 15 graph templates and also supports layout customization. Graf-FX lets you view up to eight data elements (e.g., variables) and there can be up to nine graphs (called grafs) active at any one time. Figure 9.33 shows an example of a Graf-FX display.

There are several features supported by Graf-FX that are useful during a data mining analysis. You can drill-down on any table or query and display it either through group or pivot/crosstabs tables. Graf-FX is a good after market add-on to the Access environment because it makes the data come alive and allows the analyst to interact with the data set. You can view the SQL statements or save the query from any one of the drill-down exercises. The grafs can be saved, reused, replayed, and batched according to your data analysis needs. There is also a fully callable procedures library available within Graf-FX.

TempleMVV

TempleMVV is developed by Mihalisin Associates, Inc. The fundamentals of this system are based on a patented method (U.S. Patent #5338119) of graphing multiple dimensions of data through a technique that is independent of the number of records. The graphing process is governed by the degree to which you need to bin the variables (e.g., define the range of values to partition a continuous variable). TempleMVV uses a series of embedded diagram components, such as bar graphs, which let you present several variables at once within a single display. There are a variety of visual formats associated with TempleMVV and an example is provided in Figure 9.34. The system supports drill-down to the underlying binned data sets.

Figure 9.33 A sample Graf-FX screen.

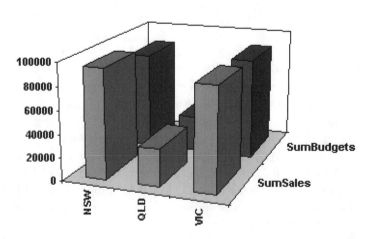

Figure 9.34 A TempleMVV display.

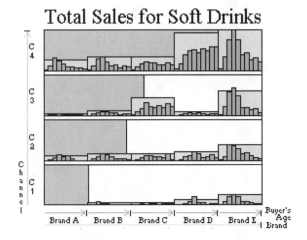

TempleMVV also supports creation of macro files that can be used to combine data sets with graph views to execute established or predefined scenarios. This feature is useful once you have defined a series of analytical steps that produce an interesting set of results. You can create the macro and then subsequently run it on different data sets. Additionally, TempleMVV has a built-in method for generating and preparing graphics for presentation. You can sequence a set of template files and play them like a video to present the results.

Summing Up

In this chapter we have reviewed several tools that can be used to perform quantitative data mining analyses. Although there are many such systems available on the market, we chose to cover Clementine, Enterprise Miner, Diamond, and CrossGraphs in detail because we felt that the combination of these four tools gives you a good idea of the range of capabilities currently available. We ended by briefly mentioning some other tools that can be considered as well. In all cases we focused our discussions on the visualization capabilities that have been developed for these systems. As you have seen, many diverse and creative approaches can be used to bring visualization to the analysis of quantitative data. In the next chapter we will present several trends in the development of data mining technologies that we feel will be of great importance in the coming years.

FUTURE TRENDS IN VISUAL DATA MINING

Introduction

We hope that by now you are convinced that there are a wide variety of ways in which data visualization may be used to facilitate the data mining process. As this section has shown, there are many commercial options available for you to choose from if you wish to incorporate visualization into your analytical process. The developments in this field have been and will continue to be fast-paced and exciting. Within a few short years, the approaches that we consider to be state-of-the-art today will seem simplistic when compared to those that are sure to develop. Anticipated advances in communications, computation, and software development are sure to revolutionize visual data mining as we now know it. Some broad areas in which innovations are likely to be most relevant include the following.

Communications. The second wave of the Internet is already being designed and implemented. Home ISDN lines and cable modems are readily available. In addition, T3 network server lines and wireless ATMs are already within price ranges that make them reasonable options. The faster we can access data, the quicker we can find the underlying patterns that may be contained within the data. Better communications will allow analysts to access and integrate more data sources. A good example of this is the LEXMAP system being developed by LEXIS-NEXIS, where huge quantities of public records can be analyzed visually at the touch of a button. Sources including tax assessor records, deed transfers, aircraft/vehicle/boat registrations, liens and judgements, tax judgement filings, and UCC filings are being made to their subscriber community for examination and inspection. Thus, you can proactively target a wide range of industry segments in a very timely manner and conduct analyses that were once beyond the reach of most analytical environments.

Computing. Systems are becoming faster and more powerful so that those tasks previously reserved for supercomputers only a few years ago are

[377]

now becoming computationally achievable on individual workstations. Computational power keeps doubling roughly every 18 months and there are off-the-shelf systems that can already process at 512 MHz and beyond. As new materials are being used for chip production and as the manufacturing processes become more refined, we can expect to continue on this trend for quite some time. This means that much larger data sets can be processed for more elaborate pattern extractions. Faster computation also facilitates the acceptance of more complex search and pattern matching. The combination of variables, permutation of values, and throughput that can be achieved with faster computing systems will significantly extend our abilities to expose much more complicated and informative patterns.

Software development. With the introduction of Java and common standard programming practices, there will be more opportunity for the creation of general purpose software that is platform independent and can grow through the addition of plug-and-play modules that are directly and automatically integrated into existing routines. Graphic programming environments and software visualizers will be in more general use. Application development processes can be distributed and results shared effectively among system users. It is here that we believe the greatest advances in computing will be realized. The expressiveness (e.g., creativity, sharing, and awareness) on the current Internet is just a sampling of things to come. A large portion, if not all, of next-generation software will have some type of standard visual component. This will make it easier for non-technical people to become involved in the design, development, and use of these systems. We have already seen inroads in this direction in several of the tools we presented in the previous chapters.

The range and scope of developments in all of these areas are sure to impact the field of data mining in ways that none of us can imagine. Nevertheless, there are some trends that seem to be gaining ground and hold great promise for improving on the methodologies that are currently in use. In this chapter we introduce some developments that are on the horizon that we feel will shape the direction of visualization as it is used for data mining. We discuss some general future trends as well as describe some systems that have already made use of some of these newer approaches. We include sections on the use of visualization for navigation, analysis of textual information using visualization and general purpose data mining tools that are being developed with future analytical needs in mind.

Visual Navigation

In addition to its application in data mining analyses, visualization can also provide a means of simply navigating large sets of information without entering into detailed analyses, per se. Although many systems have been developed to permit data manipulation and discovery of new patterns and trends, they also indirectly allow us to navigate the underlying data. Since not all forms of data interaction are necessarily directed towards discovering hidden patterns, however, new simpler tools are being developed that specialize in navigation.

To give an analogy of what we mean by information navigation, suppose you were planning to drive cross-country on a trip. Before you left you would want to look over your maps and make sure that you had coverage for all regions that you planned to go through. Chances are that you would look for interstate paths that would take you from your origin to the destination. The maps you use might contain a lot of detailed information, showing small state highways, elevation information, where major cities are located, icons representing landmarks, and so on. However, for your purposes you would not really be interested in those details. Smaller roads, for example, would not be of interest to you in this situation. Your goal would be just to hit the high points and see what broad categories of information were represented. In a similar way, the new breed of visual navigation techniques help you move through a data set to see what is there even though you are not manipulating the data in any way. The use of visual navigation techniques lets you peruse the data rather than focusing on the process used to search for the data in the first place.

Navigating the Internet

One of the most obvious uses of navigational tools is on the Internet. As anyone who has ever tried to run a search on the Internet knows, sorting through the morass to find the relevant pieces of information that you are looking for can sometimes prove to be difficult. There are, of course, browsers that have been developed to display and navigate the Internet, and they help to facilitate this process. In the past, however, Internet searches were conducted using a largely manual process. For most of us, we consider these browsers to be a standard part of interacting with the Internet and would not think of using anything else. The productivity increases realized using these modern browsers are almost immeasurable compared to the earlier versions of Internet navigation.

Despite the help that browsers provide, it can still be difficult to access the information that you want. The primary method of retrieving data on the Internet at present is through keyword search engines. These systems typically respond with a vast dump of URL addresses based on the keywords you initially provide. At this point, you pick the best URL and visit it to see whether it contains the type of information you want. As you know, however, this process produces a lot of dead ends and wasted time. As you sift through the lists of URLs, you are apt to revisit sites that you have already viewed. You can end up going around in circles, not knowing where you have been and not knowing what to expect from the next site-link.

How could this process be made easier? If we think of the Internet as a large network of interconnected sites, it becomes obvious that tools supporting link analysis could be used to facilitate this process. Quantitative and landscape visual displays could be used to good effect as well. To use existing tools for this purpose, however, the front-end data access methods required to collect and parse the data would need to be modified. This is not a difficult task, but would require some effort to retrofit them in order to respond in a timely manner. Remember that most of the systems described in Section III are used to analyze static data sets and do not necessarily function with the fluidity needed for dynamic navigation. There are, however, systems being built with this task in mind and we believe that these will be in widespread use as demand for improved search techniques increases.

Working with File, Network, and Web Visualizers

Although much of the emphasis in this book has been on applications that utilize large data sets, there are many instances in which you could use visualization to help manage data sets that you use most every day. For example, you could use visualization to help you monitor the structure of the file system on your computer, map out interactions on your computer network, or even monitor the activity on your company's web site. Over the past several years numerous systems have been developed for applying visualization to these problems because it is often the best approach to use due to the inherent complexity and volumes of information that must be managed. Any of these applications can be addressed using a well-bounded, small-scale data mining application where information is acquired, value is added, and results are presented in a way that facilitates analysis. These types of systems make it possible to see the infrastructure present in the data, which implicitly provides a navigational component. Thus, they make it easy to comprehend and interact with a wide range of data. We expect to see visual interfaces become a standard method for performing these types of functions in the not too distant future.

File Mapping Visualizations

There is a new breed of software systems that has been developed to present a graphic depiction of the directories and files on your disk drives. Systems such as DiskMapper (patent pending) provide support for these types of features. One format commonly used in supporting this type of interaction is to present the data as a series of embedded rectangles, where the size of the rectangle reflects the relative size of the file or folder. These rectangles are arranged in the window in a fairly compact format so you can get a good overview of what is contained on your disks. Through color-coding, these file mappers can indicate how far down within the directory structures you are at any one time. Any combination of folders can be expanded to different levels so it is easy to navigate around the display and check out different files. These types of systems make it easy to find large files and directories for consideration of deletion or compression. There is usually a link to a file compression scheme that can be invoked on any file. Figure 10.1 is provided courtesy of Micro Logic (www.miclog.com) and it shows a sample display of a file mapping visualization.

Figure 10.1 A DiskMapper view of the files and folders residing on a computer disk.

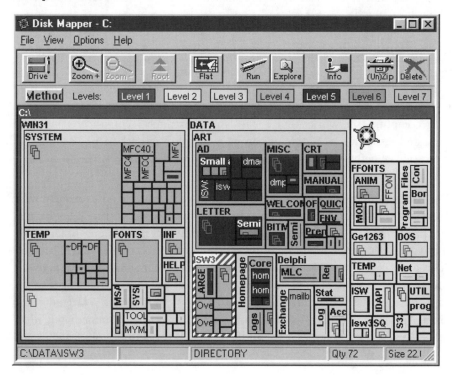

Systems such as DiskMapper also provide options for coloring the rectangles according to the owner, which is important for multiuser systems. This can help with such problems as finding missing files or determining whether there is an equitable distribution of resources across certain groups of users. The colors can be applied to other file characteristics including the read/write permissions, executables, deletion privileges, time/date stamp, and compression status. There is a special function provided by DiskMapper that reveals duplicated files by showing linkages among the different rectangles. Based on names, size, and configurations, DiskMapper can certify that files are stored in more than one subdirectory. Once duplicates are identified, you can then determine whether they should be deleted. You can also adjust DiskMapper's displays through its filter operations to show subsets of information. Any characteristic associated with a file can be used to filter the displays. This helps you navigate hard disks and see files that have not been used in a long time and gives you the option to delete or archive them accordingly.

Similar research has been conducted in other environments. In particular, the University of Maryland has a Treemap system that is used to generate file hierarchies by recursively partitioning the rectangles that represent the data. Treemap also supports zooming, enter/leave notification, select actions, and several other features. This method can obviously be applied to more than files and folders—it would work on any data set that can be structured hierarchically.

Visual Network Analyzers

Computing systems have continued to expand at ever increasing rates. Companies are taking advantage of the benefits of computers by expanding their reach to cover just about every task, process, or procedure performed in a business setting. The resulting computing networks that form can be extremely complicated and the detection and resolution of problems can be a complicated task. This need has led to the creation of network analyzers, which take on a variety of very useful and necessary functions.

The computer networks within a typical organization serve an extremely wide range of functions. They are responsible for all of the Internet traffic, e-mail transactions, printer requests, alpha-pages, faxes, disk storage, and many other tasks. When any one of these capabilities is not working or starts to misbehave, productivity can suffer. There was one situation in our own office in which several network controllers went bad and started flooding our network with extraneous packages. Within a short time, it brought the network to a crawl and affected a large number of people. A program called a network sniffer was applied and it immediately identified the problem so that it could be rectified. Due to the number of variables and volume of information that passes through our networks, it would have been next to impossible to have identified this problem using traditional methods. The sniffer allowed us to gather all of the relevant data from each of the devices in order to get an overall picture of the health of our network.

Since the visualizations used by network analyzers tend to use a combination of statistical displays and link analysis, it is easy to see the physical layout and throughput of your networks. You can therefore use these tools to determine how the network can be better designed in order to minimize disruptions in service. You could use the tools to determine who would be affected by failures in the network, verify connectivity, and determine optimal topology arrangements. Also, a wide variety of performance metrics can be reviewed to help you determine who is accessing the network, how much traffic is being generated, and where bandwidth is being consumed. Thus, navigating and analyzing your networks becomes almost a trivial task. It is as simple as looking at a picture.

Network analyzers are a great resource to have when managing complicated computing systems. Across the board for all network analysis tools, there is the ability to look at the raw data using traditional spreadsheet-like formats. However, visualization is unequivocally emerging as the primary method of conveying these results, and we expect this trend to continue. Systems such as the SGI Site Manager, netViz, Astra SiteManager, Optimal Application Insight, NetXRay, WebAnalyzer, and NetMaker XA are examples of network analyzers that support the use of visualization in helping to analyze network faults and bandwidth. Undoubtedly, there are many different systems available on the market and this selection represents only a few. Bear in mind that the capabilities of these systems are much more comprehensive than was briefly discussed in this section. It is the common use of visualization for navigation as well as analysis in these tools that captures the kind of functionality that will become more and more commonplace. Figures 10.2 through 10.4 show sample screens from some of these tools.

Visual Web Analyzers

With the explosion of the Internet, many business concerns have invested in creating and maintaining web pages that contain information about the goods and services offered by the company. The creation of a web site is only the beginning of this process. Once a web site has been made operational, the organization has a large interest in knowing the details regarding the connections *to* and *from* the site. That is, you want to keep up with the URL sites that your page points to as well as the collection of sites across the World Wide Web that point to your site. In addition, you want to monitor the activity profile of your web site in terms of how many

Figure 10.2 Example of a netViz screen.

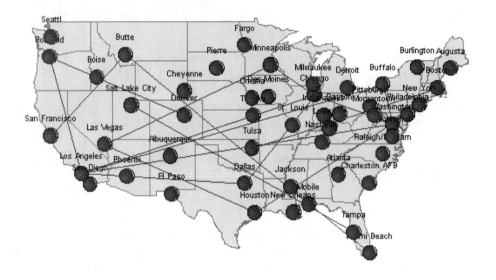

Figure 10.3 Example of a Site Manager screen.

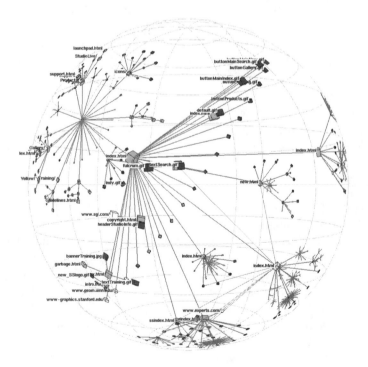

Figure 10.4 Example of a NetXRay screen.

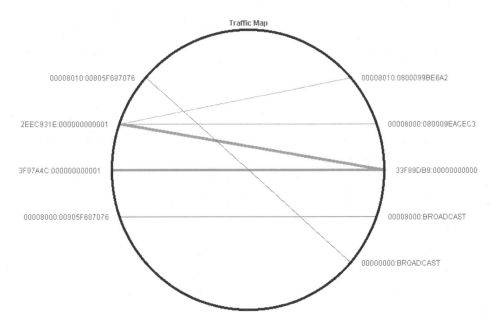

hits you are getting, where they come from, the relationship between this activity and increased revenues for your business, and so on. The growth of business participation on the Internet has spurred the creation of a whole new range of products that are specifically focused at helping you to understand the layout of your HTML pages in terms of connections as well as assess how people are using your site. Due to the complexity and volume of data involved with many of these tasks, the only viable way to manage all of the information effectively is to present it using a visual paradigm.

The approaches to using visualization in web analyzers are similar to those adopted for visual network analyzers. Web analyzers come in all shapes and sizes. There are an incredible number of web analysis packages available for looking at everything from the structure, content, and usage of web sites. Referencing all of them in this chapter would be next to impossible since there are so many new ones coming out every day. The tools being developed include research systems as well as commercial offerings. Next we present a sampling of tools intended to introduce you to different classes of visualization paradigms used to present the information. Some are better at representing structure, whereas others are more optimized for looking at content. We will leave it up to you to decide which formats are most appropriate for your needs. Additionally, as you read about these tools, you should bear in mind that many of the representation formats you will see in this section can be applied to virtually any type of data, whether those data reside on the web or not. Using these technologies in other applications would just be a matter of retrofitting the format of the data you are going to use to the format supported by the tools.

WebView WebView is a Java-based system that was developed as a proof-of-concept research project. WebView provides a simple interface in which you define a URL to be mapped. WebView collection agents then visit the specified site, parse out all of the HTML references to other pages and sites, and present the resulting network as a visual display. WebView uses a simulated annealing algorithm to organize displays. Figure 10.5 shows an example of a sample WebView display based on a single URL site.

Figure 10.5 A sample WebView display of a URL site.

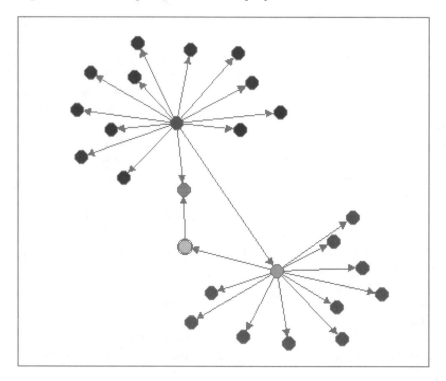

The nodes within this diagram represent the different pages that were derived from the target URL. The linkages shown between the nodes imply the direction of the connection (i.e., what pages point to what other pages). Thus, what you have is a complete mapping of a particular site. Any one of the nodes within the resulting network diagram can be selected and the text of the page will be presented within a browser. Additionally, you can map any other URL to the existing diagram by just selecting on the appropriate node and instructing WebView to collect its data. This process provides the ability to "walk the data" by literally jumping between URLs to their content.

Not only does WebView allow you to map a complete URL, but it has also been coupled to AltaVista and MetaCrawler to support key word searches. Once a set of terms is provided, the designated search engine will return a list of URLs that will then be mapped into WebView. When the display is presented, you can see an overall diagram of what the search returned. There is also a "group domains" option that will place nodes derived from similar domains (e.g., .com, .gov, and .edu) into their own segmented groupings within the display. Since WebView was only a research project, there is a lot of room for improvement. Nevertheless, it proves the point that visual navigation of complex search spaces can be very effective. This simple application sets the groundwork for introducing the other applications we are about to discuss.

Mapuccino Following the traditional link analysis approach for representing web pages, IBM has produced a simple applet called Mapuccino (previously named WebCutter), in keeping with the Java-inspired convention of coffee-related naming terminology. This is a system that provides a variety of display layouts for looking at the organization of the pages contained within a web site and how they can be navigated. To initiate Mapuccino, all you need to do is type in a URL and it will gather all the data regarding that web site and produce a visualization of it. Each page within the resulting diagrams can have either the document title or the link name as the label on the nodes. Mapuccino has several alternative schemes for presenting the data hierarchy including top-down, left-right, or as a star. Figure 10.6 shows a sample Mapuccino display.

The shape of the icons within the Mapuccino display conveys information about their content. Different symbols are used to differentiate nodes such as the root, gifs, off-site, document, and unreachable. Since pages can point back to other pages that have already been defined, these are represented in Mapuccino as backlinks and are shown as blue lines. Inclusion of them into the display is optional. There is also the ability to zoom in and out of the diagram in addition

Figure 10.6 Mapuccino web display.

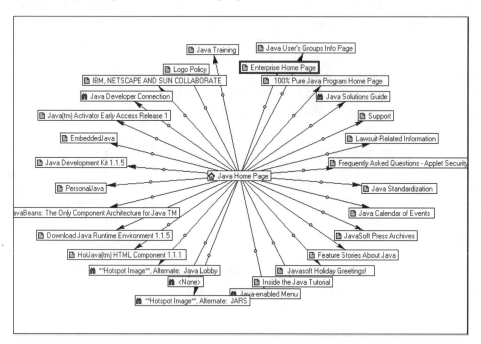

to producing minimaps that represent reduced views of the pages within the mapped web site.

MAPA One particularly popular visual web navigation tool is a system called MAPA, which is produced by Dynamic Diagrams. This application has been integrated into a wide range of commercial web pages distributed throughout the Internet. It is also written using Java, which makes it portable and applicable anywhere on the Web. MAPA takes a slightly different approach for representing the page hierarchies of a web site. Based purely on the positional structure of the diagrams (e.g., where things appear in the site), it manages the amount of information presented within one display. MAPA shows the individual pages as boxes arranged in a 3D landscape and they are positioned according to the structure of the web site. Figure 10.7 shows an example of a MAPA display for a relatively complex web site.

As you can see, it is easy to interpret the structure of a site in this visualization. When a box is selected, it will display the names/titles of the page it represents. If

Figure 10.7 Visualizing a web site using MAPA.

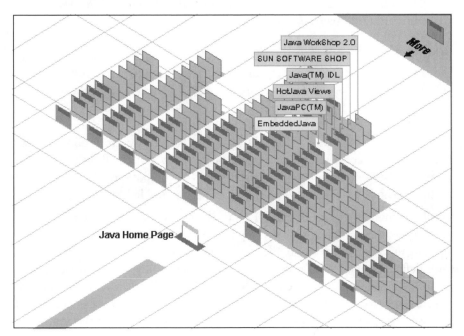

further information is desired, simply clicking on the box will take you to the desired page. Information is managed in and out of the MAPA display using some simple yet attractive Java animation. Additionally, MAPA provides site administrators with regular reports so that broken pages or timed-out links can quickly be identified and fixed. Unfortunately Dynamic Diagrams will no longer support the MAPA software by the time this text reaches press.

WebAnalyzer WebAnalyzer is developed by InContext Systems (recently merged with EveryWare Development Corp.) and it is used to help manage large web sites by providing graphic navigation and analysis techniques. WebAnalyzer presents information using what is called a Wavefront view that depicts the hierarchy of the site map as a series of rings or waves (an example is shown in Figure 10.8). The center is the main page and each successive surrounding wave represents the next level out in the set of connections. This type of display is sometimes called a starburst. WebAnalyzer lets you look at the structure of your site to see whether it has been organized properly and whether there are broken links. A variety of site statistics are also computed and presented. Using WebAnalyzer you can see the number of inbound and outbound links from any page. There are five interactive views available in WebAnalyzer: Wavefront, File, URL Tree, Site Map, and Link.

Hyperbolic Tree Toolkit Through the years, Xerox has developed a number of innovative display paradigms including user interfaces and alternative representation methods. For example, Xerox was the company that pioneered the original Cone Trees, Perspective Walls, and Hyperbolic Trees. Most recently, through a spin-off company called InXight, they have transitioned several research projects into the commercial industry. The focus of this description will be on the Hyperbolic Tree Toolkit offered through their collection of user interface components in VizControls. Depending on the type of application you are building, the Hyperbolic Tree Toolkit provides APIs that let you manipulate node images, node/link colors, text fonts, and link styles.

The Hyperbolic Tree Toolkit (HTT) has already made inroads into the web visualization world and has also been applied to product catalogs, document collections, organization charts, and file system hierarchies. Figure 10.9 shows the structure defined while looking at a set of web pages. Only a limited amount of detail can be presented at any one time. As a result, the diagrams expand and collapse accordingly to show various levels of detail. In this case, you can see one of the sublevels expanding. HTT uses an animated transition to retain the context of

Figure 10.8 The Wavefront view in WebAnalyzer.

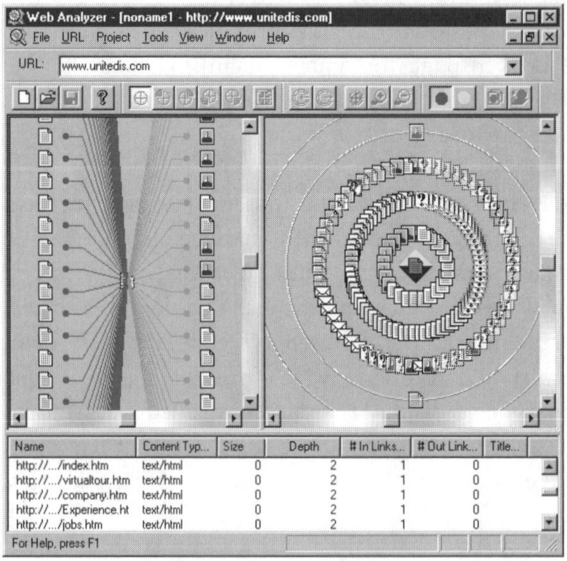

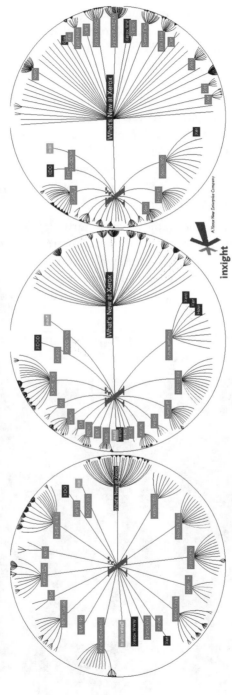

Figure 10.9 Representing web pages within the Hyperbolic Tree Toolkit (courtesy of InXight Software, Inc., a Xerox New Enterprise Company, copyright ©1996; 1998).

the environment so that you can maintain your orientation while navigating the data. HTT lets you focus on particular objects and see the proportional sizes of the different sublevels within the hierarchy.

SemioMap   SemioMap provides a way to look at the interconnected structures of web pages as well as their actual content. SemioMap displays are created from the results of keyword searches. Unlike the popular web browsers that return a list of documents in a list format, SemioMap presents its findings as a visualization. The content of the SemioMap display is not an exhaustive list of documents, but rather the concepts derived from the documents matching search conditions. Figure 10.10 provides an example of a SemioMap display for a keyword search of "visual" within its indexed document references.

The structure of a SemioMap display is fairly simple. There are two types of node classes, shallow and deep. Shallow nodes are ones that do not have any additional information available and will not be related to other concepts. Shallow nodes do not have any defined depth or associated border (e.g., a visual indicator that represents the availability of more data) so they are easy to spot

Figure 10.10 A SemioMap display representing the concepts associated with the keyword "visual".

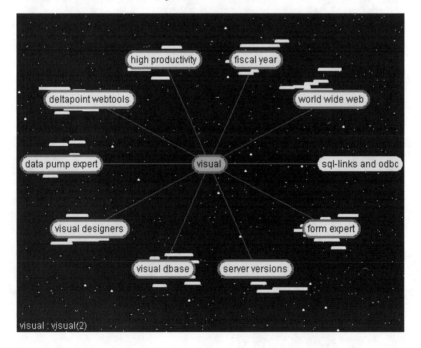

within the display. Deep nodes represent concepts that have more information returned from the search. Deep nodes can be expanded to reveal another layer of nodes (e.g., a cluster) corresponding to related concepts. Deep nodes are shown with a wide border and have satellite nodes floating in their backgrounds. Nodes are connected to one another through links that indicate that they are directly related to the content of one or more documents.

Across the bottom of a SemioMap display is the search trail, which depicts the nodes that have been selected for review. If you select one of these nodes, SemioMap will take you back to that particular point in the analysis. There is also a Web-page button that provides a view of the actual documents related to the selected nodes. SemioMap is a good example of the types of information navigation systems that are likely to be commonly available in future versions of current browsers. As you can appreciate, this facility for concept-based browsing provides a better way of managing data than the usual methods that require you to do a serial review through long lists of individual items returned from a simple search. A similar approach is provided in the PerspectaView tool described next.

A Different Perspective for Navigating Data

The systems described in the previous section were designed to present web-based information for navigational purposes. As you can imagine, these approaches can also be broadly expanded to include a more generalized way of looking at and navigating data. One of these is called Perspecta SmartContent System and it performs conceptual navigation through data. This system has a client, PerspectaView, that currently runs in Windows 95, NT, Macintosh, and Solaris configurations. PerspectaView has been largely written in Java. The company has done a superb job of designing the system to provide a very powerful and flexible data navigation system that lets you interactively fly through your data set.

PerspectaView is very straightforward in the way that it represents and displays data. Information is shown as a series of related elements, almost approximating a hierarchical notation. When PerspectaView is first loaded it appears with its top-level topic shown in the center of the display. Any other topic that is related to or can be reached from this top-level topic is shown towards the background and is connected by a set of spokes or linkages emanating from the top-level node. Figure 10.11 shows an example of the PerspectaView interface. Selecting any topic within the display will do two things. First it will present a textual summary of the topic right in the display for as long as you hold down the mouse button. This is similar to the brushing technique used in several of the tools described in this section. Second, the tool can be programmed to launch into a web page that provides a very effective form of contextual analysis by double clicking on the topic.

Figure 10.11 The PerspectaView interface.

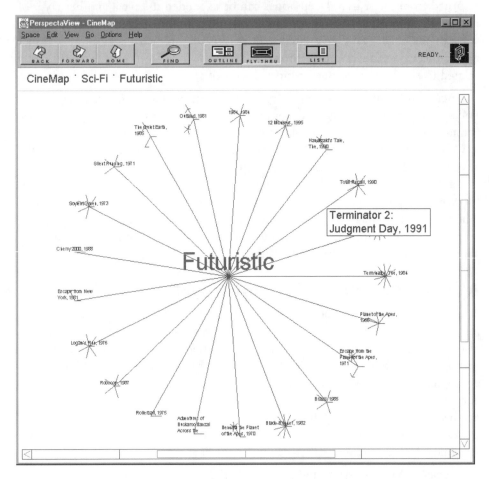

You can fly to any topic within a PerspectaView display using the mouse as your navigation control. Interaction is simple—left mouse zooms in, right mouse zooms out. All you need to do is point and click. PerspectaView takes care of everything else. As you approach a topic, it will expand its content to show you the other topics that are directly connected to it as well. At this point the display looks very similar to the view you get when you are at the top-level node. So in essence, PerspectaView provides the means to navigate through a world or worlds that are conceptually related. Figure 10.12 provides a close-up view of how the nodes expand. The closer you get to a topic, the more detail you will be able to see since

Figure 10.12 A close-up view of a topic within PerspectaView.

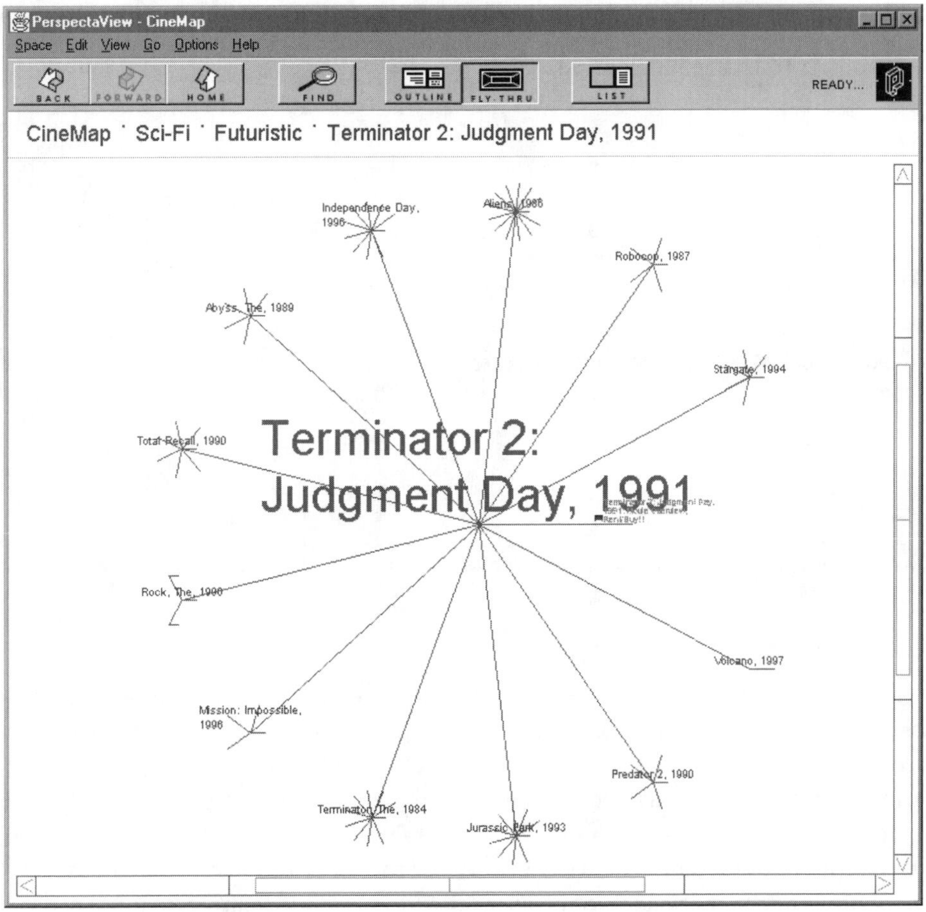

PerspectaView keeps enlarging the contents of the display as you move through the network. Flying out just reverses the process.

PerspectaView supports several different information layout formats. The preceding figures show a Radial Fly-thru perspective, but this can be changed to a Box Fly-thru view. Figure 10.13 shows an example of the PerspectaView Box Fly-thru format. So instead of showing related items as spokes emanating from the center, a series of boxes are shown to represent this information about related topics. PerspectaView also supports a third display format called an outline view. The outline view more closely resembles a textual and nonvisual representation of the data. It tends to approximate a formatted list of entries.

Figure 10.13 PerspectaView's Box Fly-thru format.

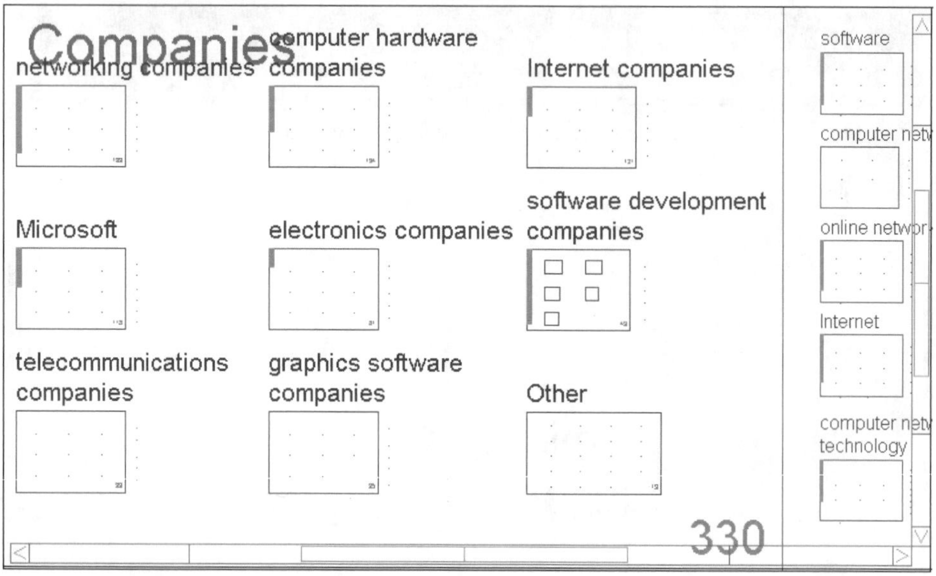

Using the PerspectaView Interface

PerspectaView is designed to be integrated directly into a browser-based application. Through JavaScript controls, a web site developer can programmatically access PerspectaView's functionality and place controls on the web page to help manage the data being visualized. There is support for buttons to move backward or forward within the structure in much the same way as you would visit sites on the Internet. Additionally, there is a history bar that provides you with a quick summary of all topics that have been traversed within the information space. This history bar contains active entries, so if you want to back up and jump to a prior topic without having to zoom out on the display, all you need to do is select the appropriate entry. PerspectaView will center the target topic in the display and show its related topics. This makes it easy to see where you have been as well as alternative pathways that might be followed through the structure.

PerspectaView also supports a function called CrossLinks, which are active pointers to other areas within the SmartContent Space. The CrossLinks show up as red lines within the display that stretch out to other areas of the space. So if there is a related topic contained within the same level as another topic, the CrossLinks option will bring in this connection. There are also methods to support RelatedTopics that represent other topics within the SmartContent space. These are shown as green lines within the space. Selection of a topic in RelatedTopics moves you over to that particular part of the space.

Within the PerspectaView interface there is also an option that can be used to present a list of the topics available within the information space as well as a text box to present related text. When a topic is selected within the main PerspectaView display, the list will contain those topics that can be derived from the selected topic. This list is a nice complement to the graphical display because it can let you see things that might not yet be visible or that have moved off the display. Double clicking on any entry in the list will bring up its related web page.

Using SmartContent Spaces in PerspectaView

To get data into PerspectaView, you use SmartContent spaces, which are representations containing metadata summaries about the underlying data sources. Essentially, they represent the topics and their relationships to one another. It also includes any source reference objects such as a URL reference. Eventually topics should point to a class of information objects that cannot be subdivided. In the main display, these information objects are presented in a different color and they will not expand when approached. Instead, they will take you outside of PerspectaView to a related URL.

The Perspecta SmartContent System offers a variety of ways to build SmartContent spaces. Data can come from sources such as relational databases as well as unstructured text documents. For database systems it is just a matter of identifying which tables and fields to use as the topic and object definitions. The same goes for news-feeds or documents that have tagged values (metadata) such as titles, dates, locations, etc. Using these formats, PerspectaView has been applied to a wide range of areas including the visual navigation of maintenance documents, technical manuals, web sites, S&T investment strategies, and live news feeds.

When dealing with large data sets or real-time feeds, PerspectaView could not possibly load all of the information at once, so the client interacts with the SmartContent System's server through the Information Streaming Transport Protocol (ISTP). This is basically a dynamic, "just-in-time" protocol that allows PerspectaView to load only those portions of the data set that are relevant to the current view or request for information. Using this approach, you can easily navigate extremely large and complex sources of information.

Text Visualization

As we discussed in Chapter 5, there are a variety of methods for dealing with textual information. Generally, text does not explicitly contain the types of coded information that would allow for a straightforward mapping based on its contents. Rather, free text does not follow any particular format or writing style. There is, however, some basic information that comes with just about any piece of free text. This is usually called its "header" and most often includes its source, creation date, and several other fundamental facts. These limited data really do not make it any easier to perform data mining, but you can calculate new information directly from the content of free text using some advanced heuristics and natural language processing techniques.

To understand the details of text documents you can either search for keywords or you can try and categorize the semantic content of the document itself. When identifying proper names in text documents, for example, you are looking at defining specific details or elements within documents that can be used to show connections or relationships with other documents. The outputs from these keyword approaches can be expressed as relational data sets that may then be analyzed using any one of the analytical techniques we have previously reviewed. Although solving this problem is not a trivial task, significant inroads have already been made in the development of these searches in both government and private industry applications. Development of methodologies for doing content-based partitions is a more complicated problem. Some progress has been made along these lines, but no standards have been established and a full definition of these approaches is beyond the scope of this book. For the purposes of these discussions, we focus on the categorization of text based on outcomes of keyword searches, particularly those aimed at the identification of proper nouns and noun phrases.

Representing Semantic Content in Topographic Maps

Generally, you can think of text categorization as comparing a document to other documents or to some predefined set of terms or definitions. The results of these comparisons can be presented visually within a semantic landscape in which similar documents are placed close together in the semantic space and dissimilar documents are subsequently placed further apart. Depending on the particular algorithms used to generate the landscape, the resulting topographic map can depict the strengths of similarities among documents in terms of Euclidean distance. This idea is analogous to the type of approach used to construct Kohonen feature maps. (Recall the unsupervised neural network learning algorithms described in Chapter 6.) Given the semantic landscape, you may then extrapolate concepts represented by documents that end up being located together (and separated from other groups of nodes) within the map. These landscapes can provide an overall roadmap to the contents of a document set.

Using Latent Semantic Analysis in Free Text Processing

Latent Semantic Analysis (LSA) is an experimental method that was originally developed to improve the accuracy and effectiveness of information retrieval techniques by focusing on semantic meaning of words across a series of usage contexts, as opposed to using simple string matching operations. LSA is a way of partitioning free text using a statistical model of word usage that is similar to eigenvector decomposition and factor analysis. Rather than focusing on superficial features such as word frequency, this approach provides a quantitative measure of semantic similarities among documents.

Using the LSA method, you first represent the text as a matrix of word occurrences. In this matrix every row represents a unique word in the text being processed and each column corresponds to a meaningful text passage or sample such as a document, paragraph, or sentence that defines a context for the word's usage. (Note that the definition of contexts in the columns is a process that may or may not be done automatically to good effect. Remember that this is still an experimental procedure in many respects.) The value of each resulting cell in the matrix is the frequency with which a word appears in the given context. Next, a preliminary weighting factor is applied to each value that codes the importance of the words within the particular context and the extent to which the word type is meaningful in the domain of general use in the document set. (Again, this may or may not be accomplished automatically, depending on the application.)

LSA then applies singular value decomposition (SVD) to the matrix. The SVD is a form of factor analysis that decomposes the matrix into a set of orthogonal factors that can be used to approximate the original matrix by linear combination. The reconstructed matrix is a least-squares fit for the orthogonal factors. This resulting matrix will contain far fewer orthogonal factors than original words, and so serves to provide a framework for semantic comparison of abstract semantic categories that subsume the individual words contained in the documents. Another way of looking at this is to note that since the number of dimensions used for comparison is smaller than the number of original words, the words themselves will not be independent. Thus, you can have situations in which two different words that are used in the same contexts across documents will have similar vectors in the LSA representation even if they never appear together in the same document.

SiteMap

There are many systems that use LSA and similar approaches to generate visual representations of the domain of discourse for navigational and analytical purposes. A display from one such system, SiteMap, is shown in Figure 10.14. This is a graphic depiction of the contents of web sites. The process used to create this map involves three steps. First, the pages contained within the site are indexed, usually using agents, spiders, or crawlers that visit the designated URL, follow all of its links, and gather as much information as possible. Second, the returned data are processed by an unsupervised neural network that sorts the items into abstract categories, and produces output specifications used to determine which subject terms will be selected from the returned data set, along with their relative weightings. Finally, a graphic map of the site is displayed in a Java applet. The individual dots in the display represent the pages that were

Figure 10.14 A SiteMap display depicting the web site at the National Library of Medicine.

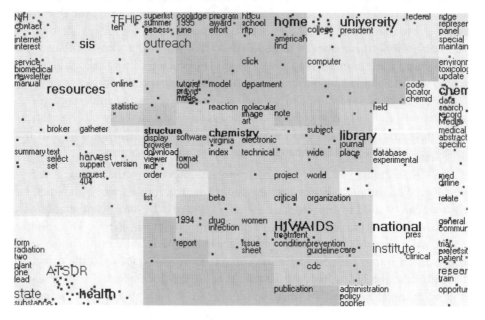

processed. The level of detail in the display can be adjusted through sliders. The prevalence of the terms in the display is based on the weights generated by the neural network. There are many different forms of these feature maps and each has a slightly different appearance and emphasis.

WEBSON

Figure 10.15 shows an example of a map generated by a system called WEBSON, which uses text processing methods much like those used in SiteMap, but employs more of a temperature gradient metaphor to construct the display of information. Notice that there are no distinct borders between the main subject terms; rather, topic areas flow into one another. The WEBSON display can be zoomed for more detail on

Figure 10.15 A WEBSON display of comp.ai.neural.nets.

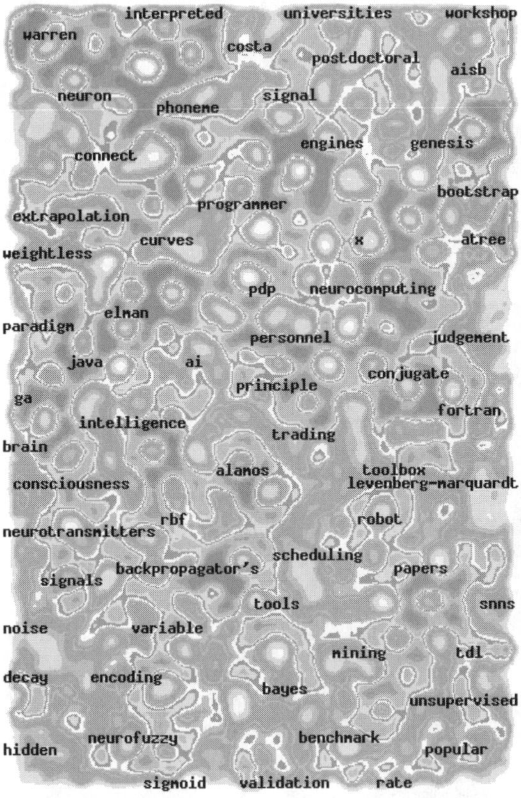

Courtesy of the Helsinki University of Technology.

any particular area. In these close-up views, the regions between the terms becomes more spread out and you can see more subject terms appear within the display.

Themescape

Themescape (a system incorporated into SPIRE) is a similar system to those just described except it uses a 3D-visualization scheme to represent information. Themescape uses a 3D representation to convey its results because it can show the relative strengths of the categorizations generated. As with the other systems, Themescape uses a self-organizing neural network algorithm to determine where individual entities should be placed within the display. Figure 10.16 shows an example of the landscape paradigm used in Themescape. The display looks like a mountainous terrain where the heights of the mountains are defined as the document clusters. Themescape can also show its workspace in a 2D representation to

Figure 10.16 A standard Themescape display.

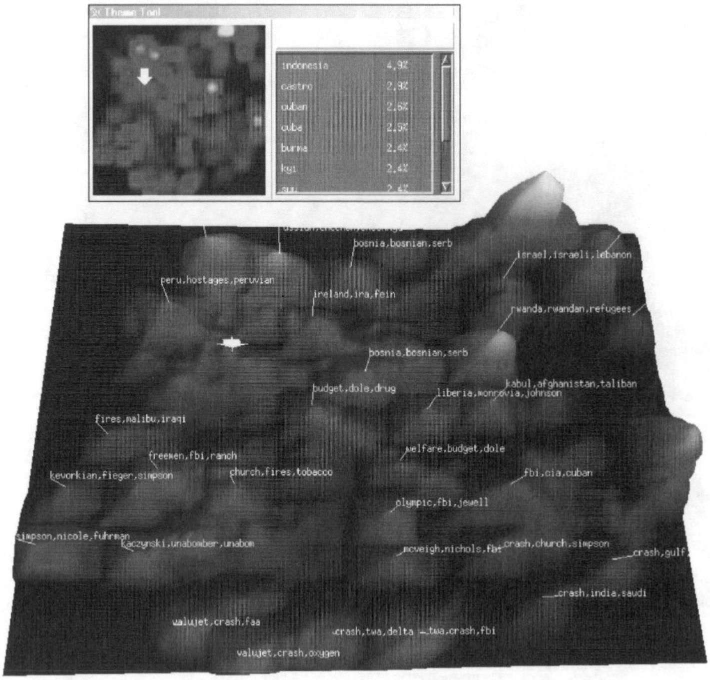

Courtesy of Battelle Pacific Northwest Laboratories.

provide a bird's eye view of the document landscape. The Themescape approach has recently been made commercially available by ThemeMedia in their SPIRIX offering.

Starlight

Starlight is an environment that supports representation of free text as well as relational and multimedia data representations. Starlight is a comprehensive system that supports a range of data mining activities. The integration and presentation of data within Starlight can facilitate the data mining process, providing opportunities for insightful analyses and interpretations of the data. Starlight is being developed by PNNL (Battelle) and in its current incarnation is operating on a Windows NT configuration. Its primary target audience has been the intelligence community, but it can realistically be applied to any environment requiring this type of data representation since its components are designed to support exploratory analyses.

Starlight supports a range of preprocessing functions that are used to populate its repositories. There are subsystems for processing free text by extracting header information and applying a variety of natural language processing techniques and statistical functions to parse for content. Header and related content are also extracted from multimedia such as pictures and video clips. Relational data are handled by CCM (continuous connection model) methods developed by a third party.

Information is stored in Starlight using an object-oriented database. There are repositories for textual, image, and geographic information. Starlight divides analysis functions for these repositories into two different types. The first is based on content and it is primarily used to understand the meaning, definition, or structure of a piece of data (e.g., document semantics). The second looks at the interrelationships that exist or are implied among various data elements by emphasizing associations or linkages. Through both 2D and 3D interfaces, Starlight provides a variety of visualizations that are used present this information. The display complexity in Starlight is managed through a combination of graph layering and interactive filtering tools.

The visualizations used by Starlight can display all of its database content within one 3D workspace. There are components that show maps, images, and the relationships among structured data. Figure 10.17 shows a typical Starlight display. As you can see there are containers that hold different types of information. Boxes represent the content of the free text documents, spheres portray the structured data, and the maps or images are shown in their native format. The workspace can be navigated interactively and multiple views can be present at any one time. These

Figure 10.17 A sample Starlight display.

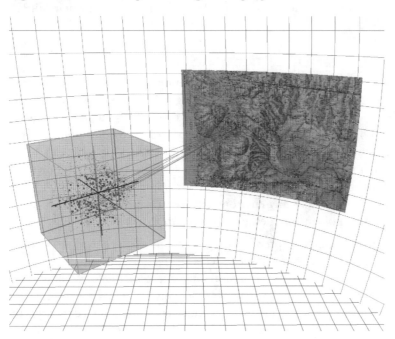

features make it easy to look at different levels of abstraction or details within the environment.

The boxes, called Similarity Plots, are used to show collections of free text documents as 3D scatter plots. Each point within a plot represents a document. The relative location of the points within these plots indicates how similar the contents of documents are with respect to one another. The closer the points, the stronger the conceptual similarity. As we discussed earlier, this type of display provides a good method for obtaining an overview about what is contained within a collection of documents. Data Spheres are used to represent the structured data within Starlight. Any value associated with a piece of data (e.g., its set of attributes) can be used to sort the data into "piles" across the surface of a sphere. It should be noted that the contents of a Similarity Plot could be placed into a Data Sphere based on one of its structured attributes (e.g., source, date, author, etc.).

Text can also be presented directly within a Starlight display. This can be done as a static representation where a text field is displayed adjacent to its associated document symbol. Alternatively, you can use a dynamic technique called *text streaming,* which continuously presents the individual words contained within a document alongside its symbol. The rate at which the words are presented can be adjusted to meet your particular processing capabilities. Since multiple text streams can be instantiated within a single Starlight display, this make it easy to depict large quantities of data using efficient presentation methods.

The structured data supported by Starlight are shown using what is called a Link Net, where the individual symbols are linked in the display. Through a wide range of query capabilities, Starlight can produce some very interesting displays using this type of approach depending on how the geometry is presented. Figure 10.18 shows an example of a Link Net within Starlight. Link Nets can also be queried by simply selecting on different attribute values, using sliders, or associating them to a map. Only those data that are relevant to the display will be presented.

As we just mentioned, linkages among data elements in a Starlight display can be intermingled. For example multimedia representations such as maps or images can have hot spots identified that will link the data elements together. An illustration is shown in Figure 10.19 in which location pointers on a map are tied directly

Figure 10.18 A Starlight Link Net representation.

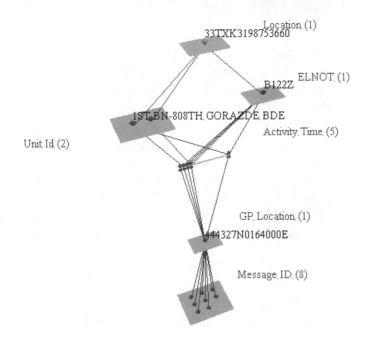

Figure 10.19 Using maps and Tie-Node linkages in Starlight.

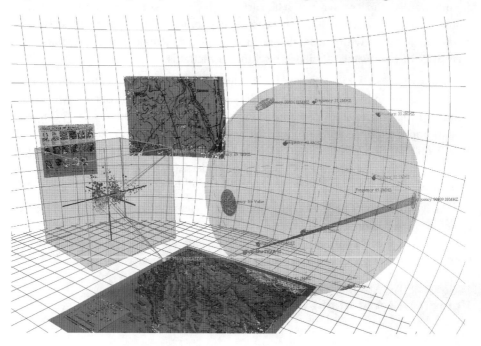

to the data objects. Abstracted data, called Tie-Nodes, can be constructed from field/value pairs used to represent specific values that are of importance to you. This feature could be used to focus the analysis in terms of relationships such as sales/dollars, product/defects, calls/durations, and so forth.

As you can see, the future of visual navigation and analysis will involve the processing and integration of information derived from disparate sources. Systems that support the integration of the three primary types of data (e.g., text, images, and relational objects) can be used to perform multidimensional analyses on a wide range of data sets. We believe that this is a general trend that will take off in the world of data mining tools, and in fact there are already several examples of systems being developed to answer this challenge. We review some of these in the next section.

Full Scope Systems

As data mining systems continue to evolve, they will become more sophisticated in their ability to support a wider array of data processing and analysis functions.

Within this framework analysts will want to be able to access multiple visualization paradigms, choosing the one most appropriate for the direction of the analysis at any point. The data mining process will be facilitated by the availability of multiple options that are interchangeable within the analytical environment. It may be that this functionality will all be bundled into a single system. Or it might be the case that the analytical environment might be composed of a set of modules that will seamlessly interact with one another. From the analyst's perspective these two are indistinguishable. The ideal situation is one in which the environment contains all functions needed to support discovery across a wide range of data models and visualization paradigms while also supporting other analytical processes (e.g., data acquisition, report writing, and presentation).

Over the past few years, several large information management systems have been developed to perform a wide range of data mining activities. Even though many data warehousing and OLAP-related systems fall within this category, they tend to be very specialized, supporting limited analyses for a small range of data types. The descriptions in this section are intended to present an overview of several large-scale systems that have been built specifically to cover a spectrum of data mining and data exploitation needs. The goal of these write-ups is to provide a general sense of the philosophy with which each system is being developed, rather than to give an exhaustive listing of all system features and capabilities. As with all other chapters in this section of the book, this listing is by no means complete. We have made selections for inclusion based on our desire to cover the range of development efforts currently underway.

Pathfinder

Pathfinder is a large-scale data mining system that was originally developed for the intelligence community by the National Ground Intelligence Center (NGIC), a division of the U.S. Army. This application currently is made available to all agencies of the U.S. government as a government-owned product, commonly referred to as GOTS. The tool is being developed by Presearch Incorporated, located in the Washington D.C. area. Presearch recently has been using the tool in a variety of open-source engagements, and a commercial version of Pathfinder is currently available.

Pathfinder's capabilities are continually being expanded through regularly sponsored Study Advisory Group (SAG) meetings in which feedback is elicited regarding the current functionality as well as future capabilities that might be included in the system. This development strategy is interesting because it ensures that the Pathfinder system evolves to reflect the real-world needs of its user base.

The system is designed to provide automated loading, manipulation, analysis, and presentation on a wide range of textual data sources, including open-source information (e.g., formatted and unformatted text messages). Pathfinder is composed of over two dozen subsystems, and a complete review of each is outside the scope of this book. In this discussion we therefore pay particular attention to the various visualization approaches that have been included to support analysis.

Pathfinder has a full set of user accounting and administrative utilities that help maintain systems-level operations. Since Pathfinder was designed to accept a wide variety of data types, there is an extensive catalogue of data management functions that can be used to clean up data fields, delete duplicated records, derive usage statistics, and much more. In particular, Pathfinder supports a Generic Load capability that provides you with the ability to create new databases from any available medium. As you can tell by its name, Generic Load supports both text and relational database feeds through input rules that define how the data should be parsed. There is also a text extraction feature that finds the names of people, facilities, equipment, and so forth. Pathfinder currently supports both Memex and Excalibur text indexing and search technologies. All search engine calls are made through an API, and Pathfinder itself is engine independent. The API-to-server calls just need to be created for any new text-search engines that are targeted for incorporation into Pathfinder. As Presearch moves the tool into a web-based environment, this new engine should become just another plug-and-play component.

As the data are populated into the system, there are many different ways in which they can be viewed. In addition to providing external hooks to systems such as the Analyst's Notebook and NETMAP, Pathfinder itself supports several unique methods for presenting data. All of these modules have been developed specifically for Pathfinder and they can be accessed through the main analytical control interface. It is here that the type of information that will be passed over to these tools is defined. The analysis window has an area where users can specify a query that will filter a portion of the data set to be selected for viewing. There are also advanced features that allow you to focus on the data you need. Next, each of these visualization tools is discussed.

CAMEO

CAMEO provides a unique perspective on visualizing information. It is a method by which you can model the trail of an analytic process or problem set through the representation of nodes and links. The nodes represent the information targeted by queries into the data set. Links between these nodes form a representation of the analytical model. This scheme can be used to help identify activities such as cocaine production triggers in counter-narcotics applications (e.g., manufacturing the coca paste) and detection of patterns in life-stage events for retail marketing (e.g., birth of a first child). Figure 10.20 shows an example of what an analytical model for cocaine production looks like in a CAMEO display.

Figure 10.20 A CAMEO screen depicting a model for cocaine production in Pathfinder.

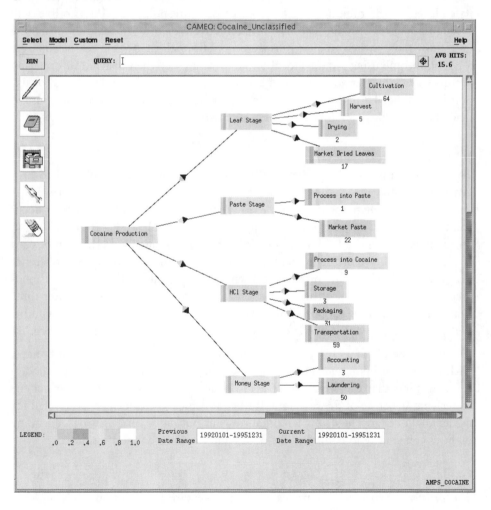

Each node within this diagram has an associated query (i.e., keywords and comparators) that retrieves information from the data set that is used in the over-all analysis. Since the individual queries reflect only a section of the model, they can be weighted independently depending on their importance. When the model is run, the nodes are ranked based on a calculation of the number of unique terms found and they also adjust their colors to code whether there is any information available in the data set that satisfies the query. Colors may also reflect ranking. The rank-ings of the nodes are then used by their parent nodes, if any, to determine their rel-evance to the model. If there is no query in a node, it uses the weighted average of its children. If the ranking of a node exceeds a threshold, CAMEO notifies you through an alert. CAMEO can be run interactively or in the background making itself known only when an alert is triggered. Additionally, CAMEO can be run over a period of time using a data-slider so that you can see when relevant information becomes available. At any time, you can select a node to see all data used to sup-port its ranking. This is vital since analytic judgments in many applications must be made based on the actual data, not just a statistical sampling.

PIM

The Personal Information Manager (PIM) is an organizational tool used to help generate and manage final outputs from Pathfinder analyses. PIM supports a link analysis format where the nodes are used to store the pointers to records or docu-ments that contain relevant information regarding an analysis. Figure 10.21 shows an example of a typical PIM diagram. Nodes have a comment field that can be used to justify how the records support the analysis. Dates are stored for each reference placed within PIM so that you can tell when something was added, deleted, or mod-ified. This framework can then be used to replay the information at a later time, similar to the features supported in CAMEO. There is even an overview window that you can use to navigate the display when the PIM diagram becomes large.

In this sample diagram, the nodes contain a variety of multimedia files, maps, URLs, and record pointers. These can be shown by profiling or viewing the nodes. Keep in mind that the structure of a PIM diagram does not actually reflect the underlying structure of the raw data. Rather, it depicts the information selected for use as final output. Thus, you can organize your output in various ways depending on how you choose to configure the nodes and the links connecting them.

Galileo

The previous two modules are used to manage different portions of your data analysis. Galileo is a module that is uses landscape visualization to show the rela-tionships among document sets through topical clustering. Thus, it provides you

Figure 10.21 A sample PIM diagram in Pathfinder.

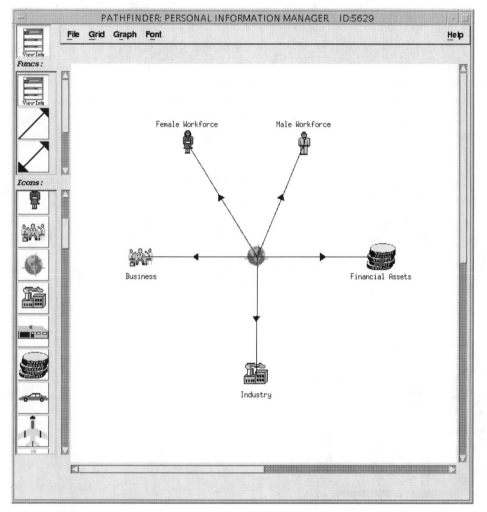

with an overall view of your data set that allows you to understand its structure and content without having to read all of the individual documents. Galileo supports many of the text processing capabilities that were presented earlier in this chapter. When producing the associated document vectors, there are several options that can be exercised. Galileo can group documents based on word sorts across entire documents (PI Vectors) or it can use only the most frequently occurring 2, 3, or 4 word phrases for forming groups (Turbo Vectors). Galileo can also present a higher level view of the document clusters using a Fixed Centroid placement technique that focuses on the cluster profile rather than on the individual documents. Figure 10.22 shows an example of a Galileo display of a topical clustering produced from a set of documents on nuclear weapons.

Documents are represented as points with the Galileo display and the physical distance between any two points corresponds to the similarity of their respective contents with similar documents placed close together in the space. Groups of closely related records (clusters) can be displayed with a large dot or cluster center. When you select any cluster, Galileo expands the cluster to show only those documents in that cluster. There are also capabilities for searching on topics within the

Figure 10.22 A Galileo display showing topical clustering of nuclear weapons documents in Pathfinder.

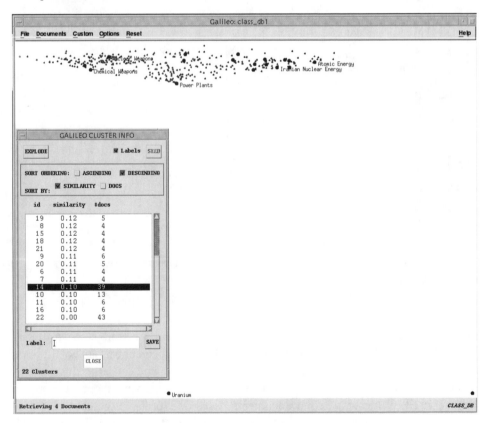

display and coding document points based on features of interest (e.g., source, language, author, etc.). As in Pathfinder's other display modes, the information within Galileo can be time sliced to show only those documents dated within a certain period. The interface for the time slice window also has a set of bar graphs that show the number of documents processed for the indicated time period.

Counts

The Counts module allows you to get a better look at the actual content of the document set. A grid is used to represent frequency of occurrence of words or phrases occurring within documents over a period of time. For instance, if a set of records concerning two countries contains the phrase "glass lined" with above-average frequency, you may start to look for records indicating chemical warfare related technology transfer activities. Each cell in the grid contains the number of occurrences of the word/phrase as well as the total number of documents in which it appeared. There is also a column for showing the total number of occurrences for all years included in the analysis. Selection of a cell within the grid will retrieve the underlying documents that were used in its construction automatically. Figure 10.23 shows an example of a typical Counts diagram.

Counts has a variety of parameters that can be set to control the type of information presented. There are methods used to select the number of words in a phrase, define stop words (e.g., and, or, the, a, is, in, etc.), and select lists of words. There are even ways to delete and merge different phrases in the resulting displays. Counts also has a 3D option in which the heights of the cells are set to reflect the frequency of occurrence (see Figure 10.24). The resulting display can be rotated and zoomed for perspective. The 3D Counts window has a set of sliders used to control the date ranges of the data being displayed.

Cross Field Matrix

Similar to the Counts diagram, the Cross Field Matrix is a two-dimensional grid for data presentation. The major difference is that the axes are defined by fielded values within the Pathfinder database. This module may be used to get a top-level view of associations occurring between variable values across the data set (see the Association Rules section of Chapter 6). Since Pathfinder supports an alias function to map different values into a single format (e.g., United States, USA, America, -> US) any one of the cells within the Cross Field Matrix can potentially represent multiple entries. The color of the individual cells is based on a ratio representing either the frequency of occurrence or a year range. For a year range ratio

Figure 10.23 A sample 2D Counts diagram in Pathfinder.

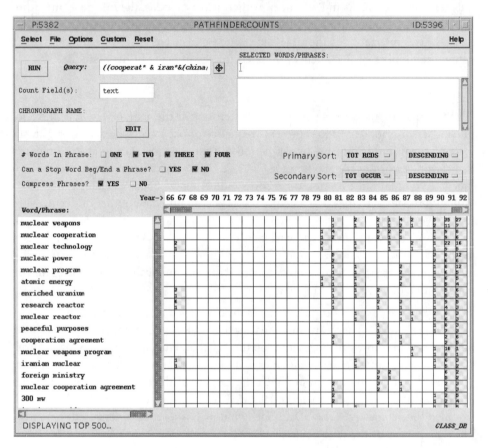

to be calculated, the Cross Field Matrix uses the longest year span of the documents. Figure 10.25 shows an example of a Cross Field Matrix showing the relationships among facilities and people.

Oil Stock

Oil Stock is yet another visual interface integrated with Pathfinder. It was originally developed by a different branch of the U.S. government and is used throughout a wide variety of agencies for both research and operational purposes. Oil Stock is a mapping package and it can either be used to identify and present data with associated geolocational coordinates or to select an area of interest (called gazetteering)

Figure 10.24 A sample 3D Counts diagram in Pathfinder.

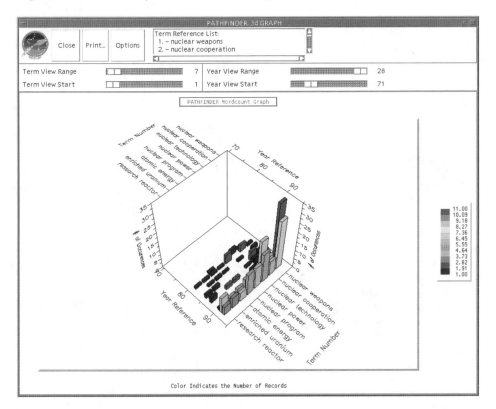

to retrieve records that contain the cities, towns, or locations identified by that region. Pathfinder is well integrated with Oil Stock. You can use this module to access all geocoordinates within a certain number of words from a target, for example, within 10 words of the term "factory." Oil Stock can also be used to display maps, zoom, pan, and generate overlays. Figure 10.26 provides an example of an Oil Stock display in Pathfinder.

Collaboration

One final point of discussion is the collaborative feature offered by Pathfinder. Pathfinder enables users to share the files associated with CAMEO, PIM, Counts, and Oil Stock with other users and groups. When you want to share one of these files, a copy of the resource is written to a common directory accessible (read-only)

Figure 10.25 A Cross Field Matrix diagram in Pathfinder.

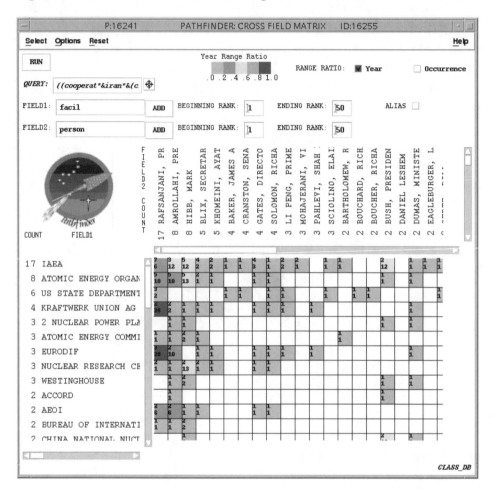

by all other Pathfinder users. Any conflicts in name are resolved before posting the resource. When the Collaboration tool is invoked, it provides you with a choice of available resources. For each entry in the list, its group, posting date, status, name/title, and any comments will be presented. Thus, choosing any one of these resources will place its content into the application in which it was originally generated in Pathfinder. By working with this type of collaborative function, you can easily share your results with other people and get valuable feedback to help refine your analysis. We believe that collaboration will become an integral part of many full-scope systems in the near future.

Figure 10.26 An Oil Stock display in Pathfinder.

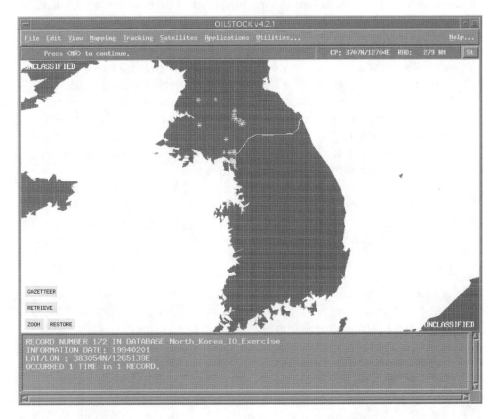

Generic Visualization Architecture (GVA)

One other future trend that we will discuss is the ability of certain systems to support multiple representations of the same data sets. As shown in many of the commercial products described in this section, it is usually possible to present data from more than one viewpoint in order to do visual data mining. In fact, the more complex the data sources, the more likely that different perspectives on the data will be required in order to fully characterize patterns and trends of interest. One tool that is being developed to address this issue head-on is called the Generic Visualization Architecture (GVA). It provides several different display paradigms that can be used to support the data mining process.

GVA is one of only a few tools written entirely in the Java programming language (see the sidebar on the Importance of Java). GVA is thus platform independent, currently running in Windows 95, NT, DEC, SUN, HP, MacIntosh, and Netscape

Browser environments. GVA is being developed by United Information Systems, Inc. as a noncommercial research project supported by the U.S. government. As such, the

The Importance of Java

Just-in-time-applications are becoming standard conventions for software designs that require the seamless integration of data, networking activities, and user interactions. Within this context, Java is a very important programming innovation. Java is an object-oriented programming language, similar to C++, that is quickly becoming a standard development environment. It is currently the only language that can be used to develop programs that can be distributed in a platform-independent manner. Java allows its software to execute regardless of the operating system being used. The object-oriented nature of Java provides powerful class libraries that can be used to structure applications using architecturally neutral code that can be run across a heterogeneous network of machines.

Java has been designed to allow the developer to write once and run anywhere. That is, you do not have to worry about what computing platform is available within your environment. Java has been ported to many different operating systems. (GVA has been verified on seven of them, all running the same underlying Java code.) Java is technically a nonproprietary language, and it is a safe and reliable choice for business programming.

One of Java's most attractive features is that it supports Dynamic Class Loading. In traditional computing environments, new code cannot be introduced into a running system without a series of steps that include exiting the system, recompiling, relinking, and re-executing the program so that the new function will be incorporated. In Java, none of these steps are necessary. You can plug new modules into an existing Java application and they will be integrated automatically into your working environment. This feature of Java supports dynamic fast-paced software development in which many people can develop code in a parallel and distributed fashion, and have their contributions immediately integrated into everyone's working version of the application.

If Java code can be updated so rapidly by Dynamic Class Loading, how can you be sure to have the most current version of an application running in your environment? Staying up to date is automatically system is available free of charge to all government agencies at both state and federal levels and is being distributed through Internet-based technologies.

guaranteed by another feature of Java, namely Object Persistence. During a typical Java application development exercise, a central site is designated as the home of the master code and all users download and post code from this location as needed. Each time your local application is launched, it automatically checks the master code site to determine whether updates have been made that need to be brought into the local environment. This feature allows you to keep track of the most recent version of your application with great ease. This turns out to be an important feature when you need to distribute new releases of a computing application to a host of users. With Java, all you would have to do is post updates to a network, and they would be picked up by all users automatically. Thus, you would not need to store the application manually on every single machine since you could let the Java application reload itself.

Another advantage of Java is that it is very secure. Although Java is in wide use, we know of no hostile applets that have caused problems within computing infrastructures. Of course, there is always the chance that some unscrupulous programmer will try and sabotage someone's ongoing operations, but Java is no more vulnerable to this sort of mischief than any other programming language. In fact, Java has features built directly into the language to help prevent these types of problems, making it less prone to security breaches than most common programming languages.

By using Java for running major applications, you can minimize the need for a complicated and elaborate computing infrastructure. Java can be structured to support a wide range of client/server configurations and does not need to be run from a massive centralized system. This fits right in with the current trend in business toward network computing (NC). NC supports "virtual offices" where any user can just plug into an NC port connected to the corporate network (whether onsite or through an Internet connection) and access his or her own work space, documents, e-mail, and other resources. The NC approach allows you to scale your computing environment down from large servers to personal digital assistants—a move that usually produces significant cost savings.

The GVA processing engine and its interface displays have been implemented in pure Java. The system is smart enough to determine whether it is being run as an application or an applet so it can adjust to different operating configurations. (Applications are run locally from the command line and have full system privileges, whereas applets are run from remote sites and executed within a restrictive mode for security purposes.) From the start GVA was designed to be very modular and flexible with the anticipation that it would be extended and customized to suit the needs of the user community. Since analytical needs differ across application domains, the system was designed to adapt to the user rather than the typical converse. GVA can be, and has already been, tailored to meet a wide variety of analytical requirements.

GVA is organized into separate modules in which you can build data models, load data, filter data for display, and display your data in one of several paradigms. Data extensions occur automatically across modules because the environment can determine when it is out of date and invoke the procedures to make the necessary upgrades. GVA's Java classes will soon be self-updating, which means that as new release versions are available, the system automatically will take advantage of any new features through intelligent update protocols built into the environment.

Modeling Data in GVA

Before any data are loaded or any analysis begins, a model of the fielded data must be specified in GVA. Since all data are treated as objects, the modeling process involves the specification of those fields that will serve as object classes in the model and fields that will provide values for attributes to be assigned to those object classes. Attributes are used to describe the features of the objects and they can include numbers, strings, dates, times, images, text documents, and sound clips. Links or relationships existing among object classes are also specified during the modeling process. Since links are treated as objects within GVA, you may specify attributes of links as well. Once specified, the modeling information is stored in a configuration file (.cfg file) that is loaded at the same time as the data set. For convenience, a graphic interface has been developed for creating and editing models. This facility allows you to alter data models on the fly, which will in turn allow you to create a wide array of visualizations with a minimum of delay and effort.

If you have a free-text file instead of a fielded database (e.g., a delimited file format), you can use GVA to sort portions of the text into fields. Using the same approach defined for fielded data, you can then select a passage of text from an editor window and create model nodes on-the-fly that are stored in configuration files.

Nodes and links can be added or deleted, attributes can be defined, and the resulting structure committed to a database. Thus, you are using the same templating methods to handle both field values and text entries.

Loading Data into GVA

As we already mentioned, data sets are loaded into GVA using a pair of files: a configuration file that specifies your model and a data file containing the information to be analyzed. The process of integrating data sets with the designated model is accomplished from GVA's Load module. GVA supports a range of data formats, including flat ASCII delimited files. GVA also has JDBC (a Java version of ODBC) foundation class libraries that can be used to overlay GVA directly onto existing databases to perform extractions. This method works well with relational, object oriented, and object-relational databases. You may load more than one data/configuration file at a time, designating one file as the working data set in the load module menu. Different load modules can be developed to handle a variety of data formats that might be encountered across different data sets.

Filtering Data in GVA

Sometimes you may want to filter the working data set so that only a portion of your information is flagged for display. GVA allows you to do this through a graphic filter interface. The graphic filter models of object classes and their linkages within the working data set are presented within the display. Selection of an object class from the main display produces a listing of all of the attributes defined for that object. You can filter on the basis of object class, attribute values, or linkage values, either for specific values or a range of values. You can also filter across the entire data set using word searches. Filter operations at the level of object classes can be performed by removing nodes and links from the display. Excluded object classes are grayed out from the filter display. If a node is excluded, any links that are connected to it will also be excluded. What is attractive about using this approach is that you are drawing your query in this interface. Figure 10.27 shows an example of the graphic filter display.

Once you have made the object, link, and attribute selections for a filter operation, you invoke the filter through a button on the interface. At this point GVA creates a new data set defined by the filter conditions. This approach helps to speed up the resulting displays and makes it easier to collaborate with other users since only a subset of the data is being processed at any time. You can easily switch back and forth between data sets within the GVA filter and the displays.

Figure 10.27 The GVA graphic filter interface.

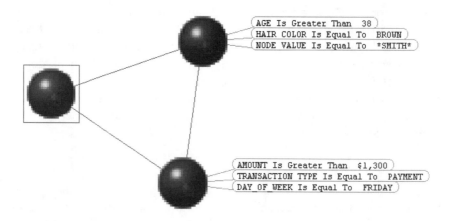

The filtered sets can also be named to provide a better reference method for recalling steps in an analysis.

GVA supports a special absolute filter algorithm for automatic detection of patterns, temporal or otherwise. Through graphic interfaces, you define a trigger event to be matched in a subsequent search. This event may be a simple representation, for instance the occurrence of a certain object with a particular attribute value (for example, sales transactions of more than $500). You then define the boundaries of the search, for example to begin and end at certain dates included in the data set. The absolute pattern detection algorithms decompose the cycle specified into a series of discrete segments of equal length. For each segment, the heuristics determine whether the trigger event you specified has occurred. The algorithm is repeated on successively smaller (or larger) intervals, finally stopping at a defined boundary. Patterns are reported for a given run if the number of intervals in which the trigger event occurs exceeds a reporting threshold (i.e., 50 percent, 75 percent, etc.). You may then inspect these findings, run the filter again with a more refined trigger event, and so on as desired.

GVA's Main Interface

As with any 3D visualization environment, users need methods that help them navigate the data effectively. GVA supports a wide range of display types, but the same general navigational aids are available in all of the different display modes. The main GVA interface has navigational controls for rotation, dragging, zooming, panning, and fitting the entire data structure to the display. There are also data manipulation functions to mark, lock, select, and profile individual data points. You can also set display parameters such as background, color, shape, labeling, and so on from this interface. This main display can be customized to include or exclude any of these navigational controls.

You can control displays in GVA in terms of the shapes, colors, and labels of objects and links. There is a transparent feature that draws the nodes in the display as wireframes. This can significantly speed up the navigation of the data since the drawing complexity will be minimized. The data labels can be used to show either node names or the values of an attribute. The display paradigm is selected from pull-down menus and there are currently four options: cluster, network, grid, and kiviat. Depending on your requirements, these displays can be turned off and never loaded into GVA if they are not used. This helps free up system resources and allows you to tailor your analytical environment individually.

Creating a Cluster Display in GVA

One of the most powerful types of positioning formats available within GVA is the *cluster* display. Its primary role is to generate clusters of data based on shared attribute values. The cluster option allows you to group data based on object classes or other attributes. The clustering display provides a suite of choices that may be used to present data in a link analysis format because it also draws links between the nodes. Using clustering, you can immediately see which nodes are linked to other nodes and how they are related. Objects may be placed in the display sorted by classes and/or attributes in several physical patterns. These include lines, circles, cylinders, grids, and other geometric formats. You can select both a main shape and a cluster shape within the display. The main shape determines how the overall display will look in terms of how the individual clusters will be positioned. The cluster shape determines how the individual objects within a particular cluster will be arranged. All of the nodes can be sorted within any cluster based on various menu selections. Very different displays will be generated for the same data set with slight variations in sorting and clustering choices. Figure 10.28 shows a sample diagram using the cluster feature.

There are several display control features, which can be used to manipulate and restructure clusters. One in particular is called *shed* because it will shed away or exclude all nodes from the display except those that have been selected and the nodes directly connected to selected nodes. This function can be used to perform a localized data walk because you can traverse from one node to the next until there are no more linkages to explore. Other features supported by the cluster display allow you to control the separation of the clusters as well as the individual nodes themselves. These

Figure 10.28 Sample cluster display generated by GVA.

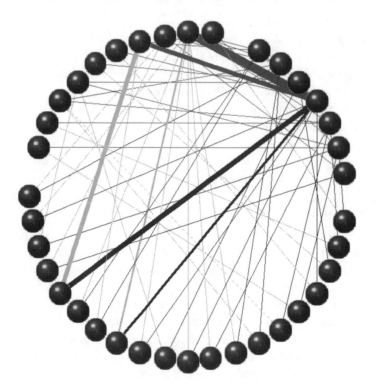

adjustments are made through sliders. There are also methods for turning links on and off, showing link labels, and showing the cluster labels (when desired).

Navigating Network Displays in GVA

The *network* display is one of the simplest and easiest to interpret within GVA. Network displays are produced by a self-organizing iterative calculation that positions data elements by the rule that links attract and objects repel each other within the display space. This display is particularly useful for data sets in which you may wish to expose isolated networks or show the extent of certain node connections. Since this particular display is threaded within GVA, it will continually adjust itself, trying to find a steady-state representation. The display moves as these adjustments occur until the number of crossing links is minimized. Figure 10.29 shows an example of a network display in which subnetworks are isolated by virtue of their modeled connections.

There are options available in this display module for setting the degree of attraction, repulsion, minimum and maximum distances, and whether a bounding box is present. By default a bounding box initially is applied to the size of the screen

Figure 10.29 A 3D GVA network display with minimal link crossings.

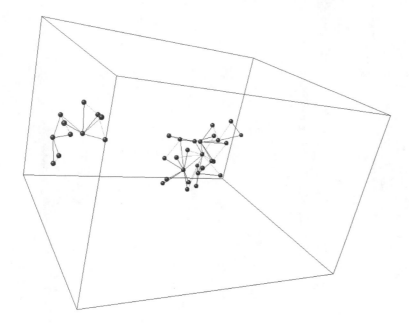

to constrain the growth of the network. There is also a 3D organization feature that allows the network to self-organize in 3D space. Thus, lines may still appear to be crossing one another when you view the display head-on, but as soon as you rotate it slightly you will see that the data have adjusted into the third dimension. The network module also supports a shed function.

Generating a Grid Display in GVA

The grid display option allows you to present data in a three-dimensional landscape grid. The representation of a grid is one of the most fundamental visualization techniques since it can be easily interpreted and it can handle a large number of dimensions. A grid metaphor is conceptually very simple but extremely powerful. The grid can be used to plot one, two, or three dimensions of the data. By making selections from the menus, you can define which variables to plot, which axes to use, how to label axes, how to shade the data, how to display the data, and how to construct the grid itself. Figure 10.30 shows a sample grid display.

One appealing feature of the grid is that you can make adjustments to the size of the cells. Data elements are depicted inside the individual cells in which they

Figure 10.30 A representative GVA grid display.

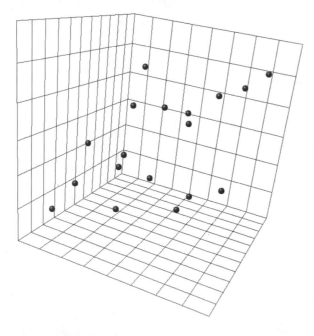

fall. The color of the cells can be set to reflect the number of data elements they contain, with brighter cells containing more data elements. This lets you quickly identify hot spots, or regions within the grid that contain the most data elements. By default, a block representation is used to fill in the grid space, although this can be changed to show x, y, or z bars within the 3D-grid space. Additionally, a point notation can be used instead of the blocks or bars within the grid (as in Figure 10.30). Depending on how you map your data into the grid, different information can be derived using these bar options. Figure 10.31 shows a bar graph option within the grid display.

Kiviat Displays in GVA

Special circular histogram displays, called *kiviats* (or radar diagrams) can also be used in GVA to present high-level summaries of the data. The kiviat is closely related to a parallel coordinate display used in some of the other visualization tools. In these displays you can present data from multiple variables with the values normalized against the mean if desired. The dimensions included in the diagram may be displayed either by value or by frequency. Actual values may be displayed to convey the range of all possible values of a numeric variable contained within a data

Figure 10.31 GVA grid display depicting bar charts.

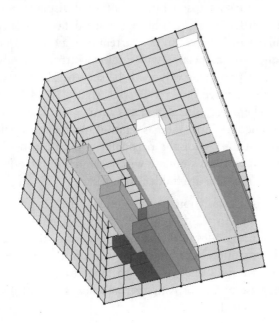

set. On the other hand, you can display by frequency in order to ascertain the distribution of values across a database. Frequency displays can be generated for either numeric or nonnumeric data.

Figure 10.32 depicts a kiviat diagram showing the same variable (e.g., amount of sale) for a range of retail transactions. The left part shows the amounts based on actual value, so the distance from the center of the display indicates the value being presented. The further away from the center, the larger the value. The right part shows the same variable by presenting the frequency of occurrence, which shows those values appearing most often. Thus, the largest peak in this figure depicts a value that has been observed more times than any other value. Only four variables are being presented here, but a kiviat can support as many variables as can be effectively interpreted.

In GVA the kiviat can also support a third dimension by specifying an attribute from the data model. This lets you slice up the display into a series of individual mini-kiviats. Each separate kiviat will reflect one of the discrete values associated with the z-dimension variable. Figure 10.33 shows an example of a 3D kiviat. This type of representation makes it easy to look for trends, especially if the third dimension is set to a time or date.

Isolating Data in GVA

There is one feature in particular that cuts across all of the different displays supported by GVA. The isolate function lets you slice through your data using any attribute to show nodes with similar values based on the current display technique being utilized. Thus, for each unique value associated with a selected attribute, only those objects or links supporting that particular value will be shown. The isolate function has an interface, which is structured like a VCR (see Figure 10.34 for a snapshot of the isolate interface). There are several features in this interface that control the behavior of the isolate function. First, there is a pull-down menu, which contains all of the attributes known to GVA for the particular application being run. You select the attribute that you want to simulate within the display. Its display flag is turned on and the rest of the data are hidden from view.

The VCR controls determine the progression of the simulation through the data. There are buttons to play, stop, step forward, step backward, reset, pause, and record. The record function accumulates nodes in the display (e.g., keeps their display flags set). The frame interval determines how fast the simulation will progress and the display window shows the unique value for the attribute currently being drawn. The isolate function is very useful and provides yet another means of discovering patterns and trends within your data sets.

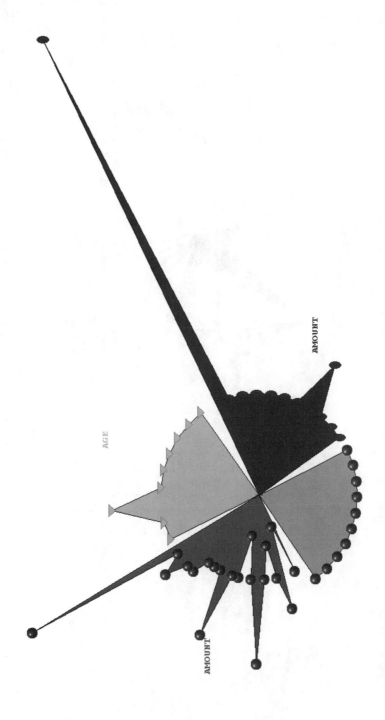

Figure 10.32 A kiviat display showing actual values versus frequency in GVA.

Figure 10.33 A 3D kiviat display shown in GVA.

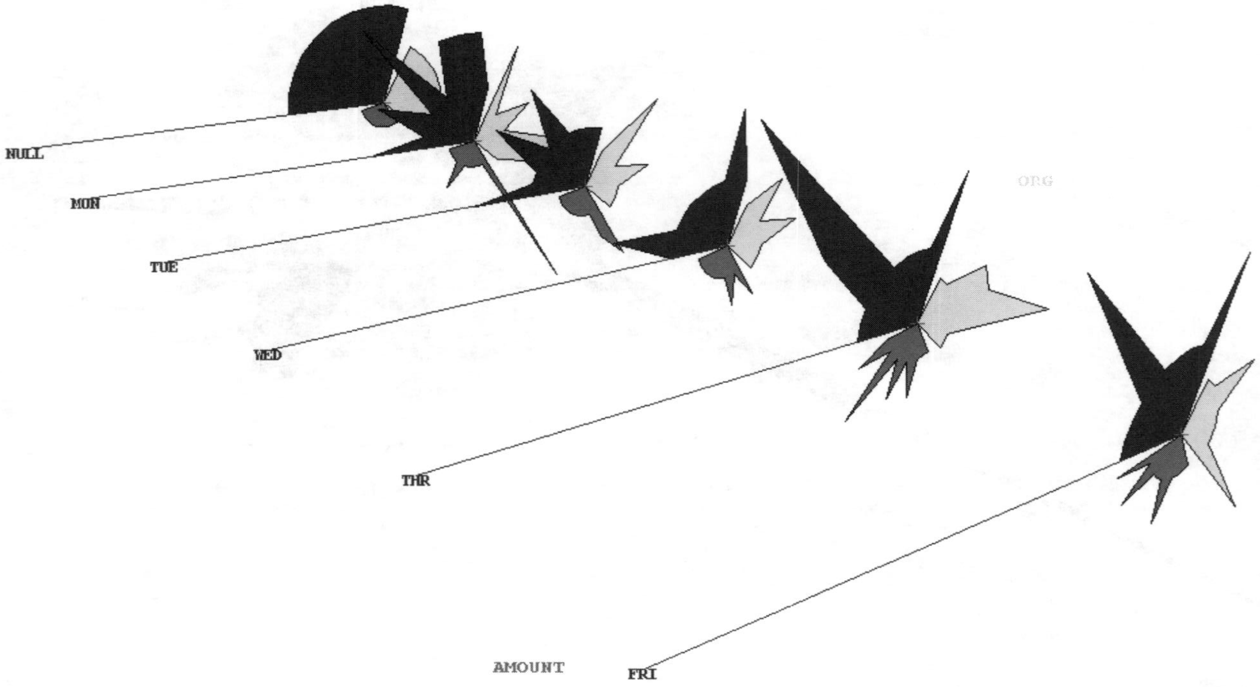

NULL

MON

TUE

WED

THR

AMOUNT

FRI

ORG

Figure 10.34 A snapshot of the isolate control interface in GVA.

Saving the State of an Analysis in GVA

Taking advantage of Java's object persistence, the GVA system provides a method for saving off its state to a file structure. What this means is that the entire configuration currently in use by GVA is captured for future recall. All of the filter conditions, display parameters, and even the viewpoint on the display can be captured. So when you finish or terminate a session with GVA, you can save the state so that you can always pick up again where you left off, reinstantiating the analysis to that particular point. As you progress through a data mining engagement, you can manually define states that are of interest to you. This could occur when there is a decision point in your analysis, before you reach out and acquire more data, or before you filter out data. When a state is saved, a thumbnail of the display is generated and put into a state-saver profile window. From this point on, you can reinstantiate that state at any time. You can save states in order to construct a storyboard of your analysis. These states can also be sent to other GVA users for remote collaboration purposes. This type of feature is just another benefit that is directly derived from the use of Java as its underlying implementation method.

Customizing the GVA Environment

A wide variety of navigation controls are available in GVA. These range from controlling the viewpoint to invoking/disabling features. Since GVA was developed using Java, it can be configured for a wide range of user preferences because it supports dynamic class loading. Sections of GVA can be loaded or unloaded from the system with great ease. If there are certain displays or features that you do not require, they can be turned off and never loaded into memory. You can also set parameters for your own preferences on such features as colors, backgrounds, fonts, and rotation and zoom increments. Thus, you can control the GVA footprint and help balance it to meet your analytical requirements. This also allows you to load in third-party functions developed by other people within the GVA user community.

A palette of images can also be specified within the GVA control menus. You can put any GIF images in this palette and use them to represent nodes in the displays. The background image within GVA can also be set as a GIF image. This is an attractive feature if you want to display maps, terrains, or other spatially oriented diagrams on the background and overlay them with data elements during the analysis. GVA can also call out to other profile methods that can override GVA's own functions. This provides a way to integrate GVA into existing applications and use their profiling mechanisms to maintain a consistent look and feel in the analytical environment.

Future Directions in GVA's Development

In future versions, GVA will automatically check to see if it is out of date to determine whether it should download new components. This capability will also provide support for the module libraries that are being developed for GVA. Since the tool is expected to become a community standard, users will be developing their own modules. As we mentioned previously, these modules could be alternative positioning techniques, new display formats, heuristic procedures, analytical algorithms, or advanced filter capabilities. Any new modules can be posted to a central library for notification and access by the community.

Remember that the overall goal of data mining is to discover new patterns and trends and present them to a target audience. In many cases these analyses will require the collective thoughts and contributions of many individuals. To help facilitate this process, data mining tool developers are beginning to explore ways of supporting collaboration among analysts. For example, the gaming market has already addressed this issue within their multiplayer worlds. The foundation for collaboration has already been incorporated into GVA's basic design and the implementation of collaboration support is being planned. The idea is to set up each running version of GVA as its own server that can handle or mediate requests for information. In the most open scenario, all registered users will be able to see what is being presented and contribute their input through annotations as well as new data. Alternatively, the system could be configured only for display. There will be mechanisms to control who sees what data, who commands the screen, and who can update the data. This can be done in real time or through a shared resource where you are granted remote access to the environment being analyzed. As with all GVA interactions, an audit log will capture all of the data manipulation for future verification, justification, or replay.

Other Systems

There are several other full-scale data mining systems that make extensive use of visualization technologies. All of these systems provide an operational framework by which to load and manipulate data using a suite of different analytical functions. Like Pathfinder and GVA, these systems let you interact with your data using a variety of alternative approaches while maintaining a consistent interface. This makes it easier to perform more complex and sophisticated analyses because you do not have to switch back and forth between different third-party systems or wrestle with their idiosyncratic data management facilities. Rather, you can spend more of your time actually performing the analysis than preparing the data. You can expect to see this trend continue as data mining systems become broader in scope and more mature in their information management capabilities. Several systems including IntelliScape, InfoSleuth, Propeller, and Minerva are heading in this direction.

Overlaying Visualization onto Existing Systems

The incorporation of visualization is expected to become a fundamental way to understand data and perform related data mining activities. In many cases this visualization capability will be overlaid onto existing systems. As data standards continue to evolve and object-oriented designs become more prevalent within the industry, we can expect to see more layered systems being developed. Thus, you will be able to actively plug-and-play components through a set of shared interfaces. This already occurs at the hardware level where there are all sorts of different configurations and peripherals that can be integrated together effort-lessly. This concept has been extended into the database world where SQL, ODBC, and CORBA standards have helped systematize information storage and retrieval protocols. We expect that this trend will continue with the introduction of more sophisticated and interactive graphics capabilities into existing analytical environments. Innovations such as Java are helping to make this a reality. Layered approaches are emerging as a standard method of doing business, most specifically in the data warehousing and Internet communities.

Layered Visualization

One offering in particular exemplifies this paradigm for the integration of visualization using a layering approach. DataVista from Visualize Inc. is a comprehensive offering of tools that can support a wide variety of two- and three-dimensional graphs with real-time updating capabilities. DataVista is a Java-based resource that can be integrated and distributed easily into virtually any application or system. DataVista has been officially certified as 100 per-cent pure Java, meaning that it can be ported into many different computing environments. This makes it an ideal candidate for performing data mining, decision support, and statistical modeling.

DataVista supports a wide range of data viewers ranging from spreadsheet for-mats to interactive displays including those identified in the following list. Overall, there are 19 different types of charts available within DataVista. Figures 10.35 through 10.40 show examples of several of these types of displays.

- Line chart (2D and 3D)
- Bar chart (2D and 3D)
- Scatter plot (2D and 3D)
- Pie chart
- Doughnut chart
- Surface plots
- High-Low-Close-Volume
- Radar
- Grid
- Scatter matrix

Figure 10.35 Sample DataVista line chart visualization.

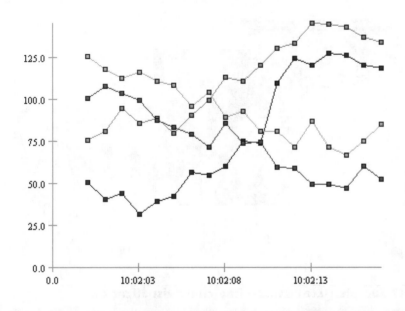

Within the DataVista system, there are built-in support methods for several data formats including HTML, ASCII, and JDBC. Moving data in and out of the displays is straightforward and there is no need for creating transport files or other intermediary representations. Through a wide range of control parameters, you can manipulate fonts, backgrounds, points, axes, legends, and labels. There are even methods to create legends, make annotations, animate display elements, and perform a variety of other functions. Thus, it is easy to customize the interfaces to reflect your specific data needs. This is most helpful when layering DataVista onto your web pages, spreadsheets, or database applications.

Data Vista also supports real-time data feeds through its Model-View-Controller architecture. The representation of the underlying data is managed separately from the graphs. Thus it is easy to work with data derived from multiple sources and have

Figure 10.36 Sample DataVista bar chart visualization.

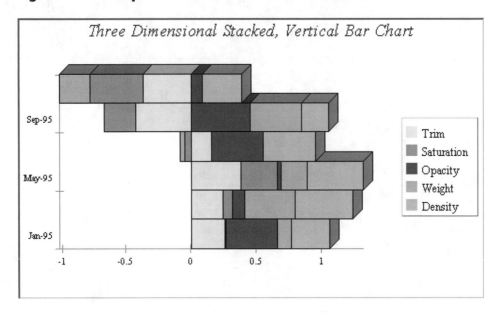

Figure 10.37 Sample DataVista 3D line chart visualization.

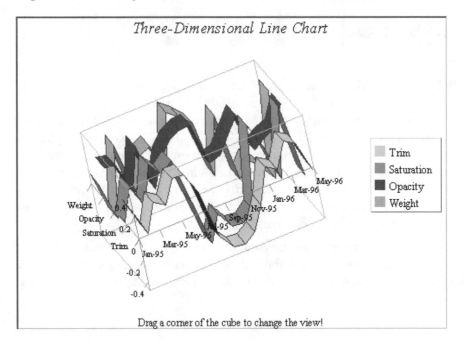

Figure 10.38 Sample DataVista 3D bar chart visualization.

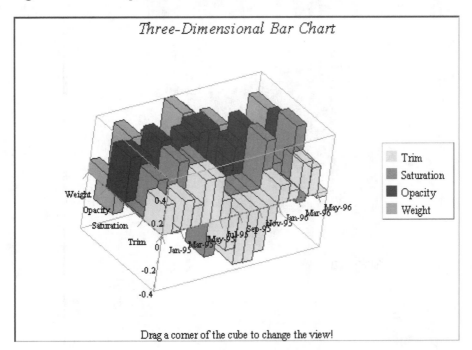

them actively viewed in more than one display at a time. There is also the ability to link the different displays together so that changes in one are immediately reflected in all of the others.

Since all of the DataVista displays are interactive, you can use them to manipulate the data where appropriate. Data in the displays can be brushed for drill-down, values can be changed to support what-if scenarios, and data such as outliers can be removed for better precision. DataVista has also been outfitted with several numerical analysis techniques that can be used to add value to the contents and presentation of your data. These techniques allow you to perform operations such as transposition, correlation, transformations, and distributions.

We can expect to see approaches like DataVista being used over a wide range of applications. Systems in the future will embrace a layered approach and the development process will be one of selecting the hardware, locking into a data repository, and choosing the visualization schema. As more web-centric tools emerge on the market, they will follow a similar approach.

Figure 10.39 Sample DataVista visualization.

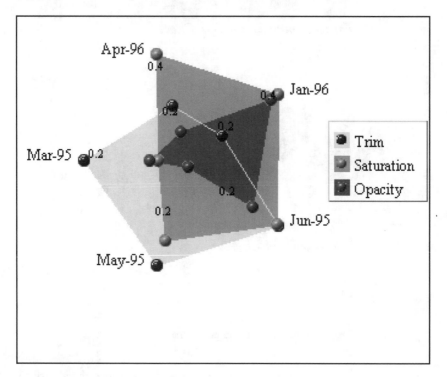

Summing Up

In this chapter we put on our psychic hats and tried to predict what some of the major trends will be for the future of data mining technology development. We summarized some of those trends that we feel are likely to be important in the coming years. We predict that navigation systems will become more commonplace, particularly in web-based settings. We described PerspectaView as one example of a tool developed for this purpose. In addition, inroads will be made in the area of text visualization. Methods for classifying large sets of documents according to their semantic content are being developed and these will be of great utility in future applications. One of the most important trends will be the development of comprehensive systems that support multiple types of analytical approaches and visualization paradigms. These full-scale systems will allow the analyst to call upon a host of techniques at various points in an analysis, all within a seamlessly

Figure 10.40 Sample DataVista grid visualization.

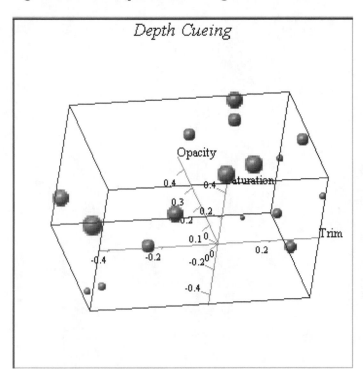

integrated analytical environment. Several systems are already being developed with this goal in mind, and we covered Pathfinder and GVA as examples. Aside from the development of these full-scale systems, an intermediate approach will be to overlay visualization capabilities onto existing data management systems. This will become popular in a variety of contexts, and we described the DataVista tool as a web-based example.

Section IV

CASE STUDIES

As you have learned from the first three sections of this book, the world of data mining can be quite complex. When you begin a data mining engagement you have to make a series of decisions concerning such issues as how to integrate data from separate sources, what types of model(s) to implement, what display paradigm(s) to use, and which tool(s) to choose for the application environment. No doubt some of these choices may be made before you begin. Nevertheless, the process of choosing options from the world of possible combinations may still require quite a bit of thought. For example, at last count there were more than 100 commercial data mining systems available on the market. These range from neural networks and decision trees to correlation matrices and visualization systems. You can get lost in this decision making process if you do not set limits for yourself. Remember that the tools you pick should reflect the type of approach and methodology that you have selected. Your knowledge of your own data and the analytical approach you want to take should drive the choice of what technology you use to help you reach those goals.

As we have illustrated, getting the data into shape at the beginning of the engagement can be the most demanding phase of the project. Once this is accomplished, you may find that you are not able to represent adequately all of the rules, situations, and circumstances that you have targeted for analysis. Once analysis begins, you have to be prepared for the direction of the investigation to change as contextual emphases shift. You should plan to have some false starts and factor them into the overall project schedule from the beginning. This whole process may be difficult initially. However, just as a doctor learns to make more accurate diagnoses as he or she sees more patients, you will become more adept at sizing up the analytical landscape of new applications as you gain experience with paradigms and data types.

The first experiences that you have with data mining can be exciting and overwhelming. You want to make a good impression, find all sorts of new and interesting patterns, and show the client that you know what you are doing. There is a tendency to over-commit and bite off more than you can chew. This usually happens when there is an overestimate of the amount and types of data that can effectively be handled in the application. Another pitfall is the temptation to explore all possible avenues of inquiry, including analytical approaches that are too ambitious for the scope of the effort. Until you actually sit down to address a particular data mining problem, you will not have an appreciation of the level of effort required to discover new patterns. For this reason, we think that you can learn a lot from reading this section in which we present case studies of real-world data mining efforts. Although each engagement was successful, the data mining practitioners had to deal with various and sundry logistical obstacles in order to achieve that success. Most of these logistical issues were not necessarily specific to the domain in which the application was developed, and so there are general-purpose lessons to be learned from each case. Taken together the case studies also serve another purpose of illustrating the breadth of the utility of the data mining approach. We hope that these examples will open up your mind to the ways in which data mining can be applied to your own environment, even if your specific application domain is not covered.

In this section we present descriptions of fielded data mining applications that are being used to solve real problems. In addition to these descriptions, we present background information describing the application area as well as a few war stories of issues faced during implementation. Where possible we have tried to describe the warts as well as the roses that are an inevitable part of every analytical effort. As you read each chapter in the section, bear in mind that in many cases we were not at liberty to provide all of the relevant details of results obtained from the analyses owing to the secure or proprietary nature of some of the information being presented. Many companies were hesitant to share their results (and their edge) with the competition. Remember, these companies have invested time and resources toward the discovery of these patterns, so they want to use them exclusively for as long as possible.

The case studies in this section are drawn from a variety of application areas including pharmaceutical research (Chapter 11), telecommunications (Chapter 12), banking (Chapter 13), retail sales and marketing (Chapter 14), stock market analysis (Chapter 15), and money laundering investigations (Chapter 16). In choosing these examples we have tried to represent a cross-section of the visualization paradigms that were covered in Section III (link analysis, landscapes, and quantitative approaches). Although we have concentrated on the use of visual data mining technologies, we tried to get a good representation from a variety of domains and tools. There are discussions ranging from very specialized engagements to more broad-level fielded applications. We hope that you enjoy reading about these applications and that these chapters give you some useful ideas that you can use in your own work.

MAPPING THE HUMAN GENOME

This chapter describes a very large commercial data mining project that has been undertaken to explore and analyze human gene sequences. As you know, the past decade has seen an explosion in genomic research that has led to the discovery of genetic causes for many diseases and disabilities. The limited progress made thus far is only the tip of the iceberg, and the drive to map the complete human genetic blueprint is thoroughly underway. The logic behind investigating the genetic causes of diseases is that once the molecular basis of diseases are known, precisely targeted medical interventions for diagnosis, prevention and treatment of the disease processes themselves can be developed. Lest you think that this area of work is an esoteric enterprise reserved for a few ivory tower scientists, be assured that genome mapping is big business. The medical implications of advances in this area are staggering. In addition to the hundreds of millions of research dollars spent each year funding basic research grants in this area, there are now billions of dollars spent by many commercial businesses working on these problems. Much of this work occurs in the context of the development of new pharmaceutical products that can be used to fight a host of diseases ranging from various cancers to degenerative disorders such as Alzheimer's Disease.

As you may already know, genes contain the DNA instructions used by the body to make proteins, which are the building blocks of life (see the sidebar entitled "What Is DNA?"). It is estimated that humans have around 100,000 genes, each one having DNA that encodes a unique protein specialized for a function or set of functions. Genes controlling production of hemoglobin, regulation of insulin, and susceptibility to Huntington's chorea are among those that have been isolated in recent years. Each gene is comprised of a series of building blocks called nucleotides. This seems simple enough in and of itself, but the real picture is very complicated. There are seemingly endless varieties of ways in which nucleotides can be ordered and sequenced to form distinct genes. Any one gene might be comprised of a sequence containing hundreds or thousands of individual nucleotides arranged in a particular order. Furthermore, the process of DNA sequencing used to extract genetic information from cells and tissues usually produces only fragments of genes. Using traditional methods, it has been difficult to tell where these fragment fit into the overall complete sequences from which they were drawn. Genetic scientists face the difficult task of trying to interpret these sequences and form hypotheses about which genes they might belong to and the disease processes that they may control.

What Is DNA?

Deoxyribonucleic acid, or DNA, forms the foundation for all living organisms. DNA contains the instructions that tell cells how to behave and is the primary mechanism that permits us to transfer our genes to our offspring. DNA sequences are all comprised of four basic building blocks called nucleotides. The four nucleotides are adenine (A), cytosine (C), guanine (G), and thymine (T). The nucleotides are always paired with one another via hydrogen bonds such that A is always paired with T, and C with G. When these nucleotides are combined, they form long sequences or chains that resemble a twisted ladder. Each "rung" of the ladder represents a bonded pair of nucleotides. A portion of a double-stranded DNA sequence might include a sequence such as A–T, C–G, T–A, G–C, A–T, G–C, A–T, C–G, and so forth. Additionally, there are regulatory proteins that bind to different parts of the DNA molecule to control how it is expressed (e.g., whether it becomes hemoglobin or controls the immune system). A complete twist in the sequence, called a gyre, occurs at every tenth step. These sequences can become quite long, such that if all of the DNA in a single cell were stretched out in a line, it would be almost a meter long.

DNA sequences form the foundation of our genetic codes and are critical for understanding how our genes behave. Unravelling these sequences has become a challenge since the 1950s when the structure of DNA was first understood. If we understand DNA sequences, theoretically we will be able to identify and predict faults, weaknesses, or other factors in our genes that can affect our lives. Getting a better grasp of DNA sequences could potentially lead to improved procedures to treat cancers, birth defects and other pathological processes. Data mining technologies are but one weapon in the arsenal used to understand these types of data, and the use of visualization is playing a crucial role in this activity.

The task of identifying good candidate gene sequences for further research and development is like finding a needle in a haystack. There can be hundreds of candidates for any given disease being studied. No drug company can pursue them all due to limitations in time and resources. Therefore, companies must decide which sequences are the most promising ones to pursue for further development. How do they determine which ones would make good therapeutic targets? Historically this has been a process based largely on trial and error. For every lead that eventually turns into a successful pharmaceutical intervention that is effective in clinical settings, there are dozens of others that do not produce the anticipated results. Chasing these red herrings is extremely costly and time consuming. This is a research area that is crying out for innovations that can help to make these analytical processes more efficient. This chapter provides an overview of a set of software applications that has been developed to address some of these problems.

The work that we describe has been undertaken by Incyte Pharmaceuticals, Inc. in cooperation with Silicon Graphics. Incyte is a publicly held company founded in 1991 and based in Palo Alto, California. The company has two wholly owned subsidiaries, Genome Systems, Inc., in St. Louis, Missouri and Synteni, in Fremont, California. Incyte is involved in high-throughput DNA sequencing and development of software and products to support the analysis of genetic information.

LifeSeq*: A Genetic Database

The first component of the application is a vast proprietary database that contains more than three million human gene sequence and expression records. The database is maintained in Oracle and Sybase and is accessed through a web interface. Clients buy a subscription to the database and receive monthly updates that include all of the new sequences identified since the last update. All of these sequences can be considered as candidate genes that might be important for future genome mapping. This information has been derived from DNA sequencing and bioanalysis of gene fragments extracted from cell and tissue samples. The tissue libraries from which these sequences were extracted contain many different types of tissues, including normal and diseased tissue. Where possible, various stages of disease development are also represented.

Organizing Knowledge in LifeSeq

The gene sequences that are stored in the LifeSeq database describe long streams of nucleotides. Interpreting these sequences can be a daunting task. What is needed is

---

*LifeSeq and LifeSeq 3D are registered trademarks and ZooSeq is a trademark of Incyte Pharmaceuticals, Inc. MineSet is a trademark of Silicon Graphic, Inc.

a methodology for finding a way of identifying sequences that might be particularly promising for certain problems. To help impose a conceptual structure on the massive amount of information contained in LifeSeq, the data have been coded and linked to several levels. Sequences can be grouped into many different categories. There is the level of the sequence or fragment itself. Above this level, sequences can be categorized according to the class of tissue from which they were derived. For example, sequences derived from a particular neurotransmitter can be linked to categories such as the protein function thought to be critical to the transmitter's action, the type of receptor that the transmitter acts upon and the type of nervous tissue from which it was originally isolated.

In addition to information about the sequences, there is information about the tissues from which the sequences were isolated. Tissue samples used for sequencing are characterized as fully as possible. For example, a prostate tumor sample from which DNA sequences are isolated might be given attributes such as human tissue, stage IV (late) cancer, originating in the center of the tumor, and so on. This information could be used to distinguish this sample from other prostate samples that might be drawn from tissue adjacent to the tumor, tissue from earlier stage tumors, or even tissue derived from animal models.

Using LifeSeq to Answer Research Questions

LifeSeq has been organized to permit comparisons of classes of sequence information within a hypothesis-testing mode. To take a straightforward example, a researcher could compare gene sequences isolated from diseased and nondiseased tissue from an organ such as the liver. The first step might be to identify which genes are turned on in the diseased tissue. You could set up a database query to return those sequences identified across the set of diseased liver tissue samples stored in LifeSeq. For each sequence identified, you might ask how many times the sequence was identified in the diseased samples, putting greater priority on those sequences identified most frequently. You could then do a comparison query to identify sequences from nondiseased samples in the same way. If there is a differential between the two tissue groups for any sequences, this might indicate that these sequences should be explored more fully. Sequences occurring more frequently in the diseased sample might reflect genetic factors in the disease process. On the other hand, sequences occurring more frequently in the nondiseased sample might indicate mechanisms that protect the body from the disease.

In a similar vein, you could do the same sorts of comparisons between human tissue samples and tissue obtained from animal models. To the degree that the sequences isolated from the two groups agree, this would tell you that the animal models are providing an accurate picture of the course of the disease in humans. This turns out to be an important question in the context of medical research because many animal models do not accurately mimic corresponding disease processes in humans.

Assessing Similarity among DNA Sequences

One of the most important types of information that is provided in LifeSeq is a measure of similarity among sequences that are derived from specified sources (organs, tumors, and so on). The power of this feature is best illustrated with an example. Suppose that you are interested in identifying gene sequences that tend to show up in cancerous prostate tumors but not in normal prostate tissue. First you can extract those sequences isolated from prostate tissue samples. Chances are that this extraction would produce a very large set of sequences that you would like to filter to include only those sequences that tend to be observed across a set of cancerous tissue samples. This can be done within LifeSeq using sequence comparison algorithms that identify sequences that are similar to one another. Calculations based on standard vector comparison methods are run across the sequences and the results are then determined using proprietary algorithms with pre-set thresholds. The resulting set of sequences is more likely to reflect gene activity in prostate cancer by virtue of the fact that they have been observed repeatedly across samples. You could then narrow this set further by excluding those sequences that matched sequences isolated from normal prostate tissue. If desired, you could further refine your results to include only sequences isolated from tumors as opposed to surrounding tissues, and so on.

Future Uses of the LifeSeq Database

LifeSeq includes a growing database application and related bioanalysis tools that are regularly updated and enhanced by Incyte. Although it has proved invaluable to the company and their clients in its current incarnation, additional features are being planned and implemented to extend the product's functionality into new areas of inquiry. A few of these are described next.

Identifying Co-Occurring Gene Sequences

As discussed earlier, much of the current usage of LifeSeq involves gene by gene (or sequence by sequence) comparisons. For example, the frequency of occurrence of a gene in a selected tissue subset might be compared to the frequency of that gene in a comparison tissue subset. Although this can be a powerful technique, it is somewhat limited because most diseases are not triggered by the activation of a single gene. Rather, many disease states are likely to be characterized in terms of combinations of genes all acting together to trigger pathological processes. For this reason, Incyte is currently exploring the application of association rule methods such as those described in Chapter 6 to identify those genes that are likely to co-occur in target samples. Analysis of the co-occurrence of gene sequences will facilitate the discovery of larger scale patterns that are likely to be more complex than those discovered with the gene by gene comparison approach.

Tying Genes to Disease Stages

Not only might more than one gene contribute to a disease process, different genes might become active at different stages of the disease. Complex diseases might be characterized by a series of steps whereby $gene_1$ is activated first, followed by $gene_2$ then $gene_3$ and so on until the activation of $gene_n$ at the end of the series. This fact has some important implications. The identification of one or two critical genes in the sequence may not provide sufficient information to allow the development of a treatment for the disease. Drugs designed on the basis of an incomplete specification of the genetic pathway might only partially address the molecular mechanisms contributing to the pathological state. On the other hand, if you know the full range of genetic activity across the sequence of steps, you can develop pharmaceutical interventions that target the different steps in the series separately. This approach should end up producing better results in the treatment of the disease. Incyte is currently developing association and path analysis methods that will facilitate identification of these ordered genetic factors.

Using LifeSeq to Predict Molecular Toxicology

Incyte is investigating ways in which to use the information within LifeSeq to aid in the drug design process. In particular they are interested in identifying potential physiological side effects that might be produced from new compounds. The fact of interest in this work is that some patients will experience certain side effects from test medications and others will not. Incyte is exploring ways of using LifeSeq during the early stages of the drug development cycle to discover attributes of molecular compounds that might be linked to toxicology well before testing with humans in clinical trials is initiated. These analyses would likely utilize information from LifeSeq as well as from ZooSeq which is another Incyte database containing data from common research animal models. This information could be used to predict toxicological profiles that might be used to redirect development of new compounds. In some cases, patient subgroups thought to be at risk could be warned of potential side effects. The characteristics used to identify these at-risk patients could be analyzed and used to guide the design of new drugs that would not produce toxic effects in these groups.

Identifying Candidates for Microarray Technology

Microarray technologies are being used to perform comparative expression analyses of thousands of genes simultaneously. To create its microarrays, Incyte attaches gene sequence clones onto glass chips. A test compound is then applied to the chip, and genes that are affected by the compound fluoresce, or light up on the chip. Thus, microarrays can be used to help researchers identify coded genes more quickly than would otherwise be possible. Specialized microarrays can be designed to detect genes of particular importance within an area of interest, for example for a particular disease. The trick is in deciding which sequences should be represented on the chip. Incyte scientists are currently analyzing the sequences contained in the LifeSeq database in order to choose those candidate sequences that are most likely to represent important indicator genes for certain applications. Once a chip has been assembled and tested, it can be used to define a proactive slice of data for an analysis. Incyte is working to create visualization tools such as the one described in the next section that can be used to analyze these data sets.

Incyte's LifeSeq 3D

Although the LifeSeq database is an invaluable research resource for Incyte and their clients, queries to the database often produce very large data sets that are difficult to analyze in text format. For this reason, Incyte was interested in using visualization to perform data mining analysis on large sets of DNA sequence information. Incyte wanted to develop an application that could be used by scientists to decide which gene sequences are interesting functionally (i.e., which sequences are tied to pharmacological target sites). LifeSeq 3D provides two visualizations that allow users to cluster and display information about genes according to protein function, tissue type, abundance of the gene as represented in LifeSeq, and the match between the gene sequence and "known" sequences already established in public domain genomic databases.

Incyte developed the LifeSeq 3D application using MineSet, a visualization tool developed by Silicon Graphics, Inc. (see Chapter 8 for an overview of MineSet's visualization capabilities). LifeSeq 3D has customized functions that let researchers explore LifeSeq and discover novel genes within the context of targeted protein functions and tissue types. MineSet is bundled with LifeSeq 3D and runs on SGI workstations. Two visualization schemes have been developed, and each is described next.

Protein Function Hierarchy

Incyte has developed a proprietary hierarchical organization that may be used to organize gene expression data according to the type of function that the protein defined by the gene performs. Protein function categories include hormones, cytokines, protease inhibitors, receptor types, and growth factors, to name a few. To get a feel for these protein functions, consider the case of protease inhibitors. Proteases are enzymes, which are proteins that break down other proteins in cells. Among other things, this mechanism is essential for the reproduction of viruses. Protease inhibitors are proteins that inhibit this breakdown process. As a result they are interesting pharmaceutical candidates for the treatment of viral diseases. In fact you may recall reading about the use of protease inhibitors in the treatment of AIDS.

The protein function hierarchy can be used to organize sets of gene sequences according to how often they have been expressed in various tissue types within LifeSeq. The visual display of this organization is presented in MineSet's Tree Visualizer in LifeSeq 3D. Each node in the tree hierarchy corresponds to a protein function category. These are displayed as horizontal bars within the MineSet display. Each of the horizontal node bars is broken up into sections of bar charts that represent tissue categories such as endocrine tissue, nervous tissue, and so on. The height of the bar charts conveys the relative gene abundance of the protein type for that tissue category.

The tissue distribution for extracellular messengers is shown in Figure 11.1. Extracellular messengers are proteins that chemically communicate information between cells through extracellular mechanisms. Examples of extracellular messengers include some neurotransmitters and hormones. Expression levels for all extracellular messengers by tissue type are shown in the foreground of Figure 11.1. In the background this overall picture is broken up into subcategories of extracellular messengers that are represented as separate nodes. In this case this second level of organization is shown for hormones. Looking at the tissue type information in the foreground, this figure shows that extracellular messengers are more commonly found in endocrine, hematopoietic/immune, and pancreatic tissues than in other tissue types. In the expansion of hormones shown in the background, we see that hormones are most often expressed in endocrine and pancreatic tissues. Using this visualization scheme, you can "fly" through the data, expanding categories as you go.

MultiGene Northern Visualization

This visualization method is an electronic version of a standard northern blot laboratory test that is commonly used to show expression of DNA sequences across

Figure 11.1 Landscape visualization display of the distribution of extracellular messenger proteins by tissue type in Life Tools 3D.

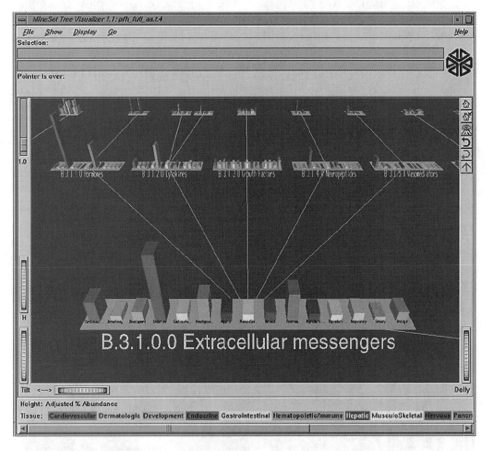

tissues. The standard lab test usually is conducted on only one gene at a time. This electronic version lets the user examine expression of multiple genes across many tissue types all in the same display. The MultiGene Northern Visualization uses MineSet's Scatter Visualizer to form a 3D plot of tissue locations for selected categories of expressed gene sequences. This visualization is particularly useful for displaying tissue distribution information about unknown genes. The three axes of the graph represent genes, tissue types, and specificity. Sequences (genes) are represented as colored cubes in the 3D space. This display supports drill-down for gene information. The user can click on any cube and display details contained in the database about the gene's identity, abundance, and tissue specificity.

Several filter and navigation functions are supported by this visualization application. Users can select from more than 100 categories of protein functions to choose information to be displayed. There are three tissue plots to choose from to display genes in terms of their tissue specificity. Additionally, four displays have been developed to show the expression level of a gene within a tissue or DNA library. LifeSeq 3D supports a variety of filter operations that can be used to focus the analysis in real time. Finally, LifeSeq 3D exploits much of the navigational functionality of MineSet, allowing users to zoom, pan, and rotate the 3D displays.

An example of a display produced in the MultiGene Northern Visualization is shown in Figure 11.2. This display shows a set of gene sequences associated with hormone protein functions and the locations of their expression in tissue libraries.

Figure 11.2 MultiGene Northern Visualization display showing tissue specificity of hormone genes in LifeSeq 3D.

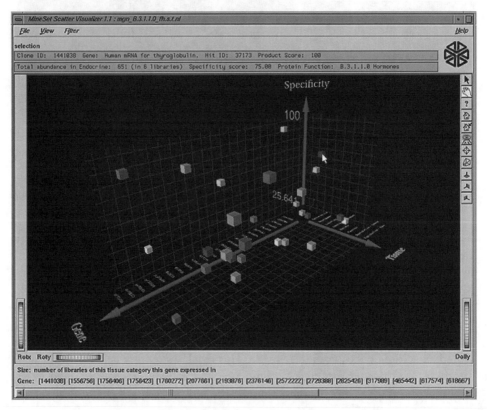

Any cube in the space is the intersection of the gene and the tissue type. The height along the other axis equates to the specificity of that gene's expression across the tissue libraries. The size of any cube reflects the number of DNA libraries in LifeSeq for that tissue type. If a cube is high (far from the bottom) on the specificity axis, that means that the gene tends to be expressed in only a small number of tissue libraries in LifeSeq. In other words, high specificity genes tend to show up in only a few places in the body. In this figure, the cursor is positioned over a gene that has been identified as a human thyroglobulin. The figure shows that this gene has a particular affinity for one type of tissue. The gene is highly specific for endocrine tissue, appearing in this category in 75 percent of its cases.

Researchers tend to use this display as a means of identifying outliers that have unusual expression profiles. You will notice that there are a lot of large cubes sitting along the bottom of the graph. These are general-purpose "housekeeping" genes that are very abundant and are found across many tissue libraries. These genes are not particularly promising as therapeutic targets because they do not discriminate among tissue types—that is, they show up everywhere. On the other hand, high specificity is a good trait with respect to the goal of identifying genes that may be good therapeutic targets. If a company is trying to develop a treatment for liver cancer, for example, they need to find a gene that is expressed in cancerous liver cells and no others if at all possible. There may be relatively few of these interesting genes as compared to the overall population, but that does not diminish their importance. This is a good example of the use of visual data mining technology to discover outliers, or exceptions, that are interesting by virtue of the fact that they do not necessarily behave like the rest of the entities in a group. As discussed many times in the first two sections of the book, this is precisely the sort of result that might be missed using traditional statistical analysis techniques.

Using LifeSeq 3D for Quality Control

As already mentioned, Incyte offers LifeSeq and LifeSeq 3D as commercial products to their clients, most of which are pharmaceutical companies. These companies report that they have used LifeSeq 3D to good effect in their own internal research activities and that the product has been instrumental in the discovery of new targets. Clients are reluctant to discuss these discoveries, however, because the pharmaceutical industry is a highly competitive one where corporate secrets are tightly held. Although these discoveries are not discussed publicly, we can write about the ways in which the LifeSeq 3D visualization application has been used internally by Incyte to help update and maintain the LifeSeq database. Next we describe two quality assurance analyses (a form of data-disambiguation) that Incyte uses to examine their own sequence and tissue data. (Note that these are internal research projects and not capabilities that ship with the LifeSeq 3D system.)

Quality Control of Gene Sequences Derived from LifeSeq Tissue Libraries

Incyte has successfully used LifeSeq 3D to analyze the quality of the DNA sequences in LifeSeq that were extracted from known tissue samples (libraries). As shown in Figure 11.3, Incyte used the MultiGene Northern Visualization to create a 3D graph plotting the gene sequences, the libraries, and the known/unknown status of the sequences on three axes. This visualization allowed them to see that there were many cases in which unknown sequences had been isolated from known tissue libraries. This finding indicated that those libraries should be resampled so that unknown sequences might be moved into known categories within the database.

Figure 11.3 LifeSeq 3D graph showing known and unknown gene sequences in LifeSeq libraries.

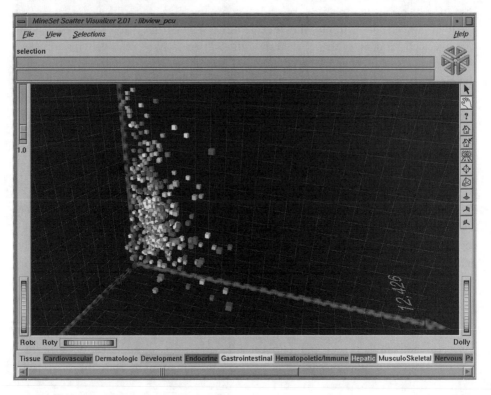

This plot allowed Incyte to identify potentially weak areas within the database that might otherwise have gone undetected.

Quality Control of Tissue Samples

Incyte maintains libraries of diseased and nondiseased tissue for any disease type represented in LifeSeq. As it happens, the tissue labeled as normal by visual microscopic inspection might not turn out to be so normal after all. The sequences derived from that tissue might more closely resemble those derived from pathological samples. Incyte has been able to identify these anomalous results using their 3D visualization application in which the specificity of genes derived from normal tissue can be shown to have higher specificity for diseased tissue.

No one would argue with the utility of the visualization methods in helping to keep the tissue libraries properly categorized. However, this example is even more exciting when you consider the larger ramifications. What has happened in these improper classifications is that DNA sequencing has been used to classify tissue properly as pathological under circumstances in which visual inspection has failed. That is, the sequencing methods can be used to detect disease before the disease reaches the stage of being detectable by visual methods. Pursuit of these findings within certain disease domains might lead to the development of tests that could be used to diagnose diseases earlier in their course than was previously possible.

Summing Up

In this chapter we have described a special-purpose data mining application developed for mining the human genome. We described a multilayered set of analytical products developed by Incyte Pharmaceuticals, Inc. The first is a very large database containing information about DNA sequences and their expression in tissue libraries maintained by Incyte. This database, called LifeSeq, is a commercial product used mainly by pharmaceutical companies. The primary use of the database is to identify genes that are specific to diseases of interest so that drugs can be targeted to those molecular functions. In addition to the LifeSeq database, we described the LifeSeq 3D data mining and visualization product that has been developed within MineSet to analyze the data contained in LifeSeq. This tool has been used to identify candidate genes associated with diseases and to assure quality control of sequencing and tissue library data.

TELECOMMUNICATION SERVICES   12

This chapter introduces a system that was developed to support an international telecommunications company (telecom) involved in the operation of low cost long distance services. With deregulation well underway within the telecom industry throughout Europe and many parts of the world, more and more companies are seeking to compete with the traditional network operators for a share of the sizeable and expanding market in international voice, fax, image, and data traffic. As a result, lower costs and more value-added services can be provided to the subscribers of telecommunication services than was previously offered by the large monopolies that once carried the day.

The demand for more progressive communications has exploded over the past several years due to the introduction of pagers, faxes, cellular phones, portable digital assistants (PDAs), voicemail, e-mail and personal computers. Therefore, in an increasingly competitive business environment, companies are now seeking new ways in which to improve the quality of service they can deliver to their customers. The telecom industry is no longer just focused on providing the best long distance calling rates, but they are aggressively marketing new and different types of advanced calling features and personalized services. Thus, managing telephone calls more effectively and efficiently has become an extremely competitive and lucrative business.

Many of our daily interactions, whether for business or private purposes, are conducted largely through a phone network. Most of us have ordered merchandise by mail, performed banking activities, bought and sold stocks, activated credit cards, and booked travel-related events all by using the phone. Therefore, when a customer's experience with dealing with an organization is based solely on phone use, the level of satisfaction received during a telephone session goes a long way toward shaping the image of the company, and could be a deciding factor in maintaining customer loyalty. The organization not only wants to enhance its image and provide better service but also to lower costs and operate with more efficient procedures in dealing with the results of the call.

Macfarlane TeleSystems (MTS) is a U.K.-based supplier of innovative switching platforms for the telecom industry. MTS has expanded its business base by making inroads into a variety of different countries by offering a comprehensive suite of telecom capabilities and products. They currently have platform customers in 12 countries and are expecting to expand to over 40 by the year 2000. A large portion of the company's installed platforms are based in the United Kingdom, which is a major telecommunications crossroads, with the actual operators located at remote sites. For instance, MTS deals with one company that has subsidiaries in several countries (both the European union and former Soviet bloc), all of which access a series of platforms located in London. This U.K.-based arrangement is important to the MTS client base because it gives them a secure location, linked to a stable currency, with reasonable telecom industry laws and competitive wholesale call rates. In this chapter we begin by describing some of the services offered by MTS as well as some of the types of problems encountered by telecom companies. We then describe ways in which data mining technologies have been applied to the solution of some of these problems.

Two systems comprise the majority of services offered by MTS. The first is CallPlus, an integrated call center used to help manage the overall telecom operations associated with a business. CallPlus offers support for everything from voice-mail to automatic call distribution. CallPlus can be used by either small or large businesses to manage their telephone interface with their customers. The second system, NetPlus, is focused on providing more competitive and cost-effective long-distance services. NetPlus determines the least-cost route of any call depending on the time of day, day of the week, and destination number. Both MTS systems are based on similar telephonic switching technologies and they can be set up and maintained virtually anywhere in the world.

The CallPlus Calling System

The MTS CallPlus CallCentre System has been designed to provide organizations with the benefits of improved call handling and management facilities. CallPlus represents a new direction in the development of CallCentre Systems, providing a complete set of Automatic Call Distribution (ACD), Voice Processing, Call Switching, and CTI (screen popping) facilities from a single standalone unit. CallPlus allows a much wider range of services to be provided from the same equipment, thereby offering significant cost savings and increased value compared to traditional systems. CallPlus is particularly suitable for small to medium installations, either as a front end or departmental level system, and does not require the upgrade or replacement of an existing office switch. CallPlus delivers a comprehensive set of features and benefits with full integration of all facilities at both an operational and management level.

Call Distribution and Queuing

The CallPlus system has a wide range of functions that can be applied by a company when dealing with the configuration of its telephone system. For instance, you can define how the calls will get distributed when they come into the main switchboard. Calls may be distributed to agents in groups according to user-defined parameters such as DDI (Direct Dialed Inwards telephone number), CLI (Calling Line Identification), or other information supplied by the caller through a front-end interactive session. Users can set up a menu of choices that direct the incoming calls to their appropriate locations or departments (e.g., press 1 for accounting, 2 for finance, 3 for support, and so forth). Many businesses now use this type of function. For example, the airline industry uses this type of automation quite extensively to allow you to check flight times, frequent flyer mileage, or travel fares.

CallPlus can also be used to implement an intelligent queuing technique. Calls can be queued with the option of playing the caller's position in the queue or an average waiting time. This helps your customer gauge how long they will have to wait in order to obtain a desired service from your company. The use of intelligent queuing is much more acceptable and appreciated than the traditional "Please hold. Your call is important to us. You will get the next available operator," which is annoying when played over and over again. CallPlus may also play other messages during the wait and the caller is always offered the option to leave to queue at any time and leave a voice message.

Voice Processing

The CallPlus system supports voice processing (e.g., audiotext). This facility allows you to create your own voice services designed to operate within the CallCentre environment. Services include audio menus and information messages, recording caller details, and screening callers. You can also obtain additional information (e.g. account numbers) before referring calls to agents—a feature used extensively in the mail-order and financial communities.

Network Processing

CallPlus has facilities to integrate the CallCentre telephone functions with the agent's data processing system using LAN-based standard protocols. Users can coordinate the progress of a call automatically with the requirements of the agent to view and update relevant information relating to that call. For example, where different telephone numbers have been assigned for calls relating to the ordering of different products, CallPlus is capable of triggering the display of the correct product information on the agent screen as the call is transferred. Similarly, using the CLI (Calling Line Identification), CallPlus can automatically cause the relevant customer account details to appear.

CallPlus switches calls between the public networks and agents, and optionally can transfer and receive calls to and from other staff via an existing office PABX (e.g., their existing phone switch). All CallCentre switching is performed within the CallPlus system and no external switch is required. This type of system can generate a large quantity of data that can be used to review the operations, throughput, and overall performance of the CallPlus network. This kind of analysis lets you find bottlenecks, inaccessible paths, system faults, and several other critical conditions that may affect your business.

The NetPlus Calling System

One of the other products offered by MTS is called NetPlus, an added-value network services system that piggy-backs on top of existing telecommunication infrastructures to provide a variety of extended calling features. NetPlus, like CallPlus, is a PC-based system, which means that it is compatible with all major telecommunications standards. A NetPlus system is essentially an industrial-grade computer with some special hardware extensions and very comprehensive software that is usually placed in a large international telecommunications exchange. This enables it to have access to the large number of dedicated lines it needs.

The basic premise for offering these types of services is roughly the same. The larger telecom companies are required by law to lease out a certain percentage of their lines at competitive rates. The more lines you purchase the better the rate you can negotiate. Once you have procured the lines, they are yours to use as you wish. Most likely, you will sell time to various target customer-market segments at very attractive rates, which is what NetPlus does. This creates an unusual situation because the main carriers become your business partners, but at the same time they are also your biggest competitors. On the one hand they will give you lower rates and on the other they are competing for the same client base. (Note that is one reason why MTS can either automatically route calls on a least cost basis or manually route them through a preferred carrier.)

Used extensively in the United Kingdom and throughout continental Europe since late 1993, NetPlus offers two primary types of calling options, CallBack and

CallThrough. CallBack exploits the telecommunications rate differentials between countries to offer lower-cost international and national calls, and CallThrough typically is used in conjunction with international freephone or local call access to route calls. NetPlus can also be used to provide full prepaid telecommunications card services.

CallBack

Finding the best rate to charge for international calls has become big business in our emerging global economy. The services provided by NetPlus allow users to benefit from the differences in call costs among various countries and the opportunities from deregulated countries for service operators to buy wholesale and sell to end users at rates significantly lower than the national operator. CallBack is thus designed to exploit the rate differentials between countries in order to offer lower cost international calls. NetPlus provides fast, reliable and easy-to-use callback services using a range of manual and autodialer protocols to control set-up and clear-down procedures. Any change to a carrier's rate table becomes effective immediately.

CallThrough

CallThrough typically is used in conjunction with international freephone or local call access, and provides an immediate and direct connection with NetPlus for the purpose of making international telephone calls. With CallThrough, users dial in to the platform and then dial on to the destination number, saving significantly on call costs. Other added value services are also provided. The most widely available form of this service is offered on a prepaid basis by means of phone cards. Increasingly these services are being introduced into tightly targeted market segments. Ancillary applications such as personal numbering, where end users are contacted automatically on alternate numbers, are also growing rapidly.

Major companies, especially those targeting consumers for promotional purposes, are also using CallThrough. Cards are given away with the product and after being registered, they can be used to make a few minutes of calls. This is expected to be a popular marketing technique in the future as it is an easy way of obtaining information about people who buy, like, or use your product.

Working within the Telecommunications Community

All operators of the NetPlus system have a common goal, which is to grow their business base continually. The way to succeed at this in the telecom industry is to improve the ratio of profits to turnover. Profits are increased with good system reliability, effective billing practices, and well-targeted marketing efforts. Profits are decreased with operator irregularities, hardware failures, and fraud. In this competitive environment, you can imagine that the introduction of services such as NetPlus elicits reactions from established players. Major European telecom operators do not like the added competition. Now that the EC and other establishments have largely deregulated the telecom industry, these operators are under severe pressure to maintain their traditional profit margins. Unfortunately, some do not always use legal means of fighting their competition.

Telecom operators can act as both the starting and delivery points of a call. This is true for both fixed (e.g., land-lines) operators such as British Telecom (BT) in the United Kingdom, Deutsche Telecom in Germany, or Telefonica in Spain, as well as mobile operators such as Cellnet in the United Kingdom. These carriers collect revenue for the carriage of calls, but they collect more if a secondary carrier such as MTS does not handle the calls. Most major carriers deal with these losses in stride and consistently fulfill their obligations to provide support services to MTS calls. However, some companies resort to less-than-legitimate tactics intended to disrupt services and gain unfair competitive advantage. For instance, just prior to its partial privatization, one major operator maliciously disrupted known CallBack operations and was dropping out (e.g., canceling) lines to the freephone numbers used to start a CallBack. This was done in spite of the fact that the practice is illegal under various international treaties.

Monitoring Operational Problems

When not combating unprincipled carriers to ensure their line leases are properly maintained, small carriers must deal with other problems created by their user community. These problems usually result from inappropriate use of the hardware platform and various patterns of fraud. Using CallBack and CallThrough systems is not as simple as using a standard telephone due to the extra dialing requirements. Inevitably, this leads to wrong numbers, usage complaints, and incorrect charging, mainly because of poor training. Often, these operational problems are specific to a particular company or even to one particular agent of that company, so it is important that faults are monitored at a user and/or company level.

CallBack and CallThrough operations are also a major target of fraudulent activities. To give an example, it is not very likely that you will be caught if you have an operation in Moldova to defraud an operator based in Germany who uses a platform in the United Kingdom. The different types of fraud that can be perpetrated within the telecom industry are commercial and technical. The following examples represent a sample of some frauds that have actually been discovered.

- A CallBack operator might sign up to route business from a former Soviet Republic providence to the rest of Europe. All goes well for a few months while the operator establishes a decent credit rating. Then the business exhibits a tremendous level of usage and the company vanishes taking with them the last month's payment, leaving the primary carrier stuck with the remainder of the bill. (This pattern is also similar to several forms of fraud exhibited by merchants within the credit card industry.)

- Some years ago, a classic fraud occurred in the United Kingdom with a premium rate number. Premium numbers are used to access information and entertainment services (e.g., 900 numbers in the United States, or 0898 or 0891 numbers in the United Kingdom). A new service established a number that offered an innovative form of "fortune-telling." The services are typical in this type of industry and this particular number gave a repeating message that owed a lot to the worst of Hollywood B films. Then one Friday night, the operator of the service allegedly broke into a vast number of business premises, dialed the number, and left the phones off the hook for the entire weekend. In this type of situation, callers are billed at premium rates and companies like MTS pay the service providers for each call. Since the breaking-and-entering activities were undetected/unprovable, the premium rate company had no choice but to pay their percentage of the fees charged for these services.

- When CallThrough is used for promotional purposes, there is always the chance that the cards will not be delivered free to the customer, but will be diverted and used for other purposes. Also, when an operator has failed to generate sufficiently random card account numbers, fraud attempts are made using PC-based power dialing to make many successive attempts to identify other valid numbers within an apparent range.

System Throughput

Each NetPlus platform system has a starting capacity of 30 line bearers, which can be increased in units of 30, which is economically viable based upon the anticipated call volume to connect. In an ideal world, these would be fully loaded with calls for 24 hours a day. As would be expected, the customer-base will only use these lines according to their personal styles and particular requirements. Obviously, there are going to be underutilized time periods as well as peak times known as the "busy hour(s)." So the actual capacity of a system is effectively capped during these busy hours when there may be few or no spare lines available for callers to connect to and make their calls. Part of what MTS customers have to manage is the utilization and throughput of these bearers.

The number of bearers utilized depends on the observed and desired Grade Of Service (GOS) ratio of success to failure to obtain a connection for the service being supplied. Too few bearers will result in a high degree of frustration for customers unable to gain access to the system. Too many bearers may produce an excellent GOS but very poor profit margins. Thus, it becomes important to know the use-behaviors associated with such a system and balance your resources accordingly.

Another main goal is to manage the calls that are placed into each system effectively. For each call, a substantial amount of detail is generated (e.g., times, dates, lines, etc.). In a typical system, there are several components, all of which must be monitored. The platform itself is often still an MTS responsibility and is managed with its own software. However, the lines and the bearers connecting the platform to the worldwide telephone network are a major cause for concern. The only indication that an incoming line is faulty is that it doesn't receive any calls. This may only happen for a few minutes at a time and so it can be difficult to spot. As you can imagine, this can affect your GOS, especially if it happens during the busy hours. Needless to say, these types of situations need to be identified and dealt with quickly before sevices are significantly degraded.

Telecom Information Management

Larger NetPlus and CallPlus users have to manage many diverse aspects of their MTS platform–based business. These include system/bearer capacity and profitable loading, service quality and call completion, routing, pricing, and management of marketing and distribution channels or re-sellers. Thus, it becomes important to understand the operations and throughput of your system through the use of traffic profiling, which is the categorization and analysis of the traffic on and between telecommunication platforms, systems, networks, and individual lines.

Each NetPlus system produces comprehensive Call Detail Records (CDRs) and associated files. In a typical day a platform may well receive and make in excess of 50,000 calls. This presents a significant amount of data that the service operator needs to be able to turn rapidly into information. Typically, an ordinary management information system might provide such things as the total number and value of calls, key routes, top spending accounts, and in some cases information on bearer failures. These traditional approaches for reporting are not enough to provide real management support. The interaction between the user and the platform together with the carrier service bearers is not captured by these measures.

As we mentioned earlier, the platforms have extensive test and monitoring programs. These are very comprehensive and check for most possible faults that can occur. The trouble is that they only check the platform and do not take into account the wider picture (e.g., calling patterns, usage, etc.). This cannot be done directly on the platform itself, due to its processing limitations. As part of setting up a system, the usage logs can be rolled up, captured, and e-mailed to an MTS data center for subsequent analysis. These data packages can be generated according to the needs of the particular platform. Thus, you could have packages being generated every hour, half-day, day, week, or month. Due to the large amount of data produced from these telephone switching systems, it takes more than just a simple print-out to get an understanding of the utilization, throughput, and potential faults occurring at the switch. Thus, MTS decided it needed a better and more reliable method of understanding their data. They needed a data mining–based approach, where the data could be processed and analyzed quickly for problems.

The Need for Data Mining

Remember that we are discussing a system that runs 24 hours, every day of the year, generating ever-changing data accordingly. The platform is also managed by non-programming staff who have a sound knowledge of the telecommunication business, but are not data mining experts. MTS therefore decided to adopt an outside approach, choosing the Daisy visual data mining system (refer to Chapter 7 for a more detailed description of Daisy). Daisy was configured to read the CDR files e-mailed to the data center and to generate a selection of charts and reports each day for review by the data management staff. These diagrams could then be compared with previous days, weeks, and months, and if there were any problems, the data associated with the chart could be retrieved and mined to better understand the cause of the problem.

A major disadvantage of the traditional management information system is that it generally is programmed to take into account known problems, strengths, and weaknesses. As you may recall from Chapter 3, this represents a typical YKYK data analysis scenario. As the business changes, the information provided is reporting on historic issues that, in all probability, have been resolved. A data mining–based approach overcomes this problem. New issues can be identified quickly (via DKYK and DKDK models) and the service adjusted to optimize quality. Equally, any potential problem that is emerging (including potentially fraudulent activity) can be investigated and dealt with before much damage has occurred. Remember that small amounts of fraud perpetrated within these types of systems can cost the operators a significant amount of their profits. Although MTS initially did not believe that fraud and failures were a particular problem, they did recognize that they could possibly exist. The following represent a set of representative patterns that were investigated during this data mining engagement within the MTS systems:

- Identification of carrier outages not otherwise identified.

- Carriers deliberately blocking CallBack and CallThrough—not all governments have strong telecommunication regulations like in the United Kingdom or the United States.

- Connecting to end users but then failing to complete destination calls due to switch or route congestion.

- Crossed lines in distant administrations.

- "Thin" routes where cheaper lower tier carriers fail to give adequate signaling response from the distant end.

- Users setting up incorrect CallBack numbers.

- Delays occurring in mobile networks in progressing a call to the handset when the network has already given a call connection signal (e.g., completing the call).

- Potentially fraudulent users with atypical usage patterns.

- Callers attempting to gain fraudulent entry to customer accounts.

- Blocking by distant operators.

- Nonoptimum set-up of inbound and outbound bearers.

- Busy hour frustrated call attempt patterns.

- "Ghost" calls from errant automatic dial-out equipment that has been improperly programmed.

- Call failure by inadequately informed end users being traced to operator-specific re-sellers.

- Destination, volume, and time of day usage patterns.

Daisy Data Mining

MTS has created a subsystem called MTS-MIS that can be used to interpret the relative performance and operation of a NetPlus system. A simple front-end has been written (in Visual Basic) that takes all of the Call Detail Records (CDRs) from a remote host platform and produces a series of charts and reports based on input defined by the user. These are then used to check the data for possible problems, strengths, and weaknesses, and then reviewed for the underlying causes. Daisy has been used as the core technology for performing these data mining activities.

MTS-MIS was written to meet several objectives:

- MTS-MIS must be simple to use, especially by inexperienced operators, and must show various anomalies within the data set.

- Due to the complexity of the total system and the number of telecom operators that might be involved in MTS calls, MTS-MIS must perform checks on all NetPlus data.

- MTS-MIS must automatically produce a comprehensive set of reports and charts as each daily CDR is received. One of the aims was to have a series of charts that could easily be compared, so that any changes could easily be determined.

- MTS-MIS must be able to produce charts and reports that track calls by individual record in the CDR, by user session, user account, and finally by such variables as individual line and time period.

- MTS-MIS reports must be capable of spotting problems, strengths, and weaknesses in hardware, network, carrier and customer performance, fraud, profitability, customer churn, and other factors contributing to the success of the system.

- MTS-MIS must be able to return to any chart or report, so that after an initial visual check by the operator and immediate management, results can then be mined in further analysis. Daisy allows further charts and reports to be made.

The technique developed for MTS-MIS is very powerful in that it takes a data file from a standard piece of hardware, creates a series of working files, extends them with extra information (e.g., metadata), and then draws a series of standard reports and charts for analysis. Using Daisy for generating this form of presentation enables exceptions or discrepancies to be identified rapidly. Any anomalies can then be reviewed in more detail.

System Faults and Capacity

To platform operators such as MTS, two of the most important operational measures are the overall fault-level of the total system and how much of the capacity is being used. Keep in mind that subscribers are responsible for managing the lines they lease from the larger carriers. You pay for the lines whether or not they are used. Therefore, you want to maximize the usage and throughput of the lines you have leased. So whether there is a fault in the system (e.g., there are down lines), hardware problems, or some other type of concern, you first need to know that it exists before you can fix it.

Figure 12.1 presents a typical Daisy circular histogram used to visualize the performance of a platform during a 24 hour period. If you recall from Chapter 7, the types of visualizations produced by Daisy are represented as a series of circular arcs, with links between them. Each arc or group of nodes is mapped to a particular field in the database and each node is linked to common values that can be aggregated and summarized. The histograms on each node are optional and can be used to show the relative values of the aggregations.

Within this diagram, there are many display dimensions being presented. Each node represents a ten minute increment throughout the day, with 144 nodes presented. The red (outer) histogram shows the maximum number of lines used in the period and the blue (inner) shows the minimum. The green line across the histograms shows the total usage in seconds for each period. The formats used in this type of chart can help to decide when to upgrade the platform. It is also a powerful check on whether any bearers or parts of the system failed. (We suggest that you consult the CD-ROM to see color versions of each of the figures presented in this chapter.)

Figure 12.1 A Daisy chart showing the load on a single platform during a 24-hour period.

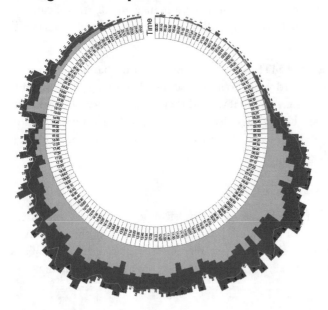

In the chart the line shows the total number of connect seconds in each time period, whereas the outer and inner histograms show the maximum and minimum number of lines used in the period. The chart offers several advantages over the standard linear presentation. It provides more detail than can be put on to a single sheet of paper, and by viewing the data in small increments (e.g., 10-minute segments), system "hiccups" or downtime can be detected. Figure 12.2 shows another example of this type of chart for a different platform. As you can see there are vast differences among the operations associated with different platforms.

These simple charts have proved invaluable in two areas; identifying faults and outages and checking capacity. The modern telephone system is usually very reliable, although it does occasionally fail. The charts shown are used to indicate gaps in the service caused by failure in equipment, carriers, or operation. It has to be mentioned that customers often do not notice small outages, as they just assume that they couldn't get through (e.g., a fast-bust signal) and will try the call later.

A quick visual check between two suitable time periods often permits detection of all relevant faults within a system. Because MTS can present these findings to the primary carriers, they have found this analysis to be invaluable when negotiating new contracts for lines and call-delivery (which can result in tangible cost savings). In each of the preceding figures, the capacity check for a system is just a simple visual examination. It is a matter for management to decide when the capacity of

Figure 12.2 A Daisy chart depicting a different platform load.

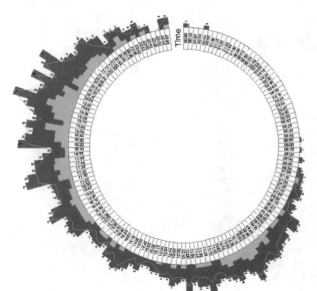

the switch should be increased. A prudent operator would increase the number of lines so that the maximum is never in use. Under normal operating conditions this would mean that there would never be a wait for an available line. Needless to say, this goes a long way towards maintaining a reliable GOS. On the other hand, operators who are more concerned with throughput and maximizing their resources might allow certain amounts of overloading at busy times. In this example, the maximum in any time period is shown as 80, well below the number of lines, which in this case is 96.

These charts do not show any specific failures, but MTS has found numerous faults not reported either by the customers or the carriers. Figure 12.3 shows a slightly different perspective on the same type of data except the values have been further accumulated. This chart shows the usage for each line on a 60-line platform. The blue histogram (the left-hand value) shows the number of calls and the green (right-hand value) shows the number of seconds connected. (Note that this type of layout was first produced and used by Florence Nightingale to highlight the problems of casualties in the Crimean War.)

MTS runs this capacity check on all of their platforms, whether owned or managed for others. By comparing a series of charts for the same platform, it is possible for managers to plan for changes in capacity. Thus, your level of activation can be adjusted to reflect the usage of your network.

Figure 12.3 A different view on platform performance.

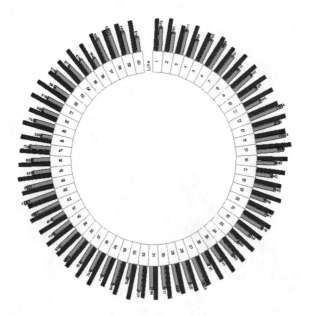

Customer Profiles

Customers in the telecom industry are often not well versed in the use of their systems (e.g., knowing all of the configuration options, features, and functions). They just want to install the system, turn it on, and have it operate with a minimal amount of intervention. However, these systems are intricate and just like any other complex system, they do require some attention from time to time.

To help address some of their customer concerns, MTS has incorporated extensive error checking on its platforms, which return the outcome of each call made within their systems. Account numbers and sessions are all tied to the information sent by the platform, so that the analysis on a customer can be very detailed. MTS-MIS can take a CDR file and calculate the number of calls, the time connected, and the status for each CallBack or CallThrough session on a NetPlus system. The resulting file can then be analyzed to discover the pattern of usage for sessions. The chart presented in Figure 12.4 is a summary of all CallBack sessions on a particular day for one of MTS' customers, who sells services to German mobile phone users.

The chart is used to analyze six fields, each of which is drawn as an arc (e.g., group). The two histograms show the number of calls (left-hand histogram) and the number of chargeable seconds (right-hand histogram). The data are derived

Figure 12.4 A summary of CallBack sessions for a selected day.

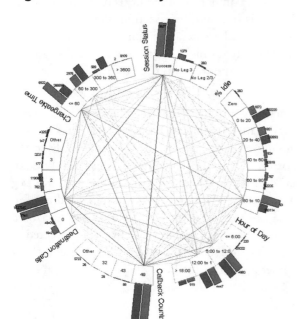

directly from the CDR maintained by the MTS platform. Each of the fields can be described as follows.

Session Status. This defines whether the user made a successful call and whether they were unable to make a full connection (No Leg 3) or whether they did not even get a successful CallBack (No Leg 2/3).

% Idle. This is a measure of how long the user was connected unproductively to the platform, without a call connected to a destination number. Note that there are a large number of sessions with a % Idle value over 80 percent and that some of these were deemed successful. This raises several questions as to whether the callers are adept at using the system and why they take so long to get connected. It may also indicate that the training offered with the system should be improved.

Hour of Day. This variable is split into four sections that cover six-hour increments (e.g., 0–6:00, 6:00–12:00, 12:00–18:00, and 18:00–24:00) This can be easily changed to accommodate different types of analyses.

CallBack Country. This is used to identify calls by code (Germany is 49).

Destination Calls. This is the number of calls made in each session. Most people appear to make only a single call.

Chargeable Time. This represents the amount of time in seconds that can be charged to an account. This arc is split into four sections that represent 0–60, 60–300, 300–3600, and 3600 and greater. The binning of this value is solely for analysis purposes. The actual time associated with a call (e.g., 15 seconds, 108 seconds, 420 seconds, and so forth) is used to assign it into its respective bin.

This type of chart is drawn each day and by comparing charts from previous days and weeks, the gradual changes that occur can be identified, tracked, and monitored. Daisy gives you the ability to mine any of these charts directly so the details can be exposed quickly. For example, suppose you are concerned about an increasing number of sessions that do not result in a full connection (e.g., No Leg 3). To get a complete description of the underlying records, all you would need to do is to select the node and those sessions are displayed as a simple grid or a Microsoft Excel worksheet. Figure 12.5 shows a sample of CDR data presented in a tabular format. Further analyses can then be performed, either by reinvoking Daisy on the data or by using another analytical method.

Figure 12.5 A tabular view of the MTS-MIS CDR format.

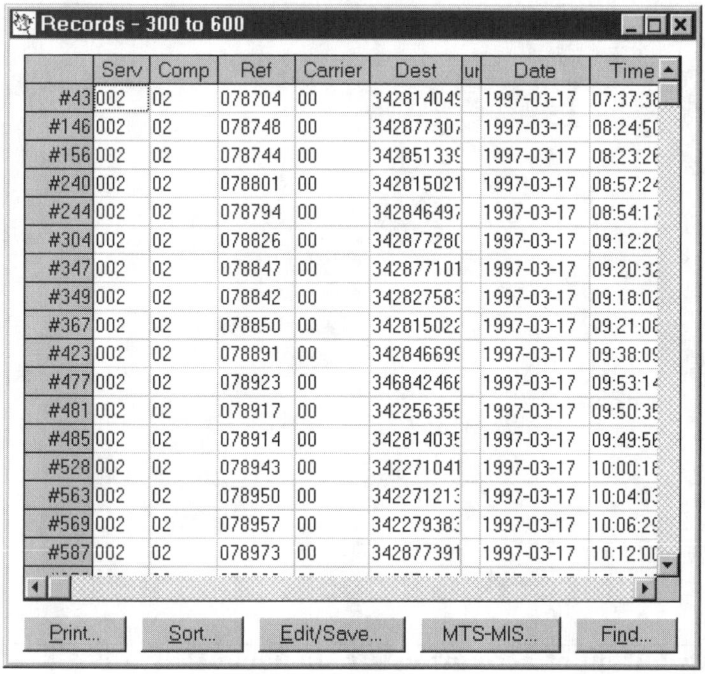

	Serv	Comp	Ref	Carrier	Dest	ur	Date	Time
#43	002	02	078704	00	342814049		1997-03-17	07:37:38
#146	002	02	078748	00	342877307		1997-03-17	08:24:50
#156	002	02	078744	00	342851339		1997-03-17	08:23:26
#240	002	02	078801	00	342815021		1997-03-17	08:57:24
#244	002	02	078794	00	342846497		1997-03-17	08:54:17
#304	002	02	078826	00	342877280		1997-03-17	09:12:20
#347	002	02	078847	00	342877101		1997-03-17	09:20:32
#349	002	02	078842	00	342827583		1997-03-17	09:18:02
#367	002	02	078850	00	342815022		1997-03-17	09:21:08
#423	002	02	078891	00	342846699		1997-03-17	09:38:09
#477	002	02	078923	00	346842466		1997-03-17	09:53:14
#481	002	02	078917	00	342256355		1997-03-17	09:50:35
#485	002	02	078914	00	342814035		1997-03-17	09:49:58
#528	002	02	078943	00	342271041		1997-03-17	10:00:18
#563	002	02	078950	00	342271213		1997-03-17	10:04:03
#569	002	02	078957	00	342279383		1997-03-17	10:06:29
#587	002	02	078973	00	342877391		1997-03-17	10:12:00

Print...   Sort...   Edit/Save...   MTS-MIS...   Find...

Another beneficial feature used on the MTS-MIS configuration is to look for common traits among the different nodes to expose similar data. Using Daisy in this configuration, you can easily see those successful calls with a large idle time that have been made after 18:00. Just click on the three nodes and the common sessions are displayed. This simple but extremely powerful selection function is invaluable in all Daisy analyses of databases. Figure 12.6 shows yet one more example of this type of diagram.

One final way to look at customer profiles is by showing all of the active accounts and their relative usage. Figure 12.7 shows an example of this type of diagram. The violet histogram placed on the outside of the nodes shows the amount of chargeable type, whereas the red line shows the percentage of calls that were successful. Note how the first 10 or so users of this platform are responsible for a large proportion of its income. However, if there was one account that had a significantly high usage rating, there would be concern about whether the operations were legitimate. Through drill-down functions, this could quickly be determined within Daisy.

Figure 12.6 Another view of callback sessions within Daisy.

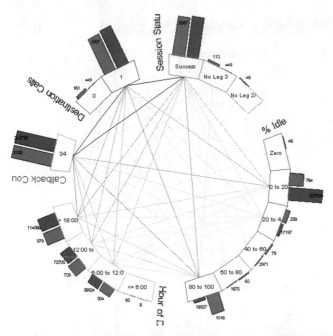

Figure 12.7 A distribution of account usage shown in Daisy.

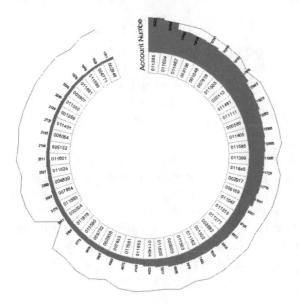

One particularly interesting feature to note in this figure can be seen near the 8:00 position. Notice the difference in the line usage for account #000004 as compared to all of the other accounts. The low success rate of this account may indicate a problem in the reliability of the bearers for that account. Alternatively it could reflect a lack of knowledge on behalf of the customer about the operations of the system. Regardless of the actual underlying issue, it is an anomaly and should be reviewed.

Summing Up

Based on a combination of recent deregulation within the telecom industry and the development of newer technologies, feature-rich phone networks and calling services have become more widespread than ever before. In an industry that sells small units of time in very large quantities, management of the data generated by the system can be a formidable task. MTS realized early on that they had to work out a better way to manage their data and improve their bottom line. In response to this issue, the MTS-MIS system was created utilizing the Daisy visual data mining package. This made it easy for MTS to interpret and understand their ever-expanding data sets. By supporting remote operations and using e-mail to send usage reports back to a central processing facility, MTS can quickly obtain the details regarding any system operating within their network. Visual analysis of this information in Daisy has permitted the company to control, adjust, and reconfigure the performance of their systems to better respond to the needs of their clients. Additionally, Daisy is used by MTS to help identify hardware faults and line problems, which are ever present in the phone-switching environment. Finally, Daisy is used to combat a wide range of fraudulent behaviors ranging from specific individuals and organized groups to dishonest providers and corrupt operators. All in all, the MTS-MIS system used in conjunction with Daisy visualization provides a comprehensive yet easy-to-use environment to understand and work with complex telecom data.

BANKING AND FINANCE

13

The following set of case studies describes a series of data mining activities that were conducted in one of America's largest banking institutions. As you will see, data mining techniques have been used in a multitude of ways in this environment. We describe several of these throughout this chapter, although the precise details of the work have been disguised to preserve anonymity.

The banking company in this case study employs a very large number of people and offers a wide variety of services to their expansive client base. Through recent deregulation, services that were once disallowed by law are now being made available through banking institutions. Not only does this bank provide standard banking and credit services such as checking, savings, transactions, and loans (mortgage, automobile, etc.), but they also provide a host of other financial services such as investment management and insurance.

As is the case with many large banking institutions, this bank frequently acquires regional banks that have their own established management information systems that can differ substantially from those maintained by the parent bank. Methods have been established over the past several years for upgrading and converting legacy databases and information systems to established standard formats that could be maintained by the parent bank. When new acquisitions occur, the existing data records of each new company must be converted to formats compatible with the existing formats currently maintained by the parent bank. There are specially trained teams of personnel who carry out these upgrades, and they complete these conversions in the most timely manner possible.

It has been a challenge for the parent bank to integrate all of this information and provide a standard experience for their clients. In particular, it is often difficult for the company to keep track of all of the interactions, services, and offerings utilized by any one customer. Due to the distribution of information across departments and individual bank branches, marketing personnel found it difficult to develop company-wide profiles for individual customers. In response to this situation, the bank has decided to evolve from a mass-marketing to a targeted-marketing approach in which particular products or services can be suggested to reflect more closely the needs of a particular customer. The ultimate goal is to find ways of integrating customer information across distributed sources so those bank associates who are dealing directly with customers can use these data.

The idea is that when employees are dealing with a client, they can do a better job if they know about the entire range of customer activities with the bank, along with other information such as the customer's various financial goals. If a customer is not satisfied with the return on investment for a CD (certificate of deposit), for example, the banking officer could refer him or her to the investment division of the company where other investment options such as money markets could be explored. This kind of service would give customers the assurance that their bank "knows" them and can provide the services that they need. This strategy is focused on both commercial and private consumers.

The decision to move to a targeted service approach was made partially in response to the increased competition within the industry. The majority of the company's competition comes from nonbanking industry companies. This includes those businesses that offer debt and credit card services, which means just about any legitimate business from airlines to car manufacturers and beyond. Discount broker services have decimated the savings holdings at most large banks through their offerings of money markets and mutual funds. Even the technology industry is taking away a share of their business through the development of electronic commerce. Officers of this bank realized that if they were going to stay competitive, they had to become a technology leader.

Technology Assessment Team

The applications described in this chapter were researched, developed, and fielded by a group within the bank called the Technology Assessment Team (TAT). Several years ago the company established the TAT in order to stay abreast of developments in computing and information technology. The TAT is tasked with identifying new and emerging technologies that might be incorporated into current or future banking operations. One of the technologies investigated by the TAT has been visual data mining.

We believe that one of the reasons that the TAT has been successful in their efforts to introduce data mining is that the company has placed great trust in their judgment, giving them the freedom to fail in some of their initial development efforts. The company does not want to restrict the kinds of technologies that the TAT can pursue.

There is an acknowledgment that in the quest to fit technological innovations to corporate problems, some approaches might not meet initial expectations. So from the onset, the company did not expect that every single data mining project was going to be a roaring success. Rather, there was an understanding that TAT personnel would continue to learn how to apply these technologies more effectively as their experience levels increased. TAT personnel were therefore free to generate test cases and prototypes to try out different approaches. Needless to say, this corporate culture fosters much more creativity, expressiveness, and motivation than one might usually expect. The company realized early on that, when it comes to data mining, you have to be willing to have a few false starts if you want to have some hits.

Having identified visual data mining as a technology that might be used to improve operations, TAT personnel conducted a review of several high-end tools. They did some preliminary prototyping with several systems and found that many of them did not quite meet their expectations. In particular the TAT determined that the majority of systems, although impressive, could not be used without significant retrofitting of their data into predefined models and landscapes that were not well suited to the planned applications. TAT wanted the freedom to tailor the visualization to meet their specific needs. With these needs in mind, they chose Discovery by Visible Decisions Inc. (VDI) as the system that offered the flexibility that they needed. The TAT worked closely with VDI personnel in developing the initial models and gained a lot of insight from these interactions. These consultations provided important information about how best to use Discovery's features to create displays for the applications. VDI personnel generated paper-scapes of screen designs and extensively reviewed the company's data for potential problems. With VDI's help, the applications we will describe were developed quickly. Generally, it took between three and six weeks to generate applications, with about 70 percent of that time spent acquiring and formatting the data. The visualizations themselves were created in under a week in most cases.

Fostering Corporate Acceptance of Data Mining

TAT personnel have been able to achieve a buy-in of data mining technology from virtually every level of the company. For example, the CEO quickly appreciated the utility and benefits of adopting this technology into the company's operations. His desire to embrace this technology facilitated its acceptance in the rest of the company. This is quite a departure from the way that technologies usually are introduced into a company. The typical path is that the technical staff are the only ones to advocate the adoption of new technology, and the acceptance and integration of new approaches into everyday practice is often a slow process with a long gestation period.

The proliferation of visual data mining approaches within the company has been strongly increasing since the TAT first introduced the concept. There are any number of reasons that data mining systems take a bit of time to be accepted and integrated fully into existing operations in any business. First, there is a tangible cost associated with development of data mining applications. This cost includes the licensing of the software as well as the actual labor time required to identify, access, and build the application itself. Hardware often adds a considerable cost as well. When the TAT first started down the data mining road, the VDI products ran only on Silicon Graphics machines, which are high-end workstations that can be quite expensive. In fact, it was only recently that the software ports produced by VDI made it available for the PC platforms currently used internally throughout the bank. There are also some socialization issues associated with the acceptance of new technologies, especially visualization, that are being addressed across the corporation. Learning to use visualization effectively requires a willingness to think "out-of-the-box," and this can sometimes be a challenge.

As we have stated repeatedly throughout the book, data mining is an iterative process. The final solution to a problem is almost never realized in the first analytic iteration. Furthermore, there may be no hard and fast rules for designing applications or defining solutions. Therefore, you may need to develop an approach to the application development cycle in a data mining project that is unlike other software development cycles. Figure 13.1 shows an example of how this process can be defined. This model was originally suggested by Richard Brath of VDI and lends itself nicely to this problem. The model assumes four stages of the development cycle: requirements generation, approach design, coding and testing, and review of results. The cycle is usually shown as a spiral, indicating that the process of development will move through these steps any number of times before completion. Note that because this cycle is vastly different from traditional software development processes, it requires special explanation before it will be accepted. There are no formal design documents or list of deliverables. In many cases, you will wind up with something completely different at the end than was envisioned at the beginning. For these reasons, those people who are very procedurally oriented and want every detail of the application spelled out from the beginning will have a difficult time adapting to this type of an approach.

Figure 13.1 A data mining development model.

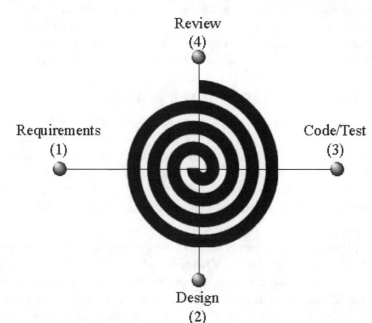

A final issue with regard to acceptance is the perceived return on investment. In this case the return on investment for data mining applications has unquestionably been tangible. Although there are no hard figures in terms of savings associated with these applications, the company clearly feels that data mining has been an extremely wise investment. At present there are several small-scale applications that are spread throughout various levels of the company, so it is difficult to quantify the exact monetary worth of this approach. Whatever this number might be, however, it is certain to increase since there are plans to expand and generalize the use of visual data mining technologies throughout the company.

Consumer Credit Policy

The first system produced was a proof-of-concept prototype developed for the CEO to demonstrate that visual data mining technologies could be applied effectively to the existing loan approval process. TAT personnel developed an application to evaluate loan policies and procedures for comparing automobile loan portfolio scorecards and credit policy overlays. The goal was to reduce the number of delinquent and defaulted car loans for the bank by correlating the incidence of bad loans with specific loan-applicant characteristics. The study was based on tens of thousands of indirect automobile loans booked in the year 1995. This time period was chosen so that payment behavior over time could be included in the evaluation. When the application was developed in 1997, payment data were available for the interceding two year interval.

Using a Geographical Landscape Paradigm

The Discovery landscape generated in this application was based on a geospatial positioning. In 1995, the bank had operations in numerous states and one question in the analysis involved a comparison of loan payment behaviors across different regions. A map of the United States was generated and the loan performance overlays were placed onto their respective states within the display. This visualization has been easily expanded to incorporate new banks purchased after this prototype was developed.

In the main display there are a series of towers placed within the landscape that represent different classes of loans (for example new and used automobiles). Data values are coded in the heights and colors of the towers. Tower height corresponds to the actual number of loans for a region. Color indicates payment behavior. The color red is used to reflect loans for which the vehicle was repossessed or charged off, yellow is for those loans that have been late one or more times (e.g., 30 days past due or delinquent), and green is used to code loans that have been paid on schedule. Figure 13.2 shows a representative example of this landscape display (refer to the CD-ROM for color versions of the figures).

A colored rectangle is drawn at the base of each tower to indicate how that state performed relative to the national average. The color of this rectangle varies along a continuous dimension from red to blue. Poor performance is shown in red and good performance is shown in blue. One of the first things that was noticed when the loan data were mapped into the display was that the Illinois loans tended to outperform those of the other states. This result agreed with other internal assessments made by credit officers in the company, and reflected the implementation of more stringent loan criteria in Illinois. This was due in part to the fact that Illinois was a new market for the company and they were being very conservative initially with respect to the Illinois dealerships chosen to sell the bank's loans. Thus, although the actual number of loans made in Illinois was small relative to the other states, the Illinois loans were less likely to be classified as "bad."

Predicting Loan Payment Performance

Within the company's credit policy group, loans are evaluated and scored according to their predicted performance. The scores are said to reflect the customer's

Figure 13.2 Automobile loans made by the bank in 1995.

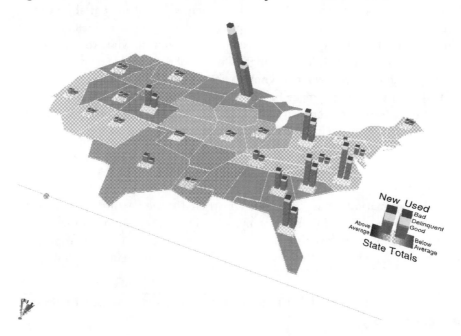

willingness to pay. The ways in which this scoring is done can be quite involved, and there are any number of variables used. Customer characteristics are acquired from loan applications and credit history information and are used to help predict payment performance. Loan scores are predictions that are based on such factors as payment histories including on-time payments, late payments, minimal payments, and general attention to overall financial obligations. The higher the score, the less the risk associated with a loan. One question of interest in this application was whether the predictions made by the loan department were in fact valid with respect to the actual loan payment performance observed in the portfolio. As it turns out, the scoring produced by the credit policy group is sometimes a good indicator of loan performance, but is not always accurate.

The predictive information for the loans is presented in another portion of the display as a set of towers corresponding to the variables used to make performance predictions. In actuality there are over 100 parameters used to determine the risk associated with a loan, including a client's ability to pay. Since the initial prototype system was developed as just a proof-of-concept, only six different variables were used originally. In future versions, all variables will be utilized to determine the optimal mix of parameters in predicting loan payment behavior. Figure 13.3 shows how the six variables are shown within the display. Each of the variables can be plotted in a matrix to determine payment performance of the loans included in the portfolio. Performance is represented in rectangles coded from white to blue to indicate poor to good repayment for the range of values of the variable contained in the data set. Therefore, if you want to know what value(s) of a certain variable was associated with the best payment behavior, all you have to do is find the bluest square(s) in the series for that variable, since that square will correspond to the value of the variable associated with the best repayment performance.

The loan-to-value ratio reflects the amount of the loan as a percent of the value (e.g., cost of the car). The visual distribution shows that the loan-to-value ranges anywhere from 70 percent up to 120 percent with the vast majority being close to the 100 percent mark. Because there was a restricted range for this variable, it did not turn out to be very useful in this analysis. A similar problem was observed for the term-of-the-loan (in months). Loan terms can range anywhere from 0–24 months up to 72 months. In this case, the majority of loans made for automobile

Figure 13.3 Using six variables to predict loan performance in the Discovery prototype.

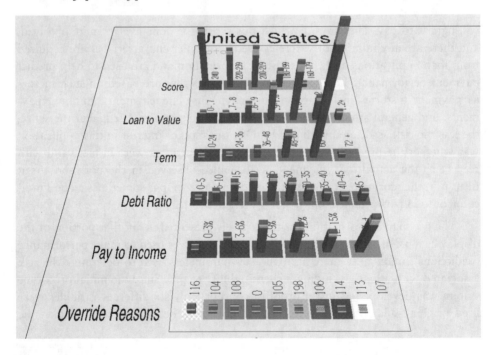

purchases are shown in the 60-72 month range, giving this variable a restricted range. The same calculations run using loans generated in more recent years would actually show a significant number at 84 months and beyond because the company has been offering seven-year loans. The visualization indicates that neither of these added much value in the loan evaluation process.

The debt ratio is yet another variable that can be used to predict the risk associated with a loan. Debt ratio is defined as the total amount of monthly debt divided by total monthly income. As it turned out, this was the most important determinant of whether loans were issued in the first place. The company has historically placed a lot of emphasis on the use of the debt ratio value and considered it to be their best predictor of performance. When evaluated in terms of actual performance, however, within the Discovery system, it can be seen that it may not be the best indicator. This was an important discovery because it clearly showed that performance could be improved by considering other variables.

The payment-to-income ratio was another variable considered in the analysis. Specifically, this represents the amount of the monthly payment as a percentage of the adjusted gross income of the borrower. This variable had a better range in the database and so served as a better predictor of payment performance. Visually, this variable provided a more complete color gradation than the debt ratio value. As a result of this type of analysis, the consumer credit policy department has replaced debt ratio with payment-to-income as one of the critical criteria to be considered when deciding whether to make a loan to a customer. Recall from Chapter 1 that the goal of data mining is to discover new trends and act on them accordingly. From this perspective, this first prototype was considered a huge success.

Changing Policies and Procedures

This prototype was also used to look at the override justifications for loans. Within most banks, the scores, ratings, and ratio analysis are all meant to serve as guidelines for whether or not a loan should be approved. Needless to say, there will be special cases or unusual circumstances that cannot be neatly classified into a quantitative value for inclusion into the scoring process. Therefore most banks authorize their loan officers to override standard approval policies. When this situation occurs, a code corresponding to the reason for the override is entered. For example, brushing on one of the very blue entries (e.g., a loan that performed well) reveals a code that indicates the customer had a previous relationship with the bank with no derogatory credit. Although the credit policy overlays may have indicated that credit should not be extended to this customer, the fact that they had a prior relationship with the bank was used to justify approval of the credit. If a lighter colored entry (e.g., white) is selected indicating a poorly performing loan, the justification is often "other" or "unknown" which does not provide much detail as to why the override actions were taken by the loan officer. Since override loans in the "other" category tended to be poor performers, the company changed their policies to disallow these types of justifications.

Within this application, individual states can also be profiled to see how loan performance in local regions corresponds to the general industry trends. For example, if Minnesota is selected, the overlays will be adjusted to show only those data from Minnesota loans. In this case it can be determined that the Minnesota distributions closely mirror the overall trends of the United States, mainly because Minnesota loans comprise an overwhelming majority of loans in the portfolio. Using Discovery, you can profile any cell and get the specific information for that state. By selecting individual cells, you can refine the focus of the analysis. In this case, a new landscape-level will appear that contains the details for any particular value. See Figure 13.4 for an example of this display.

The company has documented significant process improvements through the use of this visual data mining application. In several cases, the credit policy group

Figure 13.4 Refocusing the loan profile display to reflect the values of a selected variable.

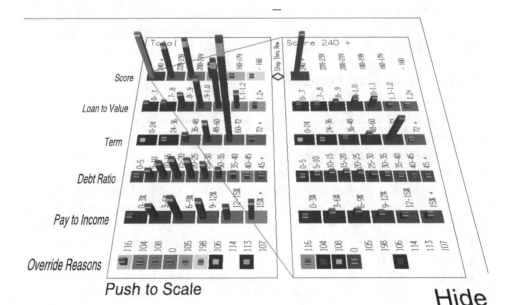

had independently realized there were some issues and problems in the way they conducted their evaluations. This recognition took several months and a significant amount of work to uncover. One of the reasons for building the initial prototype was to determine whether these types of situations would have been obvious and easy to recognize using visual data mining methods. Thus, the prototype facilitated verifications of and challenges to existing corporate policies. Certain business practices can become so entrenched within an organization that they are never questioned as to their appropriateness or timeliness. The use of visualization in this case made it obvious that certain changes needed to occur. This is a good example of a DKYK situation discussed in Chapter 3.

The system was used not only as an analysis tool but also as a communication tool. In conjunction with the development of a data mart (in production) that will be used to house all of the consumer credit policy information, the visualization application will be *productionized* to provide a standard interface into the data set. Through interactions and feedback from the user community, the TAT has compiled a list of enhancements and modifications that will be included within the productionized version. In the final system, all parameters currently used by this group will be made available for visual analysis.

Evaluating Correlations among Customer Variables

The application also supports the simultaneous evaluation of two variables. This approach allows you to determine whether there are any correlations between pairs of variables in terms of loan performance. A pop-up landscape was configured to show a cross-matrix of the selected variables. One variable is shown on the x-axis and the other on the y-axis. If two variables had a perfect positive correlation in terms of predicting loan performance, you should see a gradation of color ranging from white in one corner to blue in the opposite corner of the matrix. So, for example, if you compare score with debt ratio as presented in Figure 13.5, you can see that it is a checkerboard of values without any consistent correlational relationship. Even though it was previously determined in the other displays that debt ratio was not as good a predictor as was once thought, this view now makes it visually clear that this measure is also inconsistent. However, if you display score and payment-to-income, you can see there is a much better correlation between the variables and you can easily see where the nonperforming loans show up. Figure 13.6 shows an example of this comparison. The better a variable distributes, the more value they place on it.

The correlational matrices bring up an important point. When the TAT defined their variable classes, they were consistent in the manner in which the values were coded. The developers routinely used low values to indicate poorer quality or

Figure 13.5 Variable correlations resulting in a nonuniform checkerboard.

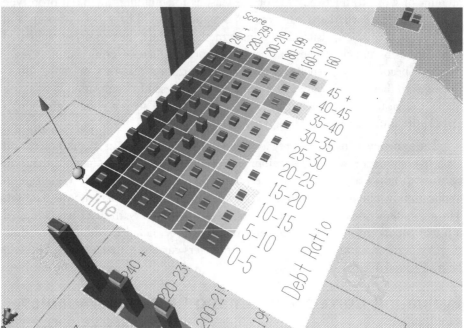

nonperformers and higher values for better or more desirable traits. For this reason they were able to construct this display and have it produce meaningful results. This may seem like an obvious approach, but it is not always followed and is an issue that should be planned out at the start of the development effort.

Industry Classification for Commercial Loans

The company not only provides loans to private consumers, but they also work with commercial companies to help them finance their businesses. Even though the number of private consumers far outweighs the commercial client base, the average size of the commercial loans is much higher. Since the company has a lot of funds tied up in commercial loans, they formulate policies regarding the allocation of loans to various industry segments. These policies can be based on any number of factors, including the strength of the economy, a variety of foreign factors, and general

Figure 13.6 Variable correlations revealing a consistent relationship.

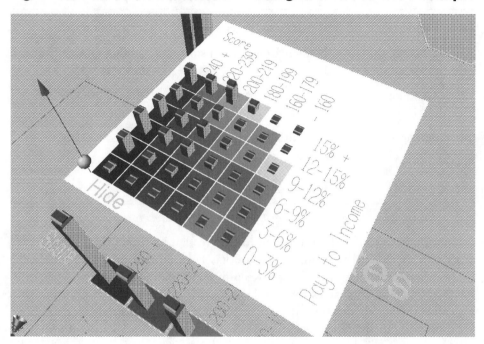

industry trends. The TAT wanted to extend their success from the automobile loan application to look at commercial loan risk in terms of industry classifications for the commercial loan portfolio.

The company has defined over 35 different industry segments representing everything from real estate to agriculture, health care, defense, computers, and electronics. A landscape visualization was developed in Discovery to convey information about performance of loans within these segments. The resulting landscape was organized to show a variety of factors about each industry including "percent criticized," which represents a percentage of those industries that are graded high-risk. The other variables that can be used to evaluate the portfolio are shown in Table 13.1. These variables are applied to the axes within the Discovery displays so that correlations can be seen. All of these variables are also presented in any of the brushing drill-downs that are performed.

The towers placed in the matrix representing each industry have two components associated with them. The first represents the total binding exposure, or the

Table 13.1 List of Terms Used in Commercial Industry Analysis

Percent criticized	Weighted average risk	Percent nonperforming
Binding 12 month growth	Binding growth from start	Binding growth from previous
Utilized 12 month growth	Utilized growth from start	Utilized growth from previous
Total binding exposure	Total utilized exposure	Utilized binding ratio
Subset utilized	Total utilized	Subset growth
Subset previous	Institution share of RMA total	

amount that the bank is legally bound to lend to that industry. The second represents how much of that binding exposure has been utilized to date. Figure 13.7 shows an example of this landscape. Keep in mind that each industry segment is made up of those companies that the bank has classified into that segment. This assignment is largely determined by their SIC (Standard Industrial Code), so that each tower actually represents a large number of different corporations. The approach adopted in this application created a level of abstraction wherein the individual behaviors of each company were aggregated into a composite representation reflecting their overall industry classification. The position of industry segment towers within the display is determined by the variables selected for the axes. Their colors can also be set to reflect values of any variable. In this case, the color is set to percent criticized with higher risk industry segments colored with brighter colors. It is clear that several of these towers fall within this category.

A unique feature of this particular application is that it can be set into motion using a VCR-like toolbar that plays a summary of segment loan performance over a designated time interval. As the system is put into motion using the industry segments previously selected, the towers start to move around the display, repositioning themselves to reflect the values for the particular time-frame (quarters) being presented. This gives the display a simulation-like look and feel. You can explicitly see different patterns, dependencies, and overall trends by stepping through time. For example, real estate and computers are big movers in this situation because they tend to be more volatile markets.

To provide additional insight into the different behaviors of the various industry segments as they progress through time, a set of tracers can be applied to show

Figure 13.7 A commercial industry analysis landscape.

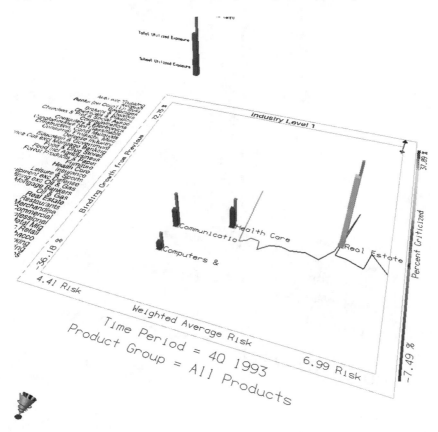

the trail or path that was taken through the performance space. This makes it easy to show the progression of an industry, relate it to other significant events (e.g., pivot dates), or compare it to other segments. By selecting on a particular industry, a side-landscape can be generated that shows the risk of loans written within that category. This provides a high-level drill-down within the selected segment where the height of the towers reflects the general risk distribution of the individual companies within that group. Figure 13.8 provides an example of this display for several industry segments.

One final feature of this particular application is that additional levels of abstraction can be exposed for any industry segment. Since different portfolio managers will be assigned to different industry segments, it would make sense to allow each operator to focus on their particular area of interest. Therefore, through a set of drill-downs built into the application, analysts can show subgroups

Figure 13.8 A landscape showing industry risk ratings.

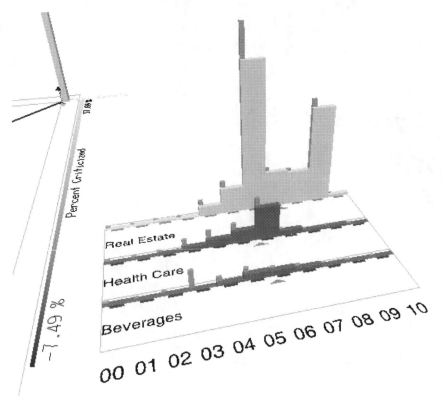

within any industry. For example, the real estate segment is made up of apartments, resorts, shopping centers, REIT (real estate investment trusts), and so forth. Figure 13.9 shows an example of this drill-down within the application. Again, this is defined by the SIC codes associated with each of the companies. A further level of drill-down could also be performed to provide yet another level of detail. As long as there is supporting information in the data set, the software will allow the user to achieve more and more focus on a particular industry segment. Since this is a portfolio management application, individual companies are not presented within the application except through brushing (i.e., the top five companies within the segment).

The TAT has looked at how this application has been used within the company. Many users want to focus on their particular area of interest. There are others that want to see their industry in the context of the other industries. Yet others

Figure 13.9 A subindustry representation for the real estate industry.

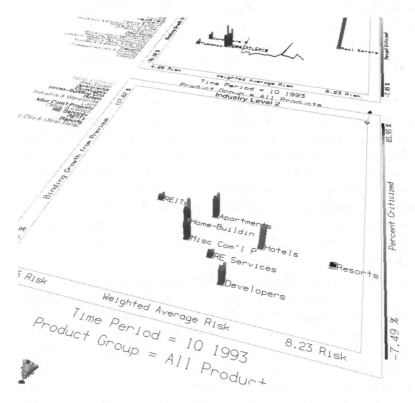

need to see every piece of supporting data. For these reasons, the TAT's decision to design the application in the way that they did has proved to be useful to a wide variety of analysts.

Analyzing Customer Clusters for Targeted Marketing Efforts

Development of this particular application was one of the company's major incentives when deciding to become involved with visual data mining technologies. They wanted to get away from mass-marketing campaigns and use a more consumer-oriented approach. To do this, they had to come up with a way of segmenting their customers into distinguishable clusters. This was done based on the behaviors exhibited by the clients, such as using similar services (e.g., channels) and products. The data used in this application were based on the behaviors of their clients in terms of balance information, maximum and minimum account balances, how many debits were conducted, how many times the client went to a teller, and so on. There were over 100 different variables analyzed across several million records.

Data Acquisition and Integration

As you might imagine, the data acquisition and integration issues encountered in this application were ponderous. First, much of the data that was to be included in the clustering analysis were not available in standard formats. The data targeted for use in the application came from various predecessor banks, all of which had their own storage and formatting conventions prior to being acquired by the company. So even if all of the targeted data were available, the data sets might not necessarily be in the same format. Across the data set there were dozens of formats used to represent the same data, each with a different layout, naming convention, and value definition.

The system developers also decided to include information from other information sources in the analysis. Demographic data sets were purchased from an external source and then integrated into the application. Demographics such as household incomes, household values, vehicle values, home values, professional status, and many others were incorporated into the clustering analysis. In addition to demographics, information was added regarding the profitability of customers for the company. For example, clients who use expensive channels (i.e., tellers) for conducting transactions are less profitable than customers who do all of their banking through ATMs. Profitability tiers (high, medium, and low) were identified and incorporated into the clustering analysis. Finally, geographical information was included regarding the customer's state of residence. As you will surmise, the integration of all of these disparate data sources was a very ambitious and extremely difficult task. It took much longer to complete this initial preparatory work than it did to do the data mining analyses.

Identifying Customer Clusters

An initial k-nearest-neighbor algorithm was run across the immense combined data set. Fourteen clusters based on customer characteristics and behaviors were identified. If you have ever used this kind of classification approach, you will appreciate that the number of clusters defined is largely arbitrary. A perfect clustering may result in several hundred clusters, but this would be far too large a number to use in devising a marketing plan. After some iteration on this issue, the bank eventually locked in on 14 strongly separated clusters, which they felt corresponded to a workable number of separable customer groups.

We should mention that the k-nearest-neighbor approach was chosen in favor of a neural network classification because the company wanted customer policies to be described in full and clear detail. As you will recall from Chapter 6, neural net classifiers produce a set of weights that cannot necessarily be recoded into clear rules that can be included in a report. The classifications produced by the k-nearest-neighbor algorithm, on the other hand, can be explicitly characterized, and so this method was the more appropriate choice in this case.

Visualizing Customer Clusters

Once the clusters were identified, the next problem was to find a way of facilitating their interpretation. An application was developed in Discovery in which each of the 14 clusters is presented as a tower within the landscape. The axes of the landscape can be used to represent variables of interest including average profitability and frequency distribution. The towers can also be broken down by their geographical regions (e.g., operating states) or by the services offered by the company including checking, savings, money markets, CDs, investment, retirement, mortgage, line of credit, retail loan, and credit card. Figure 13.10 shows an example of the cluster display.

As you can see from this figure, this data mining application provides a means of displaying and managing a tremendous amount of information at one time. The towers appearing within this landscape are stacks of embedded wafers (e.g., the 148 variables) varying in size. A larger wafer indicates there were relatively more observations of that particular variable within the cluster. (To provide normalization, size is based on the ratio to the average of that variable.) The placement of the variables is consistent across each cluster (e.g., tower) within the display. Thus, if you were to select and sort a cluster according to its variables for example, in descending value, it would form a pyramid shape. In doing so, you would also force the other clusters to reposition their variables into the same order. This provides one way in which to see similarities among the different clusters. See Figure 13.11 for an example of this type of adjustment.

Any of the wafers in the display can be brushed to show their underlying data. The actual values are shown as a percentage of how far above or below the average they are. For example, in Cluster 11, if we brush on the wafer depicting safety deposit box penetration, we can see that it is composed of 40 percent of the entries

Figure 13.10 Depicting 14 clusters with 148 variables.

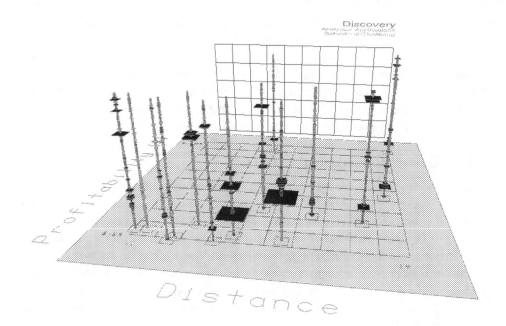

which in turn represents at 2.3 times the average. So if you wanted to sell more mortgages, you would find the cluster with the largest mortgage penetration and determine which other variables can be used to help affect the sale of mortgages. Additionally, using some of the other filters identified earlier, you can focus on specific types of information within the display.

A Generic Application

The TAT has created a generic application that can be used to display data from a wide range of data sets. This application can be used to display the contents of any multi-dimensional data file using a visual landscape. The system is configured to read in all of the different fields (separated by a default delimiter) contained within the data file. Then through a series of simple menu interfaces, it lets the user select which fields to use to populate the first level of the display. This requires the selection of three variables, one for each of three dimensions. An example of a resulting display is shown in Figure 13.12.

Figure 13.11 Sorting the variables contained within a cluster.

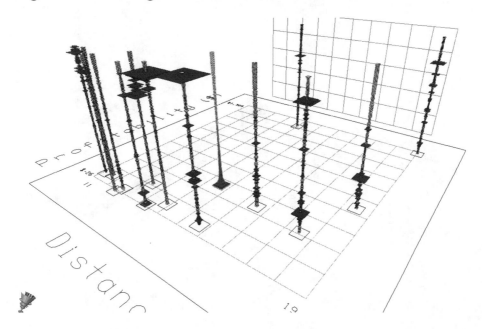

If your data set contains more than three fields, the system will expand out into separate parallel landscapes when you select on a cell within the primary grid. What happens in this case is that the next set of three variables will be presented within their own landscape (see Figure 13.13 for this expansion). This decomposition can continue until there are no longer any variables present in the data set. By design, this provides the ultimate level of drill-down because you can exhaust your data supply by constantly requesting the next, unallocated, three variables. This application has proven to be extremely valuable. It can be used to inspect new data sets and expose bad data segments, in addition to performing decision support.

One particular analysis performed with this application involved loss forecasting for the deposits made with the federal government. All banks are required by law to keep reserves against loans that are expected to go bad (e.g., default). These reserves are used as insurance for bank insolvency. Traditionally, these forecasts are not very accurate and they can fluctuate by millions of dollars at a time. If the projected losses are not calculated properly, monetary fines can be imposed against the organization. However, tying up an overage is also not profitable for the company.

Figure 13.12 A sample screen from the generic application.

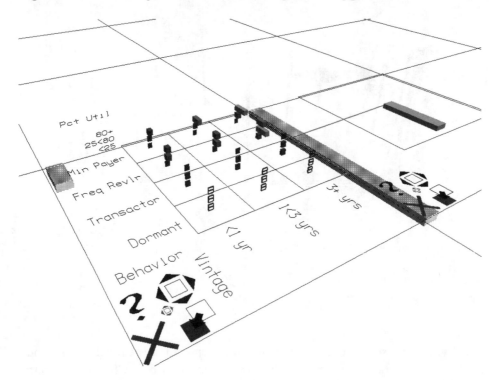

Thus, it is obviously in the bank's best interest to get a good handle on the actual losses that the bank will incur.

The company applied this generic landscape to their credit card loss data to see whether improvements could be made in loss forecasts. A facility was developed to display certain information associated with each credit card account. The information represented includes:

- The product (e.g., type of credit card)

- Vintage (e.g., how long it has been issued)

- Behavior (e.g., minimum, frequent, revolver, transactor, dormant, attritor, close-downs, default, bankrupt)

- Risk (e.g., low, medium, and high)

- APR

- Operating regions

- Market regions (e.g., in or out of states where the bank operates)

Figure 13.13 Expanding to the next level within the generic application.

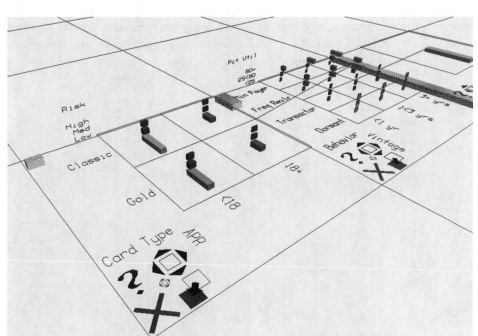

Three dimensions can be selected and presented within the generic application. Depending on what variables are selected, you can quickly identify problem areas. This greatly simplifies the problem of determining which parts of the portfolio contain bad debt and how that debt can be quantified. Once identified, this information can be used to predict losses and readjust reserves. By optimizing nonrevenue-producing reserve balances, the bank realized significant cost savings from this application in a relatively short time.

Summing Up

In this chapter we have described a series of visual data mining applications implemented in Discovery for various banking problems. The applications described include an evaluation of policies used to define criteria for automobile loan approval, evaluation of commercial loans in various industry segments, analysis of customer clusters for targeted marketing initiatives and a generic application that has been used for estimating projected losses from defaulted loans. All of the systems have been used within an operational setting. In each case, bank personnel were able to develop visual data mining applications quickly once the data were accessed and integrated. Although the use of these techniques is still relatively new in the company, benefits have already been realized. To illustrate the general utility of visual data mining in commercial applications, let us now turn to Chapter 14 in which we describe data mining applications for retail problems.

RETAIL DATA MINING

14

The first part of this chapter describes a data mining effort undertaken for a large U.S. retailer. The goal of this particular application was to use data mining to achieve better customer retention and satisfaction through more centralized marketing efforts. The second half of the chapter describes an application undertaken by a set of retailers to analyze and evaluate patterns of videocassette retail sales across geographical regions and demographic groups. The goal of this analysis was to define unique store profiles that could be used to develop more effective distribution policies. Because of the sensitive nature of some of the analyses performed during both projects, specific names and numeric details have been disguised in these descriptions. Nevertheless, the overall themes and findings of these engagements are presented in as realistic a manner as possible so that you can appreciate the approach and questions investigated.

Retail Marketing and Sales Patterns

The work described in this case has been performed during the first six months of a projected three-year project. A large data warehousing effort is also being undertaken in parallel. The overall vision of this work is that the outcomes derived from the data mining exercises will be used to help guide the design and development of the data warehouse structure that will eventually be adopted. For the initial data mining activities, the company wanted to identify and provide information to their primary business units regarding opportunities to enhance customer equity and optimize the type and value of customer contacts through focused marketing. Information about these customer classifications and contacts could then be used and maintained by the organization as a whole once the data warehouse was completed. The company's goals for this exercise were to reduce marketing costs while at the same time increase revenues (see sidebar, "Cost Reduction versus Revenue Estimation"). By doing the data mining ahead of time, the company personnel also benefit from advanced familiarization and training with any new concepts identified regarding customer classifications. Thus, the delivery of the data warehouse will not be met with skepticism within this organization, but rather with an informed attitude.

Cost Reduction versus Revenue Estimation

The company was looking for a minimum of a 10-to-1 return on investment in this data mining engagement. Generally, when dealing with a cost-reduction situation (e.g., fraud detection, marketing duplication, preventive maintenance), you have established a baseline of events which have been confirmed by the client organization (e.g., duplicate mailers). Each type of event has an associated cost (e.g., $1.00/mailer), and the total or expected number of instances of this event (e.g., 100,000) will constitute the cost reduction expected to be gained by the company. The majority of all data mining activities are focused on providing a return on investment as a cost reduction since it can be measured in quantitative values. Many companies that outsource their data mining activities (mostly fraud detection) will take their fee as a percentage of the amount of cost reduction identified, since these are real and tangible amounts.

Cost reduction can be contrasted with estimations of revenue enhancement. You can actually measure a cost reduction, but how do you estimate increased revenue? A revenue estimation is a speculated value based on how well a particular promotion does with respect to increasing sales of a product. In these cases, the calculation of return on investment is extremely difficult. There are certain factors that cannot be controlled. Storms can knock down power lines in the middle of a campaign, or a competing business can release new products or cut their prices. In an income-tax case that we once worked, over $2 million of unreported income was discovered. We considered this to be part of the revenue estimation for the agency that was sponsoring the work. However, by the time the case progressed into the investigation stages and all of the details were gathered for prosecution, the original amount was significantly diminished because of missing witnesses, altered reports, and the unavoidable plea bargaining. In the end, the final amount recovered was less than $100,000. Thus, unexpected factors can have a significant effect on this measure. There is an old saying that market share gains have multiple fathers, but market share losses are orphans.

In order to appreciate the scope of this data mining exercise, you should understand the array of retail sales areas covered by the company. Within the organization there are several distinct subunits that control various portions of the overall merchandise and service categories offered by the company. As with many modern retail companies, this particular company provides merchandise and services ranging from household appliances and furnishings to clothing and automotive parts. This "one-stop shopping" model has been adopted by many companies and provides the consumer with a consistent environment within which to have many needs met. There is one unified company that backs up all goods and services with its reputation for quality and standard guarantees on its products. For the customer, convenience, security and value are all maintained under one umbrella represented by the organization. What the retailer would like to do is to find a way of sharing information about customers among all of the business subunits so as to maximize the impact of corporate-wide marketing resources and reduce excess mail/telemarketing contacts to its customer base.

The client in this case knew that it had a lot of good customer data that could be exploited and used to help market additional products and services. However, the company as a whole is not structured in such a way as to facilitate a means of creating and sharing a comprehensive representation of the data. As part of the solution, the company wanted to put together a group that would cut across all of the different business units and pull together information that could be useful to the entire company as well as the individual business units. The company had the insight and vision to realize that it needed to change its structure in order to stay competitive within its market. In particular, the company wanted to increase its relationship marketing effectiveness, enhancing its approach to attracting and/or retaining customers (see the sidebar, "Relationship Marketing Actions"). Since there was no one central method for coordinating and controlling how the company performed its overall marketing activities, there was inevitable duplication of marketing targets maintained across the various subunits. Eventually, what happens in this type of situation is that duplication occurs in the marketing targets that have been selected. In the absence of a central coordinating authority, a single customer would receive numerous mailers, phone calls, and follow-up letters from the various subunits in the company. This is obviously overwhelming to most consumers and not an effective use of marketing resources.

Since the marketing activities of the overall corporation were fragmented among the business subunits, the company wanted to address this issue and maximize customer equity. To do this, it would have to refine its approach to marketing and develop a customer-contact strategy that would satisfy company-wide as well

Relationship Marketing Actions

Relationship marketing activities are used to persuade clients to become more associated with a business organization so that they purchase the products and services being offered because of a positive association with the company itself. There are generally four categories of actions pursued during relationship marketing:

Prospect and Acquire. This task is focused on identifying a new set of individuals or organizations that are not yet currently part of your client base. The new clients can be identified through a variety of sources, such as first-time purchases with a company, third-party customer lists, or other external sources. The goal is to offer the target set special offers or up-front discounts that will persuade them to try your products and services and become new clients. A good example of this is seen in the barrage of offers you receive from credit card companies in your mail each week.

Stimulate. This activity is aimed at persuading existing clients to increase their current expenditures for your goods and services. There are basically two methods of stimulation: The first is to try and move those clients who have a relatively low level of expenditures to a higher level of

as individual business units requirements. Part of this would be accomplished through the development of the data warehouse. However, a transition plan was required that would gradually introduce the desired concepts and, more importantly, achieve buy-in from each of the business subunits. As you can imagine, the acceptance of these concepts does not occur over a short time period, and you have to slowly build momentum toward this acceptance throughout the project.

Managing Marketing Saturation of Individual Customers

As it turns out, data entries are made in the company's marketing databases at the level of individual customers rather than households. Thus, there could be several individuals in one household who would all be considered different customers, even though they are likely members of the same immediate family. What was quickly discovered in the initial data mining efforts was that the client base was over-contacted. This was due largely to the company's policy of rewarding good customers by offering them special discounts, which were sent in various bulk mailings. If a involvement. Thus, if they are purchasing only seasonal garments, you can get them to try to get more everyday outerwear from your stores as well. The second method is to initiate a cross-sell mechanism. This entails taking worthwhile customers and trying to introduce them to other "categories" within the company that would be of interest to them. So for those individuals who only buy exercise equipment, you could try to get them interested in power tools or other home hardware products.

Retain. This method involves analysis of the purchasing histories of your clients as well as annual attrition rates in order to address the needs of "at risk" customers. In these cases, you may want to give them a special marketing plan or an offer designed to keep them as clients. Thus, if you know there is a high turnover rate in your client base, you can take proactive measures to minimize this value. The cost of retaining clients is much less than the cost of trying to identify new clients.

Reacquisition. This technique is used to try and persuade old clients to return to your business once you have determined that they have stopped utilizing your services or purchasing your goods. You need to contact them and attempt to win them back.

customer was identified for this marketing initiative across subunits in the company, that individual would receive marketing materials from all subunits in which he or she had made recent purchases. To compound this problem, since data were maintained in terms of individuals rather than households, multiple individuals in the same household could receive mailings from several departments. The data mining analysis provided evidence to the company that some clients were being contacted as many as 100 or more times in a given year.

Table 14.1 illustrates the marketing activities that were ongoing at this particular company. Including direct mailings and telemarketing calls, there were multiple offers being made to its customer base at any one time. Some clients might be contacted on average over three times per month.

During this data mining engagement, the company also looked at the revenue stream of people who were excessively contacted to see if it made a difference in their purchasing behavior. It was discovered that after approximately 45 contacts, there was no additional return on investment from sending out extra materials. Once this was discovered, the challenge was to find a way for the subunits to take advantage

Table 14.1 Sample of Marketing Activities Undertaken in One Year for Individual Customers by the Client Retail Company

	Credit Dept.	Mail Order	Services	Central
JAN	Post-holiday followup	10%-off coupon	Newsletter	Postcard
FEB	None	Direct mailing	Hardware sale	Valentine's Day
MAR	None	Direct mailing	Telemarketing call	Easter sale
APR	Statement enclosure	Direct mailing	Maintenance agreement	Store-wide mailer
MAY	None	Direct mailing	Telemarketing call	Memorial Day
JUN	Statement enclosure	Direct mailing	Newsletter	Father's Day
JUL	None	Priority mail	Telemarketing call	Fourth of July
AUG	Statement enclosure	Direct mailing	Store-wide mailer	Back to School
SEP	Statement enclosure	Telemarketing call	Maintenance agreement	Labor Day
OCT	None	Telemarketing call	Telemarketing call	Calendar
NOV	Holiday planner	Holiday gifts	Special mailer	Thanksgiving Sale
DEC	None	Direct mailing	None	Special mailer

of this information. Due to the distributed nature and financial autonomy of the individual business units, they were not explicitly instructed to refrain from mailings. Keep in mind that they are rewarded and compensated for their own performance rather than for the performance of the company as a whole. What appeals to one business subunit may not necessarily appeal to another. Thus, it was not feasible to impose a rigid structure on marketing practices. Rather, the approach was to present analytically sound evidence that would persuade those running the subunits that a change was in their own interests.

Some examples of guidelines extracted from the data mining exercise included providing a marketing history of what materials had already been sent to particular customers, together with a recommendation that no more than 10 mailers be sent to any one customer during a single quarter due to saturation and/or duplication. Additionally, a calendar of promotions throughout the year, similar to that shown in Table 14.1, was created for reference by individual business subunits so that each could determine when the other business subunits were running promotions. This calendar was made available to the entire company. Thus, if 20 mailers were about to be sent out by a business subunit, a separate subunit might opt to allow some time to pass between the contacts. These guidelines helped the company to manage the number of customer contacts in order to reduce marketing expenses and minimize customer confusion.

Using Data Mining to Investigate Customer Loyalty

The company also wanted to use the data mining exercise to examine customer loyalty. In this context, customer loyalty is defined in terms of the level of consistency of buying habits. Many retail corporations like to know the overall purchasing behaviors of their customers so that they can tailor their products and services to meet client expectations. Examination of purchasing patterns in several thousand records led to the discovery of four types of loyalty patterns (shown in Figure 14.1). The most loyal customers comprised less than 10 percent of the data set. These were people who were very consistent in their purchasing patterns, tending to repeat purchases of certain classes of goods and services. The analysts were able to characterize the purchasing habits of this group in terms of total dollar amount and number of purchases made annually. It was also noted that there was a significant amount of attrition in this group within the span of a few years. There was a second small group of loyal customers who did not show quite the same level of consistency in their purchases as the first group, although they shopped consistently and made purchases across many categories. Again, this group was characterized by the amount of money spent and the number of trips to the store in a year, as well as the number of subunits visited.

A third group of customers was identified who were far less consistent in their buying behaviors. This group comprised just under 40 percent of the customer base. They visit the store fewer times in a calendar year and utilize fewer business subunits than do the first two groups. This is the single biggest market that the company can

Figure 14.1 Purchasing trends used to characterize customer loyalty levels.

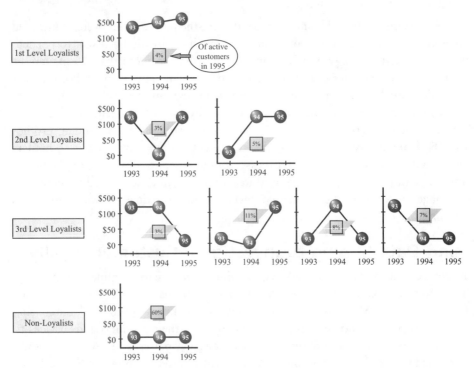

focus on to improve its profit margin. The fourth category represents the remaining client base who are, for the most part, one-time or very infrequent shoppers. They visit the store to buy a certain item because it is the only place that carries that particular brand, or because there is a sale. Alternatively, they may shop exclusively in only one category, such as appliances.

Figure 14.2 shows the buying behaviors of the four customer groups in the fourth year included in the analysis. Notice that as you move down the list from very loyal to nonloyal customers, the proportion of clients with high spending levels decreases. Since the bottom two groups are the largest and have lower proportions of high spenders, these two groups are natural targets for focused marketing efforts.

Marketing Approaches Based on Life Stages

The loyalty groups capture well-established differences among customers in terms of longer-term spending levels, number of trips to the store, and breadth of shopping.

Figure 14.2 Purchasing patterns across customer loyalty segments.

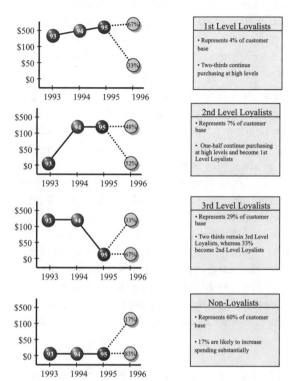

1st Level Loyalists
- Represents 4% of customer base
- Two-thirds continue purchasing at high levels

2nd Level Loyalists
- Represents 7% of customer base
- One-half continue purchasing at high levels and become 1st Level Loyalists

3rd Level Loyalists
- Represents 29% of customer base
- Two thirds remain 3rd Level Loyalists, whereas 33% become 2nd Level Loyalists

Non-Loyalists
- Represents 60% of customer base
- 17% are likely to increase spending substantially

There are also more short-term patterns that can be exploited in marketing schemes. In this data mining engagement, the pattern detection analysis also focused on life events and stages that might cause purchase cycles to peak and trough. Life events occur when specific circumstances in our lives cause us to have very distinct purchasing patterns. Thus, when you get married there are certain household items—furniture, sheets, bakeware, and other related articles—that will usually be purchased during that time. There is a limited duration to how long a life event will remain valid and an average cost can be associated with different life events. Since the term of a life event is limited from a single day to several months, it is important to pick up on the indicators and market the client appropriately.

Life stages, on the other hand, such as the birth of a baby, constitute a longer-term change that almost always entails purchases of new items not previously in the shopper's profile. In the life stage model, the company can constantly revise its marketing focus to keep up with the demands of its customers. Thus, you know that after the passage of a certain amount of time, there will be purchases of toddler clothes and toys, followed by swings, bikes, and so forth. As opposed to blindly advertising products throughout the customer base, marketing campaigns can be based on product portfolios developed to target the customer base. The life stage model helps the business understand what the customers want and when to adjust the corporate products and services portfolios to meet their needs.

Another example of a life event with purchasing implications is moving from one location to another. Inferences about moves could be made from other information sources such as local real-estate home purchasing files or change-of-address requests on credit statements. Since moves are usually accompanied by new purchases, this is a marketing opportunity for stores in the new location. Items such as window blinds and covers, carpeting, kitchen appliances, washer/dryers, paint, dishes, sheets, mattresses, and furniture are all good candidates for a new home buyer. Thus, a comprehensive offering can be provided where several of the different business subunits participate in selling their various goods. This is a good example of how the subunits gain more by participating with one another in marketing activities than they do by acting autonomously. Individually, the different business subunits do not really present much in the way of outstanding offers, but taken collectively, it becomes a very effective deal for getting the customer through the doors at their local stores. It also allows the customer to choose what is most appropriate for his or her needs.

Integrating Customer Data across Business Subunits

In order to facilitate the actual data mining process, it was decided that the set of data sources maintained by the separate business units would be combined and integrated. In order to do this, a composite view of the data needed to be generated to focus on the household rather than on specific individuals. For example, a husband and wife living at the same address would be considered one household. Roommates or other persons not sharing last names were still treated as separate individuals. The first step in the integration was to understand the file and record formats for each of these data sources (refer to Chapter 4, "Accessing and Preparing the Data," for more on this topic). In this case, the time constraints dictated that integration be based on exact matches among three different data sets obtained from three business subunits. Information maintained in common across these data sources included names, identification numbers and addresses. Based on a one-to-one matching rule, roughly 40-percent of the customer targets were found to be in agreement among the different data sets. Given that no special matching or cleansing routines were employed, this was a surprisingly high proportion of hits, although this number could obviously be improved with more advanced techniques, time and resources. However, since the goal of this exercise was to get a feel for the utility of applying data mining techniques to the data warehouse, this result worked out just fine. To handle the exceptions for the exact matches, a manual process was used to confirm the data for cases such as name variations, out-of-date addresses and different names at the same address. All of the combined information was then placed into a logical database that was based on the three separate physical files used during the integration. Since any data element represented a composite value that could potentially represent several different individuals, each record was assigned a unique household ID number. The resulting prototype data format was evaluated for its utility and acceptability by the business subunits.

Lessons Learned During Data Integration

Data integration was also taken a step further to incorporate demographic, psychographic and behavioral information from outside sources. These extra sources of information had a hit rate of over 80 percent (e.g., some portion of the name) with the integrated data set, a result that was initially met with enthusiastic response within the organization. However, the outcome was not ideal, and many important gaps remained, such as information about specific lifestyle characteristics (e.g., hobbies, household incomes, children, and so on) that would have been more useful in helping to focus marketing efforts. Thus, even though the integration of this outside information looked promising at first, it ultimately did not help with the overall marketing goal. This is an important lesson about data integration. More data do not necessarily guarantee a more interesting result. The new data have to be relevant to the overarching goal of the exercise.

There were some other lessons learned during data integration. First, it took a lot longer than had originally been anticipated to get the integration accomplished. This was due to a variety of factors, including getting the data sets delivered from the individual business subunits and converting them into a common format. It was also noted that the database administrators and the data architectures needed to be in place and well established before management and business consultants were brought into the loop to interpret the results. There were several instances in which the business consultants were required to address some tangential development issues while waiting for formatting issues to be resolved. In the early stages before all data sets were complete and integrated together, the analyses conducted by these consultants turned out to be somewhat limited because they were working with data sets that were still under construction. However, it is important to have the model designs and a general set of hypotheses established before the consultants begin in full force. That way, their time can be put to most effective use.

Using Visualization for Marketing Analyses

About half-way through this effort, the sponsor was introduced to the concept of visualization as a means to analyze the data. Up until that point, the main data mining technique had been some statistical sampling, clustering, and regression analyses. As in most statistical analyses, large-scale comparisons were performed across groups. It was soon realized, due to the large number of findings that had to be presented, that it was difficult to convey the results in a concise format. To address this problem, some data visualization approaches were explored. The initial visualizations presented were simply constructed and were prototyped to demonstrate a few different approaches. From these initial prototypes, some alternatives proved to be very worthwhile, and follow-up analyses were initiated.

Once some initial results were produced from the combined data sets, more advanced displays were introduced. One approach in particular used the representation of a 3D cube. Axes of the cube were set to represent the number of different departments visited by a shopper, frequency of trips to the store, and monetary outlay. Individual customers were presented as points within the grid. Customers were further coded according to the loyalty groups previously discussed, and this information was also conveyed in the display in terms of color coding or shaping of individual objects. The cube was set in motion by sequencing through each of the four years represented in the integrated data set. Thus, you could see how shopping patterns of customers changed during the time interval sampled. The grid showed hot spots (i.e., regions in the space representing large numbers of customers) and how these hot spots migrated through the cube space throughout the course of the sampled time cycle. At any point, a segment or cell of the grid could be reviewed to see what percentage of the data elements comprised that cell. This helped the company see how customer groups and profiles changed over time. Figure 14.3 shows a sample of the types of displays that can be produced using this method of visualization.

There was also another visualization that showed customer buying patterns as a function of geographical region. In this visualization, states were elevated within the display based on the classes of customers in those regions. The height of the state outline in the display increased with customer sales profiled in that region. As with most visualizations, the display could be interactively adjusted by using interface sliders that allowed the user to change the dates (1993–1996) as well as other parameters. Figure 14.4 shows a display representing the geographical patterns of customer buying profiles. The client was very pleased with this method of visualization as it provided a much more intuitive display paradigm than the traditional statistical and business graphs.

Figure 14.3 3D cube visualization of customer behavior patterns over time.

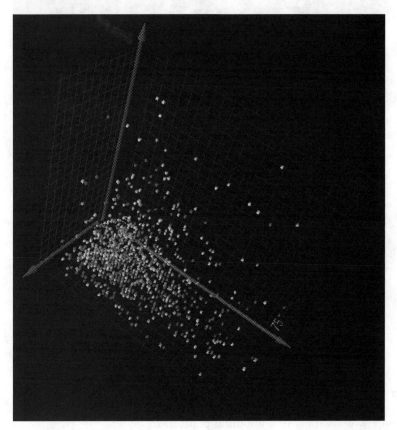

Although the prototype displays were indeed quite impressive and appeared to have a good deal of analytical potential, there were some issues in terms of the credibility of the information being presented. In some sense, the prototypes almost looked *too* good, and the client was uncertain as to how the visualization methods would perform when processing large amounts of data in more realistic settings. There were further practical reservations about using the visualization tool because it required specialized hardware and the software was specific to the hardware platform. During the visualization stage of the data mining project, the demos had to be run on special systems that had to be transported to the site. Also, the computing platform used in the Information Services department at the company was not compatible with the specialized hardware system. Thus, visualization was regarded

Figure 14.4 Geographical display of customer buying behaviors.

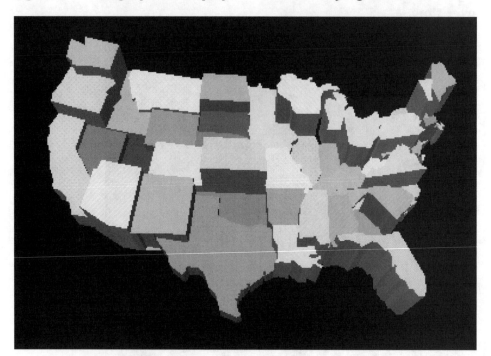

as an expensive presentation technique, and for that reason has not yet been fully accepted by the client. As reviewed in Section III of the book, however, this problem might have been avoided if the data mining team had chosen a visualization tool that runs on a wider variety of computing platforms.

This is not to say that the use of visualization within this environment was not effective nor will it be considered in the future. What occurred during this six-month effort was that the company wanted to know more about the business value of its data. Traditionally, the company was a vertically driven organization due to the strengths of the different business subunits. It needed to try and optimize the type and value of the customer contact made across the entire company. The company believed that this would help to reduce duplication as well as develop a stronger and more cohesive contact management capability which included marketing across business subunits. Finally, it wanted to maximize customer equity across the company to avoid marketing confusion and provide the necessary attention and recognition to its most highly valued customer base. The scope of the data mining efforts in this engagement proved to the company that indeed, it had the necessary resources and data to achieve its stated objectives. As the company continues to develop its infrastructure and provide additional resources to improve its analytical capabilities, visualization may start to become an integral part of its operating environment. The type of approach and software eventually selected will be based on a thorough evaluation of the market with additional prototypes developed to show and test the capabilities of each.

Videocassette Distribution

This particular case study describes data mining activities conducted in support of retail sales and distribution undertaken by two very large and successful retail organizations. In this case, a series of popular prerecorded videocassettes developed by one company (e.g., the client) was marketed and sold by a different company. The client initiated this study in order to learn more about how one particular channel of distribution, a national discount department chain, was selling its products. The client felt that the existing allocation strategy was too coarse and was resulting in inconsistent sales. The goal of this study was to gather information that would allow the client and the retail chain to target the right mix of distribution strategies and videocassettes to stores in order to maximize sales.

Traditionally, the client determined allocation of videocassettes to stores in the retail chain using sales figures from the most recent set of videos (in terms of volume). Stores were classified into high (the most sales), medium, and low (the least sales) categories. This rank determined the allotment of videocassettes to the stores in the next round of distribution. Note that the allotment was simply based on total sales; there was no categorization based on types of videos, geographical location, or other demographic factors. As you can imagine, this approach did not produce a very effective distribution of merchandise across retail outlets. As an example suppose that a store received a popular animated children's movie for a specific promotion. If the store had a lot of young family customers, this item might be in high demand, elevating the store into the high sales category. Based on the client's existing distribution process, this high-category store would receive a large shipment of the next video release, even if that movie had an adult-oriented theme. Should the store's customers not be interested in this kind of video, the store would be overstocked with the item and sales would decrease. Using this approach, the client was constantly readjusting distribution ratios to coincide with recent retail sales patterns. This readjustment had tangible costs in terms of return charges, scrap charges, airborne charges and lost sales. The client needed a better way of selectively distributing the videocassettes to stores based on actual sales data. The goal of this data mining exercise was to identify potential solutions to this problem.

In this section, we describe the development of a proof-of-principal prototype designed to address these issues. IBM performed the work through a combination of its Global Business Solutions Division and Research Division. The Global Business Solutions Division is responsible for working with Fortune 1000 businesses to define and develop data mining solutions. It identifies the applications (e.g., the problems), defines the solutions, and interfaces with the client. Its primary role in this consulting effort was to acquire the data and establish a baseline approach for developing a better allocation scheme for videocassette distribution. During the engagement, the Research Division within IBM complemented the efforts of the Global Business Solutions Division by focusing on the development of innovative and unique solutions for detecting patterns with complex data sets. The particular group involved in this activity, the Exploratory Visualization Group, is very interested in the use of visualization to support these types of tasks. More specifically, through internal research and development efforts and its contacts within the visualization community, the Exploratory Visualization Group's role in this data mining activity was to further refine the data and use visualization to help uncover and communicate critical patterns.

Sales of items offered during a special promotion, such as the release of a particular movie on video, may be described using a *decay curve* that plots sales over time. The shape of these sales decay curves will vary across industry segments. This function is referred to as a decay curve because sales are usually strong at the beginning of the interval and then drop off over time. A typical video sales cycle lasts for 45 days (on average, per store, per video). Some videos are offered as limited promotions and may only be on the shelves for a preset amount of time, whereas others might be stocked constantly. Assuming that a promotion is preceded by two weeks of advertising in local and national markets, roughly 75 percent of sales generally occur within the first 10 days of the promotion. Following that, the sales fall off (decay) substantially. Thus, there is a very narrow window in which to maximize the return on the marketing investment that has been made. Many customers come in to buy the videocassettes largely based on a combination of the advertising and general buying impulse. Videocassette sales are very profitable, so stores want to plan accurately and stock enough videos to meet demand but avoid overbuys.

Using Neural Networks to Segment Data Sets

This particular example provides a good description of how both visual and nonvisual data mining techniques can be combined to solve a problem. In this case, the Global Business Solutions Division was responsible for providing a high-level breakdown of the videocassette sales by each of the stores through the use of a Kohonen neural network algorithm. As you read in Chapter 6, "Nonvisual Analytical Methods," the Kohonen network facilitates automatic segmentation of data into categories defined by the network itself. In this example, the data given to the network were point-of-sale (POS) records provided by the distributor. The data used in the application represented the revenue and sales data of each video for each store over the past several years. These data included sales records for over 100 different video titles from over 2000 stores. There were tens of millions of records to be processed in the first round of classification. For these purposes, a set of 16 bins was artificially created for the Kohonen network to use in classifying its output. This was done to keep the number of separate categories manageable.

The data used in the study represented about three years' worth of POS records including the dates, times, amounts, stores, and videocassettes purchased. The data were collected by the distributor and provided to the client. Because this was just a proof-of-principle prototype, there was no reference to the size, profitability, or makeup of the individual stores or to the actual titles of the videos. As a result, the Kohonen classifications were based only on a limited amount of descriptive information. The data were normalized using some common statistical methods to neutralize the effect of large versus small stores sales volumes. The data were surprisingly clean and there were just a few problems with a minimal number of stores (e.g., zero sales for certain videos, less than the full three years' worth of data from certain stores, and so on). Any data not considered representative or conducive to the interests of the data mining activities were excluded from the analyses.

The outputs of the Kohonen network provided a way to better understand the general makeup of how stores clustered in terms of their sales performance patterns. Each store had a specific assignment to 1 of the 16 clusters. Although no objective rules for assignment of stores to clusters were provided within the neural net application, some categorizations were readily interpretable. As expected, some stores had better overall sales than others. Some of these were clearly mediated by other factors such as location and surrounding population. For example, stores in New York City tended to have large volumes of sales. More interesting, however, were patterns of differential sales across the sample of videocassettes. These patterns were much more complicated and this was the point in the analysis at which visual data mining techniques were introduced to provide some clarification.

Implementation of Data Visualization in Diamond

The visual data mining phase of the project was conducted by the Research Division. The particular tool chosen for the prototype was Diamond, which was developed by IBM. As described in Chapter 9, "Quantitative Data Mining Tools," Diamond can be used to look at data from a variety of different perspectives. Diamond can be run as a standalone application or it can be used as a series of callable API routines. (See the sidebar, "The Diamond API.") The Diamond API is cross-platform, and can be accessed from any user development environment (e.g., Visual Age C++, Visual C++, or Java). The API allows you to access 14 precomputed linked presentations and to create new presentations by recombining the building blocks (parts and views). The API includes an extensive mathematical function library and functions for manipulating data (e.g., joining additional data sets).

This exercise demonstrates how visualization can be integrated into an application using an API. In this particular application, IBM structured the system to take advantage of the flexibility offered through the use of the APIs provided through Diamond. The Research Division personnel were able to use a new 32-bit API version of the software in the application. Using the API routines, the Research Division was able to develop a customized interface to suit the needs of

The Diamond API

The Diamond application programming interface (API) allows you to integrate interactive visualization and analysis techniques into end-user applications. This API provides a library of visual representations of tabular data, automatically links the presentations to support color "brushing,"and provides a set of mathematical functions so that the application can include transformations and manipulations of the data. The API was designed to simplify the construction of applications incorporating interactive analysis, where all the marking, coloring, and data analysis operations are computed "on-the-fly."

An API-based approach to adding visualization addresses the problems of extensibility, customization, and data access. The Diamond API is designed to be called from applications on OS/2, Win32, and UNIX platforms. The application developer can call up predefined visual representations, create new "presentations" by mixing and matching the underlying "views" and "parts," or extend the API to include additional visual representations. In all cases, the presentations are linked in the sense that coloring or mathematical operations performed in any of the presentations are reflected automatically in all other presentations.

the client. The Research Division quickly generated a front-end data management facility written in Visual Age C++ that is used to launch the different visualizations developed in the application. The main interface developed for the client emulates what is normally found in an executive information management system. There is a simple "launch" interface developed to extract, populate, and present the data using a variety of different visualization paradigms. Since the interface is tied directly to the Diamond API, it provides a seamless integration for each of the displays that are used. As information is selected in one display (e.g., highlighted with colors), the API maintains this perspective across all of the displays through its active linking capability.

Adding Value to the Data

As already described, the neural network organized stores into groups according to similarity in sales revenues for the 100 videos. The data passed over to the Research Division contained 2000 rows (one for each store), a unique store ID, the store's

---

The API also includes an extensible library of mathematical and statistical functions that can be used to create, transform, and combine variables. The 14 precomputed presentations in the Diamond API include:

- Histograms
- Two-dimensional scatter plots
- Three-dimensional scatter plots
- Matrix of scatter plots
- Parallel coordinates
- Parametric snake plots
- Quad-wise plots
- Univariate statistics
- Bivariate statistics
- Fractal foam
- ICE: a 3D plot with glyphs encoding up to nine data parameters
- Cluster trees
- Correlation trees
- Raw data table

Figure 14.5 The structure of the data used during the videocassette analysis.

Case#	zipcode	Movie #1	Movie #2	Movie #3	Movie #4	Segment
1	20193	758	1604	1302	1201	10
2	95453	1103	875	485	594	7
3	68378	993	1291	922	852	11
4	13231	959	865	0	483	15
5	64838	357	343	949	499	4
6	10230	868	766	430	853	8
7	49494	1210	1321	985	929	2
8	68573	393	239	394	482	12
9	20393	338	495	223	0	10
10	11230	586	548	848	984	12
11	95832	887	688	348	385	3
12	49298	1012	784	1108	595	14
13	12311	499	491	944	958	11
14	12304	779	684	858	495	8
15	95858	385	432	319	394	4
16	22293	1292	1047	1020	1219	9
17	95938	868	876	592	498	2
18	33221	556	344	582	945	9
19	49392	963	954	985	394	9
20	11201	1531	1376	1034	943	13

location, and the sales data for each of the 10 best-selling videocassettes (see Figure 14.5). The models used to represent the data focused on the stores themselves. The values used to describe the videocassettes were always tied back to a store. This data set was enhanced by additional information about store locations in the hope that it might lead to the discovery of regional video preference patterns. Census data were also integrated in order to explore demographic characteristics associated with stores within particular segments. Census data can provide population-based information on age, household size, languages spoken, education, occupation, family income, and so forth. These data added information about the general make-up of shoppers in the various regions in which the stores were located. It was hoped that the integration of these external data sources would allow analysts to examine such questions as:

- Were stores with similar selling patterns located in certain geographic regions?

- Did the people shopping in stores within certain segments share demographic characteristics?

Store location information in this application was analyzed by store address. The Zip codes in these addresses were used as the key fields for joining census data into the sales record data, since the census records also contain Zip code information. Zip codes are particularly useful for this purpose because they are standardized five- or nine-digit numbers that are always used to represent the same geographical region (see the sidebar, "Using Zip Codes"). The application was also extended to include another data source from public sources that contained the geocoordinates of the Zip codes in terms of latitude and longitude. Thus the underlying data structure accessed by Diamond supported representation of Zip codes, latitude, and longitude values.

Using Zip Codes

In 1963, the U.S. Post Office came up with a new method to make the delivery of mail more efficient. It introduced the Zoning Improvement Program (ZIP) code system that assigned a five-digit Zip code number to all geographical regions in the country. Today, there are over 50,000 unique Zip codes, including military APO and FPO codes. The first digit of the Zip code designates 1 of 10 main geographical areas of the United States. Within each of these 10 zones, there are at least three states or territories. The remaining digits are used to further subdivide each of the zones into metropolitan areas and branch post offices.

More recently in 1983, the Post Office extended the Zip code to nine digits (Zip+4). This was done to define address areas more precisely, particularly in congested regions. This code is primarily used by business mailers. You can use the nine-digit code to specify an address down to its individual delivery route. Although the use of nine-digit Zip codes still remains voluntary, there are many benefits to using them. Not only are postage rates reduced for large-volume mailers, but the processing of items with nine-digit codes is more efficient. Thus, your mail is likely to be delivered more quickly if you use the nine-digit code.

Since the Zip code is such a structured, standardized, and well-accepted method of representing geographical locations, it is a good choice to use as a key variable to tie disparate data sets together. Along these lines, there is a service offered by the Postal Service called TIGER/ZIP+4 that can be used to relate the existing Zip codes to the U.S. Census Bureau's Topological Integrated Geographic Encoding and Referencing (TIGER)

Continued

Using Zip Codes (*Continued*)

database. Thus, using this capability, you can get information regarding the latitude, longitude, track, and Standard Metropolitan Statistical Area (SMSA). You can use this service to target your customers selectively by identifying desired characteristics within the census data. Then you can use the TIGER/ZIP+4 coupling to identify the specific Zip codes of interest that can then be matched against your customer databases. From here, you can send the mailers, product advertisements, or any other promotional materials to a very focused group.

Visualizing the Videocassette Retail Data

The team spent a lot of time exploring the data with the shrink-wrapped version of the software, and then designed four visual representations that it thought would be beneficial for the project. During this preliminary stage, analyses were conducted using the stand-alone Diamond product and an "API exerciser" before deciding which presentations and navigation paths to reveal to the user. The final choices included two pair-wise scatter plot displays for presenting geographic and demographic data, as well as two parallel coordinate diagrams showing the relationships between video sales and their segmentation by the neural network. All of the information presented within any of the different views is based on the same underlying data. The combination of these four views provided multiple linked perspectives on the same data, which is a trend in visualization applications that we believe will become more commonplace over the next several years (see our discussion of this and other future trends in Chapter 10, "Future Trends in Visual Data Mining").

The four navigational views of the data created for this application are called Geography, Demography, Products, and Relationships. There is also a "meta-view" showing how many stores are included in each segment. A consistent set of control interfaces is provided across these display windows. In each of these views, the user has control over brushing, variable selection, interaction method, and so on. These controls let the analyst apply any of three colors to data in any of the 16 different clusters produced by the Kohonen network. Once a segment is colored, the user can examine selling patterns in particular segments, the geographic distribution of stores in particular segments, and demographic characteristics of the people who live in (and shop in) those Zip codes where those stores are located. The interfaces also support an animation capability that steps through each of the 16 segments.

Geography The geography display shows the geographic distribution of stores colored by segment. Using a scatter plot, this application presents the stores (represented at points) plotted according to their latitude/longitude values. Just by sheer volume and placement of stores, you can easily discern the outline of the United States from the display. However, it was difficult to know exactly where the stores were located without any type of specific reference. Thus, the data were overlaid onto a map showing state boundaries. Diamond was extended to support this functionality. The vectorized maps used for this purpose were obtained from a third-party vendor. These types of maps are sold according to different levels of resolution ranging from counties to countries. In this case, high level maps of the outline of the United States and broad regions (e.g., Northeast, Southwest, Midwest, and so on) were used. If desired, this approach could have been extended as far down as Zip code areas. Figure 14.6 shows a stylized example of this type of display. (All figures used in this case study are conceptual replications of the original displays used in the application.) For these purposes, each of the vectors used in the

Figure 14.6 A modified pair-wise display used to show geopositional data in the videocassette application.

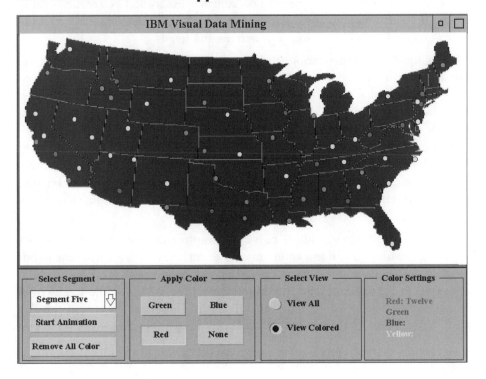

map became a plottable point within the diagram. Thus, users could achieve the appearance of an overlay by introducing a large set of points that corresponded to city, county, or state boundaries. Obviously, this technique could be applied to any type of vectorized background image or map. Very quickly, you can present the different categorizations of the data within this pair-wise display to see if there are particular biases in location.

Using the animation feature, you can have the system cycle through each value and watch to see if there are certain areas that tend to appear in certain geographical areas. For example, a lot of stores in Segment-4 tend to be located around the coastal areas of California; Segment-3 stores are more heavily represented in the Southeast; and Segment-15 appears mostly in Florida.

Demography The presentation of demographic data within this application is supported through the use of a parallel coordinates plot. Recall from our discussion in Chapter 9, "Quantitative Data Mining Tools," that a parallel coordinate breaks a record apart and shows all of its fielded values (e.g., its attributes) normalized across a set of vertical bars. Values for each record are connected as a series of lines across each of the bars—a form of connect-the-dots. Therefore, you can represent a considerable number of attributes in a parallel coordinates display and determine whether there are dependencies among their respective values. Understanding these relationships can be the key to uncovering new patterns and trends.

For simplicity, the interface of the Demography display has the same framework as the other displays (e.g., the bottom control panel). This display is used to show demographic characteristics for people living in store Zip codes colored by segment. The variables defined within the parallel coordinate display are shown as a set of vertical lines. In this application, the variables represented the proportions of families within a Zip code area with income under $25k, over $100k, proportion of individuals in a Zip code who went to college, were under 16 years of age, or were over 65. The horizontal lines intersecting these variables portrayed the data records for each of the stores encountered within the 16 segmentations.

Figure 14.7 shows an example of a demographics diagram for all Zip codes processed. The bottom and top values on any of the axes shown within the parallel coordinates diagram represent the percentage of people with the Zip code who correspond to that variable. So, for example, the .35 value for the over-$100k variable means that at least 35 percent of the families sampled within the Zip code had an income level in excess of $100k. As with all of the display interfaces

Figure 14.7 A parallel coordinates diagram showing demographic data in the videocassette application.

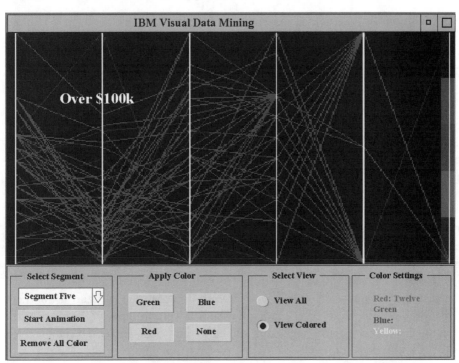

implemented for this application, the colors of the lines could be set to represent any of the 16 segments. Thus, you could dynamically color the display depending on the hypothesis being explored at any one point in time. Additionally, you could display only those segments with an assigned color. What this means is you could selectively include only those data segments of interest for an analysis.

To compare the different segments within the parallel coordinates displays, all that the user had to do was to make color assignments. Coloring Segment-12 for example, revealed a segment of mostly low-income people with some college education. Segment-3 had many more lower-income families (as many as 80 percent) and a much larger population of children under 16 and less college education (many with no advanced education). Segment-4 in comparison had higher income and higher education. Since all of the graphs were linked, it was easy to go back and forth between different views of the data. For example, the geography view showed that stores in Segment-3 tended to be located throughout the South.

Segment-4 stores, on the other hand, tended to show up more in larger metropolitan areas in the Northeast.

Relationships An alternative presentation of demographic data can be generated using the pair-wise relationships display. This display is based on the pair-wise format supported by Diamond. This display shows an x,y scatter plot of two variables from the Census data for all stores in the data set. Examination of combinations of bivariate demographic variables revealed some hidden clusters of the stores, especially when color was applied to different segments. For the purposes of the prototype, the variables used represented a percentage of families with income over $100k as a function of the individuals in the Zip code who were under 16 years of age. The variables used here were fixed, although the application could have just as easily have been outfitted with pulldown menus so that you could select the variables assigned to the different axes.

Products This display uses a parallel coordinates diagram to show sales performance for selected videos. Each entity in the display represents a different video. The Research Division narrowed their analyses down to the top 10 selling videos. In this case, each bar within the parallel coordinates became associated with the sales of a specific video; therefore, there were 10 bars. As seen in Figure 14.8, there were indeed notable differences among the sales of certain types of videos. By coloring the display to code the segment assigned to the stores, you could get a feel for what types of videos sold well in certain segments and what types had similar sales patterns across the segments.

Analyzing Allocation Strategies and Sales Patterns

The animation feature in the displays was used to better define the allocation strategy for distributing the videocassettes. For example, it was observed using a combination of the parallel coordinates for understanding demographic data and the pair-wise displays for plotting out the geographic proximity that the customer profiles in, say, California are quite diverse. One segment that was characterized by lower incomes, less formal education, and a larger percentage of children, tended to appear inland and away from the coast. Another segment with demographics of higher income and more college education was predominant along the coastlines. (There was, of course, some overlap. These are general trends.) Thus, instead of marketing videocassettes differently in Southern California than in Northern California, this analysis suggests that inland promotions should be structured differently than ones aimed at coastal areas.

Figure 14.8 A parallel coordinates diagram showing videocassette sales.

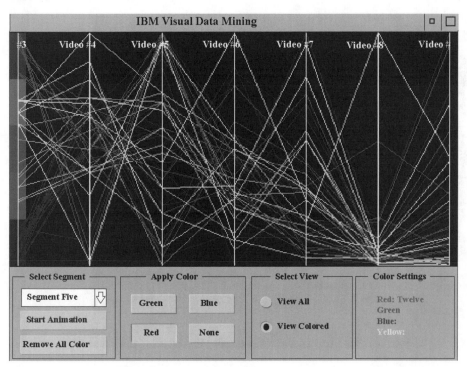

The analysts also investigated patterns of videos purchased together. It was discovered that there were indeed cassettes that sold well together; however, there were also cassettes that did *not* sell well together. There are many reasons for these findings, including a variety of demographic factors. This made it clear to the client that, for certain segments of stores, there are specific tapes that sell quite well together and others that do not. This information helped the client refine the distribution and allocation of certain tapes into stores with these categorizations. The Diamond visualization used to present these results was a directory display, which is a series of pair-wise displays. Since only the 10 best-selling tapes were used within this analysis, the resulting matrix was manageable in a single display. (If more items were included in the analysis, the Diamond interfaces could be modified to allow scrolling and other features.) Figure 14.9 shows an example of the display produced by this type of analysis.

The number of observations (stores) going into each of the segments could also be viewed within the system. This was done using a cube display. During this type

Figure 14.9 Using the Diamond directory display to expose cassette sale dependencies.

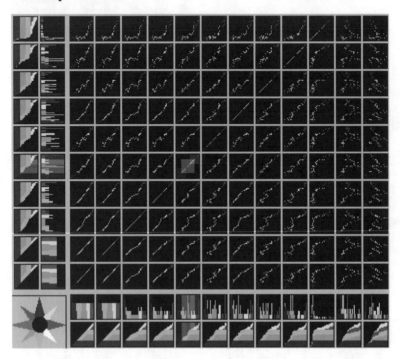

of analysis it is always important to know the number of records that go into producing a segment because that will help you determine how much weight you might want to place on any results derived using a particular segment. So, for example, Segment-0 represented a Spanish-speaking section of the population, but was defined in the Kohonen network by only about a half-dozen stores. Figure 14.10 shows an example of this cube display. It is slightly different than the cube display that ships with Diamond. (It is actually derived from another product called Ice and is part of the current API.)

Evaluating the Success of the Videocassette Sales Application

From the point of view of effort expended on development, the Diamond application was a great success. The application was created in less than a month from the time that the Research Division got the segmentation data. Some time and effort were spent acquiring the demographic data, and tying the POS records together

Figure 14.10 An Ice-Cube showing the size of the different segments.

with this data set using Zip code keys. The visualization portion of this effort took about a week to complete. Although this was an iterative process, refinements were made once there was a baseline system up and running. So after a month, the Research Division had a functioning and usable system that could be shown to the client for feedback.

As we said at the beginning of this section, the client's baseline distribution strategy was largely based on patterns of previous sales. From this exercise, however, the client was convinced of the value of segmentation in revealing geographic and demographic patterns in sales. In general, these latter types of patterns tend to be richer and more useful than the client had initially anticipated.

Of the four display types created for the application, the clients liked the geography displays the best. This was largely because this display emphasized features of the information that were not previously considered. For the most part, the clients thought that the sales of videocassettes were largely based on the region where the sale took place. The clients believed these regions would have certain characteristics in terms of the types of videos most preferred by customers. Thus, the allocation policy at the beginning of this engagement was to stock every store within a certain region in the same way. This was a gross oversimplification of the actual sales picture, as was illustrated during this data mining exercise. Once the client saw the data being presented as a set of segments, they quickly realized that the geographical region had less to do with sales than many other factors that could be represented in the application. Since there were multiple segments operating within close proximity to one another, the client could see how complex and intertwined a geographical region could actually be. In one particular example, there were two stores operating very near to one another (e.g., within a Zip code) although their segmentations (e.g., the store profiles) were completely different. Their demographic characteristics were vastly different from one another even though they were literally only a few miles apart.

The final point to note about the utility of the system was that the dynamic linking of views supported in Diamond was used to good effect in the analysis. The customer was impressed with this capability since analysts were able to get a complete picture of a segment by viewing multiple views at once. This capability greatly facilitated the process of deciding which of the relationships within or across segments were "actionable," and how widespread the effects of those actions might be.

Summing Up

This chapter presented two different types of retail data mining applications. In both cases, visualization was used to better understand the content of retail data sets and to help convey the information to the client. In the first scenario, the main emphasis was on providing more of an overall corporate marketing approach to expand the existing customer base. Much of what was discovered related to the over-stimulation and inundation of marketing contacts with customers. The engagement also focused on identifying life events and life stages to keep pace proactively with how customer needs were evolving. The second scenario had a more refined scope and was implemented as a proof-of-concept application. Specifically, it was concerned with using data mining evaluations to develop more effective distribution policies for videocassettes. The clients were surprised to learn of the diverse make-up of their distribution channels identified in the analysis, and made changes in distribution strategies to accommodate these new discoveries. From here we now turn our attention to financial data mining applications developed for use in monitoring stock market activity.

FINANCIAL MARKET DATA MINING

15

This chapter provides an overview of the use of data mining to facilitate portfolio management at a large pension fund. The company is a large U.S. institution that deals primarily in stocks, bonds, and real estate investments. The equity investments in question span many countries and industry groups to include several thousand businesses and literally millions of policy-holders. In fact, many readers whose retirement accounts were established since the early 1990s have probably been directly affected by the actions described in this case study. The total amount of money managed in the pension funds by this financial institution was over $150 billion dollars at the time of this engagement with approximately $30 billion invested in overseas markets. The portion of the portfolio involved in the data mining study was estimated to be in the neighborhood of $5 billion.

Background

As you probably know, policy holders usually choose among several options when selecting the type of investment strategies they want the corporation to pursue in managing their retirement accounts. They can opt for relatively safe approaches of putting the money into bonds and real estate (e.g., bonds floated to create new hotels, river walks, convention halls, sports stadiums, etc.). Returns on this option usually range between 8–10 percent annually. Alternatively, funds can be invested in the stock market where returns are gauged against a standard market index such as the S&P 500. Thus if the pension fund performs at 25 percent and the overall S&P performance is 20 percent, we can say that the fund outperforms the index and that the company has done a good job of portfolio management. Likewise, if the index is down 10 percent and the portfolio is down only 5 percent, the portfolio still outperforms the index. Remember that the index is an average of a large aggregate of stocks, so performing the same as the index means that you are getting only average returns (i.e., you are making Cs rather than As on your returns report card). The goal of the financial manager is to achieve the highest returns possible for the client, hopefully making more As and Bs than Cs.

What sorts of information does the financial analyst need to keep in mind when managing an investment portfolio for a client? First there are the characteristics of the individual funds themselves and the overall strategies that the analyst is using to maintain them. At a more microscopic level, there are at least 15 variables associated with each stock that are used to determine its relative position in the market at any given point in time. These variables are used to determine whether the stock should be bought or sold according to the guidelines and investment horizons specified in the portfolio. Variables to be monitored include price earnings statistics, return on equity measures, volatility statistics, results from technical analysis studies, and theoretical values on related derivatives. The money manager must determine movements in the market and other financial influences while making quick decisions to ensure that the portfolio maximizes its returns to its investors. It is difficult, however, to view so many sources of data in real time, to notice overall trends and to consider the distinct underlying characteristics of each security in a portfolio, especially when dealing with numerical formats. Now imagine that several thousand stocks and portfolios are being monitored at once and that the information is being presented in a textual and/or spreadsheet format. As we discussed in Chapter 5, the information processing demands of this situation would quickly exceed the cognitive limitations of the analyst or even a group of analysts. What is needed is a way to present information in a more manageable format that allows analysts to peruse large quantities of information and spot relevant trends. Thus, the company wanted to find ways to use visual data mining techniques to aid analysts in various aspects of their financial management activities.

Portfolio Management Operations

During this study, approximately 100 people within the institution were responsible for managing the equity portion of the business, which involves the purchase of international and domestic stocks. These people included portfolio managers, research assistants, and other support staff. Each portfolio manager within the institution was responsible for managing equities in a select region. The manager who was the focus of our case study was responsible for all markets in Asia including Japan, Thailand, Singapore, Malaysia, Indonesia, and Hong Kong. The markets within each country could potentially include hundreds and thousands of stocks. This manager was tasked with maximizing the return of this portfolio and needed to track the important changes for individual securities in order to expedite decisions about when to sell or buy them. As you can imagine, it is important to have a timely and informed decision cycle in the Asian markets because of their inherent volatility. Thus, market situation awareness was extremely important in this application.

However, it was difficult for the manager to isolate or identify the anomalies and outliers in any particular market due to the density of the information as well as the multiple decision elements that needed to be considered for each individual security.

The operating environment at that time consisted of fundamental data from a service that compiled earnings, estimates, projections, and other characteristics (e.g., dividends and book values) regarding various companies in the market. Another information source was derived from charting software that depicted stock performance over time in terms of technical indicators. There were also results from other quantitative analyses of derivative markets within Asia that affected equities of interest. Thus the portfolio manager was pulling data from news screens, technical analysis charting screens, fundamental databases on company health, performance, earnings growth, as well as their ancillary derivatives markets.

The institution had already developed a proprietary financial analytical system to fuse investment data derived from current earnings and other fundamentals, derivative aspects, price changes, historicals, and technicals. Unfortunately, the output from this integration process was presented to analysts *page by page* sorted by industry group and country in a spreadsheet format. To make matters worse, analysts also needed to consider information about future earnings such as consensus estimates generated from various brokers' opinions about the earnings projected for individual companies. Thus, the future earnings information also needed to be integrated with the other historical financial information contained in the database. As might be expected, this method of information presentation was not particularly useful to the portfolio managers because they were simply overloaded by the sheer mass of data. They could not make sense of the problem as they moved among pages. Further, they were unable to develop a "big picture" of the important trends contained within the spreadsheets. The company wanted to move from a spreadsheet format to an advanced visualization display to make the data more understandable, and to aid the managers with their analytical activities and decision support processes.

Trading firms and investment houses typically use personal computers to create graphical maps and charts as metaphors of their portfolios, and this firm was no exception. Unfortunately most of the graphical capabilities available to many analysts are very limited in their usefulness. For example, many of the systems used by the trading firm in this engagement depicted information by only limited means such as bar charts, pie diagrams, or at most, 3D surface maps. Several of these traditional, single-valued diagrams are shown in Figure 15.1. These formats could not achieve sophisticated integration and representation of data that portfolio managers could use to aid them in their analyses. Alternative means had to be

Figure 15.1 Traditional types of diagrams used to present financial data.

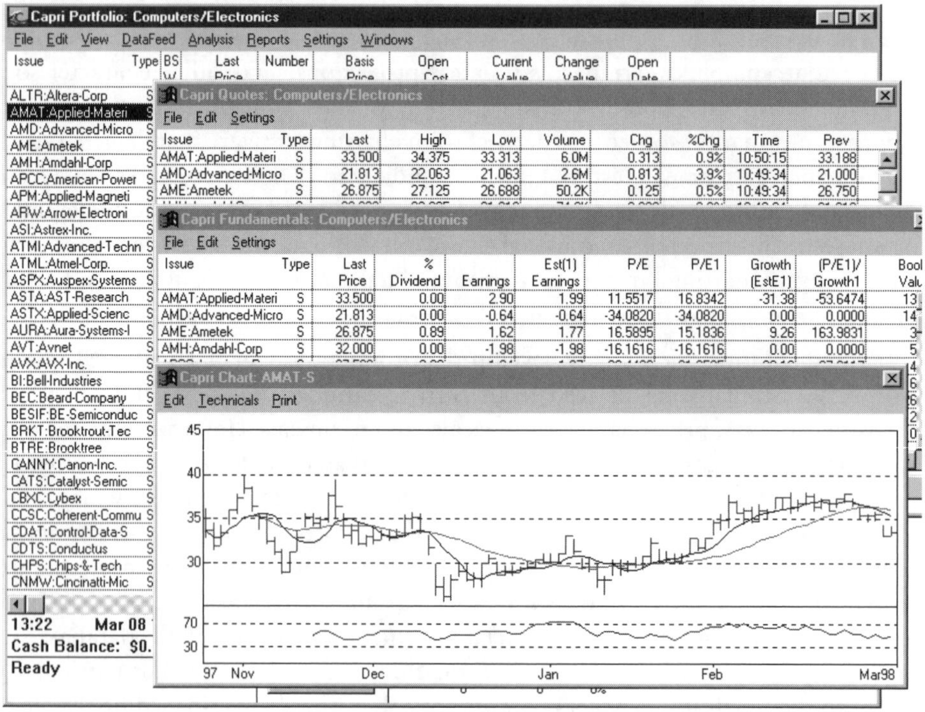

identified. The company chose Metaphor Mixer (MM) for this project because, at the time, it was the only commercial system that explicitly supported financial applications. Furthermore, MM could support a real-time virtual data mining environment, allowing the integration of both historical market data as well as up-to-date stock prices. This provided a method by which to integrate the different types of data required by the investment firm to satisfy their portfolio management needs.

Managing Investments in an Unstable Asian Banking Market

The data mining activity described here occurred between January and April of 1992 and involved investments made by the institution within the Asian markets for a particular actively managed indexed fund. For those who may remember, banks in Japan and other Asian countries became unstable and inherently volatile during that period. The prices associated with many of their stocks tumbled, producing record losses across the board. Even though the markets for all industries took a big drop, the banking industry was hardest hit. This narrative describes what happened with the Japanese banks, how this investment firm identified the weakness, and what they did to turn it into an opportunity to make record profits. Help with some of the financial terms described in this application is given in the sidebar.

Definition of Financial Investment Terms

This chapter makes mention of several terms used within the financial investment and management community. For clarity, we provide brief definitions of some of the more widely used terms. Although this list is by no means complete, it should help you gain a better understanding of the case study presented here.

Arbitrage. The buying and selling of equivalents in order to profit from a differential in price.

Bond. Security purchased as an investment for promised interest and principal payments. Straight bonds earn interest payments, called coupon payments, at regular intervals. The final interest payment and the principal are paid at a specific date of maturity. Bonds are issued by many different entities, including corporations, governments and government agencies. Bonds may be regarded as loans made by the investor with a guaranteed return. Zero Coupon bonds are purchased for less than their face value and pay no coupons.

Book Value. Stock value plus retained earnings divided by the number of outstanding shares.

Breakout. Occurs when the price of a stock falls above or below its resistance levels (prior highs/lows). Breakouts can signal a continuing trend in the direction of a stock's price, often spurring a buy or sell signal.

Convertible Bonds. Bonds that can be exchanged for stock in the issuing corporation at a specified price or conversion ratio. They have a coupon payment and their value, like all bonds, depends on the level of prevailing interest rates and the credit quality of the issuer.

Continued

Definition of Financial Investment Terms (*Continued*)

Derivative. A security whose fundamental value is derived from another underlying security. Derivatives include securities such as options or futures because they are derived from the price of the stock they represent.

Dollar Cost Averaging. A method of buying a security at regular intervals without regard to its share price. Thus, when the price is lower more shares are bought than when the price is higher. This results in the average cost per share invested with the security to be distributed out over its spread. You will see this technique often used with purchasing shares of mutual funds.

Earnings. Amount of profit or net income declared for a company during a specific period.

Earnings Per Share (EPS). Earnings reported by a company divided by its number of outstanding shares of stock for a specific time period. For example, if a company earned $5 million in one year with 1 million shares of stock outstanding, its EPS for the year would be $0.20 per share.

Fundamental Analysis. Means of evaluating stocks in terms of factors such as revenues, earnings, future growth, return on equity, and profit margins. The results from the analysis of fundamentals can be used to estimate a company's underlying value and potential for future growth.

Market Capitalization. The number of outstanding shares of a stock multiplied by the current market price.

Market Timing. An investor's attempt to time the ups and downs in the market in order to profit from purchases and sales of securities.

Market Value. The price at which investors buy or sell a security at any point in time.

Moving Average. Average value for a stock across a sample of successive temporal intervals. As an example, a 30 day moving average for a stock is calculated from 30 point measurements across successive days. A new moving average is computed for each successive point by throwing away the oldest point and including the next in sequence. The Moving Average can be used to infer the stability of the price of a stock across time.

Overbought/Oversold. Technical analysis descriptors for situations in which the price of a security has moved farther or faster in either direction than is justified by the fundamentals.

Price-to-Earnings Ratio (P/E). Sometimes called a "multiple," this measure is calculated by taking the price per share and dividing it by the earnings per share for the company's most recent four quarters. For example, if a stock sells for $15 a share and has earned $1.50 per share during the last year, then the P/E is 10 times earnings. A P/E contains little information on its own and is often used to compare a stock with other industry members.

Range. Difference between the highest and lowest price values of a security during a particular time period.

Retained Earnings. Those earnings that are not paid out in dividends by a company but are retained and used for buying down debt or other reinvestment.

Relative Strength. Ratio of a stock's price divided by a market index over a specified period of time. This measure can be used to determine how well a particular security is doing in comparison to the market as well as to other stocks.

Security. Anything of value that can be bought or sold with an expectation of making a profit. For example, notes, stocks, bonds, debentures, and certificates of interest are all securities.

Spread. The difference between the ask and bid prices of a stock.

Technical Analysis. Securities analysis based on market activity, usually involving such measures as price and volume. Results from technical analyses are used to predict future activity. *Continued*

> **Definition of Financial Investment Terms (*Continued*)**
>
> **Warrant.** A security entitling the holder to buy a specified amount of stock at some future date at a particular price.
>
> **Yield.** Income received for a security during a specified time period divided by its market price.

Metaphor Mixer (MM) was chosen for this application because its information terrain paradigm was an ideal representation for helping to manage the analysis of large quantities of complex financial data. (See Chapter 8 for a more complete description of the functionality of MM). The border elements (e.g., grid axes) defined within the application were configured to represent different target analysis groups. Along one dimension were the industry segments such as electronics, financials, construction, manufacturing, utilities, automotive, paper, and so on. On the other dimension were Asian financial markets including Japan, Thailand, Singapore, Malaysia, Indonesia, and Hong Kong. Figure 15.2 shows the border elements defined for this application. Multiple levels of abstraction could also be presented within the border elements by adjusting the breakdowns represented (e.g., various types of consumer electrical equipment, certain categories of automotive manufacturing, or even the orientation of the different financial investments used by the banks). Within each cell of the matrix produced by the border elements selected by the portfolio manager were objects that represented the individual stocks being traded within their respective markets. The objects, also referred to as chips, could be manipulated on several dimensions including color, shape, and presentation style (e.g., blinking and spinning) to convey further information about performance, behavior, and future projections.

The information terrain within this application depicted the stock data using a variety of display dimensions. The color of a particular stock in the display conveyed information about how well it was performing with respect to its market index. A red chip indicated that the stock was down in value from a previous posting (e.g., usually tied to a daily value) whereas a blue chip showed a positive value. The color gray signified no substantial change in price. The baseline of the MM display was set to the index of the market being analyzed. The height of the chips within the terrain showed how far above or below the index the particular stock was performing. A spinning chip indicated that a stock had attractive characteristics such as a low price-to-earnings ratio with high earnings potential (referred to as a low p/e-growth rate). Blinking was tied to certain arbitrage possibilities as

Figure 15.2 Information terrain border elements in Metaphor Mixer.

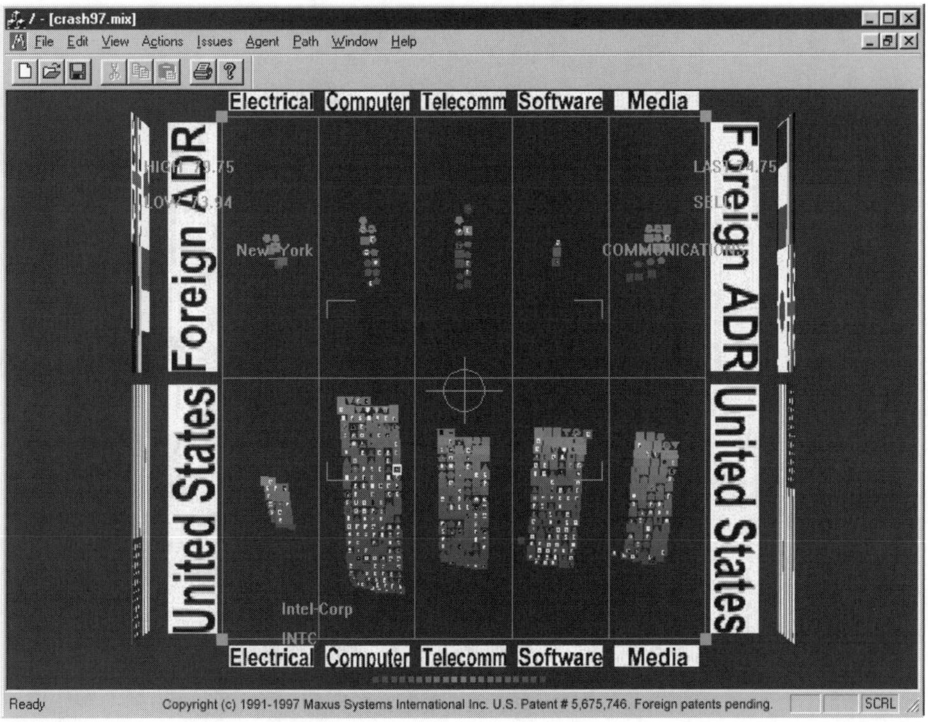

determined by the stock's options or warrants. If that same data element had an arrow vector pointing out, it would also indicate the stock had some sort of low technical indicator, such as a moving average. This provided a third decision element that reinforced the portfolio manager's judgment to buy a stock or look more closely at it because three very important outlier statistics had been flagged on that security element. Figure 15.3 presents an example of a MM display showing the different display characteristics for this type of information.

Within this MM application, the portfolio manager was able to incorporate as much knowledge as possible from the available information and make more informed and timely decisions. He was able to isolate anomalies and potential opportunities using a topsight display that allowed him to drill-down and focus on specific market indicators. This guided further investigation of various options and investment strategies. The portfolio manager also used the MM system to key in on estimates made by various brokers who were analyzing the companies in the index.

Figure 15.3 A Metaphor Mixer display showing a financial terrain.

At the same time, MM was fusing background information, real time data, and consensus estimates from brokers regarding projected earnings. Live news feeds could be scanned to look for keywords indicating earning surprises or shortfalls. As these were identified off the news service, the MM agent would pop up and drag the portfolio manager's viewpoint to that element and display the headline to the news wire story. This arrangement resulted in a decision space that integrated historical, current, and future estimates data into one model that supported situational awareness of the market at any given time. At this point, the institution had an operational visualization environment that allowed its portfolio managers to do screen searches and sorts on all of these integrated variables.

Because of their use of this MM application, the institution was one of the first firms participating in the Asian markets to identify the initial slide in 1992, identifying the price change collapse as well as other fundamental and technical analysis elements. One trend that was spotted early on involved equities and convertible bonds issued by the Bank of Tokyo. Depending on price, investors may want to trade convertible bonds like equities. A convertible bond with an "exercise price" far higher than the market price of the stock generally trades at its bond value, although the yield is usually a little higher due to its lower credit status. However, when the bond's share price is sufficiently high, traders want to use the convertible more like an equity. If the exercise price is much lower than the market price of the common shares, the holder of the convertible can convert into the stock attractively. Issuers sell convertible bonds to provide a higher current yield to investors and equity capital upon conversion. Investors buy convertible bonds to gain a higher current yield and less downside, since the convertible should trade to its bond value in the case of a steep drop in the common share price.

What happened in this case was that the investment firm saw that the equities issued by the Bank of Tokyo were decaying at the same time that convertible bond arbitrage opportunities were being made available. This was conveyed in the MM application by coding colors, heights, spins, and blinks to fuse the convertible bond information with that of the underlying bank's stocks. Analysts were able to see that market volatility was increasing by changes in the spinning and the blinking in the displays. However, there were also indicators showing that a convertible bond issue was available that could be swapped out for the stock. These behaviors were being displayed in real time in the application and when the big crash came and everything went red in MM (e.g., all the chips dropped below the baseline—see Figure 15.4), the firm had already safely ensconced most of their capital in convertible bonds. This was an important move because of the way the firm evaluated the performance of its investments. Specifically, the Japanese bank markets formed a major portion of the index against which performance was assessed. Thus, the firm wanted to participate in the banking industry because it comprised such a large portion of the index, and buying into the convertible bonds allowed them to be in the banking market without realizing losses when the stock prices dropped. In addition, the investment in the Bank of Tokyo's convertible bonds and others like it allowed the fund to maintain its currency in yen mandated for the portfolio's diversification requirements. By being alert to the growing sector instabilities and anticipating a sudden volatility spike, the portfolio manager took advantage of the situation. Below we will explain in detail how he was to surf the downside curvature of a convertible bond.

When the market crashed, the convertible bonds did not go down. Instead, they actually went up in price. This occurred because in the panic sell-off of the market, the Japanese government was forced to lower its interest rates. As with all markets, bond prices are inversely proportional to the interest rates. So when the rates are

Figure 15.4 A MM information terrain showing the 1992 collapse of the Japanese banking market.

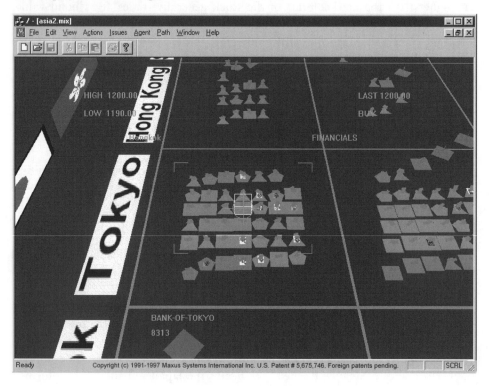

lowered, bond prices increase. On average, the Japanese stocks dropped over 15 percent in value while the convertible bonds increased 10 percent in the same time interval. This meant that the pension fund outperformed the market by 2500 basis points. (To say that this was a good outcome is a gross understatement.) Thus, it was an intelligent move in terms of identifying a weakness and finding the attractive alternative possibilities. This investment tactic would likely not have been pursued without the use of MM. That is, the firm used MM to fuse the real-time data with the arbitrage information and the historical earnings estimates into one display state in addition to sorting by industry groups and countries. This allowed them to see early on that the weakest part of the industry was the Japanese banking sector. Thus on April 8, 1992, when the market took its hit, the portfolio managers were sitting pretty because they had already been able to predict the collapse and redirect some of their Asian banking investments into convertible bonds. This resulted in an initial gain of approximately $10 million dollars. Had they not taken this action they might have lost between $30 and $40 million, so the "real" net gain approached $40–$50 million dollars. The institution has maintained their investments in convertible bonds, and over the past several years the Japanese banks have still continued to decay. However the fact that much of the investments were swapped into convertible bonds early meant that they never lost ground. The investments were always in the index with the stock, and they were earning a rate of return from convertible bond interest instead of getting nothing from equities.

Managing Declines in the Technical Sector

A crisis similar to the Japanese banking crash occurred in the summer of 1996 in the U.S. technology sector. The crisis was identified in MM using similar information fusion techniques as those employed in the Asian market application. In this case the recovery of the market was also tracked. Red icons in the MM landscape grid depicted drops in stock prices below the baseline. Quaking in the icons depicted further day-by-day drops and spinning icons showed low price-to-book ratios. Blinking was keyed to high returns on equity. Figures 15.5 and 15.6 show sample MM displays depicting the U.S. technology market information.

During the period initially following the crash, all of the stocks were below baseline and were, not surprisingly, oversold. The challenge was to determine whether anything might be salvaged from the situation. Although the stocks in question were shown to be below baseline in the MM application, analysts were able to determine that some of these stocks might be good investments because some of their other fundamental indicators (shown as arrows on the icons) started to show upward trends. That is, the analysts were able to determine that even though the technology sector had bottomed out, certain stocks showed behaviors that made them less risky for investment at that time. The type of data visualization provided by MM helped the financial managers to determine which of the hundreds of stocks merited further attention, even within a market that had recently crashed. Note that there was no magical black box that told the analyst when to buy, but the use of visualization allowed knowledgeable analysts to make the most of the information at hand.

The information maintained in the MM terrain during the technology crash episode can be replayed using MM's VCR feature. Analysts in the company can replay a movie that includes data collected over 3–4 months before, during, and after the crash. The VCR replay shows when stock prices bottomed out, identifies which interests and industry groups were most severely affected, and shows the return of certain key stocks within the overall population.

Figure 15.5 Visualizing the technology sector within U.S. markets using Metaphor Mixer.

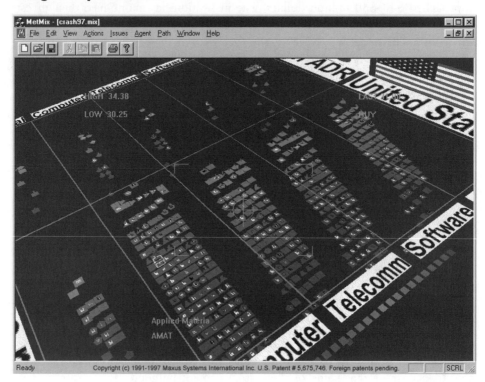

Discovery of Insider Trading Patterns

Using what would eventually become the MM inference engine, the investment firm developed an application that displayed the activity profiles of a set of stocks that were members of an Asian index. In this application the analysts were particularly interested in monitoring patterns of trading volumes of a set of Japanese stocks. One of the most salient stocks identified by the institution was a large Japanese-based corporation that was cyclically manipulated in an insider trading scam by a group of Japanese investors. Regular patterns of volume spikes were discovered in the trading data for this stock. The patterns began with an initial day of elevated trading that would move a set of stocks up 5–10 percent in value (see Figure 15.7). The elevated trading would last up to five days. This initial period was then followed three to six months later by a precipitous drop in prices. The pattern occurred with remarkable regularity and, as it turned out, signaled the operation of an insider trading scam.

Figure 15.6 The bottom of the technology market shown using Metaphor Mixer.

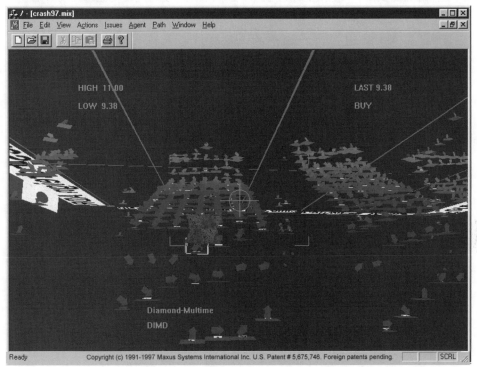

Since any of the stocks being manipulated were typically poor performers, they were likely to be underweighted within the portfolios maintained by investment managers (see the sidebar on Insider Trading). The frenzy of buying by the insider traders significantly inflated the price of the stock, thereby causing a big delta in the index ratios expected for the portfolio. Large portfolio managers then purchased the stock, the insider traders sold at the higher price, and the portfolio managers took a loss as the price eventually fell back to its true price range.

Once the pattern of insider trading was discovered using MM, the portfolio manager at the investment firm was able to avoid losses on this stock. The manager purchased only enough stock to achieve market weight, so that the investment could track with the index. However, the manager did not overpurchase the stock, thus setting himself up for a loss. That is, since the manager knew that the price was going to fall, he arranged his investments so as to shield against any index fluctuations

Figure 15.7 A volume spike of trades depicted in the MM landscape.

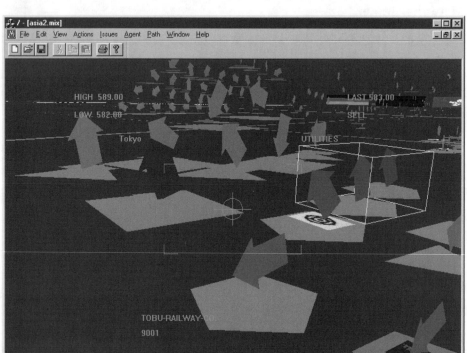

One Type of Insider Trading Scam

Certain unscrupulous firms in the early 1990s were well known for their involvement in insider trading scams. One particular scheme that was discovered by this investment firm before the plunge of the Japanese banking system was based on the ability of others to inflate the prices of individual stocks being traded within an indexed portfolio. Basically, a group of investors would illegally make organized acquisitions of certain stocks that had been historically poor performers, and would buy large quantities of these stocks at relatively low prices. This action artificially inflated the price of the stocks. The investors would then spread false rumors about the projected worth of these stocks in order to drive up their prices even more, usually on the order of 30–40 percent. Once this occurred, they would then call up pension funds to try to get them to while selling out of the stock as it hit its highest level. Thus, by discovering this pattern of insider trading, our investment company was able to beat the inside traders at their own game using legal means, thus saving their clients millions of dollars. As it turned out, the insider traders became aware of the actions of the investment firm, and believed that a pension fund manager must have been receiving leaks of inside information from someone involved in the scam. Nevertheless, they were hardly in a position to do anything about it since any complaint would have drawn attention to their own illegal activities. (Little did they know that it was sophisticated data mining analysis, rather than information leaks, that had given them away.)

commit portions of their capitol to meet or exceed index guidelines. After the buy-ins, the investors would sell out of the stock, taking all of the profits with them. The stock would then collapse since its trading price was falsely driven up, and the pension funds would be left with significant losses.

This scam works because the stocks being influenced belong to an index-rating, but they are stocks that the portfolio manager either does not want to own or wants to under-weight (i.e., buy smaller quantities of) because of their historically poor performance. Remember, the goal of the investor is to track or outperform the index. Thus, if you own shares of an indexed stock at market weight (e.g., a certain percentage of your portfolio) and that stock goes up 10 percent, your portfolio keeps up with the main index, which will have also (hypothetically) gone up 10 percent. Now let's say you are not at market weight for a particular stock (i.e., you don't own very much of it) because you do not regard it as a good performer. Should that stock suddenly have a 10 percent increase, you will still make money, but you will make less than you would have if you purchased enough of the stock to be at the market index weight. Thus, porfolio managers generally try to be at or near the market index weight with their stock investments. In the insider scam, however, the price of the low performer stock is being artificially manipulated by external factors unknown to the portfolio managers. Thus as the stock price increases, many pension fund managers might unwittingly buy more of the stock to keep their portfolios weighted with the index once they see that the stock price has started moving. However, when the bottom eventually drops out, they will lose a significant portion of their investment.

It Pays to Keep Careful Records

There is an interesting follow-up to this tale. Almost two years later, the particular Japanese company in this example along with some of their colleagues were investigated by the SEC for suspicious stock dealings. Not surprisingly, the investigation revealed that these investors were involved in a good deal of insider trading within certain markets. Once their suspicious activities had been flagged, these insider traders were anxious to share the brunt of the SEC's attentions with as many companions as possible. To deflect the investigation away from themselves, the insider traders tried to implicate the large pension fund in the scheme as well, offering as evidence the similar investment trades conducted by that fund during the interval in question.

What was not known by either the Japanese traders or the SEC was that this financial fund was legitimately trading by the numbers—they had just been smart enough to discover the stock price patterns described earlier, and to act upon them accordingly. So when the SEC visited this pension fund looking for information regarding the trading activity for a specific event that occurred over two years prior, the portfolio manager was easily able to show the MM analysis to the SEC investigators, using the same visualization application employed in the original analysis. This points out another important issue that we have discussed throughout the book regarding the justification and presentation of results. Visualization is a very powerful tool for conveying a large quantity of information in a manner that is readily apprehensible. When asked to produce a justification for their investments, the institution did not have to go through mounds of paper to produce the evidence that the SEC needed to see. You can imagine what all of the raw data would have looked like—it would have been a morass of information including company reports, price change data, select balance sheet information, historical earnings, book values, highs, lows, closes, volumes, and so forth. Instead, the portfolio manager was able to go a succinct diagram generated from MM that made the motivations for the original trades clear to the investigators. Once they understood the data mining analysis, the SEC investigators quickly refocused their efforts back on the Japanese investors.

Summing Up

Wall Street and other financial markets are increasingly turning to the use of visual data mining techniques to deal with large quantities of data. This chapter introduced a set of data mining applications in which Metaphor Mixer (MM) was used to discover and analyze some very complicated patterns of data within the Asian financial markets. One of the MM applications was used to identify a significant downward trend in the Japanese banking system by taking advantage of financial indicators that were modeled at the time. By visually presenting all of the variables within the market, the institution was able to discover this trend early and respond by moving some of their risky investments into more secure and convertible instruments. Thus the fund was well prepared when the collapse occurred. The other application was helpful in revealing a pattern of insider trading by a Japanese firm. Managers of the fund were able to take advantage of the situation legally by adjusting their own acquisitions so as to maximize profits as stock prices were artificially manipulated by this insider trading. The use of data mining was instrumental in this situation because it not only helped the fund managers to discover the pattern but was also used to justify buying and selling behaviors to the SEC when they investigated the matter several years later. We now turn to the final chapter in this section where we describe a data mining application used to identify patterns of money laundering.

MONEY LAUNDERING AND OTHER FINANCIAL CRIMES

Detecting, investigating, and prosecuting financial crimes are monumental tasks. Financial crimes in the United States range from real estate scams and loan-back schemes to dual price assets looting and cash receipt falsification. Mechanisms for identifying these crimes and others are constantly being considered and developed. One goal of investigators is to *deter* money laundering activities by seizing the profits associated with criminal activities such as drug trafficking and illegal narcotics operations, white-collar crimes including embezzlement and fraud, unreported gambling and lottery winnings, and organized crime operations. However, effective targeting of individuals and enterprises engaged in these illicit activities requires review and analysis of large volumes of information stored in federal and state data sets. The data mining process used by investigators to understand these data involves several steps. First, the data of interest in the investigation must be accessed and integrated, taking into account the fact that data formats will differ across sources. The second step usually involves visualizing, linking, and interpreting the known and implicit interactions, complex relationships, and patterns of activity contained in the data. Finally, the third goal of these data mining investigations is to produce results that will be acceptable and understandable to criminal investigators, lawyers, judges, and juries. This chapter provides an overview of a data mining system that was configured to assist in the detection and characterization of financial crimes and money laundering activities.

Background

Money laundering is a term applied to any process that is used to take the monetary proceeds of illegal activities and transform them into assets that appear to have been legitimately obtained. Money laundering usually involves the conversion of large amounts of cash into legitimate funds. Laundering this cash is essential to many ongoing criminal operations. From the law enforcement point of view, these funds are most easily detected at the point in which they first enter a legitimate financial system. Federal and state law enforcement agencies must be able to detect and identify those people and organizations that are actively involved in laundering money. Resources, systems, and procedures must be constantly enhanced to keep pace with the estimated 100–300 billion U.S. dollars that are laundered each year.

Financial Reporting Regulations

One of the ways in which money laundering activities can be discovered is through analysis of data reported by financial institutions concerning certain types of monetary transactions. Financial institutions are required to comply with federal statutes specified in the Money Laundering Control Act of 1986. Compliance with the Bank Secrecy Act (BSA) reporting requirements by regulated filing institutes such as banks, savings and loans, and credit unions has significantly improved over the past several years. This is due in part to the large number of audits that are performed—with severe fines and penalties (civil and criminal) assessed to noncompliant institutions. Since these regulations have been imposed on banks, there has been a trend for money laundering operations to move to other types of businesses that are not so tightly regulated. These tend to be businesses that routinely process large cash transactions. Some examples include currency exchange houses (casas de cambio), automotive dealerships, jewelers, security brokers, and casinos.

The regulations imposed on banks and other financial institutions were designed to generate a paper trail that could be used to track the path of money as it moves through the system. There are several different types of forms that must be filed when a cash transaction of currency for more than $10,000 is conducted. Banking related industries are required to file an IRS Form 4789—*Currency Transaction Report* (CTR). Businesses such as car dealerships, jewelry stores, and any other retailer dealing with large dollar merchandise are required to file IRS Form 8300—*Report of Cash Payments over $10,000 Received in a Trade or Business*. Additionally, casinos need to file IRS Form 8362—*Currency Transaction Report by Casinos*, and any international travelers file Customs Form 4790—*Report of International Transportation of Currency or Monetary Instruments* (CMIR). Finally, those people that maintain foreign bank accounts are required to file Treasury Form TD F 90-22.1—*Report of Foreign Bank and Financial Accounts* (FBAR). There is even a special form called a *Suspicious Activity Report* (SAR) TD F 90-22.47 that is submitted by financial institutions for any suspicious financial transactions, including those under the $10,000 trigger. It is also illegal to "structure" a series of transactions to avoid the $10,000 threshold. For example, you cannot legally fool the financial institution into failing to file a CTR report on you by making three deposits of $9000 instead of one $27,000 deposit. Figure 16.1 shows an example of a CTR form and illustrates that there is a lot of information included in these reports.

Figure 16.1 A standard Currency Transaction Report (CTR) form.

Form **4789**
(Rev. October 1995)
Department of the Treasury
Internal Revenue Service

Currency Transaction Report
Use this 1995 revision effective October 1, 1995.
For Paperwork Reduction Act Notice, see page 3.   Please type or print.
(Complete all parts that apply–See instructions)

OMB No. 1545-0183

1 Check all box(es) that apply:
a ☐ Amends prior report   **b** ☐ Multiple persons   **c** ☐ Multiple transactions

Part I Person(s) Involved in Transaction(s)

Section A–Person(s) on Whose Behalf Transaction(s) Is Conducted

2 Individual's last name or Organization's name	**3** First name / **4** M.I.
5 Doing business as (DBA)	**6** SSN or EIN
7 Address (number, street, and apt. or suite no.)	**8** Date of birth M M D D Y Y
9 City / **10** State / **11** ZIP code	**12** Country (if not U.S.) / **13** Occupation, profession, or business

14 If an individual, describe method used to verify identity:
a ☐ Driver's license/State I.D.   **b** ☐ Passport   **c** ☐ Alien registration   **d** ☐ Other.................................
e Issued by: **f** Number:

Section B–Individual(s) Conducting Transaction(s) (if other than above)
If Section B is left blank or incomplete, check the box(es) below to indicate the reason(s):

a ☐ Armored Car Service   **b** ☐ Mail Deposit or Shipment   **c** ☐ Night Deposit or Automated Teller Machine (ATM)
d ☐ Multiple Transactions   **e** ☐ Conducted On Own Behalf

15 Individual's last name	**16** First name / **17** M.I.
18 Address (number, street, and apt. or suite no.)	**19** SSN
20 City / **21** State / **22** ZIP code	**23** Country (if not U.S.) / **24** Date of birth M M D D Y Y

25 If an individual, describe method used to verify identity:
a ☐ Driver's license/State I.D.   **b** ☐ Passport   **c** ☐ Alien registration   **d** ☐ Other.................................
e Issued by: **f** Number:

Part II Amount and Type of Transaction(s). Check all boxes that apply.

26 Cash In $ _____.00   **27** Cash Out $_____.00   **28** Date of Transaction M M D D Y Y

29 ☐ Foreign Currency _____ (Country)   **30** ☐ Wire Transfer(s)   **31** ☐ Negotiable Instrument(s) Purchased

32 ☐ Negotiable Instrument(s) Cashed   **33** ☐ Currency Exchange(s)   **34** ☐ Deposit(s)/Withdrawal(s)

35 ☐ Account Number(s) Affected (if any):   **36** ☐ Other (specify)

Part III Financial Institution Where Transaction(s) Takes Place

37 Name of financial institution	Enter Federal Regulator or BSA Examiner code number from the instructions here. [ ]
38 Address (number, street, and apt. or suite no.)	**39** SSN or EIN
40 City / **41** State / **42** ZIP code / **43** MICR No.	

Sign Here

44 Title of approving official	**45** Signature of approving official	**46** Date of signature M M D D Y Y
47 Type or print preparer's name	**48** Type or print name of person to contact	**49** Telephone number ( )

Cat. No. 42004W

Form**4789**(Rev. 10-95)

Please keep in mind that moving more than $10,000 in cash is neither illegal nor prohibited. To the average person, this seems like a large quantity of money. However, for cash businesses these kinds of transactions are not unusual. Consider the cash sales of concessions (e.g., drinks, food, souvenirs, etc.) at a sporting event. If you sold 2000 cups of beer (@ $5.00) along with 1000 hot dogs (@ $3.00) plus 1000 bags of peanuts (@ $2.00) you would have $15,000 in cash to deposit. You can imagine what a stadium capacity crowd will generate. The same applies to fast food establishments, gas stations, convenience stores, amusement parks, transportation services, and so on. This money must be deposited so that it can eventually be utilized to pay bills, purchase goods, or be reinvested. When the money is generated from legitimate means, there is nothing to worry about. However, should a drug dealer try to convert cash gained from drug sales into "laundered" cash or usable assets, we have a different situation. It is these patterns of turning illegal profits into legitimate resources that law enforcement agencies try to pick up on and pursue.

BSA regulations have also been adopted that require financial institutions to aggregate multiple transactions daily among branch offices and to verify the identities of their customers to better target and structure violations and violators. The consistent filing of these forms by financial institutions is a crucial element in the detection and tracking of money laundering crimes. Federal and state agencies make regular use of the data in these forms. Thus, the role of financial institutions in filling out and submitting these forms is an important step in the identification and prosecution of money-laundering activities.

Regulatory Agencies

There are a wide variety of agencies that are involved in the detection and prosecution of financial crimes. They range from state level agencies such as the Attorney General's offices, Departments of Public Safety, and Financial Crime Task Forces all the way up to the federal government. A diverse set of federal agencies such as the DEA, FBI, Customs, and IRS are very active in this arena. More importantly, the Financial Crimes Enforcement Network (FinCEN) has been exclusively tasked to perform investigations in this particular area both domestically and internationally. FinCEN frequently enlists the support of individual states to help round out and coordinate the types of investigations being pursued.

FinCEN has developed a system called FAIS (Financial Artificial Intelligence System) that is used to analyze the tens of millions of financial transactions reported every year. FAIS is a comprehensive system that has been used to initiate a number of investigations. Since there are no formal domain models for detecting money launderers, FAIS uses a set of sophisticated rules, heuristics, weighting functions, and visualizations to identify anomalies and potential suspects from their databases. The types of patterns that FAIS has been programmed to detect are extensive. There are hundreds of rules defined within FAIS to examine factors such as frequency and volumes of transactions. For example, a corner convenience store located within a large city might be expected to do about $250,000 worth of business annually. However, if the same volume of business were observed for a rural store, this finding might be of interest and therefore weighted more heavily in FAIS models because it is unexpected. The FAIS system can also examine the frequency of cash transactions to determine whether they are consistently filed throughout the year. Since all of the rules triggered within FAIS produce a weighting (e.g. one method of defining a proactive slice of data), those individuals with a high score will be targeted for further investigation. FinCEN also looks at driver licenses, vehicle registrations, boat registrations, department of corrections records, doctors' licenses, lien files, and other information sources when conducting their investigations.

To help FinCEN and other agencies recognize the perpetrators of financial crimes, an application has been developed that uses FAIS and several other data sources. This application currently is configured to use both CTR and CMIR data. This allows analysts to observe transactions of U.S. bank accounts as well as the money moving across international borders. Many federal agencies also use the CASINO and 8300 forms as well. By presenting these data in a visual format, the analysts can quickly identify high volume accounts, closely interacting associates, and affiliations between or among people, locations, organizations, identification numbers, filing institutions, and accounts. The system also provides mechanisms to show enterprise structures, common connections, name aliases, and even the best times to move against suspect accounts.

Discovery in Financial Crimes Analysis

Money laundering is a worldwide problem. All of the leading economic countries have some sort of laws and law enforcement personnel who deal exclusively with these types of investigations. In recent years there has been increasing cooperation and involvement among countries. Much of what we will discuss in this chapter stems from input received from a variety of state, federal, and international money laundering experts. Therefore the approaches that we discuss *are not specific to any one agency*. You should remember that this domain is unique in the sense that the discovery of even one illegal action during a data mining engagement constitutes an actionable result. That is, if you can discover a set of illegal monetary transactions, a case can be made and the individuals involved can be targeted for further investigation. You do not necessarily have to amass a myriad of observations in order to show a general trend. In this context the analyst is less concerned with predicting future patterns than with detecting illegal actions that have already transpired. The examples provided in the remainder of the chapter are based on real world events that actually occurred. All names, addresses, accounts, identification numbers, and other descriptive information have been changed for this presentation although the structure of the relationships presented are valid.

Analyzing Financial Crime Data

The data mining process used by financial crime investigators to understand BSA data is identical to that used in other application areas and can be divided into three stages. The first stage, *data preparation*, subjects the data to a series of processes designed to access and integrate the various formats and structures encountered in each data set. The second stage, *information analysis*, supports a variety of analytical approaches including data visualization tools, link analysis techniques, and heuristics procedures that are used to interpret the implicit interactions and complex activities contained in the data. The third stage, *presenting results* is used to generate the final diagrams that are necessary to convey the results of the integration and analysis stages to other investigators or third-party affiliates. Figure 16.2 shows a diagram of this process.

Traditionally, much of the emphasis in this process has been placed on the collection and reporting of data with few resources applied to actually performing analysis. Ideally, the majority of time and effort should be placed on analyzing and understanding the contents of the data. Increased emphasis on analysis would improve the accuracy, reliability, and productivity of analysts and would save a

Figure 16.2 Money laundering data mining process.

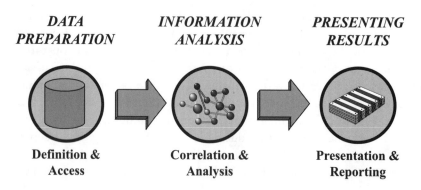

DATA PREPARATION	INFORMATION ANALYSIS	PRESENTING RESULTS
Definition & Access	Correlation & Analysis	Presentation & Reporting

considerable amount of time and money. There are a number of issues connected to each phase of the data mining process, many of which are discussed next.

Data Preparation

A domain that requires the analysis of data, including complex financial crimes and money laundering investigations, necessitates the development of formal models of interaction. These models are best derived directly from the analyst/investigator working in the domain. The format and content of the data sources also have a large influence on the type of model (or application) that can be developed. There are a series of steps that should be considered during the data preparation phase that directly contribute to the development of a functioning model that reflects the requirements of the analysts. These steps are data collection, data modeling, data integration, and data integrity and security assurance.

Data Collection

Before any system can be developed to analyze and report intelligently on data, the data must be made available. This basic requirement is not always easy to fulfill. In the majority of cases, there are online database systems and files that can be obtained directly without any special procedures, protocols, or access privileges. In the financial crimes arena these include state versions of CTR/CMIR, automobile registrations, and real property records. Most of these data sets are stored in relational structures that can be queried to access the desired information. However, there are systems in which the information is not in a usable format, either because there is no way of distinguishing (or describing) the data in order to retrieve it, or because it does not reside in available resources. For instance, CTR/CMIR forms do not indicate the gender of the person performing the transaction. It is not always possible to generate gender information from the names provided, especially when initials or abbreviations are used. In other cases access to data sources might be restricted by limited access privileges (IRS Form 8300), copyright infringements (NEXIS/LEXIS), or related security issues (NCIC).

Another problem with data access is that many systems require their users to aquire data through front-end menu facilities without any way of performing batch executions, which are back-end mechanisms used to extract large volumes of data. (We mentioned data access problems such as this in Chapter 4.) In many of these cases, data must be cut and pasted manually between systems. Furthermore, in a large number of systems, the report/query generation capabilities that are available do not meet the requirements of the analyst. Precanned reports or fixed queries tend to serve the general population of requests, which will inevitably produce too much or too little information for a particular need. When the data are available, typical proactive BSA data requests extract all records for a particular region, date frame, subject, port-of-entry, or even dollar value. These data eventually are visualized in an environment in which analysts have complete control (via a point-and-click interface) over any subfilters or inquires that are made. Furthermore, the analysts can request updates to this working set of data at any time.

Collection of BSA data is a resource-intensive process for those institutions that are required to fill out the forms. In many places, the process is still done manually. Facilitators (usually bank tellers) must complete all fields in the form by hand. As you can imagine, each facilitator does this task slightly differently and the transactions themselves have varied structures. The forms are usually reviewed for accuracy and content by the bank's compliance officer and are then entered into a computer system. Most banks generate these forms electronically, although some do not. In the latter cases, the hardcopy forms are sent directly to the U.S. Treasury Department at the Detroit Data Center where data entry clerks type them into the main BSA collection system. Several states have duplicate reporting requirements, meaning that reports must be sent to the federal as well as the state government. FinCEN eventually becomes a recipient of all of these data and has recently been making the information available, in limited quantities, to the states. To help reduce some of the workload associated with producing and maintaining these data, there are provisions for exemptions that can be made on a case-by-case basis. For example, if a local fast food store consistently puts in $18,000–$25,000 each day, the store can get an exemption from filing forms, as long as it stays under some agreed limit such as $25,000.

If a state does not have laws requiring the collection of this information, they can set up a MOU (Memorandum of Understanding) with the federal government to receive a version of their data. Extractions occur roughly on a weekly basis (sometimes more often for CTRs; sometimes monthly for CMIRs) from forms submitted to the federal government that contain a state descriptor (e.g., reference or zip code). The extracted data are stored on a 9-track tape and sent to the requesting state agency. It can take about six weeks to process the data from the time the form is filled out until it is available online. A benefit of using this approach is that if someone living in one state goes to a different state and deposits a lot of money triggering the submission of a CTR form, both states are going to receive the information.

Depending on the state, the volume of transactions can vary considerably. For example, Arizona receives anywhere from 1,000 to 10,000 forms a month. Other states such as California, Florida, and Texas have to deal with much larger volumes of transactions. In the summer, the number of filings in Arizona goes down and then increases around the holidays. At one point the Arizona officials tried to correlate the influx of funds with the harvest season for marijuana, but the data were too sporadic to establish this connection. These kinds of time cycle analyses can produce interesting results in some cases, however, as we show at the end of this chapter.

Data Modeling

Once data are made available for access, further review can reveal the layout, format, and content of the data structures. Keep in mind that a financial investigation usually involves multiple data sources. For example, the BSA data literally are comprised of half a dozen different data sets. In addition to reporting data, other data sets are often added such as automotive databases, real property assets records (e.g., real-estate property), and criminal history records. The analyst must decide what the important aspects of the data are and how these can be used to fulfill the objectives of the investigation. There are many ways to identify these structures using a variety of informal techniques and methodologies that expose critical facts, similarities, or anomalies contained within the data sets.

The NETMAP system is in use in a large percentage of government organizations involved with the proactive detection of financial crimes. As described in Chapter 7, "Link Analysis Tools," NETMAP is a software application contributing to the data mining process utilizing data integration, visualization/link-analysis, and presentation techniques. The tool has been used extensively for visualizing large quantities of complex information included in analyses. Financial crimes analysts use NETMAP to define the important parts of the transaction (e.g. nodes) and how they relate to one another (e.g., links). (Refer to Chapter 2 for a discussion of modeling techniques in data mining analyses.) BSA data are usually modeled in NETMAP by designating people, organizations, or locations as nodes or object classes. Depending upon the requirements of the analysis, you can designate other object classes as well such as occupations, values, dates, or transactions. The links among the nodes are based on some type of relationship found in the BSA data, typically between the entries on a transaction record. The internal organization of the NETMAP data structures for the nodes and links contains descriptive features respectively called attributes and qualifiers. These features are used and manipulated by the analyst to understand and reveal the important facts contained in the BSA data. Attributes characterize facts about the nodes (e.g., accounts have types, transactions have amounts and dates, people have occupations, etc.). Qualifiers describe facts about the relationships between nodes and can include dates, amounts, suspiciousness, institutions, ID-numbers, source, link type, and direction, to name a few.

The information contained in a BSA transaction can be used to help investigators identify potential money laundering activities, expose suspicious financial behavior, or focus on high-profile subjects or accounts. The most widely submitted form is the CTR. CTR transactions used to be composed of five parts, but in recent years the government has modified the form to try and make it easier to fill out. Refer back to Figure 16.1 for an overview of this form. In its current incarnation, there are three primary sections to the CTR form, as described next.

CTR Form Part I: Person(s) Involved in Transaction(s) The first part of the CTR form is actually composed of two sections. The first is called Section A, "Person(s) on Whose Behalf Transactions(s) Is Conducted," and it is used to identify the owner of the money. All information regarding the name of the individual or organization including the address, identification number (SSN or EIN), date of birth, occupation/business, and several other valuable pieces of data are collected. By default the individual or company identified in this section along with any identification numbers and addresses are designated as nodes within the NETMAP system along with the appropriate intra-transactional links.

The second portion of Part I, Section B, "Individual(s) Conducting Transaction(s)," closely resembles the structure of the previous section. The difference is that the value refers to the entity who is physically present at the financial institution to make the transaction. So if the company or person identified in Section A delegates different people to make deposits or withdrawals, they are also going to be referenced on the form. This helps identify cases in which a central figure hires others to do the "dirty work" in the hopes of avoiding discovery. The nodes created within NETMAP for Section B are directly linked to the nodes in Section A because they are defined in the same transaction. This allows the investigators to see the relationships between the various people and organizations in addition to related street addresses and identity numbers. If the transactor in Section A owns the money, then no additional information is specified in Section B.

CTR Form Part II: Amount and Type of Transaction(s) The information in Part II provides investigators with the details necessary to understand the nature of the transaction. The total dollar amount involved in the transaction is represented as cash in/out along with foreign currency amounts, wire transfers, and other negotiable instruments. Part II also shows the date of the transaction and whether it was a deposit or withdrawal. Part II also has entries for all of the account types and numbers that were used in the transaction. All entries from Parts I and II are linked to each account number provided. The entries that become NETMAP nodes are the dollar amount (currently rounded to the nearest $10,000), any account numbers, and the transaction itself based on the DCN (Document Control Number). All other data are represented as attributes (called qualifiers) on the links between the various nodes. This allows the investigators to filter the data according to very specific criteria.

CTR Form Part III: Financial Institution where Transaction(s) Takes Place

The banks, savings and loans, credit unions, securities brokers/dealers, and all other institutions required to file this form are listed in Part III. There is room for the name of the approving official as well as the preparer's name. Information about the institution type, name, address, and identity numbers (EINs) are included in this part of the form and are represented as nodes in NETMAP.

It should be noted that NETMAP handles those transactions that have multiple entries for any filing made. What this means is if there is more than one transactor listed or the funds are derived from more than one source, all information will be recorded. This supplementary information is accessed from CTR subforms. Surprisingly, there are more of these in the data sets than you would think. There are also NETMAP features that allow the user to control the types of data that are accessed and available for processing. Analysts can set up alternative models to look at subsets of data such as people and accounts, people and transactions, people and addresses, or people and identification numbers. This provides flexibility to the analyst to change the application to fit specific needs where applicable.

Data Integration

The logical and physical integration of disparate data sets is the next step required for development of a formal money laundering detection application. Once all of the important facts and structures have been identified, they need to be integrated into a single coherent representation. To accomplish this, data sets are "normalized" as they are brought into the application. This forces all underlying schemas to be managed in a consistent and useful manner. The BSA information targeted for integration and analysis to combat financial crimes can come from a variety of formats and styles. These representations influence how the data are presented and interpreted by the end user. As an example, the representations of names can differ substantially across data sources. Many are stored in first-name, last-name format, others are last-name, first-name format. Some provide for up to four name segments (e.g., Spanish surnames), and a few mix in the names of organizations with the names of individuals. These formats determine whether the integration is going to be simple or difficult. Other types of data such as addresses and identification numbers can also be used as pivot points for integration, but the use of names is more common.

Before the actual integration can occur, an incredible amount of data cleanup and disambiguation needs to be done to BSA data. The data collection mechanisms are prone to circumvention (e.g., falsified information), typos, misspellings, and load errors that all contribute to a degradation in the quality of the data. There are methods to help overcome these problems. Normalization and standardization of terms can be conducted in addition to a wide range of value-added computations. In particular you can use sound-index vectors to identify names with similar phonetic pronunciation, data decompositions to expose day-of-week and holiday schedules, as well as annotations to help expose international addresses. Even when most of the obvious inconsistencies and omissions have been addressed, there are many more that just cannot be fixed through the use of conventional programming techniques. Those inaccuracies and errors can be exposed during the visual analysis. At that point NETMAP functions can be used for further refinements.

The utility of BSA data in financial crimes and money laundering investigations can be extended further when it is coupled with other data sets to provide alternative perspectives, enhanced resolution, or more detailed descriptions. NETMAP handles these representational issues through structures that help define the nodes and links. All data are translated into internal "definition" formats using NETMAP layout files for each data set to be integrated. NETMAP has been used to integrate CTR and CMIR databases. The layout files are set up to read the formats of each database into a NETMAP definition file that is responsible for maintaining the integrity of the data. Each entity (e.g., people, addresses, ID-numbers, etc.) identified in either database is created as a unique entry in NETMAP. Any association to these nodes regardless of whether it came from CTR or CMIR are shown as a link. This is a very effective method for integrating heterogeneous data of all kinds—irrespective of the platform, structure, format, or location of the data.

Data Integrity and Security

Increasingly, financial crimes involve extremely sophisticated techniques that aim to circumvent laws and limits imposed by law enforcement agencies. With increased cooperation among federal, state, and local agencies (to include the intelligence sector), valuable data become available that must be safeguarded. Issues of data integrity and security must be addressed. NETMAP allows all data to be traced back to original sources. Data imported into NETMAP can be tagged with attributes such as time-of-load and user information. Specific data elements are provided to NETMAP with as much or little information as allowable, depending on the needs of the investigative agency using the data. The fields related to integrity and security can also be used to assist in user/account monitoring, system audits, internal security, or other related activities. Since menus within each application can be customized as data are imported, NETMAP can also be configured for security concerns to allow analysts to filter on such things as source database, issuing agency/department, or classification level.

Information Analysis

The volume of information that is accessed during financial crime investigations does not lend itself well to traditional analytical methods. New approaches beyond the association matrix and link/edge diagrams must be considered when dealing with the tens of thousands of transactions that may be reviewed for any single case. There must also be provisions to accommodate both reactive and proactive targeting techniques. Reactive analysis is used in money laundering cases where a suspect entity such as a person, organization, location, or account has been identified *a priori* through investigative methods as a probable target. All subsequent focus is then placed on that entity in the analysis. Proactive analysis is used to uncover potential money laundering activities by identifying unusual patterns of interactions or usage that would indicate suspicious behavior. Proactive targeting can uncover important trends in the data set that might otherwise go undetected.

Using the NETMAP Application

The approach used in the NETMAP application combines a series of advanced analytical tools and visualization styles to provide the investigator with unparalleled methods to identify and expose financial crimes quickly. Conversion of raw BSA data into a visual format requires that layout files be used to access and transform the data into canonical node and link structures. These structures are then used by NETMAP to manipulate and control the displays. Every node has attributes that can be used to define position, color, style, shape, size, label, and inclusion within the display. Similarly, the qualifier values control the colors, styles, widths, and inclusions of the links on the display.

The formats used by NETMAP to display BSA data are extensive. There are circles, columns, rows, row/columns, and concentric formats that are currently supported. Depending on requirements defined by the analyst, each one of these formats can be useful for understanding BSA data. To provide an example, the information contained in Parts 1–3 for a CTR form are shown in a circular NETMAP format in Figure 16.3. In this case a person has deposited money into an account. The data contained in this figure represent the transaction (DCN), person, filing institution (bank), account, and amount that were provided for a *single* CTR form (not shown are addresses and occupations). The diagram explicitly connects all entries for all parts of the form. When several hundreds or thousands of these forms are presented in

Figure 16.3 A single CTR transaction represented in NETMAP.

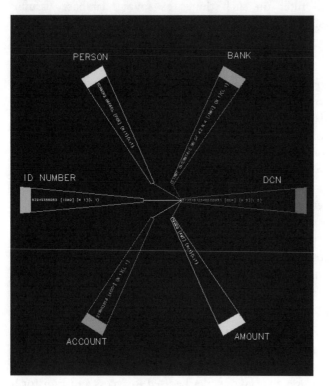

NETMAP, patterns of behavior and implicit interactions can become intuitively obvious in the displays.

The NETMAP application has specialized menus to manipulate and filter these displays. The options in the menus closely approximate the information found on the CTR and CMIR forms, allowing the investigator to peruse the data resources available for analysis. These menus are initially defined in the data mining activities of the data preparation phase and are produced automatically by the NETMAP creation routines based on the definition and layout files specified. These menus allow the analyst to control what appears in the displays and to perform the necessary link analysis activities. Since the entries on these menus approximate the types of data found on the CTR/CMIR forms, the analyst can quickly navigate through the data by selecting only those features of interest for more detailed review.

A set of basic link analysis functions in the NETMAP menus can be used to filter the BSA data set. Standard functions support the inclusion or exclusion of certain data objects, links from/to/between data classes, date/time ranges, link type filters, cluster variables, display layouts, and a variety of other control mechanisms. Depending on how these functions are combined and manipulated, the investigator can analyze the interactions and associations contained in the BSA data to target new suspects involved in suspicious patterns of activity.

Establishing Analytical Questions

As already stated, the primary goal of using the BSA data is to identify potential money laundering activities using either proactive or reactive analytical techniques. There are many levels of conceptualization and numerous inquires that can be made by the investigator using the NETMAP application to analyze BSA data including the ability to, for example:

- Recognize the individuals, organizations, or accounts associated with transactions involving non-U.S. locations. NETMAP will also show any foreign currency involved in these transactions.

- Reveal all accounts, street names, or identification numbers with multiple users. This is an effective technique to expose indirect relationships and additional targets.

- Select the type of transactions to analyze. NETMAP supports analysis of deposits, withdrawals, checks cashed, securities redeemed or purchased, wire transfers, and shipments abroad.

- Cluster the data according to the Soundex values of the names and organizations. Using the resulting grouping, duplications within the data can be identified on the basis of shared or common addresses and identification numbers. Taking these results, NETMAP can merge similar objects together into a single composite representation.

- Selectively choose the dollar amounts for a transaction. Filters are specified in NETMAP to assess total amounts derived from hundred dollar bills, foreign currencies, check-wires, coins, negotiable instruments, as well as several other values contained on the forms.

- Choose any checking, savings, securities, loan, money market, or other special account numbers to analyze. NETMAP will also show the links between these accounts and their filing institutions.

Investigators also have the option of using either the CTR or CMIR data sets, reviewing transactions with unusually large volumes of cash, or filtering the data by regions including cities, states, and zip codes. The combinations of filters are endless and can reflect many of the analytical inquiries required by the investigator. There are, however, instances where certain structures contained in the data cannot explicitly be exposed using "conventional" link analysis techniques. The NETMAP application addresses these requirements by providing special heuristics and algorithms that can help to disclose hidden money laundering patterns and implicit financial crime trends contained in the BSA data. Many of these techniques were discussed in Chapter 5 and include emergent groups, pathway analyses, and common connections.

Discovering Common Patterns in Financial Crimes Analyses

Many financial crimes and money laundering investigations are initiated by tip-offs or through active cases. Many more go undetected, however, because they are hidden in the vast amounts of data or they appear to be legitimate business transactions. Advanced analytical methods are necessary when trying to understand the complex relationships in large data sets such as the BSA information. Analysts need better targeting mechanisms that can be guaranteed only by providing better analysis and visualization tools. The sheer volume and changing nature of the BSA data can make patterns difficult to identify. Thus, many investigators look at only the most recent three months worth of data to detect patterns or look for anomalies. The types of crimes vary from case to case and can include circumvention of reporting requirements, identification of noncompliant practices, or avoidance of detection or involvement in illegal financial activities. Next we present two examples of financial crime patterns that are easy to detect using visualization methods.

Structuring Transactions under $10,000 There are many ways in which money launderers try to avoid detection. One approach mentioned earlier is called *structuring* and it occurs when someone tries to circumvent the reporting requirements by conducting multiple transactions that are under the $10,000 limit. An individual may try to use several different branches of a bank, deposit funds into different accounts, or even get various associates to conduct the trades on his/her behalf. There are explicit anti-money laundering laws prohibiting the structuring of financial transactions so as to avoid reporting requirements. Even though the limit for filing a report is $10,000, cumulative transactions exceeding this amount are reported as a set. The inspectors and officials at the financial institutions are wary of structuring and keep a watch out for any questionable or suspicious behavior. Some banks even go so far as to calculate cumulative structuring totals using an accumulation value aggregated over several days. In general, however, the level of criminal suspicion is inversely proportional to length of the time interval in which the transactions occur. Exposing a structuring pattern within NETMAP is fairly easy and routine because you can filter out any data above $10,000 and view those entities that are left behind. If there are multiple transactions (e.g., DCNs) tied to any particular person, organization, account, or address within a short time period, then a potential structuring has occurred.

Using the Same Address One of the most reliable signs of wrongdoing in a BSA data analysis is the use of one address by multiple transactors (e.g., those people identified in Part I of the CTR form). There have been several cases where upwards of 100 people conducting transactions over $10,000 have used the same reported address, although their names are recorded differently. When investigators drive by and check out the address, it is usually either an empty lot or a shell of a house with one resident at most. The same type of pattern is seen in the registration of motor vehicles owned by suspicious operations such as drug networks. There are cases in which an organization purchases several cars and registers them to different individuals. Most of the time the vehicles are not expensive because the organization wants to minimize losses if the cars are seized. Nevertheless, in order to avoid exposure, many vehicles are often registered to a single P.O. box or address. This type of pattern automatically is revealed when registration records are clustered by address in a visual display.

Presenting Results

This presentation stage of the analysis is equally as important in performing money laundering investigations as the data preparation and analysis stages. The results from the analysis are typically converted into more conventional and standard representation formats. The conversion is necessary due to a variety of factors including comprehensibility through drawing and reporting techniques and transportability for dissemination purposes. Often the results are incorporated into a presentation format that is accepted within the problem domain. As an example, the Anacapa methods discussed in Chapter 5 are a typical representation paradigm used to convey results from financial crimes analysis.

Automated Procedures for Reproducing Results

Results must be reproducible by investigators, especially when particular lines of reasoning are pursued during the course of the analysis. Typically, there are a series of inquiries that the analyst makes against the data set. These inquiries can be stored into automated procedures for recall at any time and may also be shared among investigators, either at local or remote sites, for better intelligence and targeting activities. NETMAP has several storage and recall procedures that can be used to replay the process used by investigators to analyze a case. The batch-file mechanisms supported by NETMAP can dynamically recreate and play back the sequence of filters used by the investigator. The displays automatically regenerate and present their results in a slide-show fashion. Other facilities provided by NETMAP can save the settings used by the investigator for quick recall of important menu configurations and screen layouts. The procedures used for reconstructing these analytical sessions can also be used for historical review, case generation, and even training purposes.

Drawing and Reporting

The lines of reasoning pursued during an analysis are not always the ones governing the composition of the final presentation. The analytical process is intended to work against large volumes of information, identifying the important data based on the investigator's criteria. Once these data have been derived from the analysis, they need to be cleaned up for final presentation. The NETMAP Presentation Tool (NPT) is an integral part of the NETMAP software package and is used extensively in this application. NPT is extremely useful for litigation support because it allows the analyst to display and then interactively manipulate the NETMAP diagrams. As described in Chapter 7, NPT is designed to allow the analyst to make textual annotations to the display for clarifications and/or notes, change the shape and color of nodes and links, and, where appropriate, realign nodes and links into more meaningful layouts. NPT supports all of the standard drawing routines found in many commercial systems. Figure 16.4 shows an example of a NETMAP-generated data screen processed through NPT.

Disseminating Findings

Once an investigator has accessed, analyzed, and charted the information pertaining to a money laundering case, there is a need to disseminate these results to other analysts and decision-makers. There are essentially two ways to do this—through hardcopy or electronic formats. Hardcopy output of NETMAP diagrams can be sent to standard printers and are admissible as forensic evidence in several countries. They are usually produced on plotters or other color output devices and can vary from standard letter-size paper to E-size plots that are 3x4 feet in size—a very effective medium for use in courtroom presentations. Electronic formats are useful for sending diagrams out onto a computer network for other analysts to view in addition to integrating them into other software packages or for desktop publishing.

Figure 16.4 A NPT transformation for presenting results.

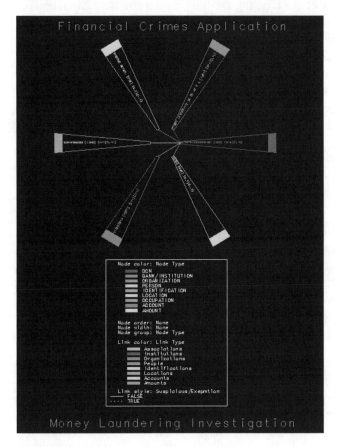

Money Laundering Examples

Cash is a liability to criminal organizations. They must identify and exploit methods to convert the cash into other negotiable instruments. Once this is done, they are less vulnerable to detection. The number of ways in which cash can be transformed are extensive. What follows are several examples of some of these methods along with the methods used by investigators to detect them.

Banking Investigations

There are certain towns along the southern border of the United States that are located in economically depressed areas where high levels of unemployment and unskilled labor abound. These same places are also home to some of the most profitable retail stores and most active banking facilities in the country. Law enforcement agencies realize that many of the dollars being used to purchase goods and services in these areas are largely illegitimate. In one particular example, a large well-established bank opened a small branch in one of these border towns. An ongoing investigation found that this branch had very unusual behavior when it came to returning cash back to the Federal Reserve. As a rule banks do not keep additional cash on hand because the cash itself does not earn interest. Rather they return it to the Federal Reserve. Investigators monitoring these cash returns in a visual data mining application noticed that this one branch was accounting for more than 80 percent of the cash that was shipped by the entire bank chain in that region. People were literally bringing in shopping bags and laundry baskets full of cash to deposit into this branch. Because the branch was shipping the cash directly to the Federal Reserve rather than routing it through the bank's headquarters, the main bank did not know this was occurring. Once notified, the internal security and compliance department put a stop to the behavior. In fact, this particular bank changed their written policies to prevent this from ever happening again. Because this pattern was hidden down in the depths of a large banking organization, it would have been difficult to detect without advanced data mining methods.

Transferring Funds by Wire

Wire transfer companies have recently seen a surge in business as money launderers utilize their services to send money. These places are also called *giros* and can offer a variety of services including answering services, beepers, pagers, and cellular communications. As a side-note, wire transfer houses are required to fill out suspicious transaction reports (SARs). In addition, many of the sanctioned wire transfer companies accepting cash deposits have an upper limit to the amount of funds they send or transfer in a single transaction. Most places restrict the amount of personal transfers to $3000. Nevertheless, more than 1 trillion dollars are wired through NYC every day, which gives you an idea of the magnitude of this business. Although the majority of these transferred funds are legitimate, there is no doubt that questionable transactions are included in the mix.

As in the case of banking transactions, the analysis of wire transfers often involves detection of commonality of addresses. Analysts often discover that although there are not a lot of wire transfers conducted by a limited set of individuals, there are addresses that have many transfers attached to them. This type of pattern is easily visualized in a link analysis diagram. This transfer behavior has been tied to money laundering operations for narcotics and alien smuggling. When illegal aliens are smuggled across the border they send back payments to cover the cost of managing their importation. What makes the pattern of alien smuggling unique is that the individuals are dispersed throughout the United States and are sending payments from all over the country to a small select set of addresses. In drug dealing a different sort of pattern occurs in which funds are wired in a more localized way. Another recent trend in illegitimate transfers involves the use of traveler's checks whereby people bring in large quantities of traveler's checks to be cashed and transferred over a period of days. Obviously this is not what you would consider a typical use of this negotiable instrument.

Using the Department of Motor Vehicles

Yet another avenue for detecting financial crimes is through analysis of records maintained by the Department of Motor Vehicles (DMV). In this case, the targets of interest are the car dealers that are not complying with requirements to report cash transactions of $10,000 or more. The cash sale of high priced items such as cars, jewelry, real estate, and electronics must be reported on a Form 8300. (Items purchased with personal checks do not need to be reported since the check itself constitutes a traceable paper trail.) In several states, the DMV retains information relating to the registration of vehicles worth at least $20,000 purchased without a lien. These records can be integrated and compared with the cash transaction reports from car dealerships in data mining applications to identify those that are not complying with reporting requirements. During the course of an investigation controlled buys might be made at targeted dealerships. In these cases law enforcement agents can purchase a car and then see whether the corresponding 8300 is filed by checking the BSA and DMV records.

Working with a Casa de Cambio

As you have probably surmised by now, the majority of small- to medium-sized drug operations use fairly unsophisticated methods of transferring funds through legitimate businesses. The casa de cambio, or house of money, is one of their preferred establishments for laundering money. Literally thousands of these establishments have been set up along the southwest border of the United States. If you have ever been in an airport or traveled internationally, you will be familiar with these currency exchange operations. Their charter is to change money from one currency to another (e.g., dollars into pesos). Their entire business base is in cash and they handle large quantities of money. For their service fee they usually take a percentage of the total amount of the conversion. Many of them also offer other financial-related services such as wire transfers, money orders, and cashier's checks.

For a long while the casas de cambio were the primary method of laundering money from drug operations in the southwest. However, in some states such as Arizona, money transmitter statutes have been enacted requiring these establishments to become a licensed trade and to keep detailed records. Of course these records can subsequently be investigated for money laundering violations. There is also a hefty licensing fee for these businesses, ensuring that fly-by-night operations will not be able to function legally without some type of collateral. As a result of these statutes, the casas de cambio are less of a threat now than they once were, but they are still operating and they do perform a significant amount of money laundering.

Traditionally, there has not been much oversight of casa de cambio businesses. Due to their large numbers and dispersed locations, they are hard to track, and each one can clear anywhere from several hundred thousand to millions of dollars a month. These casas employ a variety of methods to launder drug money. The following is a brief list of several of these techniques.

- Casas can neutralize money by using their own accounts when clearing funds into or out of a bank. What this means is that any monies transacted by the casa are transferred directly between the bank and the casa itself. All details about where the underlying money was acquired are maintained in separate records by the casa. So if anyone asks, all of the money belongs to the casa. CTR forms reference the casa as the owner instead of the individuals whose money is actually represented. Once the money is safely in the bank's accounts, the casa will transfer the funds to their different clients or to a different money clearing establishment.

- Casas can also act as brokers for their clients. Any monies deposited with the casa can be used to pay bills, purchase goods, or make payments for services rendered. Essentially, the client directs the casa to make these payments under their business name. So, for example, if you wanted to purchase an expensive piece of electronic equipment, you could have the casa call up the store and purchase the desired item. The casa would make the payment (e.g., credit card, check, or cash) to the vendor, but you would take possession of the item. The materials can never be traced back to you since the paper trail stops at the casa.

- Some casas operate with "sister" casas across the border. In these situations, only a set of books is maintained by the operation. There is no physical movement of money between the two casas. If any of their clients need to exchange or transfer funds, purchase materials, or have money made available, the casas can adjust their books to reflect these conditions. The client freely floats between the casas without the hassle of changing back and forth between two or more currencies.

- Many casas offer their clients the ability to purchase other negotiable instruments such as money orders and cashier's checks and these can be made out to any payee. This transforms a quantity of cash into a different format so that CTRs are not filed. The casas are technically required to fill out a form, but this is rarely observed because of the lack of compliance.

Working a Real Case

The following represents an actual case that was generated by a state-level agency heavily involved in the detection and prosecution of financial crimes. The agency has established a special department tasked to detect potential money laundering activities. They have employed a wide variety of technologies and have developed some unique approaches for dealing with these situations, including the special NETMAP application described earlier in the chapter. Investigators within this department probe their BSA data sets in a variety of ways, looking for interesting clues, including high velocity accounts, multiple id-number usage, suspicious addresses, or emergent group networks. Some of these patterns were illustrated in other sections of this book.

Retrieving the Proactive Slice of Data

In this example, the investigator starts off by downloading a set of data derived from reports of all financial activities occurring within a particular region known for drug activity during a six month period. Since there are several million records within the master database, it must be reduced in order to perform the analysis. This extraction defines the proactive slice of data of roughly 1200 records from the original data set. Figure 16.5 shows this data set within a standard NETMAP display format. You can see that there are nine groups presented which include, from the 3:00 position going counter-clockwise, document control numbers (DCNs), filing institutions, organizations, individuals, identification numbers, addresses, occupation codes, account numbers, and the actual dollar amount of the transaction (e.g., a conceptual object class). Thus, using this model, there is a large degree of fan-out for each record loaded. Other models exist, but for this case, this was the format used.

This initial diagram may appear a bit overwhelming. However, to the trained eye there are several important things to observe. First, the relative sizes of the

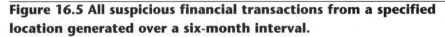

Figure 16.5 All suspicious financial transactions from a specified location generated over a six-month interval.

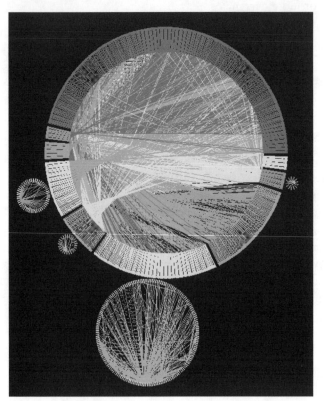

different groups tell us some things about the general construction and makeup of this slice of data. As expected, the number of DCN objects exceeds all other groups. That is because each unique DCN used to create the data set is represented. This is a good example of a transactional model. Thus, there is an object in this band for each record loaded. We consider this a one-to-one correspondence with the underlying data set. The DCNs also act as the integrating factor among all other object classes. Thus, if a drill-down (or profile as it is called within NETMAP) is performed, you can see all of the underlying attributes describing the particular transaction. The DCN also references the hardcopy document that was originally used to create the electronic entry.

We can see that the size of the bands containing the individuals and accounts are somewhat smaller than the DCN band. Immediately we know that there are many-to-one representations present. This indicates that the same people and accounts have been used across multiple transactions. Therefore, we can infer there are going to be a few "players" in this data slice that may prove to be of interest. This is one of the primary benefits of using a visualization such as NETMAP to present this type of data. You break down the barriers among unique records and view them as a collective whole in order to expose these types of patterns.

Filtering the Proactive Slice of Data

From here the investigator wanted to see the individuals who were involved in high-dollar transactions—for these purposes, over $80,000. Within NETMAP, there are a variety of ways to filter the data. In this case, there were two options to choose from. The first involved showing only those specific transactions that in of themselves exceeded $80,000. The second method used accumulated values of the transactions that existed between any two connected objects, showing those that had more than $80,000 between them. Thus, if there were 10 transactions involving a person and an account, each for $10,000, then those entities would be flagged for display. The filters were set to $80,000 for any particular transaction and the results are depicted in Figure 16.6.

The results of this action are a bit easier to interpret since fewer records are being presented. In this configuration, the data clearly show the investigator that there is only a small set of individuals playing at this level. Again the proportions of each of the bands, which essentially are relatively placed clusters, depict the degree of fan-out within the data itself. The next steps are to refine further what is being displayed to focus only on the individuals and accounts involved. Through the exclusion of specific values, NETMAP can alter the type of data being displayed. The results of this action are shown in Figure 16.7 along with the thickness of the links set to reflect the frequency of connection (e.g., number of observations across all DCNs). As a side note, the number of dimensions being presented within this figure equates to 12—extraction date (1), extraction location (2), initial object/link model (3), threshold filter (4), type filter (5), display position (6), object color (7), object size (8), object label (9), link color (10), link thickness (11), and link style (12). We could further refine this display along other dimensions, but as you can tell, there is a good deal of information being presented within such a simple display.

What you can see is that there are only two accounts present with several people using them. A closer examination of these names reveals that many of them are similar in their spelling, perhaps indicating duplicate data. Also a quick check on the account type via the profiling mechanisms shows that it is a loan account. The investigator does not concern himself with this issue for the time being. However, what attracts his attention is the link style used to convey the data. As we mentioned, the

Figure 16.6 Filtering the data using an $80,000 threshold.

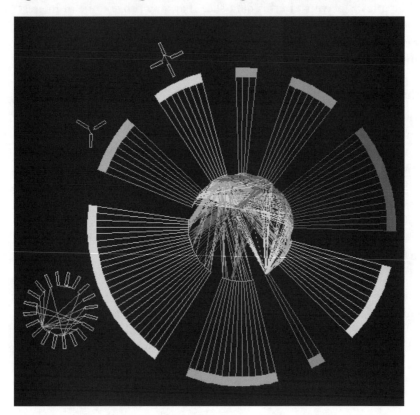

thickness of the link corresponds to the number of $80,000 transactions that exist between the two entities. Solid links signify normal DCNs, but dotted lines denote those transactions considered suspicious by the filing institution. This relationship was profiled to reveal that the amount of the transaction was in excess of $158,000 in low denomination bills—essentially a bag full of money was deposited. Rightly so, the teller marked the transaction as suspicious. The person involved in this particular transaction then becomes the current focus of this particular investigation.

Switching to a Reactive Analysis Mode

The next step in the analysis is to show all of the transactions associated with that person, not just those exceeding $80,000. This display is depicted in Figure 16.8. This diagram shows the investigator that they have locked in on a person who is

Figure 16.7 Further filter including only individuals and accounts.

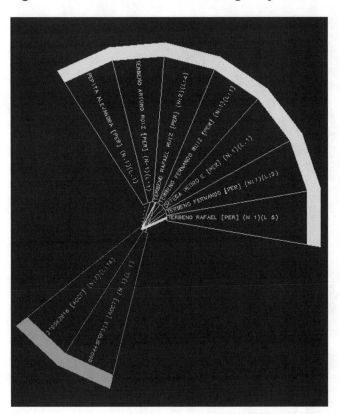

heavily involved in suspicious behavior. There are 43 transactions associated to this person with all but 4 marked as suspicious. A quick check in the occupation band of the transactor shows that there are a variety of entries all roughly indicating that the person is a "secretary of a money exchange house"—which means she is a gopher (also called grunt or mule) for a casa de cambio. What this tells the investigator is that someone else is controlling or directing her behavior and she is only serving as an intermediary in the operations of the enterprise.

There is only one other person connected to our prime lead (shown in the satellite) and he shares the same name of the organization on whose behalf the money has been deposited. This means he is probably the owner of that establishment. The investigator decides to turn his attention to this person. A request is made to "walk the data" by acquiring all the records within the master data set (e.g., the millions of records)

Figure 16.8 Display of all transactions for a targeted individual.

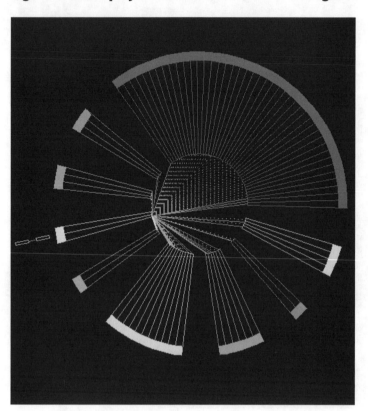

using this person's name as the search key. The results from this search are shown in Figure 16.9. The diagram contains a good deal of information that can be used to help further guide the analysis. First, the investigator sees that the suspect is well connected to a variety of other people. This can be seen in the satellite that appears outside the group (down near the 7:00 position). Each person that has been involved in a monetary transaction for the target suspect is connected within the diagram. As is obvious, this man uses a large number of people to move his money around the various financial institutions. This in and of itself tells the investigator that there is almost certain illegal activity occurring within that organization.

At this point, the investigator believes that there is enough material to warrant further investigation into the behavior of the filing patterns for this suspect. Since this state has strict seizure and forfeiture laws, it becomes necessary to understand

Figure 16.9 Display of all the connections for the new suspect.

when the transactions are occurring. By doing so, the investigator can predict when the next best opportunity for intercepting the suspect will occur. Other factors in the investigation help determine whether any action will actually be taken. For this example, we are showing only the process used for detecting and understanding the financial flow patterns of suspected money launderers.

Modeling the Transactional Components of BSA Data

Until now, the entire analysis has been based on understanding the structure of the data by exposing the relational and declarative characteristics contained within the data set. Thus, the process used to identify the suspect was based on analysis of the ways in which the specific data elements have been linked together to form different types of interesting and unusual structures. Since BSA data are transactional, the investigator refocuses his attention to include only the links that exist between the subject and the actual transactions (e.g., the DCNs) as shown in Figure 16.10. Here we can see that there are a significant number of DCNs associated with this person. Each DCN represents a completed CTR form and can be used to tell the investigator the nature of the filing.

One very important fact that can be derived from the data is when this person is conducting "business" and at what level of activity. Since the DCNs represent the actual transaction, they have been populated with all of the declarative data associated with the event. Thus, any of the details from Parts I, II, or III of the CTR form will be available as attributes from these objects. Using the NETMAP profile mechanisms, the investigator can quickly see any of these attributes. Additionally, as was mentioned in Chapter 2 under *Defining Transactional Data Models*, links generated within a transactional model can represent attributes of the transactions themselves. Thus a link can also be profiled within this application to reveal the details about the transaction.

Figure 16.10 Display of all the transactions from/to the target subject.

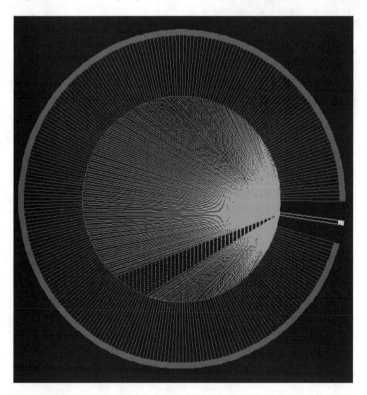

Since the unique value of the DCN does not convey much information to the investigator, he can set the label of the objects to reflect several other types of information. In this case, the date, amount, and direction of transactions are depicted within the labels for the DCNs. Since NETMAP uses relative placement when generating its clusters, these values allow you to interpret the diagram quickly without having to profile each group to see its respective value.

Conducting Temporal Analyses with BSA Data

To expose filing behavior, the investigator regroups the data based on the month in which the transactions were conducted. Individuals do not have an associated date in this context, so our suspect is placed into the 3:00 position reserved for NULL values. The rest of the data objects are then broken out into 12 distinct groups, one for each month encountered. If there were only a few transactions in this data slice, this grouping might generate fewer than 12 groups. In that event the investigator would immediately know there were nonrepresented periods within the data set selected for analysis. He could determine which months were missing by quickly scanning the labels of the DCNs since they contain the date. From here he could see if there were any particular biases or unusual filing patterns.

Figure 16.11 shows that the month grouping reveals periods of time that are more active that others. As we mentioned previously, the investigator thought that these influxes might be attributed to the various drug-harvest cycles encountered throughout the region, although this cannot officially be confirmed. You can see that the third and eleventh groups (e.g., March and November) are the most active time frames with respect to the operations of this individual suspect (shown in the figure as group 0) and his business. Figure 16.12 shows the same information depicted in Figure 16.11 using a different display format. This display gives the investigator a more explicit presentation format that highlights differences in group sizes.

These results are encouraging because they suggest two potential time frames in which to mount an operation against this individual. However, these are still very broad clusters and more resolution would be needed before any actions would be taken. At this point, the investigator requests that the transactions be regrouped based on a day-of-week breakdown. Recall from Chapter 2, there are a lot of data in data. In this case, the day-of-week values can be calculated directly from the dates themselves. This resulting metadata calculation can then be applied to the transactions as an attribute. As you can see in Figure 16.13, this analysis reveals quite a bit of detail about the filing behavior of the suspect. During this date decomposition, the investigator also changes the colors of the transactions to reflect the months in which they occurred. Each of the color bands within each of the groups depicted in Figure 16.12 code the months.

Figure 16.11 Transactions grouped according to the month of filing.

It does not take the investigator long to realize that the largest spike in this display represents Friday. Perhaps you could make the argument that it merely reflects the receipts for the business conducted for the week. Regardless, to the investigator, what it means is that he now has a window of opportunity in order to seize the accounts should the investigation reach that stage. Since the colors reflect the month, it is concluded that Fridays in March and November are the critical time periods for the movement of this suspect's money. What the diagram does not tell us is whether the funds are coming or going. It would be a bit ironic if they went in to seize the accounts and no funds were present because all of the transactions presented reflected a withdrawal instead of a deposit. So the final step of this investigation was to change the colors of the linkages to show whether the money was coming or going. This result is presented in Figure 16.14 and shows that March was a very volatile month. Even though March has the most transactions, there is a random mixture of deposits and withdrawals, clarifying that perhaps March might not

Figure 16.12 Alternate presentation format for information presented in Figure 16.11.

be the best intervention period after all. We refer you to the color figures on the CD-ROM for a better appreciation of the differences between Figures 16.12 and 16.13.

A closer inspection for November shows that virtually all of the transactions being made are deposits. The investigator was quite pleased to see this behavior and indicated this was expected since these businessmen will pad their accounts before the holiday season so they can draw on their funds while vacationing. Note that there are also filings that occurred on a Sunday. For the most part, these are not seen too often within this type of data set since most financial institutions are closed. However, these may be present because an ATM or night box was used to make a deposit. If this situation was more prevalent, it would indicate a different type of pattern to the investigator, namely one indicating that the transactor does not like to be present during the transactions. There are also many other more subtle indicators that are reviewed by the investigator during his course of analysis.

As you can see in this example, the investigator very quickly identified important relationships, disambiguated duplicate data, consolidated nodes, and exposed

Figure 16.13 Transactions grouped according to day-of-week.

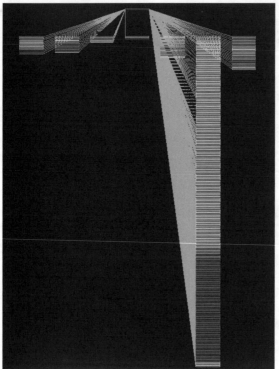

implicit patterns of activity. An investigator produces intelligence much more rapidly when using visualization during the data mining process.

Summing Up

The data mining process described in this chapter can be routinely used by virtually all financial crimes investigators, whether for telephone toll analysis, border crossings, cargo/container tracking, counter-narcotics applications, or money laundering investigations. There are three steps that are addressed in data mining analyses in this domain. The first step of data preparation is used to access, extract, and integrate the variety of data sources available to the investigator including federal, state, private, and commercial databases. Secondly, analysis is performed where visualization, link analysis, and targeting mechanisms are available to the investigator for identifying important relationships and patterns of activity. Finally, results derived

Figure 16.14 Link colors changed to reflect deposits or withdrawals.

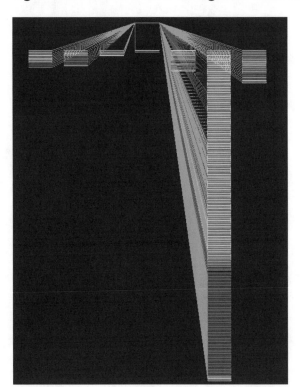

from the first two steps are refined to produce final intelligence suitable for dissemination and reporting purposes.

The tool most widely used within this domain is NETMAP because it explicitly addresses each stage of the data mining process by providing the investigator with full control over what information is accessed, the results which are generated for analysis, and finally, how it is presented. The use of NETMAP in a financial crimes domain provides a very robust environment where investigators can review thousands of transactions in a single display. These displays can be used to perform both reactive and proactive targeting activities.

We reviewed various classes of data mining activities and described ways in which these may be discovered using electronic records generated from financial transactions, many of which are reports filed for cash transactions exceeding $10,000. We ended the chapter by taking you through a money laundering investigation as it would be pursued step-by-step in a NETMAP application.

Tool and Technology Resources

A

As we have mentioned throughout the book, the world of data mining is changing at a very rapid pace. It is difficult to keep up with the variety of products and services available from the industry. Fortunately, there are several reference sites on the Internet that you can consult to receive a more up-to-date listing of the new breakthroughs and topics as they arise in the data mining community. These sites cover everything from conferences, journals, services, products, discussions, and references. It would not be possible to provide an exhaustive list of all of these sites since such a list would be obsolete in short order. We would, however, like to point out a few sites that we frequently visit and have found helpful in the past. The following sites should provide a good starting point for those who want to learn more about the data-mining field.

http://pwp.starnetinc.com/larryg/datamine.html

http://www.cs.bham.ac.uk/~anp/TheDataMine.html

http://www.cs.su.oz.au/~thierry/ckdd.html

http://www.kdd.org/

http://www.kdnuggets.com

http://www.research.microsoft.com/datamine/

http://www.santafe.edu/~kurt/dmvendors.shtml

http://www.heinz.cmu.edu/project/INSNA/soft_inf.html

In addition to these Internet references, we have assembled a partial list of companies currently offering software products for data mining. Please use the following list as a guide to help point you in the right direction. Bear in mind that we do not advocate the use of one product over another. As we argued in the book, the data mining tool(s) that you choose should depend upon your application problem and the methodology you adopt. Again, this list is not exhaustive. In many cases the vendors have offices located throughout the world and we list only the main headquarters. Be aware that the information in this list is likely to change quickly. Most of these companies maintain Web sites that you can consult for the most current information concerning their software products.

NOTE

We recommend that you visit vendor Web sites, because many have free downloads of demonstration versions of their software. Others have pictures, movies, and animations that illustrate visualization capabilities. The CD-ROM provided with this book contains only a small sample of the types of information available from these sources.

Daisy Charts

Daisy Analysis Ltd.
East Green Farm, Great Bradley
Newmarket, Suffolk CB8 9LU
tel: 44-(0)1440-783789
fax: 44-(0)1440-783791
http://www.daisy.co.uk/

Discovery / In3D

Visible Decisions, Inc.
200 Front Street West
Suite 2203, P.O. Box 35
Toronto, Ont M5V 3K2
tel: (416) 595-6282
fax: (416) 595-7292
http://www.vdi.com

MineSet

Silicon Graphics Inc.
2011 N. Shoreline Blvd.
Mountain View, CA 94043
tel: (650) 960-1980
fax: (650) 961-0595
http://www.sgi.com/Products/
software/MineSet

Metaphor Mixer

Maxus Systems International Inc.
610 River Terrace
Hoboken, NJ 07030
tel: (201) 963-3554
fax: (201) 963-3576
http://www.maxussystems.com/

Clementine

Integral Solutions Ltd
Berk House - Basing View
Basingstoke, England
Hants RG21 4RG
tel: 44-(0) 1256-355899
fax: 44-(0) 1256-363467
http://www.isl.co.uk

Generic Visualization Architecture (GVA)

United Information Systems, Inc.
10401 Fernwood Road, #200
Bethesda, MD 20817
tel: (301) 571-0240
fax: (301) 571-0264
http://www.unitedis.com/gva

NETMAP

ALTA Analytics, Inc.
929 Eastwind Drive, Suite 203
Westerville, OH 43081
tel: (614) 523-1067
fax: (614) 523-2159
http://www.alta-oh.com/

DataVista

Visualize, Inc.
1819 East Morten, Suite 210
Phoenix, AZ 85020
tel: (602) 861-0999
fax: (602) 861-1650
http://www.visualizetech.com

DIAMOND

SPSS Inc.
444 North Michigan Avenue
Chicago, IL 60611
tel: (312) 329-2400
fax: (312) 329-3668
http://www.spss.com

Data Desk

Data Description, Inc.
840 Hanshaw Road, Suite 9
Ithaca, NY 14850
tel: (800) 573-5121
fax: (607) 257-4146
http://www.datadesk.com

Analyst's Notebook

i2 Ltd.
Breaks House
Mill Court, Great Shelford
Cambridge CB2, SLD UK
tel: (44) 1233-844032
fax: (44) 1223-840632
http://www.i2.co.uk/

Watson

Harlequin Incorporated
One Cambridge Center, 8th Floor
Cambridge, MA 02142
tel: (617) 374-2400
fax: (617) 252-650
http://www.harlequin.com/

AVS/VIZ Express

Advanced Visual Systems, Inc
300 Fifth Avenue
Waltham, MA 02154
tel: (781) 890-4300
fax: (781) 890-8287
http://www.avs.com

ORIONLEADS

ORION Scientific Systems
19800 MacArthur Blvd. Suite 480
Irvine, CA 92612
tel: (714) 261-0226
fax: (714) 261-0243
http://www.orionsci.com/

CrossGraphs

Belmont Research, Inc.
84 Sherman St.
Cambridge, MA 02140
tel: (617) 868-6878
fax: (617) 868-2654
http://www.belmont.com/

Spotfire

Spotfire, Inc.
28 State Street, Suite 1100
Boston, MA 02109
tel: (617) 573-5163
fax: (617) 573-5164
http://www.ivee.com/

Crime Link

Precision Computing, Inc.
P.O. Box 1193
Sierra Vista, Arizona 85636
tel: (520) 458-5990
fax: (520) 458-5998
http://www.crimelink.com/

WinViz

Information Technology Institute
11 Science Park Road
Singapore Science Park II
Singapore 117685
tel: (65) 778 7951
fax: (65) 779 5966
http://jsaic.iti.gov.sg/projects/
vizMain.html

Enterprise Miner

SAS Institute Inc.
SAS Campus Drive
Cary, NC 27513-2414
tel: (919) 677-8000
fax: (919) 677-8123
http://www.sas.com/software/
data_mining/

Data Explorer (DX)

IBM Corporation
Almaden Research Center
650 Harry Road
San Jose, CA 95120-6099
tel: (408) 927-1080
http://eagle.almaden.ibm.com/dx/

Visual Insights

Lucent Technologies
600 Mountain Avenue
Murry Hill, NJ 07974
tel: (800) 295-3067
tel: (888) 584-6366
http://www.visualinsights.com/

SphinxVision

NCO Natural Computing
Deutschherrnufer 31
60594 Frankfurt
Germany
tel: 49-69-61992342
fax: 49-69-61992344
http://www.asoc.com/

IMAGIX 4D

Imagix Corporation
6025 White Oak Lane
San Luis Obispo, CA 93401
tel: (805) 781-6002
fax: (805) 781-6003
http://www.imagix.com/

WEBSOM

Helsinki University of Technology
Neural Networks Research Centre
P.O.Box 1000
FIN-02015 HUT - Finland
tel: +358 9 4511
http://websom.hut.fi/websom/

Tecplot

Amtec Engineering, Inc.
PO Box 3633
Bellevue, WA 98009-3633
tel: (800) 676-7568
fax: (425) 827-3989
http://www.amtec.com/

Mapuccino

IBM - Haifa Research Laboratory
Matam, Haifa 31905, Israel
tel: (972) 3 697 8500
fax: (972) 4 855 0070
http://www.ibm.com/java/mapuccino/

SpaceSQL (SpaceCharts)

Infospace, Inc.
181 2nd Avenue, Suite 218
San Mateo, CA 94401
tel: (415) 685-3000
fax: (415) 685-3001
http://www.infospace-inc.com

IDL

Research Systems, Inc.
2995 Wilderness Place
Boulder, CO 80301
tel: (303) 786-9900
fax: (303) 786-9909
http://www.rsinc.com/

Graf-FX

GR-FX Pty Limited
PO Box 2121,
Clovelly, NSW, 2031, Australia
tel: (02) 9665 2871
fax: (02) 9665 8448
http://www.gr-fx.com/

KrackPlot

Analytic Technologies
104 Pond Street
Natick, MA 01760
tel: (508) 647-1903
fax: (508) 647-3154
http://analytictech.com/

VisiGraph

The GIFIC Corporation
405 Atlantic Street
Melbourne Beach, FL 32951
tel: (800) 374-4342
http://www.gific.com/

VizControls

Inxight Software Inc.
3400 Hillview Avenue
Palo Alto, CA 94304
tel: (650) 852-0290
fax: (650) 813-7499
http://www.inxight.com/

SPIRIX

ThemeMedia Inc.
8383 158th Avenue NE, Suite 320
Redmond, WA 98052
tel: (425) 602-3550
fax: (425) 602-3570
http://www.ThemeMedia.com/

Heatmaps

NeoVision Hypersystems, Inc.
50 Broadway, 34th Floor
New York, NY 10004
tel: (212) 378-8412
fax: (212) 378-8415
http://www.neovision.com/

VisualMine

Artificial Intelligence Software SpA
Via Carlo Esterle
9 - 20132 Milano Italy
tel: 39 (0)2 280141
fax: 39 (0)2 2610853
http://www.iunet.it/ais/vis1.htm

KDD Toolset (Explorer)

SRA International, Inc.
2000 15th Street
Arlington, VA 22201
tel: (703) 558-4700
fax: (703) 558-4723
http://www.knowledgediscovery.com/

DecisionHouse

Quadstone Ltd
16 Chester Street
Edinburgh
EH3 7RA Scotland
tel: 44-(0)1312-204491
fax: 44-(0) 1312-204492
http://www.quadstone.co.uk/

Cambio

Data Junction Corporation
2201 Northland Drive
Austin, TX 78756
tel: (512) 459-1308
fax: (512) 459-1309
http://www.datajunction.com

SemioMap

Semio Corporation
1730 South Amphlett Boulevard #101
San Mateo, CA 94402
tel: (415) 638-3330
fax: (415) 638-3339
http://www.semio.com/

PV-Wave

Visual Numerics, Inc.
9990 Richmond Avenue, Suite 400
Houston, TX 77042-4548
tel: (800) 222-4675
fax: (713) 781-9260
http://www.vni.com/

PerspectaView

Perspecta, Inc.
600 Townsend Street Suite 170E
San Francisco, CA 94103-4945
tel: (415) 437-4150
fax: (415) 437-4179
http://www.perspecta.com/

MAPA

Dynamic Diagrams
12 Bassett Street
Providence, RI 02903
tel: (401) 331-2014
fax: (401) 331-2015
http://www.dynamicdiagrams.com

dbProbe

InterNetivity Inc.
1545 Carling Avenue, Suite 404
Ottawa, Ontario
K1Z 8P9 Canada
tel: (613) 729-4480
fax: (613) 729-6711
http://www.internetivity.com

Temple-MVV

Mihalisin Associates, Inc.
P.O. Box 3183
Maple Glen, PA 19002
tel: (215) 646-3814

Pathfinder

Presearch Incorporated
8500 Executive Park Avenue
Fairfax, VA 22031
tel: (703) 876-6400
fax: (703) 876-6411
http://www.presearch.com

DiskMapper

Micro Logic
P.O. Box 70
Hackensack, NJ 07602
tel: (201) 342-6518
fax: (201) 342-0370
http://www.miclog.com

XpertRule

Attar Software USA
Two Deerfoot Trail On Partridge Hill
Harvard, MA 01451
tel: (508) 456-3946
fax: (508) 456-8383
http://www.attar.com/

WebAnalyzer

InContext Systems
6733 Mississauga Road 7th floor
Mississauga, Ontario
L5N 6J5 Canada
tel: (888) 819-2500
fax: (905) 819-9245
http://www.incontext.ca/

DataScope

Cygron Research & Development, Ltd.
Szeged, Pf.: 727, H-6701 Hungary
tel: +36 62 325 928
http://www.tiszanet.hu/cygron/

NetScout

NetScout Systems, Inc.
4 Technology Park Drive
Westford, MA 01886
tel: (978) 614-4000
fax: (978) 614-4004
http://www.frontier.com

The following are additional companies that provide software products addressing preliminary stages of the data mining process dealing with data access, cleanup, and integration. We also suggest that you look at http://pwp.starnetinc.com/larryg/ for similar information.

DSS Agent

MicroStrategy, Inc.
8000 Towers Crescent Drive
Vienna, VA 22182
tel: (703) 848-8600
fax: (703) 848-8610
http://www.strategy.com/

d.b.EXPRESS

Computer Concepts Corp.
80 Orville Drive
Bohemia, NY 11716
tel: (800) 619-0757
fax: (516) 563-8085
http://www.computerconcepts.com/

SSA-NAME3

Search Software America
1445 East Putnam Avenue
Old Greenwich, CT 06870
tel: (203) 698-2399
fax: (203) 698-2409
http://www.searchsoftware.co.uk/

AutoMatch

MatchWare Technologies
Springpoint Executive Center
15212 Dino Drive
Burtonsville, MD 20866
tel: (301) 384-3997
fax: (301) 384-8095
http://www.matchware.com/

Trillium

Trillium Software System
25 Linnell Circle
Billerica, MA 01821
tel: (508) 436-8900
fax: (508) 670-5793
http://www.trilliumsoft.com/

INTEGRITY

Vality Technology
One Financial Center 6th Floor
Boston, MA 02111
tel: (617) 338-0300
fax: (617) 338-0338
http://world.std.com/~Vality/vality.html

DataRight

i.d.Centric
A Division of Firstlogic, Inc.
100 Harborview Plaza
La Crosse, WI 54601-4051
tel: (800) 551-9491
http://www.idcentric.com/

NameSearch

Intelligent Search Technology
222 Grace Church Street, #202
Port Chester, NY 10573
tel: (800) 287-0412
tel: (914) 934-0205
http://www.intelligentsearch.com/

WHAT'S ON THE CD-ROM

Book Figures

The figures used throughout the book (approximately 250) have been provided as a series of GIF images on this CD. Since the book only provides black-and-white figures, we felt it important to provide color versions for your review so that the full effect of the displays could be appreciated. This is especially important for the figures derived from screen captures of some of the visualization tools. The figures have been categorized by the section of the book in which they appear (Sections I, II, III, and IV) and have been named in correspondence with the figure numbers assigned in the book (e.g., F-07-21.gif refers to Figure 21 in Chapter 7). You will need software that is capable of presenting GIF images in order to view these figures on your computer. We have included PicViewer (http://www.strong-software.net/dronix/) as one method of viewing these GIF images. There are several settings within PicViewer that allow you to either best-fit the images or look at them in full-size. We recommend that you maximize the window when viewing the GIFS. To look at the GIFS all you need to do is double click on the file name and the GIF will be displayed within PicViewer. You can also use any variety of graphics software or one of the many popular Internet browsers to look at these images.

Visualization Software

The CD-ROM contains supplementary material describing and illustrating a subset of the visual data mining systems covered in various sections of the book. The range of programs on the CD-ROM covers both high-end and lower-end systems. Our inclusion of a particular vendor's software does not indicate any preference for one product over another. (In fact, we solicited inputs from many vendors who were unable to provide materials for this purpose.) Rather, this material is intended to give you a representative sample of the types of technologies currently available for data mining. We hope that you find this information helpful, but ask you to bear in mind that the systems included on this disk are only a small sample of the systems available. We strongly urge you to use the list of software vendors in the Appendix of the book and contact them directly to see the most up-to-date versions of their systems.

All of the software on this CD-ROM is provided solely for demonstration purposes. The vendors have either placed date/time stamps to activate the software for a fixed period of time or they have disabled certain key features (e.g., loading different data sources) in order to ensure that these packages are not used for application work. The vendors of these systems retain all rights to the software under copyright laws. If you find any of the software of interest, we ask that you contact the appropriate vendor to work out any future licensing agreements. Also mention that you saw their demo in this book—it helps them to justify the investment they made in graciously providing their software for these purposes.

Adobe Acrobat Reader

Several of the software systems on the CD-ROM have manuals or references that are stored in the PDF format. The Acrobat Reader has been installed on the CD-ROM to display PDF files automatically. If you do not already have the Acrobat Reader installed on your system, please use this version to view the PDF files. We also encourage you to visit www.adobe.com to find out about the latest Adobe products.

QuickTime

There are a few products that require the use of QuickTime to view the movies that have been included on the CD-ROM. QuickTime is an industry standard format developed by Apple that provides support for video and sound. You can visit their web page (http://www.apple.com/quicktime/) to learn more about the product. For your convenience, a QuickTime system has been installed on the CD-ROM.

Hardware Requirements

Most of the software provided on the CD-ROM will run on Windows 95/NT platforms. You should be running a minimum of a 486 with at least 16 MB of memory. Not all the software provided is compatible with Windows. Several of the systems support QuickTime, PDF, and Java. Thus, depending on your environment, you need to have the appropriate viewer/executable available to view the systems. Several of these systems will also run in a UNIX environment (as was indicated in Section III) and we ask that you contact the vendors directly to determine which platforms they support.

Installing the Software

We have created a front-end interface that you can use to launch the software programs provided on this CD-ROM. Where possible we have minimized installation procedures and maximized the space on the CD-ROM. However, there are several cases in which you will need to install programs. If you cannot get the main interface to work, you can use the file explorer included with your operating environment to individually launch each of the applications.

To install the software, follow these simple steps:

1. Start Windows (95/NT) on your computer.

2. Place the CD-ROM into your CD-ROM drive.

3. A self-executing script will run once the CD-ROM is initialized.

4. Follow the screen prompts to utilize the different software packages.

If the script does not execute as expected, it might be because you have not enabled your computer to *auto-run* CDs when they are inserted into the drive. To do this follow these instructions:

-   Right-click on the "My-Computer" icon and select "Properties."

-   Click the "Device Manager" tab.

-   Expand the tree under "CD-ROM."

-   Double-click on your CD-ROM device.

-   Click the "Settings" tab.

-   Check the box labeled "auto insert notification."

Depending on your system, you may have to restart windows in order for this change to take effect. If you do not want to change your computer settings, then just double-click on the launch.exe file located in the top directory of the CD-ROM. You can find this through the file browser or by using your desktop explorer.

Using the Software

Each piece of software on this CD-ROM has been provided at the discretion of the vendor. Each vendor has its own set of licensing conditions and it is the user's responsibility to read and comply with these requirements. The systems included on the disk are:

Analyst's Notebook

i2 Inc. has provided a comprehensive and very effective demonstration of their product line on this CD-ROM. They have produced an exceptional introduction to the Analyst's Notebook that takes you through an attention-grabbing sequence of videos. This demo provides detailed information about the Link Analysis, Case Analysis, iBase Database System, and iGlass Visual Data Mining products. The demonstration provides a thorough overview of the Analyst's Notebook with ample opportunities to look at example case studies, product features, and other recent improvements made to the software. This is a definite "must see" application. There are two versions available—one for Windows 3.1 (View Demo 16) and the other for Windows 95/NT (View Demo 32).

CrossGraphs

Belmont Research has provided a set of demonstration files that shows off their comprehensive line of data mining products. There are two slide presentations (one for CrossGraphs and the other for TableTrans) in addition to a functioning version of the CrossGraphs product itself. Be sure to read the license agreements that come with this evaluation version. There are also several PDF files that provide a set of examples discussing the different CrossGraphs displays, the release notes, as well as the complete User's Manual. We recommend that you take a close look at each of these PDF files to get an appreciation for what CrossGraphs can do.

Daisy

Included on the CD-ROM is a version of Daisy Lite 4.11 along with a suite of example PDF files. Look at each of the nine PDF files to get a feel for what Daisy has to offer. Each file provides a different perspective of data that reveals the various features and functionality of Daisy as they apply to a variety of domain areas. Please be sure to read the license conditions provided in the installation script when you are ready to install the Daisy Lite 4.11. Once the installation is complete you can use the templates and data files provided with this evaluation copy.

DataVista

There are a variety of Java-based visualizations provided by Visualize Inc. on the CD-ROM. DataVista Lite is a graphing tool provided to demonstrate some of the capabilities of the DataVista line of visual, interactive, graphing solutions. They have also included the User's Guide in a PDF format. This is not free-ware, so please read their license agreement before you use any of the DataVista products in your own work. You can also visit the web site, which has a full-blown suite of interactive demos.

Diamond

SPSS has provided an interactive version of their Diamond system. However, before you begin, please read the SPSS Diamond Limited Edition License Agreement that comes with the software. SPSS has provided online help if you have any questions or want to learn more details about any of the features. Because this is an evaluation version of Diamond, SPSS has set the maximum number of active variables to 12 and the maximum number of data cases (spreadsheet rows) to 50. There is also a 30-minute time-out that has been built into the evaluation version for any active sessions. These restrictions do not hamper your ability to get an appreciation for Diamond's functionality

GangNet

This is a PowerPoint Presentation (with the associated viewer) created by Orion Scientific Systems to demonstrate their GangNet product. This is just one in a series of investigative systems produced by Orion. The slides illustrate the features and multimedia capabilities supported by GangNet. There are slides that show pictures and link diagrams, as well as fielded data entry/search screens. See the Orion home-page for more detail about their link analysis and flow-charting systems, especially the ORIONLink System.

Graf-FX

This is a shareware version of the Graf-FX data mining system. In order to run this application, you will need to couple it up to your current version of Microsoft Access. There are three different versions on the CD-ROM, once for each Access version 2.0, 7.0, and 97. If you run into a problem launching the MDB file, double check your version of Access and make sure that you have launched the correct Graf-FX. This application has been built entirely in Access, and those familiar with Access/Office should have no problem using Graf-FX. Do not hesitate to check out the help functions or the Graf Utilities. Graf-FX is a simple and easy-to-use system.

GVA

This is a Java-based program that has been provided by UIS. In order to run the software you will need a Java virtual environment. If you are not already running a JDK or JRE on your machine, you can download one free of charge from www.javasoft.com. Since Java runs across a wide range of platforms, you need to select a version for your operating environment. This is a fully functioning version of GVA and you may use it to load in your own data sets once you get a feel for how the tool works. Many of the functions can be controlled through the defaults file, so make sure that you take a look at this file if you want to change the look and feel of the analytical environment. There is also a set of movies included with GVA. Check back often with the developers because this software is constantly being upgraded.

Imagix 4D

Imagix 4D has traditionally been a UNIX system, but a Windows 95/NT version has recently been released. Please make sure to read the Software License Agreement and Release Notes when you install this program. Imagix 4D uses TCL (Tool Command Language), which is automatically included with the software when you install it. This version includes Imagix 2000, which you can use to see how Y2K issues can be easily resolved with visual data mining technologies. As was mentioned in Section III of the book, Imagix 4D has a comprehensive and effective tutorial that we strongly recommend you consult when first using the product. The tutorial can be used to demonstrate the tool's capabilities. Do not forget to use your mouse buttons and shift keys to manipulate the diagrams.

Hyperbolic Tree Toolkit

This software is used to show off the Hyperbolic Tree Demos developed by Inxight Software. The Hyperbolic Trees are Java applets that you can use to interact with your data, performing manipulation and navigation operations. In order to make the applets work, you will need to run them within a browser such as Netscape Communicator or Microsoft Explorer. There are six Hyperbolic Tree Demos on the CD-ROM. Try clicking on object labels as well as dragging the mouse around within the display as you view the demos. You will see that the Hyperbolic Trees developed by Inxight are easy to navigate and are very responsive.

MineSet

A set of materials related to MineSet 2.0 has been provided by Silicon Graphics. SGI has provided movies that let you see how the software operates. While viewing the movies, keep in mind that MineSet is a very dynamic and interactive system. If you get the chance to use an SGI box, we strongly recommend trying out this software. Of course, you will have to work out the licensing issues with SGI. There have been many new enhancements and upgrades made to MineSet in the time it took to write this book, and you can visit their web-page to get an overview of these new capabilities (e.g., Version 2.5). As a side note, make sure that you maximize the display screen when looking at each of these movies.

Metaphor Mixer

There are several HTML pages that have been made available by Maxus Corporation to provide descriptions of the design and operation of the Metaphor

Mixer system. The HTML pages cover such topics as corporate philosophy, financial applications, configuration of terrains, functionality of intelligent agents, and a range of other data mining applications. There are no interactive demonstrations of Metaphor Mixer included on this CD-ROM because their newest release (NT version) was being developed as we went to press. However, be sure to check their web site to receive the latest update on the Metaphor Mixer software.

Spotfire Lite

This system is produced by IVEE/Spotfire and is provided on the CD-ROM with a 21-day evaluation period. Please make sure you read their license agreement before using the software. Spotfire is a very interactive system that provides some very intuitive methods of interacting with data. The sliders can be easily adjusted to set the upper and lower bounds for any variable being displayed. The colorful displays produced from the menu selections reveal patterns within the data set. Check out all of the different data files that IVEE/Spotfire has provided with this demo and make sure to experiment with axis assignments, data types, and variable values.

Tecplot

Amtec has provided a demonstration of their data visualization system called Tecplot. This is a general purpose set of visualizations that allow you to look at a wide variety of data types, structures, and formats. Although it has a lot of scientific visualization capabilities, this tool may also be used to view relational data sets. The demo is very comprehensive and covers a lot of features. There are sets of movies that you can play to see a simulation of the visualizations that can be produced using Tecplot. Try out the plots (e.g., XY, Field, 3D Volume), data enhancements, data manipulation, and animation features offered from the main overview menu. Use the menu and navigation facilities to interact with the diagram.

SeeIt-In3D (VDI)

Visible Decisions Inc., has provided a copy of their SeeIt-In3D product. This is a landscape visualization that supports a wide range of capabilities. This demo is fully interactive and comes with several different data examples. We recommend that you try out each data set to see the different types of displays that can be generated with this product. When using SeeIt-In3D, you should reassign the axis values, try out the brushing feature, set the waterlevels (baseline), and turn on the back walls. Since SeeIt-In3D relies heavily on its API, you can customize the system to accommodate a variety of application problems. VDI's homepage shows a wide range of display landscapes built using their products.

Visual Insights

Two movies (AVI format) have been provided by Visual Insights to describe their suite of software. The first movie illustrates the use of their System and Network Analysis Tools to monitor computing systems and data networks. This software lets you look at processor activities, network traffic, and system bottlenecks using visualization methods. The second video demonstrates their Year 2000 Analysis Tools that support selection of conversion strategies and estimation of software repair costs using visualization methods. Readers interested in learning more should contact the vendor directly.

User Assistance and Information

The software accompanying this book is provided as-is without warranty or support of any kind. Should you require basic installation assistance, or if your media is defective, please call the Wiley product support number at (212) 850-6194 weekdays between 9 A.M. and 4 P.M. Eastern Standard Time or send an email to **wprtusw@wiley.com**.

If you are unsure about how to use a demo or application provided on the CD-ROM, you are encouraged to contact the vendor directly using the information provided in the Appendix. Vendors may have updated releases of the software that you can download to try out new features and functions.

Make sure your display is set above 256 colors or many of the software programs will not display properly.

To place additional orders or to request information about other Wiley products, please call (800) 879-4539.

INDEX

CUSTOMER NOTE: IF THIS BOOK IS ACCOMPANIED BY SOFTWARE, PLEASE READ THE FOLLOWING BEFORE OPENING THE PACKAGE.

This software contains files to help you utilize the models described in the accompanying book. By opening the package, you are agreeing to be bound by the following agreement:

This software product is protected by copyright and all rights are reserved by the author, John Wiley & Sons, Inc., or their licensors. You are licensed to use this software as described in the software and the accompanying book. Copying the software for any other purpose may be a violation of the U.S. Copyright Law.

This software product is sold as is without warranty of any kind, either express or implied, including but not limited to the implied warranty of merchantability and fitness for a particular purpose. Neither Wiley nor its dealers or distributors assumes any liability for any alleged or actual damages arising from the use of or the inability to use this software. (Some states do not allow the exclusion of implied warranties, so the exclusion may not apply to you.)

To use this CD-ROM, your system must meet the following requirements:

IBM or compatible computer, using a Pentium processor, running Windows 3.1 or Windows 95 operating system

8 MB RAM required, 16 MB recommended. This CD uses helper applications that may require more memory. Refer to the documentation for these applications for further information.

CD-ROM Drive

Web browser installed.